P9-DNR-498

L'EUROPE

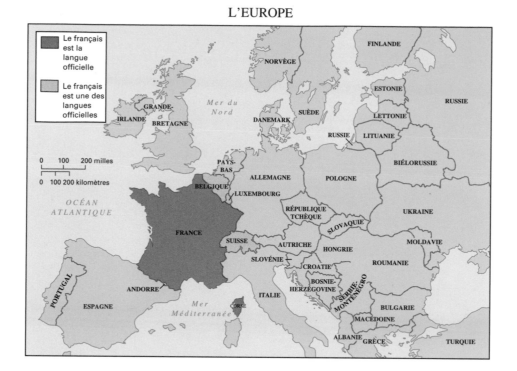

DÉPARTEMENTS ET TERRITOIRES D'OUTRE-MER

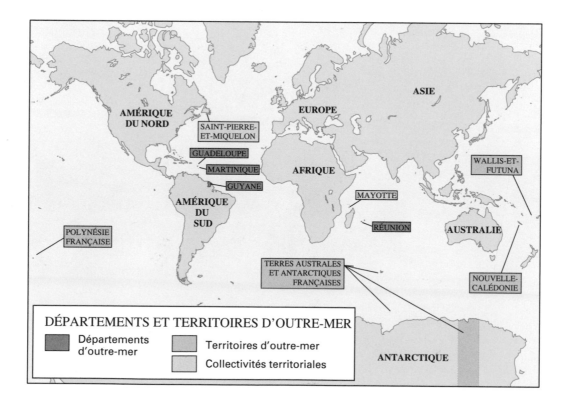

Rapports

Fifth Edition

An Introduction to French Language and Francophone Culture

JOEL WALZ
University of Georgia

JEAN-PIERRE PIRIOU
University of Georgia

HOUGHTON MIFFLIN COMPANY
Boston   New York

Publisher: Rolando Hernández
Sponsoring Editor: Randy Welch
Development Manager: Sharla Zwirek
Development Editor: Susan Abel
Assistant Editor: Judith Bach
Editorial Assistant: Patricia Osborne
Project Editors: Harriet C. Dishman, Stacy Drew
Senior Production/Design Coordinator: Carol Merrigan
Senior Manufacturing Coordinator: Priscilla J. Bailey
Associate Marketing Manager: Claudia Martínez

Cover art: "Sunday," Marc Chagall. Oil on linen. © Réunion des Musées Nationaux/Art Resource, NY

For permission to use copyrighted material, grateful acknowledgment is made to the copyright holders listed on pages 539 and 540, which are hereby considered an extension of this copyright page.

Copyright © 2003 by Houghton Mifflin Company. All rights reserved.

No part of this work may be reproduced or transmitted in any form or by any means, electronic or mechanical, including photocopying and recording, or by any information storage or retrieval system without the prior written permission of Houghton Mifflin Company unless such copying is expressly permitted by federal copyright law. Address inquiries to College Permissions, Houghton Mifflin Company, 222 Berkeley Street, Boston, MA 02116-3764.

Printed in the U.S.A.

Library of Congress Control Number: 2002110820

Student Text ISBN: 0-618-23994-4
Instructor's Annotated Edition ISBN: 0-618-23995-2

3 4 5 6 7 8 9-DOW-06 05

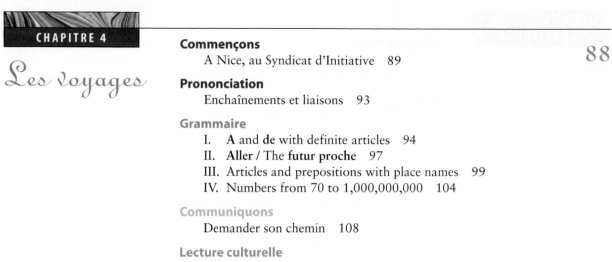

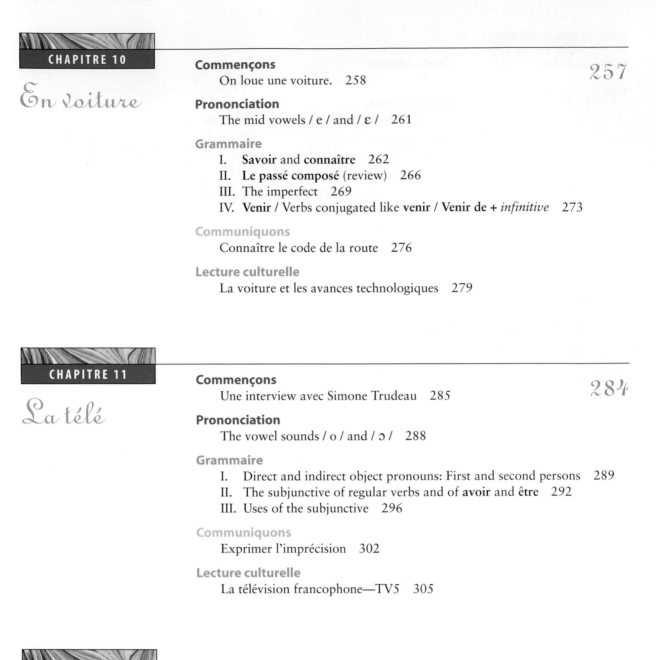

CHAPITRE 13

La santé

CHAPITRE 14

Les sports

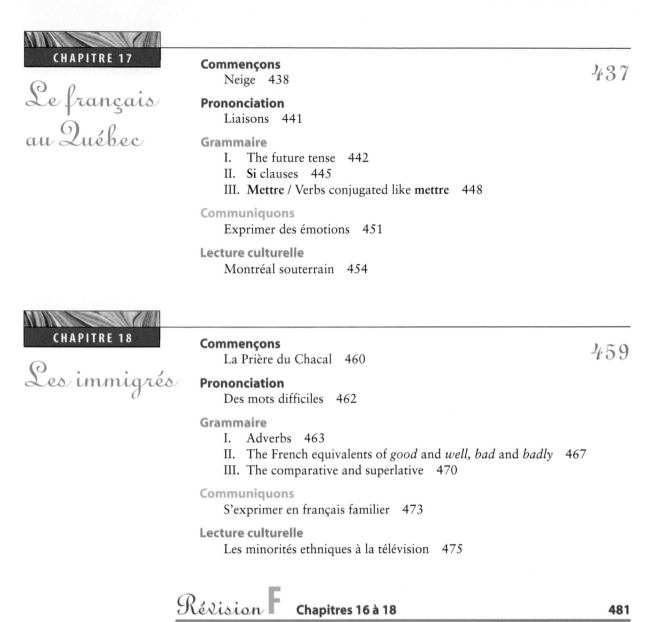

Preface

Rapports, Fifth Edition, is a complete first-year French program for college and university students. It promotes the active command of spoken French without neglecting the development of your listening, reading, and writing skills. Because *Rapports* focuses on the practical use of French for communication in context, it also emphasizes the everyday life and cultures of the French and of French speakers in other francophone countries.

The Text

Rapports consists of a brief preliminary chapter and eighteen chapters. After every three chapters, there is a review section with oral and written exercises for class work and interactive activities for pair and small group work.

The preliminary chapter enables you to begin talking in French with your fellow students on the very first day of class. In this chapter, you will learn greetings, leave-takings, and basic information about French pronunciation, and you will be introduced to the francophone world through a reading in English.

Each subsequent chapter contains the following features:

1. *Chapter Opener*   The first page of each chapter introduces you to the theme, topics, and structures you will study.

    A. **Theme**   Each chapter is centered around a theme. The chapter theme will be evident in the opening dialogue, vocabulary, language exercises and activities, functional / situational phrases, and the cultural reading. A unifying theme enhances your ability to understand and learn the language.

    B. **Objectives**   The first page of each chapter also sets forth the learning objectives for the chapter according to the textbook's three goals: *Language,* or the structures and vocabulary you will learn; *Culture,* information on the French-speaking world that provides an authentic context; and *Communication,* the notions, functions, and situational language that you will use to express yourself.

2. *Commençons*   This section provides samples of everyday language, cultural information, active vocabulary related to the chapter theme, and information on pronunciation. All these will help you integrate the structures you will be learning so that you can communicate in French.

A. **Dialogue**   Each chapter opens with a dialogue or other type of communication such as a phone conversation, a postcard, a formal letter, a poem, or a fable. The setting for each text is a situation that you might encounter or one that is typical of college-age people in francophone countries. **Etudions le dialogue** provides questions on the content of the opening text. A **Mots clés** section follows, listing all new active vocabulary from the dialogue or text. Two icons refer you to other components of the program. An earphones icon indicates that the dialogue or text is recorded in the *Audio CD Program*. The WWW symbol that appears with most chapter openers and elsewhere in the chapter means that additional information relating to the content can be accessed through the *Rapports* Web site.

B. **Faisons connaissance**   This section presents cultural information in English that will help you understand the interaction in the dialogue. It is thematically related to the rest of the chapter and especially to the reading passage in the **Lecture culturelle** at the end of the chapter.

C. **Enrichissons notre vocabulaire**   Active vocabulary appears here in drawings and in conversational exchanges. The vocabulary will recur throughout the chapter in grammar exercises and activities and in the *Workbook / Laboratory / Video Manual. Rapports* has tightly controlled vocabulary with active words appearing only in the dialogue, **Faisons connaissance, Enrichissons,** and grammar presentations when they pertain to the structure being taught. All other sections contain only passive vocabulary, which your teacher may ask you to learn.

D. **Prononciation**   This section offers detailed yet simple explanations of the major features of French pronunciation along with exercises. You may go over the exercises in class or practice them in the language laboratory, since they are recorded in the *Audio CD Program* (as the earphones icon indicates).

3. *Grammaire*   The grammar sections present structures that you can be expected to handle and use actively. The clear presentations in English allow you to prepare the lesson before coming to class and thus spend more class time using the language than discussing it.

A. **Usage statement**   Each presentation begins with a short explanation in English of *why* you would need to know the structure in order to communicate in French.

B. **Explanation**   The structure is explained in a clear fashion with numerous examples, which often come from the dialogue.

C. **Ce qu'ils disent**   Spoken French is not exactly like the more formal language taught in textbooks. While you should learn a fairly formal style, these explanations will help you to understand what you will hear in a French-speaking country.

D. **L'orthographe**   This section describes the features of the French language that appear only in writing, since written French sometimes differs from spoken French.

E. **Attention**   This section points out elements of the language that cause trouble for non-native speakers or that are easy to forget.

F. **Language / Langue**   The first group of exercises for each grammar point carries this name (the names as well as directions to all exercises, change from English to French as of Chapter 7). These exercises are all meaningful; that is, you must understand the French to produce the correct answer. Virtually all these exercises are also in a context that unifies the items, so that you practice each structure in an everyday situation.

G. **Culture**   For every point of grammar taught, *Rapports*, Fifth Edition, has at least one activity based on cultural similarities and differences between the United States and francophone cultures. You must understand not only the language but also the culture to produce a correct answer. The activities reflect a wide range of content, involving everything from famous artists and historical figures to the way French speakers conduct their daily lives. You will not know some of the information at first, but you can create sentences that seem logical, and your teacher will guide you to the correct answers.

H. **Communication**   Every grammar point is also followed by a number of activities that allow you to express your own ideas and experiences. The formats always provide suggestions to get you started, but they also encourage originality. The personal questions center around a basic context to help you interact with your teacher and classmates in a natural conversation.

4. *Communiquons*   This section introduces a notion, a function, or a situation that is important to communication. A short paragraph in English introduces the topic. Then, you learn various common phrases so you can express your thoughts appropriately in French. The **Expressions** and dialogue or **Interaction** that follows illustrate authentic usage of the phrases presented, and the communication activities allow you to practice using the new expressions in other contexts.

5. *Lecture culturelle*   Each chapter concludes with a reading passage on a topic related to the cultural theme of the chapter. The pre-reading section will give you background information, and its activities will help you develop skills so that you can read French more proficiently. The post-reading activities will check your comprehension of the reading passage and enable you to discuss what you have learned in terms of your own life.

6. *Vocabulaire*   At the end of the chapter, a list of all the active vocabulary in the chapter will help you review the new words you have learned.

End-of-Text Reference Materials

1. Appendices include the International Phonetic Alphabet, the French names of and prepositions used with the fifty American states and the provinces of Canada, supplemental grammar points, and verb conjugation charts.

2. The French-English vocabulary lists the active and passive vocabulary in *Rapports,* Fifth Edition. The English-French vocabulary lists all active words and expressions. Each entry in the vocabularies is followed by a reference indicating the chapter in which it first appears.

3. An index provides ready access to all grammatical structures, vocabulary topics, and pronunciation points presented in the textbook.

The *Rapports* Web Site

A Web site created specifically for users of *Rapports* has more than 150 links to the French-speaking world available to you. Using the World Wide Web is useful for expanding one's knowledge of the French-speaking world, obtaining up-to-date information, and increasing reading skills. We have referenced sites every time we found one corresponding to the content of this book. In order to make use of this feature, you should do the following: Look for the **WWW** symbol in your book; then visit the Houghton Mifflin College Division's site at **http://www.college.hmco.com/languages.** When you are on the *Rapports* Resource Center site, read the introduction, or scroll down to the Table of Contents. You can then click on the chapter in *Rapports,* Fifth Edition, that you are currently studying, which will display all the links to sites that correspond to the content of that chapter. Clicking on any underlined words in a contrasting color will connect you with that site. These Web sites will allow you to do such things as see the latest fashions from Paris, study the itinerary of the next Tour de France, plan a subway trip, find out what is on TV in France or Canada, or read the morning paper in French!

The Workbook / Laboratory Manual and Audio CD Program

The *Workbook / Laboratory Manual* is fully integrated with *Rapports,* Fifth Edition, to further develop your writing, speaking, and listening skills. The *Workbook* section offers a variety of exercises that require you to write in French using the structures and vocabulary of the corresponding textbook chapter. Each *Workbook* section concludes with **Ecrivons,** a section devoted to directed compositions and open-ended, personalized writing assignments. The *Laboratory* section guides you through the *Audio CD Program,* providing pronunciation explanations and exercises and cues for all of the listening-and-speaking and listening-and-writing activities that accompany each chapter. The *Workbook / Laboratory Manual* also provides workbook exercises and laboratory activities for the review sections, which appear after every three chapters.

The *Audio CD Program* provides you with forty to fifty minutes of listening material for each textbook chapter and additional listening activities for each review section. The textbook dialogues and pronunciation exercises are recorded. They are followed by a series of listening-and-speaking and listening-and-writing activities for each grammar point. Each chapter concludes with a dictation and a global listening comprehension activity tied thematically to the content of the corresponding textbook chapter.

At the end of the *Workbook / Laboratory Manual,* you will find answers to all exercises and activities that have a fixed response, including the **Dictée** and the **Compréhension.** Check these answers as you complete an activity to be aware of any errors you have made. Whenever you have questions that require a personalized response, you will see the comment "Answers will vary." In those cases, your teacher will have to grade your work. Also, watch for "Possible answers." Your response could be just as correct as the ones given; check with your teacher if you are not sure. Having answer keys will allow you to work independently, to obtain immediate feedback, and to do more than the minimum assignments your teacher gives.

Multimedia CD-ROM

The *Rapports* multimedia CD-ROM incorporates dialogues, vocabulary, and readings from each chapter as source material. This fun, interactive tool provides pronunciation practice, on-line grammar notes, word and phrase meanings, supplemental exercises, and quizzes and self-tests to help you prepare for exams. Four types of activities with sound, voice recordability, scoring, and beat-the-clock options make learning French enjoyable. The *Workbook / Laboratory Manual* will also be available in an electronic, interactive format.

Videocassette and Video Manual

This ninety-minute video is divided into modules that present authentic materials. The accompanying *Video Manual* in the Workbook contains the complete videoscript followed by video exercises for each video clip.

Acknowledgments

The authors would like to express their appreciation to the Houghton Mifflin editorial staff for their support in the development and production of this revision. We are particularly grateful to Lisa Jurkowitz, Ph.D. candidate at the University of Arizona, and André Klein, Professor Emeritus at Thunderbird, the American Graduate School of International Management, for their work in finding authentic readings for the new edition and for writing new activities to accompany them, in addition to their work in updating the cultural references throughout the text. Our thanks also to Michael Lastinger, who revised the *Testing Program* for this edition.

In addition, we would especially like to thank Valérie Boulanger, Ph.D. candidate in Linguistics at the University of Georgia, for compiling the end vocabularies, including the chapter codes that users have found so helpful. Her specialization in lexicography served us well in this respect. We could not have completed this revision without frequent contacts in France, especially with Jean-Claude Pfeffer and his family, Shane Fowler, and Daphne McConnell. We received documents and information from colleagues and students, in particular from Melanie Poudevigne, Jennifer Higdon, Teri Hernández, Denis Jamet, Andy Wallis, Michael Lindsey, Kristin Bruno, and Raymond Cormier. Our apologies to whomever we have forgotten to mention.

We would also like to thank the following reviewers, who have all used *Rapports* in the past and who have made interesting and useful comments for this revision.

John T. Booker, *University of Kansas,* Lawrence, KS
Ray Cornelius, *Daytona Beach Community College,* Daytona Beach, FL
Robert R. Daniel, *Saint Joseph's University,* Philadelphia, PA
Catherine Dunand, *Northeastern University,* Boston, MA
Richard Durán, *Baylor University,* Waco, TX
Mary E. Gutermuth, *Sam Houston State University,* Huntsville, TX
Julien Lafontant, *University of Nebraska at Omaha,* Omaha, NE
Patricia J. Siegel, *SUNY–Brockport,* Brockport, NY
Joanne J. Viano, *University of Pittsburgh at Greensburg,* Greensburg, PA
Odette Winn, *San Bernardino Valley College,* San Bernardino, CA

JOEL WALZ
JEAN-PIERRE PIRIOU

Salut! Ça va?

Bonjour!

OBJECTIVES

Language	Culture	Communication
■ Idiomatic expressions ■ Some basic information on pronunciation	■ How people greet and take leave of each other ■ The usefulness of knowing French	■ Greetings and leave-takings

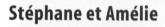

commençons

Stéphane et Amélie

STÉPHANE: Bonjour!

AMÉLIE: Salut! Ça va?

STÉPHANE: Oui, ça va bien. Et toi?

AMÉLIE: Ça va, merci.

STÉPHANE: Je m'appelle Stéphane. Et toi?

AMÉLIE: Amélie.

Laurent et Madame Dumas

MME DUMAS: Bonjour, Laurent.

LAURENT: Bonjour, Madame. Comment allez-vous?

MME DUMAS: Je vais bien, merci. Et vous?

LAURENT: Très bien, merci.

Mots clés

Bonjour!	*Hello! / Good morning!*
Salut!	*Hi!*
Ça va?	*How's it going?*
Oui.	*Yes.*
Ça va bien.	*Fine.*
Et toi?	*And you?*
Merci.	*Thank you.*
Je m'appelle...	*My name is . . .*
Madame	*Mrs.; ma'am*
Comment allez-vous?	*How are you?*
Je vais bien.	*I'm fine.*
Et vous?	*And you?*
Très bien.	*Very well.*

Faisons connaissance

The way people greet each other varies from culture to culture and depends on how well they know each other. When French people meet, they always make physical contact. Friends and business associates exchange a brief handclasp (**une poignée de main**) not only upon being introduced, but also upon seeing each other for the first time each day, and again upon parting. In France, women shake hands as often as men.

Rencontre rue de la Sorbonne

When two French people who are relatives or good friends see each other, they may embrace lightly and kiss on both cheeks (**faire une bise à...**). It is not unusual for French men to greet each other this way, especially if they are related or if they are celebrating an important occasion. In a French family, all children, no matter how old, will kiss both parents before leaving for the day or going to bed.

Relationships also influence the kind of language people use in greeting each other. For example, in the dialogue, two friends of the same age say «**Salut, ça va?**», but a young person would say to an adult: «**Bonjour, comment allez-vous?**». In general, French people are more formal than Americans, and they are less likely to act casually with new acquaintances.

Enrichissons notre vocabulaire

Faisons connaissance! *(Let's get to know each other!)*

Au revoir.	*Good-bye.*
Bonsoir.	*Hello / Good evening.*
A bientôt.	*See you soon.*
A plus tard.	*See you later.*
A tout à l'heure.	*See you later.*
—Comment ça va?	*How's it going?*
—Pas mal.	*Not bad.*
—Comme ci, comme ça.	*So-so.*
Quoi de neuf?	*What's up?*
Monsieur	*Mister; sir*
Mademoiselle	*Miss*

Communication

Using the expressions you have just learned in the dialogue, greet the student next to you, introduce yourself, and ask how things are going.

Prononciation   Some basic information

A. Although French and English use the same alphabet, the combinations of letters and the sounds that they represent can be very different. Each language contains some sounds that do not exist in the other. French has no *th* sound as in *thank,* no *ch* sound as in *children.* English has no **u** sound, as in **une,** no **r** sound as in **merci.**

B. Both languages have words containing letters that are not pronounced.

French: tar*d,* alle*z,* Madam*e*
English: *i*sland, *k*nife, ni*gh*t

C. In French, as in English, one letter or one combination of letters can be pronounced more than one way.

French: **comme, merci**
English: *c*all, *c*ircle

D. In French, as in English, one sound can be written more than one way.

French: **ça, salut, merci, professeur**
English: con*qu*er, *k*itchen, *ch*aracter

lecture culturelle

Le français, c'est utile!

The French language is a practical tool for travel and work, as it is spoken by approximately 129 million people worldwide. About half the people who use French daily live in France. The remainder live in more than forty other countries, scattered across five continents. French is the official language of France, the Canadian province of Quebec, and thirteen countries in Africa, as well as Martinique, Guadeloupe, French Guiana, and the island of Réunion. French is one of the official languages of Belgium, Luxembourg, Switzerland, Haiti, Cameroon, Mauritania, Djibouti, Rwanda, Burundi, Mauritius, and Canada. Knowledge of French is therefore useful, and can enhance your employment opportunities, both in the United States and abroad.

Along with English, French is the official working language of many international organizations, such as the United Nations, UNESCO, NATO, the Organization for Economic Cooperation and Development (OECD), the International Red Cross, the International Olympic Committee, and the European Union.

Few are aware that French companies employ more than four hundred thousand Americans. If you can speak French, you could very well find yourself working in some of the exciting fields in which France is at the forefront. Did you know that France is the world's leader in the production of luxury goods and in the area of telecommunications? It is the fourth largest producer of automobiles (Renault, Peugeot, Citroën), the world's third largest manufacturer of electronics equipment, and the European leader in the aerospace

Réunion de chefs d'Etat francophones

25 industry (Aérospatiale, Arianespace, Airbus). Among other noteworthy advances, high-definition television (HDTV) and fiber optics were both invented in France. The fastest train, the TGV (**train à grande vitesse**), is French, and so is the fastest commercial airplane, the Concorde, built in collaboration with British Airways. France is also a major world research center in the fields of high-energy physics and medical genetics (the Human Genome
30 Project is located in Paris), as well as a world leader in medical research (the AIDS virus was co-discovered by French and American scientists).

Another interesting statistic to bear in mind is that French is the second most frequently taught foreign language in the world, after English. You join a thriving community by studying French. «**Bonne chance, et**
35 **amusez-vous bien!**» *(Good luck, and have fun!)*

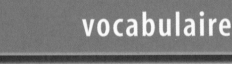

vocabulaire

Noms / Pronoms

Madame	Mrs. / Ms. / ma'am	**une poignée de main**	handshake
Mademoiselle	Miss / Ms.	**toi**	you
Monsieur	Mr. / sir	**vous**	you

Adjectifs / Adverbes

bien	well	**très bien**	very well
très	very		

Expressions

à bientôt	see you soon	**Comment ça va?**	How are you?
à plus tard	see you later	**et**	and
à tout à l'heure	see you later	**et toi**	and you
au revoir	good-bye	**et vous**	and you
bonjour	good morning / hello	**faire une bise à...**	to kiss (someone)
		Je m'appelle...	My name is . . .
bonsoir	good evening / hello	**Je vais bien.**	I'm fine.
		merci	thank you
Ça va?	How are you?	**oui**	yes
Ça va bien.	I'm fine.	**pas mal**	not bad
comme ci, comme ça	so-so	**Quoi de neuf?**	What's new?
Comment allez-vous?	How do you do?	**Salut.**	Hi.

commençons

grammaire

communiquons

lecture culturelle

vocabulaire

Travail à l'ordinateur

La vie universitaire

OBJECTIVES

Language		Culture	Communication
■ Vocabulary for the classroom	■ Subject pronouns	■ University life	■ Managing a brief conversation
■ The International Phonetic Alphabet, the French alphabet, accent marks, and punctuation	■ **-er** verbs		■ Naming things
	■ Yes-or-no questions		■ Describing actions
	■ Numbers from 0 to 20		■ Asking questions
■ Nouns and definite articles			■ Doing math problems

commençons

A l'université, en cours d'anglais

LE PROFESSEUR: Commençons! Mademoiselle, comment vous appelez-vous?

L'ÉTUDIANTE: Je m'appelle Patricia Keller.

LE PROFESSEUR: Alors, vous parlez bien anglais, n'est-ce pas?

PATRICIA: Non, juste un peu.

LE PROFESSEUR: Eh bien, ouvrez votre livre page neuf et lisez le dialogue. *(A la classe)* Ecoutez et répétez ensemble après Patricia.

Etudions le dialogue

1. Repeat the dialogue after your teacher.
2. Read the dialogue with another classmate.
3. Ask one of your classmates to act out the dialogue with you in front of the class.

Mots clés

à l'université *(f.)*	*at the university*	Eh bien	*Well then*
en cours *(m.)*	*in class*	Ouvrez votre livre.	*Open your book.*
anglais *(m.)*	*English*	une page	*page*
un professeur	*teacher*	neuf	*nine*
Commençons! (commencer)	*Let's begin!*	lisez (lire)	*read*
Comment vous appelez-vous?	*What's your name?*	un dialogue	*dialogue*
étudiant, -e *(m., f.)*	*student*	à	*to*
Alors...	*Then . . .*	une classe	*class*
parlez (parler)	*speak*	écoutez (écouter)	*listen (to)*
n'est-ce pas?	*don't you?*	répétez (répéter)	*repeat*
non	*no*	ensemble	*together*
juste un peu	*just a little bit*	après	*after*

$\mathcal{F}$aisons connaissance

French universities are state-supported. Since 1968, new universities have been created in many French cities. However, in Paris and in other major cities, the universities are so big that they are divided and have numbers. For example, the former **Sorbonne** is now **Paris IV.** In addition to having numbers, many universities also have names. For instance, **Lyon III** is also called **l'université Jean Moulin,** whereas **Montpellier III** is known as **l'université Paul Valéry.** Students use the term **la fac,** an abbreviation of **la faculté,** to refer to the university or any of its schools, such as **la faculté de Médecine** *(School of Medicine)* or **la faculté des Lettres et des Sciences humaines** *(College of Arts and Humanities).*

La Sorbonne

Most French students go to the university nearest to their home and continue to live with their families. Students who cannot return home every night often have to rent a room from individuals because universities cannot provide housing for everyone who needs it. This also helps explain why there is little campus life.

Students often go to cafés between classes and when classes are over to meet friends or simply study. Traditionally, one can stay in a café for an unlimited period of time without having to place another order. Near universities, however, a sign may indicate that orders will be taken again every two hours.

Enrichissons notre vocabulaire

Voilà la salle de classe. *(Here is the classroom.)*

le tableau
la craie
le bureau de Madame Dumas
la clé
la chaise
le stylo
le cahier
les livres
la porte
la fenêtre
le cadeau
le crayon

FRANCE
la carte

A B C D E F G
H I J K L M N
O P Q R S T
U V W X Y Z
l'alphabet *(m.)*

PARIS
l'affiche *(f.)*

le sac à dos

Expressions utiles pour le cours de français *(Useful expressions for French class)*

Continuez la leçon.
Commencez ici et **répétez avec** Patricia.
Commencez l'examen *(m.)* / vos **devoirs** *(m.)*.
Lisez de la page quatre **à** la page cinq et **répondez aux** questions.
Faites l'exercice A.
Parlez beaucoup en classe, mais **en** français!

—Qu'est-ce que c'est?
—C'est le bureau de Madame Dumas.
—Ce sont les livres de français.

Continue the lesson.
Start here and repeat with Patricia.
Start the test / your homework.

Read from page four to page five and answer the questions.
Do exercise A.
Speak a lot in class, but in French!

What is this?
It's Mrs. Dumas's desk.

They're the French books.

—Comment dit-on «good-bye»
à Paris / au Québec?
—Je ne sais pas.
—A Paris, **on dit** «au revoir»,
mais au Québec, on dit
«bonjour».

—Qu'est-ce que «salut» **veut dire**?
—**Cela** veut dire «hi».

—**Voici** le livre de français.
—Merci.
—Il n'y a pas de quoi. / De rien.

*How do you say "good-bye" in
Paris / in Quebec?*
I don't know.
*In Paris, you say "au revoir,"
but in Quebec, you say
"bonjour."*

What does "salut" mean?
It means "hi."

Here is the French book.
Thank you.
Don't mention it. / You're welcome.

Prononciation   **The International Phonetic Alphabet**

The International Phonetic Alphabet (IPA), which is used in the **Prononciation** sections of this book, simplifies learning new words because each written symbol represents one specific sound. The International Phonetic Alphabet appears in Appendix I.

The French alphabet

A. The French alphabet is the same as the English, but the names of the letters differ. The following chart gives the letters, the IPA symbols showing the pronunciation of each letter, and a short, imaginary word to help you remember the names.

a	/ a /	ah	j	/ ʒi /	ji	s	/ ɛs /	esse			
b	/ be /	bé	k	/ ka /	ka	t	/ te /	té			
c	/ se /	sé	l	/ ɛl /	elle	u	/ y /	u			
d	/ de /	dé	m	/ ɛm /	emme	v	/ ve /	vé			
e	/ ø /	euh	n	/ ɛn /	enne	w	/ du blø ve /	double vé			
f	/ ɛf /	ef	o	/ o /	oh	x	/ iks /	iks			
g	/ ʒe /	jé	p	/ pe /	pé	y	/ i gʀɛk /	i grec			
h	/ aʃ /	ache	q	/ ky /	ku	z	/ zɛd /	zed			
i	/ i /	i	r	/ ɛʀ /	erre						

B. The letters **k** and **w** are rare in French and occur only in words borrowed directly from other languages. Examples are **le week-end, le wagon, le kiosque.**

C. The letter **h** is always silent. Words that start with **h** sound as though they start with the vowel that follows. Two examples are **homme** / ɔm / and **hôtel** / o tɛl /.

Accent marks and punctuation

A. French has a system of written accent marks that are as important as the dot of an **i** or the cross of a **t**. Be sure to learn accents as part of the spelling of words.

accent	name		example
´	l'accent aigu	*acute accent*	poignée
`	l'accent grave	*grave accent*	très
^	l'accent circonflexe	*circumflex accent*	hôtel
¸	la cédille	*cedilla*	français
¨	le tréma	*dieresis*	Noël

B. Accents can indicate pronunciation.

commençons	/ kɔ mã sɔ̃ /
classe, café	/ klas /, / ka fe /

C. Accents can differentiate words.

a	*has*	ou	*or*
à	*to*	où	*where*

You will not, however, see accents on capital letters. For example, you will see **à Paris**, but **A Paris**.

D. French uses almost the same punctuation marks as English; only quotation marks look different.

.	le point	*period*
,	la virgule	*comma*
-	le trait d'union	*hyphen*
'	l'apostrophe	*apostrophe*
«»	les guillemets	*quotation marks*

E. To spell words aloud in French, say the letter and any accent mark it may have immediately after it. If the word has a double consonant, say **deux** *(two)* before the letter that is doubled. A *capital* letter is **majuscule** and a *small* letter is **minuscule**.

ça	**c** cédille, **a**	accent	**a**, deux **c**, **e**, **n**, **t**
café	**c**, **a**, **f**, **e** accent aigu	René	**r** majuscule, **e**, **n**, **e** accent aigu

---

Exercices

Ⓐ Repeat the French alphabet after your teacher.

Ⓑ In French, spell your full name, your mother's maiden name, and the name of the street where you live.

Ⓒ Team up with a classmate and ask each other to spell words from the dialogue. When giving the words, be sure your pronunciation is correct. When spelling the words, be sure to remember accents.

grammaire

I. Nouns and definite articles

You use nouns to name people, places, and things.

A. In French, all nouns, whether they represent living or nonliving things, are either masculine or feminine. Nouns referring to male human beings are generally masculine. Nouns referring to female human beings are generally feminine.

B. An article almost always accompanies a noun in French. The article indicates the gender (masculine or feminine) and the number (singular or plural) of the noun. A masculine noun is introduced by a masculine article. A feminine noun is introduced by a feminine article. French has four forms that may correspond to the English definite article *the*.

definite articles		
	singular	*plural*
masculine	**le** dialogue	**les** dialogues
	l'étudiant	**les** étudiants
feminine	**la** porte	**les** portes
	l'étudiante	**les** étudiantes

C. **Le** / lø / is used with masculine singular nouns that begin with a consonant.

le stylo	*pen*
le café	*sidewalk café; coffee*
le crayon	*pencil*
le français	*French (language)*

D. **La** / la / is used with feminine singular nouns that begin with a consonant.

la radio	*radio*	**la** leçon	*lesson*
la télévision	*television*	**la** classe	*class*

Attention!

Notice the similarity between **classe** and *class*. French and English words that are alike in sound, spelling, and meaning are *cognates*. There are, however, French words that are similar in spelling to English words but that differ in meaning. These are **faux amis**, or *false friends*. An example is **comment**, which means *how*.

E. L' is used with all singular nouns that begin with a vowel sound.

l'ami *(m.)*	/ la mi /	*friend*
l'amie *(f.)*	/ la mi /	*friend*
l'hôtel *(m.)*	/ lo tɛl /	*hotel*
l'enfant *(m. or f.)*	/ lã fã /	*child*

F. Les is used with plural nouns, masculine and feminine. It is pronounced / le / before a consonant and / lez / before a vowel sound.

les livres *(m.)*	/ le livʀ /	*books*
les femmes *(f.)*	/ le fam /	*women*
les hommes *(m.)*	/ le zɔm /	*men*
les amies *(f.)*	/ le za mi /	*friends*

Ce qu'ils disent

You are no doubt aware that people do not always use a language the way grammar books (or textbooks) describe it. For example, English has the verb *going to,* but most people say "gonna." To help you bridge the gap between written and spoken French, this section, **Ce qu'ils disent** *(What people say),* will appear throughout this book.

In conversations, French people often shorten words. Two that you have just seen are **la télévision,** which becomes **la télé** (often written **la TV**), and **le professeur,** which is shortened to **le prof.** While you normally use the masculine **le professeur** for male and female teachers, both **le prof** and **la prof** exist.

L'orthographe

As with English, there are numerous differences in French between what you say and what you write. This section, **L'orthographe** *(Spelling),* will appear throughout the book to explain forms that are present only when you write in French.

1. In French, the plural of most nouns is formed by adding an **s** to the singular noun. If the noun already ends in **s**, the singular and the plural are the same.

le stylo	les stylos	*pens*
la leçon	les leçons	*lessons*
le cours	les cours	*classes*
l'autobus	les autobus	*buses*

2. The letter **x** is used for the plural of words ending in **-eau.**

le cadeau	les cadeaux	*gifts*
le bureau	les bureaux	*desks, offices*
le tableau	les tableaux	*chalkboards*

Language

A **Les pluriels.** Make the following nouns plural.

1. l'enfant
2. la carte
3. le stylo
4. le dialogue
5. l'ami
6. la clé
7. l'étudiante
8. l'affiche

B **Les singuliers.** Make the following nouns singular.

1. les cours
2. les radios
3. les femmes
4. les étudiants
5. les exercices
6. les hommes
7. les livres
8. les amies

C **Les articles définis.** Use the correct definite article with the following nouns. (Watch for the plural marker **s** or **x**.)

1. fenêtre
2. radios
3. classe
4. hommes
5. crayon
6. ami
7. bureaux
8. alphabet
9. stylos
10. amies
11. leçon
12. femmes

Culture

D **L'hypermarché.** An **hypermarché** is a huge store that combines a supermarket and a discount store, such as Wal-Mart, under one roof. Two well-known French chains are **Carrefour** and **Mammouth**. Indicate whether or not you think the following items are available for sale in an **hypermarché** by adding a definite article and **Oui** or **Non**.

MODEL: livres   *Les livres? Oui.*
étudiants   *Les étudiants? Non!*

1. cartes
2. bises
3. sacs à dos
4. enfants
5. affiches
6. cours
7. crayons
8. livres

Communication

E **La salle de classe.** Divide into pairs. Take turns pointing to classroom or personal objects and asking, **Qu'est-ce que c'est?** Your partner will answer with **C'est,** a definite article, and a noun.

MODEL: Student 1: (Pointing to the window) *Qu'est-ce que c'est?*
Student 2: *C'est la fenêtre.*

F **Les objets.** Team up with a classmate to study the nouns you have learned. When giving the French word, use the definite article.

MODEL: Student 1: *Comment dit-on «book»?*
Student 2: *On dit «le livre».*

Then choose a French word and ask for the English equivalent.

MODEL: Student 1: *Qu'est-ce que «le stylo» veut dire?*
Student 2: *Cela veut dire «pen».*

II. Subject pronouns and *-er* verbs

A. Subject pronouns

You use pronouns to avoid repeating the names of people and things when the meaning is clear.

1. Subject pronouns replace noun subjects.

Paul chante. → **Il** chante.   *Paul sings.* → *He sings.*
Paul et Marie étudient. →   *Paul and Marie study.* →
   Ils étudient.   *They study.*

subject pronouns			
je	*I*	nous	*we*
tu	*you*	vous	*you*
il	*he, it*	ils	*they (m.)*
elle	*she, it*	elles	*they (f.)*
on	*one, we, you, they*		

2. Note that there are two French forms for *you*: **tu** and **vous**. **Tu** is the singular, informal form. Use **tu** to address a person that you know well, such as a friend or a relative, or a child.

  Tu parles français?   *Do **you** speak French?*

Vous can be singular or plural. Use **vous** to speak to one person you do not know well, or are unsure how to address, or wish to treat with respect. Also use **vous** to speak to more than one person, regardless of your relationship.

  Vous parlez anglais, Madame?   *Do **you** speak English, ma'am?*
  Philippe et Isabelle, **vous**   *Philippe and Isabelle, are **you***
    écoutez le professeur?   *listening to the teacher?*

Ce qu'ils disent

In the last few years, the French people have relaxed their constraints on the use of **tu**. Business associates who would have used **vous** in the past are now more likely to use **tu** with each other. As a foreigner, you should still use **vous** with native speakers until they use **tu** with you. It is generally acceptable, however, to use **tu** with another student.

In other parts of the French-speaking world, particularly Louisiana, rules for the **tu–vous** distinction are even more relaxed, with **tu** used for individuals and **vous** for more than one person.

3. There is no specific word in French for *it*. Since all nouns have a gender, **il** refers to masculine nouns and **elle** refers to feminine nouns.

4. **Elles** refers to two or more females or feminine nouns.

Marie et Amélie? **Elles** travaillent bien.	*Marie and Amélie? **They** work hard.*
La porte et la fenêtre? **Elles** ferment mal.	*The door and the window? **They** close badly.*

5. **Ils** refers to two or more males or masculine nouns. **Ils** also refers to a combined group of males and females or masculine and feminine nouns.

Les étudiants? **Ils** écoutent en cours.	*The students? **They** listen in class.*
La carte et le livre? **Ils** sont ici.	*The map and the book? **They** are here.*

6. There is one impersonal subject pronoun in French: **on**. It is used in a general sense and has at least four English equivalents: *we, one, they, people.*

Ici **on** parle français.

{ *Here **we** speak French.*
*Here **one** speaks French.*
*Here **they** speak French.*
*Here **people** speak French.*

Ce qu'ils disent

> In conversational French, the pronoun **on** usually replaces **nous**.
>
> | | |
> |---|---|
> | **On** regarde la télévision? | *Shall **we** watch television?* |
> | **On** commence! | *Let's begin!* |

B. Present Tense of *-er* Verbs

You use verbs to describe actions or states of being.

1. French verbs are classified by the ending of the infinitive. The infinitive consists of a stem (like **chant**) and an ending (like **-er**). The largest group of French verbs has an infinitive that ends in **-er,** like **chanter.**

infinitive: *chanter* (to sing)		
singular		
1st person	je **chante**	*I sing, I am singing, I do sing*
2nd person	tu **chantes**	*you sing, you are singing,* *you do sing*
3rd person	il **chante**	*he sings, he is singing,* *he does sing*
	elle **chante**	*she sings, she is singing,* *she does sing*
	on **chante**	*one sings, one is singing,* *one does sing*
plural		
1st person	nous **chantons**	*we sing, we are singing,* *we do sing*
2nd person	vous **chantez**	*you sing, you are singing,* *you do sing*
3rd person	ils **chantent**	*they sing, they are singing,* *they do sing*
	elles **chantent**	*they sing, they are singing,* *they do sing*

2. The present tense in French corresponds to three English forms as shown
   in the preceding verb chart.

   > En général, ils **chantent** bien,
   >   mais ce soir ils **chantent** mal.

   > *Generally, they **sing** well, but*
   >   *tonight they **are singing** badly.*

3. Conjugated **-er** verbs have only three pronunciations. The singular forms
   and the third-person plural forms (**ils / elles**) are pronounced alike. The lis-
   tener must know from the context whether / il ʃɑ̃t / is singular or plural.

je	/ ʃɑ̃t /	nous	/ ʃɑ̃ tɔ̃ /
tu	/ ʃɑ̃t /	vous	/ ʃɑ̃ te /
il	/ ʃɑ̃t /	ils	/ ʃɑ̃t /
elle	/ ʃɑ̃t /	elles	/ ʃɑ̃t /

4. When a verb starts with a vowel sound, **je** becomes **j'**, the letter **n** of **on** is
   pronounced, and the final **s** of all plural subject pronouns is pronounced.

J'invite.	/ ʒɛ̃ vit /	Vous invitez.	/ vu zɛ̃ vi te /
On invite.	/ ɔ̃ nɛ̃ vit /	Ils invitent.	/ il zɛ̃ vit /
Nous invitons.	/ nu zɛ̃ vi tɔ̃ /	Elles invitent.	/ ɛl zɛ̃ vit /

L'orthographe

1. All regular **-er** verbs are conjugated the same way. Written present-tense endings for **-er** verbs are: **-e, -es, -e, -ons, -ez, -ent.**

2. In written French, verbs that end in **-ger** add an **e** before the **-ons** ending (**nous mangeons**). Verbs that end in **-cer** add a **cédille** to the **c** before the **-ons** ending (**nous commençons**). These small changes preserve the "soft" sounds of the **g** and **c.**

Mots clés *Common and useful -er verbs*

adorer	*to love; to adore*	fermer	*to close*
aimer	*to like*	fumer	*to smoke*
arriver	*to arrive*	habiter	*to live (in a place)*
commencer	*to begin*	inviter	*to invite*
continuer	*to continue*	jouer	*to play*
danser	*to dance*	manger	*to eat*
demander	*to ask (for)*	montrer	*to show*
donner	*to give*	parler	*to speak*
écouter	*to listen (to)*	regarder	*to watch*
étudier	*to study*	terminer	*to end*
expliquer	*to explain*	travailler	*to work*

Language

A **En cours.** Make complete sentences about the following classmates with each group of words provided.

MODEL: Pierre / aimer / université
Pierre aime l'université.

1. Je / écouter / professeur
2. Stéphane / arriver / avec Marie
3. Nous / commencer / examen
4. étudiants / étudier / français
5. Hélène et Chantal / travailler / ensemble
6. Vous / terminer / devoirs

Culture

B **Le Crazy Horse.** The **Crazy Horse Saloon** is a famous Parisian nightclub. Guess what people do there by using the verbs below with either **Oui** or **Non.**

MODEL: danser *On danse? Oui.*
étudier le français *On étudie le français? Non!*

1. fumer
2. manger
3. parler
4. travailler
5. regarder les hommes et les femmes
6. écouter la radio
7. regarder la télé
8. jouer

C **J'aime ça!** Make a list of five statements about yourself using the **-er** verbs and other vocabulary you have learned. Share your list with a classmate to find differences and similarities.

MODEL: *J'aime les enfants. Je chante bien. Je danse mal. Je regarde la télévision. J'étudie le français.*

D **Questions personnelles.** A l'université.

1. Le professeur de français explique bien la leçon?
2. Vous parlez français?
3. Vous étudiez beaucoup?
4. Les étudiants travaillent bien ici?
5. Vous écoutez bien le professeur?
6. Vous aimez les cours à l'université?

>> A L'ÉTUDE

Bibliothèque de Paris VIII
2, rue de la Liberté
93100 Saint-Denis
Tél.: 01 49 40 69 69
www.univ-paris8.fr
Lun. 11h30–20h, mar.–ven. 9h–20h,
sam. 10h–17h30
M° Saint-Denis université
RER D : Saint-Denis + bus 255

III. Yes-or-no questions

You use yes-or-no questions to find out information.

A. One of three basic ways to ask a yes-or-no question in French is to use intonation. This means that you make your voice rise, rather than fall, at the end of a sentence.

Statement: Il travaille ici.   *He works here.*

Question: Il travaille ici?   *He works here?*

B. You can add the phrase **Est-ce que** to the beginning of a sentence.

Statement: Cécile parle bien.   *Cécile speaks well.*

Question: Est-ce que Cécile parle bien?   *Does Cécile speak well?*

When the subject of a sentence begins with a vowel, the **e** of **que** is not pronounced and is replaced with an apostrophe.

Est-ce **qu'il** regarde la télévision?   *Is he watching television?*
Est-ce **qu'on** parle français ici?   *Is French spoken here?*

C. You can add the phrase **n'est-ce pas?** to the end of a sentence.

Statement: Je joue bien.   *I play well.*

Question: Je joue bien, n'est-ce pas?   *I play well, don't I?*

Statement: Elle parle français.   *She speaks French.*

Question: Elle parle français, n'est-ce pas?   *She speaks French, doesn't she?*

Ce qu'ils disent

In conversation, rising intonation is the most frequently used type of question. The expression **n'est-ce pas?** is used often, to be sure that the other person is listening.

J'explique bien la situation,   *I'm explaining the situation well,*
   n'est-ce pas?   *aren't I?*
Oui, très bien.   *Yes, very well.*

Language

A Incrédule. Since you do not believe everything you hear, ask for a clarification of each of the following sentences, using yes-or-no questions.

MODEL: Patricia aime le français.
         Patricia aime le français?
         Est-ce que Patricia aime le français?
         Patricia aime le français, n'est-ce pas?

1. Les enfants étudient la carte.
2. Le prof ferme la porte.
3. Les étudiants fument beaucoup.
4. Tu aimes danser.
5. Jean et Marie habitent ici.
6. On écoute beaucoup la radio.

B Conversations interrompues. You are circulating from group to group at a party and you overhear several conversations. Ask the question that elicited the following answers. Be sure to use the correct pronoun. You have a choice as to which question form to use.

MODEL: Oui, je travaille après le cours.
         Tu travailles après le cours?
         Est-ce que tu travailles après le cours?
         Tu travailles après le cours, n'est-ce pas?

1. Oui, elles aiment la radio.
2. Oui, tu parles bien.
3. Oui, je chante bien.
4. Oui, vous mangez beaucoup.
5. Oui, on parle anglais ici.
6. Oui, elles jouent ensemble.

C **Interview.** You are going to interview someone about the francophone world. Ask questions using the pronoun **on** with the following expressions.

1. aimer les Américains
2. fumer beaucoup
3. regarder beaucoup la télé
4. aimer faire la bise
5. travailler beaucoup
6. parler anglais à Paris
7. manger bien
8. parler français au Québec

D *Tu* ou *vous*? Remember that in asking questions, you must indicate your relationship with the person to whom you are speaking by choosing between **tu** and **vous.** Use the following expressions to ask questions of your classmates and your teacher.

1. regarder beaucoup la télé?
2. aimer les étudiants?
3. adorer les enfants?
4. fumer?
5. aimer danser?
6. travailler beaucoup?

E **Questions personnelles.** Prepare five questions using -er verbs from the list on page 19. Interview a classmate in a small group or in front of the class.

IV. Numbers from 0 to 20

0 zéro	6 six	11 onze	16 seize
1 un	7 sept	12 douze	17 dix-sept
2 deux	8 huit	13 treize	18 dix-huit
3 trois	9 neuf	14 quatorze	19 dix-neuf
4 quatre	10 dix	15 quinze	20 vingt
5 cinq			

A. Numbers can be used alone, as in telephone numbers, or they can be used with nouns, for example, **trois livres.** When used with nouns, many numbers require pronunciation changes. You will study this in Chapter 4.

B. To express math problems, use the following:

Combien font deux et trois?	*How much are two and three?*
ou	*or*
Combien font deux **plus** trois?	*How much is two plus three?*
Deux plus trois font cinq.	*Two plus three is five.*
Combien font vingt **moins** six?	*How much is twenty minus six?*
Vingt moins six font quatorze.	*Twenty minus six is fourteen.*

Combien font quatre **multiplié par** trois?

Quatre multiplié par trois font douze.

Combien font seize **divisé par** quatre?

Seize divisé par quatre font quatre.

*How much is four **multiplied by** three?*

Four multiplied by three is twelve.

*How much is sixteen **divided by** four?*

Sixteen divided by four is four.

Language

Ⓐ Comptons! Count in French, continuing each series of numbers started below.

1. 1, 2, 3 . . . 20
2. 2, 4, 6 . . . 20
3. 1, 3, 5 . . . 19

4. 20, 19, 18 . . . 0
5. 20, 18, 16 . . . 0
6. 19, 17, 15 . . . 1

Ⓑ Calculons! Do the following math problems in French.

1. $12 + 3 =$
2. $11 + 2 =$
3. $2 \times 2 =$
4. $15 \div 3 =$
5. $1 + 5 =$
6. $16 - 2 =$
7. $3 \times 5 =$
8. $20 \div 2 =$

9. $9 + 8 =$
10. $5 - 5 =$
11. $4 \times 4 =$
12. $18 \div 3 =$
13. $2 + 17 =$
14. $20 - 1 =$
15. $6 \times 3 =$
16. $10 \div 2 =$

Culture

Ⓒ Au Québec. In Quebec, people say telephone numbers one digit at a time. Read the numbers for the following places you might have to call while in Quebec.

1. la Banque nationale du Canada   (800) 473-5149
2. la Bibliothèque nationale du Québec   (800) 363-9028
3. le Musée du Québec   (418) 643-2150
4. *Le Devoir*   (514) 985-3333
5. l'Hôpital général de Montréal   (514) 937-6011
6. l'Université du Québec   (418) 657-3551

Communication

Ⓓ Les maths. Divide into pairs and ask each other math problems, the answers to which range from 0 to 20.

MODEL: Student 1: *Combien font sept et deux?*
Student 2: *Sept et deux font neuf.*

Student 1: *Combien font cinq multiplié par deux?*
Student 2: *Cinq multiplié par deux font dix.*

communiquons

Commencer et terminer les conversations

The way people greet each other and manage conversations varies from culture to culture. An important consideration is the degree of familiarity between the speaker and the person being greeted. In France, people greet acquaintances (**les connaissances**) and business associates with a few words and a handshake. Good friends and relatives may embrace lightly and kiss on both cheeks (**faire la bise**). Formal situations require a word of greeting (e.g., **Bonjour**) and the title **Monsieur, Madame,** or **Mademoiselle,** but no last name.

Small talk in French involves topics similar to those of American conversations: the speakers' health, their recent activities, and the weather. Like English speakers, French speakers use a variety of expressions to end a conversation. However, the expressions **Salut!** and **Bonsoir!** can be used for both arrival and departure. In Quebec, **Bonjour** is also used in this way.

Expressions

▶ **On commence les conversations avec les amis / les connaissances.**

Salut!	*Hi!*
Tiens!	*Hey!*
Dis donc!	*Say!*

▶ **On commence les conversations avec les personnes importantes.**

Bonjour, Monsieur / Messieurs.	*Good morning / afternoon, sir / gentlemen.*
Bonjour, Madame / Mesdames.	*Good morning / afternoon, ma'am / ladies.*
Bonsoir, Mademoiselle / Mesdemoiselles.	*Good evening, miss / ladies.*

▶ **On commence les conversations avec les inconnus** *(strangers).*

Pardon, Monsieur.	*Pardon / Excuse me, sir.*
Excusez-moi, Madame.	*Excuse me, ma'am.*
Pardonnez-moi, Mademoiselle.	*Pardon me, miss.*

▶ **On continue les conversations.**

Ça va? / Comment ça va? / Ça va bien?	*How's it going?*
Comment allez-vous?	*How are you?*
Qu'est-ce que tu deviens?	*What are you up to?*
Qu'est-ce que vous faites?	*What are you doing?*
Quoi de neuf?	*What's new?*
Il fait chaud!	*It's hot!*
Il fait froid!	*It's cold!*

▶ **On termine les conversations.**

A bientôt.	*See you soon.*
A ce soir.	*See you this evening.*
A demain.	*See you tomorrow.*
A la prochaine.	*See you next time.*
A tout à l'heure.	*See you a little later.*
Bonne nuit.	*Good night. (when one is going to bed)*
Bonsoir.	*Good evening. / Good night.*
Salut.	*So long.*
Au revoir.	*Good-bye.*

Interaction

Marie rencontre (meets) *Monsieur Dupont.*

MARIE:	Bonjour, Monsieur!
M. DUPONT:	Bonjour, Marie. Comment ça va?
MARIE:	Ça va, merci. Et vous?
M. DUPONT:	Pas mal. Qu'est-ce que vous faites?
MARIE:	J'étudie l'anglais à l'université.
M. DUPONT:	Très bien. A la prochaine!

Activités

Ⓐ What would the person mentioned in the following situations be most likely to say?

1. Jacques is kissing his mother good night.
2. Patricia has just run into a friend on campus.

3. Philippe and his English teacher arrive at the classroom at the same time.
4. Cécile is leaving class, but she will see her classmates the next day.
5. Anne and Marie are going to different classes, but they have plans to study together later in the afternoon.
6. The school year is over, and you may not see your friends for several months.
7. You stop someone on the street to ask directions.
8. Marc is leaving the room, but he will be back in an hour.

Ⓑ Greet the student next to you.

Ⓒ Go to the front of the class with a classmate. Greet each other and say good-bye.

Ⓓ Write a short dialogue with a classmate involving two friends who run into each other, and then present it in front of the class.

lecture culturelle

Avant la lecture

In different francophone countries, the systems of higher education vary. A comparison of France, Canada, and Belgium, for instance, reveals that each university system has different entrance requirements. In France, students who plan to attend a university must pass the **baccalauréat** (or **bac**), a series of rigorous written and oral examinations, by the end of secondary school. French-speaking Belgian students are required to obtain a **certificat d'enseignement secondaire supérieur** (**CESS**), as well as to compile a dossier that includes their grade-point average and letters of recommendation. French-speaking students in Quebec must submit a dossier, as well as present a **diplôme d'études collégiales** (**DEC**), which they earn after thirteen to fourteen years of schooling (by comparison with the twelve years required in the United States). Other differences between American and francophone universities include the following points:

- There are more than four thousand institutions of higher learning (public and private universities, colleges, and community colleges) in the United States, compared with fewer than one hundred fifty in France, forty in Belgium, and fewer than two hundred in all of Canada.
- Most French-speaking universities in Europe are public, and tuition costs are extremely low.

Elle prépare le bac

- University campuses are not as common in French-speaking European countries. Students can therefore choose to live at home with their parents to save rent, or, if the university is not close by, they can live in dormitories or apartments in town.
- Sports are part of university life, but they do not constitute big business in Europe.
- Canada has a system of community colleges, but these do not exist in France or Belgium.

Activités

Ⓐ Skim the list of **facultés** at the Université de Liège on page 28 to find out which **faculté** someone studying Romance languages would attend.

Ⓑ Examine the course list for the **baccalauréat d'anthropologie** at the Université Laval on page 28 to determine which of the following courses are required and which are elective:

Anthropology of Native American Peoples

Introduction to Anthropology

Anthropology of Language

Qualitative Methods in Anthropology

Prehistory and Archaeology

L'université

The screen captures on page 28 are taken from the actual university Web sites. You will need the information they contain in order to complete **Activitiés A** and **B**.

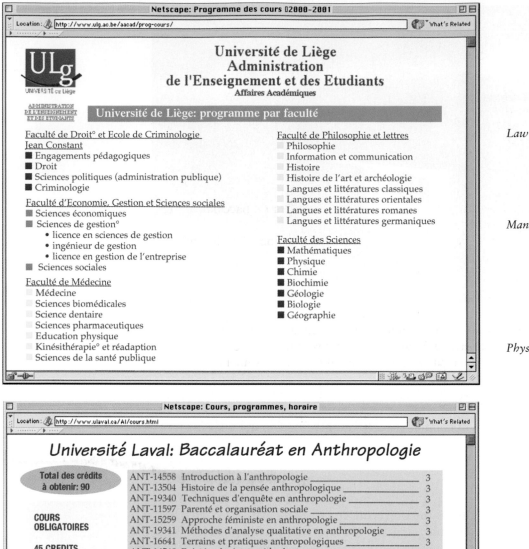

Netscape: Programme des cours ◻2000-2001

Location: http://www.ulg.ac.be/aacad/prog-cours/

ULg
UNIVERSITÉ de Liège

ADMINISTRATION
DE L'ENSEIGNEMENT
ET DES ETUDIANTS

Université de Liège
Administration
de l'Enseignement et des Etudiants
Affaires Académiques

Université de Liège: programme par faculté

Faculté de Droit° et Ecole de Criminologie
Jean Constant
◼ Engagements pédagogiques
◼ Droit
◼ Sciences politiques (administration publique)
◼ Criminologie

Faculté d'Economie, Gestion et Sciences sociales
◼ Sciences économiques
◼ Sciences de gestion°
   • licence en sciences de gestion
   • ingénieur de gestion
   • licence en gestion de l'entreprise
◼ Sciences sociales

Faculté de Médecine
▢ Médecine
▢ Sciences biomédicales
▢ Science dentaire
▢ Sciences pharmaceutiques
▢ Education physique
▢ Kinésithérapie° et réadaption
▢ Sciences de la santé publique

Faculté de Philosophie et lettres
▢ Philosophie
▢ Information et communication
▢ Histoire
▢ Histoire de l'art et archéologie
▢ Langues et littératures classiques
▢ Langues et littératures orientales
▢ Langues et littératures romanes
▢ Langues et littératures germaniques

Faculté des Sciences
◼ Mathématiques
◼ Physique
◼ Chimie
◼ Biochimie
◼ Géologie
◼ Biologie
◼ Géographie

Law

Management

Physical therapy

Netscape: Cours, programmes, horaire

Location: http://www.ulaval.ca/Al/cours.html

Université Laval: Baccalauréat en Anthropologie

Total des crédits à obtenir: 90

ANT-14558	Introduction à l'anthropologie	3
ANT-13504	Histoire de la pensée anthropologique	3
ANT-19340	Techniques d'enquête en anthropologie	3
ANT-11597	Parenté et organisation sociale	3
ANT-15259	Approche féministe en anthropologie	3
ANT-19341	Méthodes d'analyse qualitative en anthropologie	3
ANT-16641	Terrains et pratiques anthropologiques	3
ANT-14560	Epistémologie et méthode	3

COURS OBLIGATOIRES

45 CREDITS

ANT-11603	Anthropologie politique	3
ANT-11608	Anthropologie des Inuits	3
ANT-11609	Anthropologie des Amérindiens	3
ANT-11624	Idéologie et religions	3
ANT-11627	Ethnohistoire	3
ANT-13522	Minorités ethniques et nationalitaires	3
ANT-17513	Orient-Occident	3
ANT-17870	Sexualités et cultures	3
ANT-15035	Anthropologie écologique	3
ANT-15052	Anthropologie et développement	3
ANT-15778	Anthropologie urbaine	3
ANT-15965	Ethnomédecine	3

COURS A OPTION

45 CREDITS

Description du cours ANT-14558, Introduction à l'anthropologie

Comment° comprendre la diversité humaine par l'analyse comparative et l'ethnographie. L'organisation socioculturelle: économie, politique, religion, parenté, etc. Dynamique selon° l'inégalité des âges, des sexes, des nations et du pouvoir°. Apports° théoriques. Illustration par de multiples cas et étude ethnographique des participants.

How

according to power/ contributions

Après la lecture

Questions sur le texte

Ⓐ **Liège**

1. Où est Liège? Trouvez la ville *(Find the city)* sur une carte.
2. Dans quelle *(In which)* faculté étudiez-vous?
3. Quelles sont les différences et les ressemblances entre les programmes à l'Université de Liège et à votre université?

Ⓑ **Laval**

1. Où est Laval? Trouvez la ville sur une carte.
2. Quel est le nombre total de crédits nécessaires pour un baccalauréat en anthropologie à l'Université Laval?
3. A quelle heure *(At what time)* est le cours Introduction à l'anthropologie?

Activités

Ⓐ In groups, try (by using the many cognates found in the description) to reconstitute what you would learn if you were taking Introduction to Anthropology at the Université Laval. Then discuss what courses you are taking this semester. Ask your teacher for help if your department is not listed.

Ⓑ Given the differences between U.S. and francophone universities noted in the introduction, would you like to study abroad? Why or why not?

vocabulaire

Noms / Pronoms

une affiche	poster	**une classe**	classroom
alphabet *(m.)*	alphabet	**une clé**	key
ami(e)	friend	**un cours**	class / course
anglais *(m.)*	English	**une craie**	chalk
un autobus	bus	**un crayon**	pencil
un bureau	desk	**devoirs** *(m.)*	homework
un cadeau	present	**un dialogue**	dialogue
un café	café	**elle**	she / it
un cahier	notebook	**elles**	they
une carte	map	**un enfant**	child
cela	this	**un étudiant**	student
une chaise	chair	**un examen**	exam

un exercice	exercise	on	one / we / they
fac *(f.)*	university / school	une page	page
une faculté	university / school	une porte	door
une femme	woman	un professeur	teacher / professor
une fenêtre	window	une question	question
français *(m.)*	French	une radio	radio
un homme	man	un sac à dos	backpack
un hôtel	hotel	une salle de classe	classroom
il	he / it	un stylo	pen
ils	they	un tableau	board
je	I	une télévision	television
une leçon	lesson	tu	you
un livre	book	une université	university
nous	we		

Verbes

adorer	to adore	fumer	to smoke
aimer	to like / to love	habiter	to live
arriver	to arrive	inviter	to invite
chanter	to sing	jouer	to play
commencer	to begin	manger	to eat
continuer	to continue	montrer	to show
danser	to dance	ouvrir	to open
demander	to ask (for)	parler	to speak / to talk
donner	to give	regarder	to look (at) / to watch
écouter	to listen (to)	répéter	to repeat
étudier	to study	terminer	to end
expliquer	to explain	travailler	to work
fermer	to close		

Adjectifs / Adverbes

alors	then	multiplié	multiplied
beaucoup	much	neuf	nine
cinq	five	non	no
combien	how much	onze	eleven
deux	two	plus	more
divisé	divided	quatorze	fourteen
dix	ten	quatre	four
dix-huit	eighteen	quinze	fifteen
dix-neuf	nineteen	seize	sixteen
dix-sept	seventeen	sept	seven
douze	twelve	six	six
ensemble	together	treize	thirteen
huit	eight	trois	three
ici	here	un, une	one
le, la, l', les	the	vingt	twenty
mais	but	zéro	zero
moins	less		

Expressions

à	at, in	Je ne sais pas.	I don't know.
après	after	juste un peu	just a little
avec	with	lisez	read
ce soir	tonight	n'est-ce pas?	isn't it so?
c'est, ce sont	it is, they are	ou	or
Combien font... ?	How much is . . . ?	Ouvrez votre livre.	Open your book.
Comment dit-on... ?	How do you say . . . ?	par	by
Comment vous appelez-vous?	What's your name?	Qu'est-ce que _____ veut dire?	What does _____ mean?
de	of / from		
de rien	not at all	Qu'est-ce que c'est?	What is it?
eh bien	well then		
en cours	in class	répondez à / aux	answer
en français	in French		
en général	in general	voici	here is
est-ce que...	is / are / does / do	voilà	there is
faites	do		
Il n'y a pas de quoi.	Don't mention it. / You're welcome.		

commençons

grammaire

communiquons

lecture culturelle

vocabulaire

Mariage à Tahiti

La famille et les amis

OBJECTIVES

Language		Culture	Communication
■ Vocabulary for the family, friends, pastimes, and likes and dislikes	■ Vocabulary for occupations and nationalities	■ Family life	■ Describing people and things
■ Word stress	■ Descriptive adjectives	■ Pastimes	■ Counting
■ Negation	■ Numbers from 21 to 69	■ Introducing people	■ Making introductions
■ **Etre**	■ Ordinal numbers		

commençons

Au café

Gilles et Laure, deux étudiants, sont au café.

GILLES: Tiens, voilà Monique!

LAURE: Oui, elle est avec Jacques.

GILLES: C'est le dernier petit ami?

LAURE: Oui, il est sympathique et studieux.

GILLES: Et Monique, elle n'est pas studieuse?

LAURE: Si, elle est toujours première. Ils étudient l'anglais ensemble.

GILLES: L'anglais? Tu es certaine?

LAURE: Oui, quand ils ne sont pas au café!

Devant une boîte

Des jeunes gens sont devant une boîte.

MONIQUE: Où est la sœur de Patrick?

LAURE: Chantal? Elle arrive avec un copain américain.

CHANTAL: Salut! *(Elle embrasse Monique et Laure.)* Voici Jim. Il est étudiant avec Patrick; ils sont ensemble en philo à la fac.

JIM: Enchanté. Je suis très heureux de passer la soirée avec vous. *(A Chantal)* Ton frère n'est pas là?

MONIQUE: Si. Il gare la voiture.

CHANTAL: Il est toujours en retard. Entrons sans lui.

Etudions les dialogues

Ⓐ Au café

1. Est-ce que Monique est la petite amie de Gilles?
2. Elle est studieuse, n'est-ce pas? Et Jacques?
3. Est-ce que Jacques est toujours premier?
4. Jacques et Monique étudient le français, n'est-ce pas?

Ⓑ Devant une boîte

1. Est-ce que Monique est la sœur de Patrick?
2. Jim est américain, n'est-ce pas?
3. Jim et Patrick sont en philo?
4. Patrick gare la voiture, n'est-ce pas?

Mots clés

sont (être)	*are*	premier, -ère	*first*
au	*at*	es (être)	*are*
Tiens!	*Hey!*	certain, -e	*certain*
C'est (être)	*It's*	quand	*when*
le dernier, la dernière	*the latest*	ne... pas	*not*
un petit ami / une petite amie	*boyfriend / girlfriend*	devant	*in front of*
sympathique	*nice*	une boîte	*(night)club*
studieux, -euse	*studious*	des jeunes gens	*some young people*
Si.	*Yes, of course.*	où	*where*
toujours	*always*		

une sœur	*sister*	une soirée	*evening*
un copain / une copine	*friend, boyfriend / girlfriend*	ton frère *(m.)*	*your brother*
américain, -e	*American*	là	*here*
embrasse (embrasser)	*kisses*	gare (garer)	*is parking*
la philo(sophie)	*philosophy*	une voiture	*car*
Enchanté, -e.	*Delighted.*	en retard	*late*
suis (être)	*am*	Entrons (entrer)	*Let's go in*
heureux, -se	*happy*	sans	*without*
passer	*to spend*	lui	*him*

Faisons connaissance

In general, French families are much closer than American families. Many people remain in the areas where they were brought up as children, and families are not scattered all over the country as in the United States. Even after they are married, people continue to visit their parents regularly. The main meal on Sunday still provides an opportunity for family members to get together. The French calendar also has many holidays that constitute occasions for family reunions. In addition, it is not unusual for parents, married children, and sometimes grandparents to plan their summer vacations together.

Having friends is very important to French people. They tend, however, to have fewer friends than Americans do, because in their view, friendships take longer to get established and are not as casual as some relationships among Americans. The French still make a distinction between an acquaintance (**une connaissance**) and a friend (**un[e] ami[e]**). This is also true in the business world, where doing business with someone does not automatically turn the person into a friend. Most of the time, that person remains a business acquaintance (**une relation d'affaires**).

Un dîner en famille

Enrichissons notre vocabulaire

La famille de Marie *(Marie's family)*

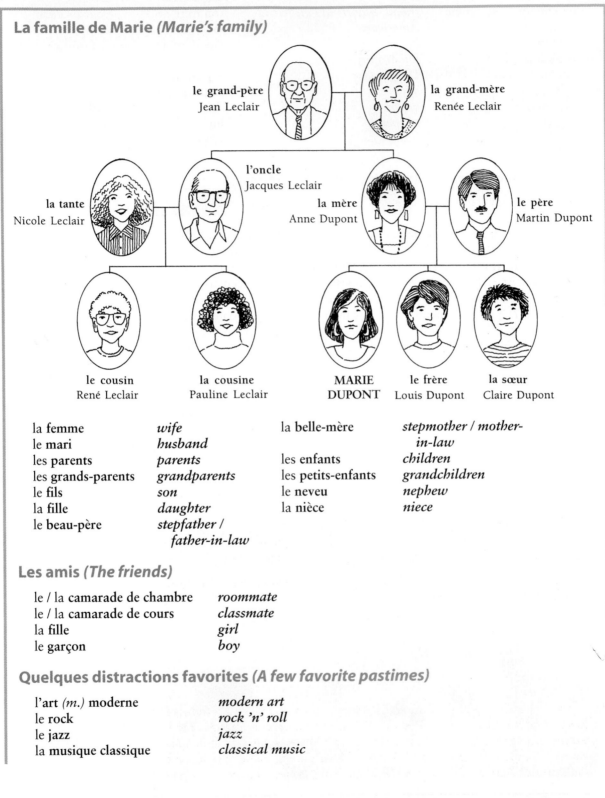

le grand-père
Jean Leclair

la grand-mère
Renée Leclair

l'oncle
Jacques Leclair

la tante
Nicole Leclair

la mère
Anne Dupont

le père
Martin Dupont

le cousin
René Leclair

la cousine
Pauline Leclair

MARIE DUPONT

le frère
Louis Dupont

la sœur
Claire Dupont

la **femme**	*wife*	la **belle-mère**	*stepmother / mother-in-law*
le **mari**	*husband*		
les **parents**	*parents*	les **enfants**	*children*
les **grands-parents**	*grandparents*	les **petits-enfants**	*grandchildren*
le **fils**	*son*	le **neveu**	*nephew*
la **fille**	*daughter*	la **nièce**	*niece*
le **beau-père**	*stepfather / father-in-law*		

Les amis *(The friends)*

le / la **camarade de chambre**	*roommate*
le / la **camarade de cours**	*classmate*
la **fille**	*girl*
le **garçon**	*boy*

Quelques distractions favorites *(A few favorite pastimes)*

l'**art** *(m.)* **moderne**	*modern art*
le **rock**	*rock 'n' roll*
le **jazz**	*jazz*
la **musique classique**	*classical music*

les **sports** (*m.*)	*sports*
les **matchs** (*m.*) de football	*soccer games*
les **films** (*m.*) à la télé	*films on TV*

J'aime / Je déteste (*I like / I dislike*)

aimer / aimer **faire**	*to love / to like **to do***
aimer bien	*to like*
aimer mieux	*to prefer*
apprécier	*to appreciate*
désirer	*to want*
détester / détester faire	*to hate / to hate to do*

—**Qu'est-ce que** tu aimes / aimes faire?	*What do you like / like to do?*
—J'adore **fréquenter** les **boîtes de nuit.**	*I love **to go to nightclubs.***
—**Moi aussi,** je fréquente souvent les **clubs** (*m.*).	*Me too, I often go to nightclubs.*
—Qu'est-ce que tu détestes?	*What do you hate?*
—Je déteste l'**hypocrisie** (*f.*) / l'**intolérance** (*f.*).	*I hate **hypocrisy / intolerance.***
—J'aime mieux la **sincérité.**	*I prefer **sincerity.***

Prononciation   Word stress in French

A. Learners of English as a foreign language often have difficulty putting stress on the proper syllables. Some words, such as *record* or *present,* can vary in pronunciation according to their meaning. Words can even vary according to region. For example, one says *laboratory* in England and *laboratory* in the United States. In French, however, all syllables receive the same stress except the last, which has a somewhat longer vowel.

Notice the difference in stress as you repeat the following pairs of English and French words after your teacher.

English	French
exam**ine**	exam**ine**
merchandise	marchan**dise**
a**part**ment	apparte**ment**

B. In French, each syllable has the same stress, and vowels maintain the same pronunciation throughout the word. This is not the case in English. For example, *Alabama* has the same written vowel throughout, but in its unaccented syllables (the second and the fourth), the vowel sound is reduced to / ə /, the "uh" sound. In French, vowel quality does not change.

Note the difference in the sound and quality of the boldface vowels as you repeat the following pairs of English and French words after your teacher.

English	French
university	université
television	télévision
laboratory	laboratoire

Exercice

Read the following sentences aloud, taking care to put equal stress on all syllables.

1. Je regarde la télévision.
2. Paul examine l'itinéraire.
3. Nous visitons le laboratoire.
4. Elle expédie les marchandises.
5. La police occupe l'appartement.
6. Le professeur est intelligent.

grammaire

I. Negation

You use the negative to indicate that something is not true or does not occur.

A. To make a statement negative in French, place the words **ne... pas** around the conjugated verb.

Est-ce qu'ils sont au café?	*Are they at the café?*
Non, ils **ne** sont **pas** au café.	*No, they aren't at the café.*

B. If there are two consecutive verbs, you still place the **ne... pas** around the conjugated verb to make the statement negative.

Ils aiment travailler ensemble?	*Do they like to work together?*
Non, ils **n'**aiment **pas** travailler ensemble.	*No they **don't** like to work together.*

C. If the verb begins with a vowel sound, you do not pronounce the **e** of **ne**, and you write **n'**.

Elle **n'**est pas studieuse.	*She isn't studious.*
Tu **n'**es pas étudiant.	*You aren't a student.*

Even before a consonant, the **e** of **ne** is rarely pronounced.

Vous n~~e~~ parlez pas bien.   *You don't speak well.*
Je n~~e~~ ferme pas la fenêtre.   *I am not closing the window.*

The pronunciation of the **s** of **pas** before a vowel is optional.

Ils ne sont pas‿au café. ⎱
Ils ne sont pas / au café. ⎰   *They aren't at the café.*

Ce qu'ils disent

In casual conversation, the French leave out the **ne** of the negation. This is particularly the case with young people. However, they would never write that way, and you must always use **ne** to maintain an appropriate style.

Speaking	**Writing**
On mange pas beaucoup.	On **ne** mange pas beaucoup.
Il écoute pas la radio.	Il **n'**écoute pas la radio.
C'est pas un stylo.	Ce **n'**est pas un stylo.

Language

Ⓐ **Mais non!** You think your friend Robert is always wrong. Contradict every sentence he says.

MODEL: Nadine joue avec les enfants.
           Nadine ne joue pas avec les enfants.

1. Je danse avec les sœurs de Louise.
2. Le frère de Jean parle beaucoup.
3. Les parents de Michelle adorent la musique.
4. Tu apprécies l'art moderne.
5. Vous travaillez bien.
6. Marthe et Jean mangent souvent.

Culture

Ⓑ **En France?** Answer the following questions based on your knowledge of life in France.

1. On parle anglais avec les copains?
2. Les femmes travaillent?
3. Les Français fument beaucoup de cigares?
4. Ils détestent la musique américaine?
5. Les parents voyagent avec les enfants?
6. Les Français fréquentent les cafés?

En famille. Complete the following statements as they apply to your family and you. If your answer is negative, give your own alternative or use one of the suggestions in parentheses.

MODEL: J'aime l'art. (la musique)
Non, je n'aime pas l'art. J'aime la musique.

1. Je travaille mal. (bien / beaucoup / souvent)
2. J'apprécie l'intolérance. (l'hypocrisie / la sincérité)
3. Mes *(My)* parents aiment le rock. (jouer / danser)
4. Mes frères / sœurs adorent étudier. (les sports / les cafés)
5. Ma *(My)* famille et moi, nous regardons les matchs de football. (écouter la radio / fréquenter les clubs)
6. Ma famille déteste mes copains. (adorer / apprécier)

C'est vrai? Divide into groups of three or four and find someone who can answer truthfully each of the following questions in the negative.

1. Tu chantes bien?
2. Tu écoutes souvent la radio?
3. Tu fumes?
4. Tu travailles beaucoup?
5. Tu fréquentes les clubs?
6. Tu aimes regarder les films à la télé?

II. The verb *être*

You use être to indicate a state of being or to describe something.

A. *Etre*

1. The verb être is irregular, so you must memorize its forms.

être *(to be)*					
je **suis**	/ ʒø sɥi /	*I am*	nous **sommes**	/ nu sɔm /	*we are*
tu **es**	/ ty ɛ /	*you are*	vous **êtes**	/ vu zɛt /	*you are*
il **est**	/ i lɛ /	*he is*	ils **sont**	/ il sɔ̃ /	*they are*
elle **est**	/ ɛ lɛ /	*she is*	elles **sont**	/ ɛl sɔ̃ /	*they are*
on **est**	/ ɔ̃ nɛ /	*we are*			

2. The final written consonant of each form of être is usually not pronounced. When the verb occurs before a vowel, however, the **t** of the third-person forms is pronounced.

Elle est͜ étudiante. *She is a student.*
Ils sont͜ en philo. *They are philosophy majors.*

3. The other final consonants may be pronounced and linked before vowels, but it is not necessary.

> Je suis_étudiant.
> Je suis / étudiant. } *I am a student.*

> Tu es_américaine.
> Tu es / américaine. } *You are American.*

B. *Etre* with occupation or nationality

1. When **être** is used with occupation or nationality, no article is used—the noun or adjective follows the verb directly.

Marie **est médecin.**	*Marie is a **doctor.*** (noun)
Christian **est allemand.**	*Christian is **German.*** (adjective)

L'orthographe

Note that adjectives of nationality are not capitalized in French. When used as nouns, however, they are capitalized.

Il invite trois **Français.**	*He is inviting three **French people.***
Les **Canadiens** travaillent beaucoup.	***Canadians** work a lot.*

2. Some occupations have one form for both the masculine and feminine.

Mme Dupont est **professeur.**	*Mrs. Dupont is **a teacher.***
L'auteur est aussi **actrice.**	*The author is also **an actress.***

Mots clés   *Professions and nationalities*

Les professions (f.)			

un acteur,
  une actrice
un agent de police
architecte *(m./f.)*
artiste *(m./f.)*
un auteur
	un avocat,
	  une avocate
	  lawyer
	diplomate *(m./f.)*
	économiste *(m./f.)*
	un écrivain
		un ingénieur
		journaliste *(m./f.)*
		un médecin
		  doctor
		un musicien,
		  une musicienne
			un président,
			  une présidente
			un programmeur,
			  une programmeuse
			secrétaire *(m./f.)*

Les nationalités (f.)			

allemand, allemande
  German
américain, américaine
	anglais, anglaise
	canadien, canadienne
		espagnol, espagnole
		  Spanish
			français, française
			italien, italienne

Ce qu'ils disent

1. In very informal conversation, the **u** of **tu** is often dropped with the verb **être.** This may occur in sentences in which the **ne** of the negative is also dropped.

   T'es certain?   *Are you sure?*
   T'es pas anglais!   *You aren't English!*

2. In Quebec, French speakers have invented the feminine form **écrivaine** because there are so many active women writers there. The **Québécois** in general are more relaxed about vocabulary than the French; one also sees **auteure** and **professeure.**

Language

Ⓐ **Les professions.** What do the following people do? Use the correct form of **être.**

MODEL: Je / étudiant(e)
       Je suis étudiant(e).

1. L'oncle de Jean / musicien
2. Les cousines de Patricia / profs
3. Vous / diplomate
4. Nous / étudiants
5. Elle / agent de police
6. La nièce de Robert / journaliste

INGÉNIEUR
TECHNICO-COMMERCIAL EXPORT
bilingue allemand

Culture

B **Des célébrités françaises.** Identify the professions of the following famous French-speaking people.

MODEL: Debussy
Il est musicien.

1. Gérard Depardieu
2. l'Inspecteur Clouseau
3. Marc Chagall
4. René Descartes
5. Juliette Binoche
6. Maurice Ravel
7. Gustave Eiffel
8. Emile Zola et Victor Hugo

C **Familles célèbres.** With a partner, try to match the following people with their famous French-speaking family members, living or dead.

MODEL: La fille de Victor Hugo?
C'est Adèle H.

1. le mari de Joséphine   a. Simone de Beauvoir
2. la femme de Louis XVI   b. Charlotte
3. le mari de Marie Curie   c. Napoléon
4. l'amie de Sartre   d. Paul
5. le frère de Camille Claudel   e. Pierre
6. la fille de Serge Gainsbourg et Jane Birkin   f. Marie-Antoinette

Communication

D **Les célébrités.** Can you think of famous people with the following occupations and nationalities? Work in groups of three or four to see which group can find the most names within the time limit given by your teacher.

MODEL: Student 1: *Qui* (Who) *est acteur?*
Student 2: *Daniel Auteuil est acteur.*

actrice	français(e)	espagnol(e)	anglais(e)
médecin	américain(e)	diplomate	journaliste
artiste	avocat	étudiant(e)	auteur
canadien(ne)	italien(ne)	musicien(ne)	agent de police

E **Mes connaissances.** Ask each other the following questions about people you know. Be sure to answer in complete sentences, and honestly!

1. Le professeur est français?
2. Est-ce que le président est intelligent? Et le vice-président?
3. Les parents de votre *(your)* copain / copine sont sympathiques?
4. Les camarades de cours sont américains?
5. Est-ce que vous êtes studieux (-euse)?
6. Vous êtes toujours premier (-ère)?

III. Descriptive adjectives

You use adjectives to describe people and things.

In French, adjectives are usually placed after the noun, and they may vary in pronunciation or spelling or both, to agree in gender and number with the nouns they describe.

A. Singular and plural forms

1. Most adjectives add a written -s to form the plural. The pronunciation does not change.

   L'étudiant **intelligent** travaille
   beaucoup.
   Les étudiants **intelligents** travaillent
   beaucoup.

   The **intelligent** student works
   a lot.
   Intelligent students work
   a lot.

   Elle n'est pas **studieuse?**
   Elles ne sont pas **studieuses.**

   She isn't **studious?**
   They aren't **studious.**

2. Masculine adjectives that end in a written -s or -x do not have a different plural form.

   Le professeur **français** est
   ambitieux.
   Les professeurs **français** sont
   ambitieux.

   The **French** professor is
   ambitious.
   The **French** professors are
   ambitious.

3. To describe a mixed group of masculine and feminine nouns, use the masculine plural form of the adjective.

   Marie et Pierre ne sont pas **italiens.**   Marie and Pierre are not **Italian.**

B. Masculine and feminine forms

1. Masculine singular adjectives that end in a silent -e do not change in pronunciation or spelling in the feminine.

   Le garçon est **sympathique.**
   La fille est **sympathique.**

   The boy is **nice.**
   The girl is **nice.**

   Some adjectives that have the same masculine and feminine forms are as follows:

agréable *pleasant*	inutile *useless*	riche
désagréable	magnifique	simple
difficile	malade *sick*	sincère
facile *easy*	optimiste	stupide
fantastique	pauvre *poor*	sympathique
formidable *great*	pessimiste	timide
hypocrite	possible	utile *useful*
impossible	rapide	

2. Masculine singular adjectives that end in a pronounced vowel or a pronounced consonant are spelled differently in the feminine, although they are pronounced the same.

> José est **espagnol**.   *José is **Spanish**.*
> Maria est **espagnole**.   *Maria is **Spanish**.*

Some adjectives that change in spelling but not in pronunciation are as follows:

compliqué, compliquée *complicated*	**impoli, impolie** *impolite*
espagnol, espagnole	**poli, polie** *polite*
fatigué, fatiguée *tired*	**seul, seule** *alone*
fermé, fermée *closed*	**vrai, vraie** *true*

3. Many adjectives end in a silent consonant in the masculine. To form their feminine, add a written **-e** and pronounce the consonant.

> Le livre **français** est magnifique.   *The **French** book is great.*
> La musique **française** est magnifique.   *French music is great.*

Some adjectives that end in a silent consonant in the masculine are as follows:

absent, absente	**indépendant, indépendante**
anglais, anglaise	**intelligent, intelligente**
charmant, charmante	**intéressant, intéressante**
chaud, chaude *hot*	**laid, laide** *ugly*
compétent, compétente	**mauvais, mauvaise** *bad (quality)*
content, contente *happy*	**méchant, méchante** *bad (character)*
fascinant, fascinante	
français, française	**ouvert, ouverte** *open*
froid, froide *cold*	**présent, présente**
incompétent, incompétente	**prudent, prudente** *careful*

4. Some adjectives end in a nasal vowel in the masculine. To create their feminine forms, add a written **-e**. If the masculine ends in **-en,** however, double the **-n** before adding the **-e**. In both cases, the vowel loses its nasality and the **-n** is pronounced.

> Il n'est pas **italien**, mais **américain**.   *He's not **Italian**, but **American**.*
> Elle n'est pas **italienne**, mais **américaine**.   *She's not **Italian**, but **American**.*

Some adjectives of this type are as follows:

-ne	**-nne**
américain, américaine	**ancien, ancienne** *old*
certain, certaine	**canadien, canadienne**
féminin, féminine	**italien, italienne**
masculin, masculine	**parisien, parisienne**
mexicain, mexicaine	

Ce qu'ils disent

> One of the adjectives used most frequently in conversations is **bien,** which means *good, great,* or *fine.* It is invariable; that is, it never changes in pronunciation or spelling.
>
> | | |
> |---|---|
> | L'hôtel est **bien!** | *It's a **good** hotel.* |
> | Ses copains sont **bien.** | *His friends are **great.*** |

5. To form the feminine of adjectives that end in **-eux,** add the sound / z / and change the **-x** to **-se.**

Le garçon est **paresseux.**	*The boy is **lazy.***
La fille est **paresseuse.**	*The girl is **lazy.***

Some adjectives ending in **-eux, -euse** are as follows:

affectueux,	**généreux, généreuse**
affectueuse *affectionate*	**heureux, heureuse** *happy*
affreux, affreuse *terrible*	**malheureux,**
ambitieux, ambitieuse	**malheureuse** *unhappy*
courageux, courageuse	**paresseux, paresseuse** *lazy*
dangereux, dangereuse	**sérieux, sérieuse**
ennuyeux, ennuyeuse *boring*	**studieux, studieuse**

L'orthographe

> Two quick rules of thumb that will work for spelling most French adjectives are as follows:
>
> *Plural:*   Add an **-s** to any letter except **s** or **x.**
> *Feminine:* Add an **-e** to any letter except unaccented **e, x,** or **en.**

Language

Ⓐ Les descriptions. Describe the following people with the definite article and the adjective provided.

MODEL: étudiant / français   *l'étudiant français*

1. actrice / formidable
2. étudiante / intelligent
3. auteur / ennuyeux
4. enfant / paresseux
5. hommes / fatigué
6. femmes / indépendant

Ⓑ C'est comment? Describe the following people and things with the verb **être** and the correct form of the adjective provided.

MODEL: garçons / fatigué   *Les garçons sont fatigués.*

1. musique / affreux
2. filles / sympathique
3. livres / facile
4. Ils / malade
5. professeurs / intéressant
6. Nous / fatigué   *(two possibilities)*
7. Je / américain   *(two possibilities)*
8. Vous / poli   *(four possibilities)*

Culture

C L'Amérique. Describe what you believe are traditional French attitudes toward Americans and American culture, using the following nouns and adjectives.

MODEL: les Américains: agréable / désagréable
Les Américains sont agréables.

1. les Américains: sympathique / froid
2. la musique: ennuyeux / fantastique
3. la télévision: fascinant / affreux
4. le café: mauvais / formidable
5. les présidents: compétent / incompétent
6. la politique *(politics):* prudent / dangereux

Communication

D Les qualités. Use the adjectives listed below to describe the following people and things. You may also provide your own adjectives if you prefer. Find a classmate who disagrees with you.

MODEL: *Les journalistes sont ambitieux et intelligents.*

sincère	ennuyeux	inutile	charmant
hypocrite	ambitieux	fantastique	intelligent
formidable	paresseux	fatigué	heureux
compliqué	utile	méchant	malheureux

1. secrétaires
2. professeurs
3. rock
4. télévision
5. université
6. Français
7. médecins
8. président
9. femmes
10. hommes
11. étudiants
12. Je

E Vos préférences. Tell your preferences by choosing one item from each of the columns and adding any necessary words. Work with a classmate to find a consensus.

MODEL: *J'aime les hommes intelligents.*
Je n'aime pas les enfants méchants.

A	B	C	
J'aime	femmes	désagréable	généreux
Je n'aime pas	hommes	compétent	stupide
	familles	incompétent	sérieux
	médecins	charmant	sympathique
	étudiants	impoli	sincère
	Français *(pl.)*	intelligent	méchant
			???

IV. Numbers from 21 to 69 / Ordinal numbers

You use cardinal numbers to count or quantify *(one, two, three . . .)* and ordinal numbers *(first, second, third . . .)* to rank people or things.

A. Cardinal numbers

A few of the cardinal numbers from 20 to 69 are as follows:

20 vingt	30 trente	40 quarante
21 vingt et un	31 trente et un	41 quarante et un
22 vingt-deux	32 trente-deux	44 quarante-quatre
23 vingt-trois	36 trente-six	47 quarante-sept

50 cinquante	60 soixante
51 cinquante et un	61 soixante et un
55 cinquante-cinq	67 soixante-sept
58 cinquante-huit	69 soixante-neuf

1. **Et** is used with the numbers 21, 31, 41, 51, and 61; the **t** of **et** is never pronounced.

2. The succeeding numbers are hyphenated.

3. The **t** of **vingt** is pronounced from 21 to 29.

4. In **soixante** (/ swa sɑ̃t /), the **x** is pronounced / s /.

5. Except for **un / une**, numbers do not agree in either number or gender with the nouns they modify.

Quatre garçons habitent ensemble.	*Four boys live together.*
Voilà **neuf** filles.	*There are nine girls.*
but: **vingt et une** pages	*twenty-one pages*

B. Ordinal numbers

1. To form ordinal numbers, in most cases simply add the suffix **-ième** to the cardinal number.

cardinal	ordinal
deux	**deuxième** *second*
trois	**troisième** *third*
dix-sept	**dix-septième** *seventeenth*
vingt	**vingtième** *twentieth*
vingt et un	**vingt et unième** *twenty-first*

C'est le **troisième** médecin de la famille.	*He / She is the **third** doctor in the family.*
Nous terminons le **quatrième** exercice.	*We are finishing the **fourth** exercise.*

2. Three exceptions are as follows:

cardinal	ordinal
un, une	premier, première
cinq	cinquième
neuf	neuvième

In addition, for **deuxième** an alternate form, **second / seconde,** is used.

L'orthographe

1. If the cardinal number ends in **-e,** you must drop the written **-e** before adding the **-ième** suffix.

cardinal	ordinal
onze	**onzième**
trente	**trentième**
cinquante-quatre	**cinquante-quatrième**

2. Ordinal numbers may be abbreviated as follows:

premier → 1er première → 1ère

cinquième → 5ème or 5e vingtième → 20ème or 20^e

Language

A **Comptons!** Count in French.

1. 30, 31, 32... 40
2. 21, 24, 27... 69
3. 25, 26, 27... 35
4. 20, 22, 24... 68
5. 21, 23, 25... 69
6. 60, 59, 58... 50

B **Calculons!** Do the following problems in French.

1. $10 + 11 =$
2. $14 + 16 =$
3. $47 - 19 =$
4. $15 + 16 =$
5. $21 - 12 =$
6. $18 + 22 =$
7. $30 + 15 =$
8. $20 + 29 =$
9. $24 + 27 =$
10. $19 + 33 =$
11. $40 - 22 =$
12. $55 - 34 =$

Culture

C **Au lycée.** The French count years of schooling in reverse order of the American system. The *sixth grade* is **la sixième,** but *seventh grade* is **la cinquième.** Give the French equivalent of the following grades. (The *senior year* is called **la terminale.**)

1. sixth grade
2. seventh grade
3. eighth grade
4. freshman
5. sophomore
6. junior

D **Au téléphone.** You are in Paris and want to plan your visits to the following places in advance. Read the names and numbers to your hotel switchboard operator.

1. Air Canada   01. 43. 20. 14. 15
2. le Centre Georges Pompidou   01. 45. 08. 25. 00
3. Notre-Dame   01. 40. 33. 22. 63
4. la tour Eiffel   01. 47. 05. 44. 13
5. La Tour d'Argent   01. 43. 44. 32. 19
6. Le Moulin Rouge   01. 42. 64. 33. 69

Communication

E **Les priorités.** Rank the following things according to how important they are to you. Use the phrases **En premier:...**, **En deuxième:...**, and so on, to do so. Find a classmate who agrees with you and one who disagrees.

les amis   la profession
être riche   la nationalité
la famille   être heureux (-euse)

communiquons

Faire les présentations

The basic rules of politeness that exist in the United States are also observed in France. You must introduce people who do not know each other, and you must pay attention to the style of language you use. To introduce someone who is older than you, use one of the following formal expressions. For friends and relatives, one of the informal expressions is appropriate.

Expressions

▶ **On présente les adultes.**

Monsieur / Madame / Mademoiselle, je voudrais vous présenter Marie.
Sir / Ma'am / Miss, I would like you to meet Marie.

Permettez-moi de vous présenter Marie.
Allow me to introduce Marie to you.

Enchanté, Monsieur / Madame / Mademoiselle.
Pleased to meet you, sir / ma'am / miss.

Très heureux (-euse) (de faire votre connaissance).
A pleasure (to meet you).

▶ **On présente les amis.**

Robert, je voudrais te présenter Marie.	*Robert, I'd like you to meet Marie.*
Robert, je te présente Marie.	*Robert, this is Marie.*
Robert, voilà Marie.	*Robert, this is Marie.*
Salut, Marie.	*Hi, Marie.*
Bonjour, Marie, ça va?	*Hello, Marie, how are you?*

Interaction

Solange et son père rencontrent un professeur sur le campus.

SOLANGE: Bonjour, M. Renaud!

M. RENAUD: Bonjour, Solange. Comment allez-vous?

SOLANGE: Très bien. Je voudrais vous présenter mon père.

M. RENAUD: Enchanté, Monsieur.

LE PÈRE DE SOLANGE: Très heureux.

Je voudrais te présenter mon ami Mamadou.

Ⓐ What would you say to introduce the following people?

1. your roommate and your
   teacher

3. your parents and your
   faculty advisor

2. your roommate and an old
   friend from high school

4. your sister and someone in
   your class

Ⓑ Divide into groups of three and practice introducing your classmates to
each other.

lecture culturelle

Avant la lecture

The twentieth century was witness to many changes in marriage practices. Until the 1960s in most European countries and in North America, a majority of couples married and had children. There were few divorces and only a small number of children born out of wedlock. In later decades, many couples chose to live together before marriage, either as a prelude to marriage or in lieu of it. France's enactment of the **Pacte civil de solidarité** in 1999 lent support to such **cohabitation** or **union libre**. The **pacte** accords unmarried couples, both heterosexual and homosexual, a range of spousal rights.

In the last several years, more couples have been choosing to marry. The year 2000 was hailed in France as "the year of marriages and babies" by the French national statistical institute INSEE. That year, more than 300,000 marriages were celebrated—the highest number in seventeen years. The French health care system is very supportive of families. Paid maternity leave has long been offered, and in an effort to enable both parents to share in the care of their newborns, the French recently instituted two weeks of paid paternity leave.

As you may know, French children are often given compound first names. Male and female names are combined in some instances: Jean-Marie (m.), Marie-Pierre (f.), Jean-Luc (m.), Marie-Thérèse (f.). Since France is a predominantly Catholic country, most French children are named after saints. It is common for children to celebrate not only their birthday but also their saint's day. Nowadays, with the number of non-Catholic families on the rise in France, parents have the option to choose nonreligious first names.

Below, you will find two announcements (**faire-part**). The birth announcement is from France; the wedding announcement is from Canada.

Activité

Skim the two **faire-part** to find the following information:

1. How much does baby Thomas weigh?
2. Who is announcing the marriage of Sandrine and Alexandre (Sandrine and Alexandre themselves, one set of parents, or both sets of parents)?
3. What were the dates of each of these life events?

La famille

Faire-part de naissance

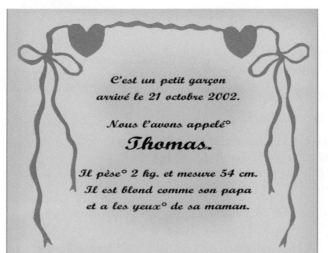

C'est un petit garçon
arrivé le 21 octobre 2002.

Nous l'avons appelé°
Thomas.

Il pèse° 2 kg. et mesure 54 cm.
Il est blond comme son papa
et a les yeux° de sa maman.

l'avons... *named him*

weighs

eyes

Faire-part de mariage

Monsieur et Madame Georges Durand
sollicitent l'honneur de votre présence
au mariage de leur fille
Sandrine
et
Alexandre
fils de Monsieur et Madame Alain Duhamel
et vous prient° d'assister° à la cérémonie nuptiale
samedi, le quatorze septembre deux mil deux
à quatorze heures trente°
en l'église° de Saint-Pierre.

Après la cérémonie, bar ouvert° à la salle du
Club Optimiste 50, rue St-Jean.

vous... *ask you /*
to attend

2:30 P.M.
church

open

Après la lecture

Questions sur le texte

Ⓐ **Faire-part de naissance**

1. Comment est-ce que Thomas ressemble à son père?
2. Comment est-ce que Thomas ressemble à sa mère?

Ⓑ **Faire-part de mariage**

1. Où est la cérémonie de mariage?
2. En quelle année *(In what year)* est la cérémonie?
3. A quelle heure est le mariage de Sandrine et Alexandre?

Activités

Ⓐ Thomas's weight and height are measured in kilograms and centimeters. Look up the conversion from the metric system to the U.S. system of weights and measures to determine Thomas's equivalent weight and height in inches and pounds.

Ⓑ Think of some French-sounding last names. Together with your classmates, compile a list.

Ⓒ Go to the French and Canadian telephone directories on the World Wide Web. Key in the common last name (**nom**) and city (**localité/ville**) for each entry listed here. Leave the rest of the blanks empty. Submit your query. Then, write down one or two first names (**prénoms**) for each last name. Next, jot down a telephone number and address for one of the people you find. Finally, with a partner, practice saying the number and address in French. Remember to say Canadian telephone numbers one number at a time and French numbers two at a time.

French directory

Last names *(Noms)*	City *(Localité)*
1. Berger	Angers
2. Dupont	

Fill in some first names:

(a) _____ (b) _____ Berger

(a) _____ (b) _____ Dupont

Canadian directory

Last names *(Noms)*	City *(Localité)*
1. Pelletier	Laval
2. LeCompte	

Fill in some first names:

(a) _____ (b) _____ Pelletier

(a) _____ (b) _____ LeCompte

vocabulaire

Noms / Pronoms

un acteur	actor	**une boîte**	club
une actrice	actress	**une boîte de nuit**	nightclub
un agent de police	policeman	**camarade de**	
architecte *(m./f.)*	architect	**chambre** *(m./f.)*	roommate
artiste *(m./f.)*	artist	**camarade de**	
un auteur	author	**cours** *(m./f.)*	classmate
un avocat	lawyer	**un club**	club / nightclub
un beau-père	stepfather /	**une connaissance**	acquaintance
	father-in-law	**un copain**	friend (male)
une belle-mère	stepmother /	**une copine**	friend (female)
	mother-in-law	**un/une cousin(e)**	cousin

diplomate *(m./f.)*	diplomat	un musicien	musician
une distraction	entertainment	une nationalité	nationality
économiste *(m./f.)*	economist	un neveu	nephew
un/une écrivain(e)	writer	une nièce	niece
une famille	family	un oncle	uncle
une femme	wife	parents *(m.)*	parents
une fille	girl / daughter	un père	father
un film	film	un/une petit(e) ami(e)	boyfriend / girlfriend
un fils	son	petits-enfants *(m.)*	grandchildren
le football	soccer	la philosophie	philosophy
un frère	brother	un/une président(e)	president
un garçon	boy	une profession	profession
une grand-mère	grandmother	un programmeur	computer programmer
un grand-père	grandfather		
grands-parents *(m.)*	grandparents	une relation d'affaires	business acquaintance
hypocrisie *(f.)*	hypocrisy		
un ingénieur	engineer	le rock	rock
intolérance *(f.)*	intolerance	une secrétaire	secretary
le jazz	jazz	la sincérité	sincerity
jeunes gens *(m.)*	young people	une sœur	sister
journaliste *(m./f.)*	journalist	une soirée	evening
lui	him	sports *(m.)*	sports
un mari	husband	une tante	aunt
un médecin	doctor	une télé	TV
une mère	mother	une voiture	car
moi	me / I		

Verbes

apprécier	to appreciate	être	to be
désirer	to desire / to wish	fréquenter	to go to / go out with
détester	to hate	garer	to park
embrasser	to kiss	passer	to spend (time)
entrer	to enter / go in		

Adjectifs / Adverbes

absent	absent	bien	nice
affectueux	affectionate	canadien	Canadian
affreux	horrible	certain	certain / some
agréable	pleasant	charmant	charming
allemand	German	chaud	hot
ambitieux	ambitious	cinquante	fifty
américain	American	cinquième	fifth
ancien	old / former	classique	classical
aussi	also	compétent	competent

compliqué	complicated	mexicain	Mexican
content	happy	ne... pas	not
courageux	courageous	neuvième	ninth
dangereux	dangerous	onzième	eleventh
le dernier	the latest	optimiste	optimistic
désagréable	unpleasant	où	where
deuxième	second	ouvert	open
difficile	difficult	paresseux	lazy
dix-septième	seventeenth	parisien	Parisian
enchanté	delighted	pauvre	poor
ennuyeux	boring	pessimiste	pessimistic
espagnol	Spanish	premier	first
facile	easy	présent	present
fantastique	fantastic	prudent	careful
fascinant	fascinating	quand	when
fatigué	tired	quarante	forty
favori	favorite	quatrième	fourth
féminin	feminine	quelque	some
fermé	closed	rapide	fast
formidable	sensational / terrific	riche	rich
froid	cold	second	second
généreux	generous	sérieux	serious
heureux	happy	seul	alone
hypocrite	hypocritical	si	yes
impoli	impolite	simple	simple
impossible	impossible	sincère	sincere
incompétent	incompetent	soixante	sixty
indépendant	independent	souvent	often
intelligent	intelligent	studieux	studious
intéressant	interesting	stupide	stupid
inutile	useless	sympathique	nice
italien	Italian	timide	shy
là	there	ton	your
laid	ugly	toujours	always
magnifique	magnificent	trente	thirty
malade	sick	trentième	thirtieth
malheureux	unhappy	troisième	third
masculin	masculine	utile	useful
mauvais	bad	vingtième	twentieth
méchant	mean, bad	vrai	true

Expressions

aimer bien	to like / to be fond of	détester faire	to hate doing
aimer faire	to enjoy doing	devant	in front of
aimer mieux	to prefer	en retard	late
art moderne	modern art	sans	without
au	at	Tiens!	Hey!

RESTAURANT LA GOULETTE

SPECIALITES TUNISIENNES

SALLE S/SOL

On va manger un couscous

CHAPITRE

3

commençons

grammaire

communiquons

lecture culturelle

vocabulaire

Au restaurant

OBJECTIVES

Language	Culture	Communication
■ Vocabulary for beverages and food	■ French restaurants	■ Ordering food
■ Silent consonants	■ North African food	■ Making commands and requests
■ Indefinite and partitive articles	■ Cajun and Creole cooking	■ Expressing quantity
■ The verb **avoir** and idiomatic expressions		
■ Use of articles		
■ The imperative		

commençons

A La Goulette

Sylvie, programmeuse à IBM, et Maude, journaliste à Elle, *sont dans un restaurant tunisien à Paris. Elles regardent la carte.*

LE GARÇON: Bonsoir. Vous désirez?

SYLVIE: Je voudrais un apéritif. Vous avez du Martini?

LE GARÇON: Oui, mademoiselle. Du rouge ou du blanc?

SYLVIE: Du rouge, s'il vous plaît.

LE GARÇON: Mademoiselle aussi?

MAUDE: Non, merci.

SYLVIE: J'ai faim ce soir. Je voudrais un couscous au mouton.

LE GARÇON: Vous aussi, mademoiselle?

MAUDE: Non, je ne mange pas de viande. Je suis végétarienne. Je voudrais un couscous aux légumes.

LE GARÇON: Qu'est-ce que vous prenez comme boisson?

SYLVIE: Apportez de l'eau minérale et un pichet de vin rouge, s'il vous plaît.

LE GARÇON: Très bien. J'apporte l'apéritif tout de suite.

Etudions le dialogue

1. La Goulette est un restaurant anglais?
2. Maude aime l'apéritif?
3. Est-ce que Sylvie et Maude demandent du vin blanc?
4. Est-ce que Sylvie a faim ce soir?
5. Maude mange un couscous au mouton aussi?
6. Le garçon est poli *(polite)* ou impoli?

Mots clés

dans	*in*	au	*with*
un restaurant	*restaurant*	le mouton	*mutton*
tunisien(ne)	*Tunisian*	de	*any*
une carte	*menu*	la viande	*meat*
un garçon	*waiter*	aux	*with*
je voudrais	*I would like*	légumes *(m.)*	*vegetables*
un apéritif	*before-dinner drink*	prenez (prendre)	*take*
avez (avoir)	*have*	comme	*for*
du	*any*	une boisson	*drink*
rouge	*red*	apportez (apporter)	*bring*
blanc	*white*	eau minérale *(f.)*	*mineral water*
s'il vous plaît	*please*	un pichet	*pitcher*
J'ai faim. (avoir faim)	*I am hungry.*	un vin	*wine*
ce soir	*this evening*	tout de suite	*immediately*
un couscous	*couscous*	un/une végétarien(ne)	*vegetarian*

Faisons connaissance

France offers a variety of restaurants that range from very elegant and expensive establishments to little **bistrots** or **cafés** where people can go for a simple meal. Fast-food places have become popular, and McDonald's is a presence in all major French cities. Unlike its American counterpart, however, McDonald's does serve wine and beer.

Restaurants featuring foreign cooking are also very popular in France. Because of France's ties to its former colonies in North Africa, Tunisian, ▶

Le fast-food en France

Algerian, and Moroccan specialties are particularly well liked. Couscous is a typical Arab dish made with a wheat product called semolina (**la semoule**), which resembles rice somewhat. On top of the grain one puts a vegetable stew and often a choice of meat. Mutton, lamb chops, or chicken are the usual choices.

Traditionally, Arabs do not drink alcohol, but North African restaurants in France do serve it. An **apéritif** usually contains alcohol and is drunk before meals to increase one's appetite. **Un pichet** would be the house wine, which is less expensive than bottled wine. Many French people order mineral water in restaurants; they rarely drink tap water.

Menus are posted in the windows of restaurants. Patrons often have a choice of ordering individual items from **la carte** or a three- or four-course meal from **le menu.** Many choose the latter because the fixed price (**prix fixe**) usually includes not only the tip (**service compris**), but often a beverage as well. The selection normally offers an appetizer (**le hors-d'œuvre**), a main course (**le plat principal**), a vegetable, and a choice of cheese, fruit, or dessert.

Enrichissons notre vocabulaire

Des boissons *(Drinks)*

du **thé**

de l'**eau**

du **café**

du **coca**

du **vin**

du **lait**

de la **bière**

du **jus de fruit**

De la nourriture *(Food)*

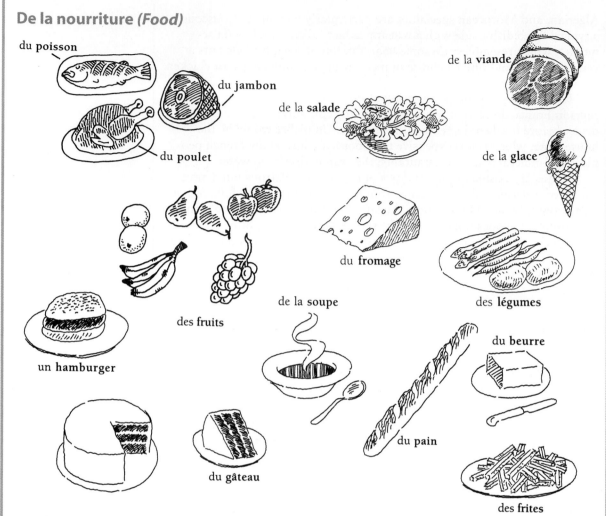

du poisson

du jambon

de la **salade**

de la **viande**

du **poulet**

de la **glace**

du **fromage**

des **légumes**

de la **soupe**

des **fruits**

du **beurre**

un **hamburger**

du **gâteau**

du **pain**

des **frites**

Quelques expressions utiles *(Some useful expressions)*

boire: je **bois,** tu **bois,** vous **buvez**	*to drink: I drink, you drink, you drink*
commander	*to order*
consommer	*to consume, to eat or drink*
déjeuner	*to have lunch*
dîner	*to eat dinner or supper, to dine*
goûter	*to taste (a food), to have a snack*
préparer	*to prepare*
recommander	*to recommend*

—Comment **trouvez**-vous le couscous à La Goulette?

*How do you **like** the couscous at La Goulette?*

—Il est **délicieux;** c'est le **plat préféré** de Sylvie.

*It is **delicious**; it is Sylvie's favorite dish.*

—Quelle **sorte de cuisine** est-ce qu'elle aime?

*What kind of **cooking** does she like?*

—La cuisine tunisienne.

Tunisian cooking.

Prononciation   Silent consonants

A. As mentioned in the preliminary chapter, a large number of written consonants are not pronounced in French.

Il est paresseux.	*He is lazy.*
Jacques et Gilles étudient l'anglais.	*Jacques and Gilles are studying English.*

B. Final written consonants are rarely pronounced.

Nous ne travaillons pas.	*We aren't working.*
Les livres sont ennuyeux.	*The books are boring.*

There are, however, exceptions to this rule.

Marc apporte un apéritif.	*Marc is bringing a drink.*
Il travaille seul.	*He works alone.*

C. In general, a final silent **e** shows that the preceding consonant is pronounced.

Elle regarde la carte.	*She is looking at the menu.*
Jean est présent; Jeanne est absente.	*Jean is present; Jeanne is absent.*

Remember that the final silent **e** marks the difference between masculine and feminine nouns and adjectives such as **étudiant / étudiante** and **froid / froide.**

Exercice

Read the following sentences aloud, paying particular attention to silent consonants.

1. Les trois Français étudient l'anglais.
2. Nous sommes très contents.
3. Jean est méchant et il n'est pas heureux.
4. Elles dansent avec le fils de Monsieur Legrand.
5. Tu es paresseux et tu n'études pas.
6. Mon amie canadienne est médecin.

PALAIS JAMAI
FES

grammaire

I. Indefinite and partitive articles

You use indefinite and partitive articles with names of people, things, and ideas to indicate something not specific or previously mentioned.

As mentioned in Chapter 1, an article almost always accompanies a noun in French. The most frequently used articles in French are *nondefinite*—they stand for a person, thing, or idea that is not specific and not defined.

There are two types of nondefinite articles because in French, as in English, there is a distinction between nouns that can be counted *(count nouns)*, and those that cannot *(mass nouns)*. *Indefinite articles* are used with count nouns. *Partitive articles* are used with mass nouns.

A. Indefinite articles

indefinite articles				
	singular		*plural*	
masculine	un ⎫	*a, an*	des ⎫	*some*
feminine	une ⎭		des ⎭	

1. Indefinite articles refer to one unspecified object or person or to an unspecified group of *countable* objects or persons.

Elles sont dans **un** restaurant tunisien.	*They are in a Tunisian restaurant.*
Je commande **des** fruits comme dessert.	*I order fruit for dessert.*

2. The indefinite articles **un** and **une** correspond to the English *a* or *an*. The masculine singular indefinite article is **un**, pronounced / ɛ̃ / before a consonant and / ɛ̃n / before a vowel.

un bureau	/ ɛ̃ by ʀo /	*a desk, **an** office*
un mur	/ ɛ̃ myʀ /	*a wall*
un stylo	/ ɛ̃ sti lo /	*a pen*
un élève	/ ɛ̃ ne lɛv /	*a (male) student*

3. The feminine singular indefinite article is **une**, always pronounced / yn /.

une carte	/ yn kaʀt /	*a map, a card, a menu*
une école	/ y ne kɔl /	*a school*
une élève	/ y ne lɛv /	*a (female) student*
une photo	/ yn fo to /	*a photograph*

4. The plural indefinite article is **des,** pronounced / de / before consonants and / dez / before vowel sounds.

des chaises *(f.)*	*(some) chairs*
des examens *(m.)*	*(some) exams*

B. Partitive articles

partitive articles		
before masculine, singular nouns	**du**	
before feminine, singular nouns	**de la**	} *some, any*
before singular nouns beginning with a vowel	**de l'**	

1. Partitive articles refer to an unspecified portion, or *part,* of an object that is measurable but not countable, such as water, wine, or meat. **Du, de la,** and **de l'** may be expressed in English as *some* or *any,* or may not be expressed at all.

Je désire **du** vin.	*I want wine. [or:]* *I want **some** wine.*
Elle mange **de la** tarte.	*She is eating pie. [or:]* *She is eating **some** pie.*
Apportez **de l'**eau minérale!	*Bring **some** mineral water!*

2. The masculine partitive article for mass nouns—those that are not counted—is **du,** pronounced / dy /.

du chocolat	*hot chocolate, chocolate candy*
du gâteau	*cake*
du sel	*salt*
du sucre	*sugar*

3. The feminine partitive article for mass nouns is **de la.**

de la confiture	*jam*
de la farine	*flour*
de la moutarde	*mustard*
de la crème	*cream*

4. The singular partitive article **de l'** is used with masculine or feminine mass nouns that start with a vowel sound.

de l'agneau *(m.)*	*lamb*
de l'alcool *(m.)*	*alcohol*
de l'argent *(m.)*	*money*
de l'huile *(f.)*	*oil*

5. When referring to a countable unit of a mass noun, such as *a bottle* of beer, *a loaf* of bread, or *two cups* of coffee, the indefinite article is used.

Mass		Count	
de la bière	*(some) beer*	**une** bière	*a bottle of beer*
du café	*(some) coffee*	**un** café	*a cup of coffee*
du couscous	*(some) couscous*	**un** couscous	*a meal of couscous*
du gâteau	*(some) cake*	**un** gâteau	*a cake*
du pain	*(some) bread*	**un** pain	*a (loaf of) bread*
de la pizza	*(some) pizza*	**une** pizza	*a pizza*

Attention!

In negative sentences, all indefinite and partitive articles change to **de** (**d'** before a vowel sound), except when the verb is **être.**

Elle mange **de la** viande.   Elle **ne** mange **pas de** viande.
Vous avez **des** frites?   Vous **n'**avez **pas de** frites?
J'ai **un** stylo.   Je **n'**ai **pas de** stylo.

but:

C'est **un** stylo.   Ce **n'**est **pas un** stylo.
Le Martini **est un** apéritif.   Le Perrier **n'**est **pas un** apéritif.

Language

Ⓐ **Des noms.** Identify the following nouns as primarily count nouns or mass nouns and provide an indefinite or partitive article as appropriate.

1. stylo	4. homme	7. sucre	10. élève
2. crayon	5. photo	8. moutarde	11. fille
3. lait	6. crème	9. eau	12. sel

Ⓑ **Au supermarché.** You are going to a supermarket and have begun a list of what you need. Finish your list by adding the correct partitive or indefinite article.

huile
confiture
lait
stylo
glace
beurre
eau minérale
bière
gâteau
apéritif

C **Je suis désagréable!** You are very unpleasant today! Contradict the following statements.

MODEL: J'invite des copains.
Je n'invite pas de copains.

1. Marc commande du fromage.
2. Ils demandent du vin.
3. Le mouton est un légume.
4. Nous invitons des amis.
5. Je mange de la viande.
6. Catherine prépare de la salade.
7. Tu bois un coca.
8. Le couscous est un apéritif.

Culture

D **A l'épicerie.** In a neighborhood grocery store in France (**une épicerie**), you may have to ask the grocer to get your supplies. What do you have on your shopping list for a party you are giving this weekend for French friends?

MODEL: *Je voudrais du pain, du beurre et du lait.*

E **Qu'est-ce qu'ils vendent?** What do the following companies headquartered in French-speaking countries sell? Can you think of others?

MODEL: Chanel? *Ils vendent du parfum.* (They sell perfume.)

1. Mouton Cadet?
2. Labatt?
3. Evian?
4. Larousse?
5. Nestlé?
6. Knorr?
7. Martini?
8. La Vache Qui Rit?
9. Godiva?
10. Bic?

Communication

F Answer the following questions, using any of the suggested words below or your own ideas.

intéressant	ennuyeux	anglais	gâteau
simple	sérieux	formidable	vin
difficile	américain	de jazz	thé
fantastique	français	de rock	lait

MODEL: Quelle sorte de livres est-ce que tu aimes regarder?
J'aime regarder des livres intéressants.

1. Qu'est-ce qu'on trouve dans votre *(your)* frigidaire?
2. Quelle sorte de boissons est-ce que vous buvez?
3. Qu'est-ce que vous aimez manger?
4. Quelle sorte de films est-ce que vous regardez à la télé?
5. Quelle sorte de CD est-ce que vous écoutez?

G Interview a classmate to find out what he or she likes to eat.

MODEL: Student 1: *Est-ce que tu aimes manger de la tarte?*
Student 2: *Non, je ne mange pas de tarte.*

Student 1: *Est-ce que tu bois du thé?*
Student 2: *Oui, je bois du thé.*

II. The irregular verb *avoir* / Expressions with *avoir*

> You use **avoir** to state possession and to describe certain conditions.

A. *Avoir*

1. **Avoir** is an irregular verb, and you must memorize its forms.

avoir	(to have)				
j' **ai**	/ ʒe /	*I have*	nous **avons**	/ nu za vɔ̃ /	*we have*
tu **as**	/ ty a /	*you have*	vous **avez**	/ vu za ve /	*you have*
il **a**	/ i la /	*he has*	ils **ont**	/ il zɔ̃ /	*they have*
elle **a**	/ ɛ la /	*she has*	elles **ont**	/ ɛl zɔ̃ /	*they have*
on **a**	/ ɔ̃ na /	*we have*			

2. The final **s** of **nous, vous, ils,** and **elles** is pronounced / z / and the **n** of **on** is pronounced / n / in the affirmative because the verb forms start with a vowel sound. The **s** of **sont** *(they are)* is pronounced as / s /: **ils sont** → / il sɔ̃ /.

3. Before a vowel sound, **je** becomes **j'** and **ne** becomes **n'**.

J'ai du talent.	*I have talent.*
Je **n'**ai pas de patience.	*I don't have any patience.*

B. Expressions with *avoir*

Avoir is used in several idiomatic expressions.

Elle a chaud; ils ont froid.	*She is hot; they are cold.*
Je ne mange pas; je n'ai pas faim.	*I'm not eating; I'm not hungry.*
Elle désire de l'eau; elle a soif.	*She wants some water; she's thirsty.*
Vous n'avez pas raison, vous avez tort!	*You aren't right, you are wrong!*
—Quel âge avez-vous?	*How old are you?*
—J'ai dix-huit ans.	*I'm eighteen.*
Il y a une carte dans la classe.	*There's a map in the classroom.*
Il n'y a pas de vin.	*There isn't any wine.*

Attention!

Voilà is used to point out something; **il y a** merely indicates existence. Both take singular or plural objects.

Voilà le père de Luc!	*There's Luc's father! (over there)*
Voilà des touristes américains!	*There are some American tourists.*
Il y a du sucre dans le café?	*There is sugar in the coffee?*
Il y a des légumes dans un couscous.	*There are vegetables in a couscous.*

Mots clés   *Expressions with avoir*

avoir faim	*to be hungry*	avoir tort	*to be wrong*
avoir soif	*to be thirsty*	avoir ____ ans	*to be ____ years old*
avoir chaud	*to be hot*	il y a	*there is, there are*
avoir froid	*to be cold*	il n'y a pas	*there isn't, there aren't*
avoir raison	*to be right*		

Ce qu'ils disent

You saw in Chapter 2 that the **u** of **tu** often disappears in informal conversation when the verb is **être.** The same is true with **avoir.**

T'as froid?	*Are you cold?*
T'as pas faim?	*Aren't you hungry?*

Language

Ⓐ **Les copains.** Chantal is talking to her friends about other people. Make complete sentences by adding any necessary words.

1. Ils / avoir / souvent / tort
2. Tu / ne / avoir / pas / faim?
3. Les enfants de Jacques / avoir / clé
4. On / ne / avoir / pas / froid
5. Tu / avoir / raison
6. Je / ne / avoir / pas / frère
7. Vous / ne / avoir / pas / 21 / ans?
8. Jeanne / avoir / amis

Ⓑ **J'ai, je n'ai pas.** Name three things that you have with you, three things a classmate has with him or her, and one thing you do not have with you.

MODEL: *J'ai un stylo, deux crayons et des livres.*
Anne et Jacqueline ont de l'argent, des photos et un sac à dos.
Je n'ai pas de nourriture.

Culture

Ⓒ **En cours.** Look at the photograph of some French university students on page 7 and state what there is and is not to be found in the classroom.

MODEL: *Il y a des étudiants.*
Il n'y a pas de café.

D Mes amis. Describe the kind of friends you have, using the suggestions provided below or your own ideas.

MODEL: *J'ai des amis sympathiques.*

intéressant	intelligent	ennuyeux	studieux
bien	paresseux	sympathique	???

E Des célébrités. Name famous people who have the following things. Can you think of someone who does not have them? See if you agree with your classmates.

MODEL: du talent? *Gwyneth Paltrow a du talent.*
  Nicole Kidman n'a pas de talent.

1. de l'argent?
2. un restaurant?
3. beaucoup d'ex-femmes?
4. beaucoup d'ex-maris?
5. beaucoup d'enfants?
6. des étudiants intelligents?

F Questionnaire. Find out more about your classmates by asking them questions using the following expressions.

1. avoir froid ou chaud?
2. avoir soif ou faim?
3. avoir des frères ou des sœurs?
4. avoir quel âge?
5. avoir souvent raison ou tort?
6. avoir de la patience?

G Questions personnelles. Parlez de vous!

1. Vous avez souvent faim? Qu'est-ce que vous mangez?
2. Quelle boisson est-ce que vous commandez quand vous avez soif?
3. Quel âge avez-vous? Quel est l'âge idéal?
4. Est-ce que vous avez du talent? Quelle sorte? *(What kind?)*
5. Est-ce que vous avez de l'argent? Qu'est-ce que vous désirez avoir?
6. Vous désirez avoir des enfants? Combien de garçons et combien de filles?

III. Use of articles

You must always use articles with nouns, which name people, things, and ideas. The type of article you use determines the nature of the noun (specific or general, previously mentioned or not).

Now that you have learned the definite, indefinite, and partitive articles, it is essential to know when to use each kind.

A. Use of definite articles

1. Definite articles refer to one specific person or thing.

Elles regardent **la** carte.	*They are looking at **the** menu. (a specific menu)*
Tu as **le** livre?	*Do you have **the** book? (referring to a book just mentioned)*

2. They also refer to all of a given item in a generalized sense.

Les enfants aiment **le** chocolat.	*Children like chocolate. (in general)*
Je déteste **la** bière.	*I hate beer. (all beer)*

Verbs that lend themselves to use in a generalized sense include **aimer, aimer mieux, adorer, apprécier, détester.**

B. Use of indefinite and partitive articles

1. Indefinite articles refer to a person or thing not previously mentioned.

Tu as **un** stylo?	*Do you have **a** pen? (any pen)*
Elles sont dans **un** restaurant tunisien.	*They are in **a** Tunisian restaurant. (an unspecified Tunisian restaurant)*

2. Partitive articles refer to an unspecified portion, or part, of an object that is measurable but not countable.

Apportez **de l'**eau minérale.	*Bring **some** mineral water. (not all of it)*
Jacques n'a pas **de** talent.	*Jacques doesn't have **any** talent. (none at all)*

Many verbs almost always imply a portion of an item and therefore take a partitive article. These include **consommer, demander, désirer, boire, manger,** and the expression **je voudrais.**

3. In the negative, all indefinite and partitive articles become **de** or **d',** but definite articles do not change.

—Vous buvez **du** lait.
—Non, je **ne** bois **pas de** lait.

—Tu aimes **le** café?
—Non, je **n'**aime **pas le** café.

Attention! ───────────────────────────────

Translating into English will *not* help you choose the proper article. In French, you must decide whether the item is considered in a general or specific sense or as a portion. For example, compare the following sentences:

*I like **wine**.* → J'aime **le** vin.
*I want **wine**.* → Je voudrais **du** vin.

4. If you modify a noun with an adverb of quantity, use only the preposition **de** (**d'** before a vowel).

Il n'a pas **assez de** talent.	*He doesn't have **enough** talent.*
Elle a **beaucoup de** devoirs.	*She has **a lot of** homework.*
Moins de sel, s'il vous plaît!	***Less** salt, please.*
Je voudrais **un peu de** crème.	*I would like **a little** cream.*
Nous avons **peu d'**argent.	*We have **little** money.*
Un peu plus de café, Madame?	***A little more** coffee, ma'am?*
Elle a **trop de** poisson.	*She has **too much** fish.*

trop de poisson

beaucoup de devoirs

pas assez de talent

Mots clés

assez de	*enough*	(un) peu de	*(a) little*
beaucoup de	*many, a lot*	plus de	*more*
moins de	*less*	trop de	*too many, too much*

Language

A **Mais non!** Contradict the following statements.

1. Il déteste la bière.
2. Ils mangent un couscous.
3. Tu aimes le pain français?
4. Nous avons du gâteau.
5. Christine et Michel demandent de la soupe.
6. Anne-Marie a de la salade.

B **Les préférences.** Make complete sentences, adding any necessary words to indicate what the following people like.

1. Catherine / désirer / fromage
2. Je / demander / mouton
3. Elles / adorer / glace
4. enfants / détester / légumes
5. Vous / ne / apprécier / pas / vin français
6. Tu / ne / bois / pas / eau

Culture

C **Les végétariens.** Some French people are extremely conscious about eating healthy foods, and some do not eat meat (**végétariens**) or do not eat anything of animal origin, such as fish, eggs, or milk (**végétaliens**). State their habits by making complete sentences from the words below.

MODEL: commander / fruits
         Ils commandent des fruits.

1. aimer / agneau
2. manger / beaucoup / légumes
3. détester / poulet
4. adorer / pain
5. désirer / salade
6. avoir / faim!

Ⓓ **Dînons dans un restaurant élégant.** Eating habits vary widely from one culture to another. Below is a list of eight items frequently associated with eating. Using the verb **avoir,** guess which ones you would have with dinner at a nice restaurant and which ones the restaurant would not have.

MODEL: eau   *Ils ont de l'eau.*
        «French dressing»   *Ils n'ont pas de «French dressing».*

1. thé froid
2. salade après la viande
3. café au lait
4. coca

5. un plat avec du sel et du sucre
6 fruits comme dessert
7. lait comme boisson
8. tarte

Communication

Ⓔ **J'ai ça!** State whether or not you have the following.

sœur	enfants	carte de France
radio	CD	camarade de chambre
frère	stylo	amis français
voiture		

Ⓕ **Mes préférences.** Tell whether you would like more or less / fewer of the following items using **plus de** or **moins de.**

1. argent
2. devoirs
3. camarades de chambre
4. cours

5. exercices
6. amies
7. français en classe
8. étudiants sur le campus

Ⓖ **Mes qualités.** Using expressions of quantity, tell to what degree you have the following qualities.

MODEL: *Je n'ai pas assez de patience.*

patience	talent	courage
ambition	énergie	tact
imagination	prestige	intelligence

Ⓗ **Mes opinions.** Express your opinions on the following subjects by completing the sentences in a logical manner.

1. Je n'aime pas...
2. J'apprécie...
3. Le professeur n'a pas...
4. Je mange...

5. Mon restaurant préféré prépare...
6. Les Français aiment...
7. Ma mère adore...
8. Mon frère / Ma sœur a...

Ⓘ **Questions personnelles.** A table!

1. Qu'est-ce que vous mangez quand vous avez faim?
2. Qu'est-ce que vous buvez quand vous avez très soif?
3. Qu'est-ce que vous aimez comme boisson?
4. Qu'est-ce que vous détestez? appréciez?
5. Vous préparez le dîner? Qu'est-ce que vous aimez préparer?
6. Est-ce que vous êtes végétarien(ne)? Pourquoi *(why)* ou pourquoi pas?

IV. The imperative

You use the imperative to give orders, advice, or suggestions.

A. Forms

1. To form the imperative, you simply drop the pronoun subject, except in the **tu** form in which the final **s** of the present indicative is also dropped.

Indicative:	**Vous apportez** un pichet de vin rouge.
Imperative:	**Apportez** un pichet de vin rouge.

Indicative:	**Vous invitez** des étudiants.
Imperative:	**Invitez** des étudiants.

Indicative:	**Tu manges** du pain.
Imperative:	**Mange** du pain.

2. There is also an imperative in the **nous** form. Equivalent to the English *Let's . . .* , it is used to suggest something.

Parlons!	*Let's talk!*
Travaillons ensemble.	*Let's work together.*

3. The negative imperative is formed with **ne... pas** like the other verb forms you have learned.

Ne regarde pas la télévision.	*Don't watch television.*
Ne parlez pas en classe.	*Don't talk in class.*
Ne mangez pas de sel.	*Don't eat salt.*

B. Irregular verbs in the imperative

The imperative forms of **être** and **avoir** are irregular.

Sois	/ swa /		**Aie**	/ e /	
Soyons	/ swa jɔ̃ /	} *Be*	**Ayons**	/ e jɔ̃ /	} *Have*
Soyez	/ swa je /		**Ayez**	/ e je /	

Sois prudent!	*Be careful!*
Ne **soyez** pas méchante!	*Don't be mean!*
Ayez de la patience!	*Have patience!*

C. Politeness

In French, as in English, one normally adds *please* to the imperative for politeness. There are two such forms in French.

Ouvrez la porte, **s'il vous plaît.**	*Open the door, **please.** (formal)*
Ferme la fenêtre, **s'il te plaît.**	*Close the window, **please.** (familiar)*

Ce qu'ils disent

The imperative is increasingly used only as a written form, often in advertising. In conversations, the French will often give directions in declarative sentences.

Vous commencez ici.	*Begin here.*
Tu donnes l'argent au garçon.	*Give the money to the waiter.*

NE MANQUEZ PAS LE FILM
DU DIMANCHE SOIR
SUR FRANCE 2
GAGNEZ
UN VOYAGE
A HOLLYWOOD
POUR DEUX
(POUR UNE SEMAINE)
ET 1500 EUROS
(Page 78)

NOUVEAU Par téléphone, consultez
le service boursier de **Capital**
● Dès 8 h 15 : la valeur du jour que nous conseillons à l'achat.
● A 8 h 30, 12 h et 18 h : le point sur la séance boursière.
● Les cours des actions du SRD (Service de règlement différé).
0 892 892 111*
* Service payant : 0,34 € la minute.

Language

Ⓐ Des ordres. Give commands with the following expressions and address them to the people indicated, being polite in doing so.

MODEL: *(to your classmate)* parler avec le professeur
  Parle avec le professeur.

1. *(to your brother)* danser avec Jacqueline
2. *(to your teacher)* fermer la porte
3. *(to a group of friends)* préparer un couscous
4. *(to your roommate)* étudier beaucoup
5. *(to your family, including yourself)* écouter la radio
6. *(to your classmates)* travailler ensemble

Culture

Ⓑ En vacances! A large proportion of the French population goes on vacation around August 1, creating throughout the country enormous traffic jams and dangerous driving conditions, often due to driver fatigue. On the radio, you hear advice constantly about what to do to be a safe driver. Form sentences in the imperative to give this type of advice, and do not forget to use the negative when appropriate.

1. consommer / alcool
2. être / prudent
3. avoir / patience
4. manger beaucoup
5. consommer souvent / café
6. être «macho»
7. étudier / carte
8. demander / apéritifs au café

C **Des conseils.** In pairs, one student will read a statement, and the other will give advice. Use the imperative of the verbs listed below or those of your own choosing in your sentences.

MODEL: J'ai chaud.
Ouvre la fenêtre.

étudier   manger   fermer   inviter   boire   écouter

1. J'ai faim.
2. La leçon est difficile.
3. J'ai soif.
4. Nous avons froid.
5. Je suis seul.
6. J'adore le rock.

D **Je suis stressé(e)!** Give advice to your classmates as to what they should do to relax and have a good time. You may refer to the following list for ideas, but feel free to add your own ideas.

MODEL: *Mangez de la glace. Ne travaillez pas.*

écouter les CD de...
regarder... à la télévision
manger...
(ne... pas) étudier...
inviter...
parler avec...
boire...
(ne... pas) travailler

communiquons

Exprimer des quantités

Being able to express quantity in French is very useful because these expressions apply to a variety of situations such as shopping for food and talking about people and objects. You have already learned adverbs of quantity; you can also use adjectives and nouns.

Expressions

▶ **On utilise des noms de quantité.**

As with adverbs of quantity, the preposition **de (d')** is used after nouns of quantity; no article is used.

Ils commandent une bouteille de vin.	*They're ordering a bottle of wine.*
Un kilo de farine, s'il vous plaît!	*A kilo (2.2 pounds) of flour, please!*
Je voudrais un litre d'eau minérale.	*I would like a liter of mineral water.*
Elle désire une livre de beurre.	*She wants a pound of butter.*
Le garçon apporte une tasse de thé.	*The waiter is bringing a cup of tea.*
Sylvie commande un verre de vin rouge.	*Sylvie is ordering a glass of red wine.*
Tu manges une tranche de pizza?	*You are eating a slice of pizza?*
L'enfant demande un morceau de gâteau.	*The child is asking for a piece of cake.*

▶ **On utilise des adjectifs de quantité.**

The adjectives **plusieurs** and **quelques** do not take the preposition **de.**

Il y a plusieurs cartes dans la salle de classe.	*There are several maps in the classroom.*
Marie invite quelques amis.	*Marie is inviting a few friends.*

Interaction

Jacques et Monique sont au café.

LE GARÇON: Vous désirez?

MONIQUE: Une tasse de thé et un verre de vin blanc.

LE GARÇON: Tout de suite.

A **La quantité.** Match up the words of quantity in the left column with the foods in the right. There are several possibilities for each one, especially if you make some nouns plural.

1. beaucoup	a. poisson
2. tasse	b. gâteau
3. verre	c. pain
4. tranche	d. café
5. kilo	e. eau minérale
6. litre	f. couscous
7. trop	g. apéritif
8. plusieurs	h. coca
9. assez	i. beurre
10. quelques	j. bière

B **La santé.** Are you eating better for your health? Use the expressions of quantity and the foods below to indicate any changes you have made in your diet.

MODEL: *Je mange moins de sel et beaucoup de fruits.*

moins de	plus de	ne... pas
peu de	beaucoup	ne... pas beaucoup

1. café
2. viande
3. chocolat
4. eau
5. sucre
6. légumes
7. poisson
8. poulet
9. crème
10. frites
11. huile
12. vin

Le Plateau Rouge
43 €

1/2 Homard frais du Canada
Langoustines roses, 1/2 Tourteau
Grosses crevettes roses et petites grises
Araignée de mer

*Prix service compris 15%

lecture culturelle

Avant la lecture

Louisiana, known the world over for the animated and graceful city of New Orleans, is the home of Cajun and Creole cuisine. The terms *Cajun* and *Creole* are both deeply rooted in the history of the state, as we shall see. The territory of Louisiana, which the French explorer La Salle claimed in 1682 for France and named in honor of King Louis XIV, originally extended from the Great Lakes to the Gulf of Mexico. The United States bought Louisiana in 1803 from Napoleon Bonaparte for $15 million in the transaction known as the Louisiana Purchase.

The term *Creole* can be applied to both the descendants of the French and Spanish nobles who settled in Louisiana in the late 1600s and the descendants of the black slaves who first arrived in the early 1700s. The term *Cajun,* a deformation of *Acadian,* refers to the descendants of farmers from northern France who, in the early part of the seventeenth century, settled in Acadia (today New Brunswick and Nova Scotia, Canada). In 1755, the British deported the Acadians to the bayous of southern Louisiana and to other parts of the thirteen colonies, a tragedy that Henry Wadsworth Longfellow recounted in his famous epic poem *Evangeline* (1847).

Cajun cooking reflects the culture and survival skills of the French who settled in Louisiana. When they arrived, the Cajuns adopted and later adapted the culinary practices of the Amerindians and other inhabitants of southern Louisiana. Hence, Cajun recipes frequently call for game, fish, and many different spices. Creole cuisine, with its savory yet delicate sauces, is said to be more refined, reflecting its aristocratic origins. Today the distinction between Cajun and Creole cuisine is less clear than it once was. Each, for example, features its own version of jambalaya and gumbo, two of the most popular traditional dishes of Louisiana.

Activités

Ⓐ What Cajun or Creole dishes are you familiar with?

Ⓑ Locate the following items in the introduction to the recipe: **salade, pain, viande, tomates, poulet, bœuf.** Identify the definite, indefinite, or partitive article that precedes each term, and look up the English translation.

Ⓒ List the various units of measurement in the jambalaya recipe. If you wanted to make this or another recipe based on the metric system, how would you convert the quantities to cups and teaspoons? Write out the quantities you would need.

La cuisine cajun et créole

Jambalaya

Temps° de préparation: 20 minutes   *time*
Temps de cuisson°: 75 minutes   *cooking*
Coût°: raisonnable   *cost*
Difficulté: très facile

5   C'est un classique de la cuisine créole, un plat unique et bien garni°   *ample, robust*
qu'on sert° avec du pain français et une salade verte.   *that one serves*

Le jambalaya, tel que décrit ci-dessous° avec des tomates, de la viande   *tel que... as described below*
et du bouillon de poulet, est une recette créole. Par contre°, si vous enlevez°   *However / si... if you remove*
les tomates, remplacez° le bouillon de poulet par un bouillon de bœuf et   *replace*
10   augmentez le Tabasco avec une pointe de cayenne, vous obtiendrez° un   *will obtain*
jambalaya cajun.

En un mot°, comme nous l'avons expliqué, dans la cuisine louisianaise, la   *word*
cuisine créole est plus riche et plus raffinée. La cuisine cajun est plus
rudimentaire et plus épicée° mais les racines° sont les mêmes°.   *spicy / roots, origins / same*

15

Ingrédients

225 g de chaurice (saucisse° épicée)   *sausage—here, chorizo*

454 g d'andouille ou de saucisse fumée

60 ml de tasso°   *a type of spice (smoked*
cayenne pepper flavor) /
500 ml d'oignon haché°   *minced, chopped /* **poivron...**
20   1 poivron vert° haché   *green pepper*

2 branches de céleri hachées

4 gousses d'ail° hachées   **gousses...** *cloves of garlic*

1 boîte de tomates en dés° en conserve° avec son jus   **en...** *diced /* **en...** *canned*

500 ml de riz°   *rice*

25   750 ml de bouillon de poulet chaud

500 ml de jambon fumé coupé° en cubes   *cut*

4 échalotes coupées en rouelles°   *rounds*

60 ml de persil ciselé°   **persil...** *parsley, snipped*

1/2 c. à thé° de thym   *(cuillerée à thé) teaspoon*

30   3 feuilles de laurier°   **feuilles...** *bay leaves*

sel, poivre

Tabasco au goût°   *to taste*

Après la lecture

1. Combien de temps faut-il *(is necessary)* pour préparer un jambalaya?
2. Est-ce que c'est difficile à préparer?
3. Quelle est la différence entre le jambalaya cajun et le jambalaya créole?
4. Quelles sont les viandes dans ce plat?
5. Quels sont les légumes?
6. Quelles sont les épices et les fines herbes?

Ⓐ Discuss some of your favorite regional or international dishes. What are the principal ingredients (in French)?

Ⓑ The capital of Louisiana is Baton Rouge. What other cities in the United States have French names?

Ⓒ Gumbo is another traditional dish from Louisiana. Find out what the ingredients are by looking on the Internet.

Ⓓ Read *Evangeline,* the poem by Longfellow about the expulsion of the Acadians to Louisiana. In a journal entry, record your reaction to and impressions of the poem.

Ⓔ Find out about the Cajun or Creole genre of music called zydeco. What instruments are used? Try to find a music sample on the Internet.

Ⓕ Try to match the following Creole French terms with their English counterparts (the standard French appears in parentheses):

1. une crème glacée (une glace)
2. pin-pi-po (am stram gram)
3. une craquette (un biscuit)
4. une gazette (un journal)
5. itou (aussi)
6. une lavette (un gant de toilette)

a. a newspaper
b. also, too
c. washcloth
d. ice cream
e. cracker
f. a rhyme game similar to "eeny meeny miney mo"

…Et fondez de plaisir

vocabulaire

Noms / Pronoms

âge *(m.)*	age	huile *(f.)*	oil
agneau *(m.)*	lamb	le jambon	ham
alcool *(m.)*	alcohol	un jus de fruit	fruit juice
un an	year	un lait	milk
un apéritif	before-dinner drink	légumes *(m.)*	vegetables
argent *(m.)*	money	un menu	menu
le beurre	butter	un merguez	merguez *(sausage)*
une bière	beer		
un bistrot	café / restaurant	la moutarde	mustard
un café	coffee	le mouton	mutton
une carte	menu	un mur	wall
un CD *(inv.)*	CD	la nourriture	food
un chocolat	chocolate	le pain	bread
un coca	cola	une photo	photo
la confiture	jam	un pichet	pitcher
un couscous	couscous	une pizza	pizza
une crème	cream	un plat	dish
une cuisine	cooking	un plat principal	main course
eau *(f.)*	water	un poisson	fish
eau minérale *(f.)*	mineral water	le poulet	chicken
une école	school	un prix fixe	fixed price *(menu)*
une école secondaire	secondary school		
		un restaurant	restaurant
un élève	pupil	une salade	salad
la farine	flour	le sel	salt
frites *(f.)*	French fries	la semoule	semolina
un fromage	cheese	un soir	evening
un fruit	fruit *(in general)*	une soupe	soup
un garçon	waiter	le sucre	sugar
un gâteau	cake	une tarte	tart
une glace	ice cream	un thé	tea
un hamburger	hamburger	la viande	meat
un hors-d'œuvre	appetizer	un vin	wine

Verbes

apporter	to bring	dîner	to have dinner
avoir	to have	goûter	to have an afternoon snack
bois	drink		
buvez	drink	préparer	to prepare
commander	to order	recommander	to recommend
consommer	to consume	trouver	to find
déjeuner	to have lunch		

Adjectifs / Adverbes

assez de	enough of	**préféré**	favorite
autant de	as much as	**rouge**	red
blanc	white	**trop**	too much / too many
délicieux	delicious	**tunisien**	Tunisian
peu	little		

Expressions

avoir ___ an(s)	to be ___ old	**Comment trouvez-vous... ?**	How do you like . . . ?
avoir chaud	to be hot		
avoir de la patience	to be patient	**dans**	in
avoir du talent	to have talent	**il y a**	there is, there are
avoir faim	to be hungry	**je voudrais**	I would like
avoir froid	to be cold	**quelle sorte de**	what kind of
avoir raison	to be right	**service compris**	tip included
avoir soif	to be thirsty	**s'il te plaît**	please
avoir tort	to be wrong	**s'il vous plaît**	please
comme	like	**tout de suite**	right away

Révision

A Chapitres 1 à 3

Class work

A Rewrite the following sentences using the cues in parentheses. Make any necessary changes.

MODEL: Il est studieux. (Elles...)
Elles sont studieuses.

Les gens *(People)*

1. Nous sommes généreux. (Madeleine...)
2. Tu as froid. (... fatigué.)
3. Vous invitez des Américains? (Luc et Jeanne... Canadienne?)
4. Ils sont tunisiens? (Marie... ?)
5. Je suis malade. (... patient.)
6. Nous sommes sérieux. (Claire, tu...)

Les boissons

7. Vous buvez du thé? (Tu... bière?)
8. J'aime les jus de fruit. (... demander...)
9. Il a soif. (Marc et Marie...)
10. Jean-Pierre n'aime pas le vin. (... commander... coca.)

Les possessions

11. Un sac à dos est utile. (... cartes...)
12. Nous adorons les enfants. (... avoir...)
13. Tu as une affiche? (Nous... plusieurs...)
14. Elles écoutent du jazz. (... avoir... radio.)

B **La nourriture.** Answer the following questions using the cues provided.

MODEL: Vous avez des légumes? (Non,...)
Non, je n'ai pas de légumes.

1. Qu'est-ce que vous mangez? (Nous... frites.)
2. Vous avez des gâteaux? (Non,...)
3. Qu'est-ce que tu détestes? (... poisson.)
4. Vous aimez le couscous? (Oui, nous...)
5. Jeanne et Sylvie ont faim? (Non,... soif.)
6. Est-ce qu'elles aiment le coca? (Oui,... demander...)
7. Qu'est-ce que Paulette prépare? (... mouton et... beaucoup... légumes.)
8. Est-ce que tu bois de la bière? (Non,... détester... alcool.)
9. Est-ce qu'il y a du lait? (Non,...)

10. Vous aimez la cuisine française?   (Non,... aimer mieux... américain...)
11. Vous mangez de la soupe?   (Non, nous... aimer mieux... salade.)
12. Est-ce que les enfants mangent assez?   (Non,... et... malade...)
13. Tu désires de la crème?   (Non,... beurre,... vin et... huile.)
14. Quand est-ce que vous demandez du chocolat?   (... avoir froid...)

C Create a complete sentence with each group of words below, making appropriate changes and adding any necessary words.

MODEL: étudiants / aimer / musique
         Les étudiants aiment la musique.

A table! *(Let's eat!)*

1. enfants / adorer / glace
2. crème / et / sel / être / mauvais
3. On / avoir / eau / chaud?
4. Paul / ne... pas / manger / fromage
5. garçon / préparer / quelques / boissons

Les gens

6. La sœur de Philippe / avoir / talent
7. Vous / avoir / tort / Monsieur
8. Françoise et Marc / avoir / CD *(pl.)* / américain
9. Est-ce que / elle / avoir / raison?
10. Robert / être / bien!

En cours

11. Nous / commencer / leçon / intéressant
12. Fermer / porte / s'il te plaît!
13. Ecouter / s'il vous plaît!
14. étudiant / avoir / examens / difficile

D Complete the following sentences according to your opinion.

1. J'adore...
2. Je déteste...
3. Les Américains aiment...
4. Je voudrais...
5. Quand j'ai soif, je...
6. Quand je suis malade, je...
7. Je ne suis pas...
8. Le professeur est...

E Translate the following sentences into French.

Bavardage *(Gossip)*

1. She likes a lawyer.
2. They watch football games.
3. Does he smoke a lot?
4. No, but he is lazy.
5. They are happy when they are together.

A la cuisine *(In the kitchen)*

6. Let's make *(préparer)* a cake!
7. You don't have any sugar?
8. We want butter and milk.
9. They hate milk and cream.
10. They are wrong. They are delicious!

F Do the following math problems in French.

1. 5 + 7 =	9. 3 × 4 =
2. 15 + 16 =	10. 15 × 3 =
3. 51 − 27 =	11. 48 ÷ 3 =
4. 69 − 8 =	12. 66 ÷ 2 =
5. 6 + 45 =	13. 11 × 3 =
6. 13 + 14 =	14. 7 × 3 =
7. 49 − 10 =	15. 42 ÷ 7 =
8. 41 − 12 =	16. 39 ÷ 3 =

G **Questions personnelles.** Qui êtes-vous?

1. Vous êtes optimiste? pessimiste? sincère? hypocrite?
2. Est-ce que vous avez beaucoup d'amis dans le cours de français?
3. Quelle sorte d'amis est-ce que vous avez?
4. Qu'est-ce que vous mangez quand vous avez faim?
5. Quelles boissons est-ce que vous aimez?
6. Est-ce que vous travaillez beaucoup? Vous avez assez de devoirs?
7. Est-ce que vous avez des frères et sœurs? Combien?
8. Vous désirez être avocat(e)? ingénieur? journaliste?   ???

Pair and small group work

A With a partner, practice spelling in French. Select ten words that you have learned thus far. Then, take turns spelling them to each other and guessing what each other's words are.

B Say a word in English to your partner and ask for its French equivalent. Then, say a French noun, and your partner will make a sentence using the noun with the correct definite, indefinite, or partitive article.

C In groups of three or four, count from 1 to 20 in French, continuing around the group so that each person must give the next number. Then count, taking turns, from 21 to 39 by odd numbers and from 40 to 60 by even numbers.

D With a partner, play the role of two people who disagree with each other. If one of you makes an affirmative statement, the other makes it negative and vice versa.

MODEL: Student 1: *J'ai du vin.*
                 Student 2: *Je n'ai pas de vin.*

                 Student 1: *Tu aimes faire la cuisine.*
                 Student 2: *Tu n'aimes pas faire la cuisine.*

E In groups of four students, take turns describing yourself, using three adjectives. Then describe one of your classmates without naming him or her, and have the members of the group guess whom you are describing.

F In groups of three or four students, take turns giving one or two students commands that they can carry out.

G Interview your classmates to find out the following information. Be prepared to report your findings to the class.

1. what they are like
2. what their likes and dislikes are
3. what they do every day and on weekends (**Le week-end...**)

H Create a brief dialogue based on the following drawing.

commençons

grammaire

communiquons

lecture culturelle

vocabulaire

L'aéroport de Nice

Les voyages

OBJECTIVES

Language	Culture	Communication
■ Vocabulary for travel and vacations ■ **Enchaînements** and **liaisons** ■ **A** and **de** with definite articles ■ Place names ■ **Aller** and **futur proche** ■ Articles and prepositions with place names ■ Numbers from 70 to 1,000,000,000	■ Travel in France ■ Vacations ■ Gauguin and the island of Tahiti	■ Finding a hotel ■ Expressing future time ■ Counting ■ Asking directions

commençons

A Nice, au Syndicat d'Initiative

Robert et Eric, deux étudiants américains, rentrent de Corse et voyagent sur la Côte d'Azur. Ils arrivent à Nice et ils cherchent un hôtel près de la plage. Ils sont maintenant au Syndicat d'Initiative, où ils demandent des renseignements.

L'HÔTESSE: Bonjour, Messieurs.

ÉRIC: Bonjour, Mademoiselle. Nous cherchons une chambre dans un hôtel près de la mer.

L'HÔTESSE: A côté de la plage, cela va être difficile!

ROBERT: Pourquoi?

L'HÔTESSE: Parce que les hôtels sont chers et parce qu'ils sont tous pleins aujourd'hui. Mais il y a de la place en ville. C'est près des restaurants et des cinémas; ce n'est pas loin du Casino et il faut dix minutes pour aller à la plage.

ROBERT: S'il n'y a pas de chambres au bord de la mer, nous n'allons pas rester à Nice. Nous allons visiter l'Italie. Est-ce que vous avez une liste des hôtels de San Remo?

L'HÔTESSE: Ah, non, pas du tout! Nous n'avons pas de renseignements sur l'Italie, mais vous avez une agence de voyages au coin de la rue.

ÉRIC: Où ça?

L'HÔTESSE: Là-bas, Monsieur. A côté de l'église.

ROBERT: Merci mille fois. Au revoir.

L'HÔTESSE: Au revoir, Messieurs.

Etudions le dialogue

1. Où sont Robert et Eric?
2. Qu'est-ce qu'ils cherchent?
3. Ils désirent être loin de la plage, n'est-ce pas?
4. Est-ce qu'il y a de la place au bord de la mer?
5. Qu'est-ce qu'il y a en ville?
6. Où est-ce que Robert et Eric vont aller s'ils ne restent pas à Nice?

Mots clés

un Syndicat d'Initiative	*Tourist Office*	mais	*but*
rentrent de (rentrer de)	*come back from*	de la place	*room*
la Corse	*Corsica*	en ville	*downtown*
voyagent (voyager)	*are traveling*	cinémas *(m.)*	*movie theaters*
sur	*on*	loin du Casino	*far from the Casino*
la Côte d'Azur	*French Riviera*	il faut	*it takes*
cherchent (chercher)	*are looking for*	minutes *(f.)*	*minutes*
près de	*near*	pour aller à	*to go to*
une plage	*beach*	s' (si)	*if*
maintenant	*now*	au bord de la mer	*at the seashore*
renseignements *(m.)*	*information*	rester	*to stay*
une hôtesse	*hostess*	visiter	*to go to*
Messieurs *(m.)*	*gentlemen*	Italie *(f.)*	*Italy*
une chambre	*room*	une liste	*list*
une mer	*sea*	ah, non	*of course not*
à côté de	*next to*	pas du tout	*not at all*
va être (aller être)	*is going to be*	une agence de voyages	*travel agency*
pourquoi	*why*	au coin de	*at the corner of*
parce que	*because*	une rue	*street*
chers (cher, -ère)	*expensive*	Où ça?	*Whereabouts?*
tous	*all*	là-bas	*over there*
pleins	*full*	une église	*church*
aujourd'hui	*today*	Merci mille fois.	*Thanks a million.*

Faisons connaissance

Upon arrival in a French city or town, the useful thing to do is to go to the **Syndicat d'Initiative,** where you will get information about points of interest and a list of hotels arranged by categories. If you wish, someone at the **Syndicat** will call hotels for you to check for vacancies. There you can also find out about other areas in France you may wish to visit. Because the service is run by the French government, it does not include information about other countries.

Nice is the largest city on **la Côte d'Azur,** one of the principal vacation areas of France. You may also have heard of Cannes because of its international film festival in May. Saint-Tropez was made famous in the 1950s as the playground of Brigitte Bardot and other screen personalities. The tiny country of Monaco is also wedged into the Mediterranean coast to the east of Nice. San Remo, an Italian city, is farther along the coast.

While **la Côte d'Azur** is known throughout the world for its splendid beaches, Americans are often surprised to find many of them covered with smooth stones (**les galets**) rather than with sand.

Sur la Côte d'Azur

Enrichissons notre vocabulaire

En ville *(In the city)*

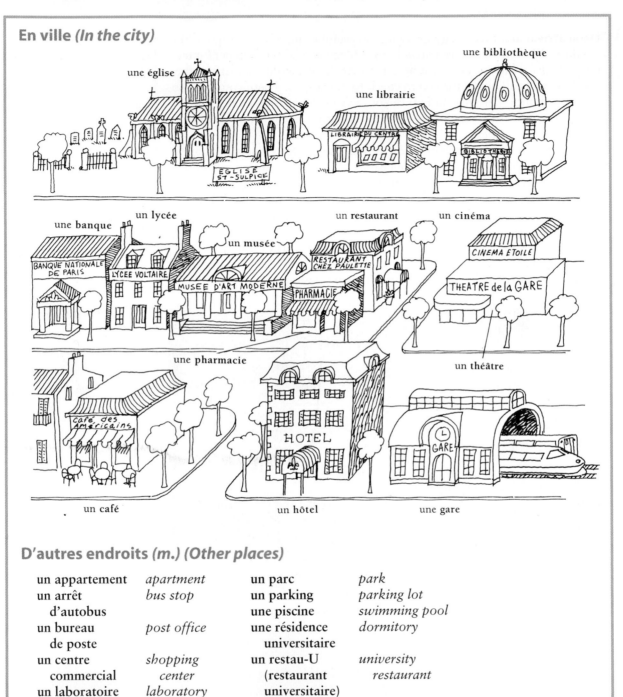

D'autres endroits *(m.)* *(Other places)*

un appartement	*apartment*	un parc	*park*
un arrêt d'autobus	*bus stop*	un parking	*parking lot*
		une piscine	*swimming pool*
un bureau de poste	*post office*	une résidence universitaire	*dormitory*
un centre commercial	*shopping center*	un restau-U (restaurant universitaire)	*university restaurant*
un laboratoire	*laboratory*		
un magasin	*store*	un stade	*stadium*
une maison	*house*	une usine	*factory*

Prononciation   Enchaînements et liaisons

A. In spoken French, words flow together very smoothly. When a word begins with a vowel sound, French speakers pronounce the last consonant of the preceding word as if it were the first letter of the next word. This is **enchaînement.**

avec elle	/ avɛ kɛl /	il a	/ i la /
sept étudiants	/ sɛ te ty djɑ̃ /	elle est	/ ɛ lɛ /

Practice **enchaînements** by repeating the following expressions after your teacher.

> neuf étudiantes / elle habite / il invite / cinq acteurs / l'artiste intelligent / le professeur intéressant

B. There is a separate category of **enchaînement** in which a written final consonant that is normally not pronounced must be sounded because a vowel sound follows it. Notice the difference in the pronunciation of: **nous travaillons** / nu tʀa va jɔ̃ / and **nous habitons** / nu za bi tɔ̃ /.

The **s** of **nous** in **nous habitons** must be pronounced because the verb begins with the vowel sound / a /. This is **liaison.** It is limited to closely linked word groups (pronoun subject–verb, adjective–noun), and most often involves the / z / sound.

Listen carefully and repeat the following paired words after your teacher, paying particular attention to the **liaisons.**

No liaison	Liaison	No liaison	Liaison
un livre	un‿ami	nous dansons	nous‿invitons
deux clés	deux‿amies	ils sont	ils‿ont
trois cafés	trois‿hôtesses	des légumes	des‿hôtels
six portes	six‿étudiants	les filles	les‿enfants
dix cartes	dix‿hommes	en France	en‿Amérique

Exercice

Practice reading these sentences aloud, while concentrating on the **enchaînements** and **liaisons.**

1. Les Américains habitent en Amérique.
2. Nous étudions avec un professeur intéressant.
3. Vous avez une opinion d'elle?
4. Les enfants sont intelligents.
5. Ils invitent des amis sympathiques.
6. Elle donne un examen aux étudiants.

grammaire

I. *A* and *de* with definite articles

You use **à** to indicate location or direction and **de** to indicate origin or possession.

A. Two very common French prepositions are **à** *(to, in, at,* or *into)* and **de** *(from* or *of)*.

Cécile habite à Paris.   Elle est **de** New York.
Ils arrivent à Nice.   J'ai le stylo **de** Robert.

B. **A** and **de** are often used with the definite articles **l'** and **la.**

Elle travaille à l'université.   C'est le livre **de** l'étudiant.
Ils sont **à la** maison.   Quel est le prix **de la** chambre?

C. When **à** and **de** come before the definite articles **le** or **les,** the two words form a contraction.

à + le = **au**   de + le = **du**
à + les = **aux**   de + les = **des**

Ils sont **au** Syndicat d'Initiative.   Il est **du** Canada.
Je donne la glace **aux** enfants.   Elles ont les cahiers **des** étudiants.

Note that the **x** of **aux** and the **s** of **des** are pronounced / z / in front of a vowel sound, just like the **s** of **les.**

Attention! ————————————————————

The preposition **de** in combination with the definite articles has the same forms as the partitive articles and the plural indefinite article, which you learned in Chapter 3, but, unlike them, the preposition **de** never changes in the negative.

Indefinite article:

J'ai **des** enfants.	*I have (**some**) children.*
Je **n'ai pas** d'enfants.	*I **don't** have (**any**) children.*

Preposition *de* and the definite article *les*:

Je parle **des** enfants.	*I'm talking **about the** children.*
Je **ne** parle **pas des** enfants.	*I'm **not** talking **about the** children.*

D. The preposition **de** is part of some prepositional expressions, subject to the same rules regarding contractions.

> Ils cherchent un hôtel **près de** la mer.
> Ils trouvent un hôtel **en face de** l'agence de voyages.
> Ce n'est pas **loin du** Casino.
> C'est **près des** restaurants.

Mots clés

Prepositions with *de*			
à côté de	*next to*	loin de	*far from*
au coin de	*at the corner of*	près de	*near*
en face de	*across from*		
Other common prepositions that do not take *de*			
chez	*at the home of*	entre	*between*
dans	*in*	sous	*under*
derrière	*behind*	sur	*on*
devant	*in front of*		

Language

Ⓐ **A la résidence.** Someone is calling your floor in the dorm, but everyone is out. Tell the caller where everyone is by forming complete sentences.

1. Marie / travailler / librairie
2. Marc / étudier / bibliothèque
3. Jacques et Jean / être / centre commercial
4. Monique / manger / restau-U
5. Jeanne et Chantal / être / près / cinéma
6. Je / être / dans / chambre de Paul

Ⓑ **Où ça?** Describe the activities and locations of the people below, using an item from each of the four columns provided.

MODEL: Je / être / à / université
         Je suis à l'université.

A	B	C	D
Les étudiants	travailler	à	bibliothèque
Je	habiter	de	cinéma
Vous	être	derrière	maison
Luc	étudier	à côté de	appartement
Mes amis	manger	devant	étudiants
Nous	parler	loin de	théâtre
Agents de police		sous	université
Mes parents		sur	magasin
		près de	parc

C Using the map in **Enrichissons notre vocabulaire**, give the locations of the following places.

MODEL: Café des Américains / musée
Le Café des Américains est près du musée.

1. cinéma Etoile / théâtre de la Gare
2. église Saint-Sulpice / Café des Américains
3. gare / hôtel
4. pharmacie / restaurant Chez Paulette
5. musée / pharmacie
6. librairie / église / bibliothèque
7. banque / lycée
8. restaurant Chez Paulette / cinéma Etoile

Culture

D **Visitons Paris.** Identify where various landmarks in Paris are located by adding **être** and a preposition to the places listed below. For help, refer to the map of Paris on page 200 of this book.

MODEL: Le parc des Expositions / le palais des Sports
Le parc des Expositions est derrière le palais des Sports.

1. La tour Eiffel / le palais de Chaillot
2. Le Louvre / la Seine
3. Notre-Dame / le Palais de Justice
4. la gare Montparnasse / le Sacré-Cœur
5. L'Arc de Triomphe / la place Charles-de-Gaulle
6. La place de la Concorde / l'avenue des Champs-Elysées et les Tuileries

a. près de
b. à côté de
c. entre
d. sur
e. en face de
f. loin de

Communication

E **Nos activités.** Interview two classmates and find out where they do the following things:

MODEL: étudier? *J'étudie dans ma chambre.*

1. jouer
2. terminer les devoirs
3. dîner
4. travailler
5. regarder la télé
6. aimer danser

F **Questions personnelles.** Votre ville *(Your town)*

1. Vous êtes de New York?
2. Où est-ce que vous habitez? C'est près de... ?
3. Qu'est-ce qu'il y a dans la ville où vous habitez?
4. Dans la ville où vous habitez, où est le musée? la gare? Où sont les cinémas? les cafés? les restaurants?
5. Vous aimez bien un restaurant? Où est-ce qu'il est?
6. Qu'est-ce que vous aimez à l'université où vous étudiez?

II. *Aller* / The *futur proche*

You use **aller** to express the idea of going somewhere, to talk about health, or to express an action or a state in the future.

A. Forms of *aller*

1. **Aller** is an irregular verb, and you must memorize its forms.

aller *(to go)*	
je **vais**	nous **allons**
tu **vas**	vous **allez**
il / elle / on **va**	ils / elles **vont**

2. **Aller** is almost never used alone as it can be in English *(I'm going!)*. It is often followed by expressions that indicate manner or direction.

Nous **allons en** France.
Je **vais au** café **avec** Marie.
Est-ce que vous **allez au** théâtre?

Pour étudier, elle **va à la** bibliothèque.

3. The formation of the imperative of **aller** is regular: **va, allons, allez.**

Allons au cinéma.

Ne va pas avec Jean.

4. You have already learned some idiomatic expressions with **aller**. Those and some other common expressions are listed below.

—**Comment ça va? Ça va?**
—**Ça va. Ça va bien.**

—**Comment allez-vous?**
—**Je vais bien.**

On y va?
Allez-y! Vas-y!
Allons-y!

Shall we go?
Go ahead!
Let's go!

B. The *futur proche*

1. One very frequent use of **aller** is to express an action in the future by using a conjugated form of **aller** + an *infinitive*. This construction is similar to the English *to be going* + an *infinitive* and is called the **futur proche** (near future). The main action is expressed by the infinitive, which directly follows the conjugated verb **aller**.

Nous **allons visiter** l'Italie.

Je **vais travailler** demain.

2. To make negative sentences with the **futur proche**, you simply place **ne... pas** around the conjugated form of **aller**.

—Tu **vas regarder** la télévision?
—Non, je **ne vais pas regarder** la télévision.

3. The **futur proche** is frequently used with expressions of time.

maintenant	*now*	demain	*tomorrow*
aujourd'hui	*today*	demain matin	*tomorrow morning*
ce matin	*this morning*	demain soir	*tomorrow evening*
cet après-midi	*this afternoon*	tous les jours	*every day*
ce soir	*tonight*		

le week-end prochain	*next weekend*
la semaine prochaine	*next week*
l'année prochaine	*next year*

Language

A **Nos destinations.** Say where the following people are going today, using the cues provided and the verb **aller.**

MODEL: Paul / cinéma   *Paul va au cinéma.*

1. Tu / université
2. Nous / arrêt d'autobus
3. Mes amis / librairie
4. Je / bureau de poste
5. Vous / centre commercial
6. Françoise / maison

B **Au futur.** Tell what will happen to the following people in the future by changing the sentences from the present tense to the **futur proche.**

MODEL: Il arrive fatigué.
       Il va arriver fatigué.

1. Je travaille en ville.
2. Elle est ingénieur.
3. Ils invitent des amis.
4. Jacques a chaud.
5. Est-ce que vous habitez ici?
6. Nous aimons le restaurant.
7. Tu vas au Canada.
8. Elles mangent un couscous.

Culture

C **A l'Office de tourisme.** This office, located on the **Champs-Elysées** in Paris, gives advice to tourists. Pretend you are working there by matching the interests of various tourists on the left with places to go on the right.

MODEL: la poésie   musée Victor-Hugo
       Allez au musée Victor-Hugo.

1. l'impressionnisme
2. l'art classique
3. l'art moderne
4. le cubisme
5. la sculpture
6. le Moyen Age *(Middle Ages)*

a. musée Cluny
b. musée Rodin
c. musée d'Orsay
d. le Louvre
e. musée Picasso
f. le Centre Pompidou

Ⓓ **En France ou aux Etats-Unis?** Form complete sentences, then state whether the action is more typical in France or in the U.S.

1. Les touristes / aller / gare pour changer de l'argent.
2. On / aller / café parce qu'on a soif.
3. Vous / aller / gare pour dîner.
4. On / aller / au supermarché pour acheter des timbres.
5. Les étudiants / aller / café pour étudier.
6. Tu / aller / librairie / parce que tu désires avoir un tee-shirt.

Communication

Ⓔ **Vos préférences.** Answer the following questions.

1. Où est-ce que vous allez aujourd'hui pour étudier? pour manger? pour regarder un film?
2. Où est-ce que vous allez pour dîner? pour danser? pour parler?
3. Vous allez regarder la télévision ce soir? écouter la radio? aller à l'église le week-end prochain?
4. L'année prochaine, est-ce que vous allez étudier le français?

Ⓕ **Mes camarades.** Ask a classmate if he or she is going to do the following things. Afterwards, present a summary to the class.

1. travailler à la maison cet après-midi?
2. aller dans une boîte ce soir?
3. rester à la résidence demain matin?
4. déjeuner chez des amis le week-end prochain?
5. être malade le jour de l'examen final?
6. trouver une profession intéressante?

Ⓖ **Mon professeur.** Ask your professor if he or she is going to do the following things.

1. donner des devoirs pour demain?
2. donner un examen facile la semaine prochaine?
3. préparer un couscous en classe?
4. être agréable ou désagréable?
5. aller à la mer l'année prochaine?
6. visiter la France?

III. Articles and prepositions with place names

You use articles, prepositions, and place names to indicate geographical location or destination.

A. Unlike English, French does not make a distinction between going *to* or being *in* a place. Instead, the correct preposition depends on the type of place name.

1. Use **à**, meaning *to* or *in,* with cities.

> Nous n'allons pas rester **à Nice.**   Robert est **à New York.**
> **A Madrid** on dîne à 22 heures.   Gilles rentre **à Québec.**

2. Use **en**, meaning *to* or *in,* with feminine countries, all continents, and countries whose names begin with a vowel. (Most countries whose names end in a written **e** are feminine.)

> Vous allez étudier **en France.**
> Nous allons aller **en Italie.**
> Ils désirent voyager **en Russie.**
> **En Asie,** on parle français.
> Le diplomate va voyager **en Israël, en Iraq,** et **en Iran.**

3. Use **au** (*pl.* **aux**), meaning *to* or *in,* with countries that are masculine. (Masculine countries have names that end in letters other than **e**, with the exceptions of **le Mexique** and **le Mozambique.**)

> Ils désirent voyager **au Canada.**
> Nous sommes **aux Etats-Unis.**
> **Au Portugal** on trouve des universités très anciennes.

B. To express *from,* use **du** with masculine singular countries, **des** with plural countries, and **de** without an article for feminine countries and cities. Some verbs often followed by **de** are **arriver, être, rentrer,** and **aller.**

> Il est **du** Canada, mais elle est **des** Etats-Unis.
> Mes parents rentrent **de** Paris la semaine prochaine.
> Nous allons aller **de** Grande-Bretagne en Belgique.

C. Use the definite article when the country is not a location but the subject or the object of the verb.

> Nous allons visiter **la France.**   J'adore **le Québec.**
> **La Chine** est en Asie.   Cherche **le Maroc** sur la carte!

Mots clés   *Cities, continents, and countries*

Des villes		Des continents	
Bruxelles	Mexico	l'Afrique	l'Asie
Genève	Moscou	l'Amérique du Nord	l'Europe
Lisbonne	La Nouvelle-Orléans	l'Amérique du Sud	
Londres	Varsovie *Warsaw*		

Des pays féminins			
l'Algérie		la Belgique	
l'Allemagne	*Germany*	la Chine	
l'Angleterre	*England*	la Côte d'Ivoire	
l'Australie		l'Espagne	
l'Autriche	*Austria*	la Finlande	

Des pays féminins			
la France		la Norvège	*Norway*
la Grande-Bretagne	*Great Britain*	la Pologne	
la Grèce		la Russie	
la Hollande		la Suède	*Sweden*
l'Irlande		la Suisse	*Switzerland*
l'Italie		la Tunisie	
Des pays masculins			
le Brésil		le Mexique	
le Canada[1]		le Mozambique	
le Danemark		les Pays-Bas	*the Netherlands*
les Etats-Unis[1]	*U.S.A.*	le Portugal	
le Japon		le Sénégal	
le Maroc	*Morocco*	le Tchad	*Chad*

Attention!

If you are not expressing *to* or *in* a place, no preposition is necessary, but the definite article *must* be used with most countries. Do not use an article with cities unless the city name already contains an article, such as **La Nouvelle-Orléans** or **La Havane**.

L'Italie est un pays fascinant.
Ils adorent **la Chine**.
Paris a des restaurants fantastiques.
Je vais visiter **La Nouvelle-Orléans** pour écouter du jazz.

CONSULATS A LA MARTINIQUE

ALLEMAGNE: Société Sodicar. Acajou. 97232 Le Lamentin. Tél.: 05 96 50 86 45.

BELGIQUE: Ets Cottrel. Z.I. La Lézarde. 97232 Le Lamentin. Tél.: 05 96 59 50 50.

ESPAGNE: Les Hauts de Frégate. 97240 Le François. Tél.: 05 96 75 03 12.

GRANDE-BRETAGNE: Ets Serge Ernoult. Route du Phare. 97200 Fort-de-France. Tél.: 05 96 61 56 30 ou 05 96 61 58 70.

ITALIE: 28, boulevard Allègre. 97200 Fort-de-France. Tél.: 05 96 70 54 75.

MEXIQUE: 31, rue Moreau de Jones. 97200 Fort-de-France. Tél.: 05 96 72 58 12.

NORVEGE: Acajou. 97232 Le Lamentin. Tél.: 05 96 58 91 02.

PAYS-BAS: 44/46, avenue Maurice Bishop. 97200 Fort-de-France. Tél.: 05 96 63 30 04.

REPUBLIQUE DOMINICAINE: Zone de Bac. 97220 Trinité. Tél.: 05 96 58 24 24.

SUISSE: Centre d'Affaires Californie. 97232 Le Lamentin. Tél.: 05 96 50 12 43.

VENEZUELA: 59, rue du Prof. Raymond Garcin. Route de Didier. 97200 Fort-de-France. Tél.: 05 96 63 34 16.

SIÈGE: Chambre de Commerce et d'Industrie. 50, rue Ernest Deproge. BP 478. 97241 Fort-de-France Cédex. Tél.: 05 96 55 28 00.

---

1. Articles and prepositions used with states of the United States and provinces of Canada are found in Appendix II.

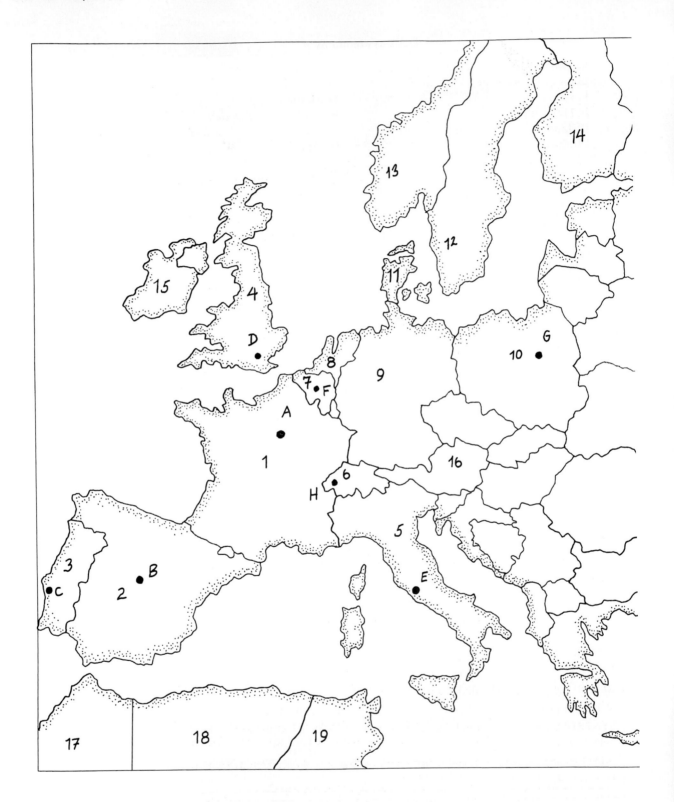

Ⓐ **Où sont-ils?** Form a sentence to describe where the people below are, based on the following model.

MODEL: Yves: Paris, France
         Yves est à Paris, en France.

1. Carlo: Rome, Italie
2. Maria: Mexico, Mexique
3. Tom: Washington, Etats-Unis
4. Mamadou: Dakar, Sénégal
5. Rachel: Tel-Aviv, Israël
6. Robert et Line: Bruxelles, Belgique
7. Paul et Claire: Montréal, Canada
8. Fatima: Casablanca, Maroc

Ⓑ **Un peu de géo.** Identify the following countries by what continent they are on.

MODEL: *La France est en Europe.*

1. Mexique
2. Angleterre
3. Chine
4. République démocratique du Congo
5. Brésil
6. Tchad
7. Portugal
8. Japon

Ⓒ **Voyages à l'étranger.** Cars crossing borders in Europe often have an oval sticker on the back that indicates the country where the car is registered. Name the country of the drivers of cars with the following stickers.

MODEL: F   *Elle est de France.*

1. D
2. B
3. I
4. DK
5. CH
6. A
7. E
8. GB

Ⓓ **Où sommes-nous?** In pairs, try to identify where you are, as another student chooses a number for a country or a letter for a city from the map of Europe on page 102.

MODEL: Student 1: *1*
         Student 2: *Nous sommes en France.*

         Student 1: *B*
         Student 2: *Nous sommes à Madrid.*

Ⓔ **Voyage en Europe.** With a classmate, plan a trip through Europe using the map on page 102. Then read your itinerary.

MODEL: *J'arrive à Paris. Je visite la France. Après, je vais en Suisse et en Italie. Je continue le voyage en Autriche et je termine à Berlin.*

Ⓕ **Un voyage idéal.** Interview a classmate to find out the information below.

1. Où est-ce que vous désirez aller en Afrique? en Europe?
2. Quelles *(Which)* villes et quels pays est-ce que vous désirez visiter?
3. Où est-ce que la vie *(life)* est agréable? désagréable? Pourquoi?
4. Quels pays est-ce que vous recommandez aux Américains? Pourquoi?

IV. Numbers from 70 to 1,000,000,000

70	soixante-dix	93	quatre-vingt-treize
71	soixante et onze	94	quatre-vingt-quatorze
72	soixante-douze	95	quatre-vingt-quinze
73	soixante-treize	96	quatre-vingt-seize
74	soixante-quatorze	97	quatre-vingt-dix-sept
75	soixante-quinze	98	quatre-vingt-dix-huit
76	soixante-seize	99	quatre-vingt-dix-neuf
77	soixante-dix-sept	100	cent
78	soixante-dix-huit	101	cent un
79	soixante-dix-neuf	108	cent huit
80	quatre-vingts	172	cent soixante-douze
81	quatre-vingt-un	199	cent quatre-vingt-dix-neuf
82	quatre-vingt-deux	200	deux cents
83	quatre-vingt-trois	231	deux cent trente et un
84	quatre-vingt-quatre	284	deux cent quatre-vingt-quatre
85	quatre-vingt-cinq	300	trois cents
86	quatre-vingt-six	400	quatre cents
87	quatre-vingt-sept	701	sept cent un
88	quatre-vingt-huit	1.000	mille
89	quatre-vingt-neuf	3.200	trois mille deux cents
90	quatre-vingt-dix	1.000.000	un million
91	quatre-vingt-onze	1.000.000.000	un milliard
92	quatre-vingt-douze		

A. Note that **et** is used with 21, 31, 41, 51, 61, and 71 (**vingt et un, trente et un,...**), but not with 81, 91, and 101 (**quatre-vingt-un, quatre-vingt-onze, cent un**).

B. Cent and **mille** are *never* preceded by **un,** but **un million** and **un milliard** *(one billion)* must be.

> 100   cent
> 1.005   mille cinq
> 1.500.000   un million cinq cent mille
> 1.003.800.000   un milliard trois millions huit cent mille

C. When counting in millions or billions, you must use the preposition **de (d')** before a noun. However, when **million** or **milliard** is followed by a number, the preposition is dropped.

un million d'habitants	*one million inhabitants*
quatre milliards d'euros	*four billion euros*
deux millions cinq cent mille dollars	*two million five hundred thousand dollars*

D. To express a distance, use the preposition **à.** For distances from one place to another, use **être à... de.** Distances would typically be in **mètres (m)** or **kilomètres (km).**

> Jacques habite à 100 m de chez moi.
> Le centre commercial est à 2 km d'ici.
> Marseille est à 778 km de Paris.

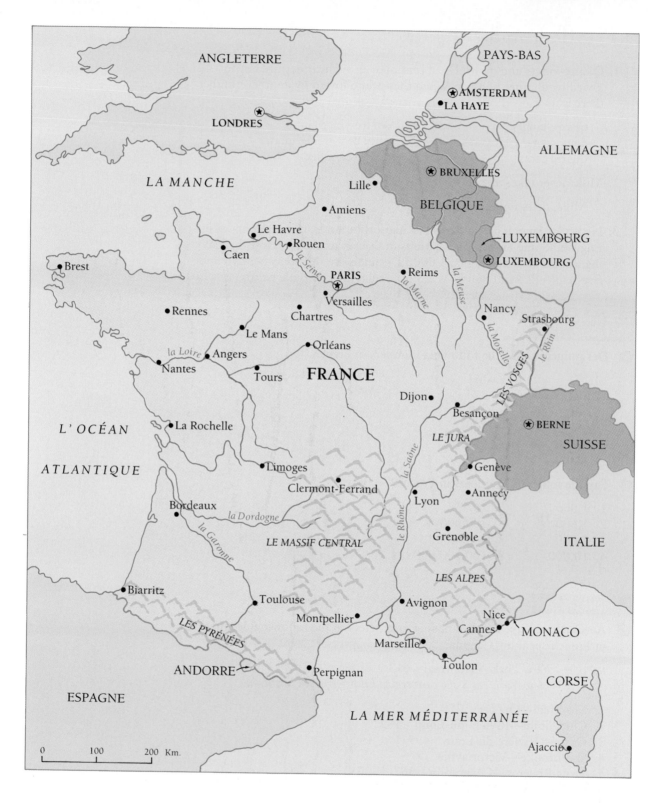

ANGLETERRE

PAYS-BAS

⊛AMSTERDAM
●LA HAYE

ALLEMAGNE

LA MANCHE

⊛ BRUXELLES

●Lille

BELGIQUE

LUXEMBOURG

●Amiens

⊛ LUXEMBOURG

●Le Havre
●Rouen

la Seine

●Reims

●Brest

PARIS
⊛

la Marne

la Meuse

●Caen

●Nancy
Strasbourg●

●Rennes

Versailles
●

●Chartres

●Le Mans

la Moselle

le Rhin

Orléans●

la Loire

LES VOSGES

●
Angers●

●Nantes

●Tours

FRANCE

L' OCÉAN

●Dijon

Besançon
●

⊛ BERNE

LE JURA

SUISSE

●La Rochelle

ATLANTIQUE

la Saône

●Limoges

●Genève

Clermont-Ferrand●

●Annecy

●Bordeaux

Lyon
●

la Dordogne

le Rhône

la Garonne

LE MASSIF CENTRAL

ITALIE

●Grenoble

LES ALPES

●Biarritz

●Toulouse

Avignon
●

●Montpellier

Nice●

LES PYRÉNÉES

Cannes●

MONACO

Marseille●

ANDORRE

●Perpignan

Toulon
●

CORSE

ESPAGNE

LA MER MÉDITERRANÉE

0   100   200 Km.

Ajaccio●

L'orthographe

1. **Quatre-vingts** and multiples of **cent** take an **s** when they are not followed by another number. When they are followed by another number, there is no **s**.

quatre-vingts	quatre-vingt-cinq
deux cents	deux cent trente-quatre
quatre cents	quatre cent dix

2. **Mille** never takes an **s**.

   Mille, deux mille, trois mille...

3. Note that French uses a period to mark thousands, not a comma as in English. (Some French publications, however, mark thousands by leaving a space between digits: 1 000.) Decimals are the opposite: two and five-tenths (2.5 in English) is **2,5** in French (**deux virgule cinq**).

Language

Ⓐ **Des numéros.** Say the following numbers in French.

1. 71	7. 151
2. 81	8. 274
3. 89	9. 391
4. 99	10. 500
5. 100	11. 544
6. 102	12. 1.000

Ⓑ Say the following numbers in French.

1. 1.000	5. 16.552
2. 1.600	6. 200.000
3. 2.000	7. 1.000.000
4. 10.000	8. 100.000.000

Culture

Ⓒ **Au Québec.** Give the distances in kilometers to the following destinations in French-speaking Canada.

MODEL: New York—Montréal   613
New York est à six cent treize kilomètres de Montréal.

1. Montréal—Québec   270
2. Chicoutimi—Rivière-du-Loup   182
3. Gaspé—Rivière-du-Loup   499
4. Sherbrooke—Victoriaville   97
5. Trois-Rivières—Chicoutimi   367
6. Québec—Ville-Marie   918

D **Les musées et les monuments les plus visités.** Below are the most visited museums and monuments in France for 1998. Put them in order of most to least frequently visited by reading the name and the number of visitors.

Orsay	2,7 millions
Louvre	5,7 millions
Tour Eiffel	6,1 millions
Cité des sciences et de l'industrie	3,3 millions
Versailles	2,7 millions

loto-quebec **Résultats**

LOTTO 6/49

Tirage du mercredi   00-08-16

9   12   13   32   34   35   no complémentaire **47**

	GAGNANTS	LOTS
Prochain tirage:	6/6	0	1 909 130,60 $
Samedi 00-08-19	5/6 +	4	180 306,70 $
	5/6	229	2 408,40 $
Prochain gros lot:	4/6	13 417	79,00 $
4 300 000,00 $	3/6	273 009	10,00 $
approx.			

Ventes totales: 15 494 672,00 $

Les modalités d'encaissement des billets gagnants paraissent au verso des billets. En cas de disparité entre cette liste et la liste officielle, cette dernière a priorité.

E **La loterie.** Answer the following questions about the results of a lottery drawing based on the newspaper report above.

1. Où est cette *(this)* loterie?
2. Quels numéros gagnent *(win)*?
3. Combien est-ce qu'on gagne avec les six numéros?
4. Combien de personnes ont quatre numéros?
5. Combien de personnes gagnent dix dollars?
6. Combien d'argent est-ce qu'on va gagner la prochaine fois *(time)*?

Communication

F **Numéros de téléphone.** Give your classmates the telephone numbers for places on campus (main library, fitness center, computer lab, bursar's office, health center). For this activity, you will probably want to consult the telephone directory for your university.

MODEL: Main library (**la bibliothèque centrale**): 887-9035
Huit cent quatre-vingt-sept, quatre-vingt-dix, trente-cinq

G **On n'est pas des numéros.** Choose a partner to ask and answer the following questions with complete French sentences.

1. Quel âge a le professeur?
2. Quel âge a le président des Etats-Unis?
3. Combien d'étudiants est-ce qu'il y a à la résidence? à l'université?
4. Combien de pages est-ce qu'il y a dans le livre de français?
5. Vous habitez à quelle distance de l'université? de vos parents?
6. Combien d'étudiants vont aux matchs de football?

communiquons

Demander son chemin

When traveling in a new place, one must be able to ask for directions (**demander son chemin**) and understand them. In this situation, you need to know how to get someone's attention on the street and then ask for directions politely. Most French people are used to seeing tourists and are glad to help.

One custom of giving directions is very different in Europe. While Americans judge distances in cities by blocks, the French generally estimate the distance in meters. A meter is about three inches longer than a yard.

Pardon, Messieurs, je cherche l'Office du Tourisme.

Expressions

▶ **On demande son chemin.**

S'il vous plaît, pourriez-vous me dire où se trouve la gare?	*Could you please tell me where the train station is located?*
Excusez-moi, pourriez-vous m'indiquer une banque?	*Excuse me, could you show me a bank?*
Pardon, où se trouve le bureau de poste?	*Pardon me, where is the post office?*

▶ **On indique le chemin.**

Tournez à droite à 200 mètres d'ici.	*Turn right 200 meters from here.*
Vous tournez à gauche au coin de la rue.	*You turn left at the corner.*
Ensuite, continuez jusqu'à la rue Pascal.	*Then, continue until Pascal Street.*
Là, vous allez tout droit.	*There, you go straight ahead.*
Traversez la rue.	*Cross the street.*

▶ **On regarde une carte de la francophonie.**

La Tunisie est à l'est de l'Algérie.	*Tunisia is east of Algeria.*
Le Sénégal est au sud de la Mauritanie.	*Senegal is south of Mauritania.*
Le Gabon est à l'ouest du Congo.	*Gabon is west of the Congo.*
Le Tchad est au nord de la République centrafricaine.	*Chad is north of the Central African Republic.*

Interaction

Robert cherche la gare.

ROBERT: Pardon, Monsieur...

UN PASSANT°: Oui?   *passer-by*

ROBERT: Pourriez-vous me dire où se trouve la gare?

PASSANT: Oui, mais c'est loin!

ROBERT: Mais, j'ai un train dans vingt minutes!

PASSANT: Alors, traversez cette rue, allez jusqu'au coin là-bas, et tournez à droite. Ensuite continuez jusqu'au coin de la rue Montaigne, à 400 mètres. Là, vous tournez à gauche et vous avez la gare en face de vous.

ROBERT: Merci beaucoup, Monsieur.

PASSANT: Je vous en prie.°   *Don't mention it.*

Ⓐ **Votre campus.** Answer the following questions about your campus.

1. Comment est-ce que vous allez de la bibliothèque au restau-U?
2. Comment est-ce que vous allez de la salle de classe à la librairie?
3. Pour aller de la salle de classe à la résidence, on va tout droit? Expliquez.
4. Le parking des étudiants est à quelle distance de la classe? Le parking des professeurs est loin ou près de la classe?

Ⓑ **Jeu de rôles.** With a classmate, prepare and act out the following situations in front of the class.

1. You are a French tourist who becomes lost in an American college town while looking for a local tourist attraction. Your partner is a French-speaking American who gives you directions to the landmark you are seeking.
2. You are an American tourist visiting the French town pictured in **Enrichissons notre vocabulaire** (page 92). Using the map, decide where you are in the town and choose a destination that you would like to visit. Your partner will play the role of the town resident whom you stop on the street to ask for directions to your chosen destination.

lecture culturelle

Avant la lecture

Tahiti, the largest of 118 islands that make up the territory of French Polynesia, is located in the South Pacific, seven and a half hours by plane from Los Angeles. Tahiti is made up of two islands, Tahiti-Nui, the larger island, and Tahiti-Iti, the smaller island. The islands have attracted many people of adventurous spirit, from Captains Wallis, Bougainville, Cook, and Bligh to one of the most noted French Postimpressionist painters, Paul Gauguin. In his youth, Gauguin spent five years in the merchant marine. In 1871, when he was twenty-three, he entered the business world as a stockbroker; he later married a Danish woman, with whom he had five children. Having initially taken up painting as a hobby, at the age of thirty-five he became a full-time artist, a decision influenced in part by an economic collapse in 1882. During the next ten years, he earned increasing respect as a painter. Then, in 1891, Gauguin gave up everything, including his family and friends, and took up residence in Tahiti, where he painted some of his most famous pieces (including *Women on a Beach*, 1891, and *Where Do We Come From? What Are We? Where Are We Going?* 1897). Although he made several voyages back to Paris to exhibit his paintings, he ultimately returned to French Polynesia, where he died in 1903.

Activités

Ⓐ Find Tahiti on a map. What is its capital? What other islands make up **la Polynésie française?**

Ⓑ Scan the text **Tahiti: «L'Ile de l'Amour»** for words related to Tahiti's climate and topography. Make a list of the terms.

Ⓒ The second text is an advertisement for the *M/S Gauguin*, a cruise ship named after the famous painter. Before reading it, make a list of the kind of vocabulary you expect to find in the advertisement. Look up the words in French.

Gauguin et Tahiti

Tahiti: «L'Ile de l'Amour»

Souvent appelée «île d'amour», Tahiti est la plus grande des 118 îles et atolls qui forment la Polynésie française. Les 1.042 km²° de la surface de Tahiti sont constitués de chaînes de montagnes survolant° des forêts de fougères° luxuriantes, des cascades, des rivières fraîches°, ainsi que° des champs° de taro et de fleurs tropicales.

5

402 square miles
towering over
ferns / cool / as well as
fields

CROISIERE° PAUL GAUGUIN

Coucher de soleil
en Polynésie française

Le *M/S Paul Gauguin* est un tout nouveau bateau de plaisance° de luxe, et dirigé° par la compagnie Radisson Seven Seas Cruises. Ce bateau propose sept nuits° de croisière à partir de° Papeete.

Le *M/S Paul Gauguin* est originaire de° France, et a été conçu pour° naviguer toute l'année à travers° la Polynésie française. Les propriétaires se sont joints à° Radisson Seven Seas Cruises pour créer cette vision et faire d'un rêve la réalité°. Tout en restant fidèle à° ses origines françaises, le *M/S Paul Gauguin* incorpore les standards six-étoiles° pour les services et conforts qui font la renommée du Radisson Seven Seas°, et propose des grandes cabines de luxe (la moitié° sont pourvues de° balcons privés), une marina ultra-moderne, des salles à manger à tables individuelles, un jacuzzi, et beaucoup d'autres aménagements°. Le navire° est construit° par la prestigieuse compagnie Chantiers de l'Atlantique à St-Nazaire, France, et a fait sa croisière de baptême en Polynésie en janvier 1998, sous le drapeau° fier° de la France.

cruise

est... comes from
a été... was designed to
throughout
joined forces with

faire... make a dream come true / *Tout en... While remaining faithful to*
stars

qui font... for which Radisson Seven Seas is renowned
half (of them) / *sont... have (as an amenity)*

amenities
ship / *built*

bateau de... pleasure boat
managed by
flag / *proud*
nights
leaving from

Après la lecture

Questions sur le texte

1. Quel est le surnom *(nickname)* de Tahiti?
2. D'où vient le bateau *M/S Gauguin* (où est-il construit)?
3. Quels aménagements a le *M/S Gauguin*?
4. Quand est-ce qu'il est possible de voyager à bord du *M/S Gauguin* (uniquement en automne, ou en toute saison)?
5. La croisière dure *(lasts)* combien de jours *(days)*?

Activités

Ⓐ Cherchez sur Internet d'autres informations sur Tahiti. Quels sont les sites touristiques? Quels sont les plats typiques servis dans les restaurants?

Ⓑ Quels autres artistes francophones connaissez-vous°? En groupes, faites une liste d'artistes francophones (musiciens, acteurs, danseurs...).

do you know

Ⓒ Le taro est une des plantes que les Polynésiens ont apporté a Hawaii. Cherchez le mot *taro sur Internet et trouvez* une recette qui utilise le taro comme ingrédient.

vocabulaire

Noms / Pronoms

Afrique *(f.)*	Africa	**la France**	France
une agence de voyages	travel agency	**un galet**	smooth stone
Algérie *(f.)*	Algeria	**une gare**	train station
Allemagne *(f.)*	Germany	**Genève**	Geneva
Amérique du Nord *(f.)*	North America	**la Grande-Bretagne**	Great Britain
Amérique du Sud *(f.)*	South America	**la Grèce**	Greece
Angleterre *(f.)*	England	**la Hollande**	Holland
une année	year	**une hôtesse**	hostess
un appartement	apartment	**Irlande** *(f.)*	Ireland
un après-midi	afternoon	**Italie** *(f.)*	Italy
un arrêt d'autobus	bus stop	**le Japon**	Japan
Asie *(f.)*	Asia	**un laboratoire**	laboratory
Autriche *(f.)*	Austria	**La Havane**	Havana
une banque	bank	**La Nouvelle-Orléans**	New Orleans
la Belgique	Belgium	**une librairie**	bookstore
une bibliothèque	library	**Lisbonne**	Lisbon
le Brésil	Brazil	**une liste**	list
Bruxelles	Brussels	**Londres**	London
un bureau de poste	post office	**un lycée**	high school
le Canada	Canada	**un magasin**	store
un casino	casino	**une maison**	house
un centre commercial	shopping center	**le Maroc**	Morocco
une chambre	bedroom	**un matin**	morning
la Chine	China	**une mer**	sea
un cinéma	cinema	**messieurs** *(m.)*	gentlemen
un continent	continent	**Mexico**	Mexico City
la Corse	Corsica	**le Mexique**	Mexico
la Côte d'Azur	French Riviera	**un milliard**	billion
		un million	million
la Côte d'Ivoire	Côte d'Ivoire	**une minute**	minute
le Danemark	Denmark	**Moscou**	Moscow
une église	church	**le Mozambique**	Mozambique
un endroit	place	**un musée**	museum
Espagne *(f.)*	Spain	**la Norvège**	Norway
Etats-Unis *(m.)*	United States	**un parc**	park
Europe *(f.)*	Europe	**un parking**	parking lot
la Finlande	Finland	**un pays**	country
		Pays-Bas *(m.)*	Netherlands
		une pharmacie	drugstore
		une piscine	swimming pool
		une place	square

une plage	beach	le Sénégal	Senegal
la Pologne	Poland	un stade	stadium
le Portugal	Portugal	la Suède	Sweden
un renseignement	information	la Suisse	Switzerland
la République centrafricaine	Central African Republic	un Syndicat d'Initiative	Tourist Office
la République démocratique du Congo	Democratic Republic of the Congo	le Tchad	Chad
		un théâtre	theater
		la Tunisie	Tunisia
une résidence universitaire	dorm	une usine	factory
		Varsovie	Warsaw
un restau-U	university cafeteria	une ville	city / town
une rue	street	un voyage	trip
la Russie	Russia	un week-end	weekend
une semaine	week		

Verbes

aller	to go	rester	to stay / remain
chercher	to look for	visiter	to visit
rentrer	to go back	voyager	to travel

Adjectifs / Adverbes

aujourd'hui	today	mille	thousand
autre	other	plein	full
cent	hundred	pourquoi	why
cher	expensive	prochain	next
demain	tomorrow	si	if
demain matin	tomorrow morning	sous	under
demain soir	tomorrow evening	sur	on
là-bas	over there	tous	all
maintenant	now		

Expressions

à côté de	next to	il faut	it is necessary
Ah non!	Oh no!	loin de	far from
allez-y	go ahead	merci mille fois	thanks a million
allons-y	let's go		
au bord de	along / by	Où ça?	Whereabouts?
au coin de	at the corner of	parce que	because
chez	at / at the home of	pas du tout	not at all
derrière	behind	(de la) place	room
en	in	pour	to / in order to
en face de	across from	près de	near
en ville	downtown	tous les jours	every day
entre	between		

CHAPITRE

5

commençons

grammaire

communiquons

lecture culturelle

vocabulaire

A Tombouctou

Le monde francophone

OBJECTIVES

Language

- Vocabulary for clothing and colors
- Vowel tension
- **Faire** and expressions using **faire**
- **Passé composé**
- Possessive adjectives
- Stressed pronouns

Culture

- The French-speaking world

Communication

- Talking about common activities
- Describing past events
- Expressing ownership
- Giving and getting information

commençons

Lise et Gaëtan Morin font leurs bagages.

Lise et Gaëtan sont québécois. Ils habitent à Montréal et, tous les ans en hiver, ils font un voyage en Martinique.

GAËTAN: Est-ce que tu as fait les valises?

LISE: Oui, mais je n'ai pas terminé les bagages à main; et toi, est-ce que tu as fait toutes tes courses?

GAËTAN: Bien sûr. Tu as pensé à mon short blanc et à mon tee-shirt de l'université de Montréal?

LISE: Si tu portes quelque chose comme cela, tu vas avoir l'air du parfait touriste!

GAËTAN: Tu as raison; ce n'est pas une bonne idée. Je vais faire des achats à Fort-de-France.

LISE: Moi aussi. Leurs maillots de bain sont super.

GAËTAN: Ça y est! Nous sommes prêts, mais où sont mes lunettes de soleil?

LISE: Dans la poche de ton veston. Fais attention; n'oublie rien!

Etudions le dialogue

1. Est-ce que Lise et Gaëtan sont français? Où est-ce qu'ils habitent?
2. Pourquoi est-ce qu'ils font leurs bagages?
3. Pourquoi Lise n'aime pas le short blanc et le tee-shirt de Gaëtan?
4. Qu'est-ce que Gaëtan va faire à Fort-de-France?
5. Qu'est-ce que Lise aime aux Antilles? Pourquoi?
6. Qu'est-ce que Gaëtan cherche?

Mots clés

font leurs bagages *(m.)*	*pack their luggage*	avoir l'air	*to look like*
(faire ses bagages)		parfait	*perfect*
québécois	*from Quebec*	touriste *(m./f.)*	*tourist*
tous les ans	*every year*	bonne (bon)	*good*
hiver *(m.)*	*winter*	une idée	*idea*
font un voyage *(m.)*	*take a trip*	faire des achats *(m.)*	*to go shopping*
(faire un voyage)		moi	*I*
as fait les valises *(f.)*	*packed the suitcases*	maillots de bain *(m.)*	*bathing suits*
(faire les valises)		super	*terrific*
bagages à main *(m.)*	*hand luggage*	Ça y est!	*That's it!*
toi	*you*	prêts	*ready*
as fait toutes tes courses *(f.)*	*did all your errands*	mes	*my*
(faire des courses)		lunettes de soleil *(f.)*	*sunglasses*
Bien sûr.	*Of course.*	une poche	*pocket*
as pensé à (penser à)	*thought of*	ton	*your*
mon *(m.)*	*my*	un veston	*coat*
un short	*shorts*	Fais attention.	*Be careful.*
un tee-shirt	*T-shirt*	(faire attention)	
portes (porter)	*wear*	N'oublie rien.	*Don't forget*
quelque chose	*something*	(oublier)	*anything.*

𝓕aisons connaissance

French is the native language of more than eight million Canadians and the official language of Quebec. Montreal is the second largest French-speaking city in the world. It has a large, cosmopolitan population and exhibits cultural features of English- and French-speaking communities and many other ethnic groups. It is often the site of international meetings and events and in 1976 hosted the Summer Olympics.

The people of Quebec love to travel, and because of the long winters, many take a vacation in a warmer climate. Some of their favorite places are the state of Florida and two French **départements** in the Caribbean, Guadeloupe and Martinique. ▶

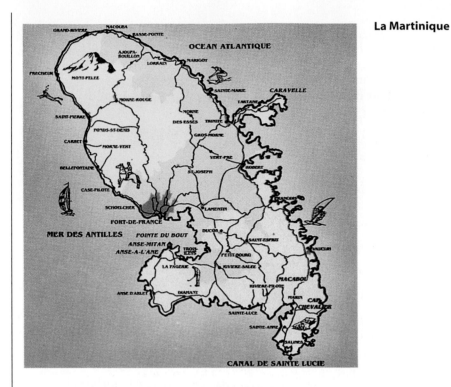

La Martinique

Discovered in 1495 by Christopher Columbus, the island of Martinique is part of the **Petites Antilles,** and it has always been a part of France except for two short periods when it was occupied by English-speaking people. Fort-de-France is its administrative, commercial, and cultural center. With its mild climate all year round and its beautiful sandy beaches, the island attracts many European and Quebecois tourists. As in Guadeloupe, French is spoken in Martinique, but **le créole** is another language spoken by the natives.

Enrichissons notre vocabulaire

Les vêtements *(m.) (Clothing)*

les bottes *(f.)*	*boots*	le manteau	*coat*
le chapeau	*hat*	le parapluie	*umbrella*
le costume	*suit*	le pull	*sweater*
l'écharpe *(f.)*	*scarf*	la robe de chambre	*robe*
l'imperméable *(m.)*	*raincoat*	les tennis *(f.)*	*tennis shoes*

Quelques expressions utiles *(Useful expressions)*

Quel polo est-ce que vous allez **acheter**?	*Which polo shirt are you going to buy?*
Combien coûte le **pyjama** / la **chemise de nuit**?	*How much are the pajamas / the nightgown?*
Quelles vestes / **ceintures** est-ce que Christine va **emporter**?	*Which jackets / belts is Christine going to take?*
Quels gants est-ce que Lise porte?	*Which gloves is Lise wearing?*

Les couleurs *(f.) (Colors)*

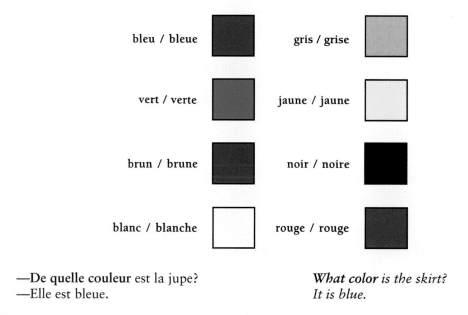

bleu / bleue	gris / grise
vert / verte	jaune / jaune
brun / brune	noir / noire
blanc / blanche	rouge / rouge

—De quelle couleur est la jupe?   *What color is the skirt?*
—Elle est bleue.   *It is blue.*

Prononciation   **Vowel tension**

French vowels are pronounced with much more tension of the muscles in the tongue, lips, and jaw than English vowels. The gliding of one vowel sound into another is common in English, and the sound produced is called a *diphthong*. You must avoid tongue movement when pronouncing French vowel sounds, so that each is distinct.

Repeat the following English and French word pairs after your teacher, being careful to avoid any unwanted movement when pronouncing the French words.

English	French		English	French
see	si		day	des
D	dit		Fay	fait
boo	bout		foe	faut
do	doux		low	l'eau

Exercices

Ⓐ Repeat the following words after your teacher, paying attention to vowel tension.

/ i /	/ u /	/ e /	/ o /
1. si	où	et	l'eau
2. dit	bout	des	beau
3. Guy	cou	les	faut
4. J	fou	mes	mot
5. oui	vous	été	tôt

Ⓑ Read the following sentences, taking care to keep your muscles tense when you pronounce the vowels.

1. Vous travaillez au café?
2. Sylvie étudie le français.
3. Hervé va aller au musée.
4. Les Anglais vont visiter l'université.
5. Le bureau est à côté du tableau.
6. J'ai oublié mon idée.
7. Vous allez téléphoner cet après-midi?
8. Nous aimons le café de Colombie.

grammaire

I. The verb *faire*

You use the verb **faire** to describe many activities and to ask other people what they are doing.

faire *(to do, make)*	
je **fais**	nous **faisons**
tu **fais**	vous **faites**
il / elle / on **fait**	ils / elles **font**
Imperative: **fais, faisons, faites**	

All singular forms are pronounced alike: / fɛ /. The **nous** form is pronounced / fø zɔ̃ /.

Il ne **fait** pas de devoirs.   **Faisons** la cuisine ensemble!

Mots clés   *Common expressions with faire*

A la maison			
faire la cuisine	*to cook*	faire la grasse matinée	*to sleep late*
des crêpes *(f.)*	*crepes*	faire la lessive	*to do the washing*
une omelette	*omelet*	faire le ménage	*to do housework*
un sandwich	*sandwich*	faire un régime	*to be on a diet*
des pâtes *(f.)*	*noodles*	faire la vaisselle	*to do the dishes*

A l'université			
faire attention à	*to pay attention to*	faire la queue	*to wait in line*
faire des devoirs	*to do homework*	faire du sport	*to play sports*

En ville	
faire les bagages *(m.)* / la valise	*to pack one's bags / a suitcase*
faire des courses *(f.)*	*to go shopping, to do errands*
faire une promenade / un tour	*to go for a walk*
faire un voyage	*to take a trip*

A l'extérieur (Outside)

*The verb **faire** is also used with the impersonal pronoun **il** to talk about the weather.*

Quel temps fait-il?   *What's the weather like?*

Il fait beau.	*It is nice.*	**Il fait chaud.**	*It is warm.*
Il fait mauvais.	*The weather is bad.*	**Il fait froid.**	*It is cold.*

Attention! ────────────────

As in English, the answer to a question using **faire** often has a different verb.

—Qu'est-ce que vous **faites** ce soir?
—Je **vais regarder** la télévision.

Language

A **Des activités.** Indicate what people are doing or asking about by filling in the blanks with the appropriate form of **faire**.

1. Nous _____ des devoirs.
2. Il _____ la vaisselle.
3. Il va _____ un tour en ville.
4. Est-ce que vous _____ les bagages de Paul?
5. Tu _____ la grasse matinée?
6. On a faim; _____ des sandwichs!

B **Interview.** You are being interviewed to find out about life in your home. Answer the following questions, using the cues provided.

1. Vous aimez faire des promenades?   (Oui, nous...)
2. Qu'est-ce que vous aimez faire le week-end?   (... des courses.)
3. Est-ce que les enfants font attention?   (Oui, mais Jacqueline ne...)
4. Vous faites la cuisine?   (Oui,... ce soir.)
5. Qu'est-ce que vous préparez?   (Nous... faire... omelette.)
6. Est-ce que vous faites la vaisselle?   (Non,... détester...)

Culture

C **Des gens célèbres.** Look at the list below. What do these French-speaking people do for a living? Can you think of other famous people and name their professions?

MODEL: *Agnès Varda fait des films.*

1. Zinedine Zidane	a. la cuisine
2. Justin Wilson et Paul Prudhomme	b. de la musique
3. Jean-Claude Killy	c. du cinéma (ancien mannequin)
4. Laeticia Casta	d. de la politique
5. Luc Plamandon	e. du ski
6. Lionel Jospin	f. du foot
7. Le professeur Luc Montagnier	g. de la recherche médicale (co-découvreur du virus du sida en 1983)

D **Les vêtements.** Match the clothes and accessories in the left column with the famous French designers that specialize in them in the right column, using the verb **faire**.

MODEL: maillots de bain   Rasurel
         Rasurel fait des maillots de bain.

1. écharpes	a. Yves Saint-Laurent
2. lunettes de soleil	b. Bally et Charles Jourdan
3. robes	c. Lacoste
4. costumes pour hommes	d. Hermès
5. chaussures	e. Vuarnet
6. polos	f. Christian Dior et Guy Laroche

Ⓔ **Mes projets.** What are your plans for next weekend? Indicate your activities for each time slot, using the suggestions provided or your own ideas.

des devoirs	la grasse matinée	aller danser
la cuisine	aller au cinéma	regarder la télévision
des courses	une promenade	travailler à la bibliothèque

1. vendredi soir *(Friday night)*
2. samedi *(Saturday)*
3. samedi soir *(Saturday night)*
4. dimanche *(Sunday)*

Ⓕ **Une interview.** Interview a classmate to find out the following information.

1. où il / elle fait des courses
2. où il / elle fait des promenades
3. s'il / si elle fait la cuisine / le ménage
4. s'il / si elle va faire un régime
5. quand il / elle aime faire le ménage
6. s'il / si elle fait attention au professeur / aux agents de police

II. The *passé composé*

You use the **passé composé** to tell what happened in the past.

A. The **passé composé** refers to actions or events that the speaker views as completed in the past. To form the **passé composé,** use the present indicative forms of **avoir** and the past participle of the main verb.

travailler	*(to work)*	
j' **ai travaillé**	nous **avons travaillé**
tu **as travaillé**	vous **avez travaillé**
il / elle / on **a travaillé**	ils / elles **ont travaillé**

J'**ai** tout **terminé** ce matin.   Tu **as acheté** un pantalon bleu?

B. To form the past participle of **-er** verbs, drop the **-er** of the infinitive and add é as in **travailler → travaillé**. (The pronunciation does not change.)

C. The **passé composé** has several English equivalents. For example, **elle a chanté** could be *she sang, she has sung,* or *she did sing.*

Elle a chanté la semaine dernière.	*She **sang** last week.*
Elle a chanté trois fois.	*She **has sung** three times.*
Elle a chanté?	***Did** she **sing**?*

D. In the negative, place the **ne... pas** around the auxiliary verb **avoir.**

Il **n'a pas** porté de costume.   Je **n'ai pas** trouvé les gants.

E. To ask a question in the **passé composé,** use the forms you learned in Chapter 1:

> **Elle a fait** du sport?
> **Est-ce que** tu as terminé les bagages à main?
> Tu as fait tous les achats, **n'est-ce pas?**

F. Many verbs have irregular past participles. Here are the ones for the verbs that you have studied so far.

avoir → eu	Il **a eu** une idée.	*He **had** an idea.*
être → été	Elle **a été** malade.	*She **has been** sick.*
faire → fait	Tu **as fait** la lessive?	***Did** you **do** the wash?*

G. Generally, expressions of time are placed either at the end or at the beginning of the sentence. Some frequent expressions indicating past time are the following:

hier	*yesterday*
récemment	*recently*
la semaine dernière	*last week*
le week-end dernier / le mois dernier	*last weekend / last month*
l'été dernier	*last summer*
l'année dernière	*last year*

> J'ai fait une promenade **hier.**
> **Hier** il a fait le ménage pendant trente minutes.
> **Le week-end dernier** nous avons fait la grasse matinée.

In contrast, many frequently used adverbs precede the past participle.

beaucoup	*a lot*	**mal**	*poorly, badly*	**souvent**	*often*
bien	*well*	**pas encore**	*not yet*	**toujours**	*always*
déjà	*already*	**peu**	*little*	**trop**	*too much, too many*

> —Vous avez **déjà** acheté des vêtements de plage?
> —Non, je n'ai **pas encore** été au magasin.

> —Ils ont **bien** dîné?
> —Oui, mais ils ont **trop** mangé.

Language

Ⓐ **Un voyage.** Replace the infinitive with the **passé composé** in the following sentences.

1. Jean-Paul (faire) un voyage en Grande-Bretagne avec Christine.
2. Pierre (donner) un cadeau à Jean-Paul.
3. —Tu (être) content du cadeau?
4. —Nous (trouver) le livre sur l'Angleterre formidable.
5. Nous (visiter) Paris aussi.
6. —Tu (manger) un couscous?
7. —On ne... pas (trouver) cela mauvais.
8. Il (faire) froid en Angleterre.

B Pas du tout! Change the following sentences to the negative to state that people did *not* do the following things.

1. Nous avons fait le ménage.
2. Il a beaucoup aimé le livre.
3. Michelle a trouvé l'hôtel.
4. Gaston a fait attention au prof.
5. Elles ont cherché une chambre.
6. On a souvent invité des amis.

C Des activités. Make complete sentences to show what happened at the times in column **A** by using these expressions with words from columns **B** and **C**.

A	B	C
hier	je	acheter une jupe
le week-end dernier	mes amis	faire froid
récemment	mes parents	avoir chaud
la semaine dernière	le professeur	visiter un parc
l'année dernière	il	être fatigué(e)(s)
l'été dernier	???	???

Culture

D Des célébrités. What did the following French-speaking people do to become famous?

MODEL: *François Mitterrand a été président de la République française.*

1. Marie Curie
2. Louis Pasteur
3. Edith Piaf
4. Auguste Rodin
5. Frédéric Auguste Bartholdi
6. Louis Malle
7. Léopold Senghor
8. Blaise Pascal

a. faire des films
b. être président du Sénégal et membre de l'Académie française
c. avoir le prix Nobel de physique et de chimie
d. développer des vaccins
e. sculpter la statue de la Liberté que la France a donnée aux Américains
f. faire des recherches géométriques et écrire *Les Pensées*
g. créer les sculptures *Le Penseur* et *Le Baiser*
h. chanter «La vie en rose»

Communication

E Ma journée. Tell your classmates one thing you did yesterday. Then, tell them something you did not do last week that you should have. Use the suggestions provided or your own responses.

MODEL: *Hier j'ai fait la lessive. La semaine dernière je n'ai pas préparé la leçon.*

préparer la leçon	faire la lessive
manger au restau-U	écouter les professeurs
parler à mes parents	terminer les exercices
faire le ménage	étudier à la bibliothèque

F **Discussion.** Divide into small groups and find out what your partners did or did not do last summer. Report your findings to the class. Some possible answers are listed below.

MODEL: *L'été dernier, Robert a étudié le français et il a visité la Floride.*

travailler à...	faire un voyage...
visiter l'état de...	inviter des amis à...
acheter...	parler au téléphone avec...
étudier...	???

G **Questions personnelles.** Mes activités récentes.

1. Où avez-vous été récemment?
2. Est-ce que vous avez acheté des vêtements? De quelle couleur?
3. Combien est-ce qu'ils ont coûté?
4. Est-ce que vous avez invité un(e) ami(e) à la maison?
5. Qu'est-ce que vous avez fait ensemble?
6. Quel pays est-ce que vous avez déjà visité?
7. Vous avez parlé avec une personne célèbre *(famous)*? Qui?
8. Quel film est-ce que vous avez regardé à la télévision récemment?

III. Possessive adjectives

You use possessive adjectives to show ownership.

A. In English, possessive adjectives show the ownership of an object (*my* coat) or of a quality (*your* honesty). They also show relationship: *his* girlfriend / *her* boyfriend.

In French, these adjectives show not only the possessor but also indicate the number (singular or plural) of the object or quality possessed. They can also show the gender (masculine or feminine) of the thing possessed.

mon pull	*my sweater*	(**pull** is *m. + sing.*)
ma ceinture	*my belt*	(**ceinture** is *f. + sing.*)
mes bottes	*my boots*	(**bottes** is *pl.*)

B. The written forms are as follows:

	singular			
person	**English equivalent**	**masculine**	**feminine**	**plural**
1st singular	*my*	mon	ma	mes
2nd singular	*your*	ton	ta	tes
3rd singular	*his, her its, one's*	son	sa	ses

plural				
person	English equivalent	masculine	feminine	plural
1st plural	*our*		notre	nos
2nd plural	*your*		votre	vos
3rd plural	*their*		leur	leurs

French identifies the gender of the item possessed, not the gender of the person who owns the item(s).

—C'est l'imperméable de Marie?
—Oui, c'est **son** imperméable.
—C'est l'imperméable de Jacques?
—Oui, c'est **son** imperméable.

—C'est la robe de chambre de Lise?
—Oui, c'est **sa** robe de chambre.
—C'est la robe de chambre de Robert?
—Oui, c'est **sa** robe de chambre.

Attention!

1. The adjectives **ma, ta,** and **sa** are not used before a vowel. You must use **mon, ton,** and **son,** even if the word is feminine.

   Vous êtes **son** étudiante?   Voilà **son** amie.

   Therefore, **ton enfant** may refer to a male or female child.

2. To identify the possessor, use **c'est** (for the singular) or **ce sont** (for plurals) as the subject of the sentence.

   —Mme Morin, **c'est** votre manteau?
   —Oui, **c'est** mon manteau.

   —**Ce sont** les chaussures de Jean?
   —Oui, **ce sont** ses chaussures.

C. The pronunciation of possessive adjectives changes according to whether the following noun starts with a consonant or a vowel sound.

1. The only final written consonant that is always pronounced is the **r** of **leur.** The pronunciation of all other possessive adjectives changes before a vowel sound.

   Où est **leur argent?**   / lœ ʀaʀ ʒɑ̃ /   Voici **leur valise.**   / lœʀ va liz /

2. The **n** of **mon, ton, son** and the **s** of **mes, tes, ses, nos, vos, leurs** are pronounced before a vowel sound because of **liaison.**

Liaison		No liaison	
leurs enfants	/ lœʀ zɑ̃ fɑ̃ /	leurs classes	/ lœʀ klas /
mon écharpe	/ mɔ̃ ne ʃaʀp /	mon frère	/ mɔ̃ fʀɛʀ /

3. The final **e** in **notre** and **votre** is not pronounced before a vowel; the adjective and noun should be pronounced as one word.

notre appartement   / nɔ tʀa paʀ tø mɑ̃ /   votre école   / vɔ tʀe kɔl /

4. Remember that **ma, ta,** and **sa** change the most: they become **mon, ton,** and **son** when the following noun begins with a vowel sound.

Ce qu'ils disent

In conversation, the **-re** of **notre** and **votre** is often dropped when it occurs before a consonant.

> Notre voiture est rouge.   / nɔt vwa tyʀ /
> Ils ont votre sac.   / vɔt sak /
>
> *but:* C'est votre imperméable?   / vɔ tʀɛ̃ pɛʀ me abl /

Language

A En cours. Replace the italicized words with each of the suggested subjects and change the possessive adjective to reflect the new subject.

1. *Il* a demandé son cahier.   (Je)
2. *Pierre* a trouvé son stylo.   (Ils)
3. *Elles* ont parlé à leurs amis.   (Vous)
4. *J'*ai oublié mon sac à dos.   (Tu)
5. *Vous* avez fait vos devoirs?   (Elles)
6. *Elle* a expliqué ses idées.   (Nous)

B Faisons la lessive! Your friends did a load of laundry, but they washed everything together, so confusion reigns as they sort out the wash. Answer their questions using possessive adjectives and the cues provided.

MODEL: C'est le chemisier de Micheline?   *Oui, c'est son chemisier.*

1. C'est la chemise de Jacques?   (Oui,...)
2. Tu as trouvé les chaussettes de Monique?   (...sont ici.)
3. Où est la jupe de Jeanne?   (Voici...)
4. Tu cherches le pyjama de mon frère?   (Oui,...)
5. Est-ce que c'est le jean de Pierre?   (Oui,...)
6. Tu as la robe de Chantal?   (Oui,...)

C A la douane. A customs agent is going through your suitcase. Answer her questions according to the cues provided.

1. Est-ce que vous avez vos bagages à main?   (Oui,...)
2. Vous êtes avec vos amis?   (Non,... famille.)
3. Ce sont vos vêtements?   (Oui,...)
4. Où est-ce que vous avez trouvé votre jean et vos chemises?
   (... à Kmart.)
5. Qu'est-ce qu'il y a dans vos chaussures?   (... chaussettes.)
6. Vous avez fait votre lessive récemment?   (Oui,... la semaine dernière.)

AIR CANADA
Téléphonez à Air Canada ou à votre agent de voyages pour des renseignements concernant nos tours-vacances.

AIR CANA

Culture

Ⓓ **Les préférences.** Try to guess the preferences of French people in the categories below.

MODEL: Vacances préférées des Français?
a. Italie   b. Espagne   c. Suisse
Leurs vacances préférées sont en Espagne.

1. Boisson préférée avec le dîner?
a. eau   b. vin   c. bière

2. Activité préférée pour les jeunes?
a. faire du sport   b. jouer   c. regarder la télé

3. Musique préférée des jeunes?
a. le rock   b. le reggae   c. le rap

4. Films préférés des Français?
a. films comiques   b. films d'amour   c. films d'aventure

5. Sport préféré des jeunes?
a. la gymnastique   b. le tennis   c. le football

6. Et avec qui est-ce que les jeunes parlent de leurs problèmes?
a. frère ou sœur   b. amis   c. mère

Communication

Ⓔ **Une décision importante.** You are stranded on a desert island. With a classmate, consult the following list and decide what three items you want to have with you.

MODEL: *Je voudrais avoir ma radio, mon short et mes tee-shirts.*

parapluie	petit(e) ami(e)	bière préférée
jean	parents	livre de français
cravates	professeurs	lunettes de soleil
radio	maillot de bain	???

F **Ma famille.** Describe the members of your family, according to the ideas below. Present your description to the class.

MODEL: *Mon frère est sympathique.*
Mes cousins habitent à New York.

Où est-ce qu'ils habitent?　　　Qu'est-ce qu'ils aiment?
Où est-ce qu'ils travaillent?　　Qu'est-ce qu'ils détestent?
Quel âge est-ce qu'ils ont?　　　Où est-ce qu'ils aiment aller?

G **Questions personnelles.** A l'université ou chez moi?

1. Où est-ce que vos parents habitent?
2. De quelle couleur est leur maison?
3. Où est votre résidence universitaire ou votre appartement?
4. Vous faites vos devoirs là ou à la bibliothèque?
5. Vous aimez mieux faire votre lessive en ville ou chez vos parents?
6. Qu'est-ce qu'il y a sur votre bureau?
7. Quand vous n'étudiez pas, qu'est-ce que vous faites avec vos ami(e)s?
8. Quel est votre restaurant préféré? Et le restaurant préféré de vos ami(e)s?

IV. Stressed pronouns

You use stressed pronouns to talk about people when you want to make it clear whom you are talking about.

	stressed pronouns	
person	**singular**	**plural**
1st	**moi** *I, me*	**nous** *we, us*
2nd	**toi** *you*	**vous** *you*
3rd	**lui** *(m.)*　*he, him*	**eux** *(m.)*　*they, them*
	elle *(f.)*　*she, her*	**elles** *(f.)*　*they, them*

A. Stressed pronouns are used without a verb, in order to ask or answer a question with one word, or in a compound subject when separated from the verb.

Et **toi?** Tu as fait tes courses?

—Qui aime le vin?
—**Moi!**

Elle et **toi,** vous n'allez pas acheter cela!

B. Stressed pronouns are also used after a preposition.

—Tu vas travailler avec **nous?**　　—Est-ce qu'ils sont en retard?
—Non, je travaille avec **elle.**　　　—Oui, le professeur a commencé
　　　　　　　　　　　　　　　　　　sans **eux.**

C. Stressed pronouns can show ownership when used with the expression **être à**. To ask to whom something belongs, use **A qui est... ?** or **A qui sont... ?**

A qui est le polo rouge?	*Whose red shirt is this?*
Il **est à moi.**	*It's mine.*
Elles **sont à vous,** les bottes?	*The boots are yours?*
Non, elles **sont à Lucie.**	*No, they're Lucie's.*

D. You also use stressed pronouns to put emphasis on a subject pronoun.

1. In French, you cannot simply emphasize a word by putting stress on it as you can in English (*I don't care!*). To emphasize a word in French, you use a stressed pronoun to repeat the subject.

—J'adore les vêtements de Madonna.
—**Moi,** je n'aime pas ses chemisiers.

—Elles sont riches, **elles.**
—Pas du tout! Elles sont professeurs.

2. This structure also allows you to contrast people:

Lui, il est médecin; **elle,** avocate.

Note that a stressed pronoun can come at the beginning or the end of a sentence, and that the intonation rises at the comma. If you want to emphasize a noun, however, the stressed pronoun must follow it.

Les Canadiens, **eux,** ils sont sympathiques.

3. Another way to emphasize a subject pronoun is to use the stressed pronoun followed by **-même(s)**. This is the equivalent of *-self* in English.

—Est-ce que vous avez fait votre robe **vous-même?**
—Oui, la semaine dernière.

—Vous mangez au restaurant?
—Non, nous faisons la cuisine **nous-mêmes.**

Ce qu'ils disent

1. Stressed pronouns appear very frequently in conversation.

   Jacques, **lui,** (il) est studieux.

2. The pronoun **moi** may appear unexpectedly to mean *in my opinion*.

   Moi, j'aime le sucre dans mon café.
   Moi, pas du tout.

3. Since **on** frequently replaces **nous** as a subject pronoun, you will hear the stressed pronoun **nous** used with it.

   On travaille beaucoup, **nous!**

A **Les possessions.** The following sentences all show possession with possessive adjectives. Change them by using the expression **être à.**

MODEL: C'est mon livre.   *Il est à moi.*

1. Ce sont leurs valises.
2. C'est ton costume.
3. Ce sont vos CD.
4. C'est la robe de Sylvie.
5. C'est mon argent.
6. Ce sont nos tennis.
7. C'est la maison des Morin.
8. C'est le pyjama de l'enfant.

B **Des opinions.** Daniel has very strong opinions about everything. How
would he make the subjects of the following sentences more emphatic?

MODEL: Elle ne va pas au cinéma.
         Elle, elle ne va pas au cinéma. / Elle ne va pas au cinéma, elle.

1. Mes amis sont très intelligents.
2. Je déteste faire des courses.
3. Nous allons acheter des vêtements formidables.
4. Mes sœurs ont du talent.
5. Tu ne travailles pas beaucoup.
6. Vous n'habitez pas une maison magnifique.

C **Les préférences.** American and French tastes are sometimes different,
sometimes similar. Form sentences from the elements below and add
stressed pronouns to indicate preferences.

MODEL: le lait avec le dîner
         Nous, nous aimons le lait; les Français, eux, ils aiment mieux l'eau.

1. aimer porter un jean
2. (ne... pas) aimer les westerns
3. avoir beaucoup d'amis
4. faire des promenades en voiture
5. commander de l'eau naturelle au restaurant
6. aimer acheter beaucoup de vêtements
7. (ne... pas) faire souvent la bise
8. (ne... pas) manger souvent du fromage

D **Les vêtements.** You are staying with a French family, and you discover
that the son / daughter is the same size as you. Using the size comparison
chart on the next page, make plans for a shopping trip by converting your
sizes for the clothing listed below.

MODELS: *(for women) Les robes? Moi, je porte un 8, elle, un 36.*
          (for men) Les costumes? Moi, je porte un 36, lui, un 38.

Les femmes	**Les hommes**
1. Les robes	1. Les costumes
2. Les collants *(pantyhose)*	2. Les chemises
3. Les chaussures	3. Les chaussures
4. Les chemisiers	4. Les tricots *(knitted wear)*

TABLE DE COMPARAISON DE TAILLES

Robes, chemisiers et tricots femmes.

F	36	38	40	42	44	46	48
GB	10	12	14	16	18	20	22
USA	8	10	12	14	16	18	20

Bas et collants femmes.

F	1	2	3	4	5
USA	8½	9	9½	10	10½

Chaussures femmes.

F	35½	36	36½	37	37½	38	39
GB	3	3½	4	4½	5	5½	6
USA	4	4½	5	5½	6	6½	7½

Chaussures hommes.

F	39	40	41	42	43	44	45
GB	5½	6½	7	8	8½	9½	10½
USA	6	7	7½	8½	9	10	11

Costumes hommes.

F	36	38	40	42	44	46	48
GB	35	36	37	38	39	40	42
USA	35	36	37	38	39	40	42

Chemises hommes.

F	36	37	38	39	40	41	42
USA	14	14½	15	15½	16	16½	17

Tricots hommes.

F	36	38	40	42	44	46
GB	46	48	51	54	56	59
USA	46	48	51	54	56	59

Communication

E **Moi et eux.** Think about a person or a group of people who do the following things and people who do not. Express the contrast using stressed pronouns.

MODEL: parler français
> *Moi, je parle français; mon camarade de chambre, lui, il parle anglais.*

1. avoir du talent
2. parler espagnol
3. aimer le vin
4. chanter bien
5. faire bien la cuisine
6. porter des vêtements super

F **Cherchez la réponse!** Question your classmates to find out the following information.

MODEL: Qui a acheté un tee-shirt récemment?
> *Robert, lui, il a acheté un tee-shirt.*

1. Qui a des chaussures rouges?
2. Qui a deux frères?
3. Qui a visité l'Europe?
4. Qui habite une maison blanche?
5. Qui adore la cuisine mexicaine?
6. Qui a fait la grasse matinée aujourd'hui?

G **Questions personnelles.** Et vous?

1. Vous habitez chez vos parents?
2. Vous parlez français avec votre professeur?
3. Est-ce que le professeur parle français avec vous?
4. Vous allez au cinéma seul(e) ou avec vos amis?
5. Est-ce que vos camarades aiment étudier avec vous?
6. Est-ce que vous pensez souvent à vos parents?

communiquons

Demander des renseignements

In Chapter 4 you learned how to ask for and give directions. There are many other types of information that you will have to ask for when traveling through or living in a French-speaking country. You will also have to clarify the meaning of what you hear and want to say, participate in basic conversations, and understand questions and provide information when it is asked of you.

S'il vous plaît, pourriez-vous me dire...

Expressions

▶ **En ville on demande...**

—Comment vous appelez-vous?	*What's your name?*
—Je m'appelle Chantal Laforge.	*My name is Chantal Laforge.*
—Comment allez-vous? / Comment ça va? / Ça va?	*How are you?*
—Je vais bien. / Ça va.	*I'm fine.*

—Quelle heure est-il?	*What time is it?*
—A quelle heure est-ce que l'autobus arrive?	*At what time does the bus arrive?*
—Il arrive à trois heures.	*It arrives at 3:00.*
—Quel temps fait-il / va-t-il faire?	*What's the weather like / going to be like?*

▶ **En cours on demande...**

—Comment dit-on *coat* en français?	*How do you say* coat *in French?*
—On dit «manteau».	*You say "manteau."*
—Qu'est-ce que ça veut dire?	*What does that mean?*
—Que veut dire «chaussures»?	*What does* chaussures *mean?*
—Ça veut dire «*shoes*».	*It means "shoes."*
—Que veut dire l'expression «à tout à l'heure»?	*What does the expression* à tout à l'heure *mean?*
—Ça veut dire «*see you soon*».	*It means "see you soon."*

▶ **Au magasin on demande...**

—Est-ce que vous avez des gants?	*Do you have gloves?*
—Oui, là-bas, au fond, Monsieur.	*Yes, over there, in the back, sir.*
—C'est combien?	*How much is it?*
—C'est 20 euros.	*It's 20 euros.*
—Combien coûte l'écharpe bleue?	*How much is the blue scarf?*
—Elle coûte 14 euros.	*It's 14 euros.*
—Combien coûtent les pulls là-bas?	*How much are the sweaters over there?*
—Le pull rouge coûte 65 euros et les blancs 83.	*The red sweater costs 65 euros, and the white ones 83.*

▶ **Chez les amis on demande...**

—Quoi de neuf?	*What's new?*
—Pas grand-chose!	*Not much!*
—Qu'est-ce qui se passe?	*What's going on?*
—Qu'est-ce qui s'est passé?	*What happened?*
—Rien d'important.	*Nothing much.*
—Qu'est-ce qu'il y a?	*What's the matter?*
—Qu'est-ce qui ne va pas?	*What's wrong?*
—Frédéric est malade.	*Fred is sick.*

Interaction

Une touriste entre dans une boutique.

L'EMPLOYÉE:	Vous désirez, Madame?
LA TOURISTE:	Vous avez des robes de chambre?
L'EMPLOYÉE:	Oui, de quelle couleur?
LA TOURISTE:	Noire, de préférence°.
L'EMPLOYÉE:	Regardez; ça vous plaît°?
LA TOURISTE:	Oui, c'est combien?
L'EMPLOYÉE:	Cent deux euros en solde°.

de... preferably

ça... do you like it?

en... on sale

Activités

Ⓐ **Interviews.** Interview a classmate to find out the following information:

1. son nom
2. son âge
3. son adresse
4. où il ou elle habite

Ⓑ **Voyage au Québec.** You are traveling in Quebec. Play the following roles with a classmate.

1. You are in Pollack's department store in Quebec and are looking for an article of clothing that you do not see.
2. You see an interesting person while going for a walk on the Terrasse Dufferin in Quebec City and want to start up a conversation with him / her.
3. You run into an old friend you haven't seen for several years.
4. You are reading the menu in the dining room of the Reine Elisabeth Hotel in Montreal, and you come across the name of a dish with which you are not familiar.
5. You want to go on a cruise on the Saint Lawrence (Saint-Laurent) but you are unsure of what weather to expect.
6. You are in the lobby of your hotel, and you see a little boy crying.

QUEBEC REALTY CORP.

MICHELE LAURANT
Realtor-Associate
Agent Immobilier

Votre place au soleil de la Floride!

Vente de condos au bord de l'océan de Ft. Lauderdale à Boca Raton.
Tous prix. Documentation gratuite sur demande.

Tel: (305) 921-0720
Res. (305) 782-8172   Fax: (305) 921-4038
1410 S. Federal Highway, Dania, Florida 33004

lecture culturelle

Avant la lecture

More and more people are familiar nowadays with the term **francophonie,** thanks in large part to the annual celebrations of the French language and French-speaking cultures (such as **La journée de la Francophonie** and **La semaine du français et de la Francophonie**) hosted by many schools across the United States. The word **francophonie** was coined in 1880 by Onésime Reclus, a French geographer, to refer to the French-speaking nations of the world; however, the designation came into widespread use only in the 1960s, when the leaders of several French-speaking countries decided to create an international association to promote the French language and the diverse peoples who speak it. **La Francophonie,** originally conceived as a purely linguistic confederation, has evolved over time into a cultural, social, economic, and political alliance comparable to the British Commonwealth of Nations.

Today, with fifty-five member states, **La Francophonie** is alive and well. Francophone heads of state attend biennial political summits; francophone festivals celebrate French-language music, theater, film, and dance; and the Francophone Games, a smaller version of the Olympics, take place every three to five years. The French-speaking West African city of Niamey, Niger, was chosen to host the Francophone Games in 2005.

As mentioned in the **Chapitre préliminaire, La Francophonie** spans five continents. You can therefore use your French all over the world. How was the French language introduced into so many places? The spread of French can be traced back to the sixteenth and seventeenth centuries, with the arrival of the explorers Jacques Cartier in Canada and Robert Cavelier de La Salle in Louisiana. French influence spread to West Africa and the Antilles during the slave-trading era. Subsequently, in the nineteenth century, France became a colonial power in North Africa, the Near East, and Southeast Asia. Many of the colonies declared their independence from France in the 1950s and 1960s, yet France has retained control of certain lands overseas known as the **DOM-TOM** (**départements d'outre-mer et territoires d'outre-mer**). The **DOM** include Martinique, Guadeloupe, French Guiana, and Réunion. The **TOM** consist of Wallis and Futuna Islands, French Polynesia, and the French Antarctic and Austral Territories. New Caledonia, formerly a **TOM,** now has a special status.

You will read here about three places where French is spoken: Switzerland, Mali, and French Guiana.

Activités

Ⓐ On what continents are Switzerland, Mali, and French Guiana found?

Ⓑ Take a look at the three readings. Which description refers to the desert? the mountains? the forests?

Ⓒ Scan the readings for four prepositions of location.

Ⓓ **Gruyère** is the name of a kind of cheese. What do you think this cheese is called in English? (Think of the country where the city of Gruyères is located.)

Ⓔ Skim the readings to find one special feature of each of the three franco-phone cities below.

La francophonie

Kourou, Guyane française

Dans le nord-est de l'Amérique du Sud, entre le Suriname et le Brésil, la Guyane, 90 000 km², terre chaude et intense au climat équatorial. La forêt qui couvre les 9/10 du département fait l'objet d'une politique° de protection de l'environnement.

La Guyane est entrée depuis bientôt quarante ans dans l'ère de la technologie spatiale. La création en 1964 du Centre spatial guyanais (CSG) [à Kourou] a en effet largement contribué à dynamiser l'économie de ce département. Ce pays équatorial convient° parfaitement à l'établissement d'un centre de lancement° d'engins spatiaux°.

L'Ariane-5 décolle du Centre spatial de Kourou

policy

is suited for launching / engins... rockets

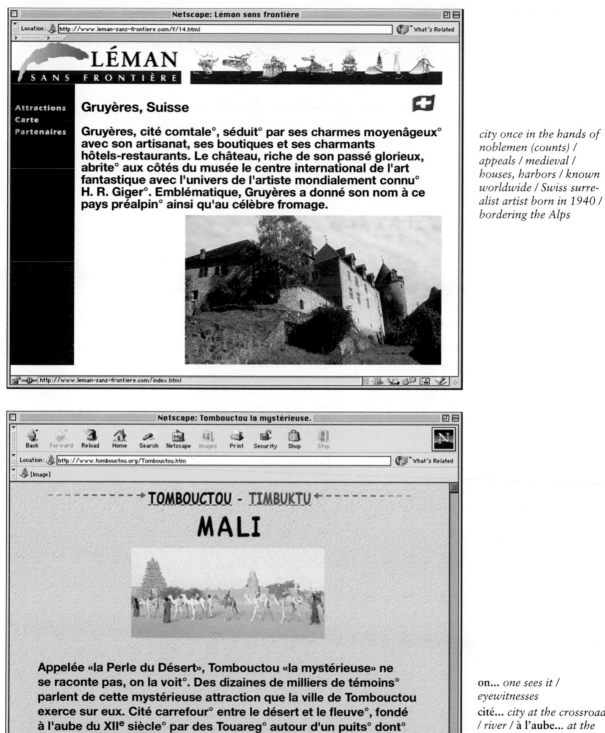

Gruyères, Suisse

Gruyères, cité comtale°, séduit° par ses charmes moyenâgeux° avec son artisanat, ses boutiques et ses charmants hôtels-restaurants. Le château, riche de son passé glorieux, abrite° aux côtés du musée le centre international de l'art fantastique avec l'univers de l'artiste mondialement connu° H. R. Giger°. Emblématique, Gruyères a donné son nom à ce pays préalpin° ainsi qu'au célèbre fromage.

city once in the hands of noblemen (counts) / appeals / medieval / houses, harbors / known worldwide / Swiss surrealist artist born in 1940 / bordering the Alps

TOMBOUCTOU - TIMBUKTU

MALI

Appelée «la Perle du Désert», Tombouctou «la mystérieuse» ne se raconte pas, on la voit°. Des dizaines de milliers de témoins° parlent de cette mystérieuse attraction que la ville de Tombouctou exerce sur eux. Cité carrefour° entre le désert et le fleuve°, fondé à l'aube du XIIe siècle° par des Touareg° autour d'un puits° dont° la gardienne se nommait° Buktu, Tombouctou «la mystérieuse» est fameuse pour ses universités et ses mosquées qui font d'elle la métropole médiévale de l'Islam et un centre religieux universitaire d'un grand renom°.

on... one sees it / eyewitnesses
cité... city at the crossroads / river / à l'aube... at the dawn of the twelfth century / a nomadic people of the African desert / well (for water) / whose / was named / d'un... highly renowned

Après la lecture

Questions sur le texte

1. Quelle est la raison pour le mouvement écologique en Guyane française?
2. Nommez une contribution économique importante en Guyane française.
3. Quels deux endroits peut-on *(can one)* visiter à Gruyères?
4. Qu'est-ce qu'on peut acheter à Gruyères?
5. Quel est le surnom de Tombouctou et quelle est l'origine du nom Tombouctou?
6. Qui a établi la ville de Tombouctou?
7. Pourquoi est-ce que Tombouctou est célèbre?

Activités

A. En plus de *(In addition to)* l'exemple de Gruyères, quelles autres villes ou régions ont le même nom qu'un produit *(product)* célèbre (e.g., Hershey, Pennsylvanie; Bordeaux, France)?

B. En paires ou en petits groupes, créez l'itinéraire d'un voyage d'été à travers la francophonie. Choisissez *(Choose)* quatre à six pays francophones. Ecrivez un petit paragraphe où vous expliquez ce que vous allez visiter et ce que vous allez faire. (Utilisez le futur proche.)

C. Quels sont les pays où l'anglais est la langue officielle? une des langues officielles? Quelle est votre opinion de l'idée d'une association de pays basée sur une langue commune? Comparez la Francophonie au British Commonwealth of Nations.

D. Quels documents et quelles immunisations sont nécessaires pour voyager en Suisse, en Guyane française et au Mali?

E. Choisissez un pays ou une région francophone. Comment est-ce que le français est arrivé là-bas? Quelles autres langues est-ce qu'on parle dans ce pays ou dans cette région? Présentez vos résultats à toute la classe.

vocabulaire

Noms / Pronoms

achats *(m.)*	purchases	**un chapeau**	hat
bagages *(m.)*	luggage	**chaussettes** *(f.)*	socks
bagages à main *(m.)*	hand luggage	**chaussures** *(f.)*	shoes
une botte	boot	**une chemise**	shirt
une ceinture	belt	**une chemise de nuit**	nightgown

un chemisier	blouse	un mois	month
un costume	suit	une omelette	omelet
une couleur	color	un pantalon	pants
courses (f.)	errands	un parapluie	umbrella
une cravate	tie	pâtes (f.)	noodles
créole	Creole	Petites Antilles (f.)	Lesser Antilles
une crêpe	crepe	une poche	pocket
un département	department	un polo	polo shirt
	(administrative	un pull	pullover
	division)	un pyjama	pajamas
une écharpe	scarf	une robe	dress
elle	her	une robe de	robe
été (m.)	summer	chambre	
eux	them	un sandwich	sandwich
un gant	glove	un short	shorts
hiver (m.)	winter	un tee-shirt	T-shirt
une idée	idea	tennis (f.)	tennis shoes
un imperméable	raincoat	touriste (m./f.)	tourist
un jean	jeans	une valise	suitcase
une jupe	skirt	une veste	coat / jacket
lunettes de soleil	sunglasses	un veston	coat
(f.)		vêtements (m.)	clothes
un maillot de bain	bathing suit	un voyage organisé	tour
un manteau	coat		

Verbes

acheter	to buy	oublier	to forget
coûter	to cost	penser à	to think
emporter	to take		about
faire	to do / to make	porter	to wear

Adjectifs / Adverbes

bleu	blue	peu	little
bon(ne)	good	prêt	ready
brun	brown	québécois	from Quebec
déjà	already	quel	what / which
gris	gray	récemment	recently
hier	yesterday	rien	nothing
jaune	yellow	sa	his / her / its
leur(s)	their	ses	his / her / its
ma	my	son	his / her / its
même	same	super	super
mes	my	ta	your
mon	my	tes	your
noir	black	trop	too
nos	our	vert	green
notre	our	vos	your
parfait	perfect	votre	your

Expressions

à l'extérieur	outside
avoir l'air	to look like
bien sûr	of course
Ça y est!	That's it!
être à	to belong to
faire attention	to pay attention
faire beau	to be nice weather
faire chaud	to be hot
faire des courses	to run errands
faire des devoirs	to do homework
faire du sport	to play sports
faire froid	to be cold
faire la cuisine	to cook
faire la grasse matinée	to sleep late
faire la lessive	to do the laundry
faire la queue	to stand in line
faire la vaisselle	to do the dishes
faire le ménage	to clean
faire les bagages	to pack
faire les valises	to pack the suitcases
faire mauvais	to be bad weather
faire un régime	to be on a diet
faire un tour	to go for a walk
faire un voyage	to take a trip
faire une promenade	to go for a walk
pas encore	not yet
quelque chose	something
tous les ans	every year

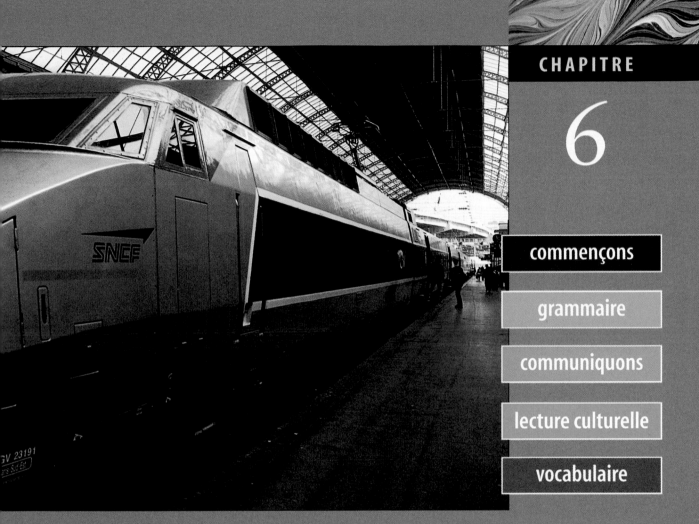

Le TGV atlantique

CHAPITRE

6

commençons

grammaire

communiquons

lecture culturelle

vocabulaire

Les transports

OBJECTIVES

Language		Culture	Communication
■ Vocabulary for means of transportation	■ Inversion and interrogative adverbs	■ The subway system of Paris	■ Expressing how to get places
■ The sounds / y /, / u /, and / ɥ /	■ **-re** verbs	■ The twenty-four-hour clock	■ Talking about events in the past
■ **Passé composé** with **être**	■ Telling time	■ **Le TGV**	■ Asking questions
			■ Telling time

commençons

Dans le métro

Un soir, Chantal a retrouvé ses amis Hélène et Richard à la station Nation. Ils ont décidé d'aller à un concert de rock au Palais Omnisport de Bercy.

CHANTAL: Salut, les copains! J'attends depuis longtemps, moi!

HÉLÈNE: Salut, Chantal! On a un gros problème. Richard a oublié nos billets dans la poche de son imperméable.

RICHARD: On a changé à Gare du Nord et quand je suis descendu, j'ai laissé mon imper sur la banquette.

HÉLÈNE: Nous sommes allés au bout de la ligne pour rien. Heureusement, le bureau des objets trouvés est ouvert le soir.

CHANTAL: C'est au métro Plaisance. Allons-y!

Au bureau des objets trouvés

Les trois jeunes gens sont arrivés au bureau et ils parlent avec l'employé.

L'EMPLOYÉ: C'est à qui?

HÉLÈNE: C'est à nous. Est-ce qu'on a rapporté un imperméable?

L'EMPLOYÉ: Comment est-il?

RICHARD: Il est beige avec une ceinture.

L'EMPLOYÉ: Est-ce qu'il est avec les manteaux là-bas?

RICHARD: Oui, justement.

L'employé donne l'imperméable à Richard. Richard cherche dans la poche et trouve les billets.

RICHARD: Quelle chance! Voilà les billets. Il est huit heures et on a encore le temps de prendre un pot avant le début du concert.

 Etudions les dialogues

Ⓐ Dans le métro

    1. Où est Chantal?
    2. Qu'est-ce qu'elle va faire avec ses amis?
    3. Quelle sorte de problème est-ce que Richard et Hélène ont?
    4. Où est-ce que Richard a laissé son imperméable?

Ⓑ Au bureau des objets trouvés

    1. Avec qui les trois amis parlent-ils au bureau des objets trouvés?
    2. Comment est l'imperméable de Richard?
    3. Est-ce que l'employé a l'imperméable?
    4. Est-ce que les billets sont toujours dans la poche de l'imperméable?

Mots clés

le métro	*subway*	laissé (laisser)	*left*
retrouvé (retrouver)	*met*	un imper	*raincoat*
une station	*metro stop*	une banquette	*seat*
ont décidé d' (décider de)	*decided*	allés (aller)	*went*
un concert	*concert*	un bout	*end*
attends (attendre)	*waited*	une ligne	*line*
depuis longtemps	*for a long time*	pour rien	*for nothing*
gros(-se)	*big*	heureusement	*fortunately*
un problème	*problem*	un bureau des	*lost and found*
billets *(m.)*	*tickets*	objets trouvés	
changé (changer)	*changed*	Allons-y!	*Let's go!*
un/une employé(e)	*employee*	Quelle chance!	*What luck!*
C'est à qui?	*Whose turn is it?*	huit heures	*eight o'clock*
rapporté (rapporter)	*brought back*	encore	*still*
Comment est-il?	*What is it like?*	le temps	*time*
beige	*beige*	prendre un pot	*to have a drink*
justement	*as a matter of fact*	avant	*before*
descendu (descendre)	*got off*	un début	*beginning*

𝓕aisons connaissance

The **métro** in Paris is a system of more than two hundred kilometers of rails connected with the **RER (Réseau Express Régional)**, a network of suburban lines. It is not only a very efficient system of transportation, it is also one of the easiest to use. Thanks to the numerous **correspondances** (stations where you can change lines), the **métro** is the fastest way to get from one point to another in Paris. Because you can go any distance on one ticket, travel is very inexpensive. Rather than buy one ticket (**un ticket**) at a time, it is more economical to buy a booklet (**un carnet**) of ten tickets or a **carte orange,** which permits unlimited travel for specified periods of time. All of these are also valid on the bus system. ▶

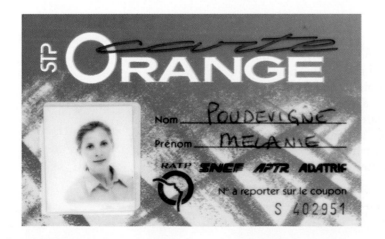

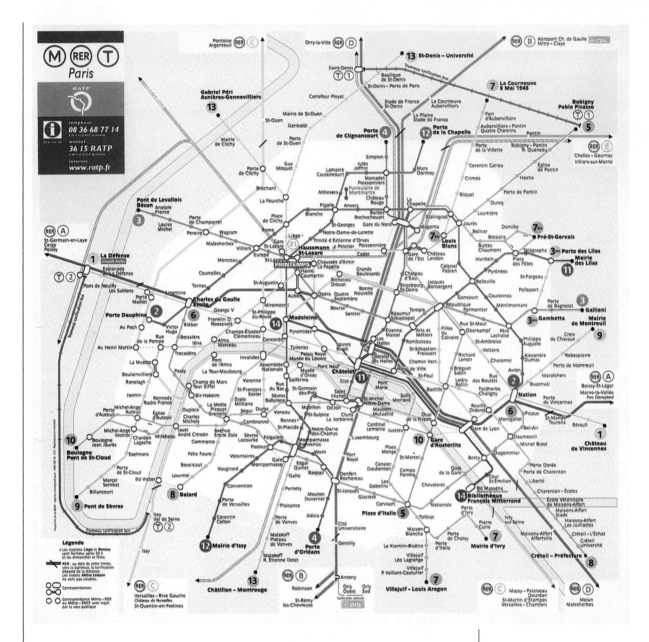

Work is constantly being done to enlarge and improve the **métro**. The old rails have been replaced, and most trains now run on rubber tires rather than on metal wheels. Some **stations** (**Louvre, Franklin Roosevelt,** and **Chaussée d'Antin**) are quite artistically decorated. Other stations (**Opéra**) are true commercial centers with many underground shops. Of course, the traditional accordion and guitar players performing for tips are still seen in the **métro**. In the near future, tickets will be replaced by cards with chips similar to the **Télécartes** currently used to make phone calls.

Enrichissons notre vocabulaire

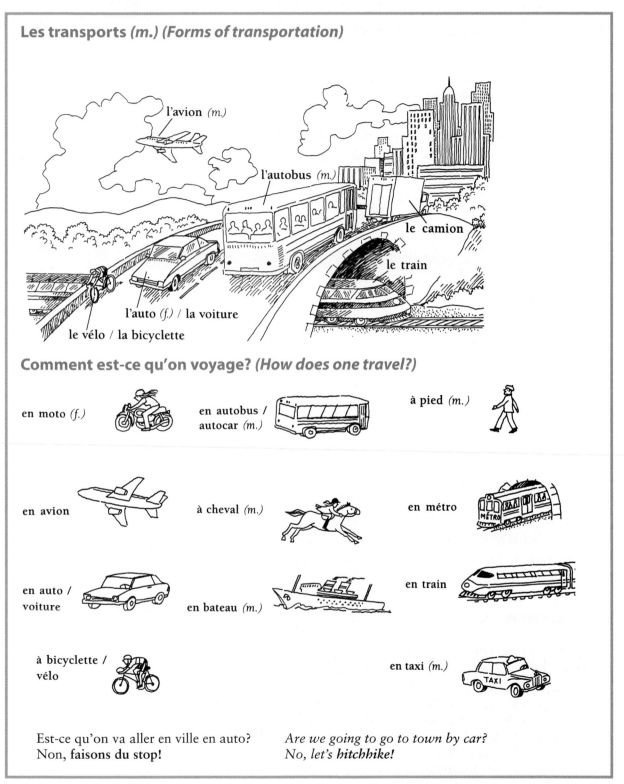

Les transports (m.) (Forms of transportation)

l'avion (m.)

l'autobus (m.)

le camion

le train

l'auto (f.) / la voiture

le vélo / la bicyclette

Comment est-ce qu'on voyage? (How does one travel?)

en moto (f.)

en autobus / autocar (m.)

à pied (m.)

en avion

à cheval (m.)

en métro

en auto / voiture

en bateau (m.)

en train

à bicyclette / vélo

en taxi (m.)

Est-ce qu'on va aller en ville en auto?
Non, **faisons du stop!**

Are we going to go to town by car?
*No, let's **hitchhike!***

Prononciation   The sounds / y /, / u /, and / ɥ /

A. You have already encountered the sound / y / several times in words such as **tu** and **du**. It is always represented in writing by the letter **u** and must not be confused with the sound / u /, written **ou** (**nous, vous**). The / y / sound is produced with the tongue forward in the mouth and lips rounded. The easiest way to say it is to pronounce the / i / sound (as in **si**) and then round your lips without moving your tongue.

Repeat the following pairs of words, which differ only in lip rounding.

/ i / (unrounded)	/ y / (rounded)
si	su
dit	du
fit	fut
J	jus
qui	Q
rit	rue

Repeat these pairs, which differ only in tongue position, after your teacher.

/ u / (back)	/ y / (front)
où	U
bout	bu
nous	nu
sous	su
tout	tu
vous	vu

B. When the / y / sound is followed by another vowel sound, it is pronounced in a shorter fashion, but still with the lips rounded and the tongue forward. Many English speakers attempting to pronounce **lui** (/ lɥi /) say / lwi / instead, which is understood as **Louis**.

Practice the / ɥ / sound, called a *semi-vowel,* by repeating the following words after your teacher.

lui / cuisine / je suis / huit / huile / ennuyeux / affectueux / tout de suite / la Suisse

Exercice

Read the following sentences aloud, paying particular attention to the vowel sounds / y / and / ɥ /.

1. Je suis curieux.
2. Tu étudies avec lui?
3. Lucie trouve vos chaussures ridicules.
4. Ils sont étudiants à l'université de Tours.
5. Luc a eu huit amis chez lui.
6. Je suis allé avec lui au Portugal.

grammaire

I. The *passé composé* with *être*

You use the **passé composé** to tell what happened in the past.

A. In the last chapter, you learned the formation of the **passé composé** using the conjugated form of **avoir** and the past participle.

> **Chantal a retrouvé ses amis.**

B. There are about twenty verbs in French that use **être** and not **avoir** as the auxiliary verb in the formation of the **passé composé**. The verb **aller** is one of them; you will learn it and five other **être** verbs in this section.

passé composé of aller	
je **suis allé(e)**	nous **sommes allé(e)s**
tu **es allé(e)**	vous **êtes allé(e)(s)**
il **est allé**	ils **sont allés**
elle **est allée**	elles **sont allées**
on **est allé(e)(s)**	

Nous **sommes allés** au bout de la ligne.

Mots clés   *Some common verbs conjugated with être*

infinitives		past participles
aller	*to go*	allé
arriver	*to arrive*	arrivé
monter	*to get on; to go up*	monté
naître	*to be born*	né
rentrer	*to return*	rentré
rester	*to stay*	resté

Les trois jeunes gens **sont arrivés** au bureau.
Il **est rentré** chez lui et **est monté** dans sa chambre.
Ma mère **est née** aux Etats-Unis.

L'orthographe

1. Note that, unlike verbs conjugated with **avoir**, verbs conjugated with **être** show agreement in number and gender between the subject and the past participle. This can lead to a number of forms with the same subject. You must use the correct agreement when writing to make your meaning clear.

Vous êtes **allé** au café?   *(if you are talking to a man)*
Vous êtes **allée** au café?   *(if you are talking to a woman)*
Vous êtes **allés** au café?   *(if you are talking to a group of men or of men and women)*
Vous êtes **allées** au café?   *(if you are talking to a group of women)*

2. The agreement of the past participle with the verbs listed above never causes a change in pronunciation: **Vous êtes arrivé** and **Vous êtes arrivées** are pronounced alike.

Attention!

With **aller** and **arriver** there is almost always a **liaison** with three forms of **être: suis, est,** and **sont.**

Je suis allée à Québec.
Il est arrivé en autobus.
Elles sont arrivées de Paris.

Language

Ⓐ **Mon retour.** Chantal has just returned from vacation. Change her sentences to the **passé composé.**

1. Je rentre de mes vacances en France.
2. Nous arrivons à Paris en autocar.
3. Nous restons quinze jours.
4. Je montre mes photos à mes amis.
5. Vous allez souvent en France?
6. Chantal est contente de ses vacances!

Ⓑ **Leurs activités.** Describe the activities of the following people by replacing the italicized words with each of the suggested phrases.

1. Jacqueline *est allée au musée.*   (visiter une église / monter à la tour Eiffel / dîner au restaurant / rentrer à l'hôtel en taxi)
2. Georges *n'a pas trouvé son parapluie.*   (chercher chez lui / aller au bureau des objets trouvés / rentrer chez lui)
3. Est-ce que tu *es arrivé en retard?*   (faire tes devoirs / rester à la biblio-thèque / avoir beaucoup à faire / rentrer à bicyclette ou en moto)

Culture

C **Personnages célèbres.** Match the famous French people with what they did.

1. Jacques Cartier
2. Charles de Gaulle
3. Napoléon Bonaparte
4. Marie Curie
5. Charlemagne
6. Clément Ader

a. aller jusqu'en Espagne
b. naître en Pologne
c. arriver au Canada en 1534
d. naître en Corse
e. monter en avion en 1890
f. rester en Angleterre

D **Les trains en France.** France is a world leader in public transportation. Form sentences with the words that follow and indicate what the French have already done (... **déjà...**) and have not yet done (**ne... pas encore...**) with trains.

MODEL: aller à 300 km/h
   On est déjà allé à trois cents kilomètres à l'heure.

1. monter de Lyon à Paris en deux heures
2. aller en Angleterre
3. préparer des dîners élégants
4. aller à Nice et rentrer à Paris dans la journée *(day)*
5. arriver de Madrid à la gare du Nord
6. aller au sommet du mont Blanc

Communication

E **Les vacances de mon professeur.** You spied on your French teacher the last time he or she was in Paris. Make a report using the following questions as a guide.

Il / Elle... rester à l'hôtel? monter à la tour Eiffel?
acheter des souvenirs? aller en métro à Pigalle?
oublier son passeport à la banque? visiter des musées?
fréquenter les bars? consommer trop de vin?
ne (n')... pas rentrer à l'hôtel?

F **Nos activités.** Tell what you, your friends, and your family did at the times given below. Add original sentences to develop a complete picture.

1. Hier, je (j')... aller à la bibliothèque? acheter... ? faire mon français? arriver en classe en retard? rester chez moi?
2. Le week-end dernier, mes amis... faire un tour en auto? aller au parc? monter à cheval? rentrer chez eux? faire du sport?
3. L'été dernier, mes parents et moi, nous... aller en vacances? rester en ville? monter en avion? voyager.... ? faire beaucoup de promenades?

G **Questions personnelles. Vos activités récentes.** Pretend you are interviewing a person on the street for a French news report and make a summary for your audience.

1. Où est-ce que vous êtes allé(e) le week-end dernier? Comment?
2. Qu'est-ce que vous avez fait?

3. Combien de temps êtes-vous resté(e) là-bas?
4. Vous êtes rentré(e) chez vos parents récemment? Quand?
5. Est-ce que vous êtes resté(e) chez vous hier?
6. Est-ce que vous êtes arrivé(e) en retard ce matin? Pourquoi?

II. Inversion and interrogative adverbs

You use interrogative adverbs to ask questions when you are seeking specific information. Inversion adds a more formal style to your questions.

A. Questions with inversion

1. In Chapter 1 you learned three ways of asking a question in French: *rising intonation*, **Est-ce que,** and **n'est-ce pas.** Another way to form a question is through *inversion*, in which you invert the pronoun subject and the verb.

   Vous travaillez ici?   **Travaillez-vous** ici?
   Ils font un régime?   **Font-ils** un régime?

2. When the subject is a noun, you add a pronoun subject of the same number and gender, in the inverted position.

   Les Français font du sport?   **Les Français font-ils** du sport?
   Jacques et Marie vont au   **Jacques et Marie vont-ils** au
      cinéma ce soir?   cinéma ce soir?

3. In the third-person singular, you must add a **t** between hyphens for all forms of verbs not ending in a written **t.**

   Parle-t-on français ici?   *but:*
   A-t-il chaud?   Etienne **est-il** arrivé à pied?
   Ecoute-t-elle la radio?

4. Inversion is usually avoided when **je** is the subject. Use **Est-ce que** instead.

   Est-ce que je suis en retard?   **Est-ce que j'**ai bien fait?

5. When there are two verbs in a sentence, as in the **futur proche** and the **passé composé,** you invert the conjugated verb and the pronoun.

   Allons-nous faire du stop?   **A-t-elle visité** la Martinique?

6. In the negative interrogative, the **ne... pas** surrounds both the conjugated verb and the pronoun subject.

> **Ne va-t-il pas faire** la vaisselle?   Les gens **ne sont-ils pas rentrés?**

7. You must pay attention to the style you use when asking questions. The most formal type would be one with inversion.

> Y a-t-il une pharmacie près d'ici?

The next most formal is the use of **Est-ce que.**

> Est-ce qu'il y a une pharmacie près d'ici?

The most informal is the use of rising intonation.

> Il y a une pharmacie près d'ici?

B. Inversion with interrogative adverbs

1. Inversion is frequently used with interrogative adverbs.

> **Combien de** frères **as-tu?**   **Pourquoi n'êtes-vous pas arrivés**
> **Comment vont-ils** à Québec?   ensemble?
> **Où faites-vous** du sport?   **Quand vont-elles** au restaurant?

Mots clés   *Interrogative adverbs*

Combien de?	*How much?, How many?*	**Pourquoi?**	*Why?*
Comment?	*How?*	**Quand?**	*When?*
Où?	*Where?*		

2. Inversion is common with **où,** and the repetition of the pronoun subject is not necessary with the present tense.

> **Où** se trouve le bureau des objets trouvés?
> **Où** habitent les Morin?

Ce qu'ils disent

1. Inversion is common in English *(Is he studying? What is he studying?),* but in French, it shows a more formal style. In conversation, rising intonation and **est-ce que** are more common:

In conversation	**More formal style**
Ils habitent à Boston?	Habitent-ils à Boston?
Est-ce qu'ils habitent à Boston?	Quand vont-ils au cinéma?

2. When speaking in a very familiar style, the French often use interrogative adverbs without inversion or **est-ce que.** They also place all the interrogative adverbs except **pourquoi** at the end of the sentence. Be

aware, however, that using this structure may be too informal for many situations you will encounter.

Tu vas où?	(*formal:* Où vas-tu?)
Il est comment, ton imper?	(*formal:* Comment est-il, ton imper?)
Tu arrives quand?	(*formal:* Quand arrives-tu?)
C'est combien?	(*formal:* Combien est-ce?)
Pourquoi vous n'allez pas au restaurant?	(*formal:* Pourquoi n'allez-vous pas... ?)

Language

Ⓐ **On va au concert.** Change the following questions with **est-ce que** to the inverted form to make them more formal.

1. Est-ce que tu vas au concert ce soir?
2. Est-ce que Monique a invité ses amis?
3. Où est-ce que nous allons aller après?
4. Comment est-ce qu'on va aller en ville?
5. Quand est-ce que vous allez arriver ici?
6. Pourquoi est-ce que vos amis ne sont pas encore arrivés?

Ⓑ **Un procès.** You are a district attorney and are charged with eliciting the following information during a trial. What questions would you ask?

1. Oui, je suis né aux Etats-Unis.
2. J'habite à New York.
3. Je suis allé au cinéma l'après-midi.
4. Parce que j'aime le cinéma!
5. Un billet coûte huit dollars.
6. J'ai trouvé le film ennuyeux.

Culture

Ⓒ **Jean-Paul et sa famille.** You have just made friends with Jean-Paul, and he has invited you home to meet his family. Ask questions to find out the information listed below. Make two sets of questions, one in an informal style for Jean-Paul, and the other in a more formal style to ask Jean-Paul's parents about him.

MODEL: aimer / télévision
(à Jean-Paul) Tu aimes la télé?
(à ses parents) Jean-Paul aime-t-il la télévision?

1. Où / naître
2. Combien / frères / sœurs
3. Pourquoi / étudier l'anglais
4. Comment / aller en cours
5. Quand / arriver à la fac
6. Où / aller en vacances

D **Une interview.** Interview a classmate. Using inversion, ask questions to elicit the following information. Present your report to the class.

MODEL: son nom
Comment t'appelles-tu?

son âge	pourquoi il / elle est à l'université
où il / elle est né(e)	comment il / elle va en classe
où il / elle habite	où il / elle est allé(e) en vacances

E **Questions personnelles.** Votre travail *(work)*.

1. Avez-vous travaillé récemment?
2. Quelle sorte de travail avez-vous fait? Où?
3. Comment êtes-vous rentré(e) chez vous après le travail?
4. Comment travaillez-vous? bien? mal?
5. Pourquoi aimez-vous / n'aimez-vous pas cela?
6. Avez-vous beaucoup travaillé avec le public? Comment sont vos clients?

III. Verbs ending in -*re*

You use verbs to describe actions or states of being.

A. Verbs with infinitives ending in **-re** drop the **-re** and add the following endings:

attendre *(to wait for)*	
j' **attends**	nous **attendons**
tu **attends**	vous **attendez**
il / elle / on **attend**	ils / elles **attendent**
Passé composé: il **a attendu**	

Mots clés

attendre	*to wait for*	**rendre**	*to give back, to return*
descendre	*to go down, come down; to get off*	**rendre visite à**	*to visit (a person)*
entendre	*to hear*	**répondre à**	*to answer*
perdre	*to lose*	**vendre**	*to sell*
perdre patience	*to lose patience*		

Où est-ce qu'on **vend** des vêtements?
Les étudiants **attendent** leur professeur.

B. The final **d** of the third-person singular of **-re** verbs has a / t / sound with inversion, so using **-t-** is not necessary.

> **Répond-il** à ta lettre?

C. The imperative of **-re** verbs is regular; the **s** is not deleted from the **tu** form.

> **Descendons** maintenant!   **Attendez** à la station.
> Ne **perds** pas ton imper!

D. The past participle is formed by dropping **-re** and adding **u.**

> J'ai **perdu** mon vélo.   Il a **vendu** sa maison.

E. **Descendre** is conjugated with **être** in the **passé composé.**

> Nous sommes **descendus** à Juan-les-Pins.

Attention! ───────────────────────────

The difference in pronunciation between the singular and plural third-person forms in the present tense is the / d / sound. You must make an extra effort to pronounce this sound when using the plural form of the verb to distinguish it clearly from the singular form.

il perd / il pɛr /	ils perdent / il pɛʀd /
elle rend / ɛl ʀɑ̃ /	elles rendent / ɛl ʀɑ̃d /

Language

Ⓐ La journée de François. Tell what François and his friends are doing by conjugating the verbs in the following sentences.

1. François (attendre) ses amis ici.
2. Ils (descendre) en ville ensemble.
3. François (vendre) des chaussures dans un magasin.
4. Moi, je (perdre) patience quand il est en retard.
5. Le soir, nous (rendre visite) à un ami malade.
6. Notre ami (entendre) nos questions, mais il (ne... pas répondre).

Ⓑ A l'aéroport. Complete the following paragraph by adding the appropriate form of **-re** verbs.

Je suis à l'aéroport Charles-de-Gaulle à Roissy, près de Paris.
J(e) _____ l'avion pour New York. J(e) _____ mon imperméable et je demande à un employé où est le bureau des objets trouvés. Il _____ :
« _____ . Vous allez le trouver en face du magasin où on _____ des vêtements.» J(e) _____ et je vois un autre employé. «Pardon, Monsieur.
J(e) _____ mon imperméable. L'a-t-on trouvé?» Il ne _____ pas et j(e) _____ patience.

C **Qui a perdu?** In the following famous confrontations with French people, tell who lost.

MODEL: Jacques Chirac / François Mitterrand en 1988
Jacques Chirac a perdu en 1988.

1. les Anglais / Guillaume le Conquérant en 1066
2. les Français / les Anglais dans la guerre de Sept Ans
3. Danton / Robespierre pendant la Révolution
4. les Français / les Prussiens en 1871
5. les Allemands / les résistants en 1945
6. Lionel Jospin / Jacques Chirac en 2002

D **J'ai perdu la tête!** Interview a classmate to discuss something each of you lost recently. Use the following questions to prepare a report to the class.

Qu'est-ce que vous avez perdu récemment? vos lunettes? votre stylo? vos clés? votre portefeuille? votre argent? votre calculatrice? votre livre de français? Pendant combien de temps l'avez-vous cherché? Où? Vous avez perdu patience?

E **Questions personnelles.** Vos habitudes.

1. Chez vous, qui répond au téléphone?
2. Quand est-ce que vous ne répondez pas?
3. Qu'est-ce que vous n'aimez pas entendre?
4. Faites-vous du sport? Dans quel sport perdez-vous souvent?
5. A qui désirez-vous rendre visite?
6. Vous rendez vos livres à la bibliothèque toujours à temps?
7. Qu'est-ce que vous avez vendu récemment?
8. Qui perd patience avec vous?

IV. Telling time

A. To ask about and tell time in French, use the following expressions.

Quelle heure est-il?	*What time is it?*
Il est une heure.	*It is one o'clock.*
Il est deux heures.	*It is two o'clock.*

B. To express minutes after the hour until the half hour, you add the minutes or the following expressions:

Il est **trois heures dix.**	*It is **ten after three.***
Il est **six heures et quart.**	{ *It is a **quarter after six.*** *It is **six fifteen.***
Il est **sept heures et demie.**	{ *It is **half past seven.*** *It is **seven thirty.***

C. To express time falling within thirty minutes of the next hour, you subtract the time from the hour.

Il est **huit heures moins vingt.**	{ *It is seven forty.* { *It is twenty to eight.*
Il est **onze heures moins cinq.**	{ *It is ten fifty-five.* { *It is five to eleven.*
Il est **neuf heures moins le quart.**	{ *It is eight forty-five.* { *It is a quarter to nine.*

D. There are special terms for *noon* and *midnight*.

Il est **midi.**	*It is noon.*
Il est **minuit.**	*It is midnight.*

L'orthographe

1. Because **heure** is feminine, **demie** following **heure** is also feminine: **une heure et demie.**

2. **Midi** and **minuit** are masculine, so **demi** does not take a final **e** with either term: **midi et demi, minuit et demi.**

3. **Demi(e)** is never plural: **trois heures et demie.**

4. When writing a time in numbers, the French separate the hours and minutes with an **h** or a period (or occasionally a colon).

   2 h 30   **deux heures et demie**   5.10   **cinq heures dix**

E. To express A.M. and P.M. in French, use **du matin** (from midnight to noon), **de l'après-midi** (from noon until about six), and **du soir** (from about six until midnight).

Il est trois heures **du matin.**	*It is 3 A.M.*
Il est quatre heures et demie **de l'après-midi.**	*It is 4:30 P.M.*
Il est onze heures **du soir.**	*It is 11 P.M.*

F. To express other time relationships, use the following expressions:

à *at, to*	**jusqu'à** *until*	**à l'heure** *on time*
de *from*	**en avance** *early*	**en retard** *late*
entre *between*		

—**A** quelle heure est-ce que vous dînez?	*At what time do you have dinner?*
—Je dîne **à** six heures et quart.	*I have dinner at 6:15.*
Je suis en cours **de** huit heures **à** trois heures.	*I'm in class from 8 to 3.*
J'étudie **jusqu'à** minuit.	*I study until midnight.*
Nous regardons la télé **entre** sept et dix heures.	*We watch TV between 7 and 10.*

—Arrivent-ils **en avance?**   *Do they arrive **early**?*
—Non, elle, elle est toujours **à l'heure;**   *No, she is always **on time**; he*
    lui, il est toujours **en retard.**   *is always **late**.*

Language

Ⓐ L'heure. Quelle heure est-il?

1.   3.   5.

2.   4.   6.

Ⓑ Robert est paresseux! Robert and Marianne go out together, but Robert is always fifteen minutes late. If Marianne arrives at the following times, when does Robert arrive?

1. 11:00 A.M.   3. 8:15 P.M.   5. 3:30 P.M.
2. 12:00 P.M.   4. 11:45 P.M.   6. 10:20 P.M.

Culture

Ⓒ Allons au cinéma. You have only two days in Paris and must make the most of your time if you want to fit in a movie. To arrive exactly at the beginning of the film (**à deux heures et demie de l'après-midi**), count back to see when you must leave the hotel.

1. le film commence (2 h 30)
2. le début de la séance (15 minutes)
3. descendre du métro, aller à pied jusqu'au cinéma (6 minutes)
4. correspondance, deuxième métro (12 minutes)
5. monter dans le métro, aller à Châtelet (12 minutes)
6. aller de l'hôtel à la station de métro (15 minutes)

Communication

Ⓓ Dans ma ville. Tell at what time of day these things occur on your campus or in town.

1. Les premiers cours de la journée commencent à...
2. Moi, j'ai des cours entre... et...
3. Les films commencent à...
4. Les matchs de football américain sont à...
5. Les bars vendent de l'alcool jusqu'à...
6. Les cafés sont ouverts jusqu'à...

Questions personnelles. Mon emploi du temps *(schedule).*

1. A quelle heure est-ce que vous arrivez en cours?
2. Arrivez-vous en avance ou en retard?
3. Jusqu'à quelle heure est-ce que vous êtes à l'université?
4. A quelle heure est-ce que vous dînez?
5. Jusqu'à quelle heure est-ce que vous étudiez le soir?
6. Vous parlez au téléphone / regardez la télé jusqu'à quelle heure?

communiquons

Utiliser l'heure officielle

The way that you just learned to tell time is called **l'heure conventionnelle,** and it is used primarily in informal conversations. In more formal situations such as those involving train or plane schedules, store hours, television schedules, and times of appointments, you will need to use **l'heure officielle,** which is based upon the twenty-four-hour clock.

In official time, times from midnight to noon are expressed as **zéro heure** to **douze heures.** To express a time from noon to midnight, continue counting the hours from twelve to twenty-four. Official time never uses the expressions **et quart, demi**(e), or **moins le quart.** You simply count the total number of minutes past the hour and use **quinze, trente,** and **quarante-cinq** respectively.

Expressions

▶ **On donne l'heure de minuit à midi.**

Le train arrive à six heures.	*The train arrives at 6 A.M.*
La classe commence à huit heures.	*The class begins at 8 A.M.*
Le camion arrive à onze heures quinze.	*The truck arrives at 11:15 A.M.*
J'attends l'autocar de neuf heures trente.	*I'm waiting for the 9:30 bus.*

▶ **On donne l'heure de midi à minuit.**

J'arrive à treize heures.	*I am arriving at 1 P.M.*
Le restau-U ferme à vingt et une heures.	*The university restaurant closes at 9 P.M.*
Le film commence à dix-neuf heures quarante-cinq.	*The film starts at 7:45 P.M.*
Le parc ferme à vingt-quatre heures.	*The park closes at midnight.*

Interaction

M. Robert va acheter un billet de train pour Marseille.

M. ROBERT: Pardon, Monsieur, à quelle heure est le prochain train pour Marseille?

L'EMPLOYÉ: Il y a un express° à quatorze heures cinq et un rapide° à quinze heures trente.   *local / express*

M. ROBERT: A quelle heure arrivent-ils?

L'EMPLOYÉ: L'express à une heure dix, mais le rapide à zéro heure vingt-cinq.

M. ROBERT: L'express arrive après le rapide?

L'EMPLOYÉ: Oui, le rapide a moins d'arrêts.

Activités

Ⓐ **L'heure officielle.** Convert the following times in the conversational style to the more formal style (**l'heure officielle**).

1. deux heures du matin
2. trois heures et quart du matin
3. onze heures et demie du matin
4. midi vingt-cinq
5. une heure moins le quart de l'après-midi
6. quatre heures cinq de l'après-midi
7. neuf heures moins dix du soir
8. minuit moins le quart

Ⓑ **L'heure conventionnelle.** Convert the following official times to the conversational style. Do not forget to indicate whether it is A.M. or P.M.

1. trois heures
2. cinq heures quinze
3. douze heures trente
4. quatorze heures quarante
5. vingt-deux heures dix
6. zéro heure quinze

Ⓒ **Le TGV Thalys.** Consult the schedule for the Thalys train on page 162 to answer the questions below.

1. Où est-ce qu'on va à Paris pour avoir un train pour Bruxelles?
2. Le train numéro 9345 arrive à Bruxelles à quelle heure?
3. Vous arrivez à quelle gare?
4. Il faut combien de temps pour aller de Paris à Bruxelles?
5. Pour aller de Paris à Amsterdam, les trains passent par quelles villes?
6. Quand est-ce que le Thalys 9357 ne circule *(run)* pas?

Paris ──○Bruxelles ─○Amsterdam

Paris - Bruxelles - Anvers - Rotterdam - **Amsterdam**

Thalys No									
	🍽		🍽	🍽		🍽	🍽	🍽	🍽	🍽
	9309	9313	9321	9333	9341	9345	9349	9353	9357	9361
	(1)	(2)			(3)		(4)		(5)	
Paris-Nord D	06:55	07:55	09:55	12:55	14:55	15:55	16:55	17:55	18:55	19:55
Bruxelles-Midi A	08:20	09:20	11:20	14:20	16:20	17:20	18:20	19:20	20:20	21:20
	🍴		🍽	🍴		🍽	🍽	🍴		
Bruxelles-Midi D	08:28	09:28	11:28	14:28	16:28	17:28	18:28	19:28	20:28	21:28
Antwerpen-Berchem (Anvers) A	09:04	10:04	12:04	15:04	17:04	18:04	19:04	20:04	21:04	22:04
Rotterdam CS A	10:08	11:08	13:08	16:08	18:08	19:08	20:08	21:08	22:08	
Den Haag HS (La Haye) A	10:27	11:27	13:27	16:27	18:27	19:27	20:27	21:27	22:27	
Schiphol (aéroport) A	10:50	11:50	13:50	16:50	18:50	19:50	20:50	21:50	22:50	
Amsterdam A	11:07	12:07	14:07	17:07	19:07	20:07	21:07	22:07	23:07	

lundi à jeudi
vendredi
samedi
dimanche

(1) ne circule pas les 1 novembre, 24, 25 décembre, 1 janvier, 1 avril, 9 et 20 mai
(2) circule les 1 novembre, 24, 25 décembre, 1 janvier, 1 avril, 9 et 20 mai
(3) circule le 31 décembre
(4) ne circule pas le 31 décembre
(5) ne circule pas les 24 et 31 décembre

lecture culturelle

Avant la lecture

The French bullet train, **le train à grande vitesse (TGV)**, travels at an average record speed of 190 miles per hour on rail beds that are said to be the smoothest in the world. Not only does the TGV serve all of France, but its service also extends beyond the country's borders. A recently inaugurated national line, the TGV Méditerranée, takes passengers across the entire country, from Calais to Marseilles, in approximately 4 hours, 30 minutes. Internationally, the TGV travels from Paris to Geneva, Switzerland, in 3 hours, 30 minutes. The Eurostar TGV connects Paris with London, England (3 hours), via the English Channel tunnel, or Eurotunnel. The Thalys TGV links Paris with Brussels, Belgium (1 hour, 25 minutes); Amsterdam, Holland (4 hours, 15 minutes); and Düsseldorf, Germany (4 hours, 30 minutes).

The TGV is so fast and comfortable that it is considered a serious competitor to the French airline industry. As a consequence, in 2001 Air France abandoned its Paris–Brussels route to its rail competitor. Because the trains move from city center to city center, passengers need not worry about transportation to and from airports. To compete, European airlines are forging alliances with the high-speed railways: Lufthansa, the German national airline, is testing the use of high-speed rail links for its short trips. It entices customers by making it easy, efficient, and comfortable to take the train to the airport and then fly from there to their final destination. One-stop check-in will be available at the train station, where luggage will be transferred automatically from the train to the airplane. At the Charles de Gaulle airport north of Paris, TGV train stations have been built to facilitate travel to destinations both within France and abroad.

The success of the TGV network is all the more striking given that the first TGV linking Paris and Lyon was launched in 1981. By 2007, two new TGV lines are scheduled to begin operation between Paris and Strasbourg and between Lyon (France) and Milan (Italy). In the future, the TGV will also link France to cities in Spain.

Un wagon de TGV

Activités

Ⓐ In small groups, discuss how train travel compares with air travel. Relate any experiences you have had taking trains.

Ⓑ Skim the text **TGV Méditerranée** to determine how long (in hours and minutes) the average trip takes between (1) Paris and Marseilles, (2) the North Sea and the Mediterranean, and (3) Lyon and Marseilles.

Ⓒ Look in both texts for the French terms for *north, east,* and *west.* How are these directions used in the text?

Ⓓ By referring to a map of France and one of western Europe, locate these cities, oceans, and seas, mentioned in the texts that follow:

Cities

Marseilles, Paris, Lyon, Brussels

Oceans and Seas

the Mediterranean Sea, the North Sea, the Atlantic Ocean

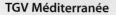

Les trains à grande vitesse (TGV)

TGV Méditerranée

Lancé° le 10 juin 2001, le TGV Méditerranée va bouleverser les habitudes° des Français. Le réseau° à grande vitesse° de la SNCF° vient s'enrichir° d'une nouvelle ligne. Marseille ne sera plus qu'à° trois heures de Paris. Une
5 étape° importante après la mise en service° du TGV Paris–Lyon en 1981, du TGV Atlantique en 1989 et du TGV Nord-Europe en 1993. Avant le TGV Est en 2006... Une véritable révolution ferroviaire° puisqu'au-delà° du temps gagné, c'est en fait° toute la France, et même° l'Europe, avec 70
10 villes et 13 régions reliées° entre elles, qui sont transformées. La Méditer- ranée est désormais° à quatre heures trente de la mer du Nord. La deu- xième et la troisième ville de France se découvrent ainsi voisines°, avec une heure quarante entre Marseille et Lyon, quinze fois par jour.

Thalys

15 Thalys, le train-éclair°, vous fait traverser le nord-ouest de l'Europe. Mais pas n'importe comment° et pas comme n'importe quel° autre train... Si Thalys bénéficie des innovations technologiques les plus modernes et relie les grandes métropoles du nord-ouest de l'Europe de centre à centre en des temps sans concurrence°, il offre aussi et surtout un nouveau concept
20 de voyage édifié° sur trois atouts° majeurs: le service, les tarifs et la fréquence. Savez-vous°, par exemple, qu'il y a 23 Thalys par jour entre Paris–Bruxelles? Et ce, en 1 h 25 seulement?

*launched / **bouleverser...** upset, dramatically change the habits / network / speed / abbreviation for Société nationale des chemins de fer français / has been en- hanced by / **ne...** will be only / stage / introduction of / relating to the railroad / since, in addi- tion / in fact / even / con- nected / henceforth, from now on / **se découvrent...** thus find themselves neighbors*

*lightning-fast train **n'importe...** anyhow / **n'importe...** any, no matter which*

competition

based on / assets, advan- tages / Do you know . . . ?

Après la lecture

Questions sur le texte

Ⓐ TGV Méditerranée

1. Pourquoi est-ce que le TGV Méditerranée va bouleverser les habitudes des Français?
2. Quelles sont les trois plus grandes villes de France?

Ⓑ Thalys

1. Où va le Thalys?
2. La publicité pour le Thalys mentionne trois avantages compétitifs. Quels sont ces atouts?
3. Combien de trains vont de Paris à Bruxelles chaque jour?

Ⓒ TGV Méditerranée, Thalys

Il y a des noms différents pour les différentes lignes de TGV. Par exemple, il y a le TGV Méditerranée, qui va de la mer du Nord à la mer Méditer- ranée. Quels sont les noms des autres TGV mentionnés dans le texte?

Activités

Ⓐ In the reading passages, you came across the terms **TGV** and **SNCF**, two commonly used French acronyms whose meaning you know. Now try to match the following French acronyms with the corresponding English version, and discuss what each one means.

French	English
1. ONU	a. EU
2. SIDA	b. IMF
3. UE	c. NATO
4. OTAN	d. AIDS
5. FMI	e. UN

Ⓑ Quels sont les différents moyens *(means)* de transport possibles aux Etats-Unis pour aller de Californie en Louisiane? Combien coûte le voyage dans chaque cas? Combien de temps dure chaque trajet *(trip)*?

Ⓒ Est-ce que vous prenez le bus ou votre voiture personnelle pour circuler en ville? Quels sont les avantages et les inconvénients de chaque moyen de transport aux Etats-Unis?

vocabulaire

Noms / Pronoms

une auto	car	un début	beginning
un autocar	bus	un/une employé(e)	employee
un avion	airplane	une heure	hour / time
une banquette	seat	un imper(méable)	raincoat
un bateau	boat	une ligne	line
une bicyclette	bicycle	un métro	subway
un billet	ticket	midi	noon
un bout	end	minuit	midnight
un bureau des	lost and found	une moto	motorcycle
objets trouvés		un pot	drink
un camion	truck	un problème	problem
un carnet	book of tickets	un quart	quarter
une carte orange	orange card	une station	stop
	(special	un taxi	taxi
	Parisian bus	le temps	time / weather
	and metro pass)	un ticket	ticket
la chance	luck	un train	train
un concert	concert	le transport	transportation
une correspondance	connection	un vélo	bicycle

Verbes

attendre	to wait for	naître	to be born
changer	to change	perdre	to lose
décider	to decide	rapporter	to bring back

descendre	to get off /
	     to go down /
	     to come down
		rendre	to give back / to
			     return (something)

		rentrer	to return
entendre	to hear	répondre à	to answer
laisser	to leave	retrouver	to find again
monter	to get on / to go up	vendre	to sell

Adjectifs / Adverbes

beige	beige	heureusement	fortunately

combien de?	how much? /
	     how many?
		justement	as a matter
			     of fact

comment	how	longtemps	for a long time
demi(e)	half	où?	where?
encore	still	pourquoi?	why?
gros(se)	big	quand?	when?

Expressions

à cheval	on horseback	en avance	early
à l'heure	on time	en retard	late
à pied	on foot	faire du stop	to hitchhike
Allons-y!	Let's go!	jusqu'à	until
avant	before	perdre patience	to lose patience
C'est à qui?	Whose turn is it?	pour rien	for nothing
de l'après-midi	P.M.	prendre un pot	to have a drink
depuis	since	Quelle chance!	What luck!
du matin	A.M.	rendre visite à	to visit (a person)
du soir	P.M.		

Révision

B

Chapitres 4 à 6

Class work

A Rewrite the following sentences using the cues in parentheses and making any necessary changes.

MODEL: Marie étudie le français. (L'année prochaine...)
L'année prochaine Marie va étudier le français.

Des activités

1. Nous attendons l'autobus. (Hier,...)
2. J'ai un examen aujourd'hui. (Demain...)
3. Lise fait une promenade en auto le week-end? (Les garçons... auto-stop... le week-end dernier?)
4. Christine a fait des courses en ville. (Nous ne... pas... souvent...)
5. Nous allons à la bibliothèque cet après-midi. (... hier.)
6. Les enfants écoutent-ils leurs parents? (Isabelle... ?)
7. Vous rendez un livre? (... demain matin?)
8. Mes sœurs étudient beaucoup. (La semaine dernière...)

En voyage

9. Claire passe un mois au Sénégal. (... l'été prochain.)
10. Il fait froid ici. (Le mois dernier... Europe.)
11. Les étudiants ne restent pas chez eux en été. (Paul... l'été dernier.)
12. Il fait un voyage en Amérique. (Vous... déjà...)

B Answer the following questions using the cues provided.

MODEL: Où allez-vous? (... université.)
Je vais à l'université.

Les possessions

1. C'est votre imper? (Oui,...)
2. Il donne des cadeaux à Mme Morin? (Non,... frère.)
3. Ton jean est français? (Non,... Etats-Unis.)
4. As-tu acheté une cravate bleue? (Non,... verte.)
5. C'est ta jupe? (Non,... ma mère.)
6. Où as-tu trouvé tes chemises? (... Angleterre.)

D'autres activités

7. Où Pierre fait-il un voyage en été? (descendre... Mexique.)
8. Où étudiez-vous le soir? (... bibliothèque.)
9. Est-ce que Sylvie visite la France? (Non,... Tunisie.)
10. Où allez-vous? (... parc.)
11. Qu'est-ce que Jean va faire? (... vendre... voiture.)
12. Tu as des amis en France? (Non, mais... Maroc.)

C Make complete sentences with each group of words below, adding any necessary words.

MODEL: Je / faire / promenade
Je fais une promenade.

Dans ma ville

1. Quand / mon / parents / aller / cinéma?
2. Tu / passer / vacances / ici?
3. Où / on / faire / lessive?
4. Marie / entendre / voitures / hier soir
5. On / faire / promenades / parc
6. Mon / fille / naître / minuit

Qu'est-ce qu'on a fait?

7. Pourquoi / Eric / rester chez lui / hier?
8. Jacques / monter / dans / voiture / et faire / tour
9. Nous / faire / ménage / hier matin
10. Elle / chercher / parapluie / sœur / et / perdre / patience
11. Nous / ne / être / pas / restaurant / récemment
12. Chantal / chercher / ceinture / pour / son / jupe / blanc

D Fill in the blanks when necessary with the appropriate article or preposition.

MODEL: ... Rome est... Italie.
Rome est en Italie.

1. ... Canada est un pays magnifique.
2. ... Madrid est une ville intéressante.
3. J'ai visité... Dakar,... Sénégal.
4. Avez-vous passé vos vacances... Japon?
5. ... Etats-Unis, les villes sont très grandes.
6. ... Florence, il y a beaucoup de musées.
7. ... Abidjan est... Côte d'Ivoire.
8. ... été prochain, mes parents vont visiter... Mexique.
9. ... Italie est un pays fantastique.
10. Je suis allé au concert... semaine dernière.
11. Je vais rendre visite... mon professeur... 4 h.
12. Marc adore répondre... questions.

E Translate the following sentences into French.

1. Where is my book?
2. It is on your table.
3. Yesterday, your mother visited my school.
4. She likes our teacher a lot.
5. Their friends have my car.
6. They lost their bicycles.
7. Her dorm is far from her parents' house.
8. She hates living at their house.

F In French, read aloud or write out the following numbers.

1. 71	6. 321	11. 1.000	16. 259.500
2. 81	7. 554	12. 1.433	17. 1.000.000
3. 95	8. 742	13. 1.982	18. 3.000.000
4. 100	9. 891	14. 2.600	19. 10.500.000
5. 214	10. 961	15. 10.971	20. 324.657.895

Pair and small group work

A Form groups of three or four students, and find out the birthdays of every-one in your group.

B Work with a partner to practice the **futur proche** and the **passé composé**. Take turns making statements in the **futur proche** and having your partner repeat your statements in the **passé composé**. Use the following verbs:

aller	inviter	acheter	descendre
oublier	rester	visiter	rendre
faire	manger	rentrer	perdre
monter	étudier	arriver	attendre

C Write a number on a slip of paper starting with one digit and adding a digit each time (**7, 17, 175...**). Your partner will read your number aloud, and then you will reverse roles. Continue until one of you makes a mistake.

D In groups of three or four, take turns identifying objects that belong to you, and point them out to your classmates using the expression **C'est...** or **Ce sont...** and possessive adjectives.

MODEL: *C'est mon stylo. Ce sont mes chaussures.*

E Using the **Est-ce que** form or inversion and the verbs **avoir** and **être**, ask a question about your partner's feelings or present state of mind.

MODEL: Student 1: *Est-ce que tu as chaud?* or *As-tu chaud?*
Student 2: *Oui, j'ai chaud.*

F With a classmate, make up a schedule of your daily activities. What things do you do at different times?

MODEL: *Notre premier cours commence à neuf heures, mais elle déjeune à midi et je déjeune à une heure.*

G Interview a classmate about the following subjects. Prepare a report of your findings for the class.

1. Qu'est-ce que tu as fait le week-end dernier?
2. Comment va-t-on chez toi?
3. Où fais-tu tes courses? ta lessive?
4. Qu'est-ce que tu aimes?
5. Quel pays as-tu visité? Où désires-tu aller?
6. Aimes-tu faire la cuisine? Quelle est ta spécialité?
7. Où es-tu allé(e) hier? Pourquoi?
8. Fais-tu toujours tes devoirs? Pourquoi ou pourquoi pas?

7

commençons

grammaire

communiquons

lecture culturelle

vocabulaire

Oui! Je suis sur mon portable!

Au téléphone

OBJECTIVES

Language	Culture	Communication
■ Vocabulary for common possessions ■ Nasal vowels ■ Interrogative and demonstrative adjectives ■ **-ir** verbs ■ Interrogative pronouns ■ **Pouvoir** and **vouloir**	■ The French telephone system ■ Mobile phones	■ Using the telephone ■ Talking about one's possessions

commençons

C'est une erreur!

Le téléphone sonne chez Elisabeth Cambon.

UNE VOIX
FÉMININE: Allô, 45.26.88.46, j'écoute.

BENJAMIN: Allô, est-ce que je peux parler à Elisabeth, s'il vous plaît?

LA VOIX: Qui est à l'appareil?

BENJAMIN: Benjamin Ducaud.

LA VOIX: Ne quittez pas, je vais voir si elle est là.

Après une ou deux minutes...

LA VOIX: Allô, je suis désolée; elle est dans sa chambre et elle dort. Voulez-vous laisser un message?

BENJAMIN: *(Il réfléchit.)* Je voudrais savoir si elle peut sortir avec moi ce soir. Est-ce que je peux rappeler plus tard?

LA VOIX: Non, ce n'est pas la peine de téléphoner, Elisabeth n'est pas libre. Au revoir.

BENJAMIN: Ne coupe pas! Elisabeth, c'est toi? Pourquoi est-ce que tu ne veux pas sortir avec moi?

1. A qui est-ce que Benjamin veut parler?
2. Pourquoi est-ce qu'il ne peut pas parler à Elisabeth?
3. Quel message veut-il laisser?
4. Qu'est-ce qu'il veut faire plus tard?
5. Pourquoi est-ce que ce n'est pas la peine?
6. A qui est-ce que Benjamin parle au téléphone?

Mots clés

une erreur	*wrong number*	voulez (vouloir)	*want*
un téléphone	*telephone*	un message	*message*
sonne (sonner)	*rings*	réfléchit (réfléchir)	*thinks*
une voix	*voice*	savoir	*know*
Allô.	*Hello.*	peut (pouvoir)	*can*
J'écoute.	*Go ahead.*	sortir	*go out*
peux (pouvoir)	*may*	rappeler	*call back*
Qui est à l'appareil?	*Who's calling?*	plus tard	*later*
Ne quittez pas.	*Hold on.*	ce n'est pas la peine	*it's no use*
voir	*to see*	téléphoner (à)	*to phone*
désolée	*sorry*	libre	*free*
une chambre	*bedroom*	Ne coupe pas.	*Don't hang up.*
dort (dormir)	*is sleeping*		

Cyber Café

Faisons connaissance

www

In France the telephone system is run by **France Télécom,** an agency that administers one of the most sophisticated telephone systems in the world. One can call anywhere in France or the rest of the world in a matter of seconds, even from public phone booths. Since more than 50% of the population now have a cell phone (**un portable**), the French use the telephone much more than in the past. Their use of it, however, still tends to be more conservative than that of Americans. The French often do not have as many phones to a home as Americans do.

To make a phone call, some people still go to a post office (**bureau de poste**) or a tobacco shop (**bureau de tabac**), where prior to the modernization of the phone system over the last twenty years, one traditionally went to use a phone. Today, however, with the installation of numerous phone booths (**cabines téléphoniques**) on the streets, in metro stations, and in other public places, the French can make a phone call from almost anywhere. French people also use car phones and cellular phones a lot.

LES HEURES FRANCE

APPELEZ AU MÊME PRIX AU COIN DE LA RUE ET AU BOUT DE LA FRANCE.

Le même prix partout en France pour joindre tous ceux que vous aimez. Et aussi nos meilleurs prix sur les autres destinations.

Le forfait qui vous va

Avec une gamme de 8 forfaits* Heures France décomptés à la seconde près, dès la première seconde, vous choisissez celui qui répond le mieux à vos besoins. Savourez ainsi chaque instant de conversation, 24h/24 et 7j/7.

- 2 h pour 7 €/mois
- 3 h pour 10 €/mois
- 4 h pour 13 €/mois
- 6 h pour 18 €/mois
- 9 h pour 26 €/mois
- 12 h pour 34 €/mois
- 16 h pour 45 €/mois
- 20 h pour 56 €/mois

Et nos meilleurs prix sur vos autres appels

Parce que vous choisissez Les Heures France sur votre ligne France Télécom, vous bénéficiez également de nos prix les plus avantageux, par exemple sur vos appels vers les mobiles** :

- 9 cts d'euro vers les mobiles Orange et SFR, en heures creuses

Pour choisir vos Heures France, contactez-nous au 1014, au ‿3000 (appels gratuits de chez vous) ou sur www.francetelecom.com

ℓ france telecom

Valable en France métropolitaine. * Hors appels vers les mobiles, les numéros spéciaux, les numéros Internet non géographiques et à partir des cartes France Télécom. ** Prix au-delà du crédit temps qui est de 23 cts d'euro pour 30 secondes en heures creuses. Pour connaître les heures creuses et le prix vers un mobile Bouygues Telecom, contactez votre agence France Télécom. Prix en France métropolitaine au 01/03/02.

Enrichissons notre vocabulaire

Mes affaires *(f.) (My things)*

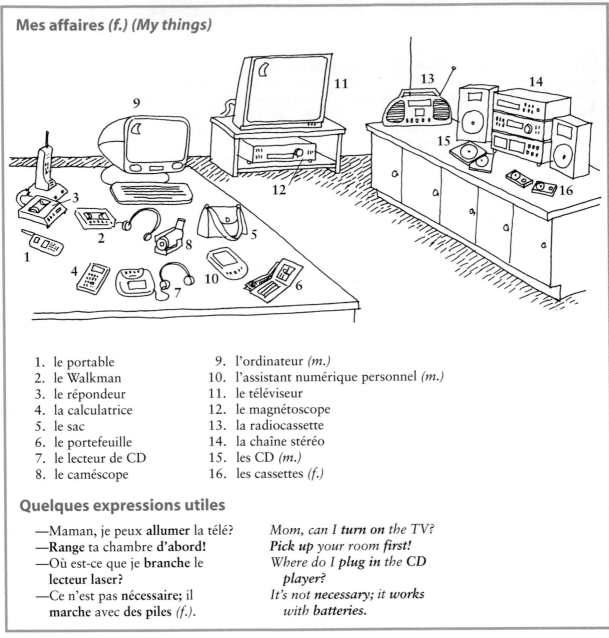

1. le portable
2. le Walkman
3. le répondeur
4. la calculatrice
5. le sac
6. le portefeuille
7. le lecteur de CD
8. le caméscope
9. l'ordinateur *(m.)*
10. l'assistant numérique personnel *(m.)*
11. le téléviseur
12. le magnétoscope
13. la radiocassette
14. la chaîne stéréo
15. les CD *(m.)*
16. les cassettes *(f.)*

Quelques expressions utiles

—Maman, je peux **allumer** la télé?   *Mom, can I **turn on** the TV?*
—**Range** ta chambre **d'abord!**   ***Pick up** your room **first!***
—Où est-ce que je **branche** le   *Where do I **plug in** the CD*
  lecteur laser?   *player?*
—Ce n'est pas **nécessaire;** il   *It's not **necessary;** it **works***
  marche avec **des piles** *(f.).*   *with **batteries.***

Prononciation   **Nasal vowels**

French has three vowel sounds that are nasalized. This means that air is allowed to pass into the nasal cavity and vibrate. If you pinch your nose and say
the words **vin** and **va,** you will feel the vibrations as you say **vin,** but not **va.**

Repeat the following words, which are grouped according to the nasal vowel sound they contain, after your teacher.

/ ã / (Your lips are slightly rounded, your tongue back.)
an / dans / gant / quand / sans / blanc / banque / chantez / changez / cent deux / je danse / il demande

/ ɔ̃ / (Your lips are more rounded, your tongue farther back.)
on / blond / ton / non / son / ils vont / ils font / elles sont / faisons / travaillons / nous avons / mon

/ ɛ̃ / (Your lips are spread, your tongue forward.)
pain / cinq / vin / bien / impossible / important / loin / Alain / sympathique

Exercices

A Repeat the following words after your teacher, paying particular attention to the nasal vowels.

allons / faisons / mes enfants / à demain / en France / invite / bonjour / sa maison / continuons / magasin / canadien / mexicain / examen / tu manges / pardon

B Repeat each sentence after your teacher, paying particular attention to the nasal vowels.

1. Chantal danse bien.
2. Combien de garçons allons-nous inviter?
3. Les Américains sont-ils sympathiques?
4. Jean et Alain vont partir en vacances en Angleterre.
5. Mes enfants vont répondre aux questions.
6. Elles ont trouvé un restaurant mexicain fantastique.

 # grammaire

I. Interrogative and demonstrative adjectives

You use interrogative adjectives to ask someone to make a choice and demonstrative adjectives to point out or choose.

A. Interrogative adjectives

1. In French, interrogative adjectives (*what?* or *which?* in English) ask for a choice. Like other French adjectives, they agree in gender and number with the nouns they modify. Either inversion or **est-ce que** is used with **quel**.

	singular	plural
masculine	quel	quels
feminine	quelle	quelles

Quel répondeur avez-vous vendu?   Vous attendez avec **quels** amis?
A **quelle** heure est-elle arrivée?   **Quelles** sont vos cassettes
                                                 préférées?

2. The plural **quels** and **quelles** call for a **liaison obligatoire**.

   Quels_artistes est-ce que tu apprécies?
   Quelles_universités vont-ils visiter?

B. Demonstrative adjectives

1. French uses several forms of **ce** as demonstrative adjectives. They are
   equivalent to *this, that, these,* and *those* in English.

	singular	plural
masculine	ce, cet	ces
feminine	cette	ces

2. **Cet** is a special form of **ce** used with masculine singular adjectives or nouns
   beginning with a vowel sound.

   Cet autocar va à Marseille.   A-t-elle invité **cet au**tre homme?

3. All the singular forms in the table above can mean *this* or *that,* and **ces** can
   mean *these* or *those*. The distinction between *this* and *that* and between
   these and *those* is rarely necessary in French.

   —Quel Walkman recommandez-vous?
   —**Ce** Walkman marche bien.

   —Quand est-ce que vous allez arriver chez nous?
   —**Cet** après-midi.

   —Tu aimes **ces** CD?
   —Quels CD?

   When a distinction in meaning is necessary, you add **-ci** to the noun to express *this* or *these* and **-là** to express *that* or *those*.

   —**Cette calculatrice-ci** est à toi?   —Vous désirez?
   —Non, elle est à mon frère.   —Montrez-moi **ce téléviseur-là**.

Ⓐ **Questions et réponses.** Employez un adjectif interrogatif et un adjectif démonstratif avec les mots suivants *(following)*.

MODÈLE: cassette
Quelle cassette? Cette cassette.

1. idées
2. saison
3. magnétoscope
4. trains
5. chaînes stéréo
6. hôtel
7. examen
8. autobus
9. piles

Ⓑ **Suivons** *(Let's follow)* **M. et Mme Ducharme à un restaurant.** Formez des phrases complètes en employant *(using)* les mots donnés et en faisant *(making)* tous les changements nécessaires.

1. Tu / penser / quel / restaurant?
2. Tu / ne... pas / laisser / ce / imper / ici?
3. hôtesse / ne... pas / recommander / restaurant-là
4. quel / heure / nous / dîner?
5. Quel / viande / et / quel / légume / nous / commander / soir?
6. Aller / chercher / le / garçon; / ce / boissons / ne... pas / être / à nous

Ⓒ **Les Dupont font une promenade.** Répondez aux questions suivantes en employant les mots entre parenthèses et des adjectifs démonstratifs.

1. Est-ce qu'on va au parc ce matin?   (Non,... après-midi)
2. Jacques a-t-il son parapluie?   (Non,... porter... imper)
3. Est-ce que Louise va porter cette robe?   (Oui, et... chaussures aussi)
4. Qu'est-ce que Pierre a oublié?   (... transistor...)
5. Michel va rester à la maison pour faire la cuisine?   (Non,... soir)
6. Est-ce que j'ai mon sac?   (Non,... sac... être à moi!)

Ⓓ **Les Français et leurs affaires.** Voilà une liste des pourcentages de familles françaises qui possèdent chacun des équipements audio-visuels suivants.

Demandez à un(e) partenaire de vous dire combien de familles possèdent chaque objet.

Téléviseur (couleurs)	99,9
Radio	99,0
Radiocassette	86,2
Autoradio	80,0
Magnétoscope	78,0
Tuner sur chaîne stéréo	77,7
Lecteur de CD	67,0
Multiéquipement couleur	40,0
Baladeur	26,8

MODÈLE: Quel pourcentage des familles a une radio?
Quatre-vingt-dix-neuf pour cent.

Communication

E **Questionnaire.** Formez des questions avec les mots suivants. Posez ces questions à un(e) camarade et préparez un résumé des réponses pour les autres.

A	B		C
Quel	appartement	musée	habites-tu?
Quelle	CD	pays	aimes-tu mieux?
Quels	ville	villes	vas-tu visiter?
Quelles	film	café	fréquentes-tu?
	cours	cinéma	
	artistes	boîtes	

F **Poursuite triviale.** Répondez aux questions suivantes avec un adjectif démonstratif si vous savez *(know)* la réponse!

MODÈLE: Quelle femme a été pilote dans les années trente?
Cette femme est Amelia Earhart.

1. Quelle actrice a joué le rôle de Scarlett O'Hara?
2. Quel maire *(mayor)* est devenu célèbre après l'attaque terroriste du 11 septembre 2001?
3. Quelle a été la première université fondée aux Etats-Unis?
4. Quel explorateur français est arrivé au Canada en 1534?
5. Quel président a acheté la Louisiane?
6. Les Américains n'ont pas élu *(elected)* quel président?

G **Questions personnelles.** Vos préférences.

1. Dans quels restaurants est-ce que vous aimez manger?
2. Quelle cuisine aimez-vous?
3. Quel vin aimez-vous beaucoup?
4. Quelle boisson aimez-vous en été? en hiver?
5. Quelle sorte de musique aimez-vous écouter dans les boîtes?
6. A quelle heure est-ce que vous rentrez de ces boîtes?

II. Verbs ending in -*ir*

You use verbs to describe actions or activities.

In Chapter 1 you learned that French verbs are categorized according to the infinitive ending. In addition to -**er** and -**re** verbs, there is a group ending in -**ir**. There are two distinct conjugations for this group.

A. -*ir* verbs conjugated like *finir*

Note the -**iss**- in the plural forms.

finir	(to finish)	
je **finis**	nous **finissons**	
tu **finis**	vous **finissez**	
il / elle / on **finit**	ils / elles **finissent**	

Mots clés *Verbs conjugated like* finir

choisir	*to choose*	**réfléchir à**	*to think (about), consider*
désobéir à	*to disobey*	**réussir (à)**	*to succeed; to pass*
obéir à	*to obey*		*(an exam)*
punir	*to punish*	**rougir**	*to blush*

Je **finis** mes cours à dix-sept heures.
Elle va **choisir** une chaîne stéréo pour son frère.
M. Dupont ne **punit** pas ses enfants.
Elles **réussissent** toujours aux examens.

1. The imperative of this group of -**ir** verbs is regular: you simply delete the subject.

   Finis tes devoirs. **Obéissez** à vos parents!

2. To form the past participle, drop the **r** of the infinitive.

   —Vous avez **choisi** votre dessert?
   —Non, nous n'avons pas **fini** notre fromage.

   —Pourquoi est-ce qu'ils ont **puni** leur fils?
   —Parce qu'il a **désobéi.**

3. Note that **obéir, désobéir,** and **réfléchir** must take the preposition **à** before a following noun. With **réussir,** however, **à** is optional.

   J'**obéis** toujours à mes parents.
   Ne **désobéissez** pas à l'agent de police.
   Je n'aime pas **réfléchir aux** problèmes difficiles.

Ⓐ **Des décisions.** Formez des phrases complètes avec les mots donnés. Faites les changements nécessaires.

1. Je / finir / ce / livre
2. Qu'est-ce que / tu / choisir / comme cours?
3. Tu / ne... / réfléchir / pas / quand / tu / étudier
4. parents / punir / enfants / quand / ils / désobéir
5. Il / ne... pas / réussir / examen
6. Tu / finir / ménage / demain

Ⓑ **Conversations à la résidence.** Refaites *(Redo)* les phrases suivantes en employant les mots donnés.

1. *Nous* finissons nos devoirs.   (Je...)
2. *Marc* ne va pas *finir* son examen ce matin.   (Vous... réussir...)
3. *Luc* obéit à *l'agent*.   (Nous... agents)
4. *Vous* finissez à huit heures?   (Jacqueline...)
5. *Ce soir,* je vais choisir le restau.   (Hier soir,...)
6. *Jean* rougit souvent en cours.   (Jean et Marie...)

B. *-ir* verbs conjugated like *servir*

Note that you drop the last consonant of the infinitive stem in the singular forms of the present tense.

servir (to serve)	
je **sers**	nous **servons**
tu **sers**	vous **servez**
il / elle / on **sert**	ils / elles **servent**

Mots clés   *Verbs conjugated like **servir***

dormir *to sleep*	je dors, nous dormons	**sentir** *to smell, to feel*	je sens, nous sentons
mentir *to lie*	je mens, nous mentons	**sortir** *to go out*	je sors, nous sortons
partir *to leave*	je pars, nous partons		

Je **sors** avec des amis après les cours.
Ce fruit **sent** mauvais.
Nous allons **dormir** tard ce week-end.
Elles **partent** aujourd'hui.
Tu ne vas pas **mentir** à ton frère.

1. The imperative of this group of -**ir** verbs is also regular.

Servons du café à nos amis.   Ne **mentez** pas à vos parents.

2. To form the past participle, drop the **r** of the infinitive.

Je n'ai pas **dormi** cette nuit.   Ils n'ont pas **servi** de vin.

3. The **passé composé** of **partir** and **sortir** take **être,** so the subject and past participle must agree.

Elles sont **parties** hier.   Nous sommes **sortis** mardi soir.

Langue

C **Les Français.** Formez des phrases complètes avec les mots donnés. Faites les changements nécessaires.

1. Les Français / servir / souvent / vin
2. Ils / partir / en vacances / à la plage
3. On / aimer / sortir / le week-end
4. enfants / dormir / huit heures
5. Les Français / réfléchir / beaucoup
6. Un jeune Français / ne... pas / mentir / parents

D **M. et Mme Morin interrogent leur fils.** Mettez les phrases suivantes au présent.

1. Tu vas sortir avec Marie ce soir?
2. Tu vas dormir cet après-midi?
3. Tu ne vas pas partir en retard?
4. Elle va servir un dîner?
5. Qu'est-ce que tu vas choisir si le dîner ne sent pas bon?
6. Tu ne vas pas mentir si tu n'aimes pas sa cuisine?

Culture

E **La France ou les Etats-Unis?** Formez des phrases avec les mots donnés et dites *(say)* si l'activité est typique des Français ou des Américains.

MODÈLE: On / servir / salade / avant / repas
          On sert la salade avant le repas. C'est typique des Américains.

1. Les jeunes gens / sortir / en groupes, / pas à deux
2. On / rougir / vite / devant la nudité
3. Les élèves / réussir / moins souvent au lycée
4. On / choisir / les restaurants avec un livre
5. Les parents / servir / vin aux enfants
6. Les gens / partir en vacances / en même temps

Communication

F **A mon avis.** Est-ce que les phrases suivantes sont vraies *(true)* ou fausses *(false)*? Si elles sont fausses, corrigez-les *(correct them)*.

1. Je dors cinq heures tous les jours.
2. Mes amis choisissent des cours difficiles.

3. Je ne mens pas à mes parents.
4. Les étudiants réfléchissent quand ils font leurs devoirs.
5. Mes amis ne servent pas d'alcool.
6. Quand je fais la cuisine, cela sent toujours bon.

G **Finissons nos phrases.** Complétez les phrases suivantes.

1. Je réussis à mes examens quand...
2. Nous sommes partis en vacances...
3. Comme restaurant, mes parents aiment choisir...
4. Je rougis toujours quand...
5. Le week-end, je dors jusqu'à...
6. Je voudrais sortir avec...

H **Que choisissez-vous?** Répondez selon le modèle suivant et justifiez vos réponses.

MODÈLE: un restaurant chinois ou américain
Moi, je choisis un restaurant chinois parce que j'adore cette cuisine.

1. un concert de musique classique ou un match de football
2. des vacances chez vos parents ou à la plage
3. du coca ou de la bière
4. un autocar ou votre voiture pour un voyage
5. la radio ou la télévision
6. une profession intéressante ou bien payée

I **Questions personnelles.** Ma vie à l'université.

1. A quelle heure partez-vous pour vos cours le matin?
2. Réussissez-vous toujours à vos examens? Et votre camarade de chambre?
3. Avez-vous rougi en cours? Quand?
4. Comment est-ce que votre professeur punit la classe quand les étudiants ne préparent pas la leçon?
5. Jusqu'à quelle heure dormez-vous le week-end?
6. Vous sortez beaucoup? Qu'est-ce que vous faites le week-end quand vous ne sortez pas?

III. Interrogative pronouns

You use interrogative pronouns to find out specific information about people and things.

In French, the form of an interrogative pronoun depends on whether the pronoun is the subject or the object of the verb. As in English, the form also varies according to whether you are asking about a person *(Who? Whom?)* or a thing *(What?).*

A. Persons

1. To ask about a person as the subject of a verb *(Who?)*, use **Qui est-ce qui** or **Qui.**

   —**Qui est-ce qui** a faim?   —**Qui** a téléphoné?
   —Moi!   —Benjamin.

2. If the person is an object of the verb *(Whom?)*, use **Qui est-ce que** or **Qui** with inversion.

   —**Qui est-ce que** vous admirez?   —**Qui est-ce que** tu as invité?
     Qui admirez-vous?   **Qui** as-tu invité?
   —J'admire mes parents.   —J'ai invité mes amis.

3. If the person is the object of a preposition *(Whom?)*, use the preposition plus **qui est-ce que** or **qui** with inversion.

   —**Avec qui est-ce qu'**ils ont joué?   —**A qui est-ce que** tu as parlé?
     Avec qui ont-ils joué?   **A qui** as-tu parlé?
   —Avec leurs enfants.   —J'ai parlé à la secrétaire.

B. Things

1. To ask about a thing as the object of a verb *(What?)*, use **Qu'est-ce que** or **Que** with inversion.

   —**Qu'est-ce que** vos frères   —**Qu'est-ce que** c'est?
     cherchent?   —C'est un téléphone portable.
   —Ils cherchent leurs clés.

   —**Qu'est-ce que** vous avez choisi?
     Qu'avez-vous choisi?
   —J'ai choisi un magnétoscope allemand.

2. A thing can be the subject of a sentence. In this case, the only interrogative pronoun that can be used is **Qu'est-ce qui** *(What?)*. This pronoun is often used with **arriver** *(to happen)* and **rester** *(to be left over; to remain).*

   —**Qu'est-ce qui** est arrivé?   —**Qu'est-ce qui** reste?
   —Mes parents sont partis.   —Un peu de coca.

3. If a thing is the object of a preposition *(What?)*, use **quoi,** which is followed by **est-ce que** or inversion.

—De **quoi** est-ce qu'ils parlent?   —A **quoi** est-ce que tu penses?
   De **quoi** parlent-ils?   A **quoi** penses-tu?
—Ils parlent de leurs affaires.   —A mes vacances!

C. Summary

	persons (who? whom?)	things (what?)
subject of verb	Qui *or* Qui est-ce qui	Qu'est-ce qui
object of verb	qui + inversion *or* qui est-ce que	que + inversion *or* qu'est-ce que
object of prep.	Prep. + qui + inversion *or* Prep. + qui est-ce que	Prep. + quoi + inversion *or* Prep. + quoi est-ce que

Langue

A **Interview avec des Français.** Vous allez interviewer des Français. Traduisez les questions suivantes en français.

1. What do you do?
2. What do you like to talk about?
3. What happened at your home last night?
4. What have you bought recently?
5. Whom do you phone often?
6. What does your family watch on TV?

B **Des questions.** Complétez les phrases suivantes avec un pronom interrogatif approprié *(appropriate)*.

1. _____ a mangé ma glace?
2. A _____ avez-vous donné l'argent?
3. _____ est arrivé ce matin?
4. Avec _____ a-t-on fait des crêpes?
5. _____ il y a dans la chambre?
6. _____ ont-ils regardé?

C **Interview avec des étudiants.** Trouvez les questions qui ont provoqué les réponses en italique *(italics)*.

1. Nous sommes *étudiants*.
2. Nous étudions *l'anglais*.
3. *Marie et Jacqueline* sont absentes aujourd'hui.
4. *La résidence* est agréable.
5. Je vais téléphoner à *mon ami Luc* ce soir.
6. Luc va acheter *un téléviseur*.

Culture

D **Des célébrités francophones.** En utilisant les mots de la colonne de gauche *(left column)*, trouvez des questions qui décrivent *(describe)* les gens célèbres de la colonne de droite *(right)*.

1. écrire des livres, avancer le féminisme	a. Catherine Deneuve
2. chanter du «rap» en français	b. Emeril Lagasse
3. explorer l'océan	c. Jacques Cousteau
4. écrire des pièces de théâtre	d. Molière
5. faire du cinéma	e. MC Solaar
6. donner des leçons de cuisine	f. Simone de Beauvoir

E **Des statistiques.** Trouvez les questions qui correspondent aux renseignements en italique, et posez *(ask)* ces questions à un(e) camarade de classe.

MODÈLE: *Les Portugais* sont les immigrés les plus nombreux en France.
            Qui sont les immigrés les plus nombreux en France?

1. 34% des Français achètent *des livres.*
2. Les Français regardent *la télévision* plus de trois heures par jour.
3. 29% des Français fument *des cigarettes.*
4. 18% des Français lisent *le journal.*
5. 30% des jeunes Français (18–24 ans) ne consomment pas *d'alcool.*

Communication

F **Enquête.** Formez des groupes et posez des questions en utilisant des pronoms interrogatifs. Consultez les verbes donnés et inventez des questions originales. Informez vos camarades de cours des résultats.

MODÈLE: *Qui admires-tu?*
            Qu'est-ce que tu as à la maison?

aimer bien	détester
porter en cours demain	ne... pas faire cette semaine
téléphoner à	manger
oublier	regarder... à la télévision
faire bien	aller faire ce week-end

G **Questions personnelles.** Votre passé.

1. Qu'est-ce que vous avez fait l'été dernier?
2. Avec qui est-ce que vous avez fait un voyage?
3. Pour qui est-ce que vos parents ont voté en 2000?
4. De quoi avez-vous parlé avec vos amis le week-end dernier?
5. A qui avez-vous téléphoné?
6. Qui avez-vous invité chez vous cette semaine?
7. Qui a fait le ménage chez vous récemment? Cette année?
8. Qu'est-ce qui est arrivé d'intéressant ce mois-ci?

IV. *Pouvoir* and *vouloir*

You use **pouvoir** to express ability or permission and **vouloir** to indicate a desire.

A. *Pouvoir*

1. **Pouvoir** *(to be able, can, may, to be allowed to)* is an irregular verb, so you must learn its forms.

je **peux**	nous **pouvons**
tu **peux**	vous **pouvez**
il / elle / on **peut**	ils / elles **peuvent**

2. **Pouvoir** is often followed by another verb in the infinitive.

—Est-ce que je **peux parler** à Elisabeth?
—**Pouvez**-vous **rappeler** plus tard?

—Est-ce que ton frère **peut partir** aujourd'hui?
—Non, tu **peux attendre** demain?

3. The past participle of **pouvoir** is **pu**.

—Qu'est-ce que vous avez?   —Vous avez **pu** parler à Elisabeth?
—Je n'ai pas **pu** dormir.   —Non, elle est sortie.

B. *Vouloir*

1. **Vouloir** *(to want)* is also irregular and must be memorized.

je **veux**	nous **voulons**
tu **veux**	vous **voulez**
il / elle / on **veut**	ils / elles **veulent**

2. Like **pouvoir, vouloir** is frequently used with an infinitive.

—Tu **veux finir** mon dessert?
—Non, je ne **peux** pas.

3. The past participle of **vouloir** is **voulu**.

—Ils n'ont pas **voulu** partir le matin?
—Non, ils ont préféré faire la grasse matinée.

4. You have already seen the expression **je voudrais**, which is a form of **vouloir** used to say *I want* politely.

Je voudrais parler au médecin.
Je voudrais du café, s'il vous plaît.

5. The expression **vouloir bien** means *to be willing.*

> —Tu veux sortir ce soir?
> —Oui, je **veux bien.**

Attention!

Pouvoir and **vouloir** share a similar pronunciation.

1. The vowel sounds are the same.

je peux / je veux	/ ʒø pø /, / ʒø vø /
nous pouvons / nous voulons	/ nu pu vɔ̃ /, / nu vu lɔ̃ /
ils peuvent / ils veulent	/ il pœv /, / il vœl /

2. Although the third-person vowels are written **eu,** the vowel sound changes from the singular to the plural. You must open your mouth wider to pronounce the sound for **eu** in the plural.

il peut, ils peuvent	/ il pø /, / il pœv /
il veut, ils veulent	/ il vø /, / il vœl /

Vous voulez passer une commande

Vous voulez régler votre facture

Vous changez d'adresse...

Nos conseillers vous accueillent du lundi au vendredi
de 8 h à 20 h et le samedi de 9 h à 17 h

0 825 837 837*

...notre service clients
est à votre écoute

Langue

Ⓐ **Jacques est difficile!** Dans les phrases suivantes, remplacez **vouloir** par **pouvoir** et vice versa.

1. Jacques ne veut pas aller en cours.
2. Vous ne pouvez pas téléphoner demain, Jacques?
3. Il n'a pas voulu parler.
4. Nous ne pouvons pas inviter des amis chez lui!
5. Ils veulent bien écouter la radio.
6. Je n'ai pas pu rester chez Jacques.

Ⓑ **Elodie et sa famille.** Formez des phrases complètes avec les mots donnés. Faites les changements nécessaires.

1. Elodie / ne... pas / pouvoir / sortir avec nous / parce que / parents / ne... pas / vouloir
2. week-end / dernier / ils / vouloir / aller / mer / ensemble
3. La semaine prochaine / ils / pouvoir / aller en ville
4. Elodie / ne... pas / vouloir / ranger / sa chambre
5. Les parents d'Elodie / vouloir / inviter / son amie Juliette
6. Juliette / ne... pas / pouvoir / rester / chez eux

Culture

C **Les élections en France.** Formez des phrases avec les mots donnés. Si une phrase est fausse, corrigez-la.

1. Les Français / pouvoir / choisir / entre plusieurs candidats
2. Ils / pouvoir / voter / deux fois *(twice)* pour un candidat
3. En France, on / vouloir / communistes dans l'administration
4. Les Français / pouvoir / voter pour le président seulement *(only)* en novembre
5. On / pouvoir / voter à dix-huit ans
6. Les Français / vouloir / voter

Communication

D **Vos préférences.** Qu'est-ce que vous voulez faire et qu'est-ce que vous ne voulez pas faire? Utilisez les suggestions données ou vos propres idées.

MODÈLE: *Je voudrais manger de la glace.*
Je ne veux pas aller au parc.

téléphoner à
écouter mon Walkman
aller à la plage
avoir une chaîne stéréo
travailler le week-end
dormir jusqu'à midi demain
acheter un lecteur laser
sortir au restaurant avec mes amis

E **Je ne peux pas.** Regardez les listes des activités et des excuses ci-dessous *(below)*. Pourquoi ne faites-vous pas chaque activité? Choisissez ou inventez une excuse.

MODÈLE: *Je ne peux pas parler français aujourd'hui parce que j'ai mal dormi hier soir.*

Activités	**Excuses**
étudier ce soir	être fatigué(e), paresseux (-euse)
aller en cours	vouloir écouter mes CD
faire le ménage	dormir mal hier soir
parler français	préparer un examen important
???	???

F **Mes activités d'hier.** Qu'est-ce que vous avez pu faire hier et qu'est-ce que vous avez voulu faire? Employez les suggestions données ou inventez des réponses originales.

MODÈLE: *Hier, j'ai pu terminer mes devoirs.*
J'ai voulu aller à la plage hier.

parler à un(e) ami(e)	oublier mes devoirs
aller en cours	acheter un vêtement
rester à la maison	téléphoner à mes parents
faire des courses	ranger mes affaires

Ⓖ **Questions personnelles.** Votre avenir.

1. Qu'est-ce que vous voulez pour votre anniversaire?
2. Où pouvez-vous aller pour vos vacances d'été?
3. Pour qui voulez-vous voter en 2004?
4. Quelle profession voulez-vous avoir?
5. Où est-ce que vous voulez habiter?
6. Combien d'enfants voulez-vous avoir?

communiquons

Donner un coup de téléphone

To make a telephone call in France, you can find a phone in post offices and some cafés, and, of course, there are telephone booths on the streets and in public buildings such as train stations. There had been a serious problem of vandalism of public phone booths, but it was solved with the introduction of the **télécarte.** This card has a set price encoded in a computer chip, and each time it is used, the phone electronically subtracts the cost of the call until the entire value is used up. You can buy a **télécarte** at all post offices and **bureaux de tabac.**

Telephone numbers in France have had ten digits since late 1996. For example, the number for the **bureau des objets trouvés** for the metro system is **01.45.31.82.10,** which is read **zéro un, quarante-cinq, trente et un, quatre-vingt-deux, dix.**

Plus de temps pour parler du pays...

5 Télécartes ACHETÉES = 1 Télécarte OFFERTE

Télécarte® 120

Expressions

▶ **On donne un coup de téléphone.**

Elisabeth donne / passe un coup de téléphone / un coup de fil.	*Elisabeth is making a phone call.*
Elle cherche le numéro de téléphone dans l'annuaire / le bottin / le Minitel.	*She looks up the phone number in the phone book / the Minitel.*
Elle compose / fait le numéro des renseignements.	*She dials the number for information.*
Elle utilise un numéro vert.	*She is using a toll-free number.*
Le téléphone sonne.	*The phone rings.*
On décroche le téléphone.	*Someone picks up the phone.*

▶ **On commence la conversation.**

Allô! *Hello!*	
Qui est à l'appareil?	*Who's calling?*
C'est de la part de qui?	*May I say who's calling?*
Est-ce que je pourrais parler à Mlle Leclerc?	*May I speak to Ms. Leclerc?*
Poste 325.	*Extension 325.*
Ne quittez pas.	*Hold the line.*
Un instant, je vous prie.	*One moment, please.*

▶ **On finit la communication.**

La ligne est occupée.	*The line is busy.*
Il / Elle n'est pas là.	*He / She isn't in.*
Il / Elle est sorti(e).	*He / She has gone / stepped out.*
Pouvez-vous rappeler dans une heure?	*Can you call back in an hour?*
Elisabeth raccroche.	*Elisabeth hangs up.*

Interaction

Jacques téléphone à son ami François Morin

MME MORIN: Allô!

JACQUES: Bonjour, Madame. Est-ce que je pourrais parler à François?

MME MORIN: C'est de la part de qui?

JACQUES: C'est Jacques Calvet.

MME MORIN: Ne quittez pas, Monsieur.

Une minute plus tard

MME MORIN: Il n'est pas là. Pouvez-vous rappeler dans une heure?

JACQUES: Bien sûr. Merci, Madame.

MME MORIN: Merci et au revoir.

JACQUES: Au revoir.

Activités

A **Le téléphone.** Répondez aux questions suivantes.

1. Avez-vous un portable? Est-ce que c'est essentiel? Pourquoi?
2. Quel est le numéro de téléphone de l'université? le numéro de la police? des renseignements?
3. En France, comment trouve-t-on un numéro de téléphone?
4. Vous êtes en France et vous voulez téléphoner à vos parents aux Etats-Unis. Que faites-vous?
5. Vos amis ont-ils la messagerie vocale *(voice mail)*?
6. Vous aimez les répondeurs? Sont-ils indispensables?

B **Jeux de rôles.** Avec un(e) camarade, inventez des dialogues adaptés aux situations suivantes.

1. Call for an appointment (**un rendez-vous**) with the doctor.
2. Call someone and ask him / her to go to the movies with you.
3. Call the train station to find out the schedule for trains from Paris to Bordeaux.
4. Call information for a phone number.
5. Call the lost and found office of your hotel to ask about your wallet, which you left in your room.
6. Call a restaurant to find out about their menu and hours.

lecture culturelle

Avant la lecture

France is at the forefront of technology in many industries, notably in the telecommunications field. **France Télécom,** France's partially privatized phone company, was in the vanguard on the "information superhighway," with its introduction in the 1980s of the free **Minitel** computer terminal, which could be hooked up to a phone line. The **Minitel** was originally an electronic telephone directory, intended to replace its bulky paper counterpart°. The idea was very successful, and in time customers also had access to thousands of paid services, such as on-line weather reports, travel information and reservations, movie schedules, stock-market updates, personal message services, and classified ads. With the growing popularity of the World Wide Web in the early 1990s, use of the **Minitel** began to decline. Although the **Minitel** is still used today, the Internet has gained a solid footing in France and has relegated the **Minitel** to a secondary role.

    France Télécom is also a leader in the cellular phone market, as it has played a key role in the growing use of mobile phones in France. In 2001, it

The paper directory, **le bottin téléphonique,** *still exists alongside the electronic* **Minitel** *version.*

Allô

was reported that more than 50 percent of the French population own and use a cell phone. A large percentage of these users subscribe to prepaid cellular phone service. **France Télécom** is currently developing a transmission system that provides users with high-speed Internet access via their cell phones.

Activités

Ⓐ For what purposes do you use the Internet?

Ⓑ Do you own a cell phone? If so, for what purposes do you use your cell phone (SMS, e-mail, Internet access, telephone calls, address book, to-do list)?

Ⓒ How many people do you know in the following age brackets who have cell phones: under 18; 19–39; 40–59; over 60?

Ⓓ As in any language, in French you will find word families (nouns, adjectives, and verbs that are related). Look up the following verbs and then try to guess the meaning of the related nouns and adjectives.

Verbs	Nouns	Adjectives
1. croître	croissance *(f.)*	croissant(e)(s)
2. s'abonner	abonné *(m.)*	abonné(e)(s)
3. s'inscrire	inscription *(f.)*	inscrit(e)(s)
4. rajeunir	jeune *(m./f.)*; jeunesse *(f.)*	jeune(s)
5. répertorier	répertoire *(m.)*	répertorié(e)(s)
6. surprendre	surprise *(f.)*	surprenant(e)(s)
7. se baser	base *(f.)*	basé(e)(s)
8. entrer	entrée *(f.)*	entré(e)(s)

Le téléphone mobile

Le téléphone au féminin

Le marché° français du téléphone mobile a connu° la plus forte croissance d'Europe en décembre 1999, passant à 11 millions d'abonnés, soit° 19% de la population. Selon The Phone House, le marché s'est féminisé: 45% de ces nouveaux clients à Noël étaient des femmes. Il a également rajeuni, les moins de 29 ans représentant désormais 47% des acheteurs contre 41% à Noël 1998.

market / experienced

that is, i.e.

Le téléphone mobile est «in»

La France vient tout juste de passer le cap des 30 millions° d'abonnés au téléphone mobile, soit plus d'un habitant sur deux. Ça fait beaucoup de nouveaux numéros. C'est pourquoi, depuis le début avril, ils ont fait leur entrée (pour la première fois) dans les annuaires de France Télécom. Contrairement aux numéros de téléphones fixes°, automatiquement inscrits, les numéros de portables ne seront répertoriés que° sur une base volontaire.

vient... *just passed the 30-million mark*

stationary
ne seront... *will be listed only*

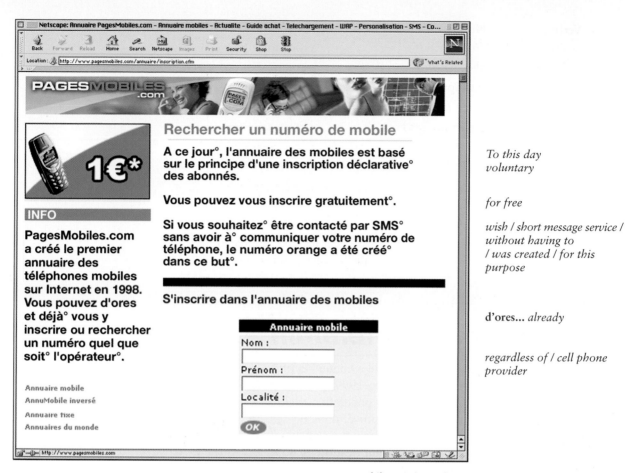

To this day
voluntary

for free

wish / short message service /
without having to
/ was created / for this
purpose

d'ores... already

regardless of / cell phone
provider

www.pagesmobiles.com/annuaire

Après la lecture

Questions sur le texte

Ⓐ Le téléphone au féminin

1. Quel groupe démographique utilise les téléphones mobiles (portables)?
2. Quel est le pourcentage d'hommes qui ont un portable?

Ⓑ Le téléphone mobile est «in»

1. Quel service unique est-ce que France Télécom offre à ses clients de téléphones portables?
2. Pourquoi est-ce que France Télécom a décidé d'offrir ce service?
3. Combien de personnes en France ont un portable?
4. Quels numéros de téléphone sont automatiquement inscrits dans l'annuaire?

Ⓒ Rechercher un numéro de mobile

1. Quel service est-ce que PagesMobiles.com offre aux clients de portables? Est-il possible d'obtenir les numéros de personnes inscrites avec des opérateurs différents?

2. Qu'est-ce que le «téléphone orange»?
3. Quelles informations est-ce qu'il faut fournir *(provide, furnish)* pour s'inscrire dans l'annuaire de PagesMobiles.com?

Ⓐ Comparez le nombre d'abonnés qui possèdent des téléphones mobiles en 1999 et en 2001. Est-ce que c'est surprenant? Expliquez. Selon vous, pourquoi est-ce que les Français achètent des téléphones mobiles?

Ⓑ Quels sont les avantages et les inconvénients des portables (par exemple, le coût, les risques pour la santé et pour la sécurité, la possibilité d'appeler en cas d'urgence, etc.)?

Ⓒ Est-ce qu'il est important pour les autres de pouvoir vous contacter 24 heures sur 24 *(around the clock)*? Dans quelles circonstances est-ce que vous éteignez *(turn off)* votre portable?

Ⓓ Que pensez-vous de l'idée d'avoir des numéros de téléphone mobile dans l'annuaire en papier et dans un annuaire sur le Web? Si vous avez un portable, aimeriez-vous *(would you like)* inscrire votre numéro dans l'annuaire? Pourquoi ou pourquoi pas?

vocabulaire

Noms / Pronoms

affaires (*f.*)	possessions	**la messagerie**	
un assistant numérique	personal digital	**vocale**	voice mail
personnel	assistant,	**un ordinateur**	computer
	handheld	**une pile**	battery
un bureau de tabac	tobacco shop	**un portable**	cellular
une cabine	phone booth		phone
téléphonique		**un portefeuille**	wallet
une calculatrice	calculator	**que**	which, that
un caméscope	camcorder	**qui**	who
une cassette	cassette	**qu'est-ce que**	what
un CD	CD	**qu'est-ce qui**	what
une chaîne stéréo	stereo system	**qui est-ce que**	whom
un courrier	e-mail	**qui est-ce qui**	who
électronique		**quoi**	what
une erreur	wrong number	**une radiocassette**	tape
une expression	expression		recorder
un lecteur de CD	CD player	**un répondeur**	answering
un magnétoscope	VCR		machine
un message	message	**un sac**	purse

un téléphone	telephone	une voix	voice
un téléviseur	TV set	un Walkman	Walkman

Verbes

allumer	to turn on	rappeler	to call back
arriver	to arrive	réfléchir	to think about
brancher	to plug in	rester	to stay
choisir	to choose	réussir	to succeed / to
couper	to disconnect		pass (a test)
désobéir	to disobey	rougir	to blush
dormir	to sleep	savoir	to know
finir	to finish	se passer	to happen
marcher	to function / to work	sentir	to feel
mentir	to lie	servir à	to be used for
obéir	to obey	sonner	to ring
partir	to leave	sortir	to go out
pouvoir	can, may	téléphoner	to telephone
punir	to punish	voir	to see
ranger	to put away, to clean up	vouloir	to want

Adjectifs / Adverbes

ce, cette, cet	this / that	libre	free
ces	these / those	nécessaire	necessary
d'abord	first	plus tard	later
désolé	sorry	quel, quelle, quels, quelles	what / which
encore	still		

Expressions

à qui	to whom
Allô, j'écoute.	Hello.
ce n'est pas la peine	it's not worth the trouble
Ne coupe pas.	Don't hang up.
Ne quittez pas.	Hold on.
Qui est à l'appareil?	Who's speaking?
vouloir bien	to be willing

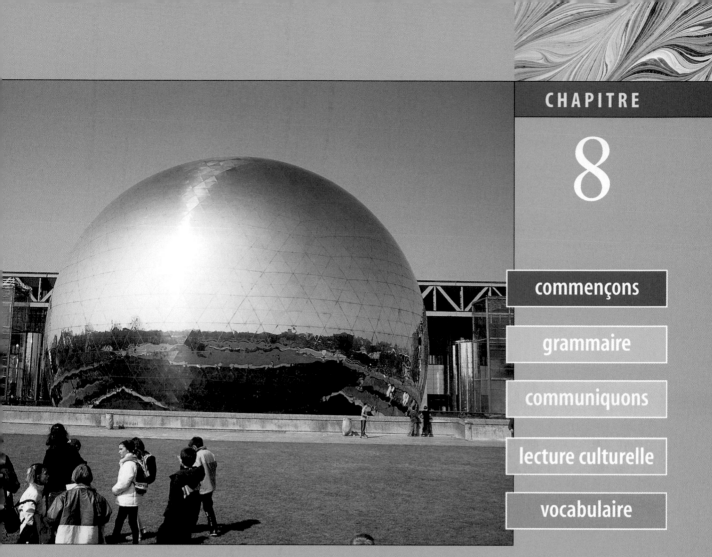

La Cité des sciences

CHAPITRE

8

commençons

grammaire

communiquons

lecture culturelle

vocabulaire

Paris

OBJECTIVES

Language	Culture	Communication
■ Vocabulary for the computer and the post office ■ Oral vowels and nasal consonants ■ The weather	■ **Suivre** and **suivre des cours** ■ Direct object pronouns: Third person ■ **Voir**	■ Studying in France ■ The post office ■ The Seine	■ Talking about the weather ■ Discussing classes and course work ■ Using the post office

commençons

Deux cartes postales

Roger Diallo est un étudiant sénégalais. Il est à Paris et il va suivre des cours à la Sorbonne pendant l'année. Deux semaines après son arrivée, il passe le week-end à la campagne et il fait une carte postale à ses parents.

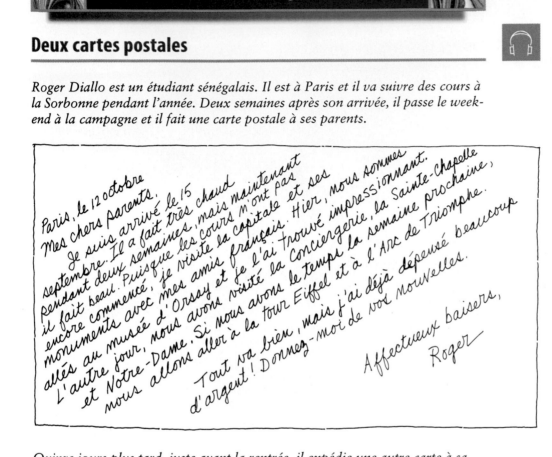

Paris, le 12 octobre

Mes chers parents,

Je suis arrivé le 15 septembre. Il a fait très chaud pendant deux semaines, mais maintenant il fait beau. Puisque les cours n'ont pas encore commencé, je visite la capitale et ses monuments avec mes amis français. Hier, nous sommes allés au musée d'Orsay et je l'ai trouvé impressionnant. L'autre jour, nous avons visité la Conciergerie, la Sainte-Chapelle, et Notre-Dame. Si nous avons le temps la semaine prochaine, nous allons aller à la tour Eiffel et à l'Arc de Triomphe.

Tout va bien, mais j'ai déjà dépensé beaucoup d'argent! Donnez-moi de vos nouvelles.

Affectueux baisers,
Roger

Quinze jours plus tard, juste avant la rentrée, il expédie une autre carte à sa sœur, Monique.

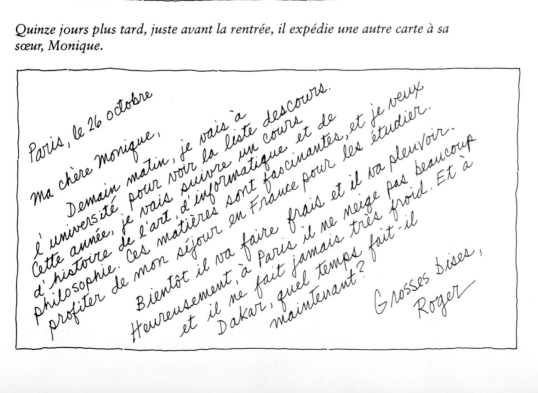

Paris, le 26 octobre

Ma chère Monique,

Demain matin, je vais à l'université pour voir la liste descours. Cette année, je vais suivre un cours d'histoire de l'art, d'informatique et de philosophie. Ces matières sont fascinantes, et je veux profiter de mon séjour en France pour les étudier.

Bientôt il va faire frais et il va pleuvoir. Heureusement, à Paris il ne neige pas beaucoup et il ne fait jamais très froid. Et à Dakar, quel temps fait-il maintenant?

Grosses bises,
Roger

Etudions les cartes postales

1. Quand Roger est-il arrivé en France?
2. Quel temps fait-il en France?
3. Avec qui Roger visite-t-il Paris?
4. Quels monuments veut-il visiter?
5. A qui expédie-t-il la deuxième carte postale?
6. Quels cours Roger va-t-il suivre cette année?

Mots clés

cartes postales (f.)	*postcards*	affectueux baisers (m.)	*hugs and kisses*
sénégalais	*Senegalese*	juste	*just*
suivre des cours	*to take courses*	la rentrée	*start of classes*
pendant	*during*	expédie (expédier)	*sends*
une arrivée	*arrival*	chère	*dear*
la campagne	*countryside*	histoire (f.) de l'art	*art history*
chers	*dear*	informatique (f.)	*computer science*
puisque	*since*	matières (f.)	*subjects*
ne... pas encore	*not yet*	profiter de	*take advantage*
une capitale	*capital*	un séjour	*stay*
monuments (m.)	*monuments*	bientôt	*soon*
l'	*it*	Il va faire frais.	*It is going to be cool.*
impressionnant	*impressive*	pleuvoir	*to rain*
avons le temps (avoir le temps)	*have the time*	Il ne neige pas. (neiger)	*It doesn't snow.*
tout	*all*	ne... jamais	*never*
ai dépensé (dépenser)	*have spent*	Quel temps fait-il?	*What's the weather like?*
Donnez-moi de vos nouvelles.	*Let me hear from you.*	grosses bises (f.)	*love and kisses*

Faisons connaissance

Paris, the capital of France, is one of the most beautiful cities in the world and is renowned for its monuments, modern and historical, which millions of tourists come to visit each year. The **musée** ▶

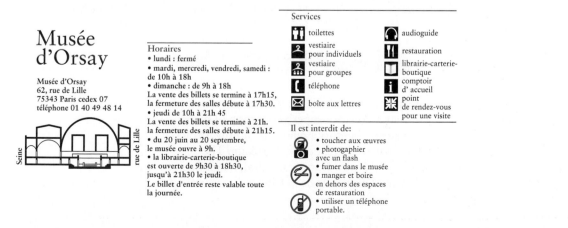

Musée d'Orsay

Musée d'Orsay
62, rue de Lille
75343 Paris cedex 07
téléphone 01 40 49 48 14

Seine / rue de Lille

Horaires
• lundi : fermé
• mardi, mercredi, vendredi, samedi : de 10h à 18h
• dimanche : de 9h à 18h
La vente des billets se termine à 17h15, la fermeture des salles débute à 17h30.
• jeudi de 10h à 21h 45
La vente des billets se termine à 21h. la fermeture des salles débute à 21h15.
• du 20 juin au 20 septembre, le musée ouvre à 9h.
• la librairie-carterie-boutique est ouverte de 9h30 à 18h30, jusqu'à 21h30 le jeudi.
Le billet d'entrée reste valable toute la journée.

Services
- toilettes
- vestiaire pour individuels
- vestiaire pour groupes
- téléphone
- boîte aux lettres
- audioguide
- restauration
- librairie-carterie-boutique
- comptoir d'accueil
- point de rendez-vous pour une visite

Il est interdit de:
• toucher aux œuvres
• photographier avec un flash
• fumer dans le musée
• manger et boire en dehors des espaces de restauration
• utiliser un téléphone portable.

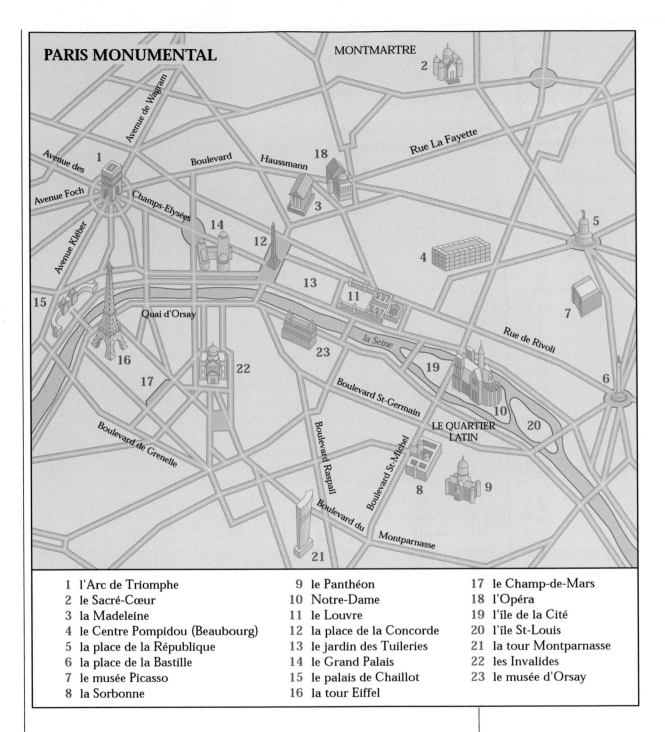

PARIS MONUMENTAL

MONTMARTRE

Avenue de Wagram

Avenue des

Avenue Foch

Avenue Kléber

Champs-Elysées

Boulevard   Haussmann

Rue La Fayette

Quai d'Orsay

la Seine

Rue de Rivoli

Boulevard St-Germain

Boulevard Raspall

Boulevard St-Michel

Boulevard de Grenelle

LE QUARTIER LATIN

Boulevard du   Montparnasse

1 l'Arc de Triomphe	9 le Panthéon	17 le Champ-de-Mars
2 le Sacré-Cœur	10 Notre-Dame	18 l'Opéra
3 la Madeleine	11 le Louvre	19 l'île de la Cité
4 le Centre Pompidou (Beaubourg)	12 la place de la Concorde	20 l'île St-Louis
5 la place de la République	13 le jardin des Tuileries	21 la tour Montparnasse
6 la place de la Bastille	14 le Grand Palais	22 les Invalides
7 le musée Picasso	15 le palais de Chaillot	23 le musée d'Orsay
8 la Sorbonne	16 la tour Eiffel	

d'Orsay is an art museum that opened in late 1986 in what used to be a train station, **la gare d'Orsay.** The museum houses a superb collection of more than four thousand pieces of nineteenth-century French art. It now attracts 2.7 million visitors a year and has received great critical acclaim. The **Conciergerie,** the **Sainte-Chapelle,** and **Notre-Dame** cathedral, magnificent examples of Gothic art, are all located on the **île de la Cité** and surrounded ▶

by the river **Seine.** Nearby is the **Quartier latin,** so named because at the **Sorbonne,** the original university of Paris, classes were once conducted in Latin.

In addition to the tourists who flock to Paris, each year thousands of foreign students come to France. Among the main centers for study are Paris, Grenoble, and Aix-en-Provence, but all universities offer special courses for foreigners to learn French. These programs may last an academic year or varying lengths of time in the summer.

Enrichissons notre vocabulaire

Un ordinateur *(A computer)*

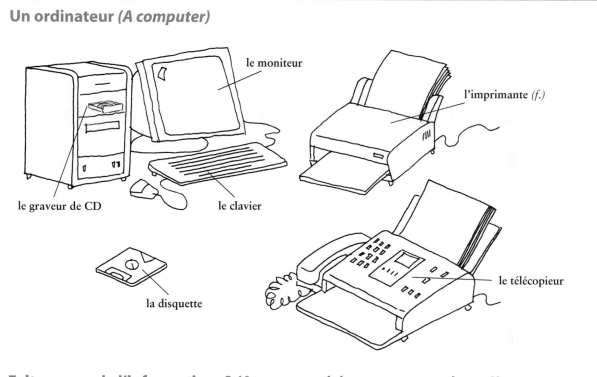

le moniteur

l'imprimante *(f.)*

le graveur de CD

le clavier

la disquette

le télécopieur

Faites-vous de l'informatique? *(Are you studying computer science?)*

—Qu'est-ce que tu penses du **matériel** IBM?	*What do you think of IBM hardware?*
—C'est formidable! J'ai acheté deux **logiciels.**	*It's fantastic! I bought two software programs.*
—Quelles sortes?	*What kind?*
—J'ai un **traitement de texte** pour mes **notes** et mes devoirs **écrits** et un **tableur.**	*I have a word processor for my notes and my written work, and a spreadsheet.*
—Avec mon **modem,** je peux consulter mon **courrier électronique** et l'**Internet.**	*With my modem, I can check my e-mail and the Internet.*
—Tu as **rencontré** des problèmes?	*Have you met with any problems?*

—Non, et je vais **gagner** de
l'argent si je **tape** les devoirs
de mes amis.
—Est-ce que je peux **emprunter**
ton matériel et tes logiciels?
—Non, je **ne** les **prête jamais;** je
les **utilise tout le temps.**

No, *and I am going to **earn**
money if I **type** my friends'
papers.*
*May I **borrow** your equipment
and your software?*
*No, I **never lend** them; I **use**
them **all the time.***

Au bureau de poste *(At the post office)*

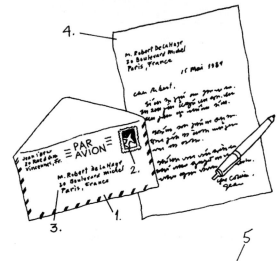

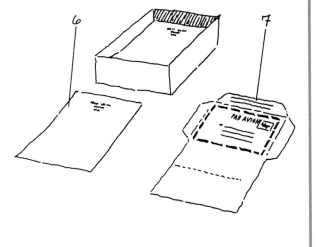

1. une **enveloppe**
2. un **timbre**
3. l'**adresse** *(f.)*
4. une **lettre**

5. un **paquet** / un **colis**
6. du **papier à lettres**
7. un **aérogramme**
8. un **télégramme**

Le **facteur:** Bonjour, Madame.
Mme Legrain: Vous avez du
courrier pour moi?
Le facteur: Oui, une lettre
recommandée et un **mandat.**
Mme Legrain: Tenez, merci
beaucoup.

*The **mailman:** Good morning, ma'am.*
*Mme Legrain: Do you have any
mail for me?*
*The mailman: Yes, a **registered**
letter and a **money order.***
*Mme Legrain: There, thanks
a lot.*

Prononciation   Oral vowels and nasal consonants

A. In Chapter 7, you learned the pronunciation of the three nasal vowels in French: / ɛ̃ / (**pain**), / ɑ̃ / (**lent**), and / ɔ̃ / (**ton**). With nasal vowels, you never pronounce the letter **n** or **m** that accompanies the written vowel.

The masculine forms of the following adjectives end in a nasal vowel, so the **n** is not pronounced. The **n** must be pronounced in the feminine, however, so the preceding vowel is oral instead of nasal.

Masculine	**Feminine**
améric**ain**	américa**ine**
canadi**en**	canadie**nne**
itali**en**	italie**nne**

B. The **n** or **m** must be pronounced if it is doubled (**so**mm**es**) or followed by a vowel (**téléphon**e).

Pronounce the following words and indicate whether the underlined vowels in boldface are oral or nasal.

je d**o**nne / t**o**n stylo / bi**e**n / **e**n ville / s**o**nne / **a**nnée / v**i**n / mat**i**n / **i**nutile / t**i**mbre / le m**o**niteur / **i**mpressi**o**nn**a**nt

Exercices

A Pronounce the following pairs of words after your teacher, making a clear distinction between the oral and nasal vowels.

1. Jean / Jeanne
2. an / année
3. matin / matinée
4. plein / pleine
5. un / une
6. vietnamien / vietnamienne
7. gens / jeune
8. brun / brune

B Read the following sentences aloud, taking care not to nasalize vowels before pronounced **n** and **m**.

1. Les usines anciennes consomment beaucoup d'énergie.
2. Elle aime un homme ambitieux.
3. Tiens! Etienne déjeune avec une Canadienne.
4. Anne et Micheline vont emprunter mon traitement de texte.
5. Jean et Jeanne ont acheté un ordinateur.
6. Yvonne expédie un télégramme à Lisbonne.

CINÉMA EN PLEIN AIR

16 JUILLET – 25 AOÛT
01 40 03 75 75
WWW.VILLETTE.COM
PRAIRIE DU TRIANGLE
M° PORTE DE PANTIN
ACCÈS LIBRE

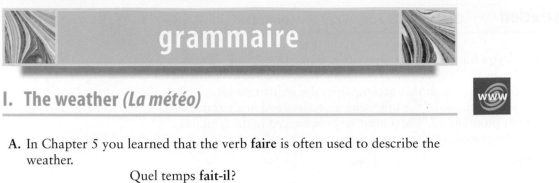

grammaire

I. The weather (La météo)

A. In Chapter 5 you learned that the verb **faire** is often used to describe the weather.

Quel temps **fait-il?**

Il fait beau.   **Il fait** chaud.
Il fait mauvais.   **Il fait** froid.

There are other descriptions of the weather that contain **faire:**

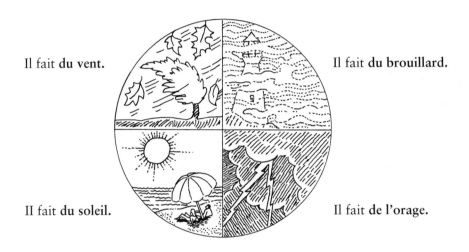

Il fait **du vent.**   Il fait **du brouillard.**

Il fait **du soleil.**   Il fait **de l'orage.**

Il fait **frais.**	*It is cool.*
Il fait **bon.**	*It is nice.*
Il fait **une chaleur insupportable!**	*The heat is unbearable!*

B. In addition to **faire,** there are other verbs and terms used to describe weather:

être: **Le ciel est couvert.**	*The sky is overcast. / It's cloudy.*
neiger: **Il neige.**	to snow: *It is snowing.*
pleuvoir: **Il pleut.**	to rain: *It is raining.*
Il y a des **nuages** *(m.).*	*There are clouds.*
Il y a **des éclairs** *(m.)* et **du tonnerre.**	*There is lightning and thunder.*
Il y a déjà beaucoup de **neige** *(f.).*	*There is already a lot of snow.*
Nous avons eu beaucoup de **pluie** *(f.)* cette année.	*We've had a lot of rain this year.*

C. The following examples show how weather expressions are used in other tenses.

> **Passé composé**
>
> Il **a fait** très chaud pendant deux semaines.
> Le week-end dernier, il **a plu** mais il **n'a pas neigé.**
>
> **Futur proche**
>
> Il **va faire frais** et il **va pleuvoir.**
> Il **va neiger** la semaine prochaine.

Attention! ────────────────────

1. **Il fait beau** is used for general weather conditions *(warm, sunny),* while **il fait bon** refers to temperature and can refer to a room indoors.

   Il fait bon dans cette chambre.

2. **Chaud** and **froid** can be used with three different verbs, depending on what is being described.

weather (**faire**):	Il **fait chaud.** Il **fait froid.**
people (**avoir**):	J'**ai chaud.** Robert **a froid.**
things (**être**):	Cette eau **est chaude.** Ma bière n'**est** pas assez **froide.**

Langue

Ⓐ **Quel temps fait-il?** Faites deux phrases pour chaque dessin *(each drawing).*

B **La météo.** Refaites les phrases suivantes en employant les mots entre parenthèses.

1. Quel temps fait-il?   (... hier?)
2. Il pleut.   (... hier.)
3. Il neige beaucoup.   (L'année dernière...)
4. Il ne fait pas froid.   (... demain.)
5. Il fait de l'orage.   (Le week-end dernier...)
6. Il va faire du brouillard.   (... hier matin.)

C **Le climat en Europe.** Caractérisez le climat des pays suivants en faisant des phrases complètes avec les mots donnés.

1. pleuvoir / beaucoup / Angleterre
2. neiger / beaucoup / Suisse
3. faire / soleil / Italie
4. Espagne / faire / chaud
5. faire / brouillard / Irlande
6. Norvège / faire / froid

Culture

D **Les prévisions de la météo.** Regardez la carte météorologique et répondez aux questions ci-dessous *(below)*.

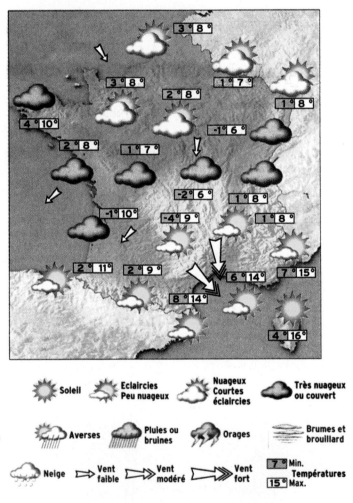

Dans le reste du monde	
(S : soleil ; N : nuageux ; C : couvert ; P : pluie ; O : orage ; * : neige)	
AFRIQUE	
Abidjan	S 32
Dakar	C 27
Le Cap	S 25
PROCHE-ORIENT	
Eilat	S 20
Jérusalem	P 10
Le Caire	S 15
ÉTATS-UNIS, CANADA	
Boston	C 8
Chicago	S 1
Houston	C 22
Los Angeles	S 14
Miami	S 26
New York	C 9
La N.-Orléans	C 21
San Francisco	P 12
Montréal	S 3

CARAÏBES	
Fort-de-France	S 27
Pointe-à-Pitre	S 28
San Juan	S 26
EXTRÊME-ORIENT	
Bangkok	C 35
Hongkong	S 24
Pékin	S 9
Saigon	S 32
Singapour	C 29
Tokyo	S 8
AMÉRIQUE CENTR. ET SUD	
Acapulco	S 30
Buenos Aires	S 33
Cancun	S 32
Lima	P 26
Mexico	S 24
Rio de Janeiro	S 30
Santiago	S 29
PACIFIQUE	
Auckland	C 24
Nouméa	C 29
Papeete	S 32
Sydney	C 23

La carte

1. Est-ce qu'il va faire du soleil en France?
2. Quel temps va-t-il faire dans les Alpes?
3. Va-t-il faire beau sur une des plages en France?

La liste des villes

4. Dans combien de villes est-ce qu'il a plu?
5. Est-ce qu'il a neigé?
6. Il a fait froid à Tokyo?

E **En vacances.** Vos camarades partent en vacances. Suggérez des activités pour les différentes conditions météorologiques.

MODÈLE: quand il fait bon
Quand il fait bon, faites une promenade!

1. quand il pleut
2. quand il neige
3. quand il fait mauvais

4. quand il fait du soleil
5. quand il fait de l'orage
6. quand il fait très froid

F **Les prévisions de la météo.** Choisissez un(e) camarade et préparez ensemble un bulletin météorologique *(weather report)* pour une des situations suivantes.

1. votre ville cet après-midi
2. votre ville l'hiver dernier
3. votre région ce week-end

4. San Diego en hiver
5. le Sénégal
6. Montréal en hiver

G **Questions personnelles.** Votre temps préféré.

1. Etes-vous content(e) quand il fait froid? quand il fait chaud?
2. Aimez-vous faire une promenade quand il pleut?
3. Quel temps a-t-il fait le week-end dernier? Qu'est-ce que vous avez fait?
4. Quel temps voulez-vous avoir pour vos prochaines vacances?
5. Où est-ce qu'on trouve un climat idéal?
6. Avez-vous visité une ville uniquement pour son climat?

II. *Suivre / Suivre des cours*

You use **suivre** to express the idea of *to follow (to follow a person; to follow an idea)* and to talk about taking an academic course.

A. *Suivre*

suivre (to follow)	
je **suis**	nous **suivons**
tu **suis**	vous **suivez**
il / elle / on **suit**	ils / elles **suivent**
Passé composé: il **a suivi**	

Nous allons **suivre** cette auto.
Suivez-moi, s'il vous plaît.
Vous **suivez** ce prof?

B. *Suivre des cours*

1. **Suivre** is often used with academic subjects (**suivre des cours, suivre un cours de...**) to express *to take a course or courses.*

   Il va **suivre des cours** à la Sorbonne.
   J'ai **suivi des cours** d'informatique.

   The following vocabulary can be used to talk about the school year: **un trimestre** *(a quarter),* **un semestre** *(a semester),* and **l'année scolaire** *(the school year).*

2. There are three ways to state the subjects you study.

suivre un cours de (d'):	Mon ami **suit un cours d'**histoire.
faire du (de la, des, de l'):	Moi, je **fais de la** physique mais j'aime mieux la psychologie.
étudier le (la, l', les):	Ma sœur **étudie le** latin et **le** grec.

Attention!

You must be sure to use the correct article with each verb.

1. **Suivre un cours** takes only the preposition **de,** not an article.

2. **Faire** takes only the articles **du, de la, de l', des.**

3. **Etudier** takes only the definite articles **le, la, l', les.**

Mots clés   *Academic subjects*

l'anthropologie *(f.)*	les langues étrangères	*foreign languages*
l'architecture *(f.)*	l'allemand *(m.)*	le grec
l'art *(m.)*	l'anglais *(m.)*	l'italien *(m.)*
la biologie	l'arabe *(m.)*	le japonais
la chimie *chemistry*	le chinois	le latin
le droit *law*	l'espagnol *(m.)*	le russe
l'éducation physique *(f.)*	le français	
la géographie	la médecine	
la géologie	la musique	
la gestion *management*	la philosophie	
l'histoire *(f.)*	la physique	
l'informatique *(f.)*	la psychologie	
le journalisme	les sciences économiques *(f.)*	
la littérature	les sciences politiques *(f.)*	
les mathématiques *(f.)*	la sociologie	

Note that all languages are masculine and all sciences are feminine.

Ce qu'ils disent

1. When French students talk about the subjects that they study, they often use abbreviations. Most of them end in **o**.

   philo   philosophie
   sciences éco   sciences économiques
   sciences po   sciences politiques

   psycho   psychologie
   socio   sociologie
   les maths   mathématiques

2. To indicate their majors, students use the verb **être** with the preposition **en**.

   Je **suis en socio** à la fac.   *I'm a sociology major* at the university.

Langue

Ⓐ **Des présentations.** Faites des phrases en remplaçant les mots en italique par les mots entre parenthèses.

   MODÈLE: Il fait du français.   (étudier)
                 Il étudie le français.

   1. Luc *étudie* le japonais.   (suivre un cours)
   2. Je *fais* du droit.   (étudier)
   3. Nous *allons suivre un cours* d'histoire.   (faire)
   4. Tu *vas étudier* la géologie.   (suivre un cours)
   5. Mon camarade de chambre *a fait* du chinois.   (suivre un cours)
   6. Julie et Kevin *ont étudié* la physique.   (être en)

Ⓑ **Les études de Juliette.** Faites une phrase complète avec les mots donnés.

   1. Juliette / suivre / cours / informatique / Etats-Unis
   2. semestre dernier / elle / étudier / grec / et / latin
   3. Sa sœur / être / sciences économiques
   4. année prochaine / elles / suivre / cours / psychologie?
   5. Non, elles / ne... pas / étudier / sciences
   6. trimestre prochain / Juliette / faire / informatique

Culture

Ⓒ **Au collège.** Un «collège» est l'équivalent d'un *junior high school* aux Etats-Unis. A la page 210 vous avez l'emploi du temps *(schedule)* de Caroline, une élève de cinquième qui habite à Lyon. Décrivez son emploi du temps en répondant aux questions ci-dessous.

   1. Qu'est-ce que Caroline étudie le lundi matin?
   2. Quand fait-elle du sport?
   3. Dans quelle salle de classe a-t-elle son instruction civique?

		LUNDI	SALLE	MARDI	SALLE	MERCREDI	SALLE	JEUDI	SALLE	VENDREDI	SALLE	
8H.15												
MATIN	I	maths	15	Sciences Naturelles 1h 30	50	maths	16	Histoire Géo	62	Français	10	I
	II	Anglais	26			Dessin	18	Enseignement religieux	23	Soutien de Français ou Hist-Géo	10 62	II
	III	musique	13	Sciences Physiques 1h 30	2	Français	36	Français	39	Hist-Géo	62	III
12H.15	IV					Français	36					IV
13H.30												
SOIR	V	Instruction Civique	62	Technologie	At			Soutien de maths		maths	27	V
	VI	Sport		Technologie	At			Anglais		Soutien d'Anglais	26	VI
15H.30	VII	sport		Français	9			Sport		Anglais	26	VII

4. Suit-elle un cours de philosophie?
5. Quelle langue étrangère Caroline étudie-t-elle? Combien d'heures par semaine?
6. Quand est-ce qu'elle n'a pas de cours?

Communication

D **De la littérature.** Votre camarade de chambre a un livre d'un des auteurs suivants. Quelle langue étudie-t-il / elle?

MODÈLE: Dante   *Il / Elle fait de l'italien.*
Il / Elle étudie l'italien.

1. Cervantes
2. Goethe
3. Jules César
4. Simone de Beauvoir
5. Homère
6. Confucius
7. Tolstoï
8. Emily Brontë

E **Questions personnelles.** Vos études.

1. Quels cours suivez-vous ce trimestre / ce semestre?
2. Qu'est-ce que vous allez étudier la prochaine année scolaire?
3. Faites-vous des sciences cette année?
4. Quels cours aimez-vous / détestez-vous?
5. Quel cours est trop difficile pour vous?
6. Qu'est-ce que vous faites quand vous n'allez pas aux cours?

III. Direct object pronouns: Third person

You use direct object pronouns to refer to someone or something already mentioned in a conversation.

A. Direct objects

1. In English, a direct object receives the action of the verb directly. In the following sentences, the words in boldface type are direct objects.

   He is buying **the apple.**　　They are going to meet **Joe** at school.
   I like **your ideas.**　　We saw **Jane** at the movies.

2. A direct object can be a person, an object, or an idea. It answers the question *whom?* or *what?* Direct object pronouns replace nouns that have already been mentioned.

   "Where is the jacket?"　　"Are they going to get Joe?"
   "He is buying **it.**"　　"Yes, they are going to get **him.**"

   "What do you think of　　"Has anyone seen Mary?"
   　his ideas?"　　"I saw **her.**"
   "I like **them.**"

B. Third-person direct object pronouns

French also has direct objects. They may be replaced by direct object pronouns that are placed *before* the verb in an affirmative or negative present-tense statement.

   Roger visite **la capitale.** → Roger **la** visite.
   Il trouve **le musée** impressionnant. → Il **le** trouve impressionnant.
   Il aime **l'informatique.** → Il **l'**aime.
   Il suit **ses cours** à la Sorbonne. → Il **les** suit à la Sorbonne.

The following chart summarizes the third-person direct object pronouns.

	singular	plural
masculine	**le, l'** *him, it*	
		les *them*
feminine	**la, l'** *her, it*	

Attention!

Remember that every French noun has a gender, so *it* is expressed by either **le** or **la,** depending on the noun for which it stands. Both **le** and **la** become **l'** before a vowel, while the silent **s** of **les** becomes the sound / z / with a **liaison.**

—Vous faites du russe?
—Je **l'**étudie, mais je ne **le** parle pas.

—Pourquoi parle-t-il aux Dupont?
—Il **les** invite chez lui.

C. Position of direct object pronouns

1. As you have just seen, the direct object pronoun precedes the verb in an affirmative or negative present tense statement.

> —Vous avez **beaucoup d'argent?**
> —Non, je **le** dépense tout de suite.

> —Vous avez utilisé **ce logiciel?**
> —Oui, mais je ne **le** trouve pas intéressant.

2. The same is true of questions, including inversion.

> —Voilà **notre étudiant sénégalais!**
> —**L'**avez-vous en cours ce trimestre?

> —Où est **la lettre de Bernard?**
> —Est-ce que vous **la** voulez maintenant?

3. In any *helping verb plus infinitive* construction, the direct object pronoun precedes the infinitive, that is, the verb of which the pronoun is a direct object.

> —Il a **beaucoup de devoirs?**
> —Oui, mais il ne peut pas **les** faire.

> —Tu as **mes aérogrammes?**
> —Non, je vais **les** apporter demain.

4. In the **passé composé,** the pronoun precedes the auxiliary verb **avoir.**

> —Tu vas suivre **un cours** sur Corneille?
> —Non, je **l'**ai déjà étudié.

> —Avez-vous **votre Walkman?**
> —Non, je **l'**ai laissé chez moi.

L'orthographe

1. In the **passé composé,** the past participle must agree in gender and in number with a direct object pronoun that precedes it. This does not change the pronunciation of most past participles.

> —Tu as acheté **cette voiture?**
> —Non, je **l'**ai empruntée à un ami.

> —Où as-tu trouvé **ces chaussures?**
> —Je **les** ai trouvées à Montréal.

2. You have learned only one past participle whose masculine and feminine forms can be *audibly* distinguished: **faire (fait / faite).**

> —Est-ce que je peux faire **la vaisselle?**
> —Non, nous **l'**avons déjà faite.

> —Ils vont faire **leurs courses** cet après-midi?
> —Non, ils **les** ont faites ce matin.

A **Changeons des phrases.** Mettez les phrases suivantes au **passé composé** et au **futur proche.**

1. Nous les empruntons tous les jours.
2. Vous la suivez.
3. Il la laisse à la gare.
4. Les porte-t-on aujourd'hui?
5. Est-ce que vous l'invitez?
6. Je la regarde le soir.

B **Qu'est-ce qu'on fait?** Remplacez les compléments d'objet direct *(direct objects)* par un pronom dans les phrases suivantes.

1. J'utilise mon ordinateur.
2. Julie emprunte-t-elle ton logiciel?
3. Jacques a fini son livre.
4. Tu vas inviter Sylvie et Monique?
5. Vous n'avez pas étudié l'allemand?
6. Henri n'aime pas prêter son imprimante.

C **Les Français et la télévision.** Répondez aux questions suivantes en employant un pronom complément d'objet direct.

1. Est-ce que les Français regardent beaucoup la télévision?
2. Aiment-ils regarder la télé l'après-midi?
3. Ils aiment Jerry Lewis?
4. Ils aiment les westerns?
5. Est-ce qu'ils apprécient les jeux télévisés *(game shows)*?
6. Ils mangent et regardent la télé en même temps?

D **Conversations interrompues.** Vous entendez *(hear)* la dernière partie d'une conversation. Dans chaque situation, imaginez le sujet de cette conversation.

MODÈLE: Je ne peux pas la faire.
          Tu ne peux pas faire la vaisselle?

1. Pouvez-vous l'expédier?
2. Il ne va pas les inviter.
3. Tu ne l'as pas préparée?
4. Nous ne l'avons pas étudié.
5. Je ne les ai pas trouvés.
6. Je n'aime pas le faire.

E **Interviews.** Posez des questions à vos camarades avec les éléments donnés ci-dessous. Ils / Elles vont répondre en employant des pronoms.

> MODÈLE: Etudiant(e) 1: *Vas-tu préparer ton dîner ce soir?*
> Etudiant(e) 2: *Oui, je vais le préparer. / Non, je ne vais pas
> le préparer.*

aller   consulter le médecin
désirer   acheter un ordinateur
pouvoir   expédier une lettre à tes grands-parents
vouloir   étudier l'arabe ou le chinois
               écouter tes parents
               expliquer tes absences
               faire la cuisine chez toi
               montrer tes photos
               oublier ton passé
               préparer ton dîner ce soir
               finir tes cours cette année
               choisir ton / ta camarade de chambre pour l'année prochaine
               suivre le cours du même professeur le trimestre prochain

F **Votre vie à l'université.** En petits groupes, préparez des réponses aux questions suivantes. Employez des pronoms et informez vos camarades de cours des résultats.

1. As-tu étudié la musique? l'informatique?
2. Aimes-tu tes cours ce trimestre?
3. Vas-tu étudier le français le trimestre prochain?
4. Où fais-tu tes devoirs?
5. Utilises-tu ton ordinateur pour faire tes devoirs?
6. Où expédies-tu ton courrier?

G **Vos opinions.** Dites *(Tell)* comment vous trouvez les personnes suivantes. Utilisez les adjectifs donnés.

super   formidable   charmant   bien
ennuyeux   insupportable affreux (-se) pas mal

> MODÈLE: *Sandra Bullock? Je la trouve charmante.*

1. Gloria Estefan   5. David Letterman
2. Jim Carrey   6. Enya
3. 'N Sync   7. Michael Jordan
4. Madonna   8. Hillary Rodham Clinton

H **Questions personnelles.** La vie moderne. Employez des pronoms compléments d'objet direct dans vos réponses.

1. Aimez-vous le jazz? le rock? le rap?
2. Quand écoutez-vous cette musique?
3. Votre camarade de chambre prête ses logiciels? ses vêtements?
4. Appréciez-vous l'art moderne?
5. Avez-vous étudié l'informatique?
6. Avez-vous utilisé les ordinateurs de votre université? Pourquoi?

IV. *Voir*

You use the verb **voir** to indicate seeing as well as understanding.

voir *(to see)*	
je **vois**	nous **voyons**
tu **vois**	vous **voyez**
il / elle / on **voit**	ils / elles **voient**

Passé composé: il **a vu**
Imperative: **vois** / **voyons** / **voyez**

—**Avez**-vous **vu** mon sac?
—Oui, nous l'**avons vu** dans ta chambre.

—Tu **as vu** mes cartes postales?
—Non, je ne les **ai** pas **vues**.

A. The forms **vois**, **voit**, and **voient** are pronounced the same / vwa /.

—Son père a 82 ans! Comment va-t-il?
—Pas mal, mais il ne **voit** pas bien.

—Ils ne sont pas contents!
—Ils ne **voient** pas pourquoi tu es toujours en retard.

Attention!

1. The expression **aller voir** means *to visit* and is used with people. **Visiter** can only be used with places.

   Quand j'**ai visité** Paris l'année dernière, je **suis allé voir** des amis.

2. **Voir un film** is used for movie theaters. For films on TV, use **regarder.**

   Ils ne veulent pas **regarder** ce film parce qu'ils l'**ont** déjà **vu** au cinéma.

B. Other verbs conjugated like **voir** are **prévoir** *(to foresee)* and **revoir** *(to see again* or *to review).*

   Il n'**a** pas **prévu** cela.   Elle va **revoir** ses leçons.

Ce qu'ils disent

The imperative form **Voyons!** changes meaning according to the speaker's tone of voice. With the simple declarative intonation, it means *Let's see,* as when someone is looking for something or trying to think of something. With a slightly exasperated intonation, it means *Come on!*

Voyons. Où est-ce que j'ai laissé mon parapluie?
Voyons! Tu n'es pas sérieux!

Langue

A **Voyage en Europe.** Faites des questions avec les mots donnés.

1. Qu'est-ce que / tu / voir / en France / été dernier?
2. Tu / revoir / amis parisiens?
3. amis / prévoir / une visite d'une semaine?
4. Vous / voir / bon film / ensemble?
5. On / prévoir / un / été / très chaud / n'est-ce pas?
6. Tu / vouloir / revoir / Paris?

B **Après les vacances.** Répondez aux questions suivantes en employant des pronoms à la place des compléments d'objet direct.

1. A-t-on bien prévu *la météo* pour tes vacances?
2. Tu as revu *ta petite amie?*
3. Tes amis ont revu *leurs parents?*
4. Tu n'as pas vu *le dernier film d'Isabelle Adjani?*
5. Est-ce que je vais voir *tes photos de vacances?*
6. Est-ce que nous allons revoir *nos leçons de français* maintenant?

Culture

C **Visitons Paris.** Vous allez visiter Paris avec votre famille. Expliquez-leur quels monuments on voit des sites donnés ci-dessous. Utilisez le plan de Paris à la page 200 pour préparer vos réponses.

MODÈLE: le boulevard Saint-Michel
Du boulevard Saint-Michel on voit le Panthéon.

1. le boulevard Montparnasse
2. le quai d'Orsay
3. la Seine
4. le boulevard Haussmann
5. le palais de Chaillot
6. le jardin des Tuileries

Communication

D **Votre avenir** *(future).* Qu'est-ce que vous voyez dans votre futur? Utilisez les suggestions suivantes et votre imagination pour interviewer un(e) camarade de cours.

MODÈLE: *Je vois cinq enfants, une profession fascinante et beaucoup d'argent.*

une maison blanche
une voiture de sport
un appartement à Nice
une femme / un mari riche
une profession intéressante
des enfants intelligents
des vacances à Tahiti
un yacht aux Antilles

Ⓔ **Au revoir!** Qui voulez-vous revoir ou ne pas revoir? Qu'est-ce que vous voulez revoir ou ne pas revoir? Cherchez en classe les étudiants qui ont les mêmes opinions que vous.

MODÈLE: *Je ne veux pas revoir mon professeur d'éducation physique.*
Je veux revoir le film Casablanca.

film	villes
ami(es)	chanteurs (-euses)
professeur(s)	émissions de télévision *(TV shows)*

Ⓕ **Questions personnelles.** Vos activités.

1. Avez-vous vu vos parents récemment? Quand?
2. Allez-vous voir un film ce week-end? Quel film?
3. Est-ce qu'on voit souvent des films français dans votre ville?
4. Vous avez passé des vacances avec votre famille? Qu'est-ce que vous avez vu ensemble?
5. Qu'est-ce qu'on peut voir dans votre ville?
6. Qu'est-ce qu'on voit de la fenêtre de votre chambre?

communiquons

Aller au bureau de poste

The post office (**le bureau de poste, la poste,** or **les PTT**) is an institution in France that every visitor should know because it plays so many roles. You not only mail things there but also make phone calls. The French use the post office even for some banking needs, such as a checking account (**un compte-chèque postal** or **CCP**).

Expressions

▶ **On expédie le courrier.**

C'est combien pour envoyer une lettre aux Etats-Unis?	*How much is it to send a letter to the United States?*
Par avion, ça coûte soixante-sept cents les cinq grammes.	*Air mail is sixty-seven cents (.67 euro) for five grams.*
Je voudrais acheter un timbre à quarante-six cents.	*I would like to buy a forty-six cent (.46 euro) stamp.*

▶ **On donne un coup de téléphone.**

Je voudrais téléphoner avec préavis à un ami à Lyon.	*I would like to make a person-to-person call to a friend in Lyon.*
L'étudiant va téléphoner à ses parents aux Etats-Unis en PCV.	*The student is going to call his parents in the U.S. collect.*
Allez dans la cabine numéro onze, Mademoiselle.	*Go into booth #11, miss.*
Je désire faire un appel interurbain / international.	*I want to make a long-distance / international call.*

▶ **On utilise la poste restante.**

En France on peut recevoir son courrier à la poste restante.	*In France, you can receive mail at general delivery.*
Le préposé demande toujours une pièce d'identité.	*The employee always asks for an ID.*
Il faut payer la surtaxe.	*You must pay a charge.*

Interaction

Un étudiant américain va au bureau de poste.

L'ÉTUDIANT: Est-ce que vous avez une lettre pour moi? Ma famille l'a envoyée à la poste restante.

LA PRÉPOSÉE: Oui, s'ils ont bien indiqué ce bureau. Je vais chercher. Vous avez une pièce d'identité avec photo? Et il va y avoir une petite surtaxe à payer.

L'ÉTUDIANT: D'accord°. Et est-ce que vous pouvez me donner un numéro de téléphone?   *O.K.*

LA PRÉPOSÉE: Ah, non, Monsieur, mais vous avez le Minitel dans le hall à gauche°.   *left*

Activités

Ⓐ **Votre correspondance.** Répondez aux questions suivantes.

1. Si vous allez en Europe, à qui allez-vous envoyer des cartes postales? des lettres?

2. Vous avez déjà envoyé des cartes postales? Avec une photo de quoi?
3. Avez-vous téléphoné d'un téléphone public? A qui? Comment avez-vous payé?
4. Où pouvez-vous recevoir du courrier en France? Et aux Etats-Unis? Est-ce que la poste restante est utile?

Ⓑ Jeu de rôles. Jouez les scènes suivantes avec un(e) camarade de cours.

1. Vous voulez envoyer des cartes postales dans plusieurs pays.
2. Vous voulez téléphoner à vos parents, mais vous n'avez pas d'argent.
3. Vous pensez avoir une lettre à la poste restante, mais l'employé ne peut pas la trouver.
4. Vous voulez envoyer un télégramme.

lecture culturelle

Avant la lecture

Paris, **"la Ville Lumière"** (the City of Light), is one of the world's richest cultural cities. In order to stay informed while you are there, it is highly recommended that you purchase one of the weekly guides to entertainment and cultural events. Two of the best weekly guides, which have coexisted for many years, are *L'Officiel des spectacles* and *Pariscope*. They are both available every Wednesday, at newsstands or kiosks, for approximately 50 cents. *Pariscope* is also available online in both French and English, as well as on the Minitel at *3615 code Pariscope*.

These guides provide information on museums, special exhibits, movie schedules, theater performances, sporting events, restaurants, concerts, and nightclub shows. One popular place for nightclub goers is along the Seine River, aboard specially remodeled barges (**péniches**). Music of all kinds is played at these floating nightclubs. The **péniches** are also available for rent for special occasions, such as weddings and birthdays.

Activités

Ⓐ When you go out with friends, where do you go? What are your favorite things to do?

Ⓑ What music do you like to listen to? Do you know any French-speaking singers or musicians?

Ⓒ If you were a nightclub owner . . .

1. what might be the advantages and disadvantages of having your nightclub on a boat along a river, as opposed to in a building in the middle of town?

2. what kinds of events would you offer, and what types of services would you provide to help defray the high costs of docking a boat along the Seine?

D Locate the Seine River on a map of Paris. What famous monuments, neighborhoods, and museums are located on the right and left banks?

Les Scènes de la Seine

Célébrée par de nombreux chanteurs, la Seine se fait désormais la scène de nombreux concerts. Sur les quais°, on continue de flâner° main dans la main, mais on y danse aussi sur des bateaux-bars qui leur° ont redonné un air de fête. Paris, quai de la Gare, 21 heures. Flâneurs et amoureux ont cédé la place° aux noctambules° branchés°. Il n'y a encore pas si longtemps°, le quai, un peu excentré, était exempt de toute vie. Il résonne aujourd'hui de toutes sortes de notes: hip-hop, techno, blues, world-music... venues des onze «bateaux-spectacles» sagement accrochés° à leurs anneaux°.

«Faire de la musique dans Paris intra-muros est toujours difficile», explique le propriétaire d'un bateau-bar. «Les voisins se plaignent° des nuisances sonores et les lieux° finissent par fermer. Ici, on est loin de toute habitation et en plus, il y a un parking.» Blues, funk, african music, salsa ou rock rappellent de bons souvenirs à ces babas° qui composent l'essentiel de la clientèle.

«Le Batofar» est l'une des seules salles parisiennes à vocation européenne: il a reçu l'avant-garde musicale berlinoise°, à son ouverture en février 1999, toujours partant dans la découverte de nouveaux talents.

Un pari° que le «Blues Café» et «La Balle au bond» ont quelque peu abandonné. Les patrons° préfèrent désormais recevoir des groupes plus connus°, histoire de° remplir la salle et de sortir la tête hors de l'eau. Ces deux bateaux louent° même régulièrement leur terrasse pour des fêtes privées. Il faut bien payer la location de l'anneau°, entre 2288€ et 3049€ ($2,300 à $3,000) par mois. Un prix prohibitif assorti de contraintes réglementaires° qui

n'ont pas découragé les gérants ou locataires° de ces bateaux-bars. Regroupés en association, le «13-ô-quai», ils ont l'intention de faire vivre aussi le quai en journée et non plus seulement le soir, et le Batofar organise déjà des après-midi à thème. Et vogue le quai!°

bank (of a river) / stroll
them (referring to «les quais»)
cédé... yielded / night owls / (fam.) cool, hip, with it / Il n'y a... not so long ago

sagement... docilely tied up / rings (to which ropes are tied to stabilize boats)

complain
places (in this case, businesses)

hippies

from Berlin, Germany

challenge, gamble

supervisors, bosses

better known / a matter of

rent out / les gérants... either the owner-managers or the renters
location... docking fees

assorti de... along with administrative constraints / Et vogue... a play on the phrase Et vogue la galére (What will be will be)

Sylvie Bullo, «Les Scènes de la Seine», *Journal Français.*

Après la lecture

1. Avant 21 heures, quelles sortes de personnes est-ce qu'on voit en général au bord de la Seine?
2. Combien de bateaux-bars existent sur la Seine?
3. Selon l'article, pourquoi est-ce que c'est difficile de «faire de la musique intra-muros»? Quels sont les avantages d'avoir une discothèque sur un bateau?
4. Quels genres de musique est-ce qu'on joue sur les bateaux-bars?
5. Quand «Le Batofar» cherche un groupe musical, il essaye de trouver du nouveau talent. Qu'est-ce que le «Blues Café» et «La Balle au Bond» préfèrent?
6. Pourquoi est-ce que les bateaux louent leurs terrasses et proposent des événements *(events)* pendant la journée?

Activités

Ⓐ Imaginez que vous êtes le propriétaire d'un nouveau bateau-bar et créez une publicité avec le nom, le prix, le genre de musique et les heures où on peut venir sur votre bateau.

Ⓑ Voici une liste de chanteurs francophones: Patricia Kaas, Francis Cabrel, Les Négresses Vertes, Henri Dikongué, Cheb Khaled, Cheb Mami, Céline Dion, Isabelle Boulay, Roch Voisine, Bruno Pelletier, MC Solaar, Kassav', et Axel Red. Allez sur le Web pour trouver de l'information et des extraits de musique de ces chanteurs. D'où viennent-ils?

Ⓒ Une des activités touristiques les plus populaires à Paris, c'est de prendre un bateau-mouche. Allez sur le Web (recherchez *bateaux-mouches*) pour trouver une compagnie de bateaux-mouches. Combien est-ce que ça coûte de prendre un bateau-mouche pendant la journée? la nuit? Qu'est-ce que vous pouvez voir? Est-ce que vous pouvez y déjeuner ou dîner?

Ⓓ Lisez les paroles de cette chanson populaire que Jacques Prévert, un célèbre poète français, a écrite au sujet de la Seine.

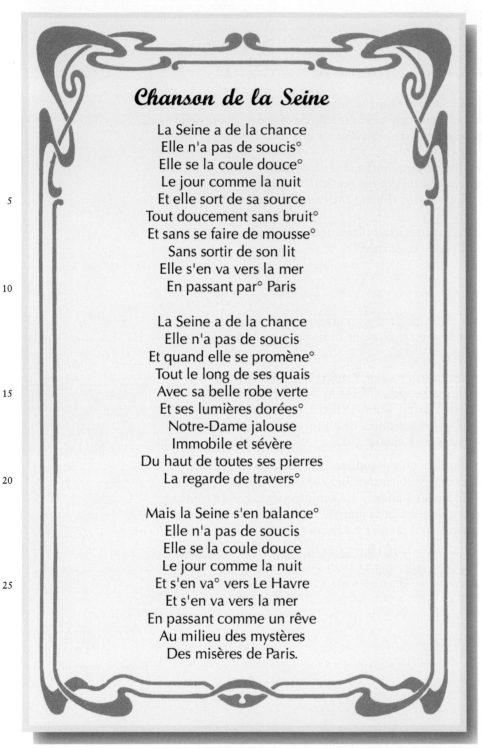

Chanson de la Seine

La Seine a de la chance
Elle n'a pas de soucis°   worries
Elle se la coule douce°   se... flows gently
Le jour comme la nuit
5   Et elle sort de sa source
Tout doucement sans bruit°   noise
Et sans se faire de mousse°   foam
Sans sortir de son lit
Elle s'en va vers la mer
10   En passant par° Paris   en... by passing through

La Seine a de la chance
Elle n'a pas de soucis
Et quand elle se promène°   se... takes a walk
Tout le long de ses quais
15   Avec sa belle robe verte
Et ses lumières dorées°   golden
Notre-Dame jalouse
Immobile et sévère
Du haut de toutes ses pierres
20   La regarde de travers°   la regarde... looks at
                                                          her scornfully
Mais la Seine s'en balance°   s'en... (fam.) doesn't care
Elle n'a pas de soucis
Elle se la coule douce
Le jour comme la nuit
25   Et s'en va° vers Le Havre   s'en... goes (away)
Et s'en va vers la mer
En passant comme un rêve
Au milieu des mystères
Des misères de Paris.

Jacques Prévert, *Spectacle, Le Point du Jour* (NRF).

vocabulaire

Noms / Pronoms

une adresse	address	Internet *(m.)*	Internet
un aérogramme	aerogram	le japonais	Japanese
une année scolaire	school year	le journalisme	journalism
anthropologie *(f.)*	anthropology	une langue	language
architecture *(f.)*	architecture	le latin	Latin
une arrivée	arrival	le, l', la, les	him, her, it, them
art *(m.)*	art	un lecteur de	disk drive
un baiser	kiss	disquettes	
la biologie	biology	une lettre	letter
une bise	kiss	la littérature	literature
la campagne	countryside	le logiciel	software
une capitale	capital	un mandat	money order
une carte postale	postcard	un match de	soccer game
la chaleur	heat	football	
la chimie	chemistry	le matériel	hardware
le ciel	sky	mathématiques *(f.)*	math
un clavier	keyboard	une matière	subject
un colis	package	la médecine	medicine
un courrier	mail	une météo	forecast
un courrier	e-mail	un modem	modem
électronique		un moniteur	monitor
une dame	lady	un monument	monument
une disquette	diskette	la musique classique	classical music
le droit	law	la neige	snow
éclair *(m.)*	lightning	notes *(f.)*	grades
éducation	physical	nouvelles *(f.)*	news
physique *(f.)*	education	un nuage	cloud
une employée	clerk *(female)*	un ordinateur	computer
une enveloppe	envelope	un papier à lettres	stationery
un facteur	mailman	un paquet	parcel
la géographie	geography	la physique	physics
la géologie	geology	la pluie	rain
la gestion	management	la psychologie	psychology
le grec	Greek	la rentrée	beginning of the
un guichet	window		school year
histoire *(f.)*	history	sciences	economics
histoire *(f.)* de l'art	art history	économiques *(f.)*	
une imprimante	printer	sciences	political science
informatique *(f.)*	computer	politiques *(f.)*	
	science	un séjour	stay

un semestre	semester	un timbre	stamp
la sociologie	sociology	le tonnerre	thunder
un tableur	spread sheet	un traitement	word processor
un télégramme	telegram	de texte	
le temps	weather	un trimestre	quarter

Verbes

dépenser	to spend	profiter de	to take advantage of
emprunter	to borrow	rencontrer	to meet
expédier	to mail	revoir	to see again
gagner	to win	suivre	to take (courses) /
neiger	to snow		to follow
pleuvoir	to rain	taper	to type
prêter	to lend	utiliser	to use
prévoir	to foresee		

Adjectifs / Adverbes

bientôt	soon	insupportable	unbearable
cher, chère, chers	dear	ne... jamais	never
couvert	overcast	ne... pas encore	not yet
écrit	written	recommandé	registered
étranger	foreign	sénégalais	Senegalese
exactement	exactly	tout	every
impressionnant	impressive		

Expressions

affectueux baisers (m.)	love
grosses bises (f.)	hugs and kisses
Donnez-moi de vos nouvelles.	Let me hear from you.
juste avant	just before
faire bon	to be nice
faire de l'orage	to be stormy
faire des économies	to save
faire du brouillard	to be foggy
faire du soleil	to be sunny
faire du vent	to be windy
faire frais	to be cool
pendant	during / for
puisque	since
tout le temps	all the time
Voyons!	Let's see. / Come on!

**Marché en plein air
en Martinique**

commençons

grammaire

communiquons

lecture culturelle

vocabulaire

La cuisine

OBJECTIVES

Language	Culture	Communication
■ Vocabulary for food and meals	■ Meals	■ Describing people and things
■ The consonant / ʀ /	■ **Les marchés en plein air**	■ Talking about food and meals
■ Prenominal adjectives	■ The Michelin **Guide Rouge**	
■ The calendar		
■ Indirect object pronouns: Third person		
■ **Prendre**		

commençons

Au marché d'Antibes

Anne Bryan passe ses vacances à Juan-les-Pins chez de bons amis de ses parents, M. et Mme Leconte. Aujourd'hui, c'est jeudi et c'est le jour du marché à Antibes. Mme Leconte va faire ses provisions et Nathalie, la fille des Leconte, a invité Anne à passer la matinée au marché.

NATHALIE: Commençons par les marchands de poissons et de fruits de mer! Tu peux prendre des photos si tu veux.

ANNE: Regarde tous ces gros poissons. Et les crevettes! Comme elles sont petites!

NATHALIE: Allons où ils vendent les fromages. Veux-tu apprendre leurs noms?

ANNE: C'est impossible, il y a trop de variétés. Est-ce qu'on peut vraiment manger un fromage différent tous les jours de l'année?

NATHALIE: Bien sûr. Est-ce que tu aimes les olives? Moi, je les mange comme des bonbons. Ici, c'est le coin de la viande. Tu vois, ça, ce sont des lapins.

ANNE: Je n'aime pas voir cela. Et les poulets, on leur a laissé la tête et les pattes!

NATHALIE: Ça, là-bas, c'est un gigot. Maman va servir cela dimanche; j'espère que tu es contente.

ANNE: Ma pauvre Nathalie, je ne mange jamais de viande; je suis végétarienne!

1. Où Anne passe-t-elle ses vacances?
2. Qu'est-ce que Nathalie et Anne vont faire?
3. Pourquoi Anne ne veut-elle pas apprendre les noms des fromages?
4. Pourquoi Anne n'aime-t-elle pas voir les poulets?
5. Qu'est-ce que les parents de Nathalie vont servir dimanche?
6. Pourquoi Anne ne mange-t-elle pas de viande?

Mots clés

un marché	*market*	**variétés** *(f.)*	*varieties*
vacances *(f.)*	*vacation*	**vraiment**	*truly*
bon(-ne)	*good*	**différent**	*different*
jeudi	*Thursday*	**olives** *(f.)*	*olives*
une matinée	*morning*	**bonbons** *(m.)*	*candy*
faire ses provisions *(f.)*	*to do her shopping*	**un coin**	*area*
marchands *(m.)*	*merchants*	**ça**	*that*
fruits *(m.)* **de mer**	*seafood*	**lapins** *(m.)*	*rabbits*
prendre	*take*	**leur**	*them*
crevettes *(f.)*	*shrimp*	**une tête**	*head*
comme	*how*	**pattes** *(f.)*	*paws*
petit(e)	*small*	**un gigot**	*leg of lamb*
vendent (vendre)	*sell*	**espère que**	*hope that*
apprendre	*to learn*	**(espérer que)**	
noms *(m.)*	*names*		

Faisons connaissance

Many French towns and villages are renowned for their open-air markets (**marchés en plein air**). They usually take place once a week and last from seven in the morning to one or two in the afternoon. **Le jour du marché** is always an important event for local people and tourists alike.

The **marché** is held on a square often named **la place du Marché,** and merchants are lined up in rows of temporary booths covered with a canopy in case of rain. The **marché** is principally a food market where people enjoy buying fresh vegetables and fruit that farmers bring and sell directly to the consumers. Although it is not as common as it used to be, it is still possible to buy live chickens and rabbits in some markets.

Southern markets, like the one in Antibes, are very picturesque. The smell of olive oil and spices used in **provençal** cooking fills the air. Other ingredients that characterize the cuisine of southern France, such as garlic, anchovies, and green and red peppers, are available in abundance at open-air booths.

▶

Des fruits de mer

   Another enjoyable experience at open-air markets is the opportunity to taste various foods. For instance, before buying cheese, it is perfectly all right to sample several varieties. This is also true with other products such as **pâtés, saucissons,** and other foods available at the delicatessen.

Enrichissons notre vocabulaire

Les repas *(Meals)*

le petit déjeuner	*breakfast*
le déjeuner	*lunch*
le dîner	*dinner*

Des hors-d'œuvre *(Appetizers)*

des carottes râpées	*grated carrots*	une salade de tomates	*sliced tomato salad*
des crudités	*raw vegetables*	une salade de concombres	*sliced cucumber salad*
un œuf, des œufs	*eggs*	du saucisson	*salami*
du pâté	*pâté*		

Des plats principaux *(Main dishes)*

du bœuf	*beef*	du porc	*pork*
un rosbif	*roast beef*	une côtelette de porc	*pork chop*
un bifteck	*steak*	un rôti de porc	*pork roast*
un filet de sole	*filet of sole*	du veau	*veal*
une truite	*trout*	une escalope de veau	*veal cutlet*

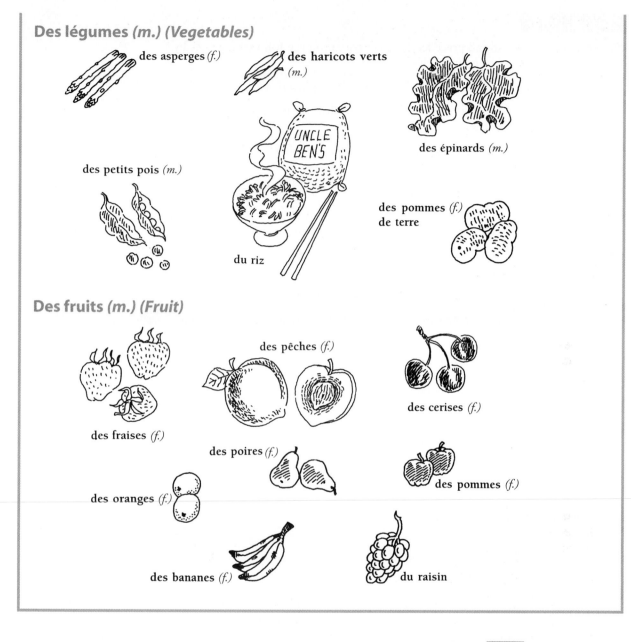

Des légumes (m.) (Vegetables)

des asperges (f.)

des haricots verts (m.)

des épinards (m.)

des petits pois (m.)

UNCLE BEN'S

du riz

des pommes (f.) de terre

Des fruits (m.) (Fruit)

des pêches (f.)

des cerises (f.)

des fraises (f.)

des poires (f.)

des pommes (f.)

des oranges (f.)

des bananes (f.)

du raisin

Prononciation   The French / ʀ / sound

To pronounce the French / ʀ / sound, tuck in the tip of your tongue behind your lower teeth, and curve the back of your tongue toward the back of the roof of your mouth. The words **gaz** (/ gaz /) and **rase** (/ ʀaz /) are almost identical, except that with the / g / sound, the back of your tongue touches the roof of your mouth, while with the / ʀ / sound, there is a small gap that causes friction.

Exercices

Ⓐ Practice the / ʀ / sound preceded by a consonant in the following words by repeating them after your teacher.

crème / cravate / grand / grammaire / groupe / crêpe / crevettes / crudités

Ⓑ Practice the / ʀ / sound in the middle of the following words by repeating them after your teacher.

Marie / admirer / africain / agréable / heureux / parapluie / différent / marché

Ⓒ Practice the / ʀ / sound at the end of the following words by repeating them after your teacher.

alors / lecture / lettre / mer / milliard / sur / porc / leur

Ⓓ Practice the / ʀ / sound at the beginning of the following words by repeating them after your teacher.

radio / rapide / regarder / regretter / rentrer / repas / riz / rosbif

Ⓔ Repeat the following sentences after your teacher, paying particular attention to the / ʀ / sound.

1. Brigitte travaille au restaurant.
2. Il va faire du brouillard à Londres.
3. Marie a perdu son portefeuille dans le parc.
4. Christine et son mari apprécient l'art moderne.
5. Beaucoup d'Américains vont avoir froid cet hiver.
6. La librairie ferme à trois heures et quart.

grammaire

I. Prenominal adjectives

You use adjectives to describe people and things.

A. As you learned in Chapter 2, an adjective agrees in gender and number with the noun it modifies, and it usually follows the noun.

Mes parents ont préparé un repas **délicieux** hier soir.
On peut manger un fromage **différent** tous les jours.

There is, however, a group of frequently used adjectives that must precede the noun. The chart on page 231 gives the most common ones.

Regarde tous ces **gros** poissons.   Ce sont de **petites** crevettes.

singular		plural		
masculine	feminine	masculine	feminine	meaning
ancien	ancienne	anciens	anciennes	*former, old*
autre	autre	autres	autres	*other*
beau	belle	beaux	belles	*beautiful, handsome*
bon	bonne	bons	bonnes	*good*
cher	chère	chers	chères	*dear, expensive*
dernier	dernière	derniers	dernières	*last*
grand	grande	grands	grandes	*big, great*
gros	grosse	gros	grosses	*big*
jeune	jeune	jeunes	jeunes	*young*
joli	jolie	jolis	jolies	*pretty*
mauvais	mauvaise	mauvais	mauvaises	*bad*
nouveau	nouvelle	nouveaux	nouvelles	*new*
pauvre	pauvre	pauvres	pauvres	*poor*
petit	petite	petits	petites	*small, little*
premier	première	premiers	premières	*first*
propre	propre	propres	propres	*own, clean*
vieux	vieille	vieux	vieilles	*old*

B. Because these adjectives precede the noun, **liaison** is obligatory when the noun begins with a vowel sound.

> J'ai téléphoné à un **bon** ami.
> Les Wright ont fait le **premier** avion.
> Elle a invité ses **bons** amis.

C. Because of **liaison,** there are some irregular adjective forms. Before masculine singular nouns that begin with a vowel, you will find:

beau → **bel**	Le Concorde est un **bel** avion.
nouveau → **nouvel**	La classe a commencé un **nouvel** exercice.
vieux → **vieil**	Il a vu un **vieil** ami.

It will help you to remember that when a masculine singular noun begins with a vowel sound, the preceding adjective sounds like its feminine form. For example, in the following phrases, **bon** and **bonne** and **vieil** and **vieille** are pronounced the same.

> un **bon** étudiant, une **bonne** étudiante
> un **vieil** ami, une **vieille** amie

D. A few adjectives may come either before or after the noun, but they change meaning according to their position.

un **ancien** professeur	*a **former** teacher*
une église **ancienne**	*an **old** church*
la **dernière** semaine	*the **last** week (of a series)*
la semaine **dernière**	***last** week*
un **pauvre** homme	*a **poor** man (unfortunate)*
un homme **pauvre**	*a **poor** man (no money)*
ma **propre** voiture	*my **own** car*
une voiture **propre**	*a **clean** car*
un **cher** ami	*a **dear** friend*
un cadeau **cher**	*an **expensive** gift*

E. Adjectives can be used alone as nouns.

Les **pauvres** ne mangent pas bien.
Les **jeunes** vont aller voir les **vieux.**

Attention!

1. Whenever the indefinite article **des** is followed by an adjective, it becomes **de.**

Ils vendent **des** cerises.	Ils vendent **de belles** cerises.
Ce sont **des** amis.	Ce sont **de vieux** amis.

but: Ce sont **des marchands désagréables.**

2. In **liaison,** the masculine form of **grand** is pronounced with a / t / sound, and the masculine form of **gros** and other adjectives ending in s (**anciens, pauvres,** etc.) are pronounced with a / z / sound.

un grand‿appartement, un grand‿homme
un gros‿œuf, les gros‿avions
de bons‿amis, de belles‿olives

Langue

Ⓐ **En ville.** Donnez le contraire de l'adjectif en italique dans les phrases suivantes.

MODÈLE: J'ai une *petite* voiture.
J'ai une grande voiture.

1. Il habite un *petit* appartement.
2. C'est un *bon* restaurant.
3. Ces *jeunes* employés travaillent beaucoup.
4. Je n'ai pas vu tes *dernières* photos de la ville.
5. Est-ce que c'est un *nouvel* hôtel?
6. Il a acheté une cravate *laide* dans ce magasin.

B **Mon ami arrive.** Ajoutez la forme appropriée des adjectifs entre parenthèses aux noms en italique dans les phrases suivantes. Faites attention à la place de l'adjectif.

MODÈLE: Nous avons voyagé dans un *avion.* (gros)
Nous avons voyagé dans un gros avion.

1. Un *ami* arrive de New York. (bon)
2. Nous avons visité des *églises.* (joli)
3. Nous avons parlé avec des *enfants.* (petit)
4. Avez-vous trouvé un *appartement* pour votre ami? (beau)
5. Il a déjà invité des *amis.* (sympathique)
6. Est-ce qu'il y a beaucoup d'*écoles* près d'ici? (bon)

Culture

C **En France ou aux Etats-Unis?** Formez des phrases avec les mots donnés et dites *(tell)* si la phrase décrit *(describes)* la France ou les Etats-Unis.

1. On / aimer / gros / voitures
2. jeune / gens / pouvoir / avoir / voiture / à seize ans
3. vieux / personnes / habiter / avec / leur / enfants
4. On / avoir / grand / universités / dans / petit / villes
5. On / prendre / bon / petit / déjeuner / tous les matins
6. «18» / être / très / bon / note
7. On / pouvoir / acheter / joli / petit / tartes / délicieux
8. nouveau / trains / être / rapide
9. On / vendre / son / propre / affaires / devant / son / maison
10. Un / ancien / maire *(mayor)* / être / président

Communication

D **Votre vie à l'université.** Donnez votre opinion en répondant aux questions suivantes. Commencez vos réponses avec «C'est... » ou «Ce sont... ».

MODÈLE: Votre cours de français est facile ou difficile?
C'est un cours facile.

1. Votre université est grande ou petite?
2. La cuisine du restaurant universitaire est délicieuse ou affreuse?
3. L'idée d'étudier l'informatique est bonne ou mauvaise?
4. Vos vêtements sont nouveaux ou vieux?
5. Votre professeur est jeune ou âgé(e)?
6. Vos réponses en cours sont bonnes ou mauvaises? intelligentes ou stupides?

E **Vos achats.** Qu'est-ce que vous avez acheté récemment? Qu'est-ce que vous avez depuis longtemps? Utilisez la liste suivante ou vos propres idées.

MODÈLE: *J'ai un nouveau vélo. J'ai une vieille voiture.*

appartement	cravate	imperméable	sac à dos
pantalon	auto	Walkman	robe
bicyclette	chaussures	chaîne stéréo	radiocassette
calculatrice	magnétoscope	cassette	répondeur

F **Questions personnelles.** Vos préférences.

1. Quels restaurants aimez-vous mieux? (simples ou chers?)
2. Quelles sortes d'amis avez-vous? (bons? sincères?)
3. Quelles sortes de villes voulez-vous visiter? (vieilles ou modernes?)
4. Quelle sorte de maison habitez-vous? (petite? grande? blanche?)
5. Quelles autos aimez-vous? (petites? grandes? économiques? chères?)
6. Quelle sorte de musique écoutez-vous? (classique? rock? reggae?)

II. *Le calendrier*

> You use vocabulary related to the calendar to situate events in time.

A. *Les jours de la semaine* (The days of the week)

lundi	*Monday*	**vendredi**	*Friday*
mardi	*Tuesday*	**samedi**	*Saturday*
mercredi	*Wednesday*	**dimanche**	*Sunday*
jeudi	*Thursday*		

1. On the French calendar, the week begins with Monday (**lundi**), not Sunday (**dimanche**). Note that in French, another way of saying *one week* (**une semaine**) is **huit jours**. **Quinze jours** is *two weeks,* but after that you say **trois semaines** and **quatre semaines** (**un mois**).

2. Do not use a preposition to express the English *on* a day of the week.

    Je vais aller au bureau lundi.   *I'm going to the office on Monday.*

3. All of the days of the week are masculine nouns. They take the article **le** only to indicate a habitual action or repeated occurrence. In English, this is expressed by a plural.

    Le bureau est ouvert **le jeudi**   *The office is open on **Thursday***
      soir.   *evenings.*
    Nous allons au marché **le mardi.**   *We go to the market on **Tuesdays.***

4. You can use **prochain** and **dernier** with the days of the week.

    Il y a un concert jeudi **prochain.**
    Ils n'ont pas travaillé mardi **dernier.**

B. *Les mois de l'année* (The months of the year)

janvier	*January*	**juillet**	*July*
février	*February*	**août**	*August*
mars	*March*	**septembre**	*September*
avril	*April*	**octobre**	*October*
mai	*May*	**novembre**	*November*
juin	*June*	**décembre**	*December*

1. August (**août**) has two acceptable pronunciations, / u / and / ut /.

2. To say *in* a month, you use **en** plus the month or **au mois de**.

> Les Français ne travaillent pas **en août**.
> Je vais aller en vacances **au mois de juin**.

3. Days of the week and months of the year are not capitalized in French.

C. *Les quatre saisons* (The four seasons)

le printemps *spring*	l'automne *(m.)* *fall*
l'été *(m.)* *summer*	l'hiver *(m.)* *winter*

> J'aime faire des promenades **au printemps**.
> Je ne suis pas de cours **en été**.
> Je vais aux matchs de football américain **en automne**.
> Je reste chez moi **en hiver**.

D. *La date*

1. To ask the date, you say:

> **Quelle est la date aujourd'hui?** *or* **Quel jour sommes-nous?**

2. To express a date in French, use a combination of the definite article **le**, the number, and then the month.

> La Saint-Valentin est **le 14 février**.
> En Belgique, la fête nationale c'est **le 21 juillet**.

3. Cardinal numbers, which you have already learned, are always used in dates, except for the first day of the month, **le premier**.

> **Le premier mai** est la fête du Travail en Europe.

4. If you wish to add the day of the week to a date, you may place it before or after the article.

> **le jeudi 12** décembre   **dimanche, le 1er** novembre

E. *Les années* (Years)

1. In French, there are two ways of expressing calendar years. Start with **mil** (a special spelling of **mille** used for years) and count in hundreds. You may also simply count in hundreds:

> 1963   **mil neuf cent** soixante-trois *or* **dix-neuf cent** soixante-trois

2. When only the year is given, the preposition **en** is used.

> Il a visité la Chine **en 2002**.

> *but:* Il est arrivé en Chine **le 22 juin 2002**.

Attention! _____

1. The **e** of **le** is not dropped before numbers that begin with a vowel.

    le huit février   **le** onze novembre

2. No prepositions are used with days of the month or with **week-end**.

    Ils vont partir le 4 octobre.   Elles travaillent beaucoup le
                                         week-end.

3. When dates are abbreviated, the day is always given before the month.

    10.3.03 → le 10 mars 2003   2.6.01 → le 2 juin 2001

Langue

Ⓐ **Des dates.** Lisez les dates suivantes en français.

1. January 1, 1918
2. March 10, 1929
3. April 23, 1776
4. Thursday, August 1, 1881
5. Friday, September 30, 2005
6. Saturday, December 25, 2004

Ⓑ **Leurs projets.** Qu'est-ce que les amis de Robert vont faire? Lisez les phrases suivantes en ajoutant *(adding)* un mot si c'est nécessaire.

1. Le copain de Robert va acheter une voiture _____ printemps.
2. Paul veut revoir l'Angleterre _____ été.
3. Sylvie va inviter Luc _____ dimanche prochain.
4. Les parents de Sylvie ne travaillent pas _____ samedi.
5. Leurs vacances commencent _____ juillet.
6. Robert dîne toujours au restaurant _____ vendredi.

Culture

Ⓒ **Examen d'histoire.** Choisissez la date qui convient *(that is appropriate)* pour chaque événement *(each event)* dans l'histoire de France.

1. Jeanne d'Arc brûlée *(burned)*
2. L'édit de Nantes
3. Naissance *(Birth)* de Louis XIV
4. Libération de la Bastille
5. Marie-Antoinette guillotinée
6. Napoléon couronné *(crowned)*

a. 14.7.1789
b. 30.5.1431
c. 5.9.1638
d. 16.10.1793
e. 13.4.1598
f. 2.12.1804

Ⓓ **Les fêtes.** Les Américains et les francophones ont souvent les mêmes fêtes, mais plusieurs fêtes ne sont pas le même jour. Comparez les fêtes en formant des phrases avec les mots donnés.

1. les Américains / les Français: avoir la fête du Travail en septembre / en mai
2. les Américains / les Canadiens: avoir *Thanksgiving* en novembre / en octobre
3. les Américains / les Français: aller en vacances en été / en août

4. les Américains / les Suisses: avoir leur fête nationale en juillet / en août
5. En janvier, les Américains / les Français: avoir la fête de Martin Luther King, Jr. / l'Epiphanie
6. Le 15 août, les Américains / les Français: travailler / ne... pas travailler (c'est l'Assomption.)

Communication

Ⓔ Mes activités. Parlez de vos activités en ajoutant les jours, les mois ou les saisons.

MODÈLE: Je n'étudie pas...
Je n'étudie pas le dimanche.

1. J'aime aller danser...
2. Mes parents vont à l'église...
3. J'aime faire mes provisions...
4. Je regarde toujours la télévision...
5. Je fais mes courses...
6. Je vais en vacances...

Ⓕ Votre agenda. Remplissez *(Fill in)* l'agenda avec une activité pour six jours différents. Ensuite *(Then)*, demandez à un(e) camarade de cours quelles choses *(things)* il / elle a faites et les dates de ces activités. Remarquez que dans les calendriers français, lundi est le premier jour de la semaine et non pas dimanche, comme aux Etats-Unis.

Exemples

passer mon dernier examen	aller chez le médecin
faire mes provisions	préparer un bon dîner
voir mes parents	acheter des bonbons pour...
expédier un colis	utiliser un ordinateur

L	M	Me	J	V	S	D
				1	2	3
4	5	6	7	8	9	10
11	12	13	14	15	16	17

Ⓖ Questions personnelles. Votre agenda.

1. Qu'est-ce que vous allez faire l'été prochain?
2. Qu'est-ce que vous avez fait samedi dernier?
3. Quel mois est votre anniversaire *(birthday)*?

4. Quand est-ce que vous faites du sport? Quel sport?
5. Allez-vous suivre un cours cet été? Quel cours?
6. Qui est-ce que vous voulez voir dimanche?
7. Quelle est votre saison préférée? Pourquoi?
8. Quel est votre jour préféré? Pourquoi?

III. Indirect object pronouns: Third person

You use indirect object pronouns to refer to people and things already mentioned in a conversation that receive the action of the verb.

A. Introduction

In Chapter 8 you learned direct object pronouns, which receive the action of the verb (**La clé? Je l'ai perdue.**). An indirect object indicates *to whom* or *to what* this action is directed.

He sold the car *to John.*   *or*   He sold the car *to him.*
He sold *John* the car.   *or*   He sold *him* the car.

In these examples, *John* is the indirect object, since the action of selling the car is directed to him. The examples also show that the indirect object noun, *John,* may be replaced with an indirect object pronoun, *him.*

B. Third-person indirect object pronouns

	singular	plural
masculine *feminine*	lui	leur

1. A pronoun can also replace the indirect object noun in French. The masculine and feminine singular form, **lui,** means *(to) him / (to) her.*

   L'étudiant répond **au professeur?** → L'étudiant **lui** répond?
   Sylvie rend les CD **à son amie.** → Sylvie **lui** rend les CD.

   The masculine and feminine plural form, **leur,** means *(to) them.*

   On a demandé **aux enfants** leur nom. → On **leur** a demandé leur nom.
   Elle téléphone **à ses copines.** → Elle **leur** téléphone.

2. Indirect objects are somewhat easier to identify in French than in English because an indirect object noun is almost always preceded by the preposition **à.**

   Il a vendu des bonbons **à Jean-Paul.** → Il **lui** a vendu des bonbons.

C. Position of indirect object pronouns

1. The position of indirect object pronouns is the same as that of direct object pronouns: they precede the verb from which the action is directed.

Present	Passé composé
Je **leur** apporte des fraises.	Nous ne **leur** avons pas téléphoné hier.
Luc ne **lui** prête pas son auto.	Elle **lui** a montré les lapins au marché.

2. Past participles do not agree with preceding indirect objects, as they do with preceding direct objects.

> A qui ont-elles donné la pomme?
> Elles l'ont donné**e** au professeur.
>
> *but:* Elles lui ont donné la pomme.

3. Indirect object pronouns follow helping verbs.

Il va **leur** servir des crudités.	Vous ne pouvez pas **lui** répondre?

4. In negative commands, indirect object pronouns precede the verb.

Ne **lui** téléphonez pas maintenant.	Ne **leur** montrez pas ma lettre.

5. The position of pronouns is irregular in affirmative commands. Both direct and indirect object pronouns are placed after the verb and joined with a hyphen.

Regarde-le!	**Apportez-lui** une pêche.
Vendez-les tout de suite!	**Servons-leur** du riz avec les crevettes.

Mots clés *Verbs that may take indirect objects*

acheter	obéir
apporter / rapporter	parler
commander	passer
demander	poser une question *to ask a question*
désobéir	préparer
donner	présenter *to introduce*
emprunter / prêter	recommander
expédier	rendre
expliquer	répéter
faire mal	répondre
indiquer *to indicate*	ressembler *to resemble*
laisser	servir
mentir	téléphoner
montrer	vendre

Attention! ───────────────

French verbs do not always take the same kind of object as their English equivalents. Translating will not always help determine whether a direct object pronoun or an indirect object pronoun should be used.

1. **Attendre, chercher, demander, écouter,** and **regarder** take a direct object in French, but are followed by a preposition in English.

   Je cherche **le métro.** → Je **le** cherche.
   Il a demandé **cette poire.** → Il **l'**a demandée.
   Nous allons écouter **la radio.** → Nous allons **l'**écouter.
   J'ai regardé **ses poissons.** → Je **les** ai regardés.

2. **Obéir à, désobéir à, téléphoner à, rendre visite à, répondre à,** and **ressembler à** take indirect objects in French but take direct objects in English.

   Ils ont obéi **à l'agent de police.** → Ils **lui** ont obéi.
   Téléphone **à Jacques.** → Téléphone-**lui.**
   Elle ressemble **à sa mère.** → Elle **lui** ressemble.

Langue

Ⓐ **A la résidence.** Répondez aux questions suivantes en utilisant des pronoms compléments d'objet indirect.

1. Est-ce que Jacques a rendu ses devoirs à son prof?   (Oui,...)
2. Vous ne servez pas de bière à vos amis?   (Non,... cocas.)
3. Tu ne veux pas parler aux autres?   (Si,...)
4. On va servir des repas aux pauvres?   (Oui,...)
5. Paul a-t-il téléphoné à son copain?   (Non,...)
6. Peux-tu demander l'adresse à Jacqueline?   (Oui,...)

Ⓑ **Vous avez invité Monique hier soir?** Refaites les phrases suivantes selon les indications entre parenthèses.

1. Vous lui servez du bifteck et des haricots verts?   (... hier soir)
2. Je lui ai montré mon ordinateur.   (... vendre... nouveau...)
3. Ne lui demandez pas de sortir samedi prochain!   *(make affirmative)*
4. Elle ressemble *à ses parents.*   *(use a pronoun)*
5. Je lui présente mes amis.   (Le week-end prochain...)
6. Nous lui donnons un beau cadeau.   *(give a command)*

Culture

Ⓒ **Les pourboires.** A qui est-ce qu'on donne un pourboire *(tip)* en France? Est-ce qu'on le donne toujours, jamais, ou uniquement pour un service spécial?

MODÈLE: garçon de café
          On ne lui donne jamais de pourboire. (Le service est compris.)

1. le marchand
2. l'ouvreuse *(usher)*
3. le facteur
4. le médecin
5. les agents de police
6. les hôtesses du Syndicat d'Initiative
7. les chauffeurs de taxi
8. les garçons de restaurant

Ⓓ Une nouvelle connaissance. Vous avez vu un très bel homme / une très belle femme et vous voulez le / la revoir. Qu'est-ce que vous pouvez faire pour arranger un rendez-vous? Utilisez les suggestions données ou vos propres idées.

MODÈLE: *Je lui demande son nom.*

parler après la classe	présenter mes amis
téléphoner ce soir	parler de son avenir *(future)*
demander s'il / si elle veut sortir	servir...
inviter chez moi	montrer mes timbres
donner mon adresse	???

Ⓔ Qui voyez-vous? Voyez-vous souvent les personnes suivantes? Leur téléphonez-vous? Tous les combien *(How often)*? Utilisez les suggestions données ou vos propres idées.

MODÈLE: votre frère
Je ne le vois pas souvent, mais je lui téléphone toutes les semaines.

vos amis	tous les jours / mois / ans
vos parents	toutes les heures / semaines
votre frère / sœur	une / deux / trois fois
votre petit(e) ami(e)	par jour / semaine / mois
vos grands-parents	souvent / pas souvent
votre camarade de chambre	rarement
votre professeur	ne... jamais

Ⓕ Des conseils. Que pouvez-vous dire *(say)* à vos amis dans les trois situations suivantes? Trouvez un(e) partenaire et créez *(create)* de bons conseils.

1. Ils ont un invité *(guest)* important.

MODÈLE: présenter vos amis *Présentez-lui vos amis.*

   servir une boisson / montrer votre appartement / ne... pas demander leur âge / ne... pas laisser seul / parler du temps

2. Leur professeur les a invités à dîner.

   apporter un cadeau / demander comment il (elle) va / admirer ton prof pour son travail / ne... pas demander d'argent / ne... pas expliquer vos absences / ne... pas parler de l'examen final

3. Ils vont visiter le campus avec des étudiants de première année.

   montrer la librairie / le laboratoire, etc. / ne... pas recommander le restaurant universitaire / parler des cours faciles / ne... pas inviter dans les bars / ne... pas vendre de billets pour la bibliothèque

Ⓖ Questions personnelles: Vos habitudes. Utilisez des pronoms compléments d'objet indirect dans vos réponses.

1. Avez-vous téléphoné à vos parents samedi ou dimanche? Pourquoi?
2. Qu'est-ce que vous allez demander au Père Noël *(Santa Claus)* cette année?
3. Prêtez-vous votre voiture à vos amis? vos CD? vos vêtements?

4. A qui vendez-vous vos livres?
5. Qu'est-ce que vous servez à vos amis quand ils dînent chez vous?
6. Qu'est-ce que vous allez apporter à vos professeurs le dernier jour de cours?

IV. *Prendre*

You use the verb **prendre** to express the idea *to take* and, when referring to food or drink, to express *to have* or *to eat*.

prendre	*(to take; to have [food])*		
je **prends**	/ pʀɑ̃ /	nous **prenons**	/ pʀə nɔ̃ /
tu **prends**	/ pʀɑ̃ /	vous **prenez**	/ pʀə ne /
il / elle / on **prend**	/ pʀɑ̃ /	ils / elles **prennent**	/ pʀɛn /

Passé composé: il **a pris**

A. Although its infinitive ends in **-re, prendre** is not conjugated like the -re verbs you learned in Chapter 6. In the present tense, **prendre** differs in the plural forms, resulting in three different vowel sounds: / pʀɑ̃ /, / pʀə nɔ̃ /, and / pʀɛn /.

On **prend** le métro pour aller au marché.
Nous **prenons** quel autobus?
Ils ne **prennent** pas le train vendredi?

B. The verb **prendre** can also mean *to have* or *to eat* when used with foods and drinks, replacing **manger**. It *must* be used with the names of meals.

Je ne **prends** pas de porc. Qu'est-ce que tu **prends**?
Ils ne **prennent** pas de petit déjeuner.
On **prend** le dîner à huit heures.

C. The past participle of **prendre** is **pris**. The feminine form is **prise**, and the s in it is pronounced.

Nous **avons pris** des poires.   Cette **photo**? Je ne l'ai pas **prise**.

D. **Apprendre** *(to learn)* and **comprendre** *(to understand)* are conjugated like **prendre**.

—Est-ce que tu **comprends** le français?
—Oui, je l'**ai appris** à l'école.

While **apprendre** means *to learn (how to)*, **apprendre à** + *a person* means *to teach*. This expression can be followed by a direct object noun or, for the subject taught, **à** plus an infinitive.

Il apprend l'italien **aux** étudiants.
Il apprend **aux** étudiants à parler italien.

Attention! ————————————————————

Since the letter **d** has a / t / sound in **liaison,** there is no need to add **-t-** with inversion of the third-person singular form of **prendre** and verbs conjugated like it.

Prend-elle l'avion ce matin?
Apprend-il le japonais?

Langue

Ⓐ **A l'université.** Substituez le verbe entre parenthèses dans les phrases suivantes.

1. On entend l'arabe à l'université?   (apprendre)
2. On vend des livres de chinois à la librairie.   (prendre)
3. Est-ce que vous avez emprunté mon livre de maths?   (prendre)
4. Etudiez l'allemand!   (apprendre)
5. Nous rendons les notes de Jean-Paul.   (ne... pas comprendre)
6. Je parle très bien l'italien.   (comprendre)

Ⓑ **Interview avec une étudiante américaine.** Répondez aux questions suivantes avec les mots donnés. Remplacez les compléments d'objet direct en italique par des pronoms.

MODÈLE: Avez-vous pris *votre voiture* ce matin?   (Oui,...)
            Oui, je l'ai prise.

1. Les étudiants comprennent-ils *leurs leçons?*   (Non, ils...)
2. Peuvent-ils apprendre *le japonais?*   (Oui,...)
3. Et vous, apprenez-vous *le chinois?*   (Non,...)
4. Comprenez-vous *l'informatique?*   (Non,...)
5. Avez-vous pris *votre petit déjeuner* ce matin?   (Non,... plus tard.)
6. Avez-vous pris *l'autobus* récemment?   (Oui, la semaine dernière...)

Culture

Ⓒ **Les habitudes gastronomiques des Français.** Les habitudes des Français sont différentes de celles *(those)* des Américains quand il est question de manger. Formez des phrases avec les mots donnés, et si la phrase ne représente pas la réalité en France, ajoutez *(add)* **ne... pas.**

1. Français / prendre / café au lait / au dîner
2. Français / prendre / toujours / asperges / froid
3. En France / on / aller / restaurant / pour / prendre / petit déjeuner
4. On / prendre / œufs / au petit déjeuner
5. On / prendre / dîner / à six heures du soir
6. Beaucoup de Français / prendre / fruit / comme dessert
7. On / prendre / vin rouge / avec / rosbif
8. On / prendre / salade / après / plat principal

Communication

Ⓓ **A table!** Décrivez *(Describe)* vos repas typiques en utilisant les suggestions suivantes ou vos propres idées. Précisez *(Specify)* l'heure, les plats et les boissons.

MODÈLE: *A midi je prends un sandwich et un coca.*

Les plats

riz	glace	pizza
bifteck	asperges	frites
veau	fromage	œufs
gâteau	salade	sandwich

Les boissons

eau	café	vin
eau minérale	thé	coca
bière	lait	jus de fruit

Ⓔ **Jeu de rôles.** Vous allez dîner au restaurant. Avec un(e) camarade, jouez une des scènes suivantes.

1. Vous êtes végétariens.
2. Votre camarade est au régime, mais vous avez très faim.
3. Vous êtes snobs.
4. Vous êtes pauvre, mais votre camarade veut dépenser beaucoup d'argent.

Ⓕ **Questions personnelles.** Vos études.

1. Quelles langues comprenez-vous? Et dans votre famille?
2. Qu'est-ce que vous apprenez à l'université?
3. Qu'est-ce que vous avez pris ce matin avant vos cours?
4. Que prenez-vous avant un examen?
5. Après vos cours, qu'est-ce que vous aimez prendre avec vos amis?
6. Qu'est-ce que vous avez appris à votre frère / à votre sœur / à votre ami(e)?

 communiquons

Prendre les repas

French people usually have three complete meals a day. Breakfast is very light, consisting of **café au lait** (half coffee, half hot milk) or tea and bread or **croissants.** Lunch is much more substantial, often consisting of meat, vegetables, cheese, and wine. The French have traditionally taken a two-hour lunch break to go home or to a restaurant while offices, banks, and stores closed. This

Menu du Jour

tradition is rapidly changing. Lunch breaks are shorter, fast-food restaurants have gained in popularity, and more and more businesses stay open during the lunch hour.

The French usually eat dinner at home and often begin as late as 8 P.M. «**A table!**» signals to everyone that a meal is ready. The first course, **les hors-d'œuvre,** can be cold cuts (**de la charcuterie**) or **des crudités,** for instance. Then the **plat principal** is served. Normally meat or fish, it is accompanied by vegetables. The last part of the meal consists of salad, cheese, and fruit or dessert.

There are many differences in eating habits between France and America. In France, you should keep both hands on the table rather than keeping one on your lap. At informal dinners in France, bread does not have a special plate, but is put directly on the table. You generally do not put butter on bread, but you do on radishes! Milk and hot beverages are not drunk with meals. Plates are changed several times during the meal, but some people wipe them with a piece of bread. Finally, French people, like all Europeans, eat with the fork in their left hand.

Expressions

▶ **On met le couvert.** *(One sets the table.)*

▶ **On parle pendant le repas.**

Passe-moi du pain, s'il te plaît.	*Pass me the bread, please.*
Tu veux encore de l'eau?	*Do you want more water?*
Merci!	*No, thanks.*
S'il te plaît!	*Yes, please.*

▶ **On est au restaurant.**

Le maître d'hôtel leur montre leur table.	*The maitre d' shows them to their table.*
Ils veulent voir la carte des vins.	*They want to see the wine list.*
Le garçon / La serveuse explique la carte et le menu.	*The waiter / The waitress explains the menu and the list of fixed-priced meals.*
Le plat du jour est délicieux.	*Today's special is delicious.*
On apporte l'addition.	*They bring the check.*
Ils donnent un pourboire au garçon.	*They give the waiter a tip.*
Boisson et service en sus.	*Drinks and tip are extra.*
Service compris.	*The tip is included.*
Payez à la caisse.	*Pay the cashier.*

Interaction

M. Marchand téléphone au restaurant Jamin pour réserver une table.

LE MAÎTRE D'HÔTEL: Allô, le restaurant Jamin.

M. MARCHAND: Bonjour, je voudrais réserver une table pour quatre ce soir.

LE MAÎTRE D'HÔTEL:	Attendez voir... Non, ce soir, nous sommes complets°. Mais je veux bien prendre votre nom. Nous allons peut-être° avoir une annulation°.	*booked* *perhaps / cancellation*
M. MARCHAND:	Et demain soir?	
LE MAÎTRE D'HÔTEL:	Oui, à quelle heure?	
M. MARCHAND:	Vingt heures trente?	
LE MAÎTRE D'HÔTEL:	C'est noté°. C'est à quel nom?	C'est... *I've got it.*
M. MARCHAND:	Monsieur Marchand.	
LE MAÎTRE D'HÔTEL:	C'est convenu°. A demain soir.	C'est... *All right*
M. MARCHAND:	A demain.	

Activités

A **Votre spécialité.** Expliquez comment vous préparez votre spécialité. Donnez votre recette *(recipe)* préférée à la classe.

MODÈLE: *Je prends du sucre, de la farine...*

B **On a faim.** En petits groupes, demandez à vos camarades quels plats ils aiment et quels plats ils détestent. Ensuite, préparez un repas idéal et un repas affreux selon vos préférences et échangez vos idées avec vos camarades de cours.

C **Jeu de rôles.** Jouez les scènes suivantes avec un(e) camarade de cours.

1. Vous êtes dans un restaurant et vous commandez un repas.
2. Vous téléphonez à votre restaurant préféré pour réserver une table.
3. Vous demandez au garçon / à la serveuse pourquoi votre repas est si *(so)* cher / froid / mauvais. (Choisissez!)

lecture culturelle

Avant la lecture

The red Michelin guide, known in French as **le Guide Rouge,** is one of the best known and most respected guides to fine cuisine in France and abroad. Being featured in the **Guide Rouge** is an honor that many seek but few achieve. Each year, a panel of culinary experts rates restaurants on the quality of their meals, service, and ambiance. A select number are then awarded either one, two, or three stars. The star system guarantees the restaurant's reputation as well as its financial success. In 2001, only twenty-one restaurants in France (of which seven were in Paris) and fewer than twenty restaurants in the rest of Europe obtained the coveted distinction of three stars.

The only chef in the world to be granted a total of six stars in the Michelin **Guide Rouge** for 2001 was Chef Marc Veyrat. He was awarded three stars for his restaurant L'Auberge de l'Eridan, located near beautiful Lake Annecy, a few miles from Geneva, Switzerland. Only a year after opening, Veyrat's second restaurant, La Ferme de mon Père, also earned three stars. La Ferme de mon Père is located in the ski resort town of Megève, in Haute-Savoie, a *département* in the French Alps.

Although the **Guide Rouge** has long appeared in book form, you can also search it on-line for famous restaurants. In addition, Michelin has recently come out with a version of the guide for personal digital assistants. Diners can choose restaurants on the basis of location, price, comfort, and quality.

Activités

Ⓐ Do you enjoy cooking? Did you use to experiment in the kitchen when you were younger?

Ⓑ What did you want to be when you grew up? Do your studies and career interests diverge from those early ambitions?

Ⓒ Locate the Alps on a map of France, and identify the *département* of Haute-Savoie.

Le chef Marc Veyrat, héritier de onze générations de paysans français

A bientôt 51 ans, le chef français Marc Veyrat, qui vient d'obtenir pour la deuxième fois trois étoiles au prestigieux guide rouge (Michelin), n'a pas changé depuis ses débuts. Cet autodidacte héritier° de onze générations de paysans° a une devise°: «Une cuisine, un homme, un lieu».

heir
small farmers / motto

5   **D**escendant d'une famille installée au cœur des Alpes, il se fait le chantre° d'une cuisine créative basée sur les herbes, les racines, les fleurs sauvages de sa région, la Savoie — pimpiolet, chénopode, aïlï aigrelet, benoîte° urbaine — apprise auprès de ses grand-pères, mais aussi d'une cuisine ouverte sur les produits du vaste monde. Son chemin° a été long et semé d'embûches°.

fervent supporter

pimpiolet... These are names of herbs and wildflowers. / path / semé... fraught with pitfalls / disruptive / renvoyé... expelled from junior high school / dreamed / shepherd / ski instructor

10   Garçon chahuteur°, il a été successivement renvoyé du collège° puis de l'école hôtelière. Il rêvait° d'être cuisinier—sa mère et sa grand-mère l'ont inspiré— il est berger° et moniteur de ski°.

   En 1978, il ouvre un bistrot en montagne sans savoir vraiment cuisiner. Il apprend par cœur 2.000 recettes, lit les livres de deux grands chefs, Michel

15   Guérard et Paul Bocuse. Un jour, avec une herbe appelée chénopode, il fait une soupe. Son aventure créative commence.

   En 1985, il quitte° sa montagne pour Annecy-le-Vieux (sud-est), où il ouvre l'Auberge de l'Eridan. Un an plus tard, il obtient sa première étoile au guide Michelin, puis en 1987 la deuxième. Cinq ans plus tard, Marc Veyrat s'installe

leaves

20   tout près, à Veyrier-du-Lac, dans une belle villa en bordure du lac d'Annecy. En 1995, il obtient enfin les trois précieux macarons°.

   Un jour, il trouve à Megève, dans les Alpes, un grand chalet. Le chef décide

Michelin stars (which look like macaroons)

d'y recréer la ferme de son enfance. En décembre 2000, La Ferme de mon Père, en hommage à un père qui n'a pas vu son couronnement°, ouvre ses portes. Il en fait un établissement d'hiver (décembre à début avril), l'Auberge de l'Eridan étant° restaurant d'été. Les cartes sont différentes, et les équipes° «migrent».

Mais il a une autre envie°: Paris. Sur son site Internet, le gourmet peut lire que le chef est à la recherche° d'un lieu dans la capitale. Pour «faire découvrir la Savoie à Paris».

crowning (achievement)

being; functioning or serving as / teams (the personnel)

wish, desire / est... is looking or searching for

Dominique Ageorges, «Le chef Marc Veyrat, héritier de onze générations de paysans français», Copyright 2001, Agence France Presse.

Après la lecture

Questions sur le texte

1. D'où vient Marc Veyrat? Décrivez les origines de sa famille.
2. Quelles sortes d'études est-ce que Veyrat a suivies? Est-ce qu'il a eu du succès?
3. Quel a été le rêve de Marc Veyrat? Quelles carrières Veyrat a-t-il eues avant de devenir chef cuisinier?
4. Comment est-ce que Veyrat a appris à cuisiner?
5. Ça lui a pris combien d'années pour obtenir trois étoiles pour l'Auberge de l'Eridan?
6. Pourquoi Veyrat a-t-il appelé le restaurant La Ferme de mon Père? A quoi ressemble le restaurant?
7. Quel restaurant est ouvert pendant l'été? Et pendant l'hiver?
8. Est-ce que les employés des deux restaurants sont différents?
9. Quel est le rêve de Marc Veyrat maintenant?

Activités

Ⓐ La devise de Marc Veyrat est «Une cuisine, un homme, un lieu». Que veulent dire les devises suivantes?

La France:	Liberté, égalité, fraternité
Le Québec:	Je me souviens
La Suisse:	Un pour tous, tous pour un
La Belgique:	L'union fait la force
L'Algérie:	Par le peuple et pour le peuple
La République du Congo:	Unité, travail, progrès

Ⓑ Inventez votre propre devise de votre vie (famille, travail etc.).

Ⓒ Quels sont vos rêves? Qui vous a inspiré(e)? Pourquoi étudiez-vous à l'université? Pourquoi avez-vous choisi votre spécialisation? Quelles ont été vos influences?

Ⓓ Lisez la description de l'Auberge de l'Eridan et répondez aux questions suivantes:

1. Pendant quels mois est-ce que l'Auberge de l'Eridan est fermée?
2. Pendant les mois où le restaurant est ouvert, est-ce qu'il est possible de dîner chaque soir de la semaine?
3. Combien de fourchettes a l'auberge? Qu'est-ce que cela veut dire?
4. Quelle est la vue du restaurant?
5. Est-ce qu'il y a un jardin de repos à l'Auberge de l'Eridan?
6. Quelles cartes de crédit sont acceptées?

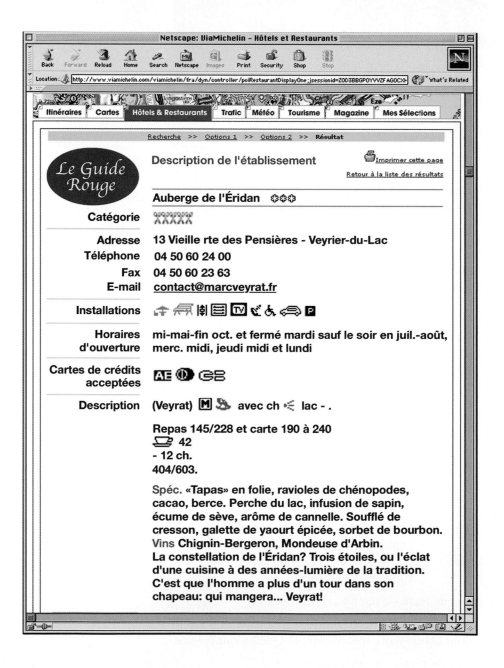

Le Guide Rouge

Légende du Guide Rouge

🏨🏨🏨🏨	XXXXX	Grand luxe
🏨🏨🏨	XXXX	Grand confort
🏨🏨	XXX	Très confortable
🏨	XX	De bon confort
🏨	X	Assez confortable
🍷		Simple mais convenable
✿✿✿		La table vaut le voyage
✿✿		La table mérite un détour
✿		Une très bonne table
		Repas soigné à prix modérés 15/20 €
☕		Petit déjeuner
enf.		Menu enfant
🏨🏨🏨🏨 ... 🏨		Hôtels agréables
XXXXX... X		Restaurants agréables
		Vue exceptionnelle
		Vue intéressante ou étendue
		Situation très tranquille, isolée
		Situation tranquille
		Repas au jardin ou en terrasse
		Salle de remise en forme
		Piscine en plein air ou couverte
	X	Jardin de repos - Tennis à l'hôtel
		Ascenseur
		Chambres pour non-fumeurs
		Air conditionné
		Téléphone direct
		Prise Modem-Minitel dans la chambre
		Accessible aux handicapés physiques
P		Parking - Garage
		Salles de conférence, séminaire
		Accès interdit aux chiens
AE 🔵		American Express - Diners Club
CB		Carte bancaire
JCB		Japan Credit Bureau

vocabulaire

Noms / Pronoms

une année	year	lui	her / him
août	August	lundi	Monday
asperges *(f.)*	asparagus	mai	May
automne *(m.)*	fall	un marchand	merchant
avril	April	mardi	Tuesday
une banane	banana	un marché en plein air	open-air market
le bifteck	steak		
le bœuf	beef	mars	March
un bonbon	candy	la matinée	morning
ça	that	mercredi	Wednesday
un calendrier	calendar	moi	me
carottes râpées *(f.)*	grated carrots	un mois	month
une cerise	cherry	un nom	name
un coin	corner / area	novembre	November
un concombre	cucumber	octobre	October
une côtelette	chop	un œuf	egg
une crevette	shrimp	une olive	olive
crudités *(f.)*	raw vegetables	une orange	orange
une date	date	le pâté	pâté
décembre	December	pattes *(f.)*	feet (animals)
un déjeuner	lunch	une pêche	peach
dimanche	Sunday	le petit déjeuner	breakfast
un dîner	dinner	petits pois *(m.)*	peas
épinards *(m.)*	spinach	une poire	pear
une escalope	cutlet	une pomme	apple
la fête du Travail	Labor Day	une pomme de terre	potato
la Fête nationale	Independence Day		
		le porc	pork
février	February	le printemps	spring
un filet	filet	un raisin	grape
une fraise	strawberry	un repas	meal
fruits *(m.)* de mer	shellfish	le riz	rice
un gigot	leg of lamb	le rosbif	roast beef
haricots verts *(m.)*	green beans	le rôti	roast
hiver *(m.)*	winter	la Saint-Valentin	St. Valentine's Day
janvier	January	la saison	season
jeudi	Thursday	samedi	Saturday
un jour	day	un saucisson	salami
juillet	July	une semaine	week
juin	June	septembre	September
un lapin	rabbit	la sole	sole
leur	them	une tête	head

une tomate	tomato	une variété	variety
la truite	trout	le veau	veal
vacances *(f.)*	vacation	vendredi	Friday

Verbes

apprendre	to learn / to teach	prendre	to take / to have
comprendre	to understand	présenter	to introduce
espérer	to hope	ressembler	to look like
indiquer	to indicate		

Adjectifs / Adverbes

beau	beautiful / nice	petit	small
bon	good	propre	clean, own
différent	different	provençal	from Provence
grand	big / tall	végétarien	vegetarian
jeune	young	vieux	old
joli	pretty	vraiment	truly
nouveau	new		

Expressions

tout comme	like
faire ses provisions	to do one's shopping
poser une question	to ask a question

Révision C

Tous ensemble!

Ⓐ Refaites les phrases suivantes selon les indications entre parenthèses.

En cours

1. Il finit ses cours à onze heures.   (Elles... midi.)
2. Elle a suivi un cours d'informatique.   (... faire...)
3. Je ne comprends pas pourquoi ils dorment en classe.   (Nous... il...)
4. Elle explique ce dialogue aux étudiants.   (... apprendre... leçon...)
5. Ils font de l'italien.   (... étudier...)

Au café

6. Ils finissent cette bière froide.   (... servir... bon...)
7. Elle présente ses vieux amis à son fils.   (... ami... fille.)
8. Nous allons voir nos copains mardi.   (... mardi dernier.)
9. Je prends du café quand il fait froid.   (Ils... pleuvoir.)
10. Demain nous allons voir nos amis anglais ici.   (Hier... bon...)

Ⓑ Répondez aux questions suivantes en employant les mots entre parenthèses.

En ville

1. Quel temps va-t-il faire demain?   (... chaud et... pleuvoir.)
2. J'ai soif. Qu'est-ce que je peux prendre?   (Prendre... eau!)
3. Qui choisit les films quand vous allez au cinéma?   (Nos parents...)
4. Est-ce que vous êtes descendu(e) en voiture?   (Non,... prendre... taxi... parce que... brouillard.)
5. Quels fruits voulez-vous?   (... choisir... pêches et... poires.)

Chez vous

6. Est-ce que tes parents ont un répondeur?   (Non... répondre eux-mêmes.)
7. Avez-vous donné de l'argent aux enfants?   (Non... petit cadeau.)
8. Vous avez fait vos provisions?   (Non...)
9. Va-t-il voir les filles?   (Non... dimanche dernier.)
10. Quelle sorte de vêtements a-t-il choisie?   (... beau...)

Ⓒ Formez des phrases complètes en employant les mots donnés.

En famille

1. Ce / homme / ressembler / mère
2. Que / vous / voir / fenêtre?
3. Mes sœurs / sortir / souvent, / mais / elles / ne... pas / dormir assez
4. Qui / pouvoir / fermer / ce / porte?
5. Je / servir / thé / chaud / mon / père / hiver

Les études

6. Quel / cours / vous / choisir?
7. Nous / réussir / examen / maths / semaine / prochain?
8. Elle / vouloir / acheter / nouveau / ordinateur
9. Nous / faire / sciences économiques / automne
10. Ce / femmes / étudier / langues / étranger

D Répondez aux questions suivantes selon les indications entre parenthèses et en remplaçant les mots en italique par des pronoms compléments.

1. Vous avez parlé *à vos amis?*   (Oui,...)
2. Avez-vous vu *son magnétophone?*   (Non,... pas encore...)
3. Elle apprend l'anglais *aux enfants?*   (Non,... le français.)
4. Est-ce que Christine veut acheter *cette robe?*   (Non,... détester.)
5. Nous allons inviter *les Ouellette* cette semaine?   (Non,... octobre.)
6. Tu vas téléphoner *à Mme Ouellette?*   (Non,... voir au bureau et... parler à midi.)
7. Est-ce qu'on fait *la vaisselle* maintenant?   (Non,... demain.)
8. Est-ce que j'ai perdu *mon livre de français?*   (Non,... oublier chez toi.)

E Complétez les phrases suivantes logiquement *(logically)*.

1. Le dimanche à six heures, je...
2. Ce cours est...
3. En cours, nous ne pouvons pas...
4. Mes amis ne veulent pas...
5. Quand il pleut,...
6. Ce trimestre, je suis des cours...
7. De ma chambre, on peut voir...
8. Je ressemble à...

F Questions personnelles

1. Quand vous mangez au restaurant, qu'est-ce que vous aimez prendre?
2. A quelle heure prenez-vous votre petit déjeuner?
3. Qu'est-ce que vous voulez apprendre?
4. Quel cours suivez-vous ce trimestre / semestre?
5. Quelles langues étrangères comprenez-vous?
6. A qui téléphonez-vous souvent?
7. Dans votre famille, qui désobéit souvent?
8. Où aimez-vous aller quand vous sortez?

Entre nous!

A Avec un(e) camarade de cours, parlez de vos études le trimestre (semestre) dernier, ce trimestre (semestre), et le trimestre (semestre) prochain.

B Interviewez un(e) camarade de cours sur ses rapports avec son / sa camarade de chambre. Utilisez les questions suivantes et des questions originales.

Vous l'aimez / le détestez?
Vous lui téléphonez souvent?
Vous lui donnez des cadeaux?
Vous lui prêtez des vêtements?

Vous l'écoutez toujours?
Vous lui avez présenté votre famille?
Vous l'avez invité(e) chez vous?

C Quels bons films avez-vous vus? Choisissez un film et racontez-le à vos camarades de cours, mais ne leur donnez pas le titre *(title)*. Ils vont le deviner *(guess)*.

D Avec un(e) autre étudiant(e), préparez un voyage pour le week-end prochain. Avec qui et comment allez-vous voyager? Qu'est-ce que vous voulez visiter? Qui est-ce que vous voulez voir?

E En groupes de trois ou quatre personnes, faites des interviews pour connaître les réponses aux questions suivantes.

1. Qu'est-ce que tu voudrais apprendre à faire?
2. Où peux-tu aller pour l'apprendre?
3. Qu'est-ce que tu peux apprendre à une autre personne?
4. A qui veux-tu apprendre quelque chose?

F **Jeu de rôles.** Jouez les scènes suivantes.

1. Vous sortez avec un(e) ami(e). Choisissez un restaurant et un film à voir.
2. Un(e) camarade de cours téléphone et il / elle veut sortir avec vous. Vous ne l'aimez pas. Trouvez des excuses.
3. Vous êtes journaliste et vous interviewez une célébrité.
4. Vous êtes au marché en plein air et vous achetez vos provisions.

La Smart

commençons

grammaire

communiquons

lecture culturelle

vocabulaire

En voiture

OBJECTIVES

Language	Culture	Communication
■ Vocabulary for the car ■ The mid vowels / e / and / ɛ / ■ **Savoir** and **connaître** ■ Review of the **passé composé** ■ The imperfect ■ **Venir** and verbs conjugated like **venir** ■ **Venir de**	■ **La Belgique** ■ Renting a car ■ Cars and new technology	■ Talking about whom and what you know ■ Describing past events and conditions ■ Driving a car

commençons

On loue une voiture.

Trois étudiants américains font un voyage en Europe pendant les grandes vacances. Ils viennent d'arriver à l'aéroport de Zaventem à Bruxelles et ils sont allés au bureau de la compagnie de location de voitures Avis.

L'EMPLOYÉE: Bonjour, vous avez besoin d'une voiture?

JANE: Oui, nous l'avons réservée aux Etats-Unis et nous l'avons payée.

L'EMPLOYÉE: Très bien. Mais vous savez, il faut régler la TVA en Belgique quand vous rendez la voiture.

JANE: Nous ne savions pas cela quand nous l'avons louée. Est-ce qu'il y a d'autres frais?

L'EMPLOYÉE: L'assurance tous risques est en plus. Elle n'est pas obligatoire, mais si vous ne connaissez pas bien les habitudes des chauffeurs européens, elle est presque indispensable.

JANE: Oui, d'accord. Je vais payer avec ma carte de crédit. Est-ce que la voiture est automatique?

L'EMPLOYÉE: Oui. C'est une Renault Laguna. Tenez, voilà les papiers à signer et les clés.

1. Que font les trois étudiants américains à l'aéroport de Bruxelles?
2. Est-ce qu'ils ont déjà réservé une voiture? Où?
3. En Belgique, qu'est-ce qu'on paye en plus du prix de la location?
4. Quand paye-t-on la TVA?
5. Quand est-il prudent de prendre une assurance tous risques?
6. Quelle sorte de voiture Jane et ses amis ont-ils louée?

Mots clés

loue (louer)	are renting	en plus	extra
grandes vacances (f.)	summer vacation	obligatoire	required
viennent d' (venir de)	have just	connaissez (connaître)	know
un aéroport	airport		
une compagnie de location	rental company	habitudes (f.)	habits
		chauffeurs (m.)	drivers
avez besoin de (avoir besoin de)	need	européens	European
		presque	almost
réservé(e)	reserved	indispensable	indispensable
payé(e)	paid for	d'accord	O.K.
régler	pay	une carte de crédit	credit card
la TVA (taxe à la valeur ajoutée)	value-added tax	automatique	automatic (transmission)
frais (m.)	costs	Tenez.	Here.
assurance (f.) tous risques	full collision insurance	papiers (m.)	documents
		signer	sign

Faisons connaissance

Renting a car is an excellent, if expensive, way to see Europe. One reason that rentals are expensive is the **TVA.** This is a tax that many European countries add to purchases; it can be 33% of the total cost, or even more for luxury items. Another major expense in renting a car is additional insurance coverage. The deductible on standard coverage is quite high, making **assurance tous risques** a good idea for renters. In general, you must be at least 21 years old to rent a car in Europe; you must also produce a valid driver's license and a major credit card.

For many years, Belgium has been a popular point of arrival for American tourists who visit Europe. Sabena, the government-operated airline, was among the first European airlines to establish gateways in major ▶

La Grand-Place à Bruxelles

American cities and to offer competitive transatlantic fares. Belgium also has a lot to offer to tourists. Cities like Brussels (**Bruxelles**), Ghent (**Gand**), Bruges, and Liège contain historical treasures. Brussels is also very well known for its fine cuisine and for the luxury shops that line its **avenue Louise,** which is often compared to the **Champs-Elysées.**

Enrichissons notre vocabulaire

Une auto *(A car)*

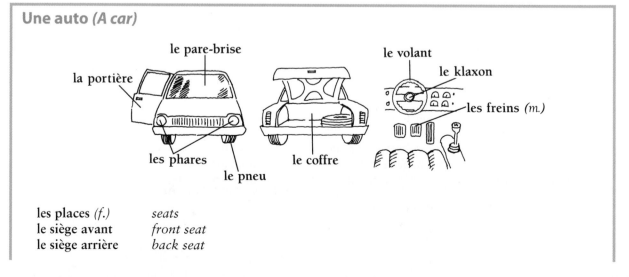

le pare-brise
la portière
les phares
le pneu
le coffre
le volant
le klaxon
les freins *(m.)*

les places *(f.)*	seats
le siège avant	front seat
le siège arrière	back seat

La circulation *(Traffic)*

conduire	*to drive*	tomber en panne	*to have a breakdown*
démarrer	*to start*	une voiture neuve	*brand-new car*
un embouteillage	*traffic jam*		
réparer	*to repair*	une voiture d'occasion	*secondhand car*
stationner	*to park*		

Un accident *(An accident)*

la ceinture de sécurité	*seatbelt*
freiner	*to brake*
les gendarmes *(m.)*	*police officers*
le permis de conduire	*driver's license*
la priorité à droite	*right of way*
rouler à... kilomètres à l'heure	*to go . . . kilometers per hour*

Prononciation   The mid vowels / e / and / ɛ /

A. French has three pairs of mid vowels, so called because the mouth is neither fully open as with the / a / sound nor closed as with the / i / sound. With all three pairs, it is important to note whether a consonant sound follows the vowel sound.

B. The mid vowel sound / ɛ / is often followed by a consonant. It is pronounced with the mouth slightly open and the tongue forward.

Practice the / ɛ / sound by repeating the following words after your teacher.

treize / faire / laisse / cette / faites / laide / Bruxelles

C. The mid vowel sound / e / is extremely tense, so you must be careful not to move your tongue or jaw when pronouncing it.

Repeat the following pairs of words after your teacher.

English	French
say	ses
day	des
bay	B

D. In French, a consonant sound never follows the / e / sound at the end of a word. Usual spellings for the / e / sound are **-é, -ez,** and **-er.** The letters **z** and **r** are silent.

Practice the / e / sound by repeating the following words after your teacher.

allé / vous arrivez / réserver / sécurité / tenez / payée

Exercices

Ⓐ Repeat the following pairs of words after your teacher.

/ e /	/ ε /
1. les	laisse
2. B	bête
3. mes	mère

Ⓑ Now, practice the / e / and / ε / sounds in words of several syllables. Be sure to avoid diphthongizing the final / e /.

céder / chercher / acceptez / préféré / fermer / préparer

Ⓒ Read the following sentences aloud, keeping all vowels very tense.

1. Daniel fait des crêpes pour la fête de sa mère.
2. Cet employé a déjà fermé la fenêtre.
3. Visitez le musée près du café.
4. Merci pour ce verre de lait frais.
5. Elle est née en janvier l'année dernière.
6. Préférez-vous aller danser ou rester chez vous?

grammaire

I. *Savoir* and *connaître*

You use **connaître** and **savoir** to indicate that you know someone or something.

A. Forms

savoir	connaître
Present: je **sais**	je **connais**
tu **sais**	tu **connais**
il / elle / on **sait**	il / elle / on **connaît**
nous **savons**	nous **connaissons**
vous **savez**	vous **connaissez**
ils / elles **savent**	ils / elles **connaissent**
Passé composé: elle **a su**	il **a connu**

B. Uses

Savoir and **connaître** are not often interchangeable.

1. **Savoir** means *to know a fact, to know very well,* or *to know how to do something.* Never use it to mean *to know people.*

   Je ne **sais** pas réparer cette voiture.
   Elle ne **sait** pas quelle sorte d'auto nous avons.
   Mais vous **savez,** il faut régler la TVA en Belgique.

Ce qu'ils disent

In conversation, the French often drop the **ne** of **Je ne sais pas.** The **je** and **sais** combine to become / ʃe pa /.

   —Quelle heure est-il?
   —J'sais pas.

2. **Connaître** means *to know, to be acquainted with,* or *to be familiar with.* Always use it to mean *to know people* or *places.*

   Je ne **connais** pas ce professeur.
   Connais-tu Bruxelles?

3. Another verb conjugated like **connaître** is **reconnaître,** *to recognize.*

   Il l'a vu mais il ne l'**a** pas **reconnu.**
   Reconnaissez-vous cette photo?

Mots clés *Words often used with **savoir** and **connaître***

	Connaître		
les étrangers *(m.)*	*foreigners*	quelqu'un	*somebody*
les gens *(m.)*	*people*	le roman	*novel*
la loi	*law*		

	Savoir ou connaître		
la chanson	*song*	la règle	*rule*
le numéro de téléphone	*phone number*	la réponse	*answer*
le poème	*poem*		

4. In some cases, both **savoir** and **connaître** can be used in similar sentences, but the meaning will then be different.

> **Connaissez**-vous cette chanson?   *Do you **know** that song? (Are you familiar with . . .)*
>
> **Savez**-vous cette chanson?   *Do you **know** that song? (Do you know the words . . .)*

Attention!

1. When implying knowledge rather than the presence or absence of an impediment, use **savoir**—not **pouvoir**. **Savoir** is the French equivalent of the verb *can* in English.

> Elle **ne sait pas** chanter.   *She **can't** sing. (That is, she has a poor voice.)*
>
> Elle **ne peut pas** chanter.   *She **can't** sing. (She has a sore throat.)*
>
> Je **ne sais pas** conduire.   *I **can't** drive. (That is, I never learned.)*
>
> Je **ne peux pas** conduire.   *I **can't** drive. (My car is in the shop.)*

2. The conjunction **que** introduces a fact; the verb **savoir** may precede it, but not **connaître**.

> Ont-ils **su** que tu n'as pas 21 ans?
> Je ne **connais** pas le professeur, mais je **sais** qu'il est sérieux.

Langue

Ⓐ **Notre prof.** Complétez les phrases suivantes avec la forme correcte du verbe **savoir** ou **connaître**, selon le cas.

1. _____-tu le nom de notre prof?
2. Oui, mais je ne _____ pas où il est né.
3. Nos camarades ne _____ pas qu'il est prof.
4. Où est-ce qu'il _____ sa femme? —Je ne _____ pas!

5. Il ne _____ pas parler italien.
6. Nous _____ ses enfants.
7. Est-ce que tu _____ ses livres?
8. Non, mais je _____ qu'ils sont difficiles.

B **Robert a changé.** Traduisez les phrases suivantes.

1. I saw Robert, but I didn't recognize him.
2. He has changed, but I don't know why.
3. Can he play music with us?
4. We know he is working this afternoon.
5. Can he go out tonight?
6. He knows a good Italian restaurant near here.

Culture

C **Des livres français.** Quel livre peut-on consulter pour connaître la France?
Choisissez entre **savoir** et **connaître** dans vos réponses.

MODÈLE: *L'Argus*
           On consulte L'Argus *pour savoir combien coûte une voiture*
              d'occasion.

1. le *Larousse*   a. de bons restaurants
2. le *Guide Michelin*   b. comment conjuguer un verbe
3. le *Quid*   c. des définitions
4. *Le Bon Usage*   d. une règle de grammaire
5. le *Bescherelle*   e. des statistiques
6. *Rapports*   f. parler français

Communication

D **Connaissez-vous... ?** Circulez parmi *(among)* vos camarades de cours pour
trouver une réponse affirmative à chaque question ci-dessous.

MODÈLE: des villes   *Oui, je connais Londres.*

1. des villes loin d'ici   5. un très mauvais restaurant
2. une autre culture   6. de bons poèmes
3. des gens célèbres *(famous)*   7. un pays européen
4. de bons films   8. des professeurs ennuyeux

E **Interview.** Formez des questions avec **Sais-tu, Connais-tu** ou **Peux-tu** et une
des expressions ci-dessous. Utilisez vos questions pour interviewer un(e)
camarade de cours; ensuite *(then)*, communiquez ses réponses aux autres.

danser   parler une langue étrangère
faire la cuisine   un numéro de téléphone
réciter un poème   important
des gens en France   stationner une grosse voiture
une chanson récente   dîner chez moi ce soir
jouer du piano ici   reconnaître toutes les voitures
                                 américaines

❶ Questions personnelles. Vos connaissances.

1. Où avez-vous connu votre petit(e) ami(e)? votre camarade de chambre?
2. Connaissez-vous des poèmes français? Quels poèmes?
3. Savez-vous votre numéro de Sécurité sociale (sans vérifier)?
4. Qui n'avez-vous pas reconnu récemment? Avez-vous été embarrassé(e)?
5. Qui connaissez-vous le mieux *(the best)*?
6. Savez-vous réparer une voiture? Quels problèmes savez-vous résoudre *(solve)*?

II. *Le passé composé* (review)

You use the **passé composé** to relate events in the past.

A. The *passé composé* with *avoir*

1. In most cases, you form the **passé composé** with the present tense of **avoir** and the past participle of the verb. The past participle is based on the infinitive.

Infinitive	Past participle
chanter	chant**é**
choisir	chois**i**
répondre	répond**u**

2. You have also learned several irregular past participles.

apprendre	**appris**	pouvoir	**pu**
avoir	**eu**	prendre	**pris**
comprendre	**compris**	reconnaître	**reconnu**
connaître	**connu**	savoir	**su**
être	**été**	suivre	**suivi**
faire	**fait**	voir	**vu**
pleuvoir	**plu**	vouloir	**voulu**

3. Remember that in the **passé composé** with **avoir** construction, the past participle agrees with the direct object that *precedes* the verb.

—Quelle **robe** avez-vous chois**ie**?
—J'ai choisi une **robe** rouge.

—Vous avez lou**é** quelle voiture?
—La rouge. Nous l'avons réserv**ée** et nous l'avons pay**ée**.

B. The *passé composé* with *être*

1. As you learned in Chapter 6, a small group of verbs forms the **passé composé** with the conjugated form of **être** and the past participle. Most of these are verbs of motion.

Mots clés   *Verbs conjugated with **être** in the **passé composé***

Infinitive		Past participle
aller	*to go*	allé
arriver	*to arrive*	arrivé
descendre	*to go down*	descendu
*devenir	*to become*	devenu
entrer (dans)	*to go in*	entré
monter	*to climb, go up*	monté
mourir	*to die*	mort
naître	*to be born*	né
partir	*to leave*	parti
passer (par)	*to pass (by)*	passé
rentrer	*to return; to run into*	rentré
rester	*to stay*	resté
retourner	*to return*	retourné
*revenir	*to come back*	revenu
sortir	*to leave*	sorti
tomber	*to fall*	tombé
*venir	*to come*	venu

2. Remember that past participles of verbs conjugated with **être** agree in gender and number with their subjects.

> **Ils** sont allés au bureau de la compagnie.
> Quand **elle** est entrée, **elle** est tombée.

Attention!

1. In spoken French, you hear past participle agreement with only one verb that takes **être**. That verb is **mourir**.

> Il **est mort** (/ i lɛ mɔʀ /) en 1967, et elle **est morte**
> (/ ɛ lɛ mɔʀt /) en 1970.

2. **Passer** can mean *to spend (time), to take (an exam),* or *to pass (something).* When it takes a direct object, it forms the **passé composé** with **avoir**.

J'**ai passé** trois jours à Paris.	*I **spent** three days in Paris.*
Elle lui **a passé** le pain.	*She **passed** him / her the bread.*

When the verb indicates motion, it cannot have a direct object, so it forms the **passé composé** with **être**.

Des amis **sont passés** chez moi hier soir.	*Some friends **came by** my house last night.*
Elle **est passée par** Marseille.	*She **went by** Marseille.*

---

*Verbs you will study later in this chapter.

3. Retourner indicates motion and is therefore conjugated with **être.**

> Elle **est retournée** à la résidence.   *She **returned** to the dorm.*

The French equivalent of *to return (an object),* **rendre,** is conjugated with **avoir.**

> Elles **ont rendu** le parapluie.   *They **returned** the umbrella.*

Langue

Ⓐ **Les vacances de Marie-Claire et de sa famille.** Formez des phrases avec les mots donnés.

1. Tu / faire / voyage / agréable?
2. Oui, / nous / aller / Belgique
3. Combien de temps / vous / rester / là-bas?
4. Nous / passer / une semaine / Bruxelles
5. Quand / vous / rentrer?
6. Jeudi dernier. / Nous / passer / par / Montréal

Ⓑ **Conversation au téléphone.** Répondez aux questions suivantes en employant les mots entre parenthèses.

1. Est-ce que Pierre est à la maison?   (Non... partir avec son frère)
2. Font-ils un voyage?   (Oui,... aller à la plage)
3. Pourquoi n'ont-ils pas pris ta voiture?   (Elle ne marche pas; je... avoir... un accident)
4. Quand est-ce qu'on va voir tes parents?   (... arriver hier soir)
5. Ton père est-il vieux?   (Oui... naître en 1923)
6. Ils ont déjà vu l'appartement de Pierre?   (Oui,... passer le voir le mois dernier)

Culture

Ⓒ **Des personnages historiques célèbres.** Identifiez les personnages historiques dans la colonne de gauche en formant une phrase avec les expressions de la colonne de droite.

MODÈLE: Rimbaud / partir pour l'Afrique
Rimbaud est parti pour l'Afrique.

1. Charles de Gaulle
2. Napoléon Bonaparte
3. Antoine de Saint-Exupéry
4. Claude Monet
5. Le Baron Haussmann
6. Paul Gauguin

a. mourir dans un accident d'avion
b. partir à Tahiti pour peindre
c. redessiner Paris
d. aller vivre à Giverny
e. naître sur une île *(island)* / mourir sur une autre île
f. devenir le chef de la Résistance française pendant la Deuxième Guerre mondiale

D **Des biographies.** Séparez-vous en petits groupes et interviewez vos camarades. Utilisez les expressions suivantes.

naître en quelle année? où?
arriver quand à l'université?
rentrer avant minuit samedi?
étudier le français au lycée?
aller au cinéma récemment?
étudier ou sortir le week-end dernier?
connaître votre petit(e) ami(e) où?
???

E **Hier.** Interviewez un(e) camarade de cours au sujet de sa journée d'hier.
Utilisez les possibilités données ci-dessous ou vos propres idées. Ensuite,
présentez un résumé à la classe.

prendre le petit déjeuner à...   voir...
   heures   rentrer chez toi à... heures
partir pour...   regarder la télévision l'après-midi
prendre l'autobus / ta voiture   faire des courses à...
attendre tes amis à...   monter dans ta chambre à...
aller à ton cours de...   téléphoner à...
répondre à... questions   ???
déjeuner avec...

F **Questions personnelles.** Vos activités extraordinaires.

1. Où êtes-vous allé(e) plusieurs fois *(several times)* en vacances?
   Pourquoi?
2. Etes-vous déjà resté(e) seul(e) chez vous tout un week-end? Qu'est-ce
   que vous avez fait?
3. Etes-vous né(e) le même jour qu'une célébrité? Quelle célébrité?
4. Etes-vous descendu(e) en Amérique du Sud? Quels pays avez-vous visités?
5. Vous êtes allé(e) à New York? Par où êtes-vous passé(e)?
6. A quel monument très haut *(high)* êtes-vous monté(e)? La tour Eiffel?
   Le monument à George Washington?

III. The imperfect

You use the imperfect when you are describing conditions in the past.

A. Formation of the imperfect

1. In addition to the **passé composé,** French has another past tense—
   l'imparfait (the imperfect). Its forms are based on the first-person plural
   (**nous** form) of the present tense: you drop the **-ons** and add the following
   endings.

parler (parl~~ons~~)	finir (finiss~~ons~~)
je parl**ais**	je finiss**ais**
tu parl**ais**	tu finiss**ais**
il / elle / on parl**ait**	il / elle / on finiss**ait**
nous parl**ions**	nous finiss**ions**
vous parl**iez**	vous finiss**iez**
ils / elles parl**aient**	ils / elles finiss**aient**

partir (part~~ons~~)	descendre (descend~~ons~~)
je part**ais**	je descend**ais**
tu part**ais**	tu descend**ais**
il / elle / on part**ait**	il / elle / on descend**ait**
nous part**ions**	nous descend**ions**
vous part**iez**	vous descend**iez**
ils / elles part**aient**	ils / elles descend**aient**

2. The imperfect of **il pleut** is **il pleuvait.**

L'orthographe

1. Because four imperfect endings begin with the letter **a**, verbs ending in -**cer** and -**ger** undergo spelling changes in those forms. For infinitives ending in -**cer,** the **c** becomes **ç** before **a** or **o**. For verbs ending in -**ger,** the **g** becomes **ge** whenever the ending begins with an **a** or an **o**:

   commen**cer** → commen**çons** → commen**çais**
   man**ger**   → man**geons**   → man**geais**

2. Verbs with infinitives ending in -**ier** (**apprécier, étudier, expédier, oublier**) will have two **i**'s in the **nous** and **vous** forms.

   Nous étudi**i**ons la gestion.
   Vous appréci**i**ez les chauffeurs prudents.

B. The imperfect of *être*

Etre has an irregular stem, **ét-.**

être	
j' ét**ais**	nous ét**ions**
tu ét**ais**	vous ét**iez**
il / elle / on ét**ait**	ils / elles ét**aient**

Attention!

Because the imperfect tense is based on the first-person plural of the present tense, you must keep the pronunciation of the stem. Be careful especially with **je faisais** (/ fø zɛ /) and **tu prenais** (/ prø nɛ /). Note that the first vowel of each verb has the same sound as in **je peux** (/ pø /).

C. Differences between the imperfect and the *passé composé*

1. The difference between these two tenses depends on your perception of the action:

   Passé composé: Events: What happened or what happened next?

   Quand j'**ai vu** l'enfant, j'**ai freiné.**
   Quand elle avait onze ans, elle **est allée** au Canada.
   Il **a perdu** son permis de conduire parce qu'il **a eu** un accident.

   Imparfait: Circumstances: What were the conditions?

Il **pleuvait** quand je suis sorti.	It *was raining* when I went out.
En 1992, nous **habitions** en Belgique.	In 1992, we *lived* in Belgium.
Quand j'**étais** petit, j'**allais** à l'école en autobus.	When I *was* young, I *used to go* to school on the bus.

2. Two actions of one person going on at the same time cannot both be in the **passé composé.** The **imparfait** shows the conditions, and the **passé composé** indicates the events.

Circumstance	Event
Je **prenais** le petit déjeuner	quand j'**ai entendu** le téléphone.
Il **était** minuit	quand Christine **est rentrée.**
Il y **avait** trop de gens chez Yves	et il **est parti.**

3. Because the difference between the **imparfait** and the **passé composé** does not exist in English, English speakers must sometimes use different verbs to establish the distinction.

Il **connaissait** la femme.	He *knew the woman.*
Il **a connu** la femme.	He *met the woman.*
Elle **savait** la réponse.	She *knew the answer.*
Elle **a su** la réponse.	She *found out the answer.*
Je ne **voulais** pas le faire.	I *didn't want* to do it.
Je n'**ai** pas **voulu** le faire.	I *refused* to do it.

Langue

Ⓐ **Mes habitudes.** Mettez le paragraphe suivant à l'imparfait. Commencez avec **L'année dernière,...**

Le dimanche, nous faisons la grasse matinée. Je prends mon petit déjeuner très tard et je sors. Je fais une promenade et je rentre à la maison.

L'après-midi, je regarde la télé ou j'écoute des disques. Ma femme téléphone à ses parents et elle leur parle de nos enfants. Nous ne travaillons
pas beaucoup le dimanche!

B **Monique et ses copines rentrent.** Dans le paragraphe suivant, mettez les
verbes au passé composé ou à l'imparfait, selon le cas. Faites les changements nécessaires.

Le week-end dernier, Monique et nous _____ (visiter) la ville où nous
_____ (habiter) quand nous _____ (avoir) dix ans. Nous _____
(chercher) nos anciennes maisons et nous _____ (voir) beaucoup de vieux
amis aussi. Nous _____ (avoir) froid quand nous _____ (retourner) à
Montfort et nous _____ (prendre) une boisson chaude. Quand Monique
_____ (partir), nous _____ (être) malheureuses. Je lui _____ (téléphoner) après qu'elle _____ (arriver) chez elle. Quand elle _____
(entendre) le téléphone, elle _____ (savoir) que c' _____ (être) moi.
Elle _____ (vouloir) parler longtemps, mais moi, j' _____ (avoir) des
courses à faire.

C **A la gare.** Mettez les verbes du paragraphe suivant au passé composé ou à
l'imparfait, selon le cas.

Samedi dernier, il _____ (pleuvoir) et il _____ (faire) du brouillard. Nous
_____ (arriver) à la gare à sept heures. Nous _____ (être) en avance car
le train pour Paris _____ (aller) partir à huit heures. Mes parents _____
(avoir) froid et ils _____ (ne... pas vouloir) rester. Nous _____ (aller) au
restaurant et nous _____ (prendre) un café bien chaud. A huit heures
moins cinq, le train _____ (entrer) en gare et il y _____ (avoir) beaucoup
de gens. Nous _____ (monter) et nous _____ (trouver) trois places ensemble. Le train _____ (partir). Nous _____ (être) contents de rentrer.

Culture

D **La France d'autrefois** *(of the past).* Qu'est-ce qui a changé en France et
qu'est-ce qui n'a pas changé?

MODÈLE: parler deux langues
*On ne parlait pas deux langues, mais beaucoup de Français
parlent deux langues maintenant.*

1. manger beaucoup à midi
2. regarder peu la télé
3. avoir des colonies en
   Afrique
4. divorcer peu
5. avoir un mauvais système
   téléphonique
6. utiliser peu le téléphone
7. avoir beaucoup d'enfants
8. consommer du coca

Communication

E **Ma jeunesse.** Quand vous étiez petit(e), que faisiez-vous pour embêter
(annoy) les gens? Utilisez les suggestions données ou vos propres idées.

manger du chewing gum
rentrer après le dîner
désobéir
étudier peu

porter des vêtements bizarres
manger des insectes
écouter un transistor
???

F **Quelles étaient les circonstances?** Décrivez le temps, les personnes, les émotions, les lieux, etc., pour les activités suivantes.

1. Votre plus long voyage en voiture
2. Un accident que vous avez eu
3. Un voyage en avion
4. La première fois que vous êtes sorti(e) avec un garçon / une fille
5. Le moment le plus embarrassant de votre vie *(life)*
6. Des vacances que vous n'allez jamais oublier

G **Questions personnelles.** Votre passé.

1. Quand vous étiez petit(e), qu'est-ce que vous aimiez faire? Est-ce que vous étiez bon(ne) élève?
2. Qui admiriez-vous?
3. Quand vous alliez au lycée, où habitiez-vous?
4. Que faisiez-vous que *(that)* vous ne faites pas maintenant?
5. Quel âge aviez-vous quand vous êtes entré(e) à l'université?
6. Qui voyiez-vous souvent l'année dernière que *(whom)* vous ne voyez pas maintenant?

IV. *Venir* / Verbs conjugated like *venir* / *Venir de* + infinitive

You use the verb **venir** to express the idea of coming or to express a recent action.

A. *Venir*

venir *(to come)*	
Présent: je **viens**	nous **venons**
tu **viens**	vous **venez**
il / elle / on **vient**	ils / elles **viennent**
Passé composé: il **est venu**	

Tu **viens** chez nous ce soir?   Je **suis venu** à huit heures.
Ils vont **venir** demain.   Elle **venait** toujours avec une amie.

B. Verbs conjugated like *venir*

1. A number of verbs are conjugated like **venir** in the present tense.

appartenir à *to belong to*	Ce transistor ne lui **appartient** pas.
contenir *to contain*	Mon *Guide Michelin* **contient** les renseignements nécessaires.
devenir *to become*	Tu **deviens** impossible!
obtenir *to obtain*	Elle **obtient** son permis.
retenir *to hold back, to remember*	Je ne **retiens** pas les dates.

revenir *to come back*	Vous **revenez** le week-end prochain?
tenir *to hold, to keep*	Tu **tiens** l'enfant?
tenir à + *noun* *to be fond of*	Ils **tiennent** à leur vieille voiture.
tenir à + *verb* *to be anxious to,* *to insist on*	Nous **tenons** à partir tout de suite.
tenir de *to take after*	Elle **tient** de son père.

2. Like **venir, devenir** and **revenir** use **être** in the **passé composé.** All other verbs conjugated like **venir** use **avoir** in the **passé composé.**

> Il **est devenu** méchant.
> Elles **sont revenues** ensemble.

> Elle **a tenu** à réparer sa voiture elle-même.
> Il n'**a** pas **obtenu** son permis de conduire.

Attention! ───────────

1. **Devenir** is often used in the expression **Qu'est-ce que tu deviens?**, meaning *What are you up to?* In the **passé composé, Qu'est-ce qu'il est devenu?** means *Whatever became of him?* Like **être, devenir** does not take an article with professions that are not modified by adjectives.

   > Elle est devenue **professeur.**   *She became a **teacher.***

2. The verb **tenir** is used in the expressions **Tenez!** and **Tiens!**, which mean *Say! Here!*

   > **Tenez!** Voilà vos papiers.
   > **Tiens!** Je n'ai pas mon permis de conduire!

C. *Venir de* + infinitive

The construction **venir de** + *infinitive* represents the **passé immédiat** and is used in two tenses: the present and the imperfect.

1. In the present tense, a conjugated form of **venir de** + *infinitive* indicates a recently completed action and is equivalent to the English *have just* + *past participle.*

Je **viens** d'avoir un accident.	*I've **just had** an accident.*
Ils **viennent** d'arriver à l'aéroport.	*They've **just arrived** at the airport.*

2. In the imperfect tense, a conjugated form of **venir de** + *infinitive* indicates an action that was completed just before another past action, which is expressed in the **passé composé.** In this case, the French **venir de** + *infinitive* is equivalent to the English *had just* + *past participle.*

Il **venait** d'arriver quand je suis rentré.	*He **had just** arrived when I got home.*
Nous **venions** d'ouvrir la porte quand le téléphone a sonné.	*We **had just** opened the door when the telephone rang.*

Langue

A **Promenade en auto.** Faites des phrases complètes avec les mots suivants.

1. Ton / voiture / contenir / combien / personnes?
2. Six, / si / on / ne... pas / tenir / beaucoup de place
3. Marc / venir / arriver / et nous / tenir / l'emprunter!
4. Marc, / qu'est-ce que / tu / devenir?
5. Je / venir / obtenir / permis de conduire!
6. Alors, / venir / avec nous / et prendre / volant!

B **Chez moi.** On téléphone pour parler avec les membres de votre famille. Mettez les phrases suivantes au passé immédiat en employant **venir de** au présent ou à l'imparfait, selon le cas.

1. Mon père part.
2. Ma sœur descend de sa chambre.
3. Robert finissait son dîner quand ma mère est arrivée.
4. Ma mère monte.
5. Elle finit son fromage.
6. Je faisais la vaisselle quand le téléphone a sonné.

Culture

C **Les anciennes colonies.** A quel pays européen est-ce que les pays africains suivants appartenaient avant leur indépendance?

MODÈLE: Le Cameroun appartenait à la France et à la Grande-Bretagne.

1. la République du Congo a. la Hollande
2. l'Algérie b. le Portugal
3. le Mozambique c. l'Italie
4. le Nigeria d. la Belgique
5. l'Ethiopie e. la Grande-Bretagne
6. l'Afrique du Sud f. la France

Communication

D **Un objet précieux.** A quoi tenez-vous? Quel objet aimez-vous beaucoup? Décrivez cet objet et expliquez pourquoi vous l'aimez beaucoup.

un vêtement (de vieilles   des livres anciens
  chaussures?)   un cadeau d'un(e) petit(e) ami(e)
une belle photo (de votre   un poème
  famille?)   ???

E **Mes activités récentes.** Séparez-vous en petits groupes et répondez à la question «Qu'est-ce que vous avez fait récemment?» Employez **venir de** et utilisez les suggestions données ou vos propres idées.

prendre le petit déjeuner   parler avec un(e) camarade
obtenir une bonne note en...   arriver sur le campus
réussir à un examen de...   sortir de mon cours de...
rentrer de...   avoir un accident
finir un coca   ???

F **Questions personnelles.** Interviewez un(e) camarade de cours et présentez un résumé de ses réponses à la classe.

1. Vous et vos amis, vous allez partir ce week-end? Quand revenez-vous?
2. Avez-vous obtenu une bonne note? Quand? Dans quelle matière?
3. Venez-vous toujours en cours? Pourquoi pas?
4. A quelles organisations appartenez-vous?
5. De qui tenez-vous?
6. Que voulez-vous devenir?

communiquons

Connaître le code de la route

In order to drive in France, you must be eighteen years old and take private lessons from an **auto-école.** The French driver's license is very difficult to obtain, but, once you have it, you never need to renew it. An American wishing to drive

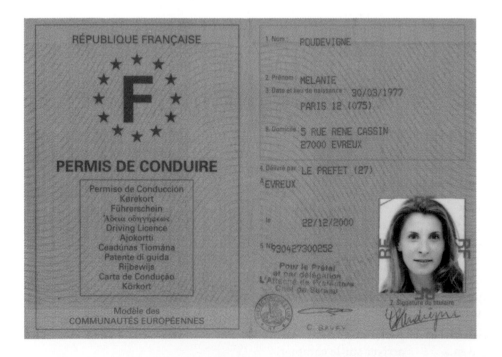

in France would do well to obtain an international driver's license before going and to become familiar with French traffic regulations (**le code de la route**).

The basic driving rules in France are the same as in North America for the most part, but there are some differences. For example, the right of way is usually given to the vehicle on the right unless otherwise indicated. In addition, to reduce noise in cities, it is forbidden to honk. Instead, drivers signal with high beams (**faire un appel de phares**) to warn others. To reduce casualties, the use of seat belts is mandatory and children under twelve are forbidden from riding in the front seat. Americans generally find French drivers very aggressive, so it is wise to be cautious when driving in France.

A campaign to reduce drunken driving involves selling individual blood-alcohol tests, called **un éthylotest**, in drugstores and cafés for use on a voluntary basis.

Expressions

▶ **On conduit sa voiture.**

Ce chauffeur fait du 100 kilomètres à l'heure.	*That driver is going 62 miles per hour.*
Ce chauffard a brûlé le feu.	*That reckless driver ran the red light.*
Ne doublez pas ici!	*Don't pass here!*
Cette auto a beaucoup de passagers (-ères) / occupants (-es).	*This car has a lot of passengers.*
J'ai pris le volant.	*I got behind the wheel.*

▶ **On entretient** *(maintains)* **sa voiture.**

J'ai besoin de prendre de l'essence / de l'huile.	*I need to get some gas / oil.*
Faites le plein, s'il vous plaît.	*Fill it up, please.*
Le garagiste vérifie les pneus / l'huile.	*The mechanic is checking the tires / the oil.*
Le mécanicien travaille à la station-service.	*The mechanic works at the gas station.*

Interaction

M. Lafont fait le plein.

M. LAFONT: Le plein de super°, s'il vous plaît. — *premium*

LA POMPISTE°: D'accord. Je vérifie l'huile? — *attendant*

M. LAFONT: Oui, et le pneu arrière droit°. — **arrière...** *right rear*

LA POMPISTE: Vous allez loin?

M. LAFONT: Oui, nous allons à Aix. C'est à combien d'ici?

LA POMPISTE: Eh bien, par l'autoroute, il faut compter° trois heures. — *plan on*

Une station-service

Activités

A En France, on utilise **les panneaux routiers** *(road signs)* internationaux.
Identifiez les panneaux correspondant aux définitions suivantes.

1. stop
2. stationnement interdit *(forbidden)*
3. chaussée glissante *(slippery)*
4. défense de *(forbidden)* tourner à droite
5. sens *(way)* unique
6. défense de doubler
7. vitesse *(speed)* limitée à cent kilomètres
8. sens interdit

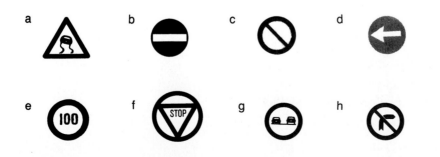

B Répondez aux questions suivantes.

1. En général, roulez-vous vite? Du combien faites-vous sur l'autoroute *(interstate)*? En ville?
2. Brûlez-vous souvent les feux? Pourquoi?
3. Etes-vous un chauffard? A quelles lois désobéissez-vous souvent?
4. Aimez-vous mieux prendre le volant ou être passager (-ère)? Pourquoi?
5. Avez-vous déjà fait du stop *(hitch-hike)*? Pour aller où? Est-ce une bonne idée?
6. Où stationnez-vous à l'université? C'est près de votre salle de cours?
7. Etes-vous tombé(e) en panne? Dans quelles circonstances?
8. Quelle station-service fréquentez-vous? Pourquoi? Connaissez-vous un(e) bon(ne) mécanicien(ne)?
9. Que faites-vous à votre voiture avant de partir en vacances? Faites une liste.

consommation-consumption-consumo	
5 l/100 km	= 56,5 mi/gal
10 l/100 km	= 28,2 mi/gal
15 l/100 km	= 18,8 mi/gal
20 l/100 km	= 14,1 mi/gal
20 mi/gal	= 14,1 l/100 km
30 mi/gal	= 9,4 l/100 km
40 mi/gal	= 7,1 l/100 km
50 mi/gal	= 5,6 l/100 km

lecture culturelle

Avant la lecture

It is difficult to imagine our lives without the automobile. Over the years, manufacturers have produced cars with radios, tape players, CD players, seat belts, air bags, and improved structural safety features designed to protect the occupants of the car in the event of an accident. One of the most recent technological breakthroughs in the French auto and telecommunications industries is the development of Visionaute, which transmits traffic information in real time. Customers can purchase the system as a feature already integrated into the dashboard of a vehicle, or they can buy the system separately and install it in their vehicle or connect it to a cell phone.

This technology gives drivers a range of helpful information before they set off for their destinations, such as the best routes to take, the amount of travel time they will need, and current road conditions. Once drivers are on the road, Visionaute also provides updates regarding problems due to bottlenecks, road repairs, road closures, and accidents. Other services continue to be added: a programmable feature now enables drivers to customize up to twenty different itineraries. Visionaute covers all of France, and the service has now been extended to Germany and England, as well.

X-TYPE 2 litres V6 10 cv.

X-TYPE, une gamme à partir de 29 490 €*

X-TYPE   L'art de la performance ▪ **JAGUAR**

Modèle présenté : X-TYPE 2L-001, option peinture métallisée, prix : **30 120 €**. *Prix TTC recommandés constructeur au 1/02/02.

Activités

A If you drive, how much time do you spend in your car each week?

B If you were to develop a system like Visionaute, what services would you provide to drivers?

C Who might benefit most from Visionaute technology (taxi drivers, commercial drivers, or others)? How could you benefit?

D Are you familiar with the Global Positioning System (GPS)? What do you know about it? What fields use GPS technology?

E What words come to mind when you think of driving, and particularly of getting from point A to point B safely and quickly? Try to predict what vocabulary you might find in the following article on Visionaute. Then match those phrases up with the terms listed below.

1. embouteillages *(m. pl.)*; bouchons *(m. pl.)*	a. road closures
2. trajet *(m.)*	b. fuel
3. cartes *(f. pl.)*	c. to avoid
4. ralentissements *(m. pl.)*	d. exhaust fumes
5. travaux *(m. pl.)*	e. trip
6. fermetures *(f. pl.)*	f. slowdowns
7. se rendre à	g. road repairs
8. carburant *(m.)*	h. road maps
9. émissions polluantes *(f. pl.)*	i. traffic jams
10. éviter	j. to go to

La voiture et les avances technologiques

80 millions. C'est le nombre d'heures perdues chaque année dans les embouteillages en Ile-de-France°, région où se produisent près de 80% des bouchons° du pays. Les heureux possesseurs d'un terminal TM 2000 de Sagem n'ont plus ce genre de souci°. Ils disposent° en effet d'un accès, par abonnement°, au Visionaute de Médiamobile (groupe France Télécom), véritable système anti-bouchons permettant de remédier aux aléas° de la circulation automobile en toutes circonstances. L'écran° monochrome affiche° des cartes à différentes échelles°, qui indiquent en permanence° et en temps réel l'état° précis de la circulation: ralentissements, bouchons, incidents, accidents, travaux, fermetures… et les moyens de les éviter.

Une autre fonction permet de connaître le temps de parcours° du trajet demandé, en tenant compte° de l'état de la circulation, et propose trois itinéraires (le plus rapide, le plus direct, et personnalisé en fonction d'étapes prédéfinies) pour se rendre d'un point à un autre. La Renault Mégane Scénic RDX équipée d'un terminal Carminat dispose en outre° d'un écran couleur à cristaux liquides, où s'affiche en permanence la position exacte de la voiture, localisée par satellite (GPS). Carminat propose aussi des informations complémentaires sur l'encombrement° des parkings en ville, l'emplacement° des stations-service ou des garages Renault, etc.

Premier objectif avoué° du Visionaute: faire gagner jusqu'à 40% de temps par trajet°, notamment° aux professionnels de la route— commerciaux, cadres dirigeants, taxis, chauffeurs routiers—premiers touchés par les aléas de la circulation. «Le temps gagné, explique Loïc Vallese, directeur des ventes sur la région parisienne chez Fuji, me permet de travailler l'équivalent de deux jours supplémentaires par mois.»

L'impact est encore plus important quand le système est décliné sur une flotte° de plusieurs véhicules. La baisse° de la consommation de carburant et des émissions polluantes est également non négligeable.

region of France that includes Paris and the surrounding area / bottlenecks

worry / have (at their disposal) / subscription

hazards, uncertainties
screen / shows
scales, sizes / constantly
state, condition

traveling time
en tenant… *taking into account*

in addition

encombrement… *congestion, obstruction; here, (lack of) availability / location*
declared
faire gagner… *to save… in travel time / notably*

décliné sur… *put into effect for a fleet / decrease*

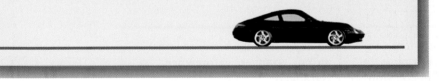

E. Thévenon «Visionaute, un système anti-embouteillages unique en Europe», *Journal Français.*

Après la lecture

Questions sur le texte

1. Selon l'article, combien de temps est gaspillé *(wasted)* à cause des embouteillages?
2. Selon l'article, comment est-ce qu'on peut avoir accès au Visionaute de Médiamobile?
3. Qu'est-ce qu'on peut voir sur l'écran?
4. Quels sont les trois types d'itinéraires qu'on peut obtenir?
5. Quels services complémentaires sont offerts par le terminal Carminat?
6. Quel est un des objectifs principaux de Visionaute?
7. Citez un avantage environnemental de Visionaute.

Activités

Ⓐ Inventez une histoire où le personnage principal se sert de la technologie de Visionaute. Utilisez le passé composé et l'imparfait. (Ecrivez 1–2 pages, à double interligne.)

Ⓑ Que faites-vous quand vous êtes dans un bouchon? Quelles recommandations avez-vous pour les gens impatients?

Ⓒ Imaginez les voitures de l'an 2010. Comment est-ce qu'elles vont être différentes?

Ⓓ Débats en classe

1. La voiture: un luxe ou une nécessité?
2. Les avantages et inconvénients des voitures électriques.

vocabulaire

Noms / Pronoms

un accident	accident	un embouteillage	traffic jam
un aéroport	airport	un/une étranger/	foreigner
assurance *(f.)* tous	full collision	étrangère	
risques	insurance	frais *(m.)*	expenses
une carte de crédit	credit card	le frein	brake
la ceinture de sécurité	seat belt	un gendarme	policeman
une chanson	song	gens *(m.)*	people
un chauffeur	driver	une habitude	habit
la circulation	traffic	un kilomètre	kilometer
le coffre	trunk	le klaxon	horn
une compagnie	rental agency	une location	rental
de location		une loi	law

un numéro de téléphone	phone number	une réponse	answer
papiers (d'identité) *(m.)*	I.D.	un roman	novel
le pare-brise	windshield	le siège arrière	back seat
un permis de conduire	driver's license	le siège avant	front seat
le phare	headlight	la TVA	VAT (value-added tax)
places *(f.)*	seats		
un pneu	tire	vacances (grandes) *(f.)*	summer vacation
un poème	poem		
une portière	door (car)	une voiture d'occasion	used car
quelqu'un *(m.)*	someone		
une règle	rule	une voiture neuve	new car

Verbes

appartenir à	to belong to	réserver	to reserve
avoir besoin de	to need	retenir	to hold back / to remember
conduire	to drive		
connaître	to know	retourner	to return
contenir	to contain	revenir	to come back
démarrer	to start	rouler à... km à l'heure	to go . . . miles per hour
devenir	to become		
freiner	to brake	savoir	to know
louer	to rent	signer	to sign
mourir	to die	stationner	to park
obtenir	to obtain	tenir	to hold
passer par	to pass by	tenir à	to be fond of
payer	to pay	tenir de	to take after
reconnaître	to recognize	tomber	to fall
régler	to pay	venir	to come
réparer	to repair	venir de	to have just

Adjectifs / Adverbes

automatique	automatic	neuf	new
étranger	foreign	obligatoire	compulsory
européen	European	presque	almost
indispensable	indispensable	quelqu'un	somebody

Expressions

d'accord	all right
d'occasion	used
en plus	in addition
priorité à droite	right of way on the right
tomber en panne	to break down

Journalistes place de
l'Hôtel de ville

La télé

OBJECTIVES

Language	Culture	Communication
■ Vocabulary for social problems, happiness, television	■ Opinion polls	■ Discussing social issues
■ The vowel sounds / o / and / ɔ /	■ Preoccupations of society	■ Expressing emotion, wishes, doubt, and judgment
■ Direct and indirect object pronouns (first and second persons)	■ French television	■ Expressing opinions and uncertainty
■ The subjunctive of regular verbs and of **avoir** and **être**		
■ Uses of the subjunctive		

commençons

Une interview avec Simone Trudeau

Simone Trudeau est journaliste à TF1. Elle prépare un reportage sur les opinions des Français sur les grands problèmes de la vie contemporaine dans le monde. Elle discute avec Claude, 25 ans, cadre dans un grand magasin parisien, et avec Marc, 20 ans, étudiant en sciences politiques.

SIMONE: Qu'est-ce qui vous préoccupe le plus?

CLAUDE: Je suis contente que vous nous posiez cette question, mais j'ai peur qu'il ne soit pas facile de répondre. Il semble que la qualité de la vie soit le plus important.

MARC: Absolument! Selon moi, les gens ont peur qu'il y ait un désastre écologique et ils ne pensent pas qu'on réussisse à rendre la société plus juste.

SIMONE: Je suis surprise que vous ne me parliez pas de l'importance de l'argent et du succès!

CLAUDE: Tous les sondages d'opinion que je consulte montrent que la santé et le bonheur viennent avant le compte en banque et le travail pour un grand nombre de Français.

SIMONE: Je vous remercie pour votre franchise. N'oubliez pas de regarder le Journal de 20 heures demain soir.

Etudions le dialogue

1. Sur quoi est-ce que Simone Trudeau fait un reportage?
2. Qui sont Claude et Marc?
3. Qu'est-ce qui préoccupe Claude?
4. Selon Marc, de quoi les gens ont-ils peur?
5. Pourquoi est-ce que Simone est surprise?
6. Qu'est-ce qui est plus important que l'argent et le succès pour Claude?

Mots clés

une interview	*interview*	selon	*according to*
un reportage	*feature story*	il y ait (avoir)	*there might be*
opinions *(f.)*	*opinions*	un désastre	*disaster*
la vie	*life*	écologique	*ecological*
contemporain(e)	*contemporary*	rendre la société	*make society more*
le monde	*world*	plus juste	*just*
discute (discuter)	*is discussing*	surprise	*surprised*
un cadre	*middle-level*	importance *(f.)*	*importance*
	manager	un succès	*success*
un grand magasin	*department store*	sondages *(m.)*	*opinion polls*
préoccupe	*preoccupies*	d'opinion	
(préoccuper)		consulte (consulter)	*consult*
le plus	*the most*	la santé	*health*
j'ai peur que	*I'm afraid that*	le bonheur	*happiness*
(avoir peur)		un compte en banque	*bank account*
soit (être)	*is*	le travail	*work*
Il semble	*It seems*	un nombre	*number*
qualité *(f.)*	*quality*	remercie (remercier)	*thank*
important	*important*	la franchise	*candor*
absolument	*absolutely*	le Journal	*news*

Faisons connaissance

WWW

French people are avid readers of public opinion polls. These appear regularly in French newspapers and magazines and vary in content from the serious (national politics) to the frivolous (reactions to an American soap opera in *Paris-Match*). The French take polls so seriously that it is forbidden to publish the results of political polls immediately before an election.

On French television, many programs are devoted to round tables (**des tables rondes**) where journalists and personalities discuss the latest contemporary issues. During an election year, it is not unusual for all the channels to present such round tables several times a week. Amazingly, the viewers rarely seem to object. ▶

Marc's fears reflect the opinions of a majority of his fellow citizens. People rank the following problems as sources of worry:

la sécurité, la délinquance
le chômage *unemployment*
la pollution
le sida *AIDS*
la drogue *drugs*

Enrichissons notre vocabulaire

Le bonheur *(Happiness)*

—Qu'est-ce qu'**il te faut** pour être **heureux**?
*What do **you need** in order to be happy?*

—**Il me faut** de l'argent; je suis **matérialiste.**
*I **need** money; I'm **materialistic.***

—Nous avons besoin de **justice** *(f.)* et de **paix** *(f.).*
*We need **justice** and **peace.***

—Qu'est-ce que le bonheur pour vous?
What is happiness for you?

—**L'amour** *(m.)* de ma famille.
***Love** of my family.*

—La sécurité d'un **emploi.**
***Job** security.*

—**L'égalité** *(f.)* dans la société.
***Equality** in society.*

—Des vacances à la **montagne.**
*A vacation in the **mountains.***

Les grands problèmes sociaux *(Major social problems)*

—Qu'est-ce qui vous **préoccupe**?
*What **worries** you?*

—**La criminalité** me **fait peur.**
***Crime** scares me.*

—Le **trafic** des drogues.
*Drug **trafficking.***

—La **politique.**
Politics.

—La **possibilité** d'une **guerre nucléaire.**
*The **possibility** of **nuclear war.***

—**L'inflation** *(f.).*
Inflation.

—Les **sans-logis** *(m.)* / sans-abri *(m.)* / SDF (sans domicile fixe) *(m.).*
*The **homeless.***

—Les **sans-papiers** *(m.).*
Undocumented aliens.

Les petits inconvénients *(Annoyances)*

—Qu'est-ce qui t'**embête** le plus?
*What **annoys** you the most?*

—Beaucoup de **choses** *(f.)*!
*Many **things**!*

—Je ne peux pas **supporter** mes **voisins** *(m.).* Ils **font du bruit.**
*I can't **stand my neighbors.** They **make noise.***

—**L'incertitude** *(f.)* de l'**avenir** *(m.).*
*The **uncertainty** of the **future.***

—Mes parents n'**arrêtent** pas de me donner des **conseils** *(m.).*
*My parents don't **stop** giving me **advice.***

La télé *(TV)*

les actualités *(f.)*	*news*	un feuilleton	*series*
la chaîne	*channel*	un jeu télévisé	*game show*
la chaîne câblée /	*cable channel*	le programme	*schedule*
le câble		la publicité	*commercials*
un dessin animé	*cartoon*	une série	*series*
les émissions *(f.)*	*shows*		
une émission de	*variety show*		
variétés			

Prononciation   The vowel sounds / o / and / ɔ /

A. The vowel sounds / o / and / ɔ / are pronounced with the tongue back and the lips very rounded. As with the sounds / e / and / ɛ /, the tongue is neither high nor low.

Repeat the following English and French word pairs after your teacher.

English	French	English	French
bow	beau	dough	dos
foe	faux	oh	eau

B. The / ɔ / sound is the same as the / o / sound, except that in the former, the mouth is held more open. You use the / o / sound when the word ends in a vowel sound. The / ɔ / sound is used when a pronounced consonant follows it.

Repeat the following pairs of words after your teacher.

/ o /	/ ɔ /	/ o /	/ ɔ /
beau	bonne	tôt	tort
faux	fort	trop	drogues
nos	notre	pot	poche

C. The spellings **au** and **ô** are almost always pronounced / o /, not / ɔ /. If the consonant that follows is a / z / sound, you also use / o /.

Repeat the following pairs of words after your teacher.

/ ɔ /	/ o /	/ ɔ /	/ o /
notre	autre	école	Côte d'Azur
botte	Claude	note	chose
pomme	pauvre	comme	cause

Exercice

Read the following sentences aloud, paying particular attention to the open / ɔ / sound and the closed / o / sound.

1. Robert veut un beau chapeau.
2. Donne-moi le téléphone!
3. A l'automne, nous faisons de bonnes promenades.
4. Paulette propose des choses idiotes.
5. Le chômage et la drogue me préoccupent.
6. Et comme fromage? —Du roquefort!

grammaire

I. Direct and indirect object pronouns: First and second persons

You use these pronouns to refer to yourself or to the person or people to whom or about whom you are speaking.

A. Direct and indirect object pronouns: First and second persons

	singular	plural
1st person	me	nous
2nd person	te	vous

You studied third-person direct object pronouns (**le, la, l'**, and **les**) in Chapter 8 and indirect object pronouns (**lui** and **leur**) in Chapter 9. In contrast, first- and second-person object pronouns do not vary in form from direct to indirect objects. Also note that **me** and **te** become **m'** and **t'** before a vowel.

Pronouns as direct objects

Tu **m'**as vu à la télévision?
Est-ce que ces problèmes **te** préoccupent beaucoup?
On ne **nous** consulte jamais quand on fait un sondage d'opinion.
Qu'est-ce qui **vous** embête le plus?

Pronouns as indirect objects

Vous **me** parlez de quelque chose d'important.
Le journaliste **t'**a posé des questions?
Tu **nous** fais peur.
Elle **vous** donne ses opinions?

B. Placement of pronouns

First- and second-person object pronouns are placed in the same position as third-person object pronouns:

1. directly before the conjugated verb in the present, imperfect, and **passé composé** tenses:

   Vous **me** posez cette question?
   Marc **me** parlait quand Sylvie **nous** a vus.

2. in front of the infinitive when there is a helping verb:

   Elle ne veut pas **vous** embêter mais est-ce qu'elle peut **vous** parler maintenant?
   Cette réponse va **vous** rendre très heureux.

3. in front of the verb in the negative imperative:

   Ne **me** parlez pas de l'importance de l'argent!
   Ne **nous** fais pas peur!

4. after the verb in the affirmative imperative and linked to the verb with a hyphen:

   Posez-**nous** des questions!

The pronoun **me** becomes **moi** in the affirmative imperative.

> Ne **me** donnez pas votre opinion → Donnez-**moi** votre opinion!
> Ne **me** laissez pas seul. → Laissez-**moi** seul.

Attention!

The distinction between direct and indirect object pronouns with **me, te, nous,** and **vous** is important only when determining past participle agreement in the **passé composé.** Only preceding *direct* object pronouns agree when the auxiliary verb is **avoir.**

Direct objects	**Indirect objects**
Elle **nous** a **regardés.**	On **vous** a **téléphoné?**
Je **vous** ai **vus** au cinéma.	Elle ne **nous** a pas **obéi.**

Langue

A **La jalousie.** Pierre a vu sa petite amie Julie en ville et il est très jaloux *(jealous).* Jouez le rôle de Julie et répondez aux questions de Pierre en employant les mots entre parenthèses.

1. Je t'ai vue au café avec Robert? (Oui, tu...)
2. Il t'a commandé une boisson? (Oui,... coca.)
3. Est-ce que vous m'avez vu? (Non, nous...)
4. Est-ce qu'il t'a parlé longtemps? (Oui,...)
5. Est-ce qu'il va te téléphoner? (Non,...)
6. Est-ce qu'il t'a donné son numéro de téléphone? (Non,...)
7. Est-ce que vous allez m'inviter demain? (Non,...)
8. Est-ce que tu m'aimes? (Non,... ne... pas pouvoir supporter.)

B **Au téléphone.** Votre sœur parle au téléphone. Imaginez des questions pour les réponses suivantes.

MODÈLE: Oui, il m'aime.
           Est-ce que Paul t'aime?

1. Oui, elle m'a parlé hier soir.
2. Oui, elles vont nous inviter.
3. Non, ils ne peuvent pas te comprendre.
4. Oui, je t'ai présenté mon nouveau petit ami.
5. Non, nous ne vous avons pas oubliées.
6. Oui, apporte-moi tes photos.

Culture

C **En famille.** Indiquez des différences culturelles entre votre famille américaine (vos parents et vous) et les familles françaises (les parents français et leurs enfants) en formant des phrases avec les mots donnés. Attention! Il y a aussi des similarités!

MODÈLE: souhaiter *(wish)* une bonne fête *(saint's day)*
           Mes parents ne m'ont jamais souhaité une bonne fête.
           Les parents français leur souhaitent une bonne fête tous les ans.

1. donner de l'argent
2. punir souvent
3. téléphoner tous les jours
4. voir tous les dimanches
5. servir du vin quand on était jeune(s)
6. embrasser tous les soirs avant de dormir

Communication

D **Une rencontre.** Vous rencontrez un garçon / une fille charmant(e) dans une boîte. Imaginez la conversation. Utilisez les suggestions données ou vos propres idées.

Est-ce que je vous ai déjà rencontré(e)?
Comment vous appelez-vous?
Vous venez souvent ici?
Je peux vous offrir une boisson?
Tu me donnes ton numéro de téléphone?
Tu veux me laisser ton adresse?
Je peux passer te voir?
Je peux t'embrasser?

E **Votre journée d'hier.** Vous êtes condamné(e) *(condemned)* et vous allez mourir demain matin. Qu'est-ce que vous demandez à la dernière minute?

MODÈLE: donner du champagne *Donnez-moi du champagne.*
laisser seul *Ne me laissez pas seul.*

servir un bon dîner   parler
donner des cigarettes   faire un gâteau
prêter une Bible   montrer un film de...
apporter du vin   oublier
laisser partir   faire mal
écouter: «Je suis innocent!» donner la clé

F **Questions personnelles.** La famille et les amis.

1. Qu'est-ce que vos amis vous ont donné comme cadeaux l'année dernière?
2. Qui vous téléphone souvent?
3. Qui est passé vous voir récemment?
4. Qui est-ce qui vous fait les repas?
5. Qu'est-ce qui vous rend heureux (-euse)? furieux (-euse)?
6. Qui est-ce qui ne peut pas vous supporter?

II. The subjunctive of regular verbs and of *avoir* and *être*

Until now, you have been using the indicative mood (**le présent, l'imparfait,** and **le passé composé**) to express facts and the imperative mood to express commands and requests. You use the subjunctive mood to express feelings, such as emotion, wishes, doubt, and judgment.

A. Introduction

Even though the subjunctive is used more frequently in French, it also exists in English:

I wish *that* he *were* home now.

As in English, the subjunctive in French is used mostly in subordinate clauses following a main clause. Both clauses are linked by **que** (that).

Emotion: Je suis contente **que** vous nous **posiez** cette question.
Wishing: Je voudrais **que** vous me **parliez** de cela.
Doubt: Les gens ne pensent pas **qu'on rende** la société plus juste.
Judgment: Il semble **que** la qualité de la vie vous **préoccupe** le plus.

B. Forms of the present subjunctive

1. The subjunctive endings are the same for the four groups of regular verbs you know. They are added to the stem of the third-person plural (**ils / elles** form) of the present indicative.

chanter (chant~~ent~~)	partir (part~~ent~~)
que je **chante**	que je **parte**
que tu **chantes**	que tu **partes**
qu'il / elle / on **chante**	qu'il / elle / on **parte**
que nous **chantions**	que nous **partions**
que vous **chantiez**	que vous **partiez**
qu'ils / elles **chantent**	qu'ils / elles **partent**

finir (finiss~~ent~~)	vendre (vend~~ent~~)
que je **finisse**	que je **vende**
que tu **finisses**	que tu **vendes**
qu'il / elle / on **finisse**	qu'il / elle / on **vende**
que nous **finissions**	que nous **vendions**
que vous **finissiez**	que vous **vendiez**
qu'ils / elles **finissent**	qu'ils / elles **vendent**

Attention!

Adding a written -**e** to the stem of -**ir** and -**re** verbs causes the final consonant to be pronounced:

dormir	→	dorm-	→	qu'il **dorme**
sortir	→	sort-	→	que tu **sortes**
attendre	→	attend-	→	qu'on **attende**
descendre	→	descend-	→	que tu **descendes**

2. Even though they are irregular in the present indicative, **connaître** and **suivre** are regular in the present subjunctive.

connaître → **connaiss-** → que je **connaisse**
suivre → **suiv-** → que tu **suives**

C. The subjunctive of *avoir* and *être*

Two irregular verbs in the subjunctive are **avoir** and **être**. You will learn other irregular verbs in the subjunctive in Chapter 12.

avoir	être
que j' **aie**	que je **sois**
que tu **aies**	que tu **sois**
qu'il / elle / on **ait**	qu'il / elle / on **soit**
que nous **ayons**	que nous **soyons**
que vous **ayez**	que vous **soyez**
qu'ils / elles **aient**	qu'ils / elles **soient**

Les gens ont peur qu'il y **ait** un désastre écologique.
Il semble que la qualité de la vie **soit** très importante.

Attention! ————————————————————————

The **nous** and **vous** forms of the subjunctive of **avoir** are pronounced with the / e / sound: **nous ayons** / nu ze jɔ̃ /, **vous ayez** / vu ze je /.

Langue

Ⓐ **Des substitutions.** Remplacez les verbes en italique par les verbes donnés dans les phrases suivantes.

1. Je veux que vous *restiez*. (répondre, partir, réussir, parler, obéir, étudier)
2. Il faut que nous *chantions* ici. (travailler, dormir, finir, attendre, descendre, être)
3. Nous désirons que tu *finisses*. (écouter, ne pas fumer, partir, finir, avoir de la patience, être à l'heure)

Ⓑ **Le succès.** Formez des phrases complètes avec les mots donnés.

1. Vous / vouloir / que / nous / être / heureux?
2. Vos parents / désirer / que / vous / trouver / travail
3. Mon père / ne... pas vouloir / que / je / avoir / trop / argent
4. Il faut / que / tu / réussir / dans / avenir
5. Nous / aimer mieux / que / vous / étudier / université
6. Mon prof / ne... pas vouloir / que / je / perdre / mon / temps

Culture

C **Connaître un pays.** Vos amis veulent visiter un pays où on parle français. Qu'est-ce qu'ils peuvent faire pour connaître la culture de ce pays? Quels conseils pouvez-vous leur donner? Commencez avec **Il faut que vous...** et choisissez la meilleure *(best)* réponse.

1. rester...
   a. dans un petit hôtel   b. dans un grand hôtel   c. avec une famille
2. aimer...
   a. parler avec des gens   b. observer les gens
   c. expliquer des traditions américaines
3. fréquenter...
   a. les musées   b. les cafés   c. les parcs
4. utiliser...
   a. le métro   b. des taxis   c. les autobus
5. passer... dans le pays.
   a. une semaine   b. un mois   c. une année
6. avoir...
   a. beaucoup de patience   b. beaucoup d'argent
   c. beaucoup de temps
7. voyager entre les villes...
   a. en voiture   b. en train   c. en auto-stop
8. étudier
   a. leur langue   b. leur art   c. leur politique

Communication

D **Pour réussir.** Pour être un(e) bon(ne) étudiant(e), qu'est-ce qu'il faut faire?

MODÈLE: étudier beaucoup
           Il faut que nous étudiions beaucoup.

écouter le professeur
passer beaucoup de temps à la bibliothèque
être studieux (-euse)
ne... pas regarder des jeux télévisés tout le temps
dormir peu
finir tous les devoirs
réussir aux examens
ne... pas sortir le soir
répondre à toutes les questions
réfléchir beaucoup
???

E **Cher monsieur.** Vous allez composer une lettre au Président des Etats-Unis pour lui donner des conseils. Utilisez les suggestions données ou vos propres idées.

MODÈLE: m'inviter à la Maison-Blanche
           Je voudrais que vous m'invitiez à la Maison-Blanche.

ne... pas oublier les pauvres
dépenser moins d'argent
écouter les femmes
voyager en autobus
avoir moins de vacances
répondre aux questions des
  journalistes

être plus patient avec les
  sénateurs
encourager les gens sans travail
penser aux problèmes des
  sans-papiers
faire attention à la Sécurité
  sociale

F **Questions personnelles.** Vos problèmes.

1. Est-ce qu'il faut que vous passiez un examen cette semaine? Dans quelle matière?
2. Combien d'heures faut-il que vous étudiiez?
3. Est-ce qu'il est important qu'un professeur soit sévère? Pourquoi ou pourquoi pas?
4. Est-ce que votre petit(e) ami(e) veut que vous sortiez avec elle / lui trop souvent?
5. Est-ce qu'il est préférable que vous gagniez beaucoup d'argent ou que vous soyez heureux (-euse)?
6. De quoi avez-vous peur?

III. Uses of the subjunctive

The verb in the main clause of a sentence determines whether you will use the indicative or the subjunctive in the subordinate clause. The indicative is used most frequently; it follows verbs indicating facts or certainty.

Ils **savent** que vous **êtes** préoccupé.
Les sondages **montrent** que le bonheur **vient** avant l'argent.

The subjunctive occurs in subordinate clauses after verbs of emotion, wishing, doubt, and uncertainty, and some impersonal expressions implying judgment.

Attention!

Note that the subjunctive is used only if the subject in the subordinate clause is different from the subject of the main clause. If the subjects in both clauses are the same, the infinitive is used.

J'ai peur qu'**elle** ait froid cet hiver.

I'm afraid (that) **she**'ll *be cold this winter.*

J'ai peur d'**avoir** froid cet hiver.

I'm afraid that I'll be cold this winter.

A. Emotion

The subjunctive mood is used in subordinate clauses starting with **que** after verbs and expressions of emotion.

Je **suis contente que vous nous posiez** cette question.
J'**ai peur qu'il ne soit** pas facile de répondre.
Je **suis surprise que vous ne me parliez** pas d'argent.

Mots clés   *Expressions of emotion*

avoir peur	*to be afraid*	être heureux (-euse)	*to be happy*
être content(e)	*to be happy*		
être désolé(e)	*to be sorry*	être surpris(e)	*to be surprised*
être étonné(e)	*to be surprised*	être triste	*to be sad*
être furieux (-euse)	*to be angry*	regretter	*to be sorry*

If the subject of the main clause does not change, use **de** plus an infinitive with all of the expressions listed above.

J'ai peur **de** conduire.
Elle regrette **de** ne pas pouvoir venir.

B. Wishing

The subjunctive is used in clauses starting with **que** after verbs expressing wishes, desire, preference, and other impositions of will.

Elle **veut que nous arrivions** à l'heure.
Tu **aimes mieux que je choisisse** le restaurant?
Nous **souhaitons que vous passiez** une bonne soirée.

Mots clés   *Verbs and expressions of will, wishing, and desire*

aimer mieux	*to prefer*	souhaiter	*to wish*
avoir envie (de)	*to feel like*	vouloir	*to want*
désirer	*to want*		

If the subject of the main clause does not change, use an infinitive with the verbs listed above. With **avoir envie,** use **de** before the infinitive.

J'aime mieux conduire.
Marc a envie **de** dormir.
Elle veut partir.

C. Doubt and uncertainty

The subjunctive is also used after verbs and expressions of doubt or uncertainty.

Je **ne pense pas** que **nous ayons** envie de beaucoup de choses.
Elle **n'est pas sûre** qu'il **soit** là.

Mots clés   *Verbs and expressions of doubt and uncertainty*

douter	*to doubt*
ne... pas penser	*not to think*
ne... pas être sûr (de)	*not to be sure, to be unsure*
ne... pas être certain (de)	*not to be certain, to be uncertain*
ne... pas trouver	*not to think / find*

If the subject of the main clause does not change, use an infinitive with **penser** and **de** plus an infinitive with **sûr** and **certain.** Sentences with **trouver** must have a change of subject.

> Ils ne pensent pas pouvoir téléphoner.
> Il n'est pas sûr **de** réussir.

Attention!

1. Because they imply certainty, **penser, trouver,** and **être sûr** in the affirmative are followed by a verb in the indicative.

   > Elle **pense** qu'il **est** beau.   *but:*   Elle **ne pense pas** qu'il **soit** intelligent.

2. The verb **savoir** is always followed by a verb in the indicative.

   > Je **sais** que **vous êtes** italien.
   > Je **ne savais pas** que **vous étiez** cadre.

3. Several other verbs that you have learned, including **apprendre, décider, espérer, expliquer, indiquer, montrer, oublier,** and **répondre,** do not imply doubt. They are therefore followed by a verb in the indicative.

   > Le journaliste **a expliqué** que le Président ne **peut** pas venir.
   > N'**oublie** pas que nous **avons** du chômage.

D. Impersonal expressions of judgment

The subjunctive is used in the subordinate clause after expressions with no specific subject, that is, without a reference to any particular person or thing, if they express a judgment or opinion on the speaker's part.

> Il **semble** que la qualité de la vie **soit** le plus important.
> Il **faut** que nous **rendions** la société plus juste.

Mots clés   *Impersonal expressions implying opinion or personal judgment*

Il est bon que	*It is good that*
Il est dommage que	*It's too bad that*
Il est faux que	*It is untrue that*
Il est important que	*It is important that*
Il est juste / injuste que	*It is fair / unfair that*
Il est nécessaire que	*It is necessary that*
Il est possible / impossible que	*It is possible / impossible that*
Il est préférable que	*It is preferable that*
Il est rare que	*It is rare that*

The expressions above take **de** with an infinitive when no specific subject is expressed.

> Il est bon **de** faire ça.

Il faut que	It is necessary that
Il semble que	It seems that
Il vaut mieux que	It is better that

The expressions above are followed directly by an infinitive when no specific subject is expressed.

Il faut partir.

| Il est peu probable que | It is unlikely that |
| Il se peut que | It may be that / Perhaps / It's possible that |

The expressions above always require a specific subject and cannot be used with an infinitive.

Attention!

The following verbs and expressions imply certainty in the speaker's mind and do *not* take the subjunctive.

Il est certain / sûr que	It is certain / sure that
Il est évident que	It is obvious that
Il est probable que	It is probable that
Il est vrai que	It is true that

Il est certain que vous n'**obéissez** pas.
Il est probable que Marc **est** très fatigué.

Langue

Ⓐ **En vacances.** Formez des phrases complètes avec les mots donnés.

1. Je / souhaiter / vous / passer / bon / vacances
2. Elle / penser / nous / partir / demain
3. Ils / avoir peur / il y a / orage
4. Tu / aimer mieux / je / être / gare / sept heures?
5. Nous / être surpris / tu / avoir / quinze / jour / de vacances
6. Il / être / certain / elles / sortir / des Etats-Unis

Ⓑ **Il faut suivre ses propres conseils!** Changez les phrases suivantes pour indiquer que la première personne pense à elle-même!

MODÈLE: Jacqueline veut qu'on parte maintenant.
Jacqueline veut partir maintenant.

1. Robert aime que nous passions chez ses amis.
2. Marie a envie que tu sortes ce soir.
3. Claire est contente que nous ayons de bonnes notes.
4. Alain aime mieux que nous pensions à l'avenir.
5. Yves n'est pas sûr qu'ils partent tout de suite.
6. Chantal veut que vous ayez de la patience.

C **Les problèmes sociaux.** Dans les phrases suivantes, remplacez les mots en italique par les mots entre parenthèses. Attention au deuxième verbe!

1. Ils *pensent* que le sida est un désastre.   (... avoir peur...)
2. Il est *vrai* que nous perdons patience avec les SDF.   (... dommage...)
3. Il est *peu probable* que nous ayons une guerre nucléaire.   (... possible...)
4. Ils *expliquent* que nous ne réfléchissons pas assez aux problèmes des pauvres.   (... regretter...)
5. Je *doute* qu'ils aient faim.   (... apprendre...)
6. Il est *évident* qu'il y a trop de criminalité.   (... certain...)

Culture

D **Connaître un pays.** Vos amis ont décidé de visiter un pays francophone, et ils veulent connaître cette culture. Donnez-leur des conseils. Faites des phrases avec les mots donnés; ensuite *(then)*, mettez les phrases dans l'ordre du plus important au moins important.

MODÈLE: Il est bon / préparer votre voyage en avance
          Il est bon que vous prépariez votre voyage en avance.

1. Il faut / goûter tous les vins
2. Il est important / choisir un bon guide
3. Il est évident / avoir besoin de parler leur langue
4. Il faut / parler avec beaucoup de gens
5. Il vaut mieux / manger avec une famille
6. Il est certain / aller chercher un bon café

Communication

E **Mes opinions.** Donnez votre opinion des sujets suivants en employant «Je pense que... » **ou** «Je ne pense pas que... ».

1. l'Amérique:
   a. Les Américains sont sympathiques.
   b. Ils parlent beaucoup de langues.
   c. Ils ne pensent pas à l'avenir.
   d. Ils sont préoccupés par l'argent.
2. les parents:
   a. Ils sont très sévères.
   b. Ils perdent souvent patience.
   c. Ils aiment mes amis.
   d. Ils ont toujours raison.
3. les grandes villes:
   a. Il y a trop de bruit.
   b. La pollution est un problème.
   c. Les habitants sont sympathiques.
   d. On dort bien en ville.
4. mes amis:
   a. Ils sont ennuyeux.
   b. Ils ont du talent.
   c. Ils réfléchissent aux problèmes importants.
   d. Ils sont préoccupés.

F **Des solutions.** Avec un partenaire, complétez les phrases avec une bonne solution aux situations suivantes. Ensuite, demandez aux autres groupes s'ils ont les mêmes idées.

1. Vous avez un examen demain matin. Il vaut mieux que vous...
   a. étudier ce soir
   b. écouter des CD
   c. sortir avec des amis
   d. ???
2. Votre frère veut sortir avec une jolie fille. Il vaut mieux qu'il...
   a. lui téléphoner à trois heures du matin
   b. l'inviter chez lui
   c. lui parler en français
   d. ???
3. Vos amis veulent aller en France cet été. Il vaut mieux qu'ils...
   a. travailler le week-end
   b. dépenser beaucoup d'argent
   c. partir maintenant
   d. ???
4. Les restaurants sont fermés et vous avez faim. Il est probable que vous...
   a. demander un sandwich à vos voisins
   b. préparer quelque chose à la maison
   c. attendre le petit déjeuner
   d. ???
5. Votre grand-mère veut venir vous voir mais une amie vous a déjà invité(e). Il vaut mieux que vous...
   a. attendre votre grand-mère chez vous
   b. expliquer le problème à votre grand-mère
   c. partir tout de suite
   d. ???

G **Mes réactions.** Dans les situations suivantes, êtes-vous content(e) ou pas content(e)?

MODÈLE: Le professeur est sévère.
Je suis désolé(e) que le professeur soit sévère.

1. Nous étudions le subjonctif.
2. Le professeur me choisit pour répondre à la question.
3. Nous donnons de l'argent aux pays pauvres.
4. Mon français (n')est (pas) très bon.
5. Il y a du chômage.
6. J'ai une voiture.

H **Questions personnelles.** Votre personnalité.

1. Avez-vous peur d'obtenir une mauvaise note? Dans quel cours?
2. Pensez-vous savoir parler français? Avec qui voulez-vous parler?
3. Est-ce qu'il est possible que vous changiez de personnalité?
4. De quoi avez-vous envie?
5. Quand êtes-vous furieux (-euse)?
6. Qu'est-ce que vous regrettez?
7. Etes-vous sûr(e) que vos études soient importantes?
8. Est-il vrai que vous pensiez aux autres?

communiquons

Exprimer l'imprécision

In English, when people are unsure of a person's name or simply wish to speak quickly without stopping to think of an exact name, they use a variety of expressions such as *What's-his-name* or *Mr. / Mrs. So-and-So*. These expressions of imprecision also exist for talking about places and things. French has similar expressions, and you will find them useful for getting your ideas across in situations where you are not sure of the precise terms to use for designating certain people, places, and things.

23.20 ON A TOUT ESSAYÉ
présenté par Laurent Ruquier

caméras cachées, les biens culturels (sites Internet, livres, films), les produits... 67014223

2 France

M. Dor, G. Miller et I. Alonso
Entouré de sa bande de « teste-tout » **(Isabelle Alonso, Claude Sarraute, Gérard Miller, Maureen Dor, Franck Dubosc, Jean-François Derec...) Laurent Ruquier** passe au crible, à travers des reportages et des

Expressions

▶ **On parle des gens.**

1. Use **on** as the subject when you cannot name a specific person.

On nous a pris notre magnétoscope.   *They took our VCR.*

On a sonné à la porte.   *They rang the doorbell.*

2. Use **quelqu'un** to express the idea of *someone*. When used with an adjective, **quelqu'un** is followed by **de (d')** and a masculine adjective.

Quelqu'un m'a déjà posé cette question.   *Somebody already asked me that question.*

J'ai vu quelqu'un dans l'auto.   *I saw somebody in the car.*

Il a rencontré quelqu'un d'important.   *He met someone important.*

3. To express *Mr. So-and-So* and *Mrs. So-and-So,* use **Monsieur Untel** and **Madame Unetelle.** When you have forgotten a person's name, or when you do not want to be bothered saying it, use the names **Machin, Machin-Chouette** *(What's-his-name),* or **Chose.**

Madame Unetelle est déjà partie.	*Mrs. So-and-So has already left.*
Machin-Chouette m'a téléphoné.	*What's-his-name phoned.*

▶ **On parle des endroits.**

1. Use **quelque part** *(somewhere),* **un coin** *(spot),* or **un endroit** *(a place)* to talk about an unspecified place.

Les enfants sont allés quelque part.	*The kids went somewhere.*
Ils ont laissé mon parapluie dans un coin.	*They left my umbrella in some spot.*

▶ **On parle des choses.**

1. Use **quelque chose** *(something)* to indicate a thing that cannot be specified. **Quelque chose** is always masculine and takes **de (d')** before an adjective.

Quelque chose a fait du bruit.	*Something made a noise.*
Je voudrais quelque chose pour ma mère.	*I'd like something for my mother.*
Vous me parlez de quelque chose d'important.	*You are talking to me about something important.*

2. There are several familiar French expressions that mean *a gadget, a thingamajig,* or *a doohickey.*

J'ai besoin d'un bidule pour ouvrir le coffre!	*I need a thingamajig to open the trunk!*
Je parle d'un engin pour réparer ma voiture.	*I'm talking about a doohickey for repairing my car.*
Qu'est-ce que c'est que ce machin?	*What's that gadget?*
Je cherche un truc pour réparer ma bicyclette.	*I'm looking for a gadget to repair my bicycle.*

3. Use **une chose** *(a thing)* for abstract nouns or ideas.

Le bonheur pour moi, c'est une chose simple.	*Happiness for me is a simple thing.*
Je voudrais vous expliquer une chose sérieuse.	*I would like to explain a serious thing to you.*

Interaction

Simon va acheter un cadeau pour son frère.

SIMON: Je cherche quelque chose de pas trop cher.

L'EMPLOYÉ: C'est pour quelqu'un de quel âge?

SIMON: Vingt-trois ans. Il aime les machins électroniques.

L'EMPLOYÉ: J'ai un truc pour prévoir l'avenir. Je viens de le poser° quelque part.   *set down*

SIMON: Non, j'aime mieux les bidules amusants.

L'EMPLOYÉ: On va en avoir beaucoup à la fin de la semaine.

SIMON: D'accord. Je vais revenir samedi.

Activités

Ⓐ Refaites le paragraphe suivant en remplaçant les mots en italique par des expressions d'incertitude.

Un *homme* m'a téléphoné hier soir. C'était *Robert Ducroc.* Il voulait emprunter *ma voiture* parce qu'il avait des problèmes *en ville* et *les gens* ne voulaient pas l'aider à réparer sa voiture. *Une femme* lui a prêté de l'argent pour téléphoner *d'un café* près de l'hôtel. Je n'avais pas envie de sortir et je lui ai demandé d'aller voir *Mme Fantaisie* à l'hôtel.

Ⓑ Répondez aux questions suivantes.

1. Avez-vous déjà rencontré quelqu'un de célèbre? Qui?
2. Etes-vous allé(e) quelque part le week-end dernier?
3. Avez-vous visité un joli coin? Où?
4. Avez-vous fait quelque chose d'intéressant récemment?
5. Est-ce qu'on vous a invité(e) quelque part ce week-end?
6. Est-ce que quelqu'un va passer vous voir ce soir? Qui?

La météo

lecture culturelle

Avant la lecture

Television plays an important role in most European countries, and France is no exception. On average, the French spend three and a half hours daily in front of their television sets. They might watch *Télématin*, a French program similar to *Good Morning America*, popular game shows such as *Des chiffres et des lettres*, cartoons, the 1 P.M. news, sports programs, sitcoms, the 8 P.M. news, talk shows, or an evening film.

If you were to peruse a weekly TV guide in France, you might find a number of foreign films and American TV series interspersed with the French programming. Interestingly, France, like most countries in the European Union (EU), has imposed a 40 percent quota on the number of non-EU programs allowed to air, in an effort to preserve and protect the national culture.

Although France does import a certain number of foreign programs, it also exports its own creations. For instance, France has been very successful in exporting TV series and cartoons to numerous European and Asian countries. In addition, France, along with Canada, Belgium, and Switzerland, has teamed up to offer francophone programming in the United States and other countries. Such programming is broadcast via the international channel TV5, created in 1984 and available in the United States since 1998. Now, with the purchase of a satellite dish, one can have access to francophone television twenty-four hours a day, seven days a week. TV5's new U.S. programming allows its viewers to choose from among five categories: news *(TV5 Infos)*, movies and drama series *(TV5 Films)*, weekend programming *(TV5 Week-end)*, children's shows *(TV5 Enfants)*, and soccer *(TV5 Soccer)*.

In the reading that follows, you will find a description of each of TV5's programming categories, as well as plot summaries for a movie and drama series shown on TV5.

Activités

Ⓐ How much television do you watch each day or every week? What kinds of television shows do you watch? What shows are your favorite and least favorite?

Ⓑ If you had access to TV5, which types of programming would you watch? Why?

C The French spoken in the francophone world varies from country to country and region to region. What other differences do you think you would find by watching news, documentaries, and films from all over the francophone world? What similarities would you anticipate?

D Without looking up any words, try to determine the gist of the plots of *Les enfants du mensonge* and *Navarro V*.

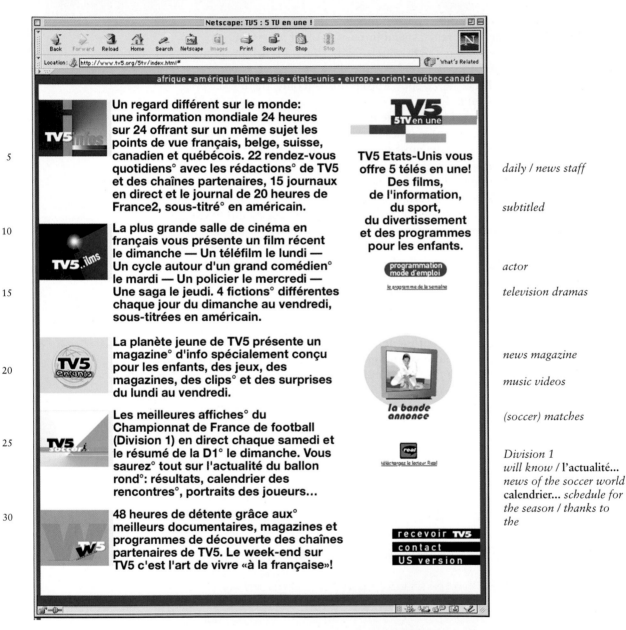

5

10

15

20

25

30

daily / news staff

subtitled

actor

television dramas

news magazine

music videos

(soccer) matches

Division 1
will know / **l'actualité...**
news of the soccer world
calendrier... *schedule for*
the season / thanks to
the

http://www.tv5.org/5tv/index.html#

Les enfants du mensonge

téléfilm sous-titré

Téléfilm de Frédéric Krivine. Avec Emmanuel Salinger, Christine Citti et François Mathouret. France. 1996. 90 min.

La veille de° son mariage, David, un jeune et brillant journaliste de 25 ans, apprend fortuitement° que son père Louis n'a jamais vraiment aimé sa mère Martine, et que la femme qu'il aime encore fera partie des° invités. Plongé dans l'angoisse°, augmentée par la pression de l'organisation matérielle de la fête, David entre en conflit avec sa future femme, Sylvie, car il est pour l'instant incapable de lui raconter ce qu'il vient d'apprendre et qui l'obsède.

On the eve of accidentally
fera... *will be among*

plongé... *full of anguish*

Navarro V

série sous-titrée

Série policière avec Roger Hanin, Sam Karmann, Christian Rauth, Jacques Martial et Catherine Allégret.

Policier hors du commun°, Navarro prend en charge les affaires les plus troublantes comme les plus émouvantes°. Avec ses quatre inspecteurs, il mène sa traque° perpétuelle des crimes et de l'injustice, agissant° toujours avec conviction, humanité et humour. Épisode 12 (de 13): Suicide d'un flic°. Un policier vient de se suicider au commissariat°. Pour° ses collègues, le surmenage°, le découragement, le manque° de reconnaissance° ont conduit Garel à ce geste de désespoir. Mais pour Navarro, il y a bien autre chose et il décide d'enquêter sur° le passé du défunt°. Ses recherches vont le mener dans le quartier chinois et au sein° de la communauté chinoise que le policier fréquentait beaucoup, soi-disant° dans le cadre° de son travail.

hors du... *out of the ordinary* / **les affaires...** *the most troubling as well as the most heart-rending cases* / **mène...** *tracks, leads the hunt* / *acting* / *cop* / *police station* / *According to* / *overwork* / *lack of* / *appreciation* / **enquêter...** *to investigate* / *dead person* / *to the heart* / *supposedly* / **dans...** *as part of*

Après la lecture

Questions sur le texte

1. Quelles perspectives sur l'information mondiale peut-on avoir grâce à *TV5 Infos*?
2. Quels sont les différents genres de programmes qui font partie de *TV5 Films*?
3. Qu'est-ce que vous pouvez apprendre en regardant *(by watching)* TV5 *Soccer*?
4. Dans la description de *TV5 Infos*, vous avez peut-être remarqué que les sous-titres sont «en américain». Citez quelques différences entre l'anglais et l'américain.
5. Selon le résumé du film *Les enfants du mensonge*, quelle est la raison pour l'angoisse de David? Quand est-ce qu'il apprend les mauvaises nouvelles?

6. Selon le résumé du film *Navarro V*, qui est Navarro? Quelle est sa personnalité? Qui s'est suicidé? Quelle est la raison de son suicide, selon ses collègues? Pourquoi est-ce que Navarro va au quartier chinois?

Activités

Ⓐ Imaginez la conversation possible entre David et Sylvie *(Les enfants du mensonge)*. Présentez votre dialogue à la classe.

Ⓑ Ecrivez les questions possibles posées par Navarro pendant son enquête dans le quartier chinois. En groupes, inventez la «vraie» raison du suicide de Garel. Ensuite, comparez votre histoire avec celles des autres groupes dans la classe.

Ⓒ Que pensez-vous du fait que la France ait un quota sur le pourcentage de programmes de télévision qui puissent venir de l'extérieur de l'Union européenne? Quels sont les avantages et les désavantages pour la France et les Français?

Ⓓ Que pensez-vous de l'idée de limiter le nombre d'heures où les enfants peuvent regarder la télé?

Ⓔ Peut-on ou doit-on censurer certaines émissions *(programs)* de télévision? Pourquoi? Pourquoi pas?

PARIS PREMIERE	ESPORT FRANCE	⊜	serieclub	CANAL JIMMY	TV5 LA TÉLÉVISION INTERNATIONALE	
20.30 **GOLF** Four Million Dollar Challenge	**20.00** **VOLLEY-BALL** Championnat de France Pro A 20e journée	**20.30** **STÉPHANE** **GRAPPELLI** 🎬 **Portrait rêvé** Documentaire (1/2)	**20.50** **FEDS** Série en VO War Against Crime	**21.00** **QUATRE EN UN** Best of Spécial Dessinateurs	**21.05** **THALASSA** Magazine Surfers Paradise 🎬	**Samedi** 17 FÉVRIER
22.30 **PARIS DERNIÈRE** Magazine	**21.30** **SUMO** Tokyo Basho au Japon	**21.25** **CINQ COLONNES** **A LA UNE** Magazine	**21.40** **ULTRAVIOLET** Série en VO Mea culpa	**21.35** **DRIVING PASSION** Document (1/4)	**22.15** **LES 16es VICTOIRES** **DE LA MUSIQUE** Spectacle	
21.00 Film **COUPS DE FEU SUR** **BROADWAY** 🎬 Comédie en VO de Woody Allen	**20.00** **LUGE** Coupe du monde sur piste artificielle 8e et dernière manche	**20.30** **PALESTINE (1/3)** 🎬 **Le Destin** **controversé d'un État** **créé de toutes pièces**	**20.40** **L'HOMME** **DE L'ATLANTIDE** Série Docteur Crawford	**21.00** **NEW YORK** **POLICE BLUES** Série en VO Une épouse indigne	**21.05** **FAUT PAS RÊVER** Magazine	**Dimanche** 18 FÉVRIER
22.35 **L'ACTOR'S STUDIO** Jessica Lange	**21.30** **ATHLÉTISME** Permit Meeting Indoor de Birmingham (GB)	**21.45** **PETER ALLEN** **Un Australien** **à Broadway**	**21.25** **LE FUGITIF** Série en VO Deux épisodes	**21.45** **RIK MAYALL** **PRESENTS...** Dancing Queen (VO)	**22.15** **ANIBAL** Téléfilm de Pierre Boutron	
21.00 Film **LES VESTIGES** **DU JOUR** 🎬🎬🎬 Drame en VO de James Ivory	**20.30** **DAYTONA 500** Winston Cup	**20.30** **LA MORT, LA HAINE,** **LE PARDON** 🎬 Documentaire	**21.00** **CONRAD BLOOM** Série en VO To Hell in a Handbag	**21.00** **LA ROUTE** Magazine Patrick Braoudé et K-Mel	**21.05** **LE POINT** Magazine	**Lundi** 19 FÉVRIER
23.10 Film **84 CHARING CROSS** **ROAD** 🎬 En VO de David Jones	**22.00** **TANT DE PAROLES** Magazine Franck Piccard	**21.30** **CARNAVAL** **A ARACATI** Documentaire	**21.25** **3e PLANÈTE** **APRÈS LE SOLEIL** Série en VO	**22.30** Film **RENDS-MOI** **LA CLE** 🎬 de Gérard Pirès	**22.15** Film **LA SYMPHONIE** **PASTORALE** 🎬🎬🎬 En NB de Jean Delannoy	

vocabulaire

Noms / Pronoms

actualités *(f.)*	news	la justice	justice
amour *(m.)*	love	le monde	world
avenir *(m.)*	future	une montagne	mountain
le bonheur	happiness	un nombre	number
le bruit	noise	une opinion	opinion
le câble	cable	la paix	peace
un cadre	middle manager	la politique	politics
la chaîne	station	la pollution	pollution
la chaîne câblée	cable station	une possibilité	possibility
le chômage	unemployment	le programme	program
une chose	thing	la publicité	ads
un compte en banque	bank account	la qualité	quality
		un reportage	report
un conseil	advice	sans-abri *(m./f.)*	homeless people
la criminalité	crime	sans-logis *(m./f.)*	homeless people
la délinquance	delinquency	sans-papiers *(m./f.)*	undocumented aliens
un désastre	disaster		
un dessin animé	cartoon	la santé	health
une drogue	illegal drug	SDF (sans domicile fixe) *(m./f.)*	homeless people
égalité *(f.)*	equality		
une émission	program	une série	series
un emploi	job	la sécurité	security
un feuilleton	series	le sida	AIDS
la franchise	frankness	la société	society
un grand magasin	department store	un sondage d'opinion	opinion poll
la guerre nucléaire	nuclear war	un succès	success
importance *(f.)*	importance	une table ronde	round table
incertitude *(f.)*	uncertainty	le trafic	(drug) traffic
un inconvénient	annoyance	le travail	work
inflation *(f.)*	inflation	variétés *(f.)*	variety shows
une interview	interview	la vie	life
un jeu télévisé	game show	un/une voisin(e)	neighbor
le Journal	TV news		

Verbes

arrêter	to stop	regretter	to regret / to be sorry
consulter	to consult	remercier	to thank
discuter	to discuss	rendre	to give back / to make
douter	to doubt		
embêter	to bother	sembler	to seem
éviter	to avoid	souhaiter	to wish
préoccuper	to preoccupy	supporter	to tolerate

Adjectifs / Adverbes

absolument	absolutely	**matérialiste**	materialistic
contemporain(e)	contemporary	**selon**	according
écologique	ecological	**social**	social
étonné	amazed	**sûr**	certain
furieux	furious	**surpris**	surprised
important	important	**triste**	sad

Expressions

avoir envie	to feel like	**il est peu probable**	it's unlikely
avoir peur	to be afraid	**il est préférable**	it's preferable
faire du bruit	to make noise	**il est probable**	it's likely
faire peur	to scare	**il est rare**	it's rare
il est bon	it's good	**il est sûr**	it's certain
il est dommage	it's too bad	**il est temps**	it's time
il est évident	it's obvious	**il faut que**	it's necessary
il est faux	it's false	**il se peut**	it's likely
il est important	it's important	**il semble**	it appears
il est injuste	it's unfair	**il vaut mieux**	it's better
il est juste	it's fair	**le plus**	the most
il est nécessaire	it's necessary		

**Aux Galeries Lafayette,
à Paris**

Les achats

OBJECTIVES

Language	Culture	Communication
■ Vocabulary for stores and shops ■ The vowel sounds / ø / and / œ / ■ **Boire, recevoir, devoir** ■ Irregular verbs in the subjunctive ■ Negatives	■ Shopping and stores ■ Money ■ The euro	■ Expressing emotions, wishes, opinions, doubts, and judgments ■ Expressing negative statements ■ Making purchases

commençons

A la charcuterie

Sophie et Annick louent un appartement au centre-ville. A midi, elles mangent au restau-U, mais le soir, comme elles ne rentrent jamais de bonne heure, elles aiment acheter des plats cuisinés dans une charcuterie et les emporter chez elles pour dîner.

LE CHARCUTIER: Bonjour, Mesdemoiselles, vous désirez?

ANNICK: Vous n'avez plus de pâté de foie?

LE CHARCUTIER: Si, nous avons reçu notre commande ce matin. Voulez-vous que j'aille le chercher?

SOPHIE: Je ne sais pas; il vaut peut-être mieux que nous prenions autre chose.

LE CHARCUTIER: J'ai de la très bonne choucroute garnie. Vous devriez l'essayer.

ANNICK: Tiens! C'est une idée. Qu'est-ce que vous nous conseillez de boire avec cela?

SOPHIE: Tu sais bien qu'avec la choucroute, il faut qu'on boive du vin blanc sec ou de la bière.

ANNICK: Très bien. Donnez-nous 500 grammes de choucroute et une bouteille de Riesling.

LE CHARCUTIER: Voilà, Mademoiselle!

SOPHIE: Combien je vous dois?

LE CHARCUTIER: Quinze euros.

A la charcuterie!

1. Est-ce que Sophie et Annick habitent à la campagne?
2. Qu'est-ce qu'elles aiment faire quand elles ne rentrent pas de bonne heure?
3. Est-ce que le charcutier a du pâté de foie?
4. Qu'est-ce qu'il recommande aussi?
5. Quelle sorte de vin va bien avec la choucroute?
6. Qu'est-ce qu'il est possible de boire aussi?

Mots clés

une charcuterie	pork butcher's shop	autre chose (f.)	something else
le centre-ville	downtown	la choucroute garnie	sauerkraut and assorted meat
de bonne heure	early		
plats cuisinés (m.)	prepared dishes	devriez (devoir)	ought
un charcutier	pork butcher	essayer	to try
Mesdemoiselles (f.)	ladies	conseillez (conseiller)	advise
n'... plus	not . . . any more	boire	to drink
le pâté de foie	liver pâté	boive (boire)	drink
reçu (recevoir)	received	sec	dry
une commande	order	grammes (m.)	grams
que j'aille (aller)	me to go	une bouteille	bottle
peut-être	perhaps	dois (devoir)	owe
prenions (prendre)	take	euro (m.)	euro

Faisons connaissance

www

Although supermarkets (**supermarchés** [*m.*]) are very popular in France, many people continue to buy food at specialty stores. They go to a neighborhood store at least once a day to pick up freshly baked bread, dairy products, or items they need for just one meal. **La charcuterie** specializes in pork products such as ham, sausages, and **pâté.** It also sells prepared dishes such as **hors-d'œuvre,** salads, and ready-to-eat foods that the shopper can warm up just before dinner. Bakeries are also specialized. You go to a **boulangerie** *(f.)* to buy bread and to a **pâtisserie** *(f.)* for pastries.

French people also go to gigantic supermarkets called **hypermarchés** *(m.).* Items that they commonly purchase include canned goods (**des conserves** [*f.*]), frozen foods (**des produits surgelés**), cleaning products, paper goods, and cases of beverages such as beer and mineral water. They also buy articles of clothing, furniture, and other items found in department ▶

stores (**les grands magasins**). In Paris, the **Galeries Lafayette** and the **Printemps** are among the most popular department stores. They have branches in large cities throughout France.

Enrichissons notre vocabulaire

Les boutiques *(Shops)*

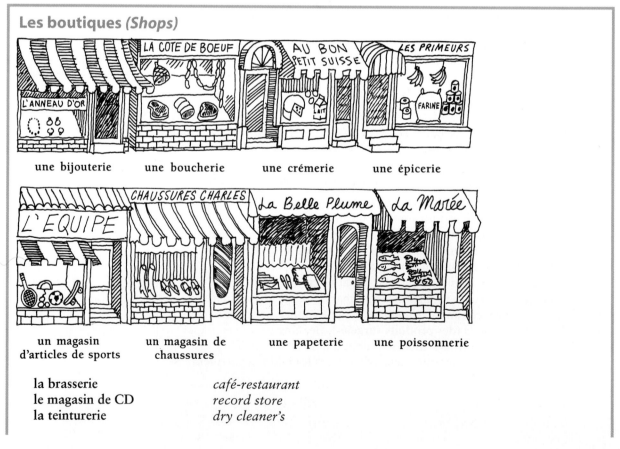

une bijouterie   une boucherie   une crémerie   une épicerie

un magasin
d'articles de sports   un magasin de
chaussures   une papeterie   une poissonnerie

la brasserie	*café-restaurant*
le magasin de CD	*record store*
la teinturerie	*dry cleaner's*

Les commerçants *(Shopkeepers)*

le boulanger / la boulangère	*baker*
le boucher / la bouchère	*butcher*
le pâtissier / la pâtissière	*pastry maker*
l'épicier / l'épicière	*grocer*
le poissonnier / la poissonnière	*fishmonger*
le marchand de... / la marchande de...	*person who sells . . .*
le / la buraliste	*tobacconist*
le / la fleuriste	*florist*

Dans un magasin *(In a store)*

le vendeur / la vendeuse	*salesperson*
le rayon	*department*
la caisse	*cashier's*
les soldes *(f.)*	*sales*
en solde	*on sale*
une remise de 10%	*10% discount*

Prononciation   The vowel sounds / ø / and / œ /

A. The third pair of mid vowels in French is / ø / and / œ /. The / ø / sound is pronounced with the mouth mostly closed, the tongue forward, and the lips rounded. It is represented by the letters **eu** and occurs in words such as **bleu** and **heureux**. The unaccented e in words such as **je, ne, ce,** and **que** approximates this sound.

B. The / ø / sound occurs when it is the last sound in a syllable. If the syllable ends in a consonant, you must pronounce the / œ / sound by opening your mouth slightly. The / œ / sound is also written **eu,** but it occurs only before a pronounced consonant in words such as **leur, veulent,** and **neuf.**

Repeat the following pairs of words after your teacher.

/ ø /	/ œ /		/ ø /	/ œ /
heureux	chauffeur		peu	peur
eux	heure		veut	veulent

C. There is only one frequent exception to the preceding rule. When the final consonant is the / z / sound, usually written **-se,** you keep the vowel sound / ø /. In the following lists, the adjectives in the right column have the same final vowel sound as those in the left column.

Repeat the following pairs of words after your teacher.

/ ø /	/ øz /		/ ø /	/ øz /
affreux	affreuse		courageux	courageuse
ambitieux	ambitieuse		délicieux	délicieuse
dangereux	dangereuse		généreux	généreuse

Exercice

Read the following sentences aloud, distinguishing between the closed / ø / sound and the open / œ / sound.

1. Je veux aller chez eux.
2. Elle a peur que tu ne sois pas à l'heure.
3. Ce vendeur ne peut pas supporter les chauffeurs furieux.
4. Cet acteur veut avoir deux répondeurs.
5. Le docteur peut venir à deux heures vingt-neuf.
6. Je suis heureuse que ma sœur soit ambitieuse et studieuse.

grammaire

I. *Boire / recevoir / devoir*

You use these verbs to express the actions of drinking and receiving and the state of having to do something, respectively.

A. The irregular French verbs **boire, recevoir,** and **devoir** have similar conjugations.

	boire *(to drink)*	recevoir *(to receive)*	devoir *(must, to have to, to be supposed to, to owe)*
présent:	je **bois** tu **bois** il / elle / on **boit** nous **buvons** vous **buvez** ils / elles **boivent**	je **reçois** tu **reçois** il / elle / on **reçoit** nous **recevons** vous **recevez** ils / elles **reçoivent**	je **dois** tu **dois** il / elle / on **doit** nous **devons** vous **devez** ils / elles **doivent**
passé composé:	j' **ai bu**	tu **as reçu**	il **a dû**
imparfait:	nous **buvions**	vous **receviez**	elles **devaient**

Qu'est-ce que vous nous conseillez de **boire?**
Nous **avons reçu** notre commande hier.
Vous **devez** partir maintenant?

B. Devoir is a frequently used verb and has many English equivalents.

1. When followed by an infinitive, **devoir** has several possible meanings:

Je **dois aller** chez le charcutier. 　　*I have to / am supposed to go to the pork butcher's.*

Elle **a dû aller** à l'épicerie. 　　*She had to go / must have gone to the grocery store.*

Nous **devions acheter** quelque chose au supermarché. 　　*We were supposed to buy something at the supermarket.*

2. Devoir + a verb in the infinitive can replace the expression **il faut que** + a verb in the subjunctive.

Il faut que tu réussisses à cet examen. 　　**Tu dois** réussir à cet examen.

3. Devoir accompanied by a noun or pronoun means *to owe.*

—C'est combien? 　　—Je **vous dois** combien?
—Vous **me devez** 14 euros. 　　—C'est 11 euros.

4. Devoir is frequently used in the conditional mood to give advice, in which case it means *should* or *ought to.*

Tu **devrais** dormir huit heures.
Je **devrais** téléphoner à ma mère.
Vous **devriez** aller à la boulangerie avant sept heures.

Langue

Ⓐ **Connaissez-vous Jacqueline?** Formez des phrases complètes avec les mots donnés.

1. Quand / elle / être / petit / elle / ne... pas / boire / lait
2. Qu'est-ce que / elle / devoir / faire / aujourd'hui
3. Le week-end dernier / sa sœur / et / elle / devoir / rester / maison
4. Hier / Jacqueline / recevoir / lettre / de sa grand-mère
5. Est-ce que / son / parents / recevoir / souvent / son / amis?
6. Chez elle / on / ne... pas boire / souvent / alcool

Ⓑ **Conseils personnels.** Dans les phrases suivantes, remplacez **Il faut que** par la forme correcte du verbe **devoir**.

1. Il ne faut pas que je mente.
2. Il faut que vous finissiez votre travail.
3. Il faut que tu sois généreux.
4. Il faut que les gens connaissent leurs voisins.
5. Il faut que nous pensions aux sans-logis.
6. Il faut qu'on ait beaucoup de patience.

Culture

C **Les boissons traditionnelles.** Qu'est-ce qu'on boit dans les régions franco-phones du monde? Faites des phrases en trouvant la bonne réponse dans la liste de possibilités.

| du cidre | du vin blanc | du bourgogne |
| de la bière | du champagne | du rhum |

1. Pour un anniversaire *(birthday)*, on...
2. A Dijon, les gens...
3. Avec les écrevisses *(crayfish)*, les Louisianais...
4. Avec une fondue, les Suisses...
5. En Bretagne, avec les crêpes, on...
6. Pour l'apéritif en Martinique, les gens...

D **Les achats.** Pour connaître la France des petits commerçants, vous devez faire vos achats d'une certaine manière. Qu'est-ce qu'on doit faire dans les situations suivantes? Trouvez la conclusion à chaque phrase dans la colonne de droite et formez une phrase avec **devoir.**

MODÈLE: Pour acheter du pain / aller à une boulangerie
Pour acheter du pain, vous devez aller à une boulangerie.

1. Si un Français vous invite à dîner chez lui, vous...
2. Si on veut servir des truites, on...
3. Quand on a envie d'un fromage, on...
4. Si les Français ont besoin d'un stylo, ils...
5. Pour acheter un plat cuisiné, on...
6. Si vous voulez goûter une belle petite tarte, vous...

a. aller à la poissonnerie
b. chercher une papeterie
c. acheter des fleurs *(flowers)* ou des bonbons
d. trouver une pâtisserie
e. aller à la crémerie
f. aller à une charcuterie

Communication

E **Donnez des conseils.** Vous êtes assistant(e) dans une résidence universi-taire et des étudiants vous parlent des problèmes suivants. Qu'est-ce que vous devriez leur recommander de faire dans ces situations?

MODÈLE: J'ai un examen de français demain.
Tu devrais étudier les verbes.

1. Il pleut beaucoup.
2. Mon / Ma camarade de chambre est très malheureux (-euse).
3. Je dois beaucoup d'argent à un(e) ami(e).
4. Mon ami(e) boit / fume trop.
5. Mon / Ma camarade de chambre et moi, nous ne recevons jamais de lettres.
6. Les étudiants font trop de bruit à la résidence.

Ⓕ **Questions personnelles.** Vos habitudes.

1. Qu'est-ce que vous aimez boire le matin? à minuit?
2. Qu'est-ce que vous buvez quand vous avez très soif? Quand vous êtes fatigué(e)?
3. De qui recevez-vous souvent des colis? du courrier électronique?
4. Aimez-vous recevoir des amis chez vous ou aimez-vous mieux sortir?
5. A qui devez-vous de l'argent? un service *(favor)*? Pourquoi?
6. Qu'est-ce que vous devriez faire que vous n'allez pas faire ou que vous n'aimez pas faire?

II. Irregular verbs in the subjunctive

A. Verbs with one subjunctive stem

Some French verbs are irregular in the present subjunctive. In all forms, they use one stem.

faire (fass-)	
que je **fasse**	que nous **fassions**
que tu **fasses**	que vous **fassiez**
qu'il / elle / on **fasse**	qu'ils / elles **fassent**

Qu'est-ce que le professeur veut que ses étudiants **fassent**?

The other verbs that are also irregular in the subjunctive and use one stem in their forms are **pouvoir** and **savoir**.

pouvoir: que je **puisse** / que nous **puissions**
savoir: que je **sache** / que nous **sachions**

Je suis étonnée qu'ils **puissent** venir.
Il faut qu'on **sache** les réponses.

Équivalences francs / euros

1/2 F = 0,08 euro	20 F = 3,05 euros
1 F = 0,15 euro	50 F = 7,62 euros
2 F = 0,30 euro	100 F = 15,24 euros
5 F = 0,76 euro	200 F = 30,49 euros
10 F = 1,52 euro	500 F = 76,22 euros

Montants en euros arrondis au deuxième chiffre après la virgule.

B. Verbs with two subjunctive stems

1. Some verbs use both the **nous** and the **ils / elles** forms of the present indicative to create two different subjunctive stems—one for the **nous** and **vous** plural forms and one for the four other forms.

boire	
present indicative: ils **boivent** nous **buvons**	*subjunctive stems:* **boiv** **buv-**
que je **boive** que tu **boives** qu'il / elle / on **boive**	que nous **buvions** que vous **buviez** qu'ils / elles **boivent**

devoir	prendre	recevoir
stems: **doiv-,** **dev-**	*stems:* **prenn-,** **pren-**	*stems:* **reçoiv-,** **recev-**
que je **doive** que tu **doives** qu'il / elle / on **doive** que nous **devions** que vous **deviez** qu'ils / elles **doivent**	que je **prenne** que tu **prennes** qu'il / elle / on **prenne** que nous **prenions** que vous **preniez** qu'ils / elles **prennent**	que je **reçoive** que tu **reçoives** qu'il / elle / on **reçoive** que nous **recevions** que vous **receviez** qu'ils / elles **reçoivent**

venir	voir
stems: **vienn-, ven-**	*stems:* **voi-, voy-**
que je **vienne** que tu **viennes** qu'il / elle / on **vienne** que nous **venions** que vous **veniez** qu'ils / elles **viennent**	que je **voie** que tu **voies** qu'il / elle / on **voie** que nous **voyions** que vous **voyiez** qu'ils / elles **voient**

Il vaut mieux qu'on **boive** du vin blanc.
Il est temps que nous **recevions** du courrier.

2. The verbs that you have already learned that are conjugated like **prendre, venir,** and **voir** in the present indicative are conjugated like those respective verbs in the subjunctive.

apprendre:	que j'**apprenne** / que nous **apprenions**
comprendre:	que je **comprenne** / que nous **comprenions**
appartenir:	que j'**appartienne** / que nous **appartenions**
contenir:	qu'il **contienne** / que nous **contenions**
devenir:	que je **devienne** / que nous **devenions**
obtenir:	que j'**obtienne** / que nous **obtenions**
retenir:	que je **retienne** / que nous **retenions**
revenir:	que je **revienne** / que nous **revenions**
tenir:	que je **tienne** / que nous **tenions**

3. The verbs **aller** and **vouloir** take one subjunctive stem from the **nous** form of the present indicative. It is used in the **nous** and **vous** forms of the subjunctive. The other subjunctive stem is irregular and is used in the other four forms.

aller	vouloir
stems: **aill-, all-**	*stems:* **veuill-, voul-**
que j' **aille**	que je **veuille**
que tu **ailles**	que tu **veuilles**
qu'il / elle / on **aille**	qu'il / elle / on **veuille**
que nous **allions**	que nous **voulions**
que vous **alliez**	que vous **vouliez**
qu'ils / elles **aillent**	qu'ils / elles **veuillent**

Voulez-vous que j'**aille** le chercher?
Il se peut qu'il **veuille** sortir ce soir.

C. *Falloir* and *pleuvoir*

1. The following verbal expressions are irregular in the subjunctive.

il faut → qu'il **faille**
il pleut → qu'il **pleuve**

Il est possible qu'il **faille** payer la TVA.
Je ne veux pas qu'il **pleuve** ce week-end.

2. In the indicative, **il faut** becomes **il a fallu** and **il fallait** in the past and **il va falloir** in the future.

Il **a fallu** que je prenne l'avion.
Il **fallait** que nous partions de bonne heure.
Il **va falloir** que tu fasses la vaisselle.

Langue

Ⓐ Des substitutions. Remplacez les mots en italique avec les expressions données.

1. Il a fallu que nous *travaillions beaucoup*.   (faire le ménage, aller à la charcuterie, boire de l'eau, voir ce film, retenir ces dates)
2. Elle a peur que vous *arriviez en retard*.   (vouloir rester longtemps, ne... pas prendre le dernier métro, devenir furieux, ne... pas pouvoir répondre, la voir)
3. Il va falloir qu'on *rentre*.   (aller à la charcuterie, faire des courses, recevoir ces gens, prendre un taxi, obtenir de bonnes notes)

Ⓑ On va faire un pique-nique. Formez des phrases complètes en employant les mots donnés.

1. Notre / amis / vouloir / nous / aller / faire un pique-nique / demain
2. Je / avoir peur / Roland / ne... pas vouloir / venir / avec nous
3. Nous / être certain / vous / pouvoir / arriver à l'heure
4. Paul / douter / faire / froid / demain
5. Nous / penser / il / pleuvoir
6. Elles / être / désolé / leurs amies / ne... pas venir
7. Marie / aimer mieux / nous / faire des courses / l'hypermarché
8. Il faut / vous / voir / ces plats!

Ⓒ Mes projets. Formez des phrases en utilisant des expressions dans les deux colonnes.

MODÈLE: *Il est possible que je fasse la grasse matinée ce week-end.*

Etes-vous désolé	apprendre à jouer de la musique
Je suis certain	aller au cinéma ce soir
Il faut	vouloir aller au concert
Je pense	faire la cuisine
Il est probable	pleuvoir cet après-midi
Nous sommes sûrs	voir un film anglais
Il vaut mieux	devoir de l'argent à la banque
Nous ne savions pas	recevoir des amis

Culture

Ⓓ Les habitudes gastronomiques des Français. Qu'est-ce que les Français ont l'habitude de faire quand ils mangent? Choisissez entre les deux possibilités dans la proposition *(clause)* principale pour former une phrase correcte.

MODÈLE: Il est probable / peu probable / / les Français / boire du vin blanc avec du fromage
   Il est peu probable que les Français boivent du vin blanc avec du fromage.

1. Il est rare / certain / / beaucoup de Français / prendre un fruit comme dessert
2. Il est vrai / faux / / les adultes en France / ne... pas boire beaucoup de lait

3. Il est probable / peu probable / / un Français / tenir à manger de la salade avant le repas
4. Il est rare / n'est pas rare / / les Français / faire leurs provisions presque tous les jours
5. Il est sûr / peu probable / / la majorité des Français / prendre des œufs au petit déjeuner
6. Il semble / Il n'est pas sûr / / il faut être un homme pour devenir un grand chef de cuisine en France

Communication

Ⓔ **Quelles sont les possibilités?** Indiquez le degré de certitude des situations suivantes.

certain   probable   possible   peu probable   impossible

MODÈLE: Il pleut ce soir.
            Il est possible qu'il pleuve ce soir.

1. Je vais en Europe cet été.
2. Les étudiants sont contents de ce cours.
3. Je deviens professeur de lycée.
4. Je bois trop de café.
5. Nous voulons aller en cours le samedi.
6. Mes amis peuvent me prêter de l'argent.

Ⓕ **Vos regrets.** Qu'est-ce que vous regrettez dans la vie? Choisissez vos réponses dans la liste suivante, ou exprimez vos propres regrets *(express your own regrets)*.

MODÈLE: Mes professeurs sont trop sérieux.
            Je regrette que mes professeurs soient trop sérieux.

Mon voisin reçoit trop d'amis.
On doit passer des examens.
Notre classe ne va pas au laboratoire tous les jours.
Mon / Ma camarade de chambre fait trop de bruit.
Il y a un pâtissier en face de chez moi.
???

Ⓖ **Vrai ou faux?** Que pensez-vous des affirmations suivantes? Doutez-vous / êtes-vous sûr(e) qu'elles soient vraies? Interviewez un(e) camarade de cours pour voir si vous avez la même opinion.

MODÈLE: Le pâté fait un bon hors-d'œuvre.
            Je suis sûr(e) que le pâté fait un bon hors-d'œuvre.

1. On doit abolir la peine capitale *(capital punishment)*.
2. On peut aller sur d'autres planètes.
3. Il y a une guerre nucléaire bientôt.
4. Nous allons connaître les causes du cancer au vingt et unième siècle *(century)*.
5. Certaines personnes prévoient l'avenir.
6. Nous ne tenons pas à notre passé.

H Questions personnelles. Vos opinions.

1. Est-il important qu'on apprenne des langues étrangères?
2. Pensez-vous qu'on voie de bons films à la télévision? de bonnes émissions?
3. Est-il nécessaire que vous alliez en classe tous les jours? Pourquoi?
4. Est-il possible que vous vouliez travailler pendant les vacances?
5. A quel âge pensez-vous qu'on puisse boire de l'alcool?
6. Est-ce qu'il vaut mieux pour l'économie que vous fassiez vos courses aux hypermarchés ou chez les petits commerçants?

III. Negatives

You use negative expressions to state that people do not do certain things or that certain situations do not exist.

A. Forms

In addition to the general negative expression **ne... pas,** French has other negative expressions.

Affirmative	**Negative**
Ils prennent **quelque chose.**	Ils **ne** prennent **rien.**
*They are having **something**.*	*They are **not** having **anything**.*
Elle a **encore** de la patience.	Elle **n'a plus** de patience.
*She **still** has patience.*	*She does **not** have **any more** patience.*
Ils reçoivent des **gens / tout le monde.**	Ils **ne** reçoivent **personne.**
*They receive **people / everyone**.*	*They do **not** receive **anybody**.*
J'ai **beaucoup** d'argent.	Je **n'ai que** deux dollars.
*I have **a lot of** money.*	*I have **only** two dollars.*
Il va **souvent / toujours** en cours.	Il **ne** va **jamais** en cours.
*He **often / always** goes to class.*	*He **never** goes to class.*

Mots clés *Negative expressions*

ne... jamais	*never, not ever*
ne... personne	*no one, nobody, not anyone*
ne... plus	*no longer, no more, not any longer, not any more*
ne... rien	*nothing, not anything*
ne... que	*only*

B. Position of negatives

1. The negative expressions **ne... jamais, ne... plus,** and **ne... rien** are used in exactly the same places in sentences as **ne... pas:** surrounding the conjugated verb and any object pronouns in declarative sentences and surrounding the verb and pronoun subject with inversion.

> Nous **n'**allons **plus** aller à cette bijouterie.
> Cette épicière **ne** m'a **jamais** servi!
> **N'**as-tu **rien** vu à la boutique?

2. The negative **ne... personne** surrounds the helping verb *and* the past participle in the **passé composé.** It surrounds the conjugated verb and the infinitive with double verbs.

> Nous **n'**avons reconnu **personne.**   Je **ne** veux oublier **personne.**

3. The **que** of **ne... que** immediately precedes the noun or preposition it modifies.

> Je n'ai pas de pâté; je **n'**ai **que** de la choucroute.
> Elles **n'**ont vu **qu'**un film français.
> Nous **n'**étudions **qu'**après les actualités.

4. **Rien** and **personne** can be the subject of a sentence. In this case, **ne** comes after them.

> **Rien n'**est arrivé.   *Nothing happened.*
> **Personne n'**est venu.   *No one came.*

5. **Jamais, personne,** and **rien** can be used alone as responses to statements or questions.

> Tu regardes les émissions de   —Jamais!
>   variétés?
> Qui vous a invité?   —Personne!
> Qu'est-ce qu'il a commandé?   —Rien.

Attention!

1. Remember that the indefinite and partitive articles all become **de** in the negative. The only exception is **ne... que,** which does not require the article to change because it does not express complete negation.

> Ils ont toujours **des** idées; ils n'ont jamais **d'**argent.
> Je n'ai pas **de** dollars; je n'ai que **des** euros.

2. While it is possible to use two or more negative expressions in the same sentence, **pas** is never used with **jamais, plus, personne,** or **rien.**

> Elle ne mange **plus rien** le matin.   *She **no longer** eats **anything** in the morning.*
>
> Je ne vois **jamais plus personne.**   *I **never** see **anyone anymore**.*

3. To contradict a negative question or statement, use the word **si.**

> —Vous **n'**avez **plus** de hors-d'œuvre?
> —**Si,** j'ai encore du pâté.

Ce qu'ils disent

1. In conversations, French speakers often drop **ne** from the negation.

   J'ai plus de patience.   Ils ont vu personne.

2. **Que** can also be used entirely by itself to mean *only.*

   Que de l'eau, s'il vous plaît!

Langue

Ⓐ **Eric n'est pas comme son ami Luc.** Remplacez **Luc** par **Eric** et mettez les phrases suivantes à la forme négative.

MODÈLE: Luc fait beaucoup de choses. *Eric ne fait rien.*

1. Luc a encore du temps pour étudier.
2. Luc a perdu quelque chose.
3. Luc a rencontré des amis à la brasserie.
4. Luc va acheter quelque chose pour sa mère.
5. Luc aime toujours recevoir ses amis.
6. Luc téléphone à quelqu'un le samedi.

Ⓑ **Interrogation.** Répondez aux questions suivantes à la forme affirmative.

1. Tu ne manges jamais dans un parc?
2. Ton frère ne veut jamais m'inviter?
3. Tu n'es plus malheureux?
4. Personne ne te comprend?
5. Tes amis ne font rien?
6. Il n'y a personne chez toi?
7. Tu ne bois plus de vin?
8. Tu ne peux rien faire?

Ⓒ **J'ai été difficile hier.** Mettez les phrases suivantes au passé composé.

1. Je ne veux rien faire.
2. Je ne bois que de l'eau minérale.
3. Je ne fais jamais la vaisselle.
4. Je ne reçois personne chez moi.
5. Je ne suis jamais content.
6. Tu n'as plus peur de moi?

Culture

Ⓓ **Les magasins en France.** Qu'est-ce qu'on trouve dans les magasins suivants? Combinez les mots donnés pour former des phrases correctes en choisissant entre les mots entre parenthèses.

MODÈLE: trouver (souvent / jamais) / lait / boucherie
          On ne trouve jamais de lait dans une boucherie.

1. (Tout le monde / Personne) / aller / pharmacie / pour acheter de la glace
2. On / aller / (souvent / jamais) / papeterie / pour acheter un stylo
3. Les charcutiers / vendre / (toujours / jamais) / poisson
4. (Les gens / Personne) / aller à l'hypermarché pour acheter des vêtements
5. Les buralistes / vendre / (toujours / jamais) / viande
6. Si on / ne chercher / que légumes, / on / trouver / (tout / rien) / dans une pâtisserie

E **Les Français et la culture.** Un sondage du ministère de la Culture montre combien de Français n'ont jamais participé aux activités suivantes. Faites des phrases en cherchant les pourcentages appropriés de la colonne de droite et les activités correspondantes dans la colonne de gauche.

MODÈLE: aller au zoo / 12%
Douze pour cent des Français ne sont jamais allés au zoo.

1. aller au cinéma   a. 83%
2. visiter un musée   b. 73%
3. aller dans une discothèque   c. 39%
4. voir une pièce de théâtre *(play)*   d. 50%
5. assister à un concert de rock   e. 19%
6. aller à l'opéra   f. 9%

Communication

F **Mes habitudes.** Qu'est-ce que vous faites **souvent, assez souvent** ou **de temps en temps** *(from time to time)*, et qu'est-ce que vous ne faites **jamais** ou **presque jamais?** Utilisez les suggestions données ou vos propres idées.

MODÈLE: étudier le samedi soir   *Je n'étudie jamais le samedi soir.*
        manger du poisson   *Je mange du poisson de temps en temps.*

avoir faim l'après-midi   écouter de la musique classique
boire de l'alcool   fréquenter les pâtisseries
faire du sport   perdre mon temps
sortir avec un footballeur   ???

G **Le snobisme.** Pour être snob, il ne faut faire ou utiliser que certaines choses. Qu'est-ce qu'on doit faire dans les situations suivantes? Préparez vos réponses avec un camarade de cours.

MODÈLE: servir / vin   *On ne sert que du vin français.*

1. porter / jean...   4. sortir avec...
2. porter / chaussures...   5. passer / vacances à...
3. aimer les... (autos)   6. faire des courses à...

MODÈLE: manger à   *Il ne faut jamais manger à McDonald's.*

7. fréquenter...   10. inviter...
8. porter...   11. passer ses vacances...
9. écouter des CD de...   12. utiliser...

H **Questions personnelles.** Votre vie personnelle.

1. Est-ce que vous allez inviter quelqu'un à dîner? Quand?
2. Est-ce que vous servez toujours du lait?
3. Quand est-ce que vous ne faites rien?
4. Quand est-ce que vous ne voulez voir personne?
5. Est-ce que vous devez de l'argent à quelqu'un?
6. Qu'est-ce que vous n'avez jamais fait?

communiquons

Parler d'argent

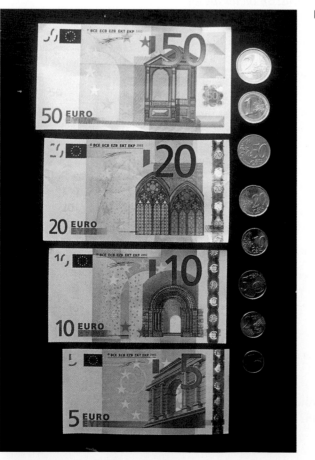

A common European currency, known as the euro, became the official legal tender of the twelve nations that make up the "euro zone" on January 1, 1999. As of that date, euros could be used in electronic financial transactions; however, individual national currencies (pesetas, francs, marks, and so on) could still be used for daily transactions. Three years later, on January 1, 2002, citizens of the zone began phasing out their national currencies and using only euros in their everyday purchases and services. A total of 14.5 billion banknotes were printed and 50 billion coins were minted to help facilitate the changeover.

In many countries, the switch to a new currency inspired mixed emotions—not least of all in France, where the French franc had been in use for more than six hundred years. During the two-month transition period between January 1 and February 28, 2002, citizens of the euro zone could pay with

L'euro

either their old national currency or the euro. To accommodate the coexistence of currencies, many stores set up two lines and separate cash registers.

As the transition period came to an end, newspapers across the euro zone reported that the changeover had gone smoothly, despite some inconveniences—notably, long lines at ATMs and frequent inability to use such coin-operated machines as parking meters, vending machines, and ticket dispensers. Throughout the zone, European citizens bade a final farewell to their national currencies with fireworks, special toasts, and symbolic ceremonies. In Italy, for instance, the mayor of Rome and other Roman citizens saved their last lire and tossed them into the Trevi Fountain. Several euro-zone nations organized exhibits around the history of their national currencies or erected statues made from old coins that had been melted down.

One of the major challenges of the historic monetary transition involved the designing of a set of bank notes that would appeal to the more than three hundred million people living in the euro zone. In the competition to select the official design, Robert Kalina of Vienna, Austria, was designated the artist. Adhering to the guidelines stating that no images associated with only one country could be used, Kalina chose as the general motif European bridges, windows, and doors. According to the artist, these symbolize connections, communication, and a perspective on the future. All euro banknotes feature the same designs, regardless of the country where they are printed. Euro coins, by contrast, reflect the country in which they were minted: one side of each coin bears a national motif, whereas a common European design appears on the other.

Expressions

▶ **On fait des achats.**

C'est combien?	*How much is it?*
Je vous dois combien?	*How much do I owe you?*
Combien coûte ce stylo / coûtent ces stylos?	*How much does this pen / do these pens cost?*
Quel est le prix de cette cassette?	*What's the price of this cassette?*
Quel est le taux de change du dollar?	*What's the exchange rate for the dollar?*
Gardez la monnaie.	*Keep the change.*
Le vendeur fait de la monnaie.	*The sales clerk is making change.*
Je vous rends la monnaie, Monsieur.	*I'm giving you the change, sir.*
Je vous remercie.	*Thank you.*
On ne marchande pas dans cette boutique.	*One doesn't bargain / haggle in this shop.*
Ça coûte un euro vingt (1,20 €).	*It costs one euro and twenty cents.*
Ce stylo coûte trente cents (0,30 €).	*That pen costs thirty cents.*
Le prix? C'est quatre euros soixante-cinq (4,65 €).	*The price? It's four euros and sixty-five cents.*

► **On parle d'argent.**

Mon père me donne de l'argent de poche chaque semaine.	*My father gives me an allowance every week.*
Il ne faut pas dépenser trop d'argent.	*One shouldn't spend too much money.*
J'économise / Je fais des économies.	*I'm saving my money.*
Je ne gaspille jamais mon argent.	*I never waste my money.*
Ce magnétoscope coûte cher.	*This VCR is expensive.*
Dix dollars pour cette chemise? C'est bon marché!	*Ten dollars for this shirt? That's cheap!*

Interaction

Un client fait des achats à la papeterie.

LE PAPETIER: Voilà vos enveloppes et votre stylo.

LE CLIENT: Merci, je vous dois combien?

LE PAPETIER: Six euros cinquante, s'il vous plaît.

LE CLIENT: Je suis désolé, monsieur, mais je n'ai qu'un billet de cent euros.

LE PAPETIER: Cela ne fait rien.° Je vais vous rendre la monnaie... Six cinquante, sept, huit, neuf, dix, trente, cinquante, et cent! Je vous remercie.

That doesn't matter.

Activités

Ⓐ Répondez aux questions suivantes.

1. Combien d'argent de poche recevez-vous chaque *(each)* mois?
2. Combien d'argent avez-vous sur vous en ce moment? Avez-vous la monnaie d'un dollar?
3. Avez-vous économisé de l'argent? Pourquoi? Qu'est-ce que vous avez fait pour avoir cet argent?
4. Qu'est-ce qui coûte trop cher? Qu'est-ce qui est bon marché?

Ⓑ Jouez les scènes suivantes avec un(e) camarade de cours.

1. Vous entrez dans une boulangerie pour acheter du pain et des croissants.
2. Vous voulez acheter un beau pantalon dans un marché aux puces *(flea market)* mais vous pensez qu'il coûte trop cher. Marchandez! *(Bargain for it!)*
3. Dans un restaurant où vous venez de dîner, le garçon vous apporte l'addition *(check)*. Vous trouvez une erreur. Expliquez-la au garçon.
4. Vous avez une interview pour un travail. Demandez combien on va vous payer (**dollars de l'heure**). Est-ce que c'est assez?

lecture culturelle

Avant la lecture

On January 1, 2002, approximately 300 million people living in the "euro zone," which includes Austria, Belgium, Finland, France, Germany, Greece, Ireland, Italy, Luxembourg, the Netherlands, Portugal, and Spain, began using euro bills and coins in their daily purchases. This day marked the culmination of years of planning for a single European currency.

Beginning in 1999, many businesses listed their prices both in their national currency and in euros, in preparation for the historic changeover. The idea behind posting the two currencies side by side was to familiarize people gradually with the euro's value, particularly in relation to the individual national currencies. Each country also participated in educational campaigns to help its citizenry understand the changes that were about to occur with the adoption of a single—and unfamiliar—monetary unit. Euro-zone countries came out with pamphlets, Web pages, posters, advertisements, lesson plans for schoolchildren, and other support materials.

During the first stage of the unified European currency, Denmark, Great Britain, and Sweden, though they are members of the European Union, declined to participate in the euro zone. As a consequence, they continue to use their national currencies, at least for the time being. Other European countries have applied for membership in the European Union. It is therefore likely that the euro community will continue to grow in the future.

The euro symbol (€) resembles a rounded E whose crossbar is composed of two parallel lines. It takes its inspiration from the Greek letter *epsilon* and thus harks back to the dawn of European civilization. The bold parallel lines are intended to represent stability.

Because the text that follows was published before January 2001, the remarks about the euro are in the future tense.

Activités

Ⓐ What do you think are the advantages of the euro for tourists traveling through Europe?

Ⓑ If you were creating a new currency, how might you design the bills and coins so that blind people could distinguish one denomination from another?

Ⓒ The following vocabulary occurs in the text. Match the French terms with their English counterparts. Familiarity with the vocabulary will facilitate your reading of the text that follows.

1. un billet	a.	weight
2. une pièce (de monnaie)	b.	thickness
3. la valeur, le montant	c.	to mint (coins)
4. les frais de change	d.	graphic design
5. la taille	e.	coin
6. imprimer	f.	size
7. le graphisme	g.	value
8. le poids	h.	commission (fee paid when
9. l'épaisseur		money is converted)
10. frapper	i.	to print
	j.	bill

L'euro: une nouvelle monnaie en France
A quoi ressemble l'euro?

L'introduction de l'euro signifie que de nouveaux billets et de nouvelles pièces seront° mis en circulation à partir du 1ᵉʳ janvier 2002. Il y aura° 7 nouveaux billets de banque et 8 nouvelles pièces de monnaie. Les billets de banque auront une valeur de 5, 10, 20, 50, 100, 200 ou 500 euros. Les billets seront de formats différents. En effet, le format° augmente avec le montant des billets. Les billets seront les mêmes pour tous les pays.

Il y aura aussi des pièces de 1 et de 2 euros, de 1, 2, 5, 10, 20 et 50 cents. 1 euro = 100 cents. Elles seront facilement reconnaissables par leur taille, leur graphisme, leur couleur, leur poids et leur épaisseur. Chaque pièce aura une face° commune et une face nationale. Une face des pièces sera donc identique dans tous les pays participants, l'autre face sera conçue par chaque Etat membre. La face nationale des pièces belges en euro portera l'effigie du Roi Albert II°.

will be / Il... There will be

size (of a bill)

side (of a coin)

portera... will bear the likeness of King Albert II (current king of Belgium)

Lors de° la conception des billets et des pièces de monnaie, on a tenu compte des aveugles et des malvoyants°: les montants sur les billets seront indiqués en grand et les aveugles reconnaîtront la valeur du billet grâce aux différents formats et à des éléments spéciaux en relief, intégrés près des bords°. Enfin, les pièces de monnaie auront chacune° un bord différent. Pour éviter la contrefaçon°, les billets et les pièces seront pourvus de° marques d'authenticité sophistiquées. Les billets seront imprimés sur un papier spécial à fibres fluorescentes, dans lequel° seront incorporés un filigrane et un fil de sécurité°. Les pièces de 1 et de 2 euros seront, quant à° elles, protégées par° des techniques particulières.

At the time of
tenu... took the blind
and seeing-impaired into
consideration / edges
each one / counterfeiting
seront... will have
dans... in which
fil... security thread
as for / protected by

Ce qui change pour les consommateurs.

L'introduction de l'euro présente des avantages pour tous les consommateurs. En effet, la valeur de tous les produits et services est affichée dans la même monnaie, l'euro. Ceci vous permet de mieux comparer les prix, que° vous fassiez vos achats en Belgique ou dans un autre pays de l'Union européenne.

whether

Bien sûr, la plupart des consommateurs continuent à faire leurs achats dans leur quartier. Certains produits importés pourront être° moins chers, grâce à la suppression° des frais de change. De plus, certains secteurs devront° tenir compte de la concurrence. Ce sera notamment le cas pour les entreprises de services comme les banques ou les assurances.

will perhaps be
elimination / will have to

Grâce à l'euro, vous pouvez donc vérifier dans quels pays les produits sont les moins chers. En voyage, l'euro vous permet de faire des économies sur les frais de change. En effet, avant l'euro, lorsque vous traversiez les différents pays de l'Union européenne, les frais de change pouvaient être très élevés. L'euro y met fin. Boire un verre à Amsterdam ou déguster° une crème glacée à la Côte d'Azur sans devoir changer d'argent? C'est, dès à présent, possible.

to eat, savor

«Bientôt l'euro remplacera le franc», Mieke van den Berghe.

Après la lecture

Questions sur le texte

1. Il y a combien de billets euro? Combien de pièces? Quelles sont les différentes valeurs?
2. Comment est-ce que les pièces sont reconnaissables entre elles?
3. Qu'est-ce qui se trouve sur une face de toutes les pièces? Et sur l'autre face?
4. Comment est-ce que les malvoyants peuvent reconnaître les différents billets? Et les différentes pièces de monnaie?
5. D'après *(According to)* le texte, quels sont les avantages principaux de l'euro pour les consommateurs?
6. Pourquoi est-ce que certains produits importés sont en principe moins chers qu'avant?

Activités

Ⓐ Dans le texte, vous avez appris que chaque pays frappe ses pièces de monnaie euro avec (sur une des deux faces) des symboles nationaux. Quels symboles trouve-t-on sur les pièces françaises, belges et luxembourgeoises? Quelle est la signification de chaque symbole?

Ⓑ Chaque état des Etats-Unis a sa propre pièce de 25 cents *(U.S. state quarters)*. Quel est le symbole sur la pièce de votre état? Est-ce que vous l'aimez? Suggérez un autre symbole approprié pour votre état.

Ⓒ Quel est le taux de change du dollar en euros? Combien coûtent les articles suivants en dollars?

Un CD	19,82 €
Un litre de lait	0,70 €
Timbre poste	0,46 €
Une voiture	18.994,49 €
Ticket de cinéma	6,86 €
Journal quotidien	1,00 €
Une baguette	0,61 €

vocabulaire

Noms / Pronoms

un article de sport	sports item / sporting goods	**une commande**	order
une bijouterie	jeweler's	**un/une commerçant(e)**	shopkeeper
un (une) boucher (-ère)	butcher	**conserves** *(f.)*	canned food
une boucherie	butcher shop	**une crémerie**	dairy store
un (une) boulanger (-ère)	baker	**une épicerie**	grocery
une boulangerie	bakery	**un (une) épicier (-ère)**	grocer
une bouteille	bottle	**euro** *(m.)*	euro
une boutique	shop	**un/une fleuriste**	florist
une brasserie	café-restaurant	**un gramme**	gram
un/une buraliste	tobacconist	**un hypermarché**	giant supermarket
la caisse	the cashier's	**Mesdemoiselles** *(f.)*	ladies
le centre-ville	downtown		
une charcuterie	pork butcher's shop	**une papeterie**	stationer's
		le pâté de foie	liver pâté
un (une) charcutier (-ère)	pork butcher	**une pâtisserie**	pastry shop
		un (une) pâtissier (-ère)	pastry maker
la choucroute garnie	sauerkraut and assorted meat	**un plat cuisiné**	prepared dish

une poissonnerie	fish market	soldes *(f.)*	sales
un (une) poissonnier (-ère)	fishmonger	un supermarché	supermarket
		une teinturerie	dry cleaner's
un produit	product	un (une) vendeur (-euse)	salesperson
un rayon	department		
une remise	discount		

Verbes

boire	to drink	essayer	to try
conseiller	to advise	falloir	must
devoir	must	recevoir	to receive

Adjectifs / Adverbes

ne... personne	nobody	ne... rien	nothing
ne... plus	no more	sec	dry
ne... que	only	surgelé	frozen

Expressions

autre chose	something else
de bonne heure	early
en solde	on sale
peut-être	maybe
tout le monde	everybody

Révision

D Chapitres 10 à 12

Tous ensemble!

Ⓐ Répondez aux questions suivantes en employant les mots entre parenthèses.

Les amis

1. As-tu vu Françoise? (Oui,... venir... hier)
2. Tu m'aimes? (Oui,...)
3. Etes-vous étonnées que vos copains ne vous téléphonent jamais? (Oui,...)
4. Qui a appris à ton ami à utiliser Internet? (Personne...)
5. Est-ce que je peux te voir ce soir? (Non, parler... demain)

Les activités

6. Est-ce que vous pouvez nous prêter votre auto? (Oui,...)
7. Avez-vous peur qu'il fasse mauvais demain? (Oui, je... pleuvoir)
8. Est-ce que vous venez me voir? (Oui,...)
9. Est-il possible que vous partiez demain? (Non, il faut que... partir aujourd'hui)
10. Est-ce que je vous ai vus à la boulangerie? (Oui,...)

Ⓑ Refaites les phrases suivantes en utilisant les mots entre parenthèses.

Qu'est-ce qu'il y a?

1. Elle part à neuf heures et elle va à la charcuterie. (Hier,...)
2. Quelque chose est arrivé au courrier. (Rien...)
3. Je les vois quand ils sortent. (... la semaine dernière.)
4. Il a attendu trois minutes. (... ne... que...)
5. Elle apprend une langue étrangère? (L'année dernière,...)

Des opinions

6. Je suis sûr qu'il ne veut pas venir. (... furieux...)
7. Il ne faut pas qu'on oublie les sans-abri. (... devoir...)
8. Je doute qu'ils soient pauvres. (... penser...)
9. Es-tu sûr que nous ayons un désastre écologique un jour? (Moi, je suis sûr...)
10. Je dois partir quand elle arrive. (... hier.)

Ⓒ Faites des phrases complètes avec les mots donnés, en faisant les changements nécessaires.

Des activités

1. Jeanne / travailler / jamais / dans / boucherie
2. Hier / nous / descendre / en ville / avec / enfants
3. Paul / boire / jamais / eau
4. Hier soir / je / recevoir / personne
5. Tu / venir / répondre / téléphone?

La famille

6. Personne / devoir / rien / mes parents
7. Il / être / peu probable / tu / voir / ton / grands-parents
8. Quand / je / habiter / Québec / je / recevoir / souvent / cousins
9. Mon / sœurs / tenir / faire / promenade
10. Mes parents / ne... pas penser / guerre / être / possible

D Complétez les paragraphes suivants avec la forme correcte des verbes donnés.

Le week-end dernier, Chantal et ses sœurs _____ (décider) d'aller au bord de la mer. Elle _____ (inviter) son petit ami Charles; il ne _____ (pouvoir) pas aller avec elles, mais il _____ (recommander) une belle plage près d'Arcachon.

Quand elles _____ (partir), il _____ (faire) du brouillard et il _____ (falloir) qu'elles _____ (faire) attention. Il _____ (être) cinq heures quand elles _____ (partir), mais dans la voiture personne ne _____ (dormir). Après deux heures, elles _____ (arriver) dans une petite ville. Il _____ (être) sept heures et tout le monde _____ (vouloir) continuer pour être à la mer avant les touristes. Mais Chantal _____ (être) fatiguée et elle _____ (vouloir) qu'on _____ (prendre) quelque chose. Elles _____ (chercher) un café ou un restaurant, mais comme il _____ (être) peu probable qu'elles _____ (pouvoir) trouver un café ouvert à cette heure, elles _____ (décider) de continuer.

Elles _____ (arriver) deux heures plus tard. Elles _____ (sortir) de la voiture et _____ (aller) sur la plage. Chantal _____ (comprendre) tout de suite pourquoi Charles aime cette plage: il n'y _____ (avoir) que des nudistes!

E Complétez les phrases suivantes de manière logique.

1. Je ne pense pas que...
2. Il est probable que...
3. Mes parents veulent que...
4. A ma résidence, nous venons de...
5. Il ne faut pas que nous...
6. Je doute que mon professeur...
7. Hier, j'ai reçu...
8. Je suis sûr(e) que...
9. Les Américains pensent que...
10. Il se peut que...

Entre nous!

A Interviewez un(e) camarade de cours et posez-lui les questions suivantes. Après, informez la classe des résultats.

1. Que veux-tu faire dans la vie?
2. Quelle sorte de travail as-tu déjà fait?
3. Où es-tu allé(e) le week-end dernier?
4. Qu'est-ce que tu as fait?
5. Qu'est-ce que tu ne fais jamais?
6. Qui te donne ton argent?

Ⓑ En petits groupes, interrogez vos camarades de cours sur leurs compétences. Qu'est-ce qu'ils savent faire? Quand est-ce qu'ils ne peuvent pas faire ces choses et pourquoi?

Ⓒ Racontez votre enfance *(childhood)* à un(e) camarade de cours. Employez les expressions suivantes ou vos propres idées.

jouer beaucoup	être méchant(e)
manger beaucoup de glace	dormir l'après-midi
regarder... à la télévision	???

Ⓓ En petits groupes, expliquez vos réactions aux situations suivantes. Utilisez les suggestions des deux colonnes ou d'autres expressions.

J'ai peur que	il y a un conflit international
Je pense que	le Président va à Moscou
Je ne pense pas que	le Canada veut coloniser les Etats-Unis
???	les jeunes peuvent influencer le gouvernement
	les athlètes russes ne sont pas compétitifs
	le Japon vend trop de voitures aux Etats-Unis
	l'inflation est un problème sérieux

Ⓔ Avec un(e) camarade de cours, faites une liste des activités que vous devez faire. Utilisez les suggestions suivantes ou vos propres idées.

étudier plus souvent?	aller à l'église / à la synagogue /
téléphoner à mes parents?	à la mosquée?
dormir moins?	réparer ma voiture?
faire une lettre à des amis?	

Ⓕ **Jeu de rôles.** Jouez les scènes suivantes avec un(e) camarade de cours.

1. Vous avez loué une voiture et vous la rendez à l'agence. Vous devez expliquer pourquoi vous êtes en retard.
2. Vous êtes journaliste. Interviewez trois personnes qui ont vu un accident de voiture.
3. Vous téléphonez au charcutier pour commander un dîner pour huit personnes. Quels plats voulez-vous servir?
4. Vous êtes dans un hypermarché et vous ne pouvez rien trouver. Demandez à un(e) employé(e) où vous pouvez trouver les choses que vous cherchez.
5. Vous cherchez du travail. Un(e) camarade de cours va prendre des renseignements sur votre identité (nom, âge, adresse...) et va vous poser des questions sur vos compétences.
6. Vous êtes journaliste et vous préparez un reportage sur les opinions des étudiants à votre université. Interrogez des camarades de cours pour voir s'ils sont optimistes ou pessimistes pour l'avenir. Qu'est-ce qui les préoccupe?

commençons

grammaire

communiquons

lecture culturelle

vocabulaire

**Médecins sans Frontières
en Somalie**

La santé

OBJECTIVES

Language	Culture	Communication
■ Vocabulary for parts of the body ■ Initial and final consonant sounds ■ Stem-changing verbs	■ Reflexive verbs in the present, **futur proche,** and infinitive ■ Reflexive verbs in the **passé composé** and imperative	■ Medical care in France ■ Nicotine addiction	■ Consulting a doctor ■ Discussing health ■ Describing one's daily routine

commençons

Chez le médecin

Paul Prévot va consulter son médecin car il dort mal et il est très fatigué depuis deux semaines.

LE MÉDECIN: Bonjour, Paul. Qu'est-ce qui ne va pas?

PAUL: Depuis quinze jours je suis très fatigué et le soir, je m'endors très tard.

LE MÉDECIN: Est-ce que vous vous couchez de bonne heure? Est-ce que vous vous réveillez tôt le matin? Vous reposez-vous dans la journée?

PAUL: Je me couche généralement vers onze heures et je ne me lève jamais avant sept heures, mais je ne ferme pas l'œil de la nuit.

LE MÉDECIN: Déshabillez-vous. Je vais vous examiner mais je ne pense pas que cela soit sérieux.

L'examen terminé, le médecin appelle Paul dans son bureau.

PAUL: Alors, docteur, j'espère que ce n'est pas une maladie grave!

LE MÉDECIN: Je ne trouve rien. Il faut que vous vous détendiez davantage. Faites-vous de l'exercice régulièrement?

PAUL: Non, mais je me promène tous les soirs après dîner.

LE MÉDECIN: Très bien. Ne vous inquiétez pas, mais suivez mon conseil: évitez de boire du café avant de vous coucher, mais si cela ne va pas mieux, il va falloir qu'on vous fasse une prise de sang.

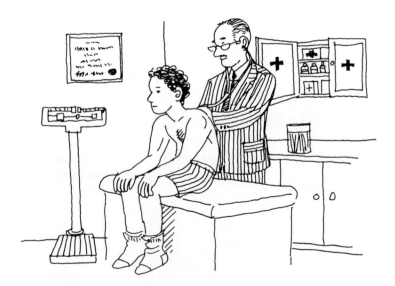

1. Pourquoi Paul Prévot va-t-il chez le médecin?
2. Combien d'heures est-ce qu'il dort?
3. Est-ce que le docteur pense que c'est grave?
4. Est-ce qu'il examine Paul?
5. Qu'est-ce que le docteur recommande?
6. Est-ce qu'il faut que Paul boive beaucoup de café?

Mots clés

consulter	*to visit*	examiner	*to examine*
Qu'est-ce qui ne va pas?	*What's wrong?*	appelle (appeler)	*calls*
		une maladie	*illness*
m'endors (s'endormir)	*fall asleep*	grave	*serious*
tard	*late*	vous détendiez (se détendre)	*relax*
vous vous couchez (se coucher)	*you go to bed*	davantage	*more*
vous vous réveillez (se réveiller)	*you wake up*	Faites-vous de l'exercice?	*Do you exercise?*
tôt	*early*	régulièrement	*regularly*
reposez-vous (se reposer)	*you rest*	me promène (se promener)	*go for a walk*
une journée	*day*		
généralement	*generally*	bien	*well*
vers	*about, around*	Ne vous inquiétez pas. (s'inquiéter)	*Don't worry.*
me lève (se lever)	*get up*		
ne ferme pas l'œil de la nuit	*can't sleep a wink all night long*	évitez (éviter)	*avoid*
		ne va pas mieux (aller mieux)	*do not feel better*
Déshabillez-vous. (se déshabiller)	*Get undressed.*	une prise de sang	*blood test*

ℱaisons connaissance

The medical profession remains a popular choice for young people in France, and medical students must go through a rigorous training that begins the year after high school. However, a surplus of physicians, particularly in the major urban centers, is beginning to create problems. Many physicians now have to compete for patients; their average income is decreasing; and the profession as a whole has lost some of its social prestige.

Many family doctors in France still follow the tradition of making house calls. A family would never go to a hospital first for an emergency—it would call the doctor. Many doctors work in their own homes and do not have secretarial help. French citizens and foreigners working in ▶

France are reimbursed by the social security system for 80 percent of their medical expenses.

In France, many people consult pharmacists rather than doctors for minor problems. A pharmacist can offer advice and sell medicines over the counter that might not be available in this country without a prescription. Pharmacies are numerous in French cities and are easily identifiable by the green cross (**la croix verte**) that hangs above the store. When a pharmacy is closed, there is always a sign hanging on the door with the address of the nearest **pharmacie de garde** or **pharmacie de nuit,** which is the pharmacy designated to stay open at night or on Sunday and holidays.

❖ ❖ ❖ ❖ ❖ ❖ ❖ ❖ ❖ ❖ ❖ ❖ ❖

**Fatiguée de courir, de toujours
se battre, plus envie de devoir
ressembler aux filles des magazines,
et parfois un peu de mal à m'endormir.
Je manquais simplement
de magnésium et vitamine C.
J'ai retrouvé qui j'étais vraiment …**

   quelqu'un de bien.

magnoscorbol

*Ceci est un médicament. Lire attentivement la notice.
Demandez conseil à votre pharmacien.*

Enrichissons notre vocabulaire

Les parties du corps *(Parts of the body)*

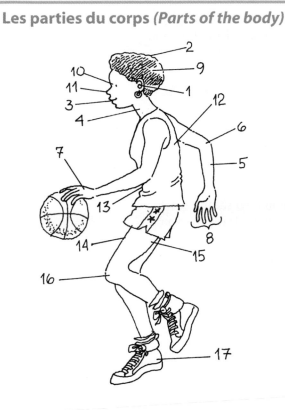

1. les oreilles *(f.)*	7. la main	12. le dos
2. la tête	8. les doigts *(m.)*	13. le ventre
3. la bouche	9. les cheveux *(m.)*	14. la jambe
4. la gorge	10. les yeux /	15. la cuisse
5. le bras	l'œil *(m.)*	16. le genou
6. le coude	11. le nez	17. le pied

La santé *(Health)*

être en bonne / mauvaise santé	*to be **in good / bad** health*
avoir **bonne mine / mauvaise mine**	*to look **good / bad***
avoir **mal à**	*to **hurt***
être **malade**	*to be ill*
avoir **de la fièvre**	*to have **a fever***
se **porter bien**	*to be **in good health***
être **au régime** / faire **un régime**	*to be **on a diet** / to follow **a diet***
aller **chez le dentiste**	*to go **to the dentist***

—Qu'est-ce qui te fait mal? /   *Where does it hurt?*
  Où as-tu mal?

—J'ai mal aux **dents** *(f.)*, au **cou,**   *My **teeth, neck, shoulder,***
  à l'**épaule** *(f.)*, à la **cheville.**   *ankle hurt.*

—Tu es **hypocondriaque!**   *You're a **hypochondriac!***

Prononciation   Initial and final consonant sounds

A. If you place your hand in front of your mouth and pronounce an English word starting with the / p /, / t /, or / k / sounds, you will feel a puff of air. This is *aspiration,* and you must avoid it in French when you pronounce such initial consonant sounds.

Listen carefully to your teacher and repeat the following pairs of words, trying to eliminate the aspiration in the French words.

English	French	English	French
Paul	Paul	two	tout
Paris	Paris	car	car

B. Final consonant sounds are stronger in French than in English. In French, it is very important to pronounce final consonant sounds clearly. As you know, some grammatical distinctions depend on the presence or absence of a final consonant sound in the oral form.

Gender: étudiant / e ty djã /
étudiante / e ty djãt /

Number: il descend / il dɛ sã /
ils descendent / il dɛ sãd /

Repeat the following pairs of words after your teacher, making the final consonant sound much stronger in French.

English	French	English	French
habit	habite	port	porte
bees	bise	long	longue
descend	descendent	mine	mine

Repeat the following words after your teacher, making sure to pronounce the final consonant sound clearly.

verte / sorte / verbe / servent / heureuse / tienne / sac / rendent / tête

Exercice

Read the following sentences aloud, avoiding the aspiration of initial consonant sounds and stressing final ones.

1. Le professeur pose une question intéressante.
2. Patrick passe l'été dans l'appartement de sa tante.
3. Au printemps, à Paris, les cafés sont pleins de monde.
4. Ces pays deviennent de plus en plus pauvres.
5. Un cours de psychologie demande beaucoup de travail.
6. Brigitte part faire des courses avec Monique.

grammaire

I. Stem-changing verbs

You use verbs to describe actions or states of being.

A. Two groups of common **-er** verbs have stem changes in the **je, tu, il,** and **ils** forms of the present indicative. These are verbs that have **é** or **e** at the end of their stem, such as **préférer** and **acheter.**

préférer	acheter
je préfère	j' achète
tu préfères	tu achètes
il / elle / on préfère	il / elle / on achète
nous préférons	nous achetons
vous préférez	vous achetez
ils / elles préfèrent	ils / elles achètent

Mots clés   *Some verbs conjugated like* **préférer** *and* **acheter**

préférer		acheter	
espérer	*to hope*	amener	*to bring*
inquiéter	*to worry*	emmener	*to take*
posséder	*to own*	enlever	*to take off / away*
répéter	*to repeat*	lever	*to raise*
sécher	*to dry*	promener	*to walk*
sécher un cours	*to cut class*		

Je **préfère** la cuisine vietnamienne. Qu'est-ce que vous **préférez?**
Eux, ils n'**achètent** jamais rien, mais nous, nous **achetons** souvent des vêtements.
Les maladies **inquiètent** beaucoup les Français.

B. Note that in the **je, tu, il,** and **ils** forms, the vowel at the end of the stem is pronounced as a more open / ɛ / sound, thus causing a change from é or e to an **accent grave** (è) before a pronounced final consonant.

préférer	→ je préfère	/ ʒø pre fɛʀ /
répéter	→ tu répètes	/ ty ʀe pɛt /
acheter	→ elles achètent	/ ɛl za ʃɛt /
lever	→ il lève	/ il lɛv /

L'orthographe

> 1. **Appeler** *(to call)* uses a double l instead of an **accent grave** to make the vowel sound / ɛ / before a final consonant. The **je, tu, il,** and **ils** forms of the present indicative show this stem change.
>
> j'appelle, ils appellent   *but:* nous appelons
>
> Le médecin appelle Paul dans son bureau.
>
> 2. In the present indicative, only the **nous** and **vous** forms keep the same pronunciation and spelling as the infinitive because these forms end in a vowel sound and not in a consonant sound.
>
> espérer → nous espérons   / nu zɛ spe rɔ̃ /
> acheter → vous achetez   / vu za ʃte /

C. Since the present subjunctive has similar endings, the vowels change as in the indicative.

Il faut que je sèche	que j'enlève
que tu sèches	que tu enlèves
qu'on sèche	qu'il / elle / on enlève
que nous séchions	que nous enlevions
que vous séchiez	que vous enleviez
qu'ils sèchent	qu'ils / elles enlèvent

D. The past participle is pronounced like the infinitive; therefore, the vowels in the stem do not change.

espérer   → espéré   lever   → levé
posséder → possédé   appeler → appelé

E. Since the imperfect has a vowel ending in all forms of the verb, the vowel in the stem does not change.

Je **possédais** une voiture, mais je l'ai vendue.
Nous **appelions** Jacques quand il est arrivé.

> Un fumeur sur trois, chaque année, essaye de s'arrêter, contre 15 % en 1981.
> Les taxes représentent 76 % du prix de vente des cigarettes.

A **En classe.** Dans les phrases suivantes, mettez les verbes au singulier au pluriel et les verbes au pluriel au singulier.

1. Répétez le dialogue!
2. N'enlève pas tes chaussures en classe!
3. Nous possédons une bonne calculatrice.
4. J'espère qu'il va réussir.
5. Lève la main si tu sais la réponse.
6. Vous appelez son professeur?
7. Elle va sécher son cours d'espagnol.
8. Achète-lui un nouveau cahier.

B **Des substitutions.** Substituez les expressions données dans les phrases suivantes.

1. Tu sèches tes cours? (préférer l'eau minérale, espérer gagner le match, enlever ton manteau, promener tes amis, inquiéter ta famille)
2. Elle appelait sa sœur. (posséder une bicyclette, espérer être heureuse, préférer aller au cinéma, répéter la question)
3. Je ne pense pas qu'elle achète une voiture. (emmener son ami, préférer mon dentiste, enlever son imperméable, appeler le docteur, amener les boissons)

C **Les distractions des Français.** Choisissez la chose ou la personne que les Français préfèrent parmi *(among)* les trois possibilités.

MODÈLE: comme distraction: la télé / les livres / les sports
          Les Français préfèrent la télé.

1. comme distraction: la radio / les cafés / le cinéma
2. comme lecture: *Télé 7 Jours* / *Paris-Match* / *L'Express*
3. à la télé: la fiction / les films / le journal / les sports
4. l'origine des films: les films français / les films américains / les films italiens
5. comme genre de film: les films d'amour / les films d'aventure / les films comiques
6. comme film américain: *La Momie* / *Les Dix Commandements* / *Tarzan*

D **Le français québécois.** Comment est-ce que les Québécois appellent les choses suivantes?

MODÈLE: un week-end? *Ils l'appellent* «une fin de semaine».

1. une voiture
2. un dîner
3. un match
4. du jambon
5. de l'auto-stop
6. un film

a. une vue
b. de la fesse
c. un char
d. un souper
e. une joute
f. du pouce

Ⓔ Vivent les différences! Etes-vous différent(e) de votre camarade de chambre? Choisissez entre les différentes possibilités. Suivez le modèle.

MODÈLE: le jazz / la musique classique / le rock
Moi, je préfère la musique classique.
Lui, il préfère le jazz.

1. cinéma / théâtre / télévision
2. lait / thé / bière / vin
3. étudier / faire une promenade / aller danser / sécher les cours
4. la plage / les parcs / le centre-ville
5. avoir une profession bien payée / avoir une profession intéressante
6. parler de grands problèmes / parler de ses amis

Ⓕ Les possessions. Trouvez quelqu'un dans la classe qui possède les choses suivantes.

MODÈLE: un vélo   *Je possède un vélo.*
une calculatrice   *Marc possède une calculatrice.*

une auto jaune	un magnétoscope
un lecteur de disques compacts	un pantalon vert
des CD des Beatles	une photo de famille
une carte du monde	un Walkman
un téléphone portable	des chaussures rouges

Ⓖ Questions personnelles. L'avenir.

1. Qu'est-ce qui vous inquiète? L'avenir? Votre santé?
2. Qu'est-ce que vous allez pouvoir acheter dans dix ans que vous ne pouvez pas acheter maintenant?
3. Combien d'enfants espérez-vous avoir? Préférez-vous des garçons ou des filles?
4. Préférez-vous un beau mari / une belle femme ou un mari / une femme intelligent(e)?
5. Qu'est-ce que vos amis espèrent avoir un jour? Et vous?
6. Quelle erreur n'allez-vous jamais répéter?

II. Reflexive verbs: Present tense, *futur proche*, and the infinitive

Reflexive verbs in French describe an action that the subject performs upon itself.

A. Present tense

1. Reflexive verbs are conjugated with a reflexive pronoun, which represents the same person as the subject. Reflexive pronouns have the same position as the other object pronouns you have learned.

se coucher *(to go to bed)*	s'amuser *(to have a good time)*
je **me** couche	je **m'**amuse
tu **te** couches	tu **t'**amuses
il / elle / on **se** couche	il / elle / on **s'**amuse
nous **nous** couchons	nous **nous** amusons
vous **vous** couchez	vous **vous** amusez
ils / elles **se** couchent	ils / elles **s'**amusent

2. In the negative, the reflexive pronoun precedes the conjugated verb.

   Je **ne me lève jamais** avant sept heures.

3. With inversion in the interrogative, the reflexive pronoun precedes the conjugated verb.

   Vous réveillez-vous tôt le matin?
   Paul **se promène-t-il** tous les soirs?

Alors, on se promène en ville?

Mots clés *Reflexive verbs*

se coucher

s'endormir

se réveiller

se lever

se laver

se brosser

s'habiller

se promener

s'amuser	*to have a good time*	s'inquiéter de	*to worry about*
s'appeler	*to be called / named*	s'occuper de	*to take care of*
se dépêcher	*to hurry*	se rappeler	*to remember*
se déshabiller	*to get undressed*	se reposer	*to rest*
se détendre	*to relax*	se sentir	*to feel*
se faire mal à	*to hurt one's . . .*	se trouver	*to be located*

Attention!

Note that definite articles, not possessive adjectives, are used with parts of the body: ownership is understood!

Elle se brosse **les** dents.   Ils se lavent **les** mains.

B. *Le futur proche*

1. To form the **futur proche,** you conjugate the verb **aller** and place the reflexive pronoun with the infinitive of the reflexive verb.

> Nous **allons nous reposer** ce soir.
> Tu **vas t'amuser** ce week-end?

2. In the negative, place the negative expression around the conjugated verb.

> Je **ne vais pas m'occuper** de la lessive.
> Nous **n'allons pas nous dépêcher** maintenant.

3. The interrogative with inversion is formed the same way as it is with other verbs in the **futur proche:**

> **Vont-elles se promener** après les cours?

C. The infinitive

With an infinitive construction, the reflexive pronoun precedes the infinitive. Reflexive pronouns must represent the same person as the subject, even if the verbs are not conjugated.

> **Je** ne peux pas **m'endormir.**
> **Tu** as besoin de **te détendre!**
> **Evitez** le café avant de **vous coucher.**
> Pour **m'amuser, j'**aime passer la journée à la plage.

Langue

Ⓐ **Une journée typique de Monique.** Mettez les phrases suivantes à la forme interrogative en utilisant l'inversion.

1. Ton amie s'appelle Monique.
2. Elle se réveille tôt.
3. Elle se lave tout de suite.
4. Elle s'habille dans sa chambre.
5. Elle s'occupe de son fils.
6. Son bureau se trouve en ville.

Ⓑ **Un week-end à Arcachon.** Mettez les phrases suivantes au futur proche.

1. Nous nous dépêchons de partir.
2. Yvette se promène sur la plage.
3. Je ne me lève pas tôt.
4. Vous ne vous inquiétez pas si Yves amène des copains?
5. Jacques ne s'occupe pas de la vaisselle.
6. Nous nous amusons là-bas.

Culture

Ⓒ **La France ou les Etats-Unis?** Formez des phrases complètes avec les mots donnés et dites si l'activité est plus typique des Français ou des Américains.

1. On / faire / bises / avant / se coucher
2. grands-mères / s'appeler / «Mamie»
3. On / pouvoir / se lever tard / 1ᵉʳ mai

4. Les personnes âgées / se promener / dans / centres commerciaux / pour leur santé
5. On / se déshabiller / sur / plage
6. On / se reposer / au déjeuner
7. Beaucoup de gens / s'inquiéter / leur poids *(weight)*
8. On / se promener / en auto / pour / se détendre

D **Les provinces françaises.** Traditionnellement, la France est divisée en provinces. Dites *(Say)* dans quelle province on trouve les villes suivantes.

MODÈLE: Bordeaux   *Bordeaux se trouve en Aquitaine.*

1. Dijon   a. Provence
2. Reims   b. Normandie
3. Brest   c. Bretagne
4. Rouen   d. Bourgogne
5. Marseille   e. Alsace
6. Strasbourg   f. Champagne

Communication

E **Une journée typique.** Racontez une journée typique dans votre vie. Ensuite, racontez une journée idéale. Si vous voulez, utilisez les mots de la liste suivante et un adverbe: **à... heure(s), tôt, tard, de bonne heure.**

se réveiller	se dépêcher	s'occuper de
se lever	partir pour les cours	se déshabiller
se laver	rentrer	se coucher
s'habiller	se reposer	???

F **Mes habitudes.** Que faites-vous pour vous amuser? vous reposer? vous endormir? vous détendre? vous réveiller? Comparez vos réponses avec les réponses d'un(e) camarade de cours et présentez les similarités et les différences à la classe.

MODÈLE: *Pour me réveiller, je bois du café.*

G **On s'inquiète.** Quand est-ce que les gens s'inquiètent? Répondez en utilisant un élément de chaque colonne avec l'expression **s'inquiéter quand.**

Je	rentrer tard
Mes parents	faire du stop
Mon petit ami	dépenser trop d'argent
Ma petite amie	sécher les cours
Mon professeur	ne pas répondre aux lettres
???	???

H **Questions personnelles.** Réfléchissons!

1. Qu'est-ce que vous vous rappelez de votre enfance *(childhood)*?
2. Vous inquiétez-vous souvent? De quoi?
3. Préférez-vous vous coucher tôt ou tard et vous lever tôt ou tard?
4. Quand est-ce que vous vous sentez triste?
5. Où se trouve votre endroit préféré?
6. Qui doit s'occuper des pauvres?

III. Reflexive verbs: *Passé composé* and imperative

You use reflexive verbs in the **passé composé** to describe personal actions in the past and in the imperative to give commands.

A. *Passé composé*

All reflexive verbs are conjugated with être in the **passé composé**.

Je **me suis levé** à sept heures.   Tu ne **t'es** pas **couché** hier soir?
Il **s'est inquiété.**   **Vous êtes**-vous déjà **lavé?**

L'orthographe

1. Unlike other verbs conjugated with être in the **passé composé,** the past participle agrees with the reflexive pronoun, which is usually a direct object and which is the same as the subject.

   Nous **nous** sommes habillés.   Elle ne **s'est** pas dépêchée.

2. There is no agreement with the past participle when a part of the body follows the verb.

   Elle s'est **lavé** les mains.   Nous nous sommes **brossé** les dents.

B. The imperative

The reflexive pronoun follows the verb in the affirmative and precedes the verb in the negative.

Déshabillez-vous!   Ne te couche pas trop tard!
Dépêchons-nous!   Ne vous inquiétez pas trop!

Attention!

The pronoun **te** becomes **toi** when it *follows* the verb.

Ne **te** dépêche pas!   →   Dépêche-**toi!**
Ne **t'**habille pas maintenant!   →   Habille-**toi** maintenant!

Langue

Ⓐ **Notre journée d'hier.** Mettez les phrases suivantes au passé composé.

1. Nous nous levons tôt.
2. Vous vous réveillez avant sept heures?
3. Nous ne nous promenons pas avant le déjeuner.
4. Robert et Julie s'amusent après notre promenade.
5. Lise se repose avant le dîner.
6. Jean se dépêche pour dîner avec nous.
7. Tu ne t'endors pas de bonne heure?
8. Je me couche tard.

B **Des conseils.** Mettez les phrases suivantes à l'impératif pour donner des conseils à vos amis.

1. Tu ne te lèves pas trop tard.
2. Vous vous dépêchez pour aller en classe.
3. Tu te reposes cet après-midi.
4. Nous nous amusons ce soir.
5. Tu ne t'endors pas au concert.
6. Vous vous déshabillez avant de vous coucher.
7. Nous ne nous détendons pas avant l'examen.
8. Vous ne vous couchez pas à deux heures du matin.

Culture

C **Des Américains ou des Français?** Avec un nom comme **Robert** ou **Michelle,** on peut être français ou américain. Formez des phrases complètes au passé pour décrire *(describe)* les activités des personnes suivantes. Ensuite dites si la personne est américaine ou française, selon l'activité.

1. Michelle / téléphoner / sa copine / avant de se coucher
2. Robert / se laver / dans sa chambre
3. Michelle / s'habiller / simplement / pour aller en cours
4. Robert / prendre un somnifère *(sleeping pill)* / et il / s'endormir
5. Michelle / se sentir / très mal / quand elle / se réveiller / et / demander au médecin / venir chez elle
6. Robert / s'amuser / faire des crêpes / 2 février

Communication

D **Expliquez-vous!** Trouvez des excuses ou des raisons pour les situations suivantes. Utilisez les suggestions données ou vos propres idées.

MODÈLE: Vous êtes très fatigué(e).
Je n'ai pas pu m'endormir.

1. Vous arrivez en cours en retard. (se lever tard / ne pas se dépêcher / se coucher à une heure / se faire mal au pied)
2. Un(e) camarade de classe n'a pas fait ses devoirs. (s'amuser hier soir / s'endormir sur ses livres / se reposer après dîner / avoir mal aux yeux / emmener un ami chez le dentiste)
3. Votre ami(e) a l'air malheureux (-euse). (s'inquiéter trop / ne pas se détendre assez / ne pas se reposer ce week-end)
4. Vos amis n'ont pas voulu vous recevoir. (ne pas se laver / ne pas s'habiller / vouloir se promener en ville)

E **Encore des conseils.** Quels conseils donnez-vous à quelqu'un pour les problèmes suivants? Si vous voulez, utilisez les verbes de la liste suivante et des adverbes: **moins, plus souvent, plus tôt, plus tard.**

se lever	se détendre	se réveiller
se coucher	s'amuser	s'endormir
se reposer	se promener	s'inquiéter

MODÈLE: Un ami ne veut pas aller en cours.
Promenons-nous!

1. Vos amis n'ont pas d'énergie.
2. Un(e) ami(e) est trop sérieux (-euse).
3. Vos ami(e)s veulent sortir avec vous.
4. Vos ami(e)s ont peur de ne pas réussir aux examens.
5. Vos parents n'ont pas le temps de prendre le petit déjeuner.
6. Votre camarade de chambre veut éviter les maladies.

F **Hier.** Interrogez un(e) camarade de cours et ensuite racontez sa journée d'hier aux autres. Utilisez les mots de la liste d'activités et des adverbes de temps (**tôt, de bonne heure, tard**) ou indiquez l'heure.

se lever	rentrer
se laver	se reposer
s'habiller	dîner avec
prendre le petit déjeuner	se coucher
partir pour l'université	s'endormir
étudier à la bibliothèque	???

G **Questions personnelles.** Le week-end dernier.

1. Est-ce que vous vous êtes réveillé(e) tôt le week-end dernier? A quelle heure?
2. A quelle heure vous êtes-vous levé(e) samedi? dimanche?
3. Vous êtes-vous détendu(e)? Comment?
4. Vos ami(e)s se sont-ils / se sont-elles bien amusé(e)s chez vous? Qu'est-ce que vous avez fait ensemble?
5. Comment est-ce que vous vous êtes habillé(e) dimanche?
6. De quoi est-ce que vous vous êtes occupé(e)?

communiquons

Parler de sa santé

The French are extremely health-conscious. For several years, eating healthful foods has been a major concern and each French person averages about six visits to the doctor a year. In addition to traditional medical care, the French believe in homeopathy, visits to health spas, and a close relationship with their pharmacist. Health spas (**stations thermales**) are so widely accepted that Social Security will reimburse a stay that was ordered by a doctor and approved by an examining board. Seeking such care is called **faire une cure** and the patients, **curistes.** Some of these spas are known in the U.S. because they also bottle their water for export (**Vichy, Evian**). Using sea water for therapy is also popular and is called **thalassothérapie.**

One tradition that remains in France is to blame a general malaise on one's liver. Because of the rich foods and alcoholic beverages that they consume, the French still complain of the stereotypical **crise de foie.**

Centre de Thalassothérapie

thalgo la baule

Dispense des cures de Thalassothérapie classiques (Médicale, Remise en Forme, Diététique) ou spécifiques (Anti-tabac, Vithalgo, Thalgo Beauté) pour prévenir ou traiter Troubles Ostéo-articulaires, Affections Cardio-vasculaires, Stress, Surmenage, Surcharges pondérales...

Hébergement privilégié à l'Hotel ROYAL**** du Groupe Lucien BARRIERE relié directement au Centre, ainsi que nombreuses possibilités hôtelières, para-hôtelières et locatives.

Possibilités forfaits séminaires sur demande.

Expressions

▶ **On parle de la santé.**

Comment allez-vous?	*How are you?*
Je vais bien.	*I'm fine.*
Je ne vais pas bien.	*I'm not well.*
Comme ci, comme ça.	*So-so.*
Mes grands-parents sont en bonne santé.	*My grandparents are in good health.*
Je suis malade.	*I'm sick.*
Vous sentez-vous bien?	*Do you feel well?*
Non, je me sens un peu fatigué.	*No, I feel a little tired.*
A tes souhaits!	*Bless you!*

▶ **On indique où on a mal.**

Les enfants ont mal au ventre.	*The children have a stomachache.*
Elle s'est cassé le bras quand elle est tombée.	*She broke her arm when she fell.*
Il s'est fait mal au genou dans un accident.	*He hurt his knee in an accident.*
Je me suis foulé le poignet.	*I sprained my wrist.*

Interaction

Monique va chez le médecin.

LE MÉDECIN: Comment allez-vous, Monique?

MONIQUE: Pas très bien. Depuis deux jours j'ai mal partout°.   *everywhere*

LE MÉDECIN: Vous avez de la fièvre? Je vais prendre votre température.

MONIQUE: J'ai mal au dos et j'ai toujours froid. Et je commence à avoir mal à la gorge.

LE MÉDECIN: C'est sans doute une petite grippe°. Déshabillez-vous; je vais   *flu*
vous ausculter°.   *examine*

Activités

Ⓐ Où est-ce que les personnages historiques suivants ont eu mal?

MODÈLE: Marie Antoinette?
Elle a eu mal au cou.

1. Van Gogh
2. Le Cyclope
3. Jesse James
4. Socrate
5. Isaac Newton
6. Pinocchio
7. Le Capitaine Crochet *(Hook)*
8. Quasimodo

Ⓑ Répondez aux questions suivantes.

1. Comment allez-vous aujourd'hui?
2. En général, êtes-vous en bonne ou en mauvaise santé?
3. Avez-vous été malade récemment? Avez-vous consulté un médecin?
4. Comment vous sentez-vous maintenant?
5. Avez-vous souvent mal? Où?
6. Est-ce que vous vous êtes déjà cassé quelque chose? Que faisiez-vous quand vous vous êtes fait mal?

Ⓒ Avec un(e) camarade de cours, jouez les scènes suivantes.

1. Vous êtes chez le médecin. Parlez-lui de vos problèmes de santé.
2. Vous avez séché votre classe de français hier. Inventez une excuse médicale et présentez-la à votre professeur.
3. Vous avez mal aux dents. Téléphonez chez le dentiste et prenez rendez-vous *(make an appointment)* avec lui / elle.
4. Vous travaillez dans une station thermale. Ecoutez les problèmes de vos curistes et donnez-leur de bons conseils.

Tourisme de santé

Les stations thermales accueillent chaque année environ 600 000 curistes, dont la moitié viennent d'Ile-de-France. La clientèle est à 70 % féminine, le plus souvent âgée de 40 à 50 ans. La tendance est à un rajeunissement et à une masculinisation, liés à l'offre de cures postnatales, antistress, ou antitabac. 200 000 personnes ont effectué en 1998 une cure de thalassothérapie, contre 150 000 en 1992 et 40 000 en 1982. 67% sont des hommes. 50% sont membres des professions libérales, chefs d'entreprises ou commerçants. 44% cherchent à lutter contre le stress, la fatigue ou le surmenage, 32% soignent des rhumatismes ou viennent en rééducation.

lecture culturelle

Avant la lecture

The tobacco industry is under attack from the European Union and from individual European countries, as well as from the United States, because of the death toll allegedly resulting from cigarette smoking, the increasing numbers of young people and women who smoke, and the health dangers to nonsmokers from secondhand smoke.

To date, the French government has no law that sets a minimum legal age for purchasing cigarettes and related tobacco products. The World Health Organization has proposed forbidding sales of tobacco to anyone under sixteen; however, former ministers of health Bernard Kouchner and Claude Evin do not feel that the law would be very effective. Instead, the French government proposed regulating advertising of tobacco products with the 1991 Evin law. Its acceptance has not been as widespread as expected, in part because tobacco has enjoyed such an important status in French society. Can one expect the French to embrace and respect the notion of nonsmoking public areas in airports, restaurants, cafés, and workplaces when the idea goes against their cherished ideals of "**liberté, égalité, fraternité**"?

Changes are indeed taking place, but very slowly. The French courts have begun to entertain tobacco-related lawsuits (on a much smaller scale than in the United States), but so far the success of the lawsuits has been limited. Furthermore, the French are increasingly calling for a healthy, smoke-free environment in the workplace and in other public areas. In 1995, the legal group called the **Comité national contre le tabagisme** was founded to help and support nonsmoking workers fighting for their right to breathe clean air. Special measures have also been introduced to educate adolescents about the risks and health consequences of smoking.

Activités

Ⓐ What have you heard about smoking trends in France as compared with those in the United States?

Ⓑ Do you think that advertising campaigns have made any headway in curbing smoking among American youth? Why or why not?

Ⓒ What would you do if you were responsible for leading an antismoking campaign?

Ⓓ Skim the following passage for statistical information. Draft tables or graphs of your findings on youth and smoking.

Le tabagisme

Netscape: Jamais la première cigarette

Location: http://www.jamaislapremiere.com/medias_actua.htm

JAMAIS LA PREMIÈRE CIGARETTE

FÉDÉRATION FRANÇAISE DE CARDIOLOGIE

ESPACE ADULTES | CONTACT

ENQUÊTE · STORYBOARD · RÉSULTATS D'ENQUÊTE · CLIP ET REPOTAGE · MEDIAS ET ACTUALITÉS · MON COEUR · SUPPORTS PÉDAGOGIQUES · AGENDA

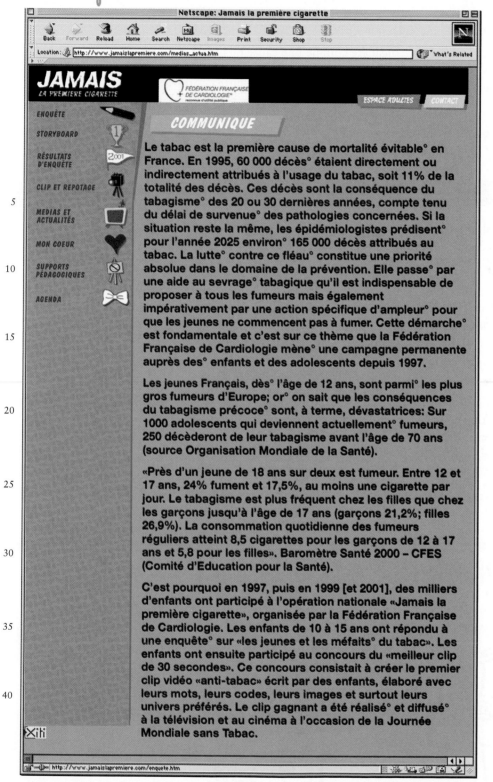

COMMUNIQUE

Le tabac est la première cause de mortalité évitable° en France. En 1995, 60 000 décès° étaient directement ou indirectement attribués à l'usage du tabac, soit 11% de la totalité des décès. Ces décès sont la conséquence du tabagisme° des 20 ou 30 dernières années, compte tenu du délai de survenue° des pathologies concernées. Si la situation reste la même, les épidémiologistes prédisent° pour l'année 2025 environ° 165 000 décès attribués au tabac. La lutte° contre ce fléau° constitue une priorité absolue dans le domaine de la prévention. Elle passe° par une aide au sevrage° tabagique qu'il est indispensable de proposer à tous les fumeurs mais également impérativement par une action spécifique d'ampleur° pour que les jeunes ne commencent pas à fumer. Cette démarche° est fondamentale et c'est sur ce thème que la Fédération Française de Cardiologie mène° une campagne permanente auprès des° enfants et des adolescents depuis 1997.

Les jeunes Français, dès° l'âge de 12 ans, sont parmi° les plus gros fumeurs d'Europe; or° on sait que les conséquences du tabagisme précoce° sont, à terme, dévastatrices: Sur 1000 adolescents qui deviennent actuellement° fumeurs, 250 décèderont de leur tabagisme avant l'âge de 70 ans (source Organisation Mondiale de la Santé).

«Près d'un jeune de 18 ans sur deux est fumeur. Entre 12 et 17 ans, 24% fument et 17,5%, au moins une cigarette par jour. Le tabagisme est plus fréquent chez les filles que chez les garçons jusqu'à l'âge de 17 ans (garçons 21,2%; filles 26,9%). La consommation quotidienne des fumeurs réguliers atteint 8,5 cigarettes pour les garçons de 12 à 17 ans et 5,8 pour les filles». Baromètre Santé 2000 – CFES (Comité d'Education pour la Santé).

C'est pourquoi en 1997, puis en 1999 [et 2001], des milliers d'enfants ont participé à l'opération nationale «Jamais la première cigarette», organisée par la Fédération Française de Cardiologie. Les enfants de 10 à 15 ans ont répondu à une enquête° sur «les jeunes et les méfaits° du tabac». Les enfants ont ensuite participé au concours du «meilleur clip de 30 secondes». Ce concours consistait à créer le premier clip vidéo «anti-tabac» écrit par des enfants, élaboré avec leurs mots, leurs codes, leurs images et surtout leurs univers préférés. Le clip gagnant a été réalisé° et diffusé° à la télévision et au cinéma à l'occasion de la Journée Mondiale sans Tabac.

http://www.jamaislapremiere.com/enquete.htm

avoidable
deaths
nicotine addiction
appearance, manifestation
predict
about, approximately
fight, struggle / scourge
Elle... *The key is; It relies on* / aide... *help in stopping*
large-scale
step
has been leading
(here) aimed at
starting at / among
yet, however
early
now, currently
survey / negative effects
produced / broadcast

«Jamais la première cigarette», www.jamaislapremiere.org.

Après la lecture

1. Pourquoi est-ce que le tabac est considéré comme une cause de mortalité évitable?
2. Comment est-ce que la Fédération Française de Cardiologie lutte contre le tabagisme?
3. Quelle est la conséquence dévastatrice du tabagisme chez les jeunes?
4. Entre douze et dix-sept ans, est-ce que les filles ou les garçons fument plus de cigarettes? Combien de cigarettes est-ce que les filles fument par jour, selon l'enquête?
5. Pourquoi la Fédération Française de Cardiologie a-t-elle organisé le concours? Pourquoi est-ce que le concours a visé *(targeted)* les jeunes de dix à quinze ans?
6. Qu'est-ce qu'il fallait faire pour participer au concours?
7. Quelle était la «récompense» pour le gagnant du concours?

Activités

A Est-ce que la fumée vous gêne? Pensez-vous que le tabagisme passif soit un risque pour les non-fumeurs?

B Comment est-ce qu'on peut faire respecter la loi Evin en France? Quelles sanctions devrait-on imposer?

C **Débats**

1. Les droits des fumeurs et des non-fumeurs
2. L'interdiction de fumer dans les restaurants ou l'existence de «coins fumeurs» (ou salles fumeurs)

D Ecrivez une liste de six recommandations/conseils pour un(e) ami(e) qui essaie de s'arrêter de fumer. Utilisez le subjonctif.

E Etes-vous en bonne santé? Que faites-vous pour être en forme? Quelles choses est-ce qu'il faut que vous changiez pour mener une vie plus saine?

vocabulaire

Noms / Pronoms

la bouche	mouth	la jambe	leg
le bras	arm	la journée	day
cheveux *(m.)*	hair	la main	hand
la cheville	ankle	une maladie	illness
le corps	body	le nez	nose
le cou	neck	la nuit	night
le coude	elbow	œil *(m.)*	eye
la croix verte	green cross	oreille *(f.)*	ear
la cuisse	thigh	une partie	part
la dent	tooth	une pharmacie	emergency
un/une dentiste	dentist	de garde	drugstore
le doigt	finger	une pharmacie	all-night
le dos	back	de nuit	drugstore
épaule *(f.)*	shoulder	le pied	foot
une fièvre	fever	une prise de sang	blood test
le genou	knee	le ventre	stomach
la gorge	throat	yeux *(m.)*	eyes

Verbes

amener	to bring	s'habiller	to get dressed
appeler	to call	s'inquiéter	to be worried
emmener	to take	s'occuper de	to take care of
enlever	to remove	se brosser	to brush
faire de l'exercice	to exercise	se coucher	to go to bed
éviter	to avoid	se dépêcher	to hurry
examiner	to examine	se déshabiller	to get undressed
inquiéter	to worry	se détendre	to relax
lever	to raise	se laver	to get washed
posséder	to own	se lever	to get up
promener	to walk	se promener	to go for a walk
répéter	to repeat	se rappeler	to remember
sécher	to dry	se reposer	to rest
sécher un cours	to cut class	se réveiller	to wake up
s'amuser	to have fun	se sentir	to feel
s'appeler	to be called	se trouver	to find oneself
s'endormir	to fall asleep		

Adjectifs / Adverbes

bien	well	**régulièrement**	regularly
davantage	more	**tard**	late
généralement	generally	**tôt**	early
grave	serious	**vers**	toward
hypocondriaque	hypochondriac		

Expressions

aller mieux	to feel better
alors	then
avoir bonne mine	to look good
avoir mal à	to hurt
avoir mauvaise mine	to look sick
être au régime	to be on a diet
être en bonne santé	to be in good health
être en mauvaise santé	to be in bad health
faire un régime	to be on a diet
ne pas fermer l'œil de la nuit	not to sleep a wink all night
se faire mal à	to hurt one's . . .
se porter bien	to be in good health

Les Bleus

commençons

grammaire

communiquons

lecture culturelle

vocabulaire

Les sports

OBJECTIVES

Language	Culture	Communication
■ Vocabulary for sports ■ The sounds / s / and / z / ■ **-ire** verbs ■ Demonstrative pronouns ■ Possessive pronouns	■ The **Tour de France** ■ Sports ■ **Le football**	■ Talking about sports ■ Expressing ownership ■ Pointing out something ■ Expressing precise quantities

commençons

Chez Ernest à l'heure du Tour de France

Robert et Jean prennent l'apéritif dans leur café préféré et ils regardent les informations à la télévision. Ils attendent le reportage sur le Tour de France. Ernest, le patron, vient de servir un pastis et lève son verre à leur santé.

ERNEST: A la vôtre, Messieurs!

ROBERT ET JEAN: A la tienne, Nénesse!

JEAN: Oh, regarde, ils vont montrer le film de l'étape d'aujourd'hui.

ROBERT: Celle d'hier était formidable! Le maillot jaune avait encore deux secondes d'avance à cent mètres de l'arrivée, mais il a perdu sa première place.

JEAN: J'ai lu dans *L'Equipe* que son contrôle anti-doping était négatif, et tout le monde dit qu'il va gagner aujourd'hui.

ERNEST: Est-ce que je vous sers un autre pastis? Vos verres sont vides.

ROBERT: Celui de Jean, oui, mais moi, je n'ai pas encore terminé le mien.

JEAN: Non, merci. J'ai soixante kilomètres à faire ce soir et il faut que je me dépêche parce que je n'aime pas conduire la nuit.

1. Où sont Robert et Jean?
2. Que font-ils?
3. Qu'est-ce que Nénesse leur dit?
4. Qu'est-ce qu'on va montrer à la télévision?
5. Qu'est-ce que le maillot jaune a fait?
6. Que boivent Robert et Jean?
7. Est-ce que Robert veut encore un pastis? Pourquoi pas?
8. Pourquoi est-ce que Jean ne veut plus de pastis?

Mots clés

informations (f.)	the news	une place	place
un patron	owner	lu (lire)	read
le pastis	anise-flavored alcoholic drink	un contrôle anti-doping	drug test
un verre	glass		
A la vôtre!	Here's to you! To your health!	négatif	negative
A la tienne!	Here's to you! To your health!	dit (dire)	says
Nénesse	(diminutive for Ernest)	gagner	to win
une étape	stage	vide	empty
celle	that	celui	that
un maillot	jersey	le mien	mine
d'avance	ahead	un kilomètre	kilometer
un mètre	meter (39.4 inches)		(0.62 miles)

Faisons connaissance

The **Tour de France,** one of the world's major bicycle races, is on the minds of many French people each year during July. The race is a succession of day-long stages called **étapes.** Some are quite long and are run over flat countryside; others are much shorter and take place across steep mountainous terrain. The leader in the race, who wears a yellow jersey (**un maillot jaune**), is determined after each stage of the race by computing who has the lowest total time of all the competitors. The final winner of the Tour de France is the cyclist who has the lowest total time at the end of the race.

L'Equipe is a daily newspaper devoted entirely to sports. True devotees of the **Tour** rely on it for information during the race. In recent years, considerable emphasis has been placed on checking for drugs. As with all major sporting events, any drugs designed to enhance performance are illegal.

French television gives extensive coverage to the race. There are live broadcasts of each day's finish and filmed highlights on the evening news. Many French people go to cafés to watch the coverage with their friends. While there, they might order a **pastis,** a very popular drink, especially in southern France. It has a strong licorice flavor and is high in alcohol content.

Une étape du Tour de France

Enrichissons notre vocabulaire

Les sports (*Sports*)

l'alpinisme (*m.*)

le base-ball

le basket-ball

le catch

le deltaplane

l'équitation (*f.*)

le football

le football américain

le golf

la gymnastique

le hockey

le jogging

le patinage

la planche
à roulettes

le roller

le ski

le ski
nautique

le snowboard

le tennis

le volley-ball

la voile

la planche
à voile

la pêche

la natation

la plongée sous-marine

Pratiquer un sport (*To play a sport*)

faire du, de la, de l'	*to do / play (a sport)*	**le champion / la championne**	*champion*
jouer à	*to play (a sport)*	**le championnat**	*championship*
		l'équipe *(f.)*	*team*
nager	*to swim*	**un/une joueur/joueuse**	*player*
patiner	*to skate*	**sportif (-ive)**	*athletic / fond of sports*

—Quels sports **pratiquez-vous?**   *What sports **do you play?***
—Je joue à la **pétanque.**   *I play **lawn bowling.***
—Je fais du **rugby.**   *I play **rugby.***
—Nous allons à la **chasse.**   *We go **hunting.***

—Nous adorons les **courses** *(f.)*   *We love **car races / bike races.***
  de voiture / de bicyclette.

—Nous ne sommes pas sportifs;   *We aren't athletic; we only play **cards!***
  nous jouons seulement aux **cartes** *(f.)*!

Prononciation   The sounds / s /, / z /, / sj /, and / zj /

A. The distinction between the sounds / s / and / z / is very clear in French. A single letter **s** between two vowels is always pronounced / z /, while a double **s** represents / s /. This permits contrasts between words such as **le désert** and **le dessert.**

Repeat the following pairs of words, which have the same meanings in English and French, but vary between the sounds / s / and / z /.

English	French	English	French
philosophy	la philosophie	disagreeable	désagréable
dessert	le dessert	disobey	désobéir
curiosity	la curiosité	resemble	ressembler

Now repeat the following words, which contain the sound / s /, the sound / z /, or both.

ils choisissent / vous finissez / qu'il désobéisse / Nénesse /
    nous réussissons / la bise / tu laisses / la phrase /
    la boisson / la chasse / ennuyeuse / mes amis

B. In French, the sounds / s / and / z / may be followed by the / j / sound, which is very similar to the initial sound in *yes*. In English, equivalent words usually have a / ʃ / sound. In French, it is important to make two distinct sounds, / s / or / z /, then the / j / sound.

Repeat the following pairs of words, which contrast the sounds / s / + / j / and / z / + / j /.

/ sj /	/ zj /	/ sj /	/ zj /
nous passions	nous faisions	traditionnel	vous lisiez
l'expression	la télévision	les sciences	les yeux
une émission	parisien	une description	une allusion

Now, pronounce the following pairs of words, which contrast the / ʃ / sound in English with the / sj / sound in French.

English	French	English	French
patience	la patience	essential	essentiel
pollution	la pollution	national	national
exceptional	exceptionnel	action	l'action

Exercice

Read aloud the following sentences, paying attention to the difference between the / s / and / z / sounds and pronouncing the sound / sj / instead of / ʃ /.

1. Ma cousine a refusé son dessert.
2. Nous allons visiter une église suisse.

3. Les Parisiens préfèrent la conversation à la télévision.
4. Les Tunisiens ont réussi à supporter l'invasion romaine.
5. Il est essentiel que vous annonciez les résultats du championnat d'équitation.
6. Nous excusons son hypocrisie et sa curiosité excessives.

grammaire

I. Verbs ending in -ire

You use verbs to describe actions.

A. Several verbs in French have infinitives that end in **-ire** and have similar conjugations.

écrire *(to write)*	conduire *(to drive)*
j' **écris**	je **conduis**
tu **écris**	tu **conduis**
il / elle / on **écrit**	il / elle / on **conduit**
nous **écrivons**	nous **conduisons**
vous **écrivez**	vous **conduisez**
ils / elles **écrivent**	ils / elles **conduisent**

B. To conjugate these verbs, you must learn which pronounced consonant appears in the plural forms. You then add the same endings used with **-ir** verbs like **servir** (Chapter 7).

Ils écrivent des poèmes.   Nous ne conduisons pas la nuit.

ECRIVEZ LE FRANÇAIS COMME LES FRANÇAIS

GRAMR

Détecteur d'erreurs grammaticales, correcteur orthographique & conjugueur

Mots clés   *-ire verbs*

conduire	to drive	nous conduisons
se conduire	to behave	nous nous conduisons
décrire	to describe	nous décrivons
dire	to say / tell	nous disons
écrire	to write	nous écrivons
lire	to read	nous lisons
produire	to produce	nous produisons
traduire	to translate	nous traduisons

Tout le monde **dit** qu'il va gagner.
Décrivez-moi l'étape d'aujourd'hui.
Ils **lisent** *L'Equipe* tous les jours.

Attention!

1. **Dire** has the irregular form **vous dites**.

2. **Dire** and **écrire** take indirect objects.

> Je vais dire cela **à mes amis**.
> Elle va écrire une lettre **au président**.

3. If a clause follows **dire, écrire,** or **lire,** you must use the conjunction **que** (**qu'**) plus the indicative.

> Elle dit **qu'**elle va faire de la gymnastique.

C. In other tenses (the imperfect and subjunctive), **-ire** verbs follow the normal rules.

> Je **conduisais** déjà quand j'avais quinze ans.
> Elle veut que nous **lisions** ce livre.

D. The past participles of **-ire** verbs vary somewhat.

(se) conduire	**conduit**	lire	**lu**
décrire	**décrit**	produire	**produit**
dire	**dit**	traduire	**traduit**
écrire	**écrit**		

Mots clés   *Words often used with -ire verbs*

On écrit et on traduit...

un conte	*tale*	la poésie	*poetry*
une phrase	*sentence*	un texte	*text*
une pièce	*play*		

On dit... | **On lit...**

une bêtise / des bêtises	*dumb thing(s)*	un journal / des journaux	*newspaper(s)*
un mensonge	*lie*	un magazine	*magazine*
la vérité	*truth*	une revue	*magazine*

Langue

A **Un voyage en Martinique.** Mettez les verbes au temps indiqué entre parenthèses.

1. On produit du sucre ici.   *(passé composé)*
2. Ils lisent un bon roman pendant le match de tennis.   *(imparfait)*
3. Elles écrivent une carte postale.   *(futur proche)*
4. Elles disent qu'elles adorent le ski nautique.   *(passé composé)*
5. A l'hôtel nous avons écrit trois lettres.   *(présent)*
6. J'ai lu le journal de Fort-de-France.   *(imparfait)*
7. Vous me décrivez votre voyage.   *(impératif)*
8. Vous avez dit que vous allez retourner en Martinique?   *(présent)*

B **De la poésie.** Faites des phrases avec les mots donnés, en faisant tous les changements nécessaires.

1. Jacques et Marie / écrire / poèmes
2. Luc / les / lire / hier
3. Je / les / traduire / français
4. Louise / dire / ils / être / bon
5. Il / être / possible / ils / écrire / pièce / aussi
6. Vouloir / vous / écrire / poésie?

Culture

C **Il n'y a pas que le vin!** Certaines régions francophones sont connues pour leurs produits. Regardez les listes, et identifiez les régions suivantes avec leur produit.

MODÈLE: En Suisse
En Suisse, on produit du chocolat.

1. En Bourgogne   a. lait / crème
2. En Normandie   b. moutarde
3. En Bretagne   c. huile d'olive
4. En Provence   d. fruits de mer
5. En Alsace   e. bière
6. En Belgique   f. choucroute

D **La lecture.** On a interrogé 1550 étudiants sur leurs lectures au cours des sept derniers jours. Faites des phrases indiquant les résultats.

MODÈLE: dictionnaire / 16%
Seize pour cent des étudiants ont lu un dictionnaire.

1. un guide pratique   a. 46%
2. des poèmes   b. 44%
3. des magazines   c. 37%
4. un journal   d. 9%
5. un livre d'art   e. 8%
6. un roman   f. 3%

E **Des descriptions.** Demandez à un(e) étudiant(e) de vous décrire les choses suivantes.

MODÈLE: ta maison
Etudiant(e) 1: *Décris ta maison.*
Etudiant(e) 2: *Ma maison est grande et blanche.*

ta chambre	tes dernières vacances
ton (ta) petit(e) ami(e)	ton sport préféré
ta voiture	ton film préféré
ton professeur	ta pièce préférée

F **Vos lectures.** Que lisez-vous? Qu'est-ce que vous avez lu récemment? Qu'est-ce que les autres personnes lisent? Donnez des titres *(titles)*.

des journaux	des magazines de sport
des romans	un livre de français
des poèmes	des contes de...

1. Moi, je...	4. Mes ami(e)s...
2. Mon (Ma) camarade de chambre...	5. Mes parents...
3. En cours, nous...	6. Mes professeurs...

G **Questions personnelles.** Vos habitudes.

1. Comment vous conduisiez-vous quand vous étiez petit(e)? Qu'est-ce que vous faisiez de méchant? Quelles bêtises disiez-vous?
2. Avez-vous écrit une lettre à une personne importante? A qui? Pourquoi?
3. Qu'est-ce que vous lisiez quand vous étiez jeune? Qu'est-ce que vous lisez maintenant?
4. Qui a écrit votre roman préféré? Votre chanson préférée?
5. Quel journal lisez-vous? Pourquoi? Quel magazine?
6. Quand avez-vous dit un mensonge?

II. Demonstrative pronouns

You use demonstrative pronouns to refer to people or things already mentioned in the conversation, often to point them out or to make a distinction.

A. Demonstrative pronouns are similar to demonstrative adjectives (**ce, cet, cette, ces**) in that they point out something, but demonstrative pronouns *replace nouns*. They have the same number and gender as the nouns they replace.

	singular	plural
masculine	celui	ceux
feminine	celle	celles

B. Demonstrative pronouns have several equivalents in English, depending on how they are used *(this one, that one, these, those, the one[s])*. These pronouns are usually followed by one of two structures:

1. the suffixes **-ci** or **-là** to indicate degree of closeness.

> **Ce** livre**-ci** est bon, mais **celui-là** est ennuyeux.
> J'aime **cette** chanson**-ci**, mais je préfère **celle-là**.
> Donnez-moi **celle-ci** et **celle-là**.

2. the preposition **de,** which can show possession.

> —Vos verres sont vides?
> —**Celui de** Jean, oui.
> Ils vont montrer l'étape d'aujourd'hui. **Celle d'**hier était formidable.
> Préférez-vous l'équipe de Lyon ou **celle de** Marseille?

Ce qu'ils disent

When demonstrative pronouns refer to people, they can have a somewhat derogatory meaning.

Oh, **ceux-là**, je ne les aime pas.	*Those guys! I don't like them.*
Celui-là, il n'est jamais à l'heure.	*That character is never on time.*

Langue

Ⓐ **A la bibliothèque.** Dans les phrases suivantes, remplacez les mots en italique avec un pronom démonstratif.

MODÈLES: Donnez-moi *ce livre-là.*
Donnez-moi celui-là.

Voilà *les CD* de Berlioz.
Voilà ceux de Berlioz.

1. Aimez-vous *les pièces* de Molière?
2. Je préfère *les poèmes* de Ronsard.
3. Nous allons traduire *ces phrases-ci.*
4. Avez-vous lu *ce roman-ci?*
5. Voltaire n'a pas écrit *ces lettres-là.*
6. Voulez-vous voir *le journal* de Montréal?
7. Où produit-on *les films* de Bertolucci?
8. Elles n'écoutent jamais *ces cassettes-ci.*

Ⓑ **Où sont nos affaires?** Dans les phrases ci-dessous, remplacez les mots en italique avec un pronom démonstratif pour indiquer la possession.

MODÈLE: Tu as perdu *le stylo* du professeur?
Tu as perdu celui du professeur?

1. *La bicyclette* de Luc est là.
2. J'ai oublié *le courrier* de Marie.

3. *La planche à roulettes* de Tim n'est pas dans la rue.
4. *Le maillot* de Robert n'est pas dans sa valise.
5. Tu as trouvé *les rollers* de ma sœur?
6. Passez-moi *le verre* de Jacqueline.
7. J'ai laissé *les devoirs* de mon copain chez moi.
8. *Le portefeuille* de Marie est dans son sac.

C **Faisons du sport.** Refaites les phrases suivantes en remplaçant les noms en italique par des pronoms démonstratifs.

1. *Ce sport-là* n'est pas très difficile.
2. *Les voitures de sport* des Italiens sont formidables!
3. *Ce joueur-là* me semble paresseux.
4. *Les montagnes* de Lyon ne sont pas assez grandes pour faire du ski.
5. *Les vêtements* des Galeries Lafayette sont excellents pour faire du sport.
6. *Ce magazine de catch-ci* est plein de bêtises.
7. Evite *les cigarettes* de mon père si tu veux jouer au football.
8. *Le français* des joueurs québécois est différent du *français* des joueurs marseillais.

Culture

D **De grands mouvements artistiques.** Les tableaux *(paintings)* des artistes ci-dessous représentent quel mouvement artistique?

MODÈLE: Matisse   *Ceux de Matisse représentent le fauvisme.*

1. David
2. Delacroix
3. Monet
4. Seurat
5. Rousseau
6. Picasso
7. Dali
8. Rouault

a. le cubisme
b. le pointillisme
c. le primitivisme
d. le classicisme
e. le romantisme
f. l'impressionnisme
g. l'expressionnisme
h. le surréalisme

Communication

E **Conversation interrompue.** Au moment où vous interrompez *(interrupt)* une conversation, vous entendez les phrases suivantes. Imaginez ce que *(what)* le pronom démonstratif peut représenter.

MODÈLE: J'ai trouvé ceux de Marc dans ma voiture.
         Il a trouvé les livres / les CD de Marc.

1. Vous avez goûté ceux-ci? Ils sont délicieux!
2. Ceux du professeur sont sur son bureau.
3. Celle-là n'est pas très économique.
4. Moi, je préfère celui-ci.
5. Celle-là n'est pas assez jolie pour aller dîner.
6. Ils ont traduit celles-là en français.

Ⓕ **Vos achats.** Qu'est-ce que vous achetez? Vous pouvez commencer la réponse avec «**Moi, j'achète...** ».

1. Les chemises de Van Heusen ou les chemises d'Hawaii?
2. Les CD de Britney Spears ou les CD de Barbra Streisand?
3. Les jeans de Calvin Klein ou les jeans de Levi Strauss?
4. Les chaînes stéréo du Japon ou les chaînes stéréo d'Allemagne?
5. Le journal de New York ou le journal de chez vous?
6. Les robes de Coco Chanel ou les robes de Sears?
7. Les ordinateurs d'Apple ou les ordinateurs d'IBM?
8. Les frites de McDonald's ou les frites de Burger King?

Ⓖ **Questions personnelles.** Vos préférences.

1. Préférez-vous les cours du matin ou les cours de l'après-midi?
2. Regardez-vous les reportages sportifs d'ABC, de CBS, de NBC, ou d'ESPN?
3. Aimez-vous mieux la musique des années quatre-vingt-dix ou la musique des années cinquante?
4. Vous voudriez passer vos vacances à la mer ou en montagne?
5. Avez-vous envie d'aller aux concerts de Pavarotti ou aux concerts des Backstreet Boys?
6. Vous aimez mieux recevoir les lettres de votre petit(e) ami(e) ou les lettres du Publishers Clearing House?

III. Possessive pronouns

You use possessive pronouns to show ownership of something already mentioned in the conversation.

A. Possessive pronouns replace possessive adjectives and the items possessed.

—**Vos verres** sont vides?
—Non, je n'ai pas encore terminé **le mien.**

	m. sing.	f. sing.	m. pl.	f. pl.	English
1st sing.	le mien	la mienne	les miens	les miennes	*mine*
2nd sing.	le tien	la tienne	les tiens	les tiennes	*yours*
3rd sing.	le sien	la sienne	les siens	les siennes	*his / hers / its*
1st pl.	le nôtre	la nôtre	les nôtres		*ours*
2nd pl.	le vôtre	la vôtre	les vôtres		*yours*
3rd pl.	le leur	la leur	les leurs		*theirs*

Mon sport préféré est la gymnastique; **le sien,** c'est l'équitation.
Elle n'aime pas cette planche à voile. Elle préfère **la sienne.**
Mes parents habitent à Paris. Et **les vôtres?**

B. Remember that possessive adjectives agree in gender and number with the thing possessed, not with the possessor as in English. The same is true of possessive pronouns.

> **son verre** = *his glass or her glass*
> **le sien** = *his or hers*

Attention!

1. Note that with all possessive pronouns, *It's . . .* and *They are . . .* translate as **C'est...** and **Ce sont... Ils** and **Elles** are not used, except with the expression of ownership in the **être à** + *noun or pronoun* and **appartenir à** constructions.

> —**C'est** celui de Pierre?
> —Oui, **c'est** le sien.
>
> —Est-ce que **ce sont** vos livres ou les leurs?
> —Ce sont **les miens.**
>
> —A qui sont ces skis?
> —**Ils** sont à moi. / **Ils** m'appartiennent.

2. Don't forget that **le** and **les** combine with any preceding **à** or **de** in the ways you studied in Chapter 4.

> As-tu téléphoné à tes parents? Moi, je vais téléphoner **aux** miens.
> Vous voulez que je parle **de** mon avenir, mais vous ne parlez pas **du** vôtre.
> Leur vélo est à côté **des** nôtres.

Langue

A **Nos possessions.** Dans les phrases suivantes, remplacez les mots en italique par des pronoms possessifs.

1. Je n'aime pas *tes vêtements.*
2. Veux-tu regarder *mes photos?*
3. *Ses chaussures* sont grandes.
4. *Mes disquettes* sont tombées dans l'eau.
5. Le facteur a oublié *celui de Jacques.*
6. Elle a retrouvé *son journal.*
7. *Vos gâteaux* sont excellents.
8. J'ai perdu *leur parapluie.*

B **Pas de chance!** Complétez les phrases suivantes avec un pronom possessif.

1. J'ai fait mes devoirs; tu n'as pas fait _____ !
2. Il n'a pas de voiture; il veut que je lui prête _____ .
3. Ils viennent de recevoir leur courrier, mais nous n'avons pas encore reçu _____ .
4. C'est son verre; donnez-moi _____ .
5. Les Baillard ont vendu leur maison, mais M. Ducharme n'a pas pu vendre _____ .
6. Garçon! Ce n'est pas ma boisson. C'est _____ .

C **Comparaison de cultures.** Comparez les phénomènes suivants comme ils existent en France et aux Etats-Unis. Utilisez les adjectifs donnés ou vos propres idées.

MODÈLES: voitures: petit / grand
Les leurs sont petites; les nôtres sont grandes.

1. églises: ancien / moderne
2. nourriture: bon marché *(cheap)* / cher
3. courses de bicyclettes: très apprécié / peu connu
4. conducteurs: prudent / agressif
5. vacances: moins long / plus long
6. billets d'avion: bon marché / cher

D **Des descriptions.** Avec un(e) camarade de cours, employez des pronoms possessifs pour décrire les choses suivantes. Indiquez les différences et les similarités aux autres étudiants.

MODÈLES: tes week-ends
Les miens ne sont pas assez longs.

ton équipe de football de lycée
La nôtre perd ses matchs.

1. ta famille
2. ton appartement
3. ton (ta) petit(e) ami(e)
4. tes CD
5. tes vacances

6. tes professeurs de lycée
7. ta résidence
8. tes sports préférés
9. tes magazines préférés
10. tes cours

E **Nos villes.** Séparez-vous en groupes de deux et comparez les villes où vous êtes né(e)s. Utilisez les suggestions données ou vos propres idées.

MODÈLES: avoir beaucoup / peu de musées
Etudiant(e) 1: *Ma ville a beaucoup de musées.*
Etudiant(e) 2: *La mienne a peu de musées.*

être calme / y avoir du bruit
Etudiant(e) 1: *Ma ville est très calme.*
Etudiant(e) 2: *Il y a beaucoup de bruit dans la mienne.*

être petite / grande
être loin / près des montagnes
avoir peu / beaucoup de cinémas
avoir de bons / mauvais restaurants
avoir beaucoup / peu de pollution
avoir beaucoup / peu de parcs
être loin / près de la plage
???

F **Questions personnelles.** Votre université.

1. Comment s'appelait votre lycée? Et celui de votre petit(e) ami(e)?
2. Est-ce que votre université est trop grande ou trop petite?
3. Il y a souvent du bruit dans les résidences, et dans la vôtre?
4. Comment est votre chambre? Petite ou grande? Bien rangée?
5. Est-ce que vos week-ends sont agréables?
6. Est-ce que vos profs sont sympathiques? Qu'est-ce qu'ils n'aiment pas?

communiquons

Utiliser le système métrique

To function in most French-speaking countries, you must be familiar with the metric system, the official system of measurement in most of the world. It was first established by the French National Assembly in 1791, and the International Bureau of Weights and Measures is still located in France, just outside Paris in Sèvres. The meter, the basic unit of length, is defined by the wavelength of krypton, whereas the kilogram, the basic unit of weight, is defined by a block of platinum that is housed at the bureau.

The following comparisons will help you do conversions from the U.S. system to the metric system and vice versa.

Expressions

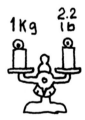

▶ **On exprime le poids** *(weight)*.

1. Here are some comparisons between metric weights and weights in the American system.

   28 grammes (g) = *1 ounce*   100 grammes = *approximately*
   454 grammes = *1 pound*   *4 ounces*
   500 grammes = une livre   1 kilogramme (kg) = *2.2 pounds*

2. To convert weights from the American system to the metric system and vice versa, use the following calculations as a guide.

   ? grammes = *3 ounces*
   Multipliez 28 par 3. Cela fait 84 grammes.

   50 kilogrammes = *? pounds*
   Multipliez 50 par 2,2. Cela fait 110 *pounds*.

3. The following expressions are used for weight.

   Je pèse quatre-vingts kilos.   *I weigh eighty kilos.*
   Ça coûte cinq euros le kilo.   *That costs five euros a kilo.*

▶ **On exprime la longueur** *(length).*

1. The following are some comparisons between metric lengths and those of the American system.

2,54 centimètres (cm) = *1 inch*   1 centimètre = *about 0.4 inches*
30 centimètres = *about 1 foot*   1 mètre = *about 39.4 inches*
0,94 mètre (m) = *about 1 yard*   1 kilomètre = *about 0.62 miles*
1,6 kilomètres (km) = *about 1 mile*

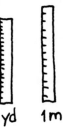

1yd   1m

2. To convert lengths from the metric system to the American system and vice versa, use the following calculations as a guide.

? mètres = *5 feet 8 inches*
5 *feet 8 inches* = 68 *inches.* Multipliez 68 par 2,54.
  Cela fait 172,72 centimètres. Divisez par 100. Cela fait 1,73 mètres ou un mètre soixante-treize.

525 kilomètres = *? miles*
Multipliez 525 par 0,62. Cela fait 325,50 ou 325 *miles* et demi.

3. These expressions are used for length or distance in French.

Paris est à 5.000 km d'ici.   *Paris is 5,000 kilometers from here.*

Ils habitent à 50 km de   *They live 50 kilometers from*
chez nous.   *our house.*

Jacques fait presque deux   *Jacques is almost two meters*
mètres.   *tall.*

Elle mesure un mètre soixante.   *She is one meter sixty centimeters tall.*

▶ **On exprime le volume.**

1. Here are some comparisons between metric measurements of volume and those of the American system.

0,95 litre (l) = *1 quart*   1 litre = *1.06 quarts*
3,8 litres = *1 gallon*   25 centilitres (cl) = *about 1 cup*

1qt   1l

2. To convert measurements of volume from the metric system to the American system and vice versa, refer to the following calculations.

? litres = *20 gallons*
Multipliez 20 par 3,8. Cela fait 76 litres.

0,75 litre = *? quarts*
Multipliez 0,75 par 1,06. Cela fait .795 *quarts.*

3. The following expression is used for miles per gallon.

Ma nouvelle voiture fait du 8   *My new car uses 8 liters (of gas)*
aux 100 km.   *per 100 kilometers.*

▶ **On exprime la température.**

1. The following are some comparisons between the Celsius and Fahrenheit scales for measuring temperatures.

0° Celsius (C) = 32° *Fahrenheit (F)*
100° C = 212° F

2. To convert temperatures from the Celsius scale to the Fahrenheit scale and vice versa, use the following formulas as guides.

40° C = ? F
degrés *Fahrenheit* = 9/5 C + 32
Multipliez 40 par 9 et divisez par 5. Cela fait 72.
  Ajoutez *(Add)* 32. Cela fait 104° F.

? C = 68° F
degrés Celsius = 5/9 (F − 32)
68° moins 32 font 36. Multipliez 36 par 5 et divisez par 9.
  Cela fait 20° C.

3. The following expressions are used with temperatures.

Ma fille a trente-neuf.	*My daughter has a temperature of thirty-nine degrees Celsius.*
Il fait trente degrés aujourd'hui.	*It is thirty degrees Celsius out today.*

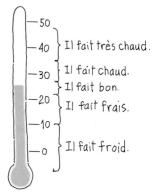

Interaction

Monsieur Gosselin et son fils font des courses à l'hypermarché.

M. GOSSELIN: Va acheter un rosbif pendant que je prends deux kilos de pommes de terre.

SON FILS: Pour nous cinq, quel poids est-ce qu'il faut?

M. GOSSELIN: Oh, entre deux kilos et deux kilos cinq cents.

SON FILS: N'oublie pas non plus un litre de lait et une demi-livre de beurre.

M. GOSSELIN: Tu as raison. Et il nous faut aussi une bouteille de vin d'Alsace et 600 grammes de gruyère.

SON FILS: Chic! Maman va faire aussi une fondue.

Activités

Ⓐ Quelle unité de mesure détermine le prix des choses suivantes en France? Choisissez parmi *(among)* les possibilités données.

MODÈLE: du café à l'épicerie
les 500 grammes

3 ou 5 centilitres	25 ou 33 centilitres	100 grammes
le litre	le kilogramme	25 centilitres
le kilomètre	75 centilitres	

1. des bananes	7. du gigot
2. une bière au café	8. du fromage
3. des bonbons	9. des crevettes
4. un vin de qualité	10. de l'essence *(gasoline)*
5. un vin de table	11. l'apéritif au café
6. un pichet de vin au restaurant	12. un billet de train

B Répondez aux questions suivantes.

1. Combien pesez-vous en kilos? Combien mesurez-vous?
2. A combien de kilomètres habitez-vous de la maison de vos parents? de l'université?
3. En Amérique, on mesure la consommation d'une voiture en *miles per gallon*. En France, c'est en litres aux 100 kilomètres. Combien est-ce que votre voiture consomme?
4. Quelle est la température normale d'une personne en degrés Celsius? Quelle température avez-vous eue quand vous étiez malade?
5. Est-ce qu'il fait beau aujourd'hui? Combien fait-il en degrés Celsius?

lecture culturelle

Avant la lecture

While soccer is popular in many parts of the world, it is the national pastime of South Americans, Africans, and Western Europeans. In 1998, France's national soccer team (**les Bleus**) gained the acclaim of the sporting world by winning the World Cup 3–0 against one of its fiercest competitors, Brazil. The winning team members were hailed as national heroes. The champions—Zinedine Zidane, Fabien Barthez, Lilian Thuram, and their coach, Aimé Jacquet—became household names and were as idolized as Michael Jordan is in the United States. French president Jacques Chirac later welcomed the team at the Elysée Palace to congratulate the Bleus.

France enjoyed another moment of pride when its national junior soccer team, known as the Mini-Bleus or Petits Bleus, won the world championship title in 2001. The Mini-Bleus, a team whose players must be less than seventeen years old, beat two-time champion Nigeria 3–0—exactly the same score as their elder counterparts, the Bleus, had achieved in 1998. It was France's first championship victory for that age category. Since the 1998 World Cup, soccer (**le foot**) has become even more popular in France, and teams from other countries are trying to entice and recruit the top French athletes.

Le foot

Activités

A Do you know any famous French-speaking athletes (in hockey, tennis, soccer, skiing, gymnastics, cycling, or ice skating, for instance)?

B Do you play sports? Who or what inspired you to participate in the particular sport?

C At what age do you believe an athlete should be able to become a professional? Explain your reasoning.

D Look up the following verbs and then try to guess the meaning of the related nouns and adjectives.

Verbs	Nouns	Adjectives
1. enregistrer	enregistrement *(m.)*	enregistré(e)(s)
2. hausser	hausse *(f.)*	haut(e)(s)
3. féliciter	félicitations *(f. pl.)*	
4. former	formation *(f.)*	formé(e)(s)
5. célébrer	célébrité *(f.)*	célèbre(s)
6. entraîner	entraînement *(m.)*	entraîné(e)(s)
7. accueillir	accueil *(m.)*	accueillant(e)(s)
8. attirer	attraction *(f.)*	attrayant(e)(s)
9. interdire	interdiction *(f.)*	interdit(e)(s)

LE FOOT

Après la victoire de la France, lors de la dernière Coupe du Monde de football, la Fédération française a enregistré une augmentation du nombre de ses licenciés° d'au moins 15% sur un an. C'est chez les jeunes de 6 à 12 ans, désireux d'imiter leurs idoles comme Zidane, Barthez ou Thuram, que la hausse est la plus spectaculaire avec une pointe° de 30%. Dans les banlieues° autour de Paris, les jeunes des cités° sont si nombreux à s'inscrire° dans des clubs que ceux-ci ont de la peine à faire face à cet afflux. C'est un vrai raz-de-marée° de footballeurs qui déferle° sur la France!

Tous les responsables du football français se félicitent de cet «effet Mondial», que les structures de formation peuvent intégrer grâce aux traditionnelles sections sport-études. Nombre des champions du monde français sont en effet de purs produits des «écoles de foot» qui peuvent conduire vers le sésame° du professionnalisme, voire° de la célébrité. L'Institut national du football (INF) de Clairefontaine (Vosges), où l'équipe de France effectue° ses entraînements, est ainsi la pépinière° la plus recherchée°. Financé par l'État et la Fédération française de football, le centre de préformation de l'INF accueille° en permanence 62 pensionnaires°, à partir de 13 ans.

Le vivier° des jeunes footballeurs français attire aussi les grands clubs étrangers. En raison de législations fiscales plus souples°, les clubs d'Italie, d'Espagne et d'Allemagne recrutent les meilleurs éléments français. Depuis peu, ces clubs s'intéressent aux jeunes encore en formation. Le cas de Jérémie Alladière, 15 ans, a ainsi provoqué l'émoi° des autorités sportives. En troisième et dernière année à l'INF, le jeune sportif a été acheté par le club britannique d'Arsenal qui lui garantit ses premiers salaires de professionnel.

Face à cette situation nouvelle, le ministère de la Jeunesse et des Sports prévoit de mettre des garde-fous° juridiques. Dans le projet de loi d'orientation sur le sport, toute transaction commerciale sera interdite sur un sportif mineur. Parallèlement, un jeune sportif issu° d'un centre de formation devra° signer son premier contrat professionnel avec le club qui l'a formé. Cette mesure, de nature à satisfaire des clubs craignant° de voir leurs centres de formation pillés°, devrait, dans l'esprit des pouvoirs publics°, préluder à une législation européenne commune.

members

surge / suburbs
housing projects / to sign up

tidal wave / is unfolding

key to success (open sesame) / even
holds / breeding ground (literally, "plant nursery") / sought-after / hosts / live-in students, boarders

breeding ground (literally, "fish tank") / permissive

a provoqué... *caused a stir*

safeguards

coming out of / will have to

fearing
plundered / **dans l'esprit...** *in the minds of the authorities*

Dominique Garraud, «L'effet Mondial attire les jeunes footballeurs français»,
Journal Français.

Après la lecture

1. Quelle a été la conséquence de la victoire française en 1998 sur les clubs de football en France?
2. Les inscriptions sont les plus nombreuses parmi quelle population? D'où viennent la plupart de ces joueurs?
3. Pour quelles raisons est-ce qu'un joueur irait *(would go)* à une école de foot?
4. Où est-ce que l'équipe de France s'entraîne? Trouvez les Vosges (une chaîne de montagnes) sur une carte de France.
5. Qui est Jérémie Alladière? Pour quel pays va-t-il jouer, selon l'article?
6. Qu'est-ce que le ministère de la Jeunesse et des Sports veut essayer de faire, et pourquoi?

Activités

A. Quelles sont les qualités d'un bon modèle *(role model)*? Est-ce que les sportifs aux Etats-Unis sont de bons modèles pour les jeunes? Expliquez.

B. Quels sont les avantages et les inconvénients de la participation des enfants aux sports compétitifs? Quels sont les effets sur leur développement?

C. Dessinez une carte de France avec les cinq chaînes de montagnes, les cinq fleuves *(rivers)*, ainsi que les villes principales suivantes: Paris, Strasbourg, Nantes, Lyon, Marseille, Toulouse, Bordeaux et Nice.

D. Choisissez un(e) athlète francophone et préparez une petite présentation pour la classe.

vocabulaire

Noms / Pronoms

alpinisme *(m.)*	mountain climbing	le championnat	championship
le base-ball	baseball	la chasse	hunting
le basket-ball	basketball	un conte	tale
une bêtise	dumb thing	un contrôle	test
cartes *(f.)*	cards	une course de bicyclettes	bicycle race
le catch	wrestling	une course de voitures	car race
celle	the one	le deltaplane	hang gliding
celui	the one	une équipe	team
ceux	those	équitation *(f.)*	horseback riding
un/une champion(ne)	champion	une étape	stage

le football	soccer	une pièce	play
le football américain	football	une place	place
le golf	golf	la planche à roulettes	skateboarding
la gymnastique	gymnastics	la planche à voile	sailboarding
le hockey	hockey	la plongée sous-marine	scuba diving
informations (f.)	the news		
le jogging	jogging	la poésie	poetry
un/une joueur/ joueuse	player	une revue	review
le Journal	TV news	le roller	in-line skating
(le) leur	theirs	le rugby	rugby
un magazine	magazine	(le) sien	his / hers
un maillot	jersey	le ski	skiing
un mensonge	lie	le ski nautique	water-skiing
un mètre	meter	le snowboard	snowboarding
(le) mien	mine	le tennis	tennis
la natation	swimming	un texte	text
(le) nôtre	ours	(le) tien	yours
le pastis	pastis (licorice- flavored drink)	le Tour de France	Tour de France
		la vérité	truth
le patinage	skating	un verre	glass
un patron	owner	la voile	sailing
la pêche	fishing	le volley-ball	volleyball
la pétanque	lawn bowling	(le) vôtre	yours
une phrase	sentence		

Verbes

conduire	to drive	nager	to swim
décrire	to describe	patiner	to skate
dire	to say / to tell	pratiquer	to practice
écrire	to write	produire	to produce
gagner	to win	se conduire	to behave
jouer à	to play	traduire	to translate
lire	to read		

Adjectifs / Adverbes

négatif	negative
sportif	athletic
vide	empty

Expressions

A la tienne!	Cheers!	contrôle anti-doping	drug testing
A la vôtre!	Cheers!	d'avance	ahead

commençons

grammaire

communiquons

lecture culturelle

vocabulaire

A la FNAC

Les arts

OBJECTIVES

Language	Culture	Communication
■ Vocabulary for musical instruments and fine arts ■ Intonation ■ Verbs followed by infinitives ■ Verbs followed by nouns ■ The pronouns **y** and **en**	■ The status of the French language ■ Comic strip art	■ Talking about the arts and other activities ■ Writing letters

commençons

Le français en péril?

La revue française L'Express a consacré un reportage à la question suivante: «Sait-on encore parler le français?» Dans plusieurs articles, des journalistes ont critiqué l'état du français parlé et écrit. Quelques semaines après, la revue a publié la lettre d'un lecteur furieux. En voici un extrait.

```
Messieurs:
    Qu'est-il arrivé à la langue de Voltaire et de Gide?
[...] Moi, je pense que le mal vient surtout d'un en-
seignement insuffisant et je dois dire que les fautes de
français entendues à la radio et à la télévision me font
souffrir, comme des atteintes à la beauté de notre
langue. [...]
    Je pense qu'il s'agit d'une volonté de certains mi-
lieux de contribuer à la destruction d'une société par
celle de sa langue. Parler et enseigner un français
correct est «bourgeois». Donc,... !
    Moi, je dis que nous devons défendre notre langue car
elle est vivace, généreuse, et elle peut servir à toutes
sortes d'usages.
    Veuillez agréer, Messieurs, l'expression de mes salu-
tations distinguées.

                                        André Florion
```

Adapté du *Débat des lecteurs*, *L'Express*, numéros 1735 et 1736.

Etudions la lettre

1. De quoi est-ce qu'on parle dans cette lettre à *L'Express?*
2. D'où vient le problème selon le lecteur?
3. Comment est-ce que la radio et la télévision contribuent au problème?
4. Est-ce que le lecteur pense qu'on a tort ou qu'on a raison d'être «bourgeois»?
5. Finissez la phrase «Donc,... !».
6. Pourquoi faut-il défendre la langue française?

Mots clés

en péril	*in danger*	publié (publier)	*published*
consacré (consacrer)	*devoted*	un/une lecteur/lectrice	*reader*
plusieurs	*several*	en	*of it*
articles *(m.)*	*articles*	un extrait	*excerpt*
critiqué (critiquer)	*criticized*	arrivé (arriver)	*happened*
un état	*state*	mal	*damage*

surtout	*above all*	contribuer	*contribute*
enseignement *(m.)*	*teaching*	la destruction	*destruction*
insuffisant	*insufficient*	enseigner	*to teach*
fautes *(f.)*	*mistakes*	correct	*correct*
souffrir	*suffer*	bourgeois	*bourgeois*
atteintes *(f.)*	*affronts*	donc	*therefore*
la beauté	*beauty*	défendre	*defend*
il s'agit d'	*it's about / it's a question of*	vivace	*alive*
la volonté	*will*	usages *(m.)*	*uses*
milieux *(m.)*	*circles*		

Faisons connaissance

The French language is a constant preoccupation for the people who speak it daily. In France, many feel that their language has deteriorated: there is too much slang; people do not follow grammar rules; and too many words have been borrowed from English. Others think that languages are in a constant state of change and that it is useless to try to stop the process. The majority of the readers responding to that issue of *L'Express* agreed that the situation is deplorable. Yet a move to simplify French spelling, promoted by the government and endorsed by the **Académie française**, has been abandoned. ▶

The French language is also an issue in other countries. Belgium is administratively divided into areas where one of two languages is official—French or Dutch, with the city of Brussels being the only officially bilingual area. A conflict exists between French and Dutch speakers, and it is so intense that it has led to riots in the past.

The province of Quebec in Canada has undergone profound changes. While the country is bilingual, the province has established French as its official language. For example, non-English-speaking immigrants must send their children to schools where classes are taught in French.

In Louisiana, several active groups have been working for years to reestablish the value of using French. The body of poetry, prose, music, and journalism in French is quite significant.

Enrichissons notre vocabulaire

Des instruments de musique *(Musical instruments)*

un orchestre / les instruments *(m.)*

un violon

une guitare

une flûte

un violoncelle

le chef d'orchestre

une trompette

un piano

—De quel instrument **jouez-vous**?   *What instrument do you play?*
—Je joue du trombone.   *I play the trombone.*

Des métiers *(m.)* artistiques *(Careers in the arts)*

Les **musiciens** *(m.)* écrivent des **opéras** *(m.)* et des **symphonies** *(f.)*.

Musicians write operas and symphonies.

Les **écrivains** *(m.)* produisent des **œuvres** *(f.)* **littéraires**.

Writers produce literary works.

Les **auteurs** *(m.)* **dramatiques** font des **pièces**: des **drames** *(m.)*, des **comédies** *(f.)*, des **tragédies** *(f.)*, et des **comédies musicales**.

Playwrights write plays: dramas, comedies, tragedies, and musicals.

Les **danseurs** et les **danseuses** font de la **danse classique** (du **ballet**).

Dancers perform ballet.

Les **peintres** *(m.)* font des **tableaux** *(m.)*: des **peintures** *(f.)* à l'**huile** *(f.)* et des **aquarelles** *(f.)*.

Les **sculpteurs** *(m.)* font des **sculptures** *(f.)* en **pierre** *(f.)* et en **bronze** *(m.)*.

Painters make paintings: oil paintings and watercolors.

Sculptors make stone and bronze sculptures.

Prononciation   Intonation

A. Intonation is the change in the pitch of the voice. It enables a speaker to distinguish between sentences such as *She's going to the movies.* and *She's going to the movies?* French intonation is not radically different from that of English. The two basic kinds are rising intonation and falling intonation.

B. With rising intonation the pitch of the voice rises in yes-or-no questions and sentences when you pause for a breath at the end of a group of related words.

Repeat the following yes-or-no questions after your teacher.

Aimez-vous ce tableau?

Est-ce qu'il est parti?

Vous avez un violon?

Repeat the following sentences with pauses after your teacher.

Elle n'est pas venue parce qu'elle est malade.

J'ai acheté un parapluie, mais je l'ai perdu.

Nous sommes allés au cinéma et nous avons dîné après.

C. With falling intonation, the pitch of the voice drops in declarative and imperative sentences and in information questions (those that start with an interrogative adverb or pronoun).

Repeat the following declarative sentences after your teacher.

Il va faire beau. / Marie n'est pas là.

Nous sommes très fatigués.

Repeat the following imperative sentences after your teacher.

Dépêche-toi. / Venez avec nous. / Allons au théâtre.

Repeat the following information questions after your teacher.

Qu'est-ce que vous allez faire? / Comment allez-vous?

Pourquoi fait-il cela?

Exercice

Read the following sentences aloud, paying particular attention to rising and falling intonation.

1. Voulez-vous danser?
2. Passez-moi le sucre.
3. Qui n'a pas pris de dessert?
4. Monique fait de la danse moderne.
5. J'ai lu un livre et j'ai téléphoné à un ami.
6. Couchez-vous plus tôt!

grammaire

I. Verbs followed by infinitives

Verbs describe actions or states of being.

A. Verbs followed directly by an infinitive

You have learned that it is possible to use two consecutive verbs in a sentence in French. Verbs and verbal expressions you already know that take an infinitive directly after the conjugated verb are as follows.

adorer	devoir	préférer
aimer	espérer	savoir
aimer mieux	il faut	sembler
aller	laisser	souhaiter
désirer	penser	il vaut mieux
détester	pouvoir	vouloir

Je **dois dire** que les fautes me font souffrir.
Sait-on encore **parler** le français?
Je **ne peux pas répondre**.

B. Verbs followed by *à* and an infinitive

Some verbs that take the preposition **à** before an infinitive are as follows.

s'amuser à	continuer à
apprendre à	hésiter à *to hesitate*
avoir du mal à *to have a hard time*	inviter à
	réussir à
chercher à *to try*	tenir à
commencer à	

Nous **avons du mal à nous lever** tôt.
Il **ne réussit pas à comprendre** la danse moderne.
Avez-vous **commencé à lire** cette comédie?

C. Verbs followed by *de* and an infinitive

Here are some examples of verbs that take the preposition **de** before an infinitive.

accepter de	essayer de
avoir besoin de	être + *adjective* + de
avoir envie de	éviter de
avoir peur de	finir de
avoir raison / tort de	oublier de
cesser de *to stop*	refuser de
choisir de	regretter de
décider de	rêver de *to dream*
se dépêcher de	venir de

As-tu **envie d'aller** au théâtre?
Alors, **dépêche-toi de t'habiller!**
J'ai décidé de faire une sculpture.

Attention!

1. If you use object pronouns with two verbs, remember that the pronoun precedes the verb of which it is an object. For example, in the first sentence below, **amis** is the object of **inviter**, and **orchestre** is the object of **écouter**.

   J'ai invité **mes amis à écouter cet orchestre**.
   Je **les** ai invités **à l'écouter**.

   Je vais essayer de téléphoner **aux lecteurs**.
   Je vais essayer de **leur** téléphoner.

2. Note that the prepositions **à** and **de** *do not* combine with the direct object pronouns **le** and **les**,

   Il regrette de vendre **ce tableau**.
   Il regrette **de le** vendre.

   Je n'ai pas encore commencé à faire **mes devoirs**.
   Je n'ai pas encore commencé **à les faire**.

A **Vos activités.** Complétez les phrases suivantes avec une préposition, s'il y a lieu *(if necessary)*.

1. Détestez-vous _____ étudier?
2. Elle regrette _____ arriver en retard.
3. Nous continuons _____ regarder la télévision.
4. Je viens _____ terminer le roman.
5. Mes voisins s'amusent _____ jouer de la guitare.
6. Mon père tient _____ écouter cet orchestre.
7. Notre professeur ne nous laisse jamais _____ partir tôt.
8. Ils vont _____ essayer _____ nous téléphoner ce soir.

B **En famille.** Formez des phrases avec les mots donnés.

1. Mon mari / cesser / travailler / année / dernier
2. Notre fils / adorer / aller à la pêche avec lui
3. En semaine / nous / finir / dîner / huit heures
4. Notre fille / apprendre / jouer du violon
5. Nous / aimer mieux / se coucher / tôt
6. On / aller / visiter / Paris / printemps
7. Je / avoir du mal / décrire / nos vacances
8. Ma sœur / décider / aller voir / nos parents / Canada

C **Au lycée.** Formez des phrases complètes avec les mots donnés et dites si la phrase est vraie ou fausse selon la vie des lycéens *(high school students)* français.

1. On / pouvoir / apprendre / conduire / au lycée
2. lycéens / adorer / écouter / musique américaine
3. On / devoir / étudier la religion
4. Ils / rêver / acheter / surtout / voiture
5. lycéens / ne... pas / chercher / travailler / après / classes
6. Parmi *(Among)* les langues étrangères, / ils / préférer / étudier / espagnol
7. Ils / avoir peur / passer le bac
8. La majorité des jeunes / obtenir le bac / et / choisir / aller / université

D **Mes activités.** Qu'est-ce que vous préférez faire?

J'aime...	J'accepte...
Je déteste...	Je refuse...

me lever tôt	écrire des lettres
préparer le petit déjeuner	lire des pièces / des romans
sortir quand il pleut	conduire vite
aller en classe en autobus	jouer à / de...
suivre des cours le matin	???

E **L'avenir.** Posez des questions à un(e) camarade de cours sur ses projets pour l'avenir en employant un élément de chaque *(each)* colonne. Ensuite, faites un résumé de ses réponses.

aller	suivre des cours pendant dix ans
tenir	gagner peu / beaucoup d'argent
décider	avoir peu / beaucoup de responsabilités
rêver	faire du cinéma / du théâtre
hésiter	devenir professeur / médecin
espérer	faire du deltaplane
avoir envie	écrire de la poésie
devoir	???

F **Questions personnelles.** Vos préférences.

1. Préférez-vous aller au cinéma ou au théâtre?
2. Avez-vous choisi d'habiter dans une résidence universitaire ou dans un appartement? Pourquoi?
3. Qu'est-ce que vous voulez apprendre à faire?
4. Qu'est-ce que vous avez du mal à faire?
5. Qu'est-ce que vous avez envie de faire ce week-end?
6. Où pensez-vous aller pour vos vacances?

II. Verbs followed by nouns

> Verbs describe actions or states of being.

A. Verbs are either transitive or intransitive. A transitive verb takes a direct object. An intransitive verb has no direct object, or it requires a preposition.

Transitive	Intransitive
Les peintres font **des tableaux.**	Elle est rentrée tôt.
On a critiqué **le président.**	Nous allons **chez** le dentiste.

B. There are a number of verbs that are transitive in French but intransitive in English. The following are some transitive French verbs that you know.

attendre	demander	payer
chercher	écouter	regarder

Ils demandent du gâteau.   *They are asking for cake.*
J'attends l'autobus.   *I'm waiting for the bus.*

C. There are also verbs that take **à** before a noun in French. Most of the following verbs are transitive in English.

désobéir à	obéir à
échouer à *to fail*	penser à
entrer à / dans	rendre visite à
faire peur à	répondre à
jouer à + *name of a sport*	ressembler à

réussir à	téléphoner à
s'intéresser à *to be interested in*	tenir à

Ne désobéissez pas à vos parents!	*Don't disobey your parents!*
Tenez-vous à ce vieux violon?	*Are you fond of this old violin?*

D. Several verbs in French must take the preposition **à** before a person and **de** before an infinitive.

conseiller **à** quelqu'un **de** faire quelque chose	*to advise someone to do something*
demander **à** quelqu'un **de** faire quelque chose	*to ask someone to do something*
dire **à** quelqu'un **de** faire quelque chose	*to tell someone to do something*
écrire **à** quelqu'un **de** faire quelque chose	*to write someone to do something*
rappeler **à** quelqu'un **de** faire quelque chose	*to remind someone to do something*
recommander **à** quelqu'un **de** faire quelque chose	*to recommend to someone to do something*

Conseillez **aux** étudiants **d'**apprendre à taper.
J'ai demandé **à** Mme Leblanc **de** jouer de la guitare.

E. Some verbs take the preposition **de** before a noun or a pronoun.

avoir besoin de	il s'agit de
avoir envie de	jouer de + *musical instrument*
avoir peur de	s'inquiéter de
changer de	s'occuper de

Il **s'occupe du** courrier des lecteurs.
Il **s'agit d'**une volonté de certains milieux.

Attention!

1. **Penser** takes the preposition **à** when it means *to have something in mind.* When **penser** means *to have an opinion,* it takes **de** and is almost always used in a question. You answer the question with **penser que...** .

    Je n'aime pas **penser aux** examens.

    —Que **pensez**-vous **de** l'art moderne?
    —Je **pense que** c'est fascinant.

2. When a verb that takes the preposition **de** is followed by a noun, the noun does not take an article if it is used in a general sense.

    Il **change** souvent **de vêtements!**
    Elle **s'occupe d'étudiants** étrangers.

3. **Il s'agit de** cannot take a noun subject. Use a prepositional phrase with **dans** instead.

Dans ce magazine, il **s'agit de** la langue française.	*This magazine deals with the French language.*

Ce qu'ils disent

Se rappeler takes a direct object, but in daily speech, many French speakers add de.

Je ne me rappelle pas cela. → Je ne me rappelle pas de cela.

Langue

Ⓐ **Faisons attention au professeur.** Complétez les phrases suivantes avec une préposition ou un article, ou avec les deux s'il y a lieu.

1. Pour être professeur, on a besoin _____ patience.
2. Mon professeur a recommandé _____ étudiants _____ bien préparer la leçon.
3. Il a conseillé _____ ses étudiants _____ étudier le latin aussi.
4. Il leur a demandé pourquoi ils ont échoué _____ examen.
5. Moi, je vais réussir _____ examens de l'année prochaine.
6. J'écoute toujours _____ conseils du professeur.

Ⓑ **Un agent de police donne des conseils aux touristes.** Formez des phrases complètes avec les mots donnés.

1. Dire / votre / amis / entrer / musée / avant six heures
2. Je / rappeler / gens / obéir / lois
3. Entrer / bureau de poste / pour / téléphoner / votre / famille
4. Je / donner / adresse / du Louvre / étudiants
5. Recommander / amis / regarder / ce / beau / église
6. Je / conseiller / Américains / visiter / musée d'Orsay

Ⓒ **Conversation avec votre camarade de chambre.** Répondez aux questions suivantes en utilisant les mots donnés.

1. Est-ce que c'est ton violoncelle? (Non... appartenir... Marie)
2. Tu pars pour l'université? (Non... revenir... supermarché)
3. Est-ce que tu as froid? (Oui... demander... Robert... fermer... fenêtre)
4. Tu veux écouter de la musique? (Non... préférer... regarder... film)
5. Alors, tu veux aller au cinéma? (Oui... chercher... journal)
6. Qu'est-ce qu'on va faire après? (... s'occuper... ménage)

Culture

Ⓓ **Au lycée.** Formez des phrases complètes avec les mots donnés et dites si la phrase est vraie ou fausse selon la vie des lycéens français.

1. Quand / deux lycéens / aller au cinéma, / garçon / payer / places
2. lycéens / regarder / souvent / télévision / l'après-midi
3. La majorité / lycéens / échouer / bac
4. On / demander / lycéens / étudier / deux langues étrangères
5. La majorité des lycéens / penser / football / et / penser / jouer / football
6. cours d'anglais / ressembler / cours de français aux Etats-Unis
7. beaucoup de lycéens / chercher / leurs amis / cafés / après les cours
8. Ils / jouer / flûte / et / guitare / comme instruments de musique préférés

Communication

E **Vos activités.** Racontez vos activités pendant une journée typique. Utilisez les verbes suivants ou vos propres idées.

téléphoner	s'occuper
écrire	parler
regarder	revenir
écouter	jouer
chercher	fréquenter
penser	changer

F **Mes rêves.** Séparez-vous en petits groupes et complétez les phrases. Ensuite expliquez à la classe les similarités et les différences entre vos réponses.

1. J'ai besoin _____ pour être heureux.
2. Je cherche _____ dans la vie.
3. Je pense souvent _____.
4. Avec mes amis, je parle _____.
5. Je tiens beaucoup _____.
6. Pour l'avenir, je ne demande que _____.

G **Questions personnelles.** Décrivez-vous.

1. A quoi vous intéressez-vous?
2. A qui ressemblez-vous?
3. A qui téléphonez-vous souvent? A qui écrivez-vous?
4. A quoi pensez-vous en ce moment?
5. De qui ou de quoi avez-vous peur?
6. Quelle sorte de musique aimez-vous écouter?
7. Quels sports pratiquez-vous?
8. De quel instrument jouez-vous?

III. The pronouns *y* and *en*

Pronouns replace nouns. You use **y** when referring to places and things when the reference is clear, and you use **en** for things and occasionally people.

A. The pronoun *y*

1. The pronoun **y** replaces prepositional phrases indicating a place. It means *there* and has the same position as the object pronouns you have already learned.

—Il habite **à Paris?**
—Oui, il **y** habite.

—Sylvie nous invite **chez elle.**
—**Allons-y** tout de suite!

—Ils vont travailler **au cinéma?**
—Oui, ils vont **y** travailler.

—Etes-vous allées **en France?**
—Oui, nous **y** sommes allées.

2. **Y** is also used with verbs taking the preposition **à** whenever the object is *not* a person.

—Avez-vous répondu **à sa lettre?**
—Oui, nous **y** avons répondu.

—Ils ne s'intéressent pas **à la sculpture?**
—Si, ils s'**y** intéressent.

Attention!

1. If the object of the preposition **à** is a person, you cannot use **y**; you must use an indirect object pronoun, **lui** or **leur**.

J'ai répondu **à la question.** → J'**y** ai répondu.
J'ai répondu **au professeur.** → Je **lui** ai répondu.

2. Two verbs you have learned require **à** plus the stressed pronoun when referring to people: **penser** and **s'intéresser.**

Elle pense souvent **à son frère.** → Elle pense souvent **à lui.**
Je m'intéresse **aux musiciens de jazz.** → Je m'intéresse **à eux.**

3. **Y** is used to indicate location. With some verbs, a place name receives the action of the verbs. In these cases, you must use a direct object pronoun.

Ils ont visité **la France.** → Ils l'ont visitée.
J'adore **le Québec.** → Je l'adore.

B. The pronoun *en*

1. The pronoun **en** replaces any direct object modified by an indefinite or a partitive article. It is the equivalent of the English *some* or, in negative sentences, *any.*

—Elle va écrire **des lettres?**   —Tu ne bois jamais **de vin?**
—Non, elle **en** a déjà écrit.   —Non, je n'**en** bois jamais.

2. **En** can replace a noun modified by a number or an adverb of quantity. The number or adverb remains after the verb in the sentence.

—Est-ce qu'elle connaît **beaucoup**   —Ne donnez pas **trop de devoirs!**
    d'écrivains?   —Je n'**en** donne jamais **trop.**
—Oui, elle **en** connaît **beaucoup.**

—Les Ducharme ont **deux voitures?**
—Non, ils **en** ont **trois.**

3. **En** is also used when the object is preceded by the preposition **de.**

—Tu as besoin **de vacances,** n'est-ce pas?
—Oui, j'**en** ai besoin.
—Je peux lui parler **de son travail?**
—Non, elle n'aime pas **en** parler.

Ce qu'ils disent

If the object of the preposition **de** is a person, you do not use **en**; you must use **de** plus a stressed pronoun (**lui, elle, eux,** etc.). In casual conversation, however, **en** is often used for people.

Des enfants? Oui, il s'occupe **d'eux.**
Mon prof? Je n'**en** ai pas peur.

Attention!

1. There is no agreement between **y** or **en** and a past participle.

Ils ont habité **en Angleterre.** → Ils y ont habité.
Il a acheté **des romans.**   → Il en a acheté.

2. **Liaison** is always obligatory between pronouns and **y** and **en.** The verbs that normally drop the **s** in the **tu** form of the imperative add it back in order to make a liaison possible.

Ils y sont allés l'année dernière.
Elles en ont trouvé au supermarché.
Vas-y. Achètes-en.

3. When **y** and **en** are used with a reflexive verb, they follow the reflexive pronoun.

Elle s'intéresse **à la musique classique.** → Elle s'y intéresse.
Il s'occupe **de la vaisselle.**   → Il s'en occupe.

4. When **en** is used with **il y a,** it follows **y.**

Il y a des stylos dans le bureau.   → **Il y en a** dans le bureau.
Y a-t-il des montagnes au Maroc? → **Y en a-t-il** au Maroc?

Langue

Ⓐ **Quelle bonne élève!** Remplacez les mots en italique par les pronoms **y** ou **en,** selon le cas.

1. Elle monte *dans l'autobus.*
2. Elle va *à l'école.*
3. Elle fait *des maths.*
4. Elle suit sept *cours.*
5. Elle s'intéresse *aux sciences.*
6. Elle n'échoue pas *aux examens.*
7. Elle rentre *chez elle* à l'heure.
8. Elle s'occupe *de ses devoirs.*

Ⓑ **Un voyage à Bruxelles.** Dans les phrases suivantes, remplacez les mots en italique par un pronom.

1. Nous sommes allés *en Belgique.*
2. Nous avons visité *la Grand-Place.*
3. Je m'intéresse *à cette architecture.*
4. On a bu trop *de bière.*
5. Laure a perdu *de l'argent.*
6. J'ai prêté quinze euros *à Laure.*
7. On a joué *au tennis* dans un parc.
8. Tu veux parler *de tes vacances?*

C **Un week-end à la résidence.** Votre camarade de chambre revient après un week-end chez ses parents et il / elle vous pose des questions. Répondez aux questions suivantes en utilisant les mots entre parenthèses et en remplaçant les noms par des pronoms.

1. As-tu répondu à la lettre de ta mère?   (Oui,...)
2. As-tu mangé une pizza?   (Non,...)
3. Tout le monde a obéi aux règles de la résidence?   (Non,... pas du tout...)
4. Tes amis et toi, vous avez écouté mes cassettes?   (Oui,...)
5. As-tu rencontré d'autres étudiants?   (Oui,... trois...)
6. On a pensé à moi?   (Non, personne... !)

Culture

D **Les sports dans le monde francophone.** Certains endroits sont connus pour le sport qu'on y pratique. Identifiez les endroits suivants du monde francophone selon ce sport.

MODÈLE: Chamonix   *On y fait du ski.*

1. Roland-Garros
2. Le Mans
3. le stade Olympique à Montréal
4. Dakar
5. les bayous de Louisiane
6. les Ardennes

a. aller à la pêche
b. jouer au tennis
c. faire des courses de voitures de Formule I
d. aller à la chasse
e. finir une course de voitures
f. jouer au base-ball

E **Les arts dans le monde francophone.** Répondez aux questions suivantes en employant le pronom **en.**

MODÈLE: Qui a écrit des romans?   *Camus en a écrit.*

1. Qui a fait des sculptures?
2. Qui joue de la flûte?
3. Qui a fait des tableaux?
4. Qui a écrit des opéras?
5. Qui a écrit des chansons?
6. Qui joue de l'accordéon?

a. Clifton Chenier
b. Camille Claudel
c. Edith Piaf
d. Jean-Pierre Rampal
e. Claude Monet
f. Georges Bizet

F **Vos activités.** Que faites-vous très souvent? de temps en temps? rarement? jamais?

MODÈLE: dîner au restaurant *J'y dîne souvent. / Je n'y dîne jamais.*

1. boire du champagne
2. manger du caviar
3. aller à la chasse
4. jouer d'un instrument
5. écrire des poèmes
6. échouer aux examens
7. penser aux vacances
8. faire des tableaux

G **Combien en avez-vous?** Interrogez vos camarades pour trouver qui a le plus grand nombre de...

MODÈLE: frères et sœurs *Marc en a six.*

1. camarades de chambre
2. instruments de musique
3. dollars dans son portefeuille
4. robes / pantalons
5. examens cette semaine
6. CD
7. tableaux
8. petit(e)s ami(e)s

H **Questions personnelles.** Vos pensées.

1. Vous intéressez-vous à la littérature?
2. Connaissez-vous des auteurs français? Que pensez-vous d'eux?
3. Allez-vous au restaurant universitaire? Qu'est-ce que vous en pensez?
4. Quand pensez-vous à vos parents?
5. Vous avez visité le musée d'art de votre ville? Pourquoi pas?
6. Est-ce que vous réfléchissez souvent à votre avenir? Etes-vous optimiste ou pessimiste?

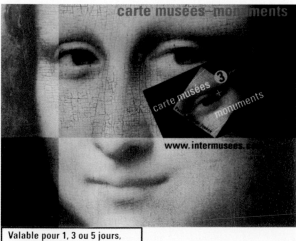

Valable pour 1, 3 ou 5 jours, la carte offre un accès libre et direct aux collections permanentes de 70 musées et monuments de Paris et de la région parisienne. En vente dans les musées et monuments, les stations de métro, à l'Office du Tourisme de Paris.

communiquons

Ecrire des lettres

The French observe a certain style when writing letters. The two basic types of letters, business and personal, are described below. Business letters are usually typed, but it is acceptable to write by hand if a typewriter is not available. A personal letter, however, should never be typed.

Elle écrit des cartes postales.

Expressions

▶ **On écrit des lettres d'affaires.**

1. To start a business letter, write or type your own name and address in the upper left corner. In the upper right corner, put your city and the date. Below them, you write the title and address of the person to whom you are writing. Note that the place of these elements is the reverse in English.

```
Jean-Michel Boirond        Paris, le 3 septembre 2003
22, rue du Bac
75007 Paris

                           Monsieur Henri Paulin
                           56, avenue Wagram
                           75017 Paris
Monsieur,
```

2. To begin the letter, use the person's title or simply **Monsieur, Mademoiselle,** or **Madame.** The standard English salutation *Dear* is generally not used in French business letters.

`Monsieur le Directeur,`	*(Dear) Director,*
`Madame la Directrice,`	*(Dear) Director,*
`Monsieur le Maire,`	*(Dear) Mr. Mayor,*
`Madame la Présidente,`	*(Dear) Madam President,*

3. The first sentence of a business letter is often a form of politeness.

`J'ai l'honneur de vous...`	*It's my privilege to . . .*
`J'ai le plaisir de vous...`	*I have the pleasure of . . .*
`Je vous serais`	*I would be grateful if . . .*
`  reconnaissant(e) de...`	
`Je vous prie de...`	*I beg you to . . .*
`Je vous remercie pour / de...`	*I thank you for . . .*
`Je vous suis`	*I thank you for . . .*
`  reconnaissant(e) de...`	

4. The closing sentence is usually a set expression in a very formal style. The person to whom you are writing must be addressed in the same way as in the opening.

```
Veuillez agréer, Monsieur le Directeur, l'expres-
   sion de mes sentiments distingués.
Veuillez agréer, Madame la Présidente, l'expression
   de mes sentiments les meilleurs.
Veuillez agréer, Mademoiselle, l'expression de mes
   salutations distinguées.
```

▶ **On écrit des lettres personnelles.**

1. To begin a personal letter, choose a heading that reflects how well you know the person to whom you are writing and his/her age. The following expressions progress from salutations used with people you do not know well to those used with friends and relatives.

Monsieur, / Madame, / Mademoiselle,	*Sir, / Madam, / Miss,*
Cher Monsieur,	*Dear Sir,*
Chère Madame, / Mademoiselle,	*Dear Madam, / Miss,*
Cher Monsieur, Chère Madame,	*Dear Mr. and Mrs._____ ,*
Cher Jacques, / Cher ami,	*Dear Jacques,*
Chère Maman,	*Dear Mom,*
Chers tous, / tous deux,	*Dear folks,*

2. To conclude a personal letter, you can use a number of closing phrases. The following expressions progress from closures used with people you do not know well to those used with friends and relatives.

Amitiés,	*Fondly,*
Amicalement,	*Sincerely,*
Cordialement,	*Cordially,*
Je t'embrasse, / Je vous embrasse,	*Love,*
Affectueux baisers,	*Hugs and kisses,*
Grosses bises,	*XXX,*

Interaction

Jacqueline écrit une lettre à sa mère.

> Toulouse, le 7 juillet, 2005
>
> Chère Maman,
>   J'espère que tout va bien à la maison. La semaine prochaine, je vais venir passer le pont° du 14 juillet avec vous. Dis à Papa que je voudrais que nous fassions un pique-nique° et que nous invitions les Fromentin.
>   Tout va bien au travail. Mon nouvel appartement est formidable. A bientôt!
>
>   Affectueux baisers,
>   Jacqueline

long weekend

picnic

Activités

A Comment allez-vous commencer et terminer une lettre dans les situations suivantes?

1. à vos grands-parents: Vous voulez aller les voir.
2. à votre voisin: Il joue de la trompette à minuit.

3. à votre concierge: Vous n'avez pas d'eau.
4. au doyen *(dean)*: Votre prof est formidable.
5. à PBS: Vous aimez leurs émissions.
6. à votre cousin: Vous l'invitez à venir.

B Ecrivez une des lettres suivantes.

Destinataire	Sujet
1. secrétaire général de la faculté	cours pour les étrangers
2. une organisation charitable	pourquoi vous admirez leur travail
3. une revue	pourquoi vous n'êtes pas d'accord avec eux
4. votre journal préféré	leur usage de l'anglais
5. votre petit(e) ami(e)	vos activités du week-end dernier
6. vos parents	pourquoi vous avez besoin d'argent

lecture culturelle

Avant la lecture

Belgium is renowned for its beautiful lace, gourmet chocolates, and fine beers. Its capital, Brussels, is also the capital of comic strip art. Brussels has an entire museum consecrated to its comic strip heroes and creators. Moreover, Brussels sponsors walking tours of the city's "comic strip route," featuring murals and statues of comic strip characters. Not surprisingly, one of Brussels' subway stations, Stockel, is adorned with two murals, each 146 yards long, representing characters from twenty-two albums of the famous comic strip *Tintin*. The author of *Tintin* was the great Brussels-born artist Georges Remi, known by his pen name, Hergé. He was the Belgian pioneer of this art form, known today in Europe as **le huitième art**. Hergé's best-known character, Tintin, is a reporter whose adventures take him, his dog Snowy (Milou), and his friend Captain Haddock to all parts of the world. The *Tintin* series has sold more than 200 million copies in sixty languages.

The French are no strangers to the passion for comic strips, either: a comic strip festival is held in the city of Angoulême each year. Furthermore, Paris is home to a popular comic-strip theme park celebrating France's famous strip *Astérix*. Over the years, the Parc Astérix has become increasingly popular, to the point of rivaling Disneyland Paris. Finally, Cheverny Castle in the Loire Valley recently unveiled a new permanent Tintin exhibition. Clearly, **le huitième art** is thriving in the twenty-first century!

Activités

Ⓐ Did you use to read comic strips when you were younger? Which ones?

Ⓑ Remi's parents noticed their son's creativity at an early age. Were your talents (in art, music, language, and so on) recognized early? If so, did you pursue them? Why or why not?

Ⓒ Georges Remi chose Hergé as his pen name. By skimming paragraph 3 of his biography, can you figure out what he did to his first and last names in order to create his pseudonym? What other writers do you know who have used pseudonyms? Do you know how the authors chose their **noms de plume**?

Ⓓ In the first paragraph of the biography of Hergé that follows, you will find instances of the formal past tense (**le passé simple**). You may want to glance at Appendix IV in your book for a brief introduction to this tense. Then, guess what each of the following verbs means.

   1. créa   2. compléta   3. fut

Ⓔ Hergé began working for the newspaper *Le Vingtième Siècle* at the age of eighteen. He later obtained a position writing for an offshoot of the same newspaper. What was that newspaper called? What was its audience?

La bande dessinée

Biographie d'Hergé (Georges Remi, 1907–1983)

Tintin est l'œuvre d'un homme, dessinateur° et scénariste°, qui a influencé toute la bande dessinée du XXᵉ siècle: le Belge Georges Remi, né en 1907 à Bruxelles. L'enfant témoigne° très jeune d'un don° réel pour le dessin, même si son père exerce une activité° sans grand lien° dans cet art: employé de con-
5 fection°. Les parents du petit Georges, bien que° sans attache religieuse particulière, vont le confier° à un collège religieux et à la Fédération des Scouts catholiques de Belgique. A l'évidence°, cette formation forgera° la fibre humaniste du père de Tintin, qu'on retrouvera dans nombre des aventures du héros.

    A 18 ans, Georges Remi entre comme employé au service des abonne-
10 ments du journal *Le Vingtième Siècle*, de ligne politique nettement° marquée à droite, et dirigé par l'abbé Wallez. Cette petite porte lui donne très rapidement accès à l'illustration de diverses rubriques° du journal. Au même moment, sous la signature d'Hergé, ses initiales inversées (R.G.), il publie dans le *Boy-scout belge* une première série: «Totor, C.P. (chef de patrouille°) des
15 Hannetons»°.

    Le dessin est plutôt sommaire° et le texte figure° sous l'image, comme dans la quasi-totalité des bandes dessinées européennes de l'époque, lesquelles ignorent le phylactère (la "bulle"° par laquelle s'expriment les personnages). Séduit par le talent de son jeune employé, l'abbé Wallez dé-
20 cide en 1928 de lui confier, à 21 ans, la rédaction en chef° du supplément hebdomadaire° jeunesse du *Vingtième Siècle, Le Petit Vingtième*. Influencé par Alain Saint-Ogan qui, en France, réalise depuis 1925 «Zig et Puce», avec usage systématique des bulles, Hergé conçoit dès janvier 1929 *Les aventures de Tintin, reporter du Petit Vingtième, au pays des Soviets*.

cartoonist / scriptwriter (in this case, the person who writes the comic strip text) / demonstrates / gift, talent / exerce... has a job or career / link, connection / clothing industry / although / to place in the care of / Obviously / will mold (someone's character)

clearly

sections or categories (of a newspaper)

patrol (in this case, boy scout troop) / June bugs (here, the name of the scout troop) / rough, basic / appears / "bubble" containing characters' speech in a comic strip / rédaction... post of editor-in-chief / weekly

© Hergé / Moulinsart 2003

A propos By the way   *J'ai hâte* I'm eager, excited   *me disant* telling me   *écrirait* would write   *Je m'étonne* I'm surprised   *Ça, par exemple!* My word!   *A qui ai-je l'honn...* The character was cut off; he meant to say, "A qui ai-je l'honneur de parler?"   *qui est au bout du fil?* who's on the line?   *olibrius* strange fellow   *Patagon* someone from Patagonia (i.e., someone with a foreign accent)   *Si nous jetions un coup d'œil* What if we took a quick look   *aérer* to air out (the room)

Après la lecture

Ⓐ Biographie d'Hergé

1. Quel âge avait Hergé quand il a publié son premier album de *Tintin?*
2. Que faisait le père d'Hergé comme travail?
3. Quelles deux expériences ont influencé Hergé et son personnage Tintin?
4. Qu'est-ce qu'Hergé a fait pour le journal *Le Vingtième Siècle?*
5. Quand Hergé a publié «Totor, C.P. des Hannetons», où est-ce qu'il a mis le texte par rapport aux images? Puis, dans les albums suivants, où est-ce qu'il a mis le texte? Qui lui a donné l'idée de changer l'endroit où mettre les paroles *(words)* des personnages?

Ⓑ Objectif lune

1. Où habite Nestor?
2. Qu'est-ce que Nestor dit au Capitaine Haddock quand Haddock demande des nouvelles de Monsieur Tournesol?
3. Qui est au téléphone? Qu'est-ce qu'il dit ou demande au capitaine?
4. Que propose Tintin, et pourquoi?
5. Pourquoi est-ce que Milou grogne *(growls)* quand il s'approche de la chambre de Monsieur Tournesol? (Devinez!)

Ⓐ Décrivez chaque personnage dans cet extrait de *Tintin*, «Objectif lune»: Qui sont Nestor, le Capitaine Haddock, Tintin et Milou? Comment sont-ils? (Faites la description de leur apparence physique et de leur personnalité.)

Ⓑ Qu'est-ce qui va arriver après? Imaginez la suite de la bande dessinée.

Ⓒ Dans le monde francophone, deux autres bandes dessinées sont très célèbres: *Astérix* (de René Goscinny et Albert Uderzo) et *Lucky Luke* (de Maurice De Bevere). Qui sont les personnages principaux de chaque série? Quels sont les thèmes généraux des albums d'*Astérix?* Et de *Lucky Luke?*

Ⓓ Est-ce qu'il est important d'enseigner *(teach)* l'art et la musique aux enfants à l'école? Si votre école décidait d'annuler ces programmes pour des raisons financières, qu'est-ce que vous diriez *(would say)* pour convaincre l'école de garder ces programmes?

Ⓔ En France, il existe un ministère de la Culture. Le ministre est responsable pour tout ce qui concerne les relations gouvernementales et les arts (musique, danse, architecture, musées, théâtre...) ainsi que la communication. Est-ce que cela existe aux Etats-Unis? Dans votre ville, est-ce qu'il existe un organisme qui s'occupe de la promotion culturelle?

vocabulaire

Noms / Pronoms

une aquarelle	watercolor	un/une lecteur/ lectrice	reader
un article	article	mal	damage
une atteinte	affront	un métier	career
un auteur dramatique	playwright	un milieu	circle
le ballet	ballet	une œuvre	work
la beauté	beauty	opéra *(m.)*	opera
bronze	bronze	un orchestre	orchestra
un chef d'orchestre	conductor	un/une peintre	painter
la comédie	comedy	une peinture à l'huile	oil painting
la comédie musicale	musical	le piano	piano
la danse classique	ballet	une pierre	stone
un/une danseur/ danseuse	dancer	un/une sculpteur	sculptor
la destruction	destruction	la sculpture	sculpture
le drame	drama	la symphonie	symphony
en	some, of it	un tableau	painting
enseignement *(m.)*	teaching	la tragédie	tragedy
un état	state	le trombone	trombone
un extrait	excerpt	la trompette	trumpet
une faute	mistake	un usage	use
la flûte	flute	le violon	violin
la guitare	guitar	le violoncelle	cello
un instrument	instrument	la volonté	will
un instrument de musique	musical instrument	y	there / of / to it

Verbes

accepter (de)	to accept	défendre	to forbid
apprendre (à)	to learn / to teach	demander (à)	to ask
arriver	to happen	dire (à)	to tell
cesser (de)	to stop	échouer (à)	to fail
changer (de)	to change	écrire (à)	to write
chercher (à)	to try	enseigner	to teach
choisir (de)	to choose	essayer (de)	to try
commencer (à)	to begin	éviter (de)	to avoid
continuer (à)	to continue	finir (de)	to finish
contribuer	to contribute	hésiter (à)	to hesitate
critiquer	to critique	inviter (à)	to invite

jouer (à)	to play (sport)	**refuser (de)**	to refuse
jouer (de)	to play (musical instrument)	**regretter (de)**	to regret / be sorry
		réussir (à)	to succeed
oublier (de)	to forget	**rêver (de)**	to dream
penser (à)	to think about / have in mind	**souffrir**	to suffer
		s'amuser (à)	to have a good time
penser (de)	to think of / have an opinion		
		s'inquiéter (de)	to worry
rappeler (à)	to remind	**s'intéresser (à)**	to be interested
recommander (à)	to recommend	**se dépêcher (de)**	to hurry

Adjectifs / Adverbes

artistique	artistic	**littéraire**	literary
bourgeois	bourgeois	**publié**	published
consacré	devoted	**surtout**	above all
correct	correct	**vivace**	lively
insuffisant	insufficient		

Expressions

avoir du mal à	to have trouble	**donc**	therefore
avoir raison de	to be right	**en péril**	endangered
avoir tort de	to be wrong	**il s'agit de...**	it's about . . .

Révision

Tous ensemble!

Ⓐ **Les vacances de Christine et d'Eric.** Répondez aux questions suivantes en employant les mots entre parenthèses et des pronoms pour les mots en italique.

1. Comment vous appelez-vous? (... Eric et Christine.)
2. Etes-vous déjà allés *en France?* (... 2000.)
3. Est-ce que vous avez dû vous occuper de *vos billets d'avion?* (Oui,...)
4. Christine, t'es-tu promenée *dans Paris?* (Oui,... déjà...)
5. Eric, tes parents étaient contents quand tu as voyagé? (Non,... s'inquiéter beaucoup.)
6. Le soir, qu'est-ce que vous aviez envie de faire? (... se détendre.)
7. Avez-vous fait du roller? (Oui,... à Paris.)
8. Quand il a plu, qu'est-ce que vous avez fait? (... lire... magazines et... écrire... lettres.)
9. Quand vous êtes en voyage, vous achetez beaucoup de choses? (Oui,... acheter des vêtements.)
10. Etes-vous allés *à l'Opéra?* (Oui,... aller trois fois.)

Ⓑ Faites des phrases avec les mots donnés.

La détente

1. Je / avoir / besoin / se détendre
2. Entrer / maison / et / se reposer!
3. Papa, / écouter / maman! / Cesser / travailler / tard!
4. Elles / ne... pas / se dépêcher / parce que / elles / ne... pas / tenir / arriver / à l'heure
5. Nous / venir / se coucher

Au travail!

6. Nous / choisir / faire / métier / artistique
7. Nous / commencer / traduire / poème / hier
8. Elles / écrire / romans / et / contes
9. Je / venir / lire / ce / revue
10. Je / dire / enfants / continuer / étudier / piano

Ⓒ **Mes amis écrivains.** Remplacez les mots en italique par un pronom d'objet direct, un pronom démonstratif, un pronom possessif ou un pronom adverbial.

1. Victor et Suzanne passent tout l'été *sur la Côte d'Azur.*
2. *Leur résidence* de Paris est petite, mais *leur résidence* de Nice est énorme.
3. Avez-vous lu *leurs livres?*
4. J'ai traduit *le poème* de Victor et *les poèmes* de sa femme aussi.
5. Lui, il parle quelquefois *de la mer;* elle, elle ne parle jamais *de cela.*

6. Voulez-vous que je vous montre *les poèmes de Suzanne?*
7. A Noël, j'ai acheté *le dernier livre* de Victor, et puis Suzanne m'a offert un *autre livre* pour mon anniversaire.
8. Je ne pense pas qu'ils aient beaucoup *d'argent.*
9. Ils s'intéressent *à la musique classique* aussi.
10. Ils invitent souvent *leurs amis* à écouter *des CD* avec eux.

D **La matinée d'Anne-Marie.** Complétez le paragraphe suivant avec la forme correcte des verbes donnés et avec des prépositions, s'il y a lieu.

Hier, Anne-Marie _____ (se réveiller) à sept heures et _____ (se lever) quelques minutes après. Elle _____ (se laver) et _____ (aller chercher) le journal. Elle l(e) _____ (lire) rapidement parce qu'il n'y _____ (avoir) rien d'intéressant et elle _____ (se dépêcher) s'habiller. Elle _____ (appeler) un taxi et l' _____ (attendre) pendant vingt minutes. Elle _____ (demander) au chauffeur _____ la conduire au bureau. Dans le taxi elle _____ (écrire) des lettres à ses employés. Quand elle _____ (arriver) au bureau, elle _____ (appeler) sa secrétaire; elle _____ (vouloir) qu'elle _____ (commencer) taper ses lettres. Elle _____ (inviter) son amie Andrée _____ déjeuner avec elle. Elles _____ (décider) _____ finir _____ travailler à 11 h 30 parce qu'elles _____ (avoir) faim.

E **Réactions personnelles.** Complétez les phrases suivantes de manière logique.

1. J'aime lire...
2. J'espère être...
3. Pour le week-end, nous avons besoin...
4. Mon ami(e) a du mal...
5. Mon / Ma camarade de chambre se dépêche quand...
6. T'inquiètes-tu quand... ?
7. Pour me détendre...
8. Je refuse...

Entre nous!

A **Ma journée.** Avec un(e) camarade de cours, décrivez une journée typique d'un(e) étudiant(e). Employez les suggestions données et vos propres idées.

se réveiller	lire le journal	rentrer
se lever	commencer	acheter
se laver	s'amuser	changer de vêtements
prendre le petit déjeuner	décider	écrire
s'habiller	jouer à / de	se coucher
partir	se détendre	s'endormir

B **Mes projets.** Dans un petit groupe de trois ou quatre, parlez de vos projets pour demain, pour ce semestre et pour l'avenir. Parlez aussi des choses que vous n'allez pas faire. Ensuite, informez les autres des résultats de votre discussion.

MODÈLE: *Je tiens à apprendre le français.*
J'ai décidé de devenir médecin.
Je vais éviter de dépenser trop d'argent.

souhaiter	aller	éviter	tenir à	s'amuser
rêver	commencer	refuser	il faut que	vouloir
chercher	avoir envie	choisir	avoir peur	devoir

C **Ginger ou Mary Ann?** Un(e) camarade de cours et vous, vous vous trouvez sur une île *(island)* déserte. Qu'est-ce qu'il faut que vous ayez pour être heureux (-euse)? De quoi n'avez-vous pas besoin? Quelles personnes préférez-vous avoir avec vous?

MODÈLE: *J'ai besoin d'une radio.*
Nous n'avons pas besoin d'argent.

D **Que font-ils?** Donnez le nom d'un(e) athlète ou d'un(e) musicien(ne) à votre camarade de cours. Ensuite, demandez-lui quel sport il / elle pratique ou de quel instrument il / elle joue.

MODÈLE: Venus Williams   *Elle joue au tennis.*
Miles Davis   *Il jouait de la trompette.*
David Douillet   *Il fait du judo.*

E **Questions personnelles.** Vos pensées.

1. Que pensez-vous...

MODÈLE: des westerns?   *Je pense qu'ils sont ennuyeux.*

a. des Beatles?
b. du Président des Etats-Unis?
c. des Français?
d. de la télévision?
e. de votre cours de français?
f. ???

2. Quand vous vous trouvez dans les situations suivantes, à quoi ou à qui pensez-vous?

MODÈLE: Vous êtes en cours.
Quand je suis en cours, je pense à mes vacances.

a. Vous téléphonez à votre petit(e) ami(e).
b. Vous vous reposez.
c. Vous êtes en cours.
d. Vous êtes seul(e).
e. Vous passez un examen.
f. Vous recevez un télégramme.
g. Vous partez en vacances.
h. ???

F **Jeu de rôles.** Jouez les scènes suivantes avec un(e) camarade de cours.

1. Vous êtes chez le médecin. Expliquez-lui vos problèmes. Le médecin vous donne des conseils.
2. Un journaliste français va vous interviewer. Il veut savoir comment est la journée typique d'un étudiant américain. Décrivez-lui la vôtre.
3. Vous jouez le rôle de votre athlète préféré. Un(e) autre étudiant(e) va vous interviewer après une compétition importante.
4. Vous êtes écrivain. Un(e) camarade de cours est journaliste et va vous interviewer. Parlez de vos créations littéraires.
5. Vous travaillez à la télévision. Faites de la publicité pour une marque *(brand name)* qui a une équipe dans le Tour de France.
6. Vous êtes guide dans un musée. Décrivez vos œuvres d'art *(works of art)* préférées. Un(e) camarade est touriste et va vous poser des questions.

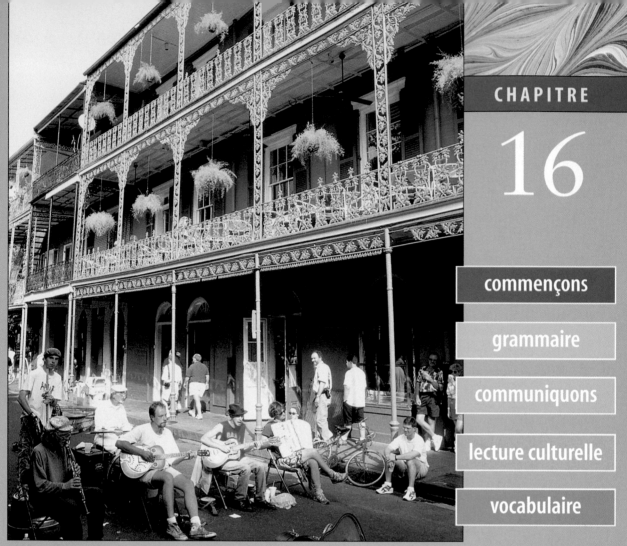

Le Vieux Carré à La
Nouvelle-Orléans

CHAPITRE

16

commençons

grammaire

communiquons

lecture culturelle

vocabulaire

Le français aux États-Unis

OBJECTIVES

Language		Culture	Communication
■ Vocabulary for rooms of the house and furniture	■ Expressing time with **pendant, depuis,** and **il y a**	■ Lodging in France	■ Finding a place to live
■ Mute **e**		■ The francophone press	■ Expressing hypothetical statements
■ The relative pronouns **qui, que,** and **où**		■ Alexis de Tocqueville	■ Expressing continuous and completed actions
■ The conditional mood			

commençons

Réponse à une petite annonce

Un étudiant américain qui vient de Louisiane et qui s'appelle Daniel est à Lyon depuis une semaine. Il lit les petites annonces dans Le Progrès. *Il a trouvé des chambres à louer qui l'intéressent et il a téléphoné aux propriétaires pendant toute la matinée. Quelqu'un répond enfin.*

DANIEL: Allô, bonjour, Madame. J'ai lu la petite annonce que vous avez placée dans le journal et j'aimerais avoir des renseignements sur la chambre que vous voulez louer.

MME LUCAS: Bien sûr! C'est une grande chambre meublée qui donne sur le parc de la Tête d'Or et que je loue tous les ans à des étudiants étrangers. J'ai trouvé quelqu'un il y a un mois, mais il a dû rentrer chez lui.

DANIEL: Quel est le prix du loyer?

MME LUCAS: Trois cents euros par mois, charges comprises. Voudriez-vous aller voir la chambre maintenant?

DANIEL: Oui, mais je ne sais pas où elle se trouve. Pourriez-vous m'indiquer le chemin?

MME LUCAS: Connaissez-vous le musée Guimet? C'est juste en face, au numéro vingt et un. C'est au sixième étage, la troisième porte à gauche. Demandez la clé à la concierge.

DANIEL: Très bien, je vais y aller tout de suite et je vais vous rappeler dans la soirée.

L'IMMOBILIER A LYON, C'EST A
L'ESPACE TÊTE D'OR!
103 BOULEVARD DE STALINGRAD LYON VILLEURBANNE

5 pièces

EXCEPTIONNEL
Dans imm. gd stand. superbe appart. vue Rhône prox Parc Tête d'Or 120M² 3 ch + 2 sdb gd séjour 2000€+ Charges. 78.37.70.44 de 9 à 13H ou 04.78.89.90.91 ap 19H
16B24907

LYON 5e, à louer ds St-Jean site prestigieux appt neuf 98m² env prest. de gd stand. séj. 42m² 3 ch park. privé asc. loyer 950€/ms + charges. SAVIE 04.78.83.26.63
10AC4069

F4 98m² interph. gge ts bon stand. 500€
O.P.L. 04.78.60.33.83
10AC4087

A louer F4 tout confort 2942 CC.
04.78.58.14.14
BEP (700)
10A46059

Studios

PART loue Lyon1er 2 stud nfs mezz rez chaus s/cour 33m² 375€ 31m² 300€ ptes ch 04.75.34.43.94
16B44635

2 pièces

Joli F2 60m² jard. cour park. 1 mois caution. 320€ CC
O.P.L. 04.78.60.33.83
10AC4086

LYON 2e Ainay part loue F2 50 m² ds imm anc clair calme 5e ét av asc interph 400€ TCC Tél. 04.78.25.50.66
16B44617

PROPRIETAIRES LOUEZ ENTRE PARTICULIERS
- Diffus. de vos offres
- Assistance juridique
- Baux de location
- Assur. loy. impayés
- locat. saisonnière
HESTIA
04.78.42.00.20

LOUER A LYON
36.15 LOGEZ
NE CHERCHEZ PLUS!
avec la CNAB (Confédération Nationale des Administrateurs de Biens)
498225

1. Qu'est-ce que Daniel lit? Pourquoi?
2. A qui téléphone-t-il?
3. Décrivez la chambre.
4. Quel est le prix du loyer?
5. Où se trouve la chambre?
6. Est-ce que Daniel la prend tout de suite?

Mots clés

qui	*who*	donne sur (donner sur)	*looks out on*
la Louisiane	*Louisiana*	il y a	*ago*
petites annonces *(f.)*	*classified ads*	le loyer	*rent*
qui	*that*	charges comprises	*utilities included*
intéressent (intéresser)	*interest*	Voudriez-vous... ? (vouloir)	*Would you like . . . ?*
propriétaires *(m. / f.)*	*owners*	Pourriez-vous... ? (pouvoir)	*Could you . . . ?*
enfin	*finally*	un chemin	*way*
que	*that*	juste	*just*
avez placée (placer)	*placed*	un étage	*floor*
aimerais (aimer)	*would like*	à gauche	*on the left*
meublée	*furnished*	un/une concierge	*concierge*

Faisons connaissance

WWW

Many French families rent rooms to students in their own homes or apartments or in property they own for purely financial reasons. This is particularly true of widows and older couples whose children have left home. They use the rent money to pay taxes and to supplement their incomes. This is a fortunate situation for students because few universities have enough student housing.

A **concierge,** such as the one mentioned in the dialogue at the beginning of the chapter, is usually a woman responsible for distributing mail, helping visitors, and keeping the building clean. **Concierges** are rapidly disappearing, however, as building owners install automatic locks and individual mailboxes.

French people have a different way of counting floors. The first floor is **le rez-de-chaussée,** the second floor, **le premier étage,** and so on. In Quebec, however, people use the word **plancher,** which also means floor, for **étage,** and they count the floors the same way Americans do. Thus, to a person from Quebec or the United States, in the dialogue, the room **au sixième étage** would be on the seventh floor. On the top floor of many apartment buildings (**un immeuble**) there are maids' rooms (**des chambres de bonne**), which are often rented to students. ▶

Une maison en construction

Enrichissons notre vocabulaire

Les pièces de la maison *(The rooms of the house)*

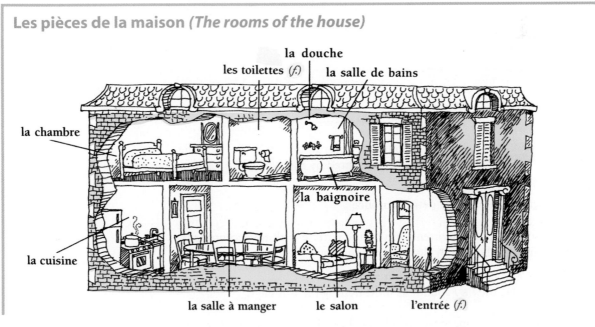

Les meubles et les appareils électro-ménagers
(Furniture and appliances)

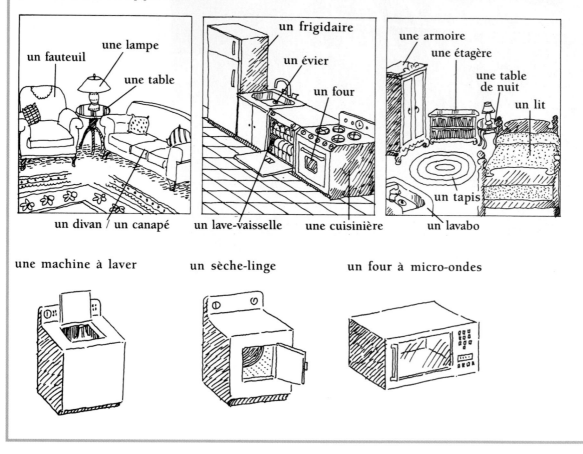

Prononciation   Mute *e*

A. Mute **e** may or may not be pronounced, according to its position in the sentence. When pronounced, it is represented by the symbol / ə / and is pronounced as the / ø / of **peu.**

> une p<u>e</u>tite annonce / la p<s>e</s>tite annonce

B. Mute **e** is identified in written form by the letter **e** with no accent mark, and it is never followed by double consonants.

> D<u>e</u>voirs and b<u>e</u>soin both contain mute **e.**
> D<u>e</u>rrière has the / ɛ / sound, as indicated by the double **r.**

C. In casual conversation, most French speakers drop as many mute **e**'s as possible, short of creating a string of unpronounceable consonants. One important rule is that mute **e** is never pronounced before a vowel sound.

> quatr<s>e</s> heures / votr<s>e</s> appartement / un autr<s>e</s> étudiant /
>   notr<s>e</s> ami / une tabl<s>e</s> immense / un pauvr<s>e</s> homme

D. In general, a mute **e** is also dropped if it is preceded by only one pronounced consonant. For example, **trop de gens** is pronounced / tʀo dʒã /. The / ʒ / is preceded by **d,** but **p** is not pronounced.

> beaucoup dé livres / sans cé livre / un kilo dé beurre / dans lé bureau / assez dé travail / Vous lé savez. / pas dé place / Tu né bois pas.

E. If a mute **e** follows two pronounced consonants, however, it is better to keep the sound.

> Il ne̲ sait pas. / Regarde le̲ garçon. / avec le̲ couteau /
> Elles me̲ connaissent. / Jeanne te̲ voit / une pauvre̲
> femme / le gouverne̲ment / quatre̲ semaines de̲ vacances

Exercice

Read the following sentences aloud, dropping as many mute **e**'s as possible.

1. Je ne sais pas si je veux cette table de nuit.
2. Beaucoup de gens se reposent le matin.
3. Elle me donne trop de travail.
4. A quatre heures nous décidons de préparer le dîner.
5. Qu'est-ce que vous allez me montrer?
6. Mon appartement se trouve au rez-de-chaussée près de la cuisine.

grammaire

I. The relative pronouns *qui, que,* and *où*

> You use relative pronouns to connect two sentences or clauses into a single sentence.

A. Uses of relative pronouns

In English, relative pronouns are used to combine two sentences or clauses into a single sentence. The relative pronoun introduces the second clause and refers to a word in the main clause. This word is called the *antecedent.*

> Here is the book. I read the book.
>
>   antecedent rel. pro.
>   ↓   ↓
> Here is the *book that* I read.
>
> Did you see the man? The man drove a red car.
>
>   antecedent rel. pro.
>   ↓   ↓
> Did you see the *man who* drove a red car?

B. The relative pronoun *qui*

1. **Qui** *(who, which, that)* may refer to people or things and serves as the subject of the verb that follows it.

> Nous avons demandé des renseignements à **Paul. Paul** connaît bien la ville.
> Nous avons demandé des renseignements à Paul **qui** connaît bien la ville.

> C'est **une grande chambre. La chambre** donne sur un parc.
> C'est une grande chambre **qui** donne sur un parc.

2. The verb following **qui** agrees with the antecedent.

> C'est **moi** qui **suis arrivé** à l'heure.   C'est **elle** qui **est montée.**

C. The relative pronoun *que*

1. **Que** *(whom, which, that)* also refers to people or things and serves as the direct object of the verb that follows it.

> Je cherche **la chambre.** Vous louez **la chambre.**
> Je cherche la chambre **que** vous louez.

> Elle n'aime pas **l'émission.** Ils regardent **l'émission.**
> Elle n'aime pas l'émission **qu'**ils regardent.

2. **Que** becomes **qu'** before a vowel sound.

> Ma mère lit le roman **qu'**elle a trouvé sur le fauteuil.

L'orthographe

> If the clause following **que** is in the **passé composé,** the past participle agrees with the antecedent of **que,** which is the preceding direct object.
>
> > Elle s'intéresse à **la robe** que tu lui as montrée.
> > Nous n'avons pas vu **les meubles** qu'ils ont achetés.
> > J'ai lu **les petites annonces** que vous avez placées dans le journal.

D. The relative pronoun *où*

1. **Où** *(where)* is used when the second clause indicates a place.

> Il n'a pas dit **où** il allait.

> Voilà la chambre **où** ils dorment.

2. If the antecedent is a place but is the *direct object* of the verb in the second clause, use **que** instead of **où.**

> L'Espagne est un pays **que** nous n'avons jamais visité.
> Le parc de la Tête d'Or est un parc **que** les Lyonnais fréquentent beaucoup.

E. In Chapter 15, you learned that demonstrative pronouns (**celui, celle, ceux, celles**) must be followed by **-ci, -là,** or the preposition **de.** They can also be followed by relative pronouns.

> Elle n'aime pas ceux **que** j'ai achetés.
> Prenez celui **qui** est sur la table.
> Regardez cette maison. C'est celle **où** je suis née.

Ce qu'ils disent

1. French intonation and rhythm do not allow a speaker to emphasize a word in a sentence simply by saying it louder, as we do in English. To emphasize a word, you must put it just before a new clause. Relative pronouns are frequently used in this construction, which you hear very often in casual conversation. In the following examples, the word in boldface in the first sentence is emphasized in the second.

Jean cherche un appartement.	C'est Jean qui cherche un appartement.
Je n'aime pas **tes meubles.**	Ce sont tes meubles que je n'aime pas.
Madeleine travaille **là.**	C'est là où Madeleine travaille.

2. In this construction, stressed pronouns replace subject pronouns, and the verb in the second clause agrees with its subject in the first.

Tu achètes un lave-vaisselle?	**Il** ne va pas conduire!
C'est **toi** qui **achètes** un lave-vaisselle?	Ce n'est pas **lui** qui **va** conduire!

Langue

Ⓐ Dans notre appartement. Complétez les phrases suivantes avec un pronom relatif.

1. J'adore les appartements _____ il y a beaucoup de fenêtres.
2. Apportez-moi le verre _____ j'ai laissé dans la cuisine.
3. L'appartement _____ ma petite amie habite est derrière celui-ci.
4. Je préfère les salons _____ n'ont pas trop de meubles.
5. Nous n'apprécions pas les voisins _____ font du bruit.
6. Le lit _____ ils veulent me prêter est trop petit.

Ⓑ Une promenade en ville. Complétez les phrases suivantes.

1. Nous avons acheté des CD que...
2. Je vous recommande un film qui...
3. J'ai visité une ville où...
4. Le restaurant sert des repas qui...
5. Allez-vous acheter les vêtements que... ?
6. Ils passent leur temps dans un magasin où...

C **L'appartement de Corinne.** Pour mettre en relief *(to emphasize)* les mots en italique dans les phrases suivantes, refaites les phrases en plaçant les mots en italique au début et en utilisant un pronom relatif. Suivez le modèle.

MODÈLE: Corinne habite *un grand appartement.*
C'est *un grand appartement* que Corinne habite.

1. Corinne habite *avec ses deux sœurs.*
2. *Sa sœur Caroline* s'occupe du ménage.
3. Elles dorment *dans cette chambre.*
4. Elles font leurs devoirs *là.*
5. *Leur sœur Claude* n'est pas étudiante.
6. Elle aime se détendre *sur ce canapé.*

Culture

D **Le français cajun.** Le français parlé en Louisiane a beaucoup de mots qui n'existent pas en France. Quels mots est-ce que les Cajuns utilisent pour les choses suivantes?

MODÈLE: Il est mort.
«Il est gone» est l'expression que les Cajuns utilisent
pour «Il est mort.»

1. maintenant	a. affreux
2. un bal *(a dance)*	b. bleu
3. un dollar	c. un grand char
4. très	d. asteur
5. triste	e. un fais-dodo
6. un train	f. une piasse

Communication

E **Mes préférences.** Formez des phrases logiques avec un élément de chaque colonne.

J'admire les gens	qui	être intéressant
Je ne peux pas supporter les gens	que	parler trop
J'aime visiter des pays	où	ne pouvoir rien faire
Je déteste les villes		être trop difficile
Je voudrais avoir un métier		donner mal à la tête
Je n'écoute jamais les gens		ne rien apprendre
Les étudiants s'intéressent aux cours		travailler beaucoup
On n'aime pas s'occuper de problèmes		être sincère
???		???

F **Mes préférences (suite).** Complétez les phrases suivantes logiquement.

1. J'aime les filles / les garçons qui...
2. Je préfère les maisons qui...
3. J'adore les appartements où...
4. Je m'intéresse aux journaux que...

5. J'apprécie les étudiants qui...
6. Je tiens aux meubles que...

G **Questions personnelles.** Votre logement.

1. Dans quelle sorte de ville habitez-vous?
2. Habitez-vous dans une résidence, dans une maison, ou dans un appartement?
3. Décrivez votre chambre.
4. De quels meubles avez-vous besoin?
5. Vous avez cherché un(e) camarade de chambre? Qu'est-ce que vous avez demandé?
6. Vous aimez quelles sortes de voisins?

II. The conditional mood

You use the conditional mood to express an occurrence that would exist under certain circumstances or to make a polite request.

A. Formation of the conditional: Regular verbs

aimer	descendre
j' aim**erais**	je descend**rais**
tu aim**erais**	tu descend**rais**
il / elle / on aim**erait**	il / elle / on descend**rait**
nous aim**erions**	nous descend**rions**
vous aim**eriez**	vous descend**riez**
ils / elles aim**eraient**	ils / elles descend**raient**

choisir	écrire
je chois**irais**	j' écr**irais**
tu chois**irais**	tu écr**irais**
il / elle / on chois**irait**	il / elle / on écr**irait**
nous chois**irions**	nous écr**irions**
vous chois**iriez**	vous écr**iriez**
ils / elles chois**iraient**	ils / elles écr**iraient**

J'aimerais avoir des renseignements sur la chambre.

1. You form the conditional mood by adding the endings of the imperfect tense to the infinitive. If the infinitive ends in **-re,** you drop the **e** before adding the endings.

2. If the infinitive ends in **-r,** you pronounce the **r.**

aimer → **j'aimerais**   louer → **tu louerais**

B. Formation of the conditional: Irregular verbs

1. Several verbs that you already know have irregular conditional stems:

aller	j'**ir**ais	pouvoir	elles **pourr**aient
avoir	tu **aur**ais	recevoir	vous **recevr**iez
devenir	on **deviendr**ait	savoir	elle **saur**ait
devoir	il **devr**ait	tenir	nous **tiendr**ions
être	nous **ser**ions	valoir	il **vaudr**ait (mieux)
faire	vous **fer**iez	venir	il **viendr**ait
falloir	il **faudr**ait	voir	tu **verr**ais
mourir	il **mourr**ait	vouloir	je **voudr**ais
pleuvoir	il **pleuvr**ait		

2. Stem-changing verbs use the **accent grave** or double consonant in the last syllable of the stem to keep the / ɛ / sound. Verbs with an **accent aigu** in the last syllable of the stem keep the / e / sound.

acheter	→	elle ach**è**terait
se lever	→	nous nous l**è**verions
appeler	→	vous appe**ll**eriez

but: préférer → je préférerais
répéter → tu répéterais

C. Uses of the conditional

1. The conditional mood softens a request or a statement. Use it instead of the present or the imperative when you want to be polite.

> **Voudriez**-vous aller voir la chambre?
> Vous **devriez** consulter une carte.

2. The conditional mood expresses a possible occurrence that would exist under certain conditions.

> Nous **aimerions** habiter en Louisiane.
> A ce prix-là, ce **serait** trop cher.
> Il ne **viendrait** pas sans son ami.

3. Several expressions are frequently used with the conditional mood to show a condition that does not exist.

à ta / votre / sa place:	A ta place, je **choisirais** un autre divan.
sans / avec cela:	Sans cela, nous ne **finirions** jamais.
si j'étais / si vous étiez:	Si vous étiez riche, vous ne **feriez** pas le ménage.

Langue

Ⓐ **A la bibliothèque.** Formez des phrases plus polies en mettant les phrases suivantes au conditionnel.

1. Pouvez-vous m'indiquer le bureau des renseignements?
2. Je veux savoir où se trouvent les revues.

3. Mon copain aime lire des journaux.

4. Où est-ce qu'on trouve les films?

5. Je suis heureux de pouvoir utiliser un ordinateur.

6. Avez-vous le temps de m'expliquer tout cela?

B **Sans argent.** Formez des phrases avec les mots donnés. Mettez les verbes au conditionnel.

1. Sans argent / vous / ne... pas / pouvoir / acheter / fauteuil

2. A votre place, je / ne... pas / entrer / ce / magasin

3. Il / avoir peur / louer / voiture

4. Ce / enfants / ne... pas / pouvoir / aller / cinéma / sans adulte

5. Nous / ne... pas / appeler / médecin

6. Moi, / je / ne... pas / aller / ce / restaurant

C **On invite nos voisins.** Répondez aux questions en employant les mots entre parenthèses et en mettant le verbe au conditionnel.

1. Vous voulez quelque chose?   (... vouloir du thé)

2. Que feriez-vous à ma place?   (... acheter un nouveau divan)

3. Est-ce que je peux ouvrir la fenêtre?   (Non,... avoir froid)

4. Est-ce que votre amie aimerait partir?   (Oui, mais... revenir tout de suite)

5. Est-elle en retard?   (Oui,... devoir se dépêcher)

6. Aimeriez-vous rester dîner?   (Non,... préférer rentrer)

Culture

D **La politesse.** Si un Français vous invitait à un dîner officiel, que feriez-vous pour être poli(e)? Qu'est-ce que vous ne feriez pas?

MODÈLE: demander aux gens d'allumer la télé
          Je ne demanderais pas aux gens d'allumer la télé.

1. apporter des bonbons

2. arriver bien en avance

3. amener un ami

4. faire des bises à tout le monde

5. enlever mes chaussures

6. avoir les mains sous la table

7. demander encore de la viande

8. partir avant 11 heures

9. manger des choses que je n'aime pas

10. placer mes coudes sur la table

Communication

E **Si les choses étaient différentes.** Avec les petits changements suivants dans votre vie, que feriez-vous? Finissez les phrases.

1. Avec beaucoup d'argent,...

2. Si j'étais au / en [pays],...

3. Avec une voiture de sport,...

4. Avec de longues vacances,...

5. Sans ma famille,...

6. Sans ce cours,...

F **Recommençons!** Si vous pouviez refaire votre vie, que feriez-vous de différent? Utilisez les suggestions données ou vos propres idées.

MODÈLE: *J'étudierais beaucoup plus. / J'habiterais en Europe.*

suivre plus / moins de cours de...   dépenser moins d'argent
aller à l'université de...   être plus / moins sympathique
apprendre à jouer du / de la...   louer un appartement
acheter un four à micro-ondes   ???

6 **Questions personnelles.** Votre avenir.

1. Sans diplôme, que feriez-vous?
2. Quand est-ce que vous devriez commencer à travailler? Qu'est-ce que vous préféreriez faire?
3. Qu'est-ce que vous n'accepteriez jamais de faire?
4. Qu'est-ce que vous pourriez faire pour trouver une solution à un problème social?
5. Que faudrait-il que vous ayez pour être heureux (-euse)?
6. Avec un tapis volant *(flying carpet)*, où iriez-vous?

III. Expressing time with *pendant, depuis,* and *il y a*

> You use time expressions to indicate when an action or a state began and whether or not it is still going on.

A. *Pendant*

Use **pendant** or no preposition at all to express the amount of time an action or a condition lasts. The English equivalent is *for*.

> J'ai téléphoné **pendant** toute la matinée.
> *or:* J'ai téléphoné toute la matinée.

> Les élèves attendent l'autobus **pendant** une heure.
> *or:* Les élèves attendent l'autobus une heure.

B. *Depuis*

1. To describe the duration of an action that started in the past but is still going on, use the *present tense* of the verb and **depuis**. The English equivalent is *has / have been* or *has / have been doing.*

Daniel **est** à Lyon **depuis** une semaine.	*Daniel **has been** in Lyon **for a** week.*
Il **cherche** une chambre **depuis** longtemps.	*He **has been looking** for a room **for** a long time.*

2. **Depuis** may also be used with a specific time. In this case, its English equivalent is *since.*

Bouteflika est président de l'Algérie **depuis 1999.**	*Bouteflika has been president of Algeria **since 1999**.*
Elle attend une lettre **depuis lundi.**	*She has been waiting for a letter **since Monday**.*

3. To express how long it has been since something happened, use a negative, the **passé composé,** and **depuis.**

> Je **n'ai pas fait** la vaisselle **depuis** trois jours.
> Le concierge **n'a rien fait depuis** une semaine.

C. *Il y a... que* and *Voilà... que*

Il y a... que and **Voilà... que** also express the duration of an action that started in the past but is still going on. They are used only with amounts of time. These two structures often show more impatience on the part of the speaker than **depuis** and must precede the subject and verb.

> **Il y a** trois jours **qu'**on n'a pas d'eau.
> *We haven't had water **for three days.***

> **Voilà** une heure **que** nous téléphonons au propriétaire.
> *We have been phoning the landlord **for an hour.***

D. *Il y a*

To describe the amount of time that has passed since an action took place, use **il y a** and a verb in a past tense. It may precede or follow the verb. The English equivalent is *ago*.

> J'**ai trouvé** un appartement **il y a** un mois.
> *I **found** an apartment a month **ago**.*

> **Il y a** trois jours, elle **était** encore en Europe.
> *Three days **ago**, she **was** still in Europe.*

Attention!

There are two differences between **il y a** meaning *for* and meaning *ago*. When **il y a** means *ago*, a past tense is used and there is no **que.**

> **Il y a** trois minutes, il **était** là.
> *He **was** here three minutes **ago**.*

> **Il y a** trois minutes **qu'**il **est** là.
> *He's **been** here for three minutes.*

E. Other useful time expressions

1. **Dès** and **à partir de** *(from . . . on, as of . . . , beginning with . . .)* can be used at the beginning or at the end of the sentence.

> **Dès** maintenant, il faut que vous utilisiez un ordinateur.
> Les Français ont eu des vacances payées **à partir des** années 30.

2. **Pour** *(for)* is used with time only for projection into the future with a verb of motion.

> Il est parti **pour** trois mois en Afrique.
> Elle va sortir **pour** une heure.

3. **Dans** *(in)* describes the amount of time before you do something; **en** *(in)* describes the amount of time it takes to do something.

> Je vais passer un examen **dans** trois jours.
> Je dois passer cet examen **en** 50 minutes.

Ⓐ **Robert utilise les petites annonces.** Complétez les phrases suivantes en traduisant le(s) mot(s) entre parenthèses.

1. Robert achète le journal ici _____ deux ans. *(for)*
2. Il lit les petites annonces _____ quelques minutes. *(in)*
3. _____ trois semaines _____ il cherche une voiture. *(for)*
4. _____ une semaine, il pensait en avoir trouvé une. *(ago)*
5. Il a téléphoné au propriétaire _____ plusieurs jours. *(for)*
6. Sa femme lui a dit qu'il venait de partir _____ une semaine en Angleterre. *(for)*
7. Il peut retéléphoner _____ mardi prochain. *(from Tuesday on)*
8. Il décide de chercher une autre voiture _____ demain. *(as of)*

Ⓑ **Ma première année à l'université.** Traduisez les phrases suivantes.

1. I have been here since September.
2. Classes started four weeks ago.
3. Every day, I stay in the lab for one hour.
4. From three o'clock on, I am in the library.
5. I have known my roommate for eight months.
6. I am going to have my last exam in three weeks.

Ⓒ **Le nouvel an.** C'est le 31 décembre à midi, et vous préparez les festivités pour le nouvel an. Depuis quand ou depuis combien de temps faites-vous les choses suivantes? Ou bien, vous les avez faites il y a combien de temps?

1. attendre ce jour / des années
2. téléphoner / amis / mardi dernier
3. préparer / plats / huit heures du matin
4. choisir / musique / mois
5. acheter le champagne / semaine dernière
6. répéter «Ce n'est qu'un *au revoir*» / toute la matinée

Ⓓ **Prenons le train.** Vous êtes à Montréal et vous décidez de prendre le train pour aller à Ottawa. Consultez l'horaire *(schedule)* et répondez aux questions page 429.

Connecting Train No. Correspondance ferroviaire		km						21 Ex. Sa. Su. Sauf sa. di.	23	23	
Québec, QC (Gare du Palais) 🔲		0	Dp					06 45	11 50	11 50	
Montréal, QC (Central Stn./Gare Centrale)		272	Ar					09 55	15 00	15 00	
Montréal, QC ET/HE 60 (Central Stn./Gare Centrale)		0	Dp	07 20	09 30	13 05		16 30	17 50	19 40	
Dorval 31 60		19		07 40	09 50	13 26		16 51	18 10	20 01	
Coteau, QC		63				F 13 51				F 20 26	
Alexandria, ON 🔳		100		F 08 32	F 10 35	F 14 16		F 17 36	F 18 55	F 20 58	
Maxville		117		F 08 46	F 10 49					F 21 12	
Casselman		140				F 14 41					
Ottawa, ON 🔲		187	Ar	09 29	11 32	15 22		18 40	19 49	21 58	

1. On peut aller de Montréal à Ottawa en combien de temps?
2. Vous êtes dans le train de Montréal de 7 h 20 et vous venez de partir de Maxville. Vous voyagez depuis combien de temps?
3. Vous allez arriver à Ottawa dans combien de temps?
4. A Montréal vous montez dans le train de 13 h 05. Il y a combien de temps que les gens qui sont montés à Québec sont dans le train?
5. Ils ont attendu à la Gare Centrale à Montréal pendant combien de temps?
6. Vous arrivez à la gare de Montréal à huit heures du soir. Le dernier train est parti pour Ottawa il y a combien de temps?

Communication

E **Mes études.** Complétez les phrases suivantes.

1. J'étudie le français depuis...
2. J'ai reçu mon diplôme de lycée il y a...
3. Il y a... que je suis étudiant(e) à cette université.
4. Je vais rentrer dans...
5. Je vais commencer à chercher du travail dans...
6. J'ai préparé cette leçon pendant...

F **Questions personnelles.** Votre logement.

1. Depuis combien de temps est-ce que votre famille habite votre maison?
2. Vous êtes parti(e) de chez eux il y a combien de temps?
3. Combien de temps avez-vous passé à chercher votre appartement / votre chambre?
4. Vous êtes là depuis combien de temps?
5. Vous faites le ménage en combien de temps?
6. Dans combien de temps pensez-vous acheter une maison?

 communiquons

Consulter la presse francophone

In France, most newspapers and news magazines can be associated with major political movements. For example, in Paris *Le Figaro* is rather conservative, but *Libération* is to the political left. One of the most respected dailies, *Le Monde,* has a liberal point of view, while *Le Canard Enchaîné,* a weekly newspaper, specializes in political satire. It uses many puns, innuendos, and allusions that only people who follow the daily political scene understand. Although these and other major Parisian newspapers are available throughout France, each region has its own paper. For example, Lyon has *Le Progrès,* Toulouse *La Dépêche du Midi,* and Rennes *Ouest-France.*

Other francophone countries have their own daily papers in French, such as *Le Devoir,* which is published in Montréal, or *Le Soir* (Belgium). In many areas, residents have a choice of languages for their papers: French or Dutch in Belgium, French or German in Switzerland, French and English in Quebec. Many newspapers now appear on-line.

In addition to daily papers (**les quotidiens**), there are also several types of weekly magazines (**les hebdomadaires**) and monthly publications (**les mensuels**). On a weekly basis, *L'Express, Le Point,* and *Le Nouvel Observateur* cover the news on the national and international scenes, while *Paris-Match,* the most widely read news magazine, provides lighter, general information, emphasizing photographs and gossip about popular figures. Monthly magazines include those for fashion (**les journaux de mode**), such as *Marie-Claire* and *Marie-France,* or publications, such as *Femme,* that represent the feminist point of view. *Elle* and *Femme Actuelle* are magazines for women.

Numerous publications appeal to specific interests (**la presse spécialisée**). You have already learned that *L'Equipe* is a daily newspaper for sports fans and that *Télé 7 Jours* and *TV Magazine* provide information on television programming, and are the most widely read French publications by far. Other types of specialized publications include the Parisian magazines *Pariscope* and *L'Officiel des Spectacles,* which give a complete listing of the current movies, plays, and nightclub acts. In addition, most French hobbyists and sports lovers have publications for their individual interests. There is even a periodical for users of the **Minitel!**

Expressions

▶ **On parle des rubriques d'un journal.**

Les enfants lisent les bandes dessinées.	*Children read the comic strips.*
Je voudrais lire le courrier du cœur.	*I would like to read the advice column.*
Maman regarde l'économie.	*Mom reads the business section.*
Papa préfère l'éditorial.	*Dad prefers the editorial.*
Mon frère lit les faits divers.	*My brother reads human interest stories.*
Ma sœur lit seulement les gros titres.	*My sister reads only the headlines.*
Passe-moi l'horoscope.	*Pass me the horoscope.*
Il y a des mots croisés difficiles.	*There are difficult crossword puzzles.*
Les petites annonces ne m'intéressent pas.	*The classified ads don't interest me.*
J'ai vu le film décrit dans les spectacles.	*I saw the film described in the entertainment section.*
Tout le monde lit les sports.	*Everyone reads the sports section.*
Cette histoire est à la une.	*That story is on the front page.*

▶ **On emploie d'autres expressions journalistiques.**

Un(e) abonné(e) à *L'Express* a écrit une lettre à la revue.	*A subscriber to* L'Express *wrote a letter to the magazine.*
J'ai un abonnement à *Paris-Match.*	*I have a subscription to* Paris-Match.
Tu t'abonnes à un magazine?	*Do you subscribe to a magazine?*
J'achète le journal au kiosque de journaux.	*I buy the paper at the newspaper stand.*
Le vendeur de journaux y travaille.	*The news dealer works there.*

Interaction

Monsieur et Madame Legrand lisent le journal.

M. LEGRAND:	Tu as vu le journal?
MME LEGRAND:	François l'a laissé sur le divan.
M. LEGRAND:	Qu'est-ce qu'il y a d'intéressant à la une?
MME LEGRAND:	Pas grand-chose°. Le président a parlé de l'économie.
M. LEGRAND:	Je veux regarder les sports.
MME LEGRAND:	François a cette page dans la salle à manger. Il cherche aussi une moto dans les petites annonces.
M. LEGRAND:	Dans ce cas°-là, j'espère qu'il trouve du travail aussi!

Pas... *Not much*

case

Activités

Ⓐ Quel journal ou quelle revue faut-il acheter dans les situations suivantes en France?

1. Vous voulez aller au cinéma.
2. Vous voulez savoir qui a gagné le match de football.
3. Vous voulez connaître la nouvelle mode.
4. Vous voulez des renseignements sur les événements *(events)* internationaux de la semaine.
5. Vous voulez regarder la télévision.

Ⓑ Quelle rubrique faut-il consulter dans les situations suivantes?

1. Vous cherchez un appartement.
2. Vous voulez connaître votre avenir.
3. Vous voulez savoir quelles sortes de problèmes personnels ont les Français.
4. Vous voulez vous détendre.
5. Vous voulez savoir qui a gagné l'étape du Tour de France.
6. Vous avez envie de sortir.

C **Où on travaille.** Comme aux Etats-Unis, les journaux français font référence aux organisations gouvernementales françaises par le nom du bâtiment *(building)* où elles se trouvent. Trouvez le bâtiment pour chaque organisation.

MODÈLE: (aux Etats-Unis) la Maison-Blanche
C'est là où le Président travaille.

1. Matignon
2. l'Elysée
3. le palais Bourbon
4. l'Hôtel de Ville
5. le palais du Luxembourg
6. le quai d'Orsay

a. le maire de Paris
b. le ministre des Affaires étrangères
c. le président
d. le Premier ministre
e. l'Assemblée nationale
f. le Sénat

D Répondez aux questions suivantes.

1. Quel journal lisez-vous? Quelles revues? Depuis quand?
2. Où se trouve votre vendeur de journaux préféré?
3. A quelles revues vous êtes-vous abonné(e)? Pour combien de temps?
4. Aimez-vous faire les mots croisés? Dans quel journal y a-t-il des mots croisés très difficiles? très faciles?
5. Lisez-vous votre horoscope? Souvent? Qu'est-ce que vous en pensez?
6. Avez-vous écrit une lettre au courrier du cœur? Pourquoi?
7. Avez-vous consulté les petites annonces? Que cherchiez-vous?
8. Quelle bande dessinée préférez-vous? Pourquoi? Quel journal a de bonnes bandes dessinées?

lecture culturelle

Avant la lecture

Even though France and the United States have not always seen eye to eye, a special bond exists between the two countries. Over the course of their histories, they have shared many of the same ideals and beliefs and have influenced each other in many respects. On the one hand, approximately forty years before the French Revolution of 1789, the French writer and philosopher Montesquieu introduced the principle of separation of powers that plays such an important role in the U.S. Constitution. On the other hand, Thomas Jefferson helped the Marquis de Lafayette write the French Declaration of the Rights of Man and of the Citizen (1789), which is modeled on the American Declaration of Independence and the constitutions of the American states.

One particularly enduring example of Franco-American influence is to be found in the work of Alexis de Tocqueville, considered one of the greatest political philosophers of the nineteenth century. Tocqueville saw the United States as the country of the future and believed that the democratic system established in the United States after the American Revolution would eventually prevail in Europe as well. His two-volume work *Democracy in America* was an immediate success and remains to this day one of the most influential books on political thought ever written.

Activités

(A) Have any French people contributed to or influenced your academic field of study?

(B) What do you know about the French Revolution of 1789? What kind of a government was in place before the Revolution?

(C) How do you see the differences between a political democracy and a social democracy, as alluded to in the next-to-the-last paragraph of the text?

De Tocqueville

Les idées de Tocqueville sont celles d'un grand libéral épris° de justice et dont le souci° est à la fois° de rester fidèle à sa famille et à ses origines, et de rechercher constamment ce qui après la Révolution serait le régime le plus juste. Il a été toute sa vie marqué par l'horreur des révolutions et de toute forme de tyrannie.

enamored
concern / at the same time

L'évolution sociale

Tocqueville part de° l'idée selon laquelle le monde évolue spontanément vers l'inégalité des conditions. C'est pourquoi il n'y a dans l'avenir, selon lui, que deux gouvernements possibles: ou bien «un état de société dans lequel tout le monde prendrait plus ou moins part aux affaires», c'est-à-dire un Etat démocratique, ou bien la tyrannie, l'asservissement° de tous à un seul, comme l'Empire° en a donné un exemple.

starts from (an idea)

subjugation
the regime of Napoléon I (1804–1814) / short-comings

Pour remédier aux carences° de sa vie politique, la France ne peut pas s'inspirer de l'Angleterre, où subsiste alors une forte aristocratie jouant un rôle considérable sur le plan° de l'administration des affaires. Il convient° donc de trouver une voie originale, en partant de la distinction entre démocratie et révolution. En cela, le modèle américain vaut la peine° d'être étudié. Car, s'il faut à tout prix° éviter une nouvelle révolution, l'apport de celle de 1789, en particulier l'œuvre des deux premières Assemblées— suivie certes° de l'horreur des massacres et de la tyrannie—reste° irremplaçable. La spécificité américaine réside dans le fait qu'aux Etats-Unis la démocratie règne dans la société civile comme dans le domaine politique, alors que la France ne connaît de démocratie que dans la société civile; le domaine politique y repose sur l'aristocratie.

with regard to / It is important

vaut... *is worth*
at all costs

admittedly, to be sure / remains

25

L'exemple américain

Tocqueville emprunte à Montesquieu le concept de caractère national:
l'Angleterre est une nation ancienne, dont le régime repose sur l'aristocratie. Les Etats-Unis sont une nation neuve; en passant sur le nouveau
continent, les Anglais ont perdu cet aristocratisme pour trouver ce qui va
30 constituer le fond du caractère national américain: l'esprit calculateur, le
goût de l'argent, l'orgueil° de la réussite°. La grande valeur des Etats-Unis   *pride / success*
par rapport à l'Angleterre et par rapport à la France, c'est qu'ils représen-
tent une révolution démocratique radicale sans violence.

«Révolution et démocratie», in «Charles Alexis Henri Clérel de Tocqueville»,
Encyclopédie Hachette, copyright © 2001 Hachette Multimédia / Hachette Livre,
all rights reserved.

Après la lecture

Questions sur le texte

1. Après la Révolution française, qu'est-ce que Tocqueville a toujours recherché?
2. Quels sont les deux gouvernements possibles dans l'avenir, d'après Tocqueville?
3. Selon lui, pourquoi est-ce que la France ne peut pas s'inspirer de l'Angleterre comme modèle de gouvernement?
4. Pourquoi est-ce que Tocqueville voit les Etats-Unis comme modèle de système gouvernemental?
5. Quel est le caractère national américain selon Tocqueville?

Activités

A Dans le texte, on parle du «caractère national américain». Etes-vous d'accord avec la liste des caractéristiques mentionnées? Donnez des exemples
de ces traits dans la vie de tous les jours. Quelles autres qualités est-ce que
vous attribueriez aux Américains? Selon vous, quel est le caractère national
français?

B Décrivez le système de gouvernement français aujourd'hui. Comment est-
ce que les pouvoirs sont divisés? Qui est le président? Et le premier ministre? Sont-ils du même parti politique? Comparez le système de gouvernement français au système américain.

C Les grandes idées des philosophes français, comme Montesquieu et
Voltaire, ont inspiré la Déclaration d'indépendance des Etats-Unis
d'Amérique de 1776. Par la suite, la Déclaration d'indépendance a
inspiré le contenu du document français la Déclaration des droits de
l'homme et du citoyen (26 août 1789). Puis, le 10 décembre 1948,

l'Assemblée générale des Nations unies a adopté la Déclaration universelle des droits de l'homme. Quels sont les droits naturels des êtres humains selon ces trois documents? Quelles sont les ressemblances et les différences entre les documents?

vocabulaire

Noms / Pronoms

un appareil électro-ménager	appliance	une lampe	lamp
une armoire	armoire	un lavabo	sink
une baignoire	bathtub	un lave-vaisselle	dishwasher
un canapé	sofa	un lit	bed
une chambre de bonne	maid's room	la Louisiane	Louisiana
		le loyer	rent
charges *(f.)*	utilities	une machine à laver	washing machine
un chemin	way	meubles *(m.)*	furniture
un/une concierge	concierge, caretaker	où *(pron. rel.)*	where
		petites annonces *(f.)*	classified ads
une cuisine	kitchen	une pièce	room
une cuisinière	stove	le plancher	floor
un divan	sofa	un/une propriétaire	owner
une douche	shower	que *(pron. rel.)*	whom / that / which
une entrée	entrance		
un étage	floor	qui *(pron. rel.)*	who / that
une étagère	shelf	un rez-de-chaussée	ground floor
un évier	kitchen sink	une salle à manger	dining room
un fauteuil	armchair	une salle de bains	bathroom
un four	oven	un salon	living room
un four à micro-ondes	microwave oven	un sèche-linge	dryer
		une table	table
un frigidaire	refrigerator	une table de nuit	bedside table
un immeuble	apartment building	un tapis	carpet
		toilettes *(f.)*	bathroom

Verbes

intéresser	to interest	placer	to place

Adjectifs / Adverbes

compris	included	juste	just
enfin	finally	meublé(e)	furnished

Expressions

à gauche	on the left	en	in (time)
à partir de	starting from	il y a	ago
à ta / votre / sa place	in your / his / her place	il y a... que	it has been . . . that
dans	in (time)	pour	for
dès	from	voilà... que	it has been . . . that
donner sur	to look out on		

Place Ville-Marie à Montréal

Le français au Québec

OBJECTIVES

Language	Culture	Communication
■ Vocabulary for nature and the environment ■ **Liaisons** ■ The future tense ■ **Si** clauses ■ **Mettre** and verbs conjugated like **mettre**	■ The Quebec poet Robert Mélançon ■ Montreal and its underground	■ Talking about events in the future ■ Expressing hypothetical situations ■ Expressing emotions

commençons

Neige

Un poète évoque un ballet de couleurs créé par le contact du soleil et de la neige sur la nature québécoise.

Le soleil ondoie sur le blanc,
Jour couché entre les troncs
Que le gel a noircis, délivrés
Des feuilles, des oiseaux, des rumeurs.
Le soleil coule sur la neige
Comme une eau plus vive que l'eau.
Terre lucide d'où jaillit la forêt
Intelligible (colonnes de raison,
Idées dont la rigueur inclut l'écorce,
Que la main touche), la neige méditative
Où passent les reflets du jour rose,
Jaune, bleu, où se dispersent des étoiles
Moins nombrables que la Voie lactée,
La neige incarne la lumière, elle est
Sa seule forme, sa seule matière.

Robert Mélançon

Dans la campagne québécoise

Etudions le poème

1. Comment expliquez-vous le deuxième vers *(line)*: «Jour couché entre les troncs»?
2. Quels sont les mots du poème qui évoquent l'hiver?
3. Que signifie «colonnes de raison» au vers 8?
4. Aux vers 11 et 12, «les reflets du jour rose, / Jaune, bleu...» évoquent quelle heure de la journée?
5. Quelle impression de la nature québécoise est-ce que ce poème vous donne?

Mots clés

un/une poète	*poet*	la nature	*nature*
évoque	*evokes*	ondoie	*shimmers*
créé	*created*	troncs *(m.)*	*trunks*
le contact	*contact*	le gel	*frost*

noircis	*blackened*	écorce *(f.)*	*bark*
délivrés	*freed*	méditative	*pensive*
feuilles *(f.)*	*leaves*	reflets *(m.)*	*reflections*
rumeurs *(f.)*	*rumors*	rose	*pink*
vive	*lively*	se dispersent	*scatter*
lucide	*lucid*	nombrables	*countable*
jaillit	*springs*	la Voie lactée	*Milky Way*
colonnes *(f.)*	*columns*	incarne	*embodies*
la raison	*reason*	la lumière	*light*
dont	*of which*	la matière	*matter*
inclut	*includes*		

Faisons connaissance

Robert Mélançon is a Quebec poet born in Montreal in 1947. A professor at the University of Montreal, he spent some time writing literary editorials for the newspaper *Le Devoir*. He also served on the editorial board of the review *Liberté*. His poetry has often been labeled classical. Among his works, one might note a collection of poems, *Inscriptions,* published in 1978, and *Peinture aveugle,* which appeared a year later.

The people of Quebec have always been very proud of their origins, their language, and their customs. Their profound attachment to their land is in evidence throughout their literature. For generations **québécois** poets have sung the beauty of the countryside and of the Quebec soul.

Today, Quebec and the rest of Canada are not just looking backward at their past; they are also oriented toward the future. Two examples of Canadian technological achievements are Hydro-Québec, one of the largest hydroelectric networks in the world, and the robotic arm (**le bras spatial**) used to manipulate objects outside the American space shuttle.

Québec, Montréal, même pays

A Québec, cité-refuge des valeurs francophones, et surtout à Montréal, on est en « presque Amérique ». Mais tout est dans ce « presque ».

Enrichissons notre vocabulaire

Le paysage *(The countryside)*

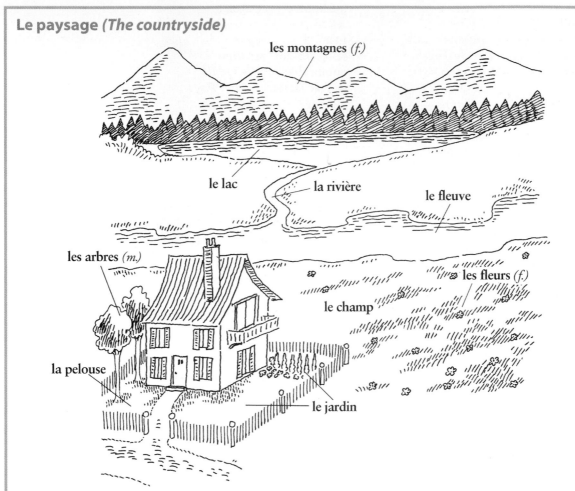

les montagnes *(f.)*

le lac

la rivière

le fleuve

les arbres *(m.)*

les fleurs *(f.)*

le champ

la pelouse

le jardin

L'environnement *(m.) (The environment)*

l'écologie *(f.)* / les écologistes *(m., f.)*	*ecology / ecologists*
l'énergie *(f.)* solaire / nucléaire	*solar / nuclear energy*
les espaces *(m.)* habitables	*livable spaces*
la pluie acide	*acid rain*
La pollution **augmente / diminue.**	*Pollution **is increasing / decreasing.***
le recyclage	*recycling*

Le futur *(The future)*

la biotechnologie	*biotechnology*
la lune, les planètes *(f.)*	*moon, planets*
la navette spatiale	*space shuttle*
la station spatiale	*space station*

Prononciation   Liaisons

A. You learned in Chapter 4 that **liaisons** occur when a normally silent, final written consonant is pronounced because a word starting with a vowel follows. Often, a certain amount of flexibility is allowed when deciding whether or not to pronounce the consonant, but sometimes you must make a **liaison.**

B. **Liaisons** that you must make are called **liaisons obligatoires.** They fall into the following categories:

1. article + noun / article + adjective + noun

mes_amis	un petit_homme	des_efforts
mon_ordinateur	un grand_appartement	deux_autres_exemples
un_habitant	de vieilles_églises	dix_étudiants

2. pronoun + verb / verb + pronoun / pronoun + pronoun

ils_habitent	Nous_en voudrions.	Nous_y allons.
Il va les_inviter.	Donnez-en.	Vont-ils les_acheter?
On_en_a.	Vous_en_avez vu.	Elles les_ont.

Do not pronounce, however, the **liaison** between subject pronouns and verbs with inversion.

Sont-ils / arrivés?
Voulez-vous / en acheter?
Peuvent-elles / ouvrir?

3. after many one-syllable prepositions and adverbs

chez_eux	trop_aimable	dans_un restaurant
très_utile	sous_un_arbre	bien_aimé

C. Some **liaisons,** called **liaisons facultatives,** are optional. Generally, you should make more of them when speaking in a formal style. Some categories are as follows:

negation

pas_avec moi	*or*	pas / avec moi
jamais_au théâtre	*or*	jamais / au théâtre
plus_à Paris	*or*	plus / à Paris

verbs + verbs / verbs + prepositions / verbs + articles

je dois_aller	*or*	je dois / aller
il faut_appeler	*or*	il faut / appeler

But with **est** and present-tense verbs ending in **-ont, liaison** is very frequent:

Il est_arrivé.
Ils font_une erreur.
Elles ont_un_appartement.

two-syllable prepositions and adverbs

devant͜ une église	*or*	devant / une église
beaucoup͜ aimé	*or*	beaucoup / aimé
souvent͜ excellent	*or*	souvent / excellent

Exercice

Read the following sentences aloud, making all **liaisons obligatoires.**

1. Ils en ont un.
2. Montrez-en aux enfants.
3. Elles y sont allées sans eux.
4. Je les ai emmenés avec leurs amis.
5. Etes-vous allés en Irlande cet été?
6. Les bons étudiants adorent étudier sous les arbres.

grammaire

I. The future tense

You use the future tense to talk about events and states that will occur in the future, but with a degree of uncertainty.

A. Forms

1. In French, the most frequent way of expressing a future action in conversation is by using the **futur proche,** but there is also a future tense that uses only one verb form. To conjugate a verb in the future tense, you add the following endings to the stems you learned for the conditional mood.

parler	finir	répondre
je parler**ai**	je finir**ai**	je répondr**ai**
tu parler**as**	tu finir**as**	tu répondr**as**
il / elle / on parler**a**	il / elle / on finir**a**	il / elle / on répondr**a**
nous parler**ons**	nous finir**ons**	nous répondr**ons**
vous parler**ez**	vous finir**ez**	vous répondr**ez**
ils / elles parler**ont**	ils / elles finir**ont**	ils / elles répondr**ont**

Nous **construirons** une maison ici.	We **will build** a house here.
Tu me **diras** le nom de ce vin?	**Will** you **tell** me the name of this wine?
Ils **apprendront** le recyclage aux enfants.	They **will teach** recycling to the children.

L'orthographe

> Note that in the preceding examples you drop the **e** from infinitives ending in **-re** before you add the future endings: **répondre → ils répondront.**

2. All verbs that have irregular stems in the conditional mood also have the same irregular stems in the future tense. For these irregular stems, refer to the section on the formation of the conditional in Chapter 16.

B. Use

There is a slight difference in meaning between the **futur** and the **futur proche.** The **futur proche** expresses actions that are more certain than those in the **futur.**

Elle va avoir un enfant.	*(She's pregnant.)*
Elle aura un enfant.	*(She hopes to have a child.)*
Je vais écrire un poème.	*(Now!)*
J'écrirai un poème.	*(When I have time.)*

C. Expressions of time

1. French has four expressions that are frequently used to introduce events in the future:

quand / lorsque	*when*
dès que / aussitôt que	*as soon as*

2. When you use these expressions in a sentence with both actions in the future, you must use the **futur** in *both* clauses, even though you would use the present tense in English.

Je lui demanderai **quand il arrivera.**	*I will ask him **when he comes.***
Dès qu'elle partira, nous nous coucherons.	***As soon as she leaves,** we shall go to bed.*

3. An imperative used in the main clause of a sentence with an expression of time implies a future action; therefore, you must use the future tense.

Téléphonez **quand vous aurez le temps.**	*Call **when you have time.***

Langue

Ⓐ **Une promenade à la campagne.** Dans les phrases suivantes, mettez les verbes au futur.

1. Allez-vous faire un voyage?
2. Oui, nous allons partir samedi.
3. Je vais aller à la campagne.
4. Mais, il va pleuvoir!
5. Nos amis vont nous emmener en auto.
6. Nous allons voir de vieilles maisons.

Ⓑ La visite d'une vieille amie. Dans les phrases suivantes, changez les verbes du passé au futur.

1. Aussitôt que nous avons reçu sa lettre, nous avons su qu'elle revenait.
2. Quand elle a téléphoné de la gare, j'ai commencé à faire le ménage.
3. Dès qu'elle est arrivée, elle a sonné à la porte.
4. Dès que je l'ai vue, je l'ai embrassée.
5. Quand on a fini de parler, elle est allée se reposer.
6. J'ai été malheureux quand elle a dû partir.

Ⓒ Notre avenir. Formez des phrases complètes avec les mots donnés.

1. Nous / ne... pas / devenir / vieux
2. On / pouvoir / aller / sur la lune
3. Il / ne... plus / y / avoir / cancer
4. Président / recevoir / lettre / d'une autre planète
5. Il / falloir / vous / utiliser / énergie / solaire
6. Il / ne... plus / pleuvoir

Culture

Ⓓ Que faire? Vous irez en France un jour. Que ferez-vous dans les situations suivantes? Trouvez la meilleure *(best)* solution.

MODÈLE: aller de Paris à Lyon / prendre le TGV
Quand j'irai de Paris à Lyon, je prendrai le TGV.

1. acheter des vêtements
   a. aller chez Chanel   b. aller à un hypermarché
   c. aller à une poissonnerie
2. mourir de soif
   a. entrer dans un café   b. chercher une fontaine
   c. chercher un distributeur de boissons
3. avoir mal à la gorge
   a. aller chez le médecin   b. aller au supermarché
   c. aller à la pharmacie
4. quelqu'un éternue *(sneezes)*
   a. dire «Mon Dieu!»   b. dire «Gesundheit!»
   c. dire «A vos souhaits!»
5. aller à Disneyland Paris valoir mieux prendre
   a. le R.E.R.   b. le métro
   c. l'autobus
6. prendre l'apéritif
   a. demander un coca   b. dire «A la vôtre!»
   c. boire directement à la bouteille

Communication

Ⓔ Votre avenir. Que ferez-vous...

1. aussitôt que le week-end arrivera?
2. quand vous serez en vacances?
3. lorsque vous pourrez avoir un appartement?

4. lorsque vous serez vieux / vieille?

5. dès que ce cours finira?

6. aussitôt que vous aurez beaucoup d'argent?

F **Le futur.** Imaginez la vie en 2020. Utilisez les suggestions données ou vos propres idées.

MODÈLE: *On passera le week-end sur la lune.*
Nous ne travaillerons plus.
Les gens resteront jeunes.

ne plus aller chez le dentiste conduire des voitures électriques
avoir des robots pour... ne plus avoir besoin de médecins
ne jamais être fatigué(e) voir les gens au téléphone
ne plus faire la vaisselle vouloir retourner en 1990
falloir parler plusieurs langues (le bon vieux temps!)
avoir des ordinateurs partout dans ???
 la maison

G **Questions personnelles.** Votre avenir.

1. Où irez-vous cet été?

2. Quand commencerez-vous à travailler?

3. Quand aurez-vous trente ans?

4. Qu'est-ce que vous ferez ce jour-là?

5. Quand aurez-vous des enfants? Combien?

6. A quelle université iront-ils? A celle-ci?

II. *Si* clauses

> You use **si** clauses to state the conditions under which things happen, even if only hypothetically.

Both French and English have sentences in which one action depends on a certain condition. In French, there is a sequence of verb tenses used in sentences that state a condition with **si.** At this point, you can construct three types.

A. Use the sequence **si** + *present tense / present tense* with general rules or typical conditions.

S'il **fait** beau, j'**emmène** mes enfants au parc.
Il **fait** ses devoirs s'il n'y **a** rien à la télé.

B. Use the sequence **si** + *present tense / futur* for a specific event.

S'il **fait** beau ce soir, on **regardera** la lune.
Les élèves s'**endormiront** si le prof **est** ennuyeux.

C. Use the sequence **si** + *imperfect / conditional* for hypothetical situations.

S'il **faisait** attention, il **réussirait.**
La pollution **augmenterait** si nous ne l'**arrêtions** pas.

Langue

Ⓐ **Ce soir...** Dans les phrases suivantes, ajoutez l'expression **ce soir** et mettez le verbe en italique au futur.

MODÈLE: Si tu pars, je *viens* avec toi.
Si tu pars ce soir, je viendrai avec toi.

1. S'il pleut, on *reste* à la maison.
2. Si nos amis veulent entrer, ils *peuvent* sonner.
3. Si on est fatigué, on *se couche* de bonne heure.
4. Si quelqu'un appelle, nous ne *répondons* pas.
5. Si tu ne travailles pas maintenant, *peux*-tu finir à l'heure?
6. Je ne *reviens* pas s'il n'y a pas d'autobus.

Ⓑ **Mais, ce n'est pas le cas!** Faites des phrases hypothétiques en mettant *(by putting)* les verbes à l'imparfait et au conditionnel, selon le cas.

MODÈLE: Si Marie est malade, nous irons sans elle.
Si Marie était malade, nous irions sans elle.

1. S'il fait beau, ils iront à la montagne.
2. S'il y a des nuages, nous ne verrons pas les étoiles.
3. Nous ne prendrons pas la voiture s'il neige.
4. Tu auras mal à la tête si tu bois trop.
5. Si vous aimez la musique classique, nous irons au concert.
6. Nous n'irons pas dans la forêt si nous prenons ce chemin.

Ⓒ **Des projets pour ce soir.** Faites deux phrases avec chaque groupe de mots.

MODÈLE: Si / nous / finir / ménage / nous / pouvoir / s'occuper / pelouse
Si nous finissons le ménage, nous pourrons nous occuper de la pelouse.
Si nous finissions le ménage, nous pourrions nous occuper de la pelouse.

1. Je / lui / écrire / si / je / recevoir / son / lettre
2. Si / elle / nous / poser / question, / nous / ne... pas / savoir / réponse
3. Les autres / ne... pas / vouloir / venir / si / je / inviter / Luc
4. Si / tout le monde / être en retard, / il / falloir / attendre
5. Si / elle / ne... pas / se dépêcher, / elle / ne... jamais / être / à l'heure
6. Si / il / ne... pas / arriver à l'heure, / il / valoir mieux / partir / sans lui

Si le français vous intéresse...
...Le Québec vous passionnera!

① **Allons au cinéma!** Voilà un extrait de *Pariscope,* qui décrit les films au cinéma Rex cette semaine (l'explication des symboles et des abréviations se trouve à droite). Regardez l'extrait et répondez aux questions.

1. Si on prend le métro, à quelle station est-ce qu'on descendra?
2. Qui peut bénéficier d'un tarif réduit au cinéma Rex?
3. Vous êtes étudiant(e): vous n'avez qu'un billet de dix euros ce jour-là; combien allez-vous recevoir en monnaie?
4. Si vous aviez un petit garçon de 8 ans avec vous, quel film choisiriez-vous?
5. Quels films pourriez-vous voir, si vous ne pouviez y aller qu'après 21 heures?
6. Si vous étiez là, quel film choisiriez-vous?

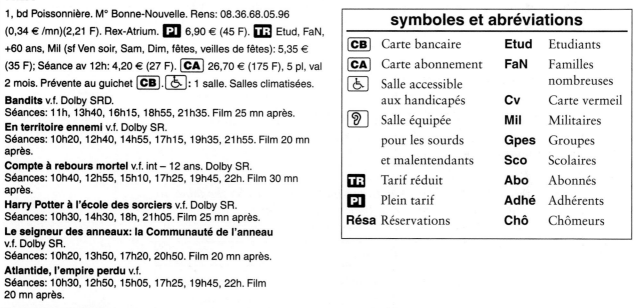

REX

1, bd Poissonnière. M° Bonne-Nouvelle. Rens: 08.36.68.05.96 (0,34 € /mn)(2,21 F). Rex-Atrium. **Pl** 6,90 € (45 F). **TR** Etud, FaN, +60 ans, Mil (sf Ven soir, Sam, Dim, fêtes, veilles de fêtes): 5,35 € (35 F); Séance av 12h: 4,20 € (27 F). **CA** 26,70 € (175 F), 5 pl, val 2 mois. Prévente au guichet **CB**. ♿: 1 salle. Salles climatisées.

Bandits v.f. Dolby SRD.
Séances: 11h, 13h40, 16h15, 18h55, 21h35. Film 25 mn après.
En territoire ennemi v.f. Dolby SR.
Séances: 10h20, 12h40, 14h55, 17h15, 19h35, 21h55. Film 20 mn après.
Compte à rebours mortel v.f. int – 12 ans. Dolby SR.
Séances: 10h40, 12h55, 15h10, 17h25, 19h45, 22h. Film 30 mn après.
Harry Potter à l'école des sorciers v.f. Dolby SR.
Séances: 10h30, 14h30, 18h, 21h05. Film 25 mn après.
Le seigneur des anneaux: la Communauté de l'anneau v.f. Dolby SR.
Séances: 10h20, 13h50, 17h20, 20h50. Film 20 mn après.
Atlantide, l'empire perdu v.f.
Séances: 10h30, 12h50, 15h05, 17h25, 19h45, 22h. Film 20 mn après.

symboles et abréviations

CB	Carte bancaire	**Etud**	Etudiants
CA	Carte abonnement	**FaN**	Familles nombreuses
♿	Salle accessible aux handicapés	**Cv**	Carte vermeil
🦻	Salle équipée pour les sourds et malentendants	**Mil**	Militaires
		Gpes	Groupes
TR	Tarif réduit	**Sco**	Scolaires
Pl	Plein tarif	**Abo**	Abonnés
Résa	Réservations	**Adhé**	Adhérents
		Chô	Chômeurs

① **Mes habitudes.** Formez des phrases avec **si** pour décrire ce que *(what)* vous faites en général. Employez **si** et un élément de chaque colonne pour former des phrases logiques.

je	avoir froid / chaud
mes amis	avoir soif
ma famille	être fatigué(e)
mon copain	le prof est absent
???	faire beau
	avoir trop de travail
	pleuvoir
	échouer à un examen
	avoir de l'argent
	???

F **Un peu d'imagination!** En quoi votre vie serait-elle différente...

1. si vous n'alliez pas à l'université?
2. si vous aviez / n'aviez pas de camarade de chambre?
3. si vous aviez une auto? / n'aviez pas d'auto?
4. si vous aviez des cours faciles?
5. si vous ne saviez pas lire?
6. si vous étiez très paresseux (-euse)?

G **Questions personnelles.** Imaginez!

1. Si vous receviez vos amis, qu'est-ce que vous feriez pour vous amuser?
2. Où habiteriez-vous si vous pouviez choisir?
3. Si vous étiez président, quelle serait votre première décision?
4. Si vous alliez prendre votre dernier repas, qu'est-ce que vous préféreriez manger?
5. Si vous pouviez voyager sans payer, où iriez-vous?
6. Si vous pouviez prévoir le futur, qu'est-ce qui vous intéresserait le plus?

III. *Mettre* / Verbs conjugated like *mettre*

> You use these verbs to describe activities, such as placing something somewhere, putting on clothes, turning on the TV, giving permission, and making promises.

The irregular verb **mettre** means *to put, to put on (clothing), to set the table, to turn on (a TV),* or *to take (an amount of time to do something).*

mettre		
présent:	je **mets**	nous **mettons**
	tu **mets**	vous **mettez**
	il / elle / on **met**	ils / elles **mettent**
futur et conditionnel:	je **mettrai**	nous **mettrions**
passé composé:	il **a mis**	elles **ont mis**
subjonctif:	que je **mette**	que nous **mettions**
impératif:	mets	mettons mettez

Où est-ce que je peux **mettre** mon parapluie?
Elle **a mis** sa robe neuve.
On ne **met** que trois heures et demie pour aller à Paris en Concorde.

Mots clés   *Verbs conjugated like **mettre***

permettre	*to permit* *to allow*
promettre	*to promise*
remettre	*to postpone* *to hand in* *to hand back* *to put back*
se mettre à	*to begin*

Une navette nous **permettra** d'aller à une station spatiale.
Il **s'est mis** à pleuvoir.

Attention!

1. **Permettre** and **promettre** take **à** before a person and **de** before an infinitive.

   Elle ne **permet** pas **aux** enfants **de** jouer dans la rue.
   Je **lui** ai **promis d'**acheter des fleurs.

2. To promise *not* to do something, put both parts of the negation (**ne pas**, **ne plus**, etc.) before the infinitive.

   Ils ont promis de **ne pas augmenter** la pollution.
   On promet de **ne plus contribuer** à la pluie acide.

Langue

Ⓐ **Faisons la cuisine.** Formez des phrases complètes avec les mots donnés.

1. Je / ne... pas / mettre / lait / dans / gâteau
2. Tu / remettre / viande / dans le frigidaire / ce matin?
3. Ils / promettre / ne pas mettre / sel
4. Ne... pas / permettre / enfants / utiliser / cuisinière
5. Elle / se mettre / préparer / dîner
6. Nous / mettre / table / sept heures

Ⓑ **Habillons-nous.** Refaites les phrases suivantes en employant les mots entre parenthèses.

1. Cet automne nous mettrons des vêtements chauds.   (L'hiver dernier...)
2. Je n'aimerais pas que mon frère porte mes vêtements.   (... permettre... mettre)
3. Tous les magasins vous recommandent d'essayer leurs vêtements. (... permettre...)
4. Si tu mets ton imperméable, il ne pleuvra pas.   (... pleuvrait...)
5. Les enfants n'ont pas porté de chaussettes.   (... mettre...)
6. Regarde cette jupe; maman m'a promis de l'acheter.   (Mettre... permettre...)

Culture

C **Le code de la route.** Vous préparez un voyage au Canada en voiture et vous avez besoin de connaître les différences entre les lois au Québec et celles des Etats-Unis. Qu'est-ce qu'on vous permet de faire et qu'est-ce qu'on ne vous permet pas?

MODÈLE: conduire à l'âge de seize ans?
On vous permet de conduire à l'âge de seize ans.

1. conduire et boire de l'alcool
2. conduire sans mettre sa ceinture de sécurité
3. transporter un jeune enfant sans siège de bébé
4. rouler à 105 à l'heure *(65 m.p.h.)*
5. tourner à droite à un feu *(light)* rouge
6. entrer dans le pays sans assurance
7. tourner à droite sans signaler
8. utiliser un détecteur de radar

Communication

D **Tenez-vous vos promesses?** Qu'est-ce que vous avez promis de faire que vous avez fait, et que vous n'avez pas fait? Utilisez un élément de chaque colonne et suivez le modèle.

MODÈLE: *J'ai promis à mon petit ami de lui téléphoner plus souvent.*
(Je le fais.)
J'ai promis au professeur de venir en cours tous les jours.
(Je ne le fais pas.)

à	de
parents	faire moins de bruit
petit(e) ami(e)	écrire toutes les semaines
camarade(s) de chambre	l' / les inviter au restaurant
voisin(e)(s)	être patient(e)
agents de police	rentrer le week-end
???	???

E **Des enfants dans votre avenir?** Quand vous aurez des enfants, qu'est-ce que vous leur permettrez de faire et qu'est-ce que vous ne leur permettrez pas de faire?

MODÈLE: *Je leur permettrai de faire du vélo.*
Je ne leur permettrai pas de jouer à table.

manger du gâteau	mettre les pieds sur la table
jouer au football	regarder la télévision
sortir le soir	avoir un(e) petit(e) ami(e)
se promener sans vêtements	avoir une voiture
fumer	boire du... / de la...
partir le week-end	???

F **Questions personnelles.** Chez vous.

1. Quels CD mettez-vous le plus souvent? Et votre camarade de chambre?
2. Permettez-vous aux gens de fumer chez vous?
3. Quand est-ce qu'on met la radio?
4. Remettez-vous toujours une partie du ménage à plus tard?
5. Quels vêtements mettez-vous quand vous êtes seul(e)?
6. Qu'est-ce que vous avez promis de faire cette semaine?

Exprimer des émotions

In conversations, it is often necessary to express emotional reactions to statements or events. The following groups of words will help you express yourself in an authentic manner in French, particularly in informal situations.

Expressions

▶ **On exprime l'étonnement** *(surprise).*

Ça alors!	*I'll be darned!*
C'est pas vrai!	*No?!*
Comment?	*What?*
Quoi?	*What?*
Tiens!	*Hey!*
Nous avons du mal à croire qu'elle a dit cela.	*We have a hard time believing that she said that.*
Je suis étonnée qu'il refuse de le faire.	*I am surprised that he refuses to do it.*
Elle est surprise qu'ils n'en sachent rien.	*She is surprised that they don't know anything about it.*
Il s'étonne que la pluie acide soit si mauvaise.	*He is astonished that the acid rain is so bad.*
Tu ne sais pas que Jean a eu un accident?	*You don't know that John had an accident?*

▶ **On exprime la déception** *(disappointment).*

(Quel) dommage!	*That's too bad! / What a shame!*
Tant pis!	*Too bad!*
Zut alors!	*Darn!*
Nous sommes déçus qu'il n'y ait pas de jardin.	*We are disappointed that there isn't a yard.*
Il est désolé que nous n'allions pas à la rivière.	*He is sorry that we aren't going to the river.*
Je suis navrée que mon mari ne puisse pas venir.	*I'm sorry that my husband can't come.*
Je regrette que le lac soit si loin.	*I'm sorry that the lake is so far away.*

▶ **On exprime la satisfaction.**

Bon!	*Good!*
Chouette alors!	*Great!*
Fantastique!	*Fantastic!*
Formidable!	*Great!*
Parfait!	*Perfect!*
Tant mieux!	*Good!*
Terrible!	*Super!*
Ils sont contents que nous nous promenions dans la forêt.	*They are happy we are walking in the forest.*
Vous êtes heureux que vos enfants arrêtent leurs plaintes?	*Are you happy that your children have stopped complaining?*
Je suis ravie que tu sois là!	*I am delighted that you are here!*
Elles sont satisfaites que tu réussisses.	*They are satisfied that you are passing.*

▶ **On exprime la colère** *(anger).*

Arrête!	*Stop!*
Ça suffit!	*Enough!*
Ça (ne) va pas, non?	*Are you crazy?*
Fiche-moi la paix! / Laisse-moi!	*Leave me alone!*
J'en ai assez!	*I've had it!*
J'en ai marre! / J'en ai ras le bol!	*I've had it up to here!*
Tu me casses les pieds!	*You really annoy me!*
Il est fâché que tu mentes.	*He is angry that you are lying.*
Elle est furieuse que les enfants jouent sur la pelouse.	*She is furious that the children are playing on the lawn.*

▶ **On exprime l'indifférence.**

Ça m'est égal. / Je m'en fiche.	*I don't care.*
Ça ne fait rien.	*It doesn't matter.*
Ce n'est pas grand-chose.	*It's no big deal.*
Ce n'est pas grave.	*It's not serious.*
Comme ci, comme ça.	*So-so.*
Et après?	*So what?*
Ça m'est égal si tu fais cela.	*I don't care if you do that.*
Peu m'importe si tu ne viens pas.	*It doesn't matter if you don't come.*

Interaction

Jean-Paul et Anne-Marie cherchent quelque chose à faire.

JEAN-PAUL: Qu'est-ce que tu veux faire cet après-midi?

ANNE-MARIE: Ça m'est égal.

JEAN-PAUL: On peut aller au ciné.

ANNE-MARIE: Les films qu'on joue en ce moment ne sont pas terribles.

JEAN-PAUL: Tiens! Les étudiants vont avoir un débat sur l'énergie nucléaire.

ANNE-MARIE: J'en ai assez de la politique!

JEAN-PAUL: Alors, tant pis. Je vais y aller tout seul.

ANNE-MARIE: Chouette alors. Il y a Jean-François qui m'a invitée au café!

Activités

Ⓐ Quelqu'un va proposer quelque chose. Indiquez si la deuxième personne veut le faire ou non.

1. MARIE: On va aller au cinéma!
   ROBERT: Super!
2. PIERRE: J'ai acheté deux billets pour le concert de Patricia Kaas.
   YVONNE: Elle est terrible!
3. MARIE-ANNE: Tu veux étudier à la bibliothèque?
   CHANTAL: Ça m'est égal!
4. JEAN-PAUL: On va écouter encore un CD.
   CLAUDE: Moi, j'en ai marre!
5. MME MORIN: Il reste encore un petit gâteau.
   SABINE: Tant mieux!
6. M. GILBERT: Nous avons loué un appartement à la plage et il y a un lit pour toi.
   ÉRIC: Formidable!

Ⓑ Que pourriez-vous dire dans les situations suivantes?

1. Votre camarade de chambre met la radio à minuit.
2. Vos ami(e)s veulent aller voir un western.
3. Vous trouvez cent dollars dans la rue.
4. Vous rencontrez un(e) ami(e) que vous n'avez pas vu(e) depuis trois ans.
5. Vous perdez votre Walkman.
6. Vos voisins parlent des problèmes de la pluie acide.
7. Quelqu'un veut que vous parliez de l'énergie solaire.
8. Un ami vous invite à passer le week-end au lac.

lecture culturelle

Avant la lecture

Many countries in the world have developed innovative uses of underground space, from indoor cities in which to bury the nation's rulers and their families to subway lines, tunnels, parking structures, and modern sewer systems. Avant-garde architects have further envisioned underground space as a means of extending the limited surface area of structures above ground. A striking recent example is the underground entryway to the Louvre in Paris, which former French president François Mitterrand commissioned the American architect I. M. Pei to design in 1985. This entryway more effectively serves the twenty thousand people a day who visit the world-renowned museum. After entering the imposing pyramid-shaped structure, visitors take escalators down to a central hall, in which information booths, ticket counters, a gift shop, and a bookstore are located and from which they can gain access to the various wings of the museum as well. The Louvre metro stop, a mini-museum in its own right, leads to a gallery of shops and boutiques and acts as another point of entry to the museum.

In addition to designing the Louvre pyramid and more than fifty other architectural projects in the United States and abroad, I. M. Pei was instrumental in the construction of the first underground pedestrian mall (1962), known as Place Ville-Marie, in Montreal, Quebec. Following on its success, other underground sites have been constructed. The original mall has turned into an indoor city that now boasts nineteen miles of indoor pedestrian corridors, among the longest in the world, which are interconnected with major subway stops.

Activités

Ⓐ Does the weather affect your mood? What about your activities? What do you like to do when it is very hot outside, or when it is raining heavily or snowing?

B If you could give your input regarding what should be included in an underground city, what would you suggest? Make a list and compare it with those of your classmates.

C Scan the second paragraph of the article below and convert the list of *places* that are a part of underground Montreal (such as hotels or movie theaters) to a list of *action verbs* describing what you can do in those places.

MODÈLES: [une gare ferroviaire]   *On peut prendre le train.*
          [sept hôtels]   *On peut réserver une chambre.*

Montréal souterrain

D e passage° à Montréal cet hiver, oublions ce qu'on appelle ici les «tuques» (bonnets) et les «mitaines» (moufles°), puisqu'il est possible de traverser les froids sibériens des hivers montréalais en petite tenue° dans la ville souterraine.

Passing through
mittens

light clothing

5   Né en 1962 avec la construction de la place Ville-Marie par l'architecte Pei, à qui l'on doit entre autres° la pyramide du Louvre, le Montréal souterrain couvre maintenant près de 4 millions de mètres carrés. Il relie une gare ferroviaire°, deux gares d'autocars, quarante succursales° bancaires, treize stations de métro, 1.600 appartements, 10.000 espaces de
10   stationnement, sept hôtels, une université, des salles de spectacle, une vingtaine de salles de cinéma, une patinoire, deux grands magasins, et 1.600 boutiques.

among other things

train station / branches (of a business)

Tourisme hivernal

Il fait −30° C (−22° F), ce qui n'est pas inhabituel à Montréal en janvier.
15   En arrivant en train à la gare centrale, on n'a qu'un ascenseur° à prendre pour gagner° la réception de l'hôtel Reine Elizabeth. Si on les préfère, un réseau de couloirs et d'escaliers mécaniques nous conduit soit à l'hôtel Hilton Bonaventure, soit au Marriott Château Champlain. En empruntant° le métro, le choix d'hôtels s'élargit et comprend l'hôtel Wyndham Montréal,
20   l'hôtel Delta centre-ville, l'hôtel Intercontinental, et l'hôtel des Gouverneurs place Dupuis.

elevator
(in this case) to get to

(in this case) By taking

      Confortablement installé dans une chambre avec vue, on peut contempler la ville peuplée de piétons° pressés° qui se hâtent° d'accéder à la chaleur de la ville intérieure. Ce qu'on nomme le Montréal souterrain est
25   tout sauf sombre° et triste. Les Montréalais ne se terrent° pas, moroses, dans des tunnels pendant six mois sans voir la lumière du jour. Les gratte-ciel° qui y sont reliés sont baignés° de soleil et dans les souterrains, on joue avec différents types d'éclairage° artificiel pour recréer un environnement qui se rapproche le plus possible de la lumière naturelle.

pedestrians / in a hurry / rush
tout... *anything but dark, depressing / bury themselves*
skyscrapers / bathed
lighting

Tout y est possible

Si par malheur, après le froid venait la tempête°, on serait d'autant plus heureux° de ne pas avoir à circuler en voiture pour faire un peu de tourisme. Une bordée° de trente centimètres de neige ne nous empêchera°

storm
d'autant... *all the happier*
heavy snowfall / will (not) prevent

pas d'assister à une conférence à l'Université de Québec, de visiter un sa-
35 lon, de «magasiner», de passer à la gym, au spa ou chez le coiffeur, de
nous baigner ou de patiner, de croquer une bouchée sur le pouce° ou de
nous attabler° devant un bon repas dans quelques-uns des meilleurs
restaurants de la ville, de voir un match de hockey, de prendre un verre sur
le toit de Montréal, d'aller au théâtre, au concert ou à l'opéra, et de casser
40 la croûte° à 2 heures du matin. Un mal de dents surgit°? Facile de trouver
une clinique bien à l'abri°. Un talon aiguille° se brise? Le chemisier de
soie° est taché? Il y a des cordonniers° et des boutiques de nettoyage à
sec°. Envie de s'évader? Vite, à l'agence de voyages.

Tout ce que l'on manquera°, finalement, ce sera le froid mordant° qui
45 pique° les joues, les escaliers enneigés°, les voisins qui déneigent° leur
voiture un lendemain de tempête et le ballet bien réglé des déneigeuses°,
mais ça, c'est une autre histoire.

Louise Gaboury, «A Montréal sans mettre le nez dehors»,
Journal Français

croquer... *to have a quick bite to eat / to sit down at the (dinner) table*

to have a snack / occurs shelter / high heel (shoe) silk / cobblers
nettoyage... *dry cleaning*
The only thing missing / biting cold / stings / snow-covered / remove snow from / snow plows

La ville intérieure

Après la lecture

Questions sur le texte

1. Que veut dire le titre de l'article, «A Montréal sans mettre le nez dehors»? Pourquoi est-ce que c'est un titre approprié?
2. Comment est-ce qu'on peut s'habiller dans le Montréal souterrain?
3. Selon le deuxième paragraphe de l'article, qu'est-ce qu'il y a dans le Montréal souterrain? Faites une liste de ce qu'on peut y trouver.

4. Est-ce qu'on doit aller dehors pour aller de la gare à un hôtel? Quelles sont les possibilités?
5. Est-ce que le Montréal souterrain est sombre? Expliquez pourquoi ou pourquoi pas.
6. Quelles sont les seules choses qui manquent dans cet environnement souterrain?

Activités

Ⓐ Trouvez une biographie de I. M. Pei et présentez un rapport sur cet architecte célèbre. Qu'est-ce qu'il a construit et dans quels pays?

Ⓑ Connaissez-vous d'autres villes ou espaces souterrains dans le monde? Croyez-vous que ce soit une bonne idée? Est-ce que ça peut poser des problèmes (en cas d'incendie, par exemple)?

Ⓒ Vous êtes agent de tourisme et vous proposez des vacances d'hiver à Montréal à des personnes qui aiment la nature. Mentionnez quelques-uns des sports suivants.

Randonnée à calèches *(excursion in horse-drawn carriages)*
Randonnée à raquettes *(snowshoes)*
Randonnée à moto-neige
Patinage à glace *(à l'extérieur)*
Promenade en traîneau *(sled)* à chiens
Ski de fond

Ⓓ Avez-vous jamais assisté au Carnaval de Québec, le plus grand carnaval d'hiver au monde? Aimeriez-vous le faire? Pourquoi? Pendant quel mois a-t-il lieu? Qui est «Bonhomme»? Assisteriez-vous au bal masqué?

vocabulaire

Noms / Pronoms

un arbre	tree	**un espace**	space
la biotechnologie	biotechnology	**une feuille**	leaf
un champ	field	**une fleur**	flower
une colonne	column	**un fleuve**	river
un contrat	contract	**une forêt**	forest
dont	whose, of which	**le futur**	future
écologie *(f.)*	ecology	**le gel**	frost
un/une écologiste	ecologist	**un jardin**	yard / garden
écorce *(f.)*	bark	**un lac**	lake
énergie *(f.)*	energy	**la lumière**	light
environnement *(m.)*	environment	**la lune**	moon

la matière	matter	la raison	reason
la nature	nature	le recyclage	recycling
une navette	shuttle	un reflet	reflection
la nature	nature	une rivière	river
le paysage	countryside	une rumeur	rumor
la pelouse	lawn	une station	station
la planète	planet	un tronc	trunk
la pluie acide	acid rain	la Voie lactée	Milky Way
un/une poète	poet		

Verbes

augmenter	to increase	noircir	to blacken
créer	to create	ondoyer	to shimmer
diminuer	to diminish	permettre	to allow
évoquer	to evoke	promettre	to promise
incarner	to embody	remettre	to postpone / to hand in / to put or hand back
inclure	to include		
jaillir	to spring		
mettre	to put (on) / to set / to turn on / to take (time to do something)	se disperser	to scatter
		se mettre à	to begin

Adjectifs / Adverbes

délivré	freed	nucléaire	nuclear
habitable	livable	rose	pink
lucide	lucid	solaire	solar
méditatif	pensive	spatial	space
noirci	blackened	vif	lively
nombrable	countable		

Expressions

aussitôt que	as soon as
dès que	as soon as
lorsque	when

Arrivée d'immigrants

CHAPITRE

18

commençons

grammaire

communiquons

lecture culturelle

vocabulaire

Les immigrés

OBJECTIVES

Language	Culture	Communication
■ Vocabulary for animals ■ **Des mots difficiles** ■ Adverbs ■ The French equivalents of *good* and *well*, *bad* and *badly* ■ Comparatives and superlatives	■ North Africa ■ Ethnic minorities on French television	■ Describing the manner in which you do something ■ Comparing and contrasting people and things ■ Using colloquial French

La Prière du Chacal

Voici un conte populaire du Maghreb.

Un matin, le Chacal voit le Coq qui chante sur une branche. Il s'approche et lui dit: «Que tu chantes bien! Quand je t'ai entendu, j'ai eu envie de devenir bon et de prier Dieu. Je suis venu tout de suite. Descends! Viens faire la prière avec moi.

    —Oncle Chacal, répond le Coq, tu vois bien que j'appelle les gens à la prière!

    —Oui, je vois, mais maintenant que tu as fini d'appeler, descends faire la prière avec moi!

    —D'accord, dit le Coq. Mais j'attends l'imam.

    —Qui est votre imam ici? demande le Chacal.

    —Tu ne le connais pas? C'est le Chien de chasse.

    —Au revoir! Au revoir! dit le Chacal. J'ai oublié de me laver avant la prière. J'y cours.»

From Jean-Paul Tauvel, *Contes et histoires du Maghreb*. Paris: Hachette.

Etudions la fable

1. A quelle sorte de personne est-ce qu'on pense quand on parle d'un chacal?
2. Comment le Chacal essaye-t-il de devenir ami avec le Coq?
3. Pourquoi est-ce que le Chacal veut que le Coq descende? Pour prier?
4. Qui est-ce que le Coq attend?
5. Pourquoi le Chacal décide-t-il de partir? Quelle raison donne-t-il?
6. Qui est plus intelligent, le Chacal ou le Coq? Pourquoi?

Mots clés

une prière	*prayer*	s'approche (s'approcher)	*gets closer*
un chacal	*jackal*	Que	*How*
populaire	*popular*	prier	*pray*
le Maghreb	*the Maghreb (Morocco, Algeria, Tunisia)*	Dieu	*God*
un coq	*rooster*	un imam	*Muslim prayer leader*
une branche	*branch*	un chien	*dog*
		cours (courir)	*am running*

Faisons connaissance

Maghreb is an Arabic word meaning *sunset;* it is the name used to refer to the northern part of Africa, the area now occupied by Morocco, Algeria, and Tunisia. In France these countries are also known as **l'Afrique du Nord,** and because they were once French colonies, French is still used, together with Arabic, as an administrative and literary language.

There are now 4 million foreigners residing in France. Approximately one-third come from the **Maghreb,** including **Algériens, Marocains,** and **Tunisiens.** Since 1954 the number of new European immigrants has decreased while the number of **Maghrébins** has constantly increased. They bring with them their ways of life and their Islamic religion.

La Prière du Chacal is set in a Muslim context where public prayer is conducted five times a day. The one who calls the faithful to assemble to pray is called the **muezzin,** but the **imam** is the one who leads the prayer.

This popular tale is reminiscent of the animal fables written by Jean de La Fontaine in the seventeenth century. Like those fables, its intent is to teach a lesson using animals as protagonists, a device used in literature since ancient times and featured in the fables of Aesop (ancient Greece), the *Roman de Renard,* popular in the Middle Ages, and more recently, in this country, the stories of Joel Chandler Harris.

Le Sésame Café
RESTAURANT DE NUIT - BAR CLUB - DISCOTHEQUE

A 2 pas de l'Arc de Triomphe
Sce jusqu'à 4h du matin
Spécialités marocaines dans un palais des mille et une nuits
Tous les vendredis soirées orientales avec orchestre - Menu

24, rue de tilsitt parís 17e
res: 01 56 68 97 03 - f. dim et lun

Enrichissons notre vocabulaire

Un animal / des animaux *(An animal / animals)*

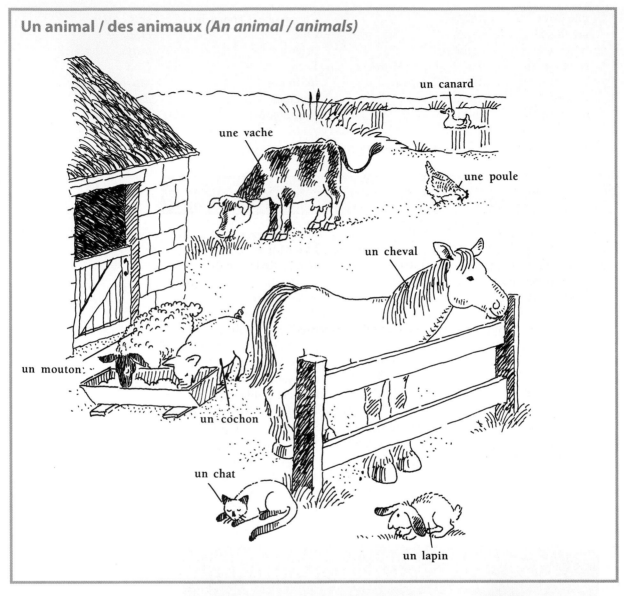

un canard

une vache

une poule

un cheval

un mouton

un cochon

un chat

un lapin

Prononciation   **Des mots difficiles**

At this point you have learned all the main features of French pronunciation.
There always remain a few individual words that are difficult to pronounce,
however. One problem for people learning French is that they rely on spelling
too much when they try to determine the correct pronunciation of a word.
French spelling, as does English, represents the pronunciation of the language
as it was spoken hundreds of years ago. The following words and phrases are
among the most difficult to pronounce that you have learned in this book.

Repeat the following verbs after your teacher.

> il peut, ils peuvent / je fais, nous faisons / tu achètes, vous achetez / je verrai, je ferai, je serai / que j'aille, que nous allions / qu'il veuille / soyons / choisissez, réussissez / ayez, aie / gagner / elle prend, elles prennent / j'aime

Repeat the following adjectives after your teacher.

> un, une / ancien, ancienne / ennuyeux / bon, bonne / utile, inutile / ambitieux

Repeat the following nouns after your teacher.

> les gens / un examen / ma sœur / la peur / le pays / mille, ville, fille / juin, juillet, août / un cours, un corps / monsieur, messieurs / une famille tranquille / la faim, la femme / l'Allemagne / la gare, la guerre / la psychologie / l'école / l'hiver, l'automne / un œil, des yeux / la campagne, la montagne / deux heures / Jean, Jeanne / un an, une année / les Etats-Unis / un œuf, des œufs / vingt-cinq, quatre-vingt-cinq

Exercice

Read the following sentences aloud, taking care to pronounce each word correctly.

1. Monsieur Martin utilise de l'huile et du beurre et sa cuisine est fantastique.
2. Je ne pense pas que Jean veuille gagner le match.
3. Nos familles prennent des vacances magnifiques en juin et en juillet.
4. Il est inutile de chercher un pays où les gens ne sont pas ambitieux.
5. Nous faisons une promenade ennuyeuse entre la gare et l'école.
6. En automne et en hiver ils peuvent suivre un cours de psychologie ou d'anthropologie.

 grammaire

I. Adverbs

You use adverbs to describe actions and to qualify descriptions.

A. Introduction

Adverbs are words that modify verbs, adjectives, or other adverbs. They usually indicate manner or degree and answer the questions *How?, How much?, When?,* and *Where?*

1. The following adverbs indicate manner or degree.

assez *rather*	**ensemble**	**surtout**
beaucoup	**mal** *badly*	**très**
bien	**mieux** *best*	**trop**
encore	**peu**	**vite** *quickly*
	presque	

Le Coq chante **bien**.   Je l'aime **beaucoup**.

2. The following indications of time and place are also adverbs.

ailleurs *elsewhere*	**ici**	**quelquefois** *sometimes*
aujourd'hui	**là**	**souvent**
bientôt	**là-bas**	**tard** *late*
déjà	**longtemps**	**tôt**
demain	**maintenant**	**toujours**
hier	**partout** *everywhere*	**tout de suite**

Demain il va appeler les gens à la prière.   Il chante **là-bas**.

B. Adverbs created from adjectives

Other adverbs may be created from adjectives by adding the ending **-ment**
(/ mã /).

1. Adjectives ending in a written vowel take **-ment** directly.

    facile → **facilement**
    nécessaire → **nécessairement**
    probable → **probablement**
    rapide → **rapidement**
    rare → **rarement**
    vrai → **vraiment**

2. Most adjectives that end in a written consonant add **-ment** to the feminine form.

    certain, certaine → **certainement**
    complet, complète → **complètement**
    général, générale → **généralement**
    heureux, heureuse → **heureusement** *fortunately*
    lent, lente → **lentement** *slowly*
    malheureux, malheureuse → **malheureusement** *unfortunately*
    parfait, parfaite → **parfaitement**
    seul, seule → **seulement** *only*
    sûr, sûre → **sûrement**
    tel, telle → **tellement** *so*
    traditionnel, traditionnelle → **traditionnellement**

3. Most adjectives ending in **-ent** or **-ant** (/ ã /) change those letters to **em** or **am**, respectively, then add **-ment**. In both cases, / ã / becomes / amã /. The following list shows examples.

-ant	-ent
brillant → **brillamment**	évident → **évidemment**
indépendant → **indépendamment**	fréquent → **fréquemment**
insuffisant → **insuffisamment**	intelligent → **intelligemment**
méchant → **méchamment**	prudent → **prudemment**
suffisant → **suffisamment**	récent → **récemment**
sufficiently	

C. Position of adverbs

1. As a general rule, short, frequently used adverbs precede the words they modify, including past participles and infinitives, while longer adverbs follow the words they modify.

Il est **déjà** parti.   *but*   Elle a conduit **lentement.**
Je vais **vite** sortir.   Je suis venu **tout de suite.**

2. While there are exceptions to the above rule, two other rules always hold true.

a. In French, a subject and conjugated verb are *never* separated by an adverb, as in English.

Ils rentrent **souvent** tard.   *They **often** get home late.*
(s.) (v.)   (adv.)   (s.) (adv.)   (v.)

b. In French, most adverbs of time and place always precede or follow the subject-verb group. Adverbs of time and place *never* occur between those elements.

Nous allons commencer **demain.**   **Ici,** il n'y a pas de cafés.
  (s.-v. group)   (adv.)   (adv.)   (s.-v. group)

Langue

Ⓐ On dîne chez Christine. Changez les adjectifs entre parenthèses en adverbes, et ajoutez-les aux phrases données.

1. Christine nous a préparé du poisson.   (récent)
2. Il n'était pas bon.   (tel)
3. Tu m'en parles!   (méchant)
4. Vous avez mangé.   (rapide)
5. Nous ne reviendrons pas.   (certain)
6. J'ai d'autres amis.   (heureux)

Ⓑ A la résidence. Mettez les phrases suivantes au passé composé et faites attention à la place des adverbes.

1. Mon camarade de chambre parle beaucoup.
2. Nous finissons les cours aujourd'hui.
3. Hélène s'habille rapidement.
4. Jacques étudie peu.
5. Mes copains viennent me voir souvent.
6. Ils arrivent déjà.

Culture

C **La société algérienne change.** La vie en Algérie a beaucoup changé depuis un certain temps. Caractérisez ces changements en parlant des choses qu'on fait **traditionnellement** et qu'on fait **aujourd'hui** dans ce pays. Employez les adverbes indiqués.

MODÈLE: boire de l'alcool (quelquefois)
> *Traditionnellement on ne buvait pas d'alcool. Aujourd'hui on*
> *en boit quelquefois.*

1. mettre les garçons et les filles ensemble à l'école (ne... plus)
2. avoir l'enseignement primaire en français / en arabe (surtout)
3. voir un voile *(veil)* sur toutes les femmes (moins souvent)
4. rencontrer des femmes avec des responsabilités professionnelles (assez souvent)
5. faire son service militaire obligatoirement (encore)
6. séparer la politique et la religion (moins)

Communication

D **Ces jours-ci.** Comment faites-vous les activités suivantes?

MODÈLE: étudier (bien, longuement, rarement, vite)
> *J'étudie vite.*

1. faire le ménage (souvent, rapidement, mal, fréquemment, demain)
2. faire vos devoirs (sérieusement, tranquillement, attentivement, vite, bientôt)
3. dormir (peu, beaucoup, bien, longtemps)
4. s'habiller (simplement, curieusement, traditionnellement, bien)

Et l'année prochaine?

5. parler français (bien, mal, fréquemment, rarement)
6. voyager (souvent, partout, sûrement, longuement)
7. chercher un appartement (partout, peut-être, certainement, sérieusement, prudemment)
8. faire du sport (souvent, rarement, sûrement, régulièrement)

E **Hier.** Comment avez-vous fait ces choses hier?

MODÈLE: se réveiller
> *Je me suis réveillée lentement.*

1. se lever
2. manger
3. faire vos devoirs
4. conduire votre auto
5. s'habiller
6. lire le journal
7. travailler
8. s'endormir

F **Questions personnelles.** Votre vie à l'université.

1. Où allez-vous tout de suite après ce cours?
2. A qui avez-vous écrit récemment?
3. Qu'est-ce que vous faites particulièrement bien ou mal ce semestre / trimestre?
4. Allez-vous préparer suffisamment l'examen final?

5. Quelle note *(grade)* allez-vous probablement avoir dans ce cours?
6. Allez-vous étudier régulièrement le semestre / trimestre prochain?

II. The French equivalents of *good* and *well, bad* and *badly*

You use these adjectives and adverbs to make value judgments about people, things, ideas, and activities.

A. When expressing the equivalents of *good / well* and *bad / badly* in French, it is important to distinguish between adjectives and adverbs.

1. The adjectives **bon** and **mauvais** modify only nouns.

C'est un **bon** vin.	*It's a **good** wine.*
Cette bière est **mauvaise.**	*This beer is **bad.***

2. The adverbs **bien** and **mal** modify verbs or adjectives.

Ce professeur parle **bien.**	*This teacher speaks **well.***
Mais il s'habille **mal.**	*But he dresses **badly.***

Ce qu'ils disent

You learned in Chapter 2 that in conversation, **bien** is used as an adjective to describe a person ("a fine person") or a thing ("a good thing").

Ton copain est **bien.**   Je connais un restaurant très **bien.**

B. To make a comparison, English uses *better* for both the adjective *good* and the adverb *well.* French, however, keeps the distinction between the adjective and the adverb. The comparative of the adjective **bon(ne)(s)** is **meilleur(e)(s).** The comparative of the adverb **bien** is **mieux.**

C'est un **bon** vin. → C'est un **meilleur** vin.
Il parle **bien.** → Il parle **mieux.**

C. To complete a comparison, use **que** *(than).*

M. Lebrun est un **très bon** professeur.
M. Ducharme est un **bon** professeur.
M. Lebrun est un **meilleur** professeur **que** M. Ducharme.

Les vins français sont **très bons.**
Les vins de Californie sont **bons.**
Les vins français sont **meilleurs que** les vins de Californie.

J'aime **bien** la viande.
J'aime **aussi** le poisson.
J'aime **mieux** la viande **que** le poisson.

Louise chante **très bien.**
Marc chante **bien.**
Louise chante **mieux que** Marc.

D. French also distinguishes between adjective and adverb forms to express the idea of *worse*. The adjective is **plus mauvais(e)(es)**, the adverb **plus mal**. To complete the comparison, use **que**.

> Robert a de **très mauvaises** idées.
> Jacqueline a de **mauvaises** idées.
> Robert a de **plus mauvaises** idées **que** Jacqueline.

> Je dors **très mal**.
> Mon camarade de chambre dort **mal**.
> Je dors **plus mal que** lui.

E. To form the superlative *(best)*, use **le, la,** or **les** with **meilleur(e)(s)** and **le** with **mieux**. To express the idea of *in*, use **de**.

> Pavarotti est **le meilleur** chanteur **du** monde.
> Non, c'est Domingo qui chante **le mieux**.

Langue

A Au théâtre. Ajoutez le mot entre parenthèses aux phrases suivantes. Faites attention à l'accord des adjectifs.

1. Michel est un acteur.   (bon)
2. Il a joué hier.   (bien)
3. Il est dans une pièce anglaise.   (mauvais)
4. J'ai entendu les acteurs.   (mal)
5. Moi, j'aime aller au cinéma.   (mieux)
6. J'adore voir des films étrangers.   (bon)

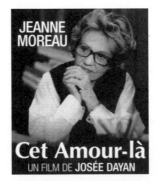

B Nos devoirs d'anglais. Complétez les phrases suivantes avec la forme correcte de **bon, bien, mauvais, mal, meilleur** ou **mieux,** selon le cas.

1. Je viens de lire un _____ roman pour mon cours d'anglais.
2. L'auteur écrit _____.
3. Mon prof pense qu'il écrit _____ que Hemingway.
4. Certains étudiants ont _____ compris les intentions de l'auteur.
5. C'est le _____ roman du semestre.
6. Je vais faire le _____ de toute la classe au prochain examen!

C **Dînons ensemble.** Formez des phrases complètes avec les mots donnés.

1. Nous / s'amuser / bien / hier
2. Je / trouver / bon / restaurant / en ville
3. On / prendre / mon / voiture, / je / conduire / bien / toi
4. Ce / restaurant-là / être / bon / celui-ci
5. On / manger / bien / ici / là-bas
6. Nous / commander / bon / lapin

Culture

D **Vos impressions.** Qui produit les meilleures choses, la France ou les Etats-Unis? Donnez votre opinion pour les catégories suivantes.

MODÈLE: le café   *Le café français est meilleur que le café américain.*
la bière   *La bière américaine est meilleure.*

1. la musique
2. le vin
3. les voitures
4. les vêtements
5. les films
6. les avions
7. la cuisine
8. les trains
9. les ordinateurs
10. les émissions de télévision

Communication

E **Etes-vous sexiste?** Pensez-vous qu'il y ait des choses que les hommes font mieux que les femmes, ou vice versa?

MODÈLE: *Les femmes jouent au tennis mieux que les hommes.*
Les hommes font mieux les courses.

conduire
faire la cuisine
jouer au football
réussir aux examens
???

nager
comprendre les mathématiques
apprendre les langues étrangères
retenir les dates
faire des économies

F **Votre santé.** Est-ce que les choses suivantes sont bonnes ou mauvaises pour la santé?

MODÈLE: l'alcool   *Un peu d'alcool est bon pour la santé.*

les cigarettes
le vin
le sport

le sucre
le sel
les œufs

le café
le poisson
l'eau de votre ville

G **Questions personnelles.** Vos souvenirs.

1. Quel moment de votre vie vous rappelez-vous le mieux?
2. Que pensez-vous de votre lycée? Vous êtes mieux préparé(e) à l'université que d'autres étudiants?
3. Aimez-vous mieux votre vie au lycée ou votre vie ici?
4. Avez-vous connu un meilleur professeur que le vôtre?
5. Quand avez-vous mal dormi? Pourquoi?
6. Combien de très bons amis / bonnes amies avez-vous eu(e)s?

III. The comparative and superlative

You use the comparative and superlative to rank people, places, things, and activities.

A. Comparative of adjectives and adverbs

1. With the exception of **bon** and **bien,** French adjectives and adverbs form the comparative with the expression **plus... que** or **moins... que.**

   Ce chat est **plus gros que** le mien. *This cat is **bigger than** mine.*
   Ils sortent **plus souvent que** nous. *They go out **more often than** we do.*
   Je comprends **moins bien que** toi. *I understand **less well than** you.*

2. To express equality, use **aussi... que** *(as . . . as)* with adjectives and adverbs and **autant... que** *(as much . . . as)* with verbs.

   Il est **aussi** intelligent **que** sa sœur.
   Elle tape **aussi** mal **que** nous.
   Je travaille **autant que** vous!

B. Comparative of nouns

To compare nouns, you use the following expressions: **plus de... que** *(more . . . than),* **autant de... que** *(as much / many . . . as),* and **moins de... que** *(less / fewer . . . than).*

   Elle a **plus de** patience **que** lui. Nous avons **moins d'argent qu'**eux.
   J'ai **autant de** talent **que** Marc.

C. Superlative of adjectives and adverbs

1. To form the superlative, use the *definite article* before **plus** or **moins** followed by the adjective or adverb. Use **de** to express the idea of *in* or *of.*

   Anne-Marie est **la plus artistique**   *Anne-Marie is **the most artistic***
   de sa famille.   ***in** her family.*
   Pierre est **le moins insupportable**   *Pierre is **the least annoying** of*
   de tes amis.   *your friends.*
   Jean-Paul travaille **le plus**   *Jean-Paul works **the most***
   régulièrement de tous mes   ***consistently** of all my*
   étudiants.   *students.*

2. If an adjective normally follows the noun it modifies, its superlative form uses the definite article twice, keeping the same number and gender.

   J'habite **la** ville **la plus** intéressante de mon pays.
   Ce sont **les** étudiants **les plus** sérieux de l'université.

3. If the adjective precedes the noun, the superlative does also.

   C'est **le plus bel** enfant de la famille.
   Voilà **la plus vieille** église de la ville.

Attention!

1. Note that in comparative constructions, you use **de,** not **que,** with numbers.

Nous avons moins **d'**une heure pour finir.
Il faut plus **de** deux cent mille dollars pour acheter cette maison.

2. The superlative of adverbs always takes **le** because adverbs have no number or gender.

Marie-France répond **le** moins souvent de toute la classe.
Nous habitons **le** plus loin de l'université de tous nos amis.

Langue

Ⓐ **Les impressions des touristes.** Formez des phrases complètes avec les mots donnés. Les symboles +, − et = représentent **plus, moins** et **aussi,** respectivement.

1. Les voitures / français / être / + petit / nôtre
2. théâtre / être / + cher / cinéma
3. hôtels / être / − grand / aux Etats-Unis
4. agents de police / être / = sympa / nôtre
5. Ce / église / être / + vieux / de la ville
6. pain / français / être / + bon / pain / américain
7. Le Louvre / être / musée / + connu / monde
8. La France / avoir / − McDonald's / Etats-Unis!

Ⓑ **Deux manières de dire la même chose.** Changez l'ordre des comparaisons sans changer le sens *(meaning)* de la phrase.

MODÈLE: Je suis plus riche que Paul. *Paul est moins riche que moi.*

1. Il parle plus vite qu'eux.
2. Tu as plus de problèmes que les autres.
3. Son français est moins bon que le tien.
4. Robert est aussi ennuyeux que Monique.
5. Jean travaille autant que ses camarades.
6. Son fils est plus laid que le mien.

Culture

Ⓒ **La France: le pays et ses habitants.** Répondez aux questions suivantes sur la France en choisissant la bonne réponse.

1. Quelle est la plus grande montagne?
   a. le pic du Midi   b. le mont Cenis   c. le mont Blanc
2. Quel est le plus long fleuve?
   a. la Loire   b. la Seine   c. le Rhône
3. Quel est le pays d'origine du plus grand nombre d'immigrés?
   a. l'Algérie   b. le Maroc   c. le Portugal
4. Ce sont les Français qui ont le plus grand nombre d(e) _____.
   a. accidents de voiture   b. résidences secondaires   c. enfants
5. Quel est l'animal qu'on trouve le plus souvent dans une maison française?
   a. le chat   b. le chien   c. l'oiseau

6. Quelle est l'activité la plus fréquente des Français quand ils ne travaillent pas?
    a. lire   b. faire une promenade   c. regarder la télévision
7. Quel est le journal qu'on achète le plus?
    a. *L'Equipe*   b. *Le Monde*   c. *Le Figaro*
8. Quel âge avait la plus vieille personne à avoir fait un CD de rap?
    a. 50 ans   b. 60 ans   c. 120 ans

Communication

Ⓓ **Des comparaisons.** Séparez-vous en groupes de deux. Comparez-vous en employant les expressions suivantes. Présentez quelques différences importantes aux autres.

MODÈLE: Etudiant(e) 1:   *Es-tu aussi grand(e) que moi?*
           Etudiant(e) 2:   *Je suis plus grand(e) que toi.*

avoir des sœurs / frères   lire des romans
habiter loin de l'université   aller au cinéma
se coucher tard   être sérieux
travailler bien   dépenser de l'argent
conduire vite   ???

Ⓔ **A votre avis.** Quel(le) est / Qui est, à votre avis,...

1. le plus grand écrivain?
2. la langue la plus difficile?
3. la plus mauvaise voiture?
4. la ville la plus agréable de votre pays?
5. l'homme politique le moins honnête?
6. le cours le plus intéressant de votre université?
7. la profession la plus difficile?
8. la meilleure pizza de votre ville?

Ⓕ **Comparez-vous.** Dans votre cours, qui a autant d(e)... que vous?

cousins   cours aujourd'hui
dollars dans son portefeuille   examens finals
chiens   disques compacts
camarades de chambre   petit(e)s ami(e)s

Ⓖ **Questions personnelles.** Rêvez un peu.

1. Quel a été le jour le plus fantastique de votre vie?
2. Quelle personne admirez-vous le plus? Qui admirez-vous presque autant qu'elle?
3. Aimeriez-vous avoir autant d'argent que Bill Gates? Qu'est-ce que vous en feriez?
4. Vous voudriez être aussi beau / belle / riche / connu(e) que quelle personnalité?
5. Préféreriez-vous avoir plus d'amis? Quelles qualités font les meilleur(e)s ami(e)s?
6. Quelle est la chose la plus importante que vous avez entendue récemment?

communiquons

S'exprimer en français familier

Although the **Ce qu'ils disent** sections of this textbook have shown you many ways in which spoken French differs from the formal language, the French you have been studying is the standard variety used in more formal speech. If you go to a francophone country, you are more likely to hear colloquial, or popular, French (**le français familier**) in casual conversation. One characteristic of colloquial French is the frequent use of conversational fillers (**des remplisseurs de pause**) similar to words like *well, like,* or *ya know*. French speakers also omit or elide sounds (**élision**), just as English speakers replace *I am going to* with *I'm gonna*. Because so many sounds are dropped, this level of speech is often harder for foreigners to understand. In addition, colloquial French, like English, abounds in popular vocabulary. The following sections will review some features and describe others that characterize rapid, casual speech.

©1991   *Nicole Lambert*

Expressions

▶ **On remplit les pauses.**

—Euh	*Uh*
—Ben	*Um*
—M'enfin	*Well*
—M'alors	*So*
—Eh bien / Eh ben	*So*

▶ **On fait des élisions.**

1. More mute e's than usual are dropped.

Jе̸ te verrai dе̸main.	*See ya tomorrow.*
Cе̸la nе̸ sе̸ fait pas.	*That isn't done.*

2. The **u** of **tu** is dropped.

T'es vraiment stupide.	*You're a dope.*
T'as fini?	*You done?*

3. The **l** of **il** and **ils** is not pronounced before a consonant.

Il̸s sont partis.	*They left.*
Il̸ ne̸ sait pas.	*He doesn't know.*
but Il_est bon.	*It's good.*

4. The **ne** of negations is not used.

Je̸ peux pas ve̸nir.	*I can't come.*
Je̸ veux pas me̸ coucher.	*I don't wanna go to bed.*
C'est pas vrai!	*It isn't true!*

5. The consonant group **-re** at the end of words before a word beginning with a consonant is not pronounced.

Donne-moi l'autre̸ stylo.	*Gimme the other pen.*
Il a quatre̸ chiens.	*He's got four dogs.*
Le pauvre̸ garçon!	*The poor guy!*

▶ **On emploie un vocabulaire familier.**

1. Following are some popular words for common things.

C'est sa bagnole.	C'est son auto.
Il n'aime pas son boulot.	Il n'aime pas son travail / emploi.
De la flotte? J'en bois jamais!	De l'eau? Je n'en bois jamais!
J'ai pas de fric.	Je n'ai pas d'argent.
Où sont mes godasses *(f.)*?	Où sont mes chaussures?
C'est un bon pinard.	C'est un bon vin.

2. There are popular words used to talk about people.

Voilà des flics.	Voilà des agents de police.
T'as vu les gosses?	Tu as vu les enfants?
Elle parle avec un type / mec.	Elle parle avec un homme.
Il sort avec une nana.	Il sort avec une jeune femme.
C'est mon pote.	C'est mon ami.
Son père est toubib.	Son père est médecin.

3. The following expressions describe actions.

Ils bouffent au restau-U.	Ils mangent au restaurant universitaire.
Ta gueule! *[vulgar]*	Tais-toi! *(Shut up!)*

4. Several popular words are adjectives used to describe people or things.

T'es dingue?!	Tu es fou?! *(Are you nuts?!)*
C'est dégueulasse! *[vulgar]*	C'est dégoûtant! *(That's disgusting!)*
Il est moche.	Il est laid.

Interaction

Julie et Etienne sont au restaurant universitaire.

JULIE: Qu'est-ce qu'on a à bouffer aujourd'hui?

ÉTIENNE: Ben, les mêmes choses dégueulasses!

JULIE: Tu me cherches de la flotte?

ÉTIENNE: Pas moi! Je vais acheter du pinard.

JULIE: T'es dingue? C'est toi qui as la bagnole!

Activités

Ⓐ   Mettez les phrases suivantes en français standard.

1. I' veut pas m' donner d' fric.
2. L' pauv' mec peut pas ach'ter d' bagnole.
3. T'as vu l'aut' nana?
4. Tu vas pas porter ces godasses au boulot?
5. T'es dingue? J'aime pas la flotte!
6. T'as pas encore fini d' bouffer?

Ⓑ   Dans les phrases suivantes, remplacez autant de mots que possible avec du vocabulaire familier.

1. Les Américains sont fous. Ils mangent dans leur voiture!
2. Mon ami n'a jamais d'argent parce qu'il n'a pas de travail.
3. Qui a mis de l'eau dans mon vin? C'est dégoûtant!
4. Voilà un homme et une femme qui jouent avec leurs enfants.
5. Tais-toi! Tes chaussures sont beaucoup plus laides que les miennes.
6. Les agents de police ont trouvé la voiture de mon ami en ville.

lecture culturelle

Avant la lecture

Throughout history, many groups in the world have experienced some form of discrimination due to race, gender, religion, or other factors. In 1961, U.S. President John F. Kennedy signed a bill to fight racial discrimination with the government's controversial "affirmative action" measures. Three years later, the Civil Rights Act made it illegal to deny equal employment opportunities to any American.

With its diverse ethnic population, France is also struggling with problems of discrimination. Blacks, North Africans (**Maghrébins**), and other minorities are fighting to claim their legal right to equality, as promised by the motto of the French Republic, "**Liberté, Egalité, Fraternité.**" To achieve equality, the practice of **discrimination positive** has been unofficially instituted in certain sectors in France. This notion, which resembles affirmative action, is gaining acceptance, yet it is not wholeheartedly embraced by the French government.

Applying further pressure on the authorities, various French lobbying organizations—SOS Racisme being one of the better known—are working to eliminate racism in all its forms. Additionally, the French media have begun studying ways to combat discrimination. Recently, the minister of culture and communication proposed changes to encourage more minority representation on public television. The nongovernmental organization Collectif Egalité has likewise been fighting for this cause. The article presented here describes the efforts of Collectif Egalité.

Activités

Ⓐ What are the top ten television shows that people in your age group watch? How many of them represent the many minority groups living in the United States? Do national newscasters in the United States come from a variety of ethnic backgrounds?

Ⓑ Do you think that typecasting of minority actors is an issue in today's film and television industries? Explain.

Ⓒ Are racial tensions prevalent on your campus? What are some solutions to fighting racism and other forms of discrimination in your community?

Ⓓ Scan the first paragraph to determine how France compares with Germany, the Netherlands, and Great Britain with regard to minority representation on television.

Les minorités ethniques à la télévision

L e monde de la télévision en France fait pâle figure°. En effet, les minorités ethniques sont très peu représentées dans les médias français. A en croire° un rapport sur l'intégration des minorités
5 dans la télévision européenne,* la France se situe dans les derniers, loin derrière des pays comme l'Allemagne, les Pays-Bas ou bien la Grande-Bretagne. Cet état de fait° est si flagrant qu'une association qui répond au nom de Collectif Egalité a vu le jour°, afin° d'imposer aux médias une représentation plus équitable des minorités.

Lorsqu'on sait que 11 millions de Français, à savoir° 18% de la po-
10 pulation, sont d'origine africaine, et que l'on se rend compte° qu'à l'heure actuelle, Nagui (d'origine maghrébine) est l'un des rares présentateurs «non-blancs» à connaître les faveurs des producteurs, on ne peut que regretter un tel manque de diversité dans ce qui est supposé refléter notre société.

Suite à° ces constatations°, plusieurs artistes d'origine africaine—la
15 romancière° Calixthe Beyala, le musicien Manu Dibango, le metteur en

makes a poor showing (literally, is pale-faced)
If we are to believe

state of affairs
was created / in order

that is to say
se rend... realizes

Following / findings
novelist

More color in the media, employment and access of ethnic minorities to TV industry in Germany, Finland, France, Great Britain, and the Netherlands, The European Institute of the Media, Dusseldorf.

scène° Luc Saint-Eloi et l'acteur Dieudonné—ont donc décidé de créer, en *director*
décembre 1998, le Collectif Egalité, une association qui se bat° pour l'in- *is fighting for*
tégration des minorités ethniques à la télé. Ils relèvent°, par exemple, que *raise (the issue)*
les fictions montrant des Français d'origine africaine ou antillaise sont
20 rares. Ils ont également recueilli° les témoignages° d'acteurs d'origine *gathered / testimonies*
africaine ou arabe qui disent la difficulté d'obtenir des premiers rôles et
d'éviter, lors des castings, des personnages caricaturaux. Forte de 6.000
membres°, cette association a demandé au CSA (Conseil supérieur de **Forte...** *Six thousand mem-*
l'audiovisuel) l'instauration° d'un quota de «gens de couleur» dans le *bers strong / establishment*
25 monde de la télévision. Ils appellent au boycott des téléphones mobiles
de la compagnie Bouygues, actionnaire° principal de la chaîne privée TF1. *shareholder*
Cette dernière°, d'après l'association, serait particulièrement «méprisante° *The latter / contemptuous*
envers les minorités».

   Pour expliquer l'apparente xénophobie de la télé française, certains
30 dirigeants° évoquent le manque de candidats et, surtout, rappellent que les *leaders*
promotions d'écoles de journalisme ont la peau° très blanche. Pourtant°, *skin / However*
les témoignages sur la discrimination ne manquent pas. Elizabeth Tchoungui, animatrice° sur France2 (première chaîne publique) s'étonne: «Il m'est *TV presenter*
arrivé souvent de passer des castings, d'avoir l'impression que ça avait bien
35 marché et puis de ne pas être retenue°. A deux reprises°, on m'a avoué° *kept (in this case, selected) /*
que je représentais une prise de risque° à l'antenne°». Ou encore Morad *occasions / admitted /*
Ait-Habbouche, grand reporter à la rédaction de France3, qui se souvient: **prise...** *risk / TV station*
«Au début, on me prenait parfois pour l'assistant quand on partait en re-
portage, l'interlocuteur n'imaginait pas que je pouvais être journaliste.»

40   France raciste? «Les Français ont gardé ce complexe colonisateur de
vouloir imposer leur culture, de n'accepter la diversité que dans la mesure
où elle renvoie° au modèle culturel français. A la télé, il faut donc renvoyer *reflects*
une image parfaite, idéale» explique Michel Lob Ewane, ancien du *Monde
diplomatique.*

45   On peut tout de même° féliciter l'initiative du Collectif Egalité d'avoir *in any case*
pris position et fait réagir° Hervé Bourges, directeur du CSA. Ce dernier *gotten a reaction from*
n'est pas pour l'instauration d'un quota de minorités à l'écran car° ce *for, because*
serait contraire à l'esprit républicain universaliste d'unicité° de la nation, *uniqueness*
de laïcité°, mais il a néanmoins° fait en sorte que° l'association soit reçue *secularism / nonetheless /*
50 par Lionel Jospin. Affaire à suivre°. *so that / to be continued*

Nicolas Guillou, «Vive la télé en couleur!» Journal Français.

Après la lecture

Questions sur le texte

1. Que dit le rapport sur l'intégration des minorités dans la télévision européenne?
2. Qu'est-ce que le groupe Collectif Egalité? Quel est son but? Combien
   de membres a-t-il?
3. Quel est le pourcentage de personnes d'origine africaine en France?

4. Combien de présentateurs «non-blancs» sont à la télé en France?
5. De quel pays vient le présentateur Nagui?
6. Lors des «castings», quelle est l'expérience des acteurs d'origine africaine et arabe?
7. Quelle est la première raison donnée pour l'apparente xénophobie à la télé française?
8. Quelle a été l'expérience d'Elizabeth Tchoungui? Qu'est-ce que la direction lui a avoué?
9. Quelle a été l'expérience de Morad Ait-Habbouche?
10. Quel est «le complexe colonisateur» de la France?
11. Pourquoi est-ce que Hervé Bourges n'est pas d'accord pour avoir des quotas?

Activités

Ⓐ Pensez-vous que la publicité américaine soit représentative de la société américaine?

Ⓑ Est-ce que la France devrait adopter des quotas à la télévision pour assurer une représentation plus équitable de tous les groupes ethniques en France? En groupes, participez à un débat. La moitié de la classe représentera le

Manifestation contre le racisme.

Collectif Egalité. L'autre moitié de la classe représentera Hervé Bourges, directeur du CSA (Conseil supérieur de l'audiovisuel).

C L'expression américaine *affirmative action* et l'expression française «discrimination positive» représentent le même idéal, mais les termes sont très différents. Que pensez-vous de la connotation de chaque expression? Laquelle préférez-vous?

D Etes-vous pour ou contre la discrimination positive? Expliquez.

vocabulaire

Noms / Pronoms

Afrique du Nord *(f.)*	North Africa	**un/une immigré(e)**	immigrant
un/une Algérien(ne)	Algerian	**le Maghreb**	the Maghreb
un animal	animal		(Morocco,
une branche	branch		Algeria,
un canard	duck		Tunisia)
un chacal	jackal	**un/une Maghrébin(e)**	person from
un chat	cat		the Maghreb
un cheval	horse	**un/une Marocain(e)**	Moroccan
un chien	dog	**un muezzin**	muezzin
un cochon	pig	**une poule**	hen
un coq	rooster	**une prière**	prayer
Dieu	God	**un/une Tunisien(ne)**	Tunisian
un imam	imam (Muslim prayer leader)	**une vache**	cow

Verbes

courir	to run
prier	to pray
s'approcher	to get closer

Adjectifs / Adverbes

ailleurs	elsewhere	**complet**	complete
algérien	Algerian	**complètement**	completely
assez	rather	**évidemment**	obviously
aussi... que	as . . . as	**facilement**	easily
autant	as much, as many	**fréquemment**	frequently
brillamment	brilliantly	**fréquent**	frequent
brillant	brilliant	**général**	general
certainement	certainly	**heureusement**	fortunately

indépendamment	independently	**prudemment**	carefully
insuffisamment	insufficiently	**que**	how, than
intelligemment	intelligently	**quelquefois**	sometimes
lent	slow	**rapidement**	rapidly
lentement	slowly	**rarement**	rarely
mal	badly	**récent**	recent
malheureusement	unfortunately	**seulement**	only
marocain	Moroccan	**suffisamment**	sufficiently
méchamment	out of meanness	**suffisant**	sufficient
meilleur	better	**sûrement**	surely
mieux	best	**tard**	late
nécessairement	necessarily	**tel(le)**	such / like
parfaitement	perfectly	**tellement**	so / so much
partout	everywhere	**traditionnel**	traditional
populaire	popular	**traditionnellement**	traditionally
probablement	probably	**vite**	fast

Révision

Tous ensemble!

Ⓐ Répondez aux questions suivantes en employant les mots entre parenthèses.

Conversation avec mes parents quand je rentre tard

1. A ta place, est-ce que nous rentrerions après minuit? (Non,... ne... pas faire cela.)
2. Qu'est-ce que vous avez fait ensemble? (Nous... danser... pendant... heures)
3. Qu'est-ce que tu as promis? (... revenir avant minuit.)
4. Vous êtes rentrés lentement? (Non,... vite...)
5. Quand nous téléphoneras-tu? (... aussitôt que... je... savoir quand je... arriver)

Un vieil ami

6. A qui ressemble-t-il? (... tenir... son père.)
7. Depuis quand êtes-vous amis? (... 1998.)
8. Est-ce qu'il sait parler français? (Oui,... + bien... que moi.)
9. Vous allez voyager ensemble pendant les vacances? (Oui,... partir... quinze jours.)
10. Est-ce qu'il est très riche? (Oui,... promettre... payer le voyage!)

Ⓑ **Parlez-moi de votre chambre.** Refaites les phrases suivantes en employant les mots entre parenthèses.

1. Il faut que tu viennes la voir. (Demain... vous...)
2. Je la loue depuis trois mois. (Il y a... que...)
3. Je ne veux pas faire le ménage. (... avoir envie...)
4. Mon frère est arrivé il y a peu de temps. (récemment)
5. On met dix minutes pour aller en ville. (L'année prochaine,...)

Ⓒ **Connaissez-vous l'amie mystérieuse de Jacques?** Combinez les phrases suivantes.

1. Vous ne connaissez pas la jeune femme? La jeune femme sort avec Jacques.
2. Il refuse de me présenter cette femme fascinante. Il vient de décrire la femme.
3. Elle habite un village formidable. Il y a trois ans, j'ai passé mes vacances dans ce village.
4. Elle sait bien faire de la planche à voile. Jacques ne sait pas aussi bien en faire.
5. Elle joue très bien au tennis. Jacques joue moins bien.

D **Robert.** Formez des phrases complètes avec les mots donnés. Le symbole = représente **aussi**.

Allons voir Robert

1. Si / nous / avoir / temps / nous / aller voir / Robert
2. Il / permettre / gens / passer le voir / sans téléphoner
3. Il / ne... pas / être / = / sympa / Jean
4. Son / chien / être / = / méchant / tien

Chez Robert

5. Vouloir / vous / je / mettre / musique?
6. Regarder / divan / je / venir / acheter
7. Si / vous / avoir / faim / je / pouvoir / vous / servir / mouton
8. Dire / moi / quand / vous / avoir envie / partir

E **Mes opinions.** Complétez les phrases suivantes de manière logique.

1. Je n'aime pas les gens qui...
2. Je pense que...
3. J'aime les animaux qu(e)...
4. Je ne sais pas où...
5. Si j'étais en retard...
6. Je partirai vendredi, dès que...
7. Je ferai mieux si...
8. J'ai plus de talent...

Entre nous!

A Avec un(e) camarade de cours, comparez des gens que vous connaissez. Employez un élément de chaque colonne, mais n'hésitez pas à utiliser vos propres idées.

je	être	plus	bien	moi
mes amis	avoir	moins	mauvais	vous
mon	conduire	aussi	mal	mes amis
professeur	comprendre	autant	beau	la ville
mes voisins	manger		brillant	l'université
mes parents	jouer		talent	le cours
mon frère /	danser		???	???
ma sœur	???			

B Interviewez un(e) camarade de cours. Parlez des sujets suivants.

1. la ville où tu habites
2. les cours que tu suis
3. les gens que tu aimes
4. les choses les plus importantes de ta vie
5. le genre de film que tu préfères
6. les endroits où tu vas
7. les animaux que tu as eus
8. les gens qui t'ont influencé(e)

C En groupe de trois ou quatre étudiants, imaginez votre vie quand vous aurez cent ans.

MODÈLE: se lever à cinq heures du matin
Nous nous lèverons à cinq heures du matin.

ne pas se rappeler les gens	ne pas bien entendre / voir
manger peu	ne plus rien remettre à plus tard
ne pas sortir	se coucher de bonne heure
ne boire que du lait	prendre beaucoup d'aspirine

D Interrogez vos camarades de cours. Demandez-leur depuis quand ils font les choses suivantes ou pendant combien de temps ils les ont faites.

s'occuper d'un chien / d'un chat	être étudiant(e) dans cette
se coucher à huit heures	université
jouer au docteur	connaître ton / ta meilleur(e)
posséder une voiture	ami(e)
habiter la ville où tu es né(e)	savoir nager

E Avec un(e) camarade de cours, imaginez ce que *(what)* vous feriez si vous étiez de l'autre sexe.

mettre une robe / cravate	dire aux personnes du sexe opposé
(ne plus) jouer au football	qu(e)...
(ne plus) faire la cuisine	trouver... formidable / affreux
payer au restaurant	(-euse)
avoir les cheveux plus / moins longs	???

F Dans un petit groupe, décrivez comment vous avez fait les choses le semestre / trimestre dernier.

vite	méchamment	brillamment
souvent	horriblement	le mieux
bien	fréquemment	le plus mal
mal	rarement	???

G **Jeu de rôles.** Jouez les scènes suivantes avec un(e) camarade de cours.

1. Vous êtes journaliste pour une revue spécialisée. Choisissez le sujet (sports, mode *[fashion],* pêche, etc.) et interviewez un(e) camarade qui le connaît mieux que vous.
2. Vous voulez louer un appartement. Téléphonez au / à la propriétaire et posez-lui des questions.
3. Vous venez de gagner 15.000 euros dans un jeu télévisé. Discutez avec votre femme / mari ce que *(what)* vous allez faire avec cet argent.
4. Vous avez besoin d'emprunter de l'argent à un(e) ami(e). Faites beaucoup de compliments.
5. Vous voulez que votre camarade s'engage *(makes a commitment)* pour une cause. Expliquez-lui celle que vous préférez.
6. Vous êtes guide dans un musée de l'avenir. Décrivez la vie qu'on y représente.
7. Essayez d'être plus snob que votre ami(e). Mentionnez toutes les choses que vous achetez qui sont de la meilleure qualité.
8. Vous êtes professeur de français, et vous parlez avec un étudiant qui n'est pas sérieux. Expliquez-lui comment il peut réussir dans votre cours.

Appendices

I. International Phonetic Alphabet

Consonants

/ p /	*P*ierre	/ v /	*v*ous
/ t /	*t*u	/ z /	bi*s*e
/ k /	*c*omme	/ ʒ /	bon*j*our
/ b /	*b*onjour	/ l /	*l*a
/ d /	*d*e	/ ʀ /	ga*r*çon
/ g /	*g*arçon	/ m /	*m*ain
/ f /	*f*ille	/ n /	A*nn*e
/ s /	mer*c*i, profe*ss*eur	/ ɲ /	poi*gn*ée
/ ʃ /	*ch*ez		

Vowels

/ i /	b*i*se	/ y /	*u*ne
/ e /	caf*é*	/ ø /	d*e*, p*eu*
/ ɛ /	app*e*lle	/ œ /	h*eu*re
/ a /	v*a*	/ ɛ̃ /	bi*en*, *un*, m*ain*
/ ɔ /	c*o*mme	/ ɑ̃ /	connaiss*an*ce
/ o /	*au*	/ ɔ̃ /	fais*ons*
/ u /	v*ou*s		

Semivowels

/ j /	P*i*erre
/ w /	*ou*i
/ ɥ /	n*u*it

Mute e

/ ə /	*je*, f*e*rai

485

II. Les Etats-Unis et le Canada

A. Les Etats-Unis

ETAT	in or to	ETAT	in or to
l'Alabama *(m.)*	dans l'Alabama / en Alabama	le Maine	dans le Maine
l'Alaska *(m.)*	dans l'Alaska / en Alaska	le Maryland	dans le Maryland
l'Arizona *(m.)*	dans l'Arizona / en Arizona	le Massachusetts	dans le Massachusetts
		le Michigan	dans le Michigan
l'Arkansas *(m.)*	dans l'Arkansas / en Arkansas	le Minnesota	dans le Minnesota
		le Mississippi	dans le Mississippi
la Californie	en Californie	le Missouri	dans le Missouri
la Caroline du Nord	en Caroline du Nord	le Montana	dans le Montana
la Caroline du Sud	en Caroline du Sud	le Nebraska	dans le Nebraska
le Colorado	dans le Colorado / au Colorado	le Nevada	dans le Nevada
		le New Hampshire	dans le New Hampshire
le Connecticut	dans le Connecticut	le New Jersey	dans le New Jersey
le Dakota du Nord	dans le Dakota du Nord	l'état de New York	dans l'état de New York
le Dakota du Sud	dans le Dakota du Sud	le Nouveau-Mexique	au Nouveau-Mexique
le Delaware	dans le Delaware	l'Ohio *(m.)*	dans l'Ohio
la Floride	en Floride	l'Oklahoma *(m.)*	dans l'Oklahoma
la Géorgie	en Géorgie	l'Oregon *(m.)*	dans l'Oregon
Hawaii *(m.)*	à Hawaii / aux îles Hawaii	la Pennsylvanie	en Pennsylvanie
		le Rhode Island	dans le Rhode Island
l'Idaho *(m.)*	dans l'Idaho	le Tennessee	dans le Tennessee
l'Illinois *(m.)*	dans l'Illinois / en Illinois	le Texas	au Texas
		l'Utah *(m.)*	dans l'Utah
l'Indiana *(m.)*	dans l'Indiana	le Vermont	dans le Vermont
l'Iowa *(m.)*	dans l'Iowa	la Virginie	en Virginie
le Kansas	dans le Kansas	la Virginie-Occidentale	en Virginie-Occidentale
le Kentucky	dans le Kentucky	l'état de Washington	dans l'état de Washington
la Louisiane	en Louisiane	le Wisconsin	dans le Wisconsin
		le Wyoming	dans le Wyoming

B. Le Canada

PROVINCE	in or to	TERRITOIRE	in or to
l'Alberta	dans l'Alberta	les Territoires du Nord-Ouest	dans les Territoires du Nord-Ouest
la Colombie britannique	en Colombie britannique	le Yukon	au Yukon
l'île du Prince-Edouard	dans l'île du Prince-Edouard		
le Manitoba	au Manitoba		
le Nouveau-Brunswick	au Nouveau-Brunswick		
la Nouvelle-Ecosse	en Nouvelle-Ecosse		
l'Ontario	dans l'Ontario		
le Québec	au Québec		
le Saskatchewan	au Saskatchewan		
Terre-Neuve	à Terre-Neuve		

III. Double Object Pronouns

A. Statements and negative commands

If you use two object pronouns in a sentence or a negative command, you must keep the following order:

me te se nous vous	le la les	lui leur	y	en

Il prête ses livres à ses amis. → Il **les leur** prête.
J'ai donné de l'argent aux enfants. → Je **leur en** ai donné.
Nous allons vendre l'auto à notre voisin. → Nous allons **la lui** vendre.

B. Tonic pronouns

Object pronouns in the first and third columns above cannot be used together. Use a tonic pronoun instead.

Il m'a présenté à Robert.   Il m'a présenté **à lui.**

C. Affirmative commands

In affirmative commands, use the following order:

verb	le la les	moi / m' toi / t' lui nous vous leur	y	en

D. The pronouns *me* and *te*

Me and **te** become **moi** and **toi** when they are the final elements of the command. If **y** or **en** is included, **me** and **te** become **m'** and **t'**.

Donnez-moi trois stylos. → Donnez-**m'en** trois.
Montrez-moi vos photos. → Montrez-**les-moi.**

Apportez-nous le journal. → Apportez-**le-nous.**

IV. Le passé simple

A. Endings for regular verbs

This tense may replace the **passé composé** in formal writing. There are three sets of endings:

-er verbs	-ir verbs	-re verbs
je chant**ai**	je part**is**	je vend**is**
tu chant**as**	tu part**is**	tu vend**is**
il chant**a**	il part**it**	il vend**it**
nous chant**âmes**	nous part**îmes**	nous vend**îmes**
vous chant**âtes**	vous part**îtes**	vous vend**îtes**
ils chant**èrent**	ils part**irent**	ils vend**irent**

B. Endings for irregular verbs

Irregular verbs add the following endings to their stems:

-s -^mes
-s -^tes
-t -rent

C. Verbs with irregular stems

The irregular stems of the verbs you know are:

avoir → eu-	être → fu-	prendre → pri-
boire → bu-	faire → fi-	savoir → su-
conduire → conduisi-	lire → lu-	suivre → suivi-
connaître → connu-	mettre → mi-	venir → vin-
devoir → du-	mourir → mouru-	voir → vi-
dire → di-	naître → naqui-	vouloir → voulu-
écrire → écrivi-	pouvoir → pu-	

Annibal **voulut** traverser les Alpes.	*Hannibal **wanted** to cross the Alps.*
Il **fit** ses devoirs.	*He **did** his homework.*
Nous **vîmes** un accident.	*We **saw** an accident.*
Napoléon **naquit** en Corse;	*Napoleon **was born** in Corsica;*
il **mourut** à Sainte-Hélène.	*he **died** on St. Helena.*
Elles ne **dirent** jamais la vérité.	*They never **told** the truth.*

V. Conjugaison des verbes

REGULAR VERBS

–er chanter

	Indicatif				Impératif	Subjonctif	Conditionnel
	Présent	Passé Composé	Imparfait	Futur			
je/j'	chante	ai chanté	chantais	chanterai		chante	chanterais
tu	chantes	as chanté	chantais	chanteras	chante	chantes	chanterais
il/elle/on	chante	a chanté	chantait	chantera		chante	chanterait
nous	chantons	avons chanté	chantions	chanterons	chantons	chantions	chanterions
vous	chantez	avez chanté	chantiez	chanterez	chantez	chantiez	chanteriez
ils/elles	chantent	ont chanté	chantaient	chanteront		chantent	chanteraient

–ir servir

	Indicatif				Impératif	Subjonctif	Conditionnel
	Présent	Passé Composé	Imparfait	Futur			
je/j'	sers	ai servi	servais	servirai		serve	servirais
tu	sers	as servi	servais	serviras	sers	serves	servirais
il/elle/on	sert	a servi	servait	servira		serve	servirait
nous	servons	avons servi	servions	servirons	servons	servions	servirions
vous	servez	avez servi	serviez	servirez	servez	serviez	serviriez
ils/elles	servent	ont servi	servaient	serviront		servent	serviraient

–ir finir

	Indicatif				Impératif	Subjonctif	Conditionnel
	Présent	Passé Composé	Imparfait	Futur			
je/j'	finis	ai fini	finissais	finirai		finisse	finirais
tu	finis	as fini	finissais	finiras	finis	finisses	finirais
il/elle/on	finit	a fini	finissait	finira		finisse	finirait
nous	finissons	avons fini	finissions	finirons	finissons	finissions	finirions
vous	finissez	avez fini	finissiez	finirez	finissez	finissiez	finiriez
ils/elles	finissent	ont fini	finissaient	finiront		finissent	finiraient

REGULAR VERBS

–re vendre

	Présent	Passé Composé	Imparfait	Futur	Impératif	Subjonctif	Conditionnel
je/j'	vends	ai vendu	vendais	vendrai		vende	vendrais
tu	vends	as vendu	vendais	vendras	vends	vendes	vendrais
il/elle/on	vend	a vendu	vendait	vendra		vende	vendrait
nous	vendons	avons vendu	vendions	vendrons	vendons	vendions	vendrions
vous	vendez	avez vendu	vendiez	vendrez	vendez	vendiez	vendriez
ils/elles	vendent	ont vendu	vendaient	vendront		vendent	vendraient

–ire conduire

	Présent	Passé Composé	Imparfait	Futur	Impératif	Subjonctif	Conditionnel
je/j'	conduis	ai conduit	conduisais	conduirai		conduise	conduirais
tu	conduis	as conduit	conduisais	conduiras	conduis	conduises	conduirais
il/elle/on	conduit	a conduit	conduisait	conduira		conduise	conduirait
nous	conduisons	avons conduit	conduisions	conduirons	conduisons	conduisions	conduirions
vous	conduisez	avez conduit	conduisiez	conduirez	conduisez	conduisiez	conduiriez
ils/elles	conduisent	ont conduit	conduisaient	conduiront		conduisent	conduiraient

–ire écrire

	Présent	Passé Composé	Imparfait	Futur	Impératif	Subjonctif	Conditionnel
j'	écris	ai écrit	écrivais	écrirai		écrive	écrirais
tu	écris	as écrit	écrivais	écriras	écris	écrives	écrirais
il/elle/on	écrit	a écrit	écrivait	écrira		écrive	écrirait
nous	écrivons	avons écrit	écrivions	écrirons	écrivons	écrivions	écririons
vous	écrivez	avez écrit	écriviez	écrirez	écrivez	écriviez	écririez
ils/elles	écrivent	ont écrit	écrivaient	écriront		écrivent	écriraient

AUXILIARY VERBS

avoir

	Indicatif				Impératif	Subjonctif	Conditionnel
	Présent	Passé Composé	Imparfait	Futur			
j'	ai	ai eu	avais	aurai		aie	aurais
tu	as	as eu	avais	auras	aie	aies	aurais
il/elle/on	a	a eu	avait	aura		ait	aurait
nous	avons	avons eu	avions	aurons	ayons	ayons	aurions
vous	avez	avez eu	aviez	aurez	ayez	ayez	auriez
ils/elles	ont	ont eu	avaient	auront		aient	auraient

être

	Indicatif				Impératif	Subjonctif	Conditionnel
	Présent	Passé Composé	Imparfait	Futur			
je/j'	suis	ai été	étais	serai		sois	serais
tu	es	as été	étais	seras	sois	sois	serais
il/elle/on	est	a été	était	sera		soit	serait
nous	sommes	avons été	étions	serons	soyons	soyons	serions
vous	êtes	avez été	étiez	serez	soyez	soyez	seriez
ils/elles	sont	ont été	étaient	seront		soient	seraient

REFLEXIVE VERBS

se laver

	Indicatif				Impératif	Subjonctif	Conditionnel
	Présent	Passé Composé	Imparfait	Futur			
je	me lave	me suis lavé(e)	me lavais	me laverai		me lave	me laverais
tu	te laves	t'es lavé(e)	te lavais	te laveras	lave-toi	te laves	te laverais
il/elle/on	se lave	s'est lavé(e)	se lavait	se lavera		se lave	se laverait
nous	nous lavons	nous sommes lavé(e)s	nous lavions	nous laverons	lavons-nous	nous lavions	nous laverions
vous	vous lavez	vous êtes lavé(e)(s)	vous laviez	vous laverez	lavez-vous	vous laviez	vous laveriez
ils/elles	se lavent	se sont lavé(e)s	se lavaient	se laveront		se lavent	se laveraient

VERBS WITH STEM CHANGES

acheter

	Indicatif				Impératif	Subjonctif	Conditionnel
	Présent	Passé Composé	Imparfait	Futur			
j'	achète	ai acheté	achetais	achèterai		achète	achèterais
tu	achètes	as acheté	achetais	achèteras	achète	achètes	achèterais
il/elle/on	achète	a acheté	achetait	achètera		achète	achèterait
nous	achetons	avons acheté	achetions	achèterons	achetons	achetions	achèterions
vous	achetez	avez acheté	achetiez	achèterez	achetez	achetiez	achèteriez
ils/elles	achètent	ont acheté	achetaient	achèteront		achètent	achèteraient

appeler

	Indicatif				Impératif	Subjonctif	Conditionnel
	Présent	Passé Composé	Imparfait	Futur			
j'	appelle	ai appelé	appelais	appellerai		appelle	appellerais
tu	appelles	as appelé	appelais	appelleras	appelle	appelles	appellerais
il/elle/on	appelle	a appelé	appelait	appellera		appelle	appellerait
nous	appelons	avons appelé	appelions	appellerons	appelons	appelions	appellerions
vous	appelez	avez appelé	appeliez	appellerez	appelez	appeliez	appelleriez
ils/elles	appellent	ont appelé	appelaient	appelleront		appellent	appelleraient

posséder

	Indicatif				Impératif	Subjonctif	Conditionnel
	Présent	Passé Composé	Imparfait	Futur			
je/j'	possède	ai possédé	possédais	posséderai		possède	posséderais
tu	possèdes	as possédé	possédais	posséderas	possède	possèdes	posséderais
il/elle/on	possède	a possédé	possédait	possédera		possède	posséderait
nous	possédons	avons possédé	possédions	posséderons	possédons	possédions	posséderions
vous	possédez	avez possédé	possédiez	posséderez	possédez	possédiez	posséderiez
ils/elles	possèdent	ont possédé	possédaient	posséderont		possèdent	posséderaient

IRREGULAR VERBS

	Indicatif				Impératif	Subjonctif	Conditionnel
	Présent	Passé Composé	Imparfait	Futur			
aller							
je/j'	vais	suis allé(e)	allais	irai		aille	irais
tu	vas	es allé(e)	allais	iras	va	ailles	irais
il/elle/on	va	est allé(e)	allait	ira		aille	irait
nous	allons	sommes allé(e)s	allions	irons	allons	allions	irions
vous	allez	êtes allé(e)(s)	alliez	irez	allez	alliez	iriez
ils/elles	vont	sont allé(e)s	allaient	iront		aillent	iraient
boire							
je/j'	bois	ai bu	buvais	boirai		boive	boirais
tu	bois	as bu	buvais	boiras	bois	boives	boirais
il/elle/on	boit	a bu	buvait	boira		boive	boirait
nous	buvons	avons bu	buvions	boirons	buvons	buvions	boirions
vous	buvez	avez bu	buviez	boirez	buvez	buviez	boiriez
ils/elles	boivent	ont bu	buvaient	boiront		boivent	boiraient
connaître							
je/j'	connais	ai connu	connaissais	connaîtrai		connaisse	connaîtrais
tu	connais	as connu	connaissais	connaîtras	connais	connaisses	connaîtrais
il/elle/on	connaît	a connu	connaissait	connaîtra		connaisse	connaîtrait
nous	connaissons	avons connu	connaissions	connaîtrons	connaissons	connaissions	connaîtrions
vous	connaissez	avez connu	connaissiez	connaîtrez	connaissez	connaissiez	connaîtriez
ils/elles	connaissent	ont connu	connaissaient	connaîtront		connaissent	connaîtraient

IRREGULAR VERBS

devoir

	Indicatif				Impératif	Subjonctif	Conditionnel
	Présent	Passé Composé	Imparfait	Futur			
je/j'	dois	ai dû	devais	devrai		doive	devrais
tu	dois	as dû	devais	devras	dois	doives	devrais
il/elle/on	doit	a dû	devait	devra		doive	devrait
nous	devons	avons dû	devions	devrons	devons	devions	devrions
vous	devez	avez dû	deviez	devrez	devez	deviez	devriez
ils/elles	doivent	ont dû	devaient	devront		doivent	devraient

dire

	Indicatif				Impératif	Subjonctif	Conditionnel
	Présent	Passé Composé	Imparfait	Futur			
je/j'	dis	ai dit	disais	dirai		dise	dirais
tu	dis	as dit	disais	diras	dis	dises	dirais
il/elle/on	dit	a dit	disait	dira		dise	dirait
nous	disons	avons dit	disions	dirons	disons	disions	dirions
vous	dites	avez dit	disiez	direz	dites	disiez	diriez
ils/elles	disent	ont dit	disaient	diront		disent	diraient

faire

	Indicatif				Impératif	Subjonctif	Conditionnel
	Présent	Passé Composé	Imparfait	Futur			
je/j'	fais	ai fait	faisais	ferai		fasse	ferais
tu	fais	as fait	faisais	feras	fais	fasses	ferais
il/elle/on	fait	a fait	faisait	fera		fasse	ferait
nous	faisons	avons fait	faisions	ferons	faisons	fassions	ferions
vous	faites	avez fait	faisiez	ferez	faites	fassiez	feriez
ils/elles	font	ont fait	faisaient	feront		fassent	feraient

IRREGULAR VERBS

		Indicatif				Impératif	Subjonctif	Conditionnel
		Présent	*Passé Composé*	*Imparfait*	*Futur*			
falloir								
	il	faut	a fallu	fallait	faudra		faille	faudrait
mettre								
	je/j'	mets	ai mis	mettais	mettrai		mette	mettrais
	tu	mets	as mis	mettais	mettras	mets	mettes	mettrais
	il/elle/on	met	a mis	mettait	mettra		mette	mettrait
	nous	mettons	avons mis	mettions	mettrons	mettons	mettions	mettrions
	vous	mettez	avez mis	mettiez	mettrez	mettez	mettiez	mettriez
	ils/elles	mettent	ont mis	mettaient	mettront		mettent	mettraient
pleuvoir								
	il	pleut	a plu	pleuvait	pleuvra		pleuve	pleuvrait
pouvoir								
	je/j'	peux	ai pu	pouvais	pourrai		puisse	pourrais
	tu	peux	as pu	pouvais	pourras		puisses	pourrais
	il/elle/on	peut	a pu	pouvait	pourra		puisse	pourrait
	nous	pouvons	avons pu	pouvions	pourrons		puissions	pourrions
	vous	pouvez	avez pu	pouviez	pourrez		puissiez	pourriez
	ils/elles	peuvent	ont pu	pouvaient	pourront		puissent	pourraient

IRREGULAR VERBS

prendre

	Indicatif				Impératif	Subjonctif	Conditionnel
	Présent	Passé Composé	Imparfait	Futur			
je/j'	prends	ai pris	prenais	prendrai		prenne	prendrais
tu	prends	as pris	prenais	prendras	prends	prennes	prendrais
il/elle/on	prend	a pris	prenait	prendra		prenne	prendrait
nous	prenons	avons pris	prenions	prendrons	prenons	prenions	prendrions
vous	prenez	avez pris	preniez	prendrez	prenez	preniez	prendriez
ils/elles	prennent	ont pris	prenaient	prendront		prennent	prendraient

recevoir

	Indicatif				Impératif	Subjonctif	Conditionnel
	Présent	Passé Composé	Imparfait	Futur			
je/j'	reçois	ai reçu	recevais	recevrai		reçoive	recevrais
tu	reçois	as reçu	recevais	recevras	reçois	reçoives	recevrais
il/elle/on	reçoit	a reçu	recevait	recevra		reçoive	recevrait
nous	recevons	avons reçu	recevions	recevrons	recevons	recevions	recevrions
vous	recevez	avez reçu	receviez	recevrez	recevez	receviez	recevriez
ils/elles	reçoivent	ont reçu	recevaient	recevront		reçoivent	recevraient

savoir

	Indicatif				Impératif	Subjonctif	Conditionnel
	Présent	Passé Composé	Imparfait	Futur			
je/j'	sais	ai su	savais	saurai		sache	saurais
tu	sais	as su	savais	sauras	sache	saches	saurais
il/elle/on	sait	a su	savait	saura		sache	saurait
nous	savons	avons su	savions	saurons	sachons	sachions	saurions
vous	savez	avez su	saviez	saurez	sachez	sachiez	sauriez
ils/elles	savent	ont su	savaient	sauront		sachent	sauraient

IRREGULAR VERBS

	Indicatif				Impératif	Subjonctif	Conditionnel
	Présent	Passé Composé	Imparfait	Futur			
suivre							
je/j'	suis	ai suivi	suivais	suivrai		suive	suivrais
tu	suis	as suivi	suivais	suivras	suis	suives	suivrais
il/elle/on	suit	a suivi	suivait	suivra		suive	suivrait
nous	suivons	avons suivi	suivions	suivrons	suivons	suivions	suivrions
vous	suivez	avez suivi	suiviez	suivrez	suivez	suiviez	suivriez
ils/elles	suivent	ont suivi	suivaient	suivront		suivent	suivraient
tenir							
je/j'	tiens	ai tenu	tenais	tiendrai		tienne	tiendrais
tu	tiens	as tenu	tenais	tiendras	tiens	tiennes	tiendrais
il/elle/on	tient	a tenu	tenait	tiendra		tienne	tiendrait
nous	tenons	avons tenu	tenions	tiendrons	tenons	tenions	tiendrions
vous	tenez	avez tenu	teniez	tiendrez	tenez	teniez	tiendriez
ils/elles	tiennent	ont tenu	tenaient	tiendront		tiennent	tiendraient
venir							
je	viens	suis venu(e)	venais	viendrai		vienne	viendrais
tu	viens	es venu(e)	venais	viendras	viens	viennes	viendrais
il/elle/on	vient	est venu(e)	venait	viendra		vienne	viendrait
nous	venons	sommes venu(e)s	venions	viendrons	venons	venions	viendrions
vous	venez	êtes venu(e)(s)	veniez	viendrez	venez	veniez	viendriez
ils/elles	viennent	sont venu(e)s	venaient	viendront		viennent	viendraient

IRREGULAR VERBS

voir

	Indicatif				Impératif	Subjonctif	Conditionnel
	Présent	Passé Composé	Imparfait	Futur			
je/j'	vois	ai vu	voyais	verrai		voie	verrais
tu	vois	as vu	voyais	verras	vois	voies	verrais
il/elle/on	voit	a vu	voyait	verra		voie	verrait
nous	voyons	avons vu	voyions	verrons	voyons	voyions	verrions
vous	voyez	avez vu	voyiez	verrez	voyez	voyiez	verriez
ils/elles	voient	ont vu	voyaient	verront		voient	verraient

vouloir

	Indicatif				Impératif	Subjonctif	Conditionnel
	Présent	Passé Composé	Imparfait	Futur			
je/j'	veux	ai voulu	voulais	voudrai		veuille	voudrais
tu	veux	as voulu	voulais	voudras	veuille	veuilles	voudrais
il/elle/on	veut	a voulu	voulait	voudra		veuille	voudrait
nous	voulons	avons voulu	voulions	voudrons	veuillons	voulions	voudrions
vous	voulez	avez voulu	vouliez	voudrez	veuillez	vouliez	voudriez
ils/elles	veulent	ont voulu	voulaient	voudront		veuillent	voudraient

Vocabulaires

Français-anglais

The French-English vocabulary contains all the French words in this text except obvious cognates that are not active vocabulary items.

A number following a definition of a word indicates the chapter in which it first appears as an active vocabulary item. (P) indicates **Chapitre Préliminaire.**

A number-letter combination indicates the appearance of a new word in a chapter's **Lecture culturelle** (L) or **Communiquons** (C) section. Your instructor may or may not require you to include these entries in your active French vocabulary. Passive vocabulary has no chapter reference.

abrév. indicates that the word is the abbreviation of another word.

fam. indicates colloquial language.

Voir followed by a word indicates a reference to another entry.

All nouns have gender markers (*m.* or *f.*). All adjectives appear in the masculine form followed by the feminine ending or feminine form. Plural forms of nouns or adjectives are indicated by the abbreviation *pl.*

Irregular verbs are followed by chapter references indicating when each verb first appears. If the infinitive or a verb form appears in the textbook prior to the presentation of the complete conjugation of the verb, the chapter in which the conjugation of the verb form appears is indicated by the reference forms + chapter number. An asterisk (*) indicates aspirate **h.**

(Vocabularies are based on lists compiled by Valérie Boulanger, Ph.D. candidate, University of Georgia.)

A

à at, in, to (1); *contraction avec* le, les: **au, aux** (2)
abonné(e) *m., f.* subscriber (16-C)
abonnement *m.* subscription (10-L)
s'abonner (à) to subscribe (to) (16-C)
abord
  d'~ first (7)
abri *m.* shelter (17-L)
abriter to shelter, to house (5-L)
absent(e) absent (2)
absolument absolutely (11)
accent *m.* accent
  ~ aigu acute accent
  ~ circonflexe circumflex accent

  ~ grave grave accent
  mettre l'~ sur to emphasize (17-L)
accepter (de) to accept (15)
accident *m.* accident (10)
accord *m.* agreement
  d'~! OK!, (all) right (8-C; 10)
  être d'~ to agree
accueillir to welcome, to host (14-L)
achat *m.* purchase (5)
  faire des ~s to go shopping, to run errands (5)
acheter to buy (5)
acteur *m.* actor (2)
actionnaire *m., f.* shareholder (18-L)
activité *f.* activity

actrice *f.* actress (2)
actualités *f. pl.* news (11)
actuellement now (13-L)
addition *f.* check *(in a restaurant)* (9-C)
adorer to adore (1)
adresse *f.* address (8)
adulte *m.* adult (2-C)
aérer to air out (15-L)
aérogramme *m.* air letter (8)
aéroport *m.* airport (10)
affaire *f.* business, affair, case (11-L)
  ~s *f. pl.* belongings, things (7)
affectueux (-euse) affectionate (2)
affiche *f.* poster (1)
afficher to show (10-L)
affreux (-euse) horrible (2)

afin de in order to (18-L)

africain(e) African

Afrique *f.* Africa (4)

~ **du Nord** North Africa (18)

âge *m.* age (3)

quel ~ avez-vous? how old are you? (3)

agence de voyages *f.* travel agency (4)

agenda *m.* calendar

agent de police *m.* policeman (2)

agir to act (11-L)

il s'agit de it's about (15)

agneau *m.* (*pl.* -eaux) lamb (3)

agréable pleasant (2)

agréer to accept (15-C)

ah non! oh no! (4)

aide *f.* assistance

ail *m.* garlic (3-L)

ailleurs elsewhere (18)

aimer to like, to love (1)

~ **bien** to like, to be fond of (2)

~ **faire** to enjoy doing (2)

~ **mieux** to prefer (2)

ainsi que as well as (4-L)

air *m.*

avoir l'~ to look, to appear to be (5)

ajouter to add (14-C)

alcool *m.* alcohol (3)

aléa *m.* hazard, uncertainty (10-L)

Algérie *f.* Algeria (4)

algérien(ne) Algerian (18)

Allemagne *f.* Germany (4)

allemand(e) German (2)

aller to go; (+ *infin.*) to be going to (4)

~ **mieux** to feel better (13)

~ **voir** to visit (8)

allez-y! go ahead! (4)

allons-y! let's go! (4)

ça va? how are you? (P)

ça va bien I'm fine (P)

ça va pas, non? are you crazy? (17-C)

comment allez-vous? how do you do? (P)

comment ça va? how are you? (P)

je vais bien I'm fine (P)

on y va? shall we go? (4)

on y va let's go (4)

vas-y! go ahead! (4)

Allô, j'écoute Hello (7)

allumer to turn on (light, TV) (7)

alors then (1); well (13)

~ **que** while

ça ~! I'll be darned! (17-C)

m'~ *(fam.)* so (18-C)

alphabet *m.* alphabet (1)

alpinisme *m.* mountain climbing (14)

ambitieux (-euse) ambitious (2)

améliorer to improve

aménagement *m.* amenity (4-L)

amener to bring (13)

américain(e) American (2)

Amérique *f.* America (4)

~ **du Nord** North America (4)

~ **du Sud** South America (4)

ami(e) *m., f.* friend (1)

amicalement sincerely (15-C)

amitiés *f. pl.* fondly (15-C)

amour *m.* love (11)

amusant(e) funny (11-C)

s'amuser (à) to have a good time, to play (13)

an *m.* year (3)

ancien(ne) old, former (2)

anglais *m.* English (language) (1)

anglais(e) English (1)

Angleterre *f.* England (4)

angoisse *f.* anguish (11-L)

anglophone English-speaking

animal *m.* (*pl.* -aux) animal (18)

animateur (-trice) *m., f.* presenter (18-L)

anneau *m.* ring (8-L)

année *f.* year (4)

~ **scolaire** school year (8)

anniversaire *m.* birthday

~ **de mariage** wedding anniversary

annonce *f.*

petite ~ classified ad (16)

annuaire *m.* phone book (7-C)

annulation *f.* cancellation (9-C)

antenne *f.* TV station (18-L)

anthropologie *f.* anthropology (8)

anti-doping

contrôle ~ drug testing (14)

août *m.* August (9)

apéritif *m.* before-dinner drink (3)

apostrophe *f.* apostrophe

apparaître to appear

appareil *m.*

~ **électro-ménager** appliance (16)

à l'~ on the phone (7)

qui est à l'~? who's speaking? (7)

appartement *m.* apartment (4)

appartenir (à) to belong (to) (10)

appel *m.* phone call (8-C)

~ **international** international call (8-C)

~ **interurbain** long-distance call (8-C)

faire un ~ de phares to flash the high beams (10-C)

appeler to call (2-L; 13)

comment vous appelez-vous? what's your name? (1)

je m'appelle my name is (P)

s'~ to be called (13)

apport *m.* contribution (1-L)

apporter to bring (3)

apprécier to appreciate (2)

apprendre (à) to learn, to teach (9)

s'approcher (de) to get closer (to) (18)

après after (1)

d'~ according to (12-L)

et ~? so what? (17-C)

après-midi *m.* afternoon (4)

de l'~ P.M. (6)

aquarelle *f.* watercolor (15)

arabe Arabic (8); Arab

arbre *m.* tree (17)

architecte *m.* architect (2)

architecture *f.* architecture (8)

argent *m.* money (3); silver

~ **de poche** allowance (12-C)

armoire *f.* armoire (16)

arrêt *m.* stop

~ **d'autobus** bus stop (4)

arrêter to stop (11)

arrière rear, back (10-C)

arrivée *f.* arrival (8)

arriver to arrive (1); to happen (7)

art *m.* art (8)

~ **moderne** modern art (2)

article *m.* (newspaper) article (15)

~ **défini** definite article

~**s de sport** *m. pl.* sporting goods (12)

artiste *m., f.* artist (2)

ascenseur *m.* elevator (17-L)

Asie *f.* Asia (4)

asperge *f.* asparagus (9)

asservissement *m.* subjugation (16-L)

assez rather (18)
  ~ de enough (3)
  j'en ai ~! I've had it! (17-C)
assiette *f.* plate (9-C)
assis(e) sitting
assistant numérique personnel *m.* personal digital assistant
assister (à) to attend (2-L); to witness
association *f.* association
assurance *f.* insurance
  ~ tous risques full collision insurance (10)
atout *m.* advantage (6-L)
s'attabler to sit down at the table (17-L)
attacher to fasten
atteinte *f.* affront (15)
attendre to wait, to wait for (6)
attention *f.* attention
  faire ~ to pay attention (5)
attirer to attract
attribuer to attribute
au *voir* à
aube *f.* dawn (5-L)
aucun(e) no, not any
au-delà beyond (6-L)
audiovisuel(le) audiovisual (11-L)
augmenter to increase (17)
aujourd'hui today (4)
auprès with
ausculter to examine (13-C)
aussi also, too (2)
  ~... que as . . . as (18)
aussitôt que as soon as (17)
autant as much, as many (18)
auteur *m.* author (2)
  ~ dramatique playwright (15)
auto *f.* car (6)
autobus *m.* bus (1)
autocar *m.* intercity bus (6)
auto-école *f.* driving school (10-C)
automatique automatic (10)
automne *m.* fall (9)
autour around
autre other (4)
  ~ chose something else (12)
Autriche *f.* Austria (4)
avance *f.* advance
  d'~ ahead (14)
  en ~ early (6)
avant before (6)
avec with (1)

avenir *m.* future (11)
  à l'~ in the future
aveugle blind (12-L)
avion *m.* airplane (6)
avocat(e) *m., f.* lawyer (2)
avoir to have (3)
  ~... an(s) to be . . . year(s) old (3)
  ~ hâte to be eager
  ~... (degrees) to have a temperature of . . . (14-C)
avouer to declare (10-L); to admit (18-L)
avril *m.* April (9)

B

baba *m.* hippie (8-L)
bac *abrév. de* **baccalauréat**
baccalauréat *m.* exam at the end of high school
bachot *abrév. de* **baccalauréat**
bagages *m. pl.* luggage (5)
  ~ à main hand luggage (5)
  faire les ~ to pack (5)
bagnole *f. (fam.)* car (18-C)
baigné(e) bathed (17-L)
baignoire *f.* bathtub (16)
baiser *m.* kiss (8)
baisse *f.* decrease (10-L)
bal *m.* dance
balayer to sweep
balcon *m.* balcony (4-L)
ballet *m.* ballet (15)
ballon *m.* ball
  ~ rond soccer (11-L)
banane *f.* banana (9)
bande dessinée *f.* comic strip (16-C)
banlieue *f.* suburb (14-L)
banque *f.* bank (4)
banquette *f.* seat (6)
bas(se) low
base-ball *m.* baseball (14)
basket-ball *m.* basketball (14)
basque *m.* Basque language
bateau *m. (pl. -eaux)* boat (6)
bâtiment *m.* building
bavardage *m.* gossip
beau (bel, belle, beaux, belles) handsome, beautiful, nice (9)
  faire ~ to be nice (weather) (5)
beau-père *m. (pl.* **beaux-pères**) stepfather, father-in-law (2)

beaucoup much, many, a lot of (1)
beauté *f.* beauty (15)
beige beige (6)
Belgique *f.* Belgium (4)
belle *voir* **beau**
belle-mère *f. (pl.* **belles-mères**) stepmother, mother-in-law (2)
ben *(fam.)* uh (18-C)
berger *m.* shepherd (9-L)
besoin *m.* need
  avoir ~ (de) to need (10)
bêtise *f.* dumb thing (14)
Beur *(fam.)* child of Arab immigrants
beurre *m.* butter (3)
bibliothèque *f.* library (4)
bicyclette *f.* bicycle (6)
bidule *m. (fam.)* thingamajig (11-C)
bien *m.* good
bien well (P); nice (2)
  ~ entendu of course
  ~ sûr of course (5)
bientôt soon (8)
  à ~ see you soon (P)
bière *f.* beer (3)
bifteck *m.* steak (9)
bijouterie *f.* jewelry store (12)
billet *m.* ticket (6)
  ~ de banque bank note (12-C)
biologie *f.* biology (8)
biotechnologie *f.* biotechnology (17)
bise *f.* kiss (8)
  faire une ~ à to kiss *(someone)* (P)
  grosses ~s hugs and kisses (8)
bistrot *m.* café, restaurant (3)
blanc(he) white (3)
blessé(e) *m., f.* injured person
bleu(e) blue (5)
bœuf *m.* beef (9)
boire to drink (12)
  je, tu bois I, you drink (3)
  vous buvez you drink (3)
bois *m.* wood
  en ~ wooden
boisson *f.* drink (3)
boîte *f.* club (2)
  ~ de nuit nightclub (2)
bon(ne) good (5)
  ~ marché cheap (12-C)
  faire ~ to be nice *(temperature)* (8)

bonbon *m.* candy (9)

bonheur *m.* happiness (11)

bonjour good morning, hello (P); *(in Quebec)* bye (1-C)

bonne nuit goodnight (1-C)

bonsoir good evening, good night, hello (P)

bord *m.* edge, shore (12-L)

  à ~ de aboard (4-L)

  au ~ de along, by (4)

  ~ de la mer seaside (4)

bordée de neige *f.* heavy snowfall (17-L)

botte *f.* boot (5)

bottin *m.* phone book (7-C)

bouche *f.* mouth (13)

boucher (-ère) *m., f.* butcher (12)

boucherie *f.* butcher shop (12)

bouffer *(fam.)* to eat (18-C)

boulanger (-ère) *m., f.* baker (12)

boulangerie *f.* bakery (12)

boules *f. pl.*

  partie de ~ bowling game

bouleverser to upset, to change dramatically (6-L)

boulot *m. (fam.)* job (18-C)

bourgeois(e) bourgeois, middle-class (15)

Bourgogne *f.* Burgundy

bout *m.* end (6)

bouteille *f.* bottle (3-C; 12)

boutique *f.* shop (12)

branche *f.* branch (18)

branché(e) *(fam.)* cool, hip (8-L)

brancher to plug in, to connect (7)

bras *m.* arm (13)

brasserie *f.* café-restaurant (12)

Brésil *m.* Brazil (4)

breton *m.* Breton language

brillamment brilliantly (18)

brillant(e) brilliant, shiny (18)

britannique British

bronze *m.* bronze (15)

se brosser to brush (13)

brouillard *m.*

  faire du ~ to be foggy (8)

bruit *m.* noise (11)

  faire du ~ to make noise (11)

brûlé(e) burned

brûler un feu to run a red light (10-C)

brun(e) brown (5)

Bruxelles Brussels (4)

bulle *f.* bubble (15-L)

bulletin météorologique *m.* weather report

buraliste *m.* tobacconist (12)

bureau *m. (pl. -eaux)* desk, office (1)

  ~ de change currency exchange (12-C)

  ~ de poste post office (4)

  ~ des objets trouvés lost and found (6)

  ~ de tabac tobacco shop (7)

but *m.* purpose (7-L)

C

ça that, it (9)

cabine *f.* booth (8-C)

  ~ téléphonique phone booth (7)

câble *m.* cable (11)

cadeau *m. (pl. -eaux)* gift (1)

cadre *m.* middle manager; framework (11)

café *m.* café (1); coffee (3)

  ~ au lait *m.* coffee with milk (9-C)

cahier *m.* notebook (1)

caisse *f.* cashier's (9-C; 12)

calculatrice *f.* calculator (7)

calculer to calculate

calèche *f.* horse-drawn carriage (17-L)

calendrier *m.* calendar (9)

camarade *m., f.* friend (2)

  ~ de chambre roommate (2)

  ~ de cours classmate (2)

caméscope *m.* camcorder

camion *m.* truck (6)

campagne *f.* country (8); campaign

campus *m.* campus

Canada *m.* Canada (4)

canadien(ne) Canadian (2)

canapé *m.* sofa (16)

canard *m.* duck (18)

capitale *f.* capital (6-L; 8)

car for (18-L)

caractère *m.* nature

Caraïbes *f. pl.* Caribbean

carence *f.* deficiency, shortcoming (16-L)

carnet *m.* book (of tickets) (6)

carotte *f.* carrot (9)

  ~s râpées grated carrots (9)

carré(e) square (4-L)

carrefour *m.* crossroad(s) (5-L)

carrière *f.* career

carte *f.* map (1); menu (3); card (14)

  ~ de crédit credit card (10)

  ~ des vins wine list (9-C)

  ~ orange orange card (6)

  ~ postale postcard (8)

cas *m.* case

casino *m.* casino (4)

casser to break

  ~ la croûte *(fam.)* to have a snack (17-L)

  se ~ le (la, les)... to break one's . . . (13-C)

  tu me casses les pieds! you really annoy me! (17-C)

cassette *f.* cassette (7)

catalan *m.* Catalan language

catch *m.* wrestling (14)

cause *f.*

  à ~ de because of

CD *m.* CD (7)

ce this, that, it (1)

  ~ qui, que what

  ~ sont they are (1)

  c'est it is (1)

  c'est à qui? whose turn is it? (6)

  c'est-à-dire that is

ce (cet, cette) this, that (7)

cédille *f.* cedilla

ceinture *f.* belt (5)

  ~ de sécurité seat belt (10)

cela this, that, it (1)

célèbre famous (5-L)

celui (celle) the one; this (that) one; that (14)

censure *f.* censorship

cent hundred (4)

centimètre (cm) *m.* centimeter (14-C)

centre *m.* center

  ~ commercial *m.* shopping center (4)

centre-ville *m.* downtown (12)

cependant however

cerise *f.* cherry (9)

certain(e) certain, some (2)

certainement certainly (18)

certes admittedly, to be sure (16-L)

ces these, those (7)

cesser (de) to stop (15)

cet *voir* ce

ceux (celles) these, those; the ones (14)

chacal *m.* jackal (18)

chacun(e) each one (12-L)

chaîne *f.* channel, station (11)

~ **câblée** cable station (11)

chaise *f.* chair (1)

chaleur *f.* heat (8)

chambre *f.* bedroom (4)

~ **de bonne** maid's bedroom (16)

champ *m.* field (4-L)

champagne *m.* champagne

champion(ne) *m., f.* champion (14)

championnat *m.* championship (14)

chance *f.* luck (6)

quelle ~! how lucky! (6)

changement *m.* change

~ **d'avis** change of mind

changer (de) to change (6)

chanson *f.* song (10)

chanter to sing (1)

chapeau *m. (pl.* -eaux) hat (5)

chapitre *m.* chapter

chaque each

charcuterie *f.* cold cuts (9-C); pork butcher's shop (12)

charcutier (-ère) *m., f.* pork butcher (12)

se charger to be responsible

charges *f. pl.* utilities (16)

charmant(e) charming (2)

chasse *f.* hunting (14)

chassé(e) de forced out of

chat *m.* cat (18)

chaud(e) hot (2)

avoir ~ to be hot (3)

faire ~ to be warm *(weather)* (5)

il fait ~ it's hot (1-C)

chauffard *m.* reckless driver (10-C)

chauffeur *m.* driver (10)

chaussette *f.* sock (5)

chaussure *f.* shoe (5)

chef *m.*

~ **d'Etat** *m.* head of state

~ **d'orchestre** *m.* conductor (15)

chemin *m.* path, way (9-L)

chemise *f.* shirt (5)

~ **de nuit** nightgown (5)

chemisier *m.* blouse (5)

chèque de voyage *m.* traveler's check (12-C)

cher (-ère) dear (8); expensive (4)

chercher to look for (4)

~ **à** to try (15)

cheval *m. (pl.* -aux) horse (18)

à ~ on horseback (6)

cheveux *m. pl.* hair (13)

cheville *f.* ankle (13)

chez at the house of (4)

chien *m.* dog (18)

chimie *f.* chemistry (8)

Chine *f.* China (4)

chinois(e) Chinese (8)

chocolat *m.* chocolate (3)

choisir (de) to choose (7)

choix *m.* choice

chômage *m.* unemployment (11)

chose *f.* thing (11)

choucroute garnie *f.* sauerkraut and assorted meat (12)

chouette alors! great! (17-C)

ci-dessous below

ci-dessus above (17-L)

ciel *m.* sky (8)

cinéma *m.* cinema, movie theater (4)

cinq five (1)

cinquante fifty (2)

cinquième fifth (2)

circulation *f.* traffic (10)

cité *f.* high-rise project (14-L)

classe *f.* classroom (1)

classique classical (2)

clavier *m.* keyboard (8)

clé *f.* key (1)

client(e) *m., f.* customer (12-C)

clip *m.* music video (11-L)

club *m.* club *(association)* (2)

coca *m.* Coca-Cola (3)

cochon *m.* pig (18)

code *m.* code

~ **de la route** *m.* traffic regulations (10-C)

~ **postal** *m.* zip code (2-L)

cœur *m.* heart

coffre *m.* trunk (10)

coin *m.* corner, area (9)

au ~ **de** at the corner of (4)

colère *f.* anger (17-C)

colis *m.* package (8)

collège *m.* junior high (9-L)

colline *f.* hill

colonne *f.* column (17)

combien how many, how much (1)

c'est ~? how much is it? (5-C)

~ **de** how many, how much (6)

~ **de temps?** how long?

~ **font... ?** how much is . . . ? (1)

comédie *f.* comedy (15)

~ **musicale** musical (15)

comédien(ne) *m., f.* actor (11-L)

commande *f.* order (12)

commander to order (3)

comme as, like (3); how (9); as well as (11-L)

~ **ci,** ~ **ça** so-so (P)

tout ~ like (9)

commencer (à) to begin (to) (1)

comment how (1-L)

~? what? (17-C)

~ **dit-on... ?** how do you say . . . ? (1)

~ **est-il?** what is it like? (6)

commerçant(e) *m., f.* shopkeeper (12)

commissariat *m.* police station (11-L)

communication *f.* phone call (7-C)

communiquer to communicate

compagnie de location *f.* rental agency (10)

compétent(e) competent (2)

complet (-ète) complete, full (18)

complètement completely (18)

compliqué(e) complicated (2)

composer to make up

~ **un numéro de téléphone** to dial a number (7-C)

comprendre to understand (9)

compris(e) included (16)

compte en banque *m.* bank account (11)

compter to plan on (10-C); to count

concert *m.* concert (6)

concevoir to devise, to conceive, to intend (4-L)

concierge *m., f.* concierge, caretaker (16)

concombre *m.* cucumber (9)

concurrence *f.* competition (6-L)

conduire to drive (10; 14)

se ~ to behave (14)

confection *f.* clothing industry (15-L)

confier to entrust, to place in the care (15-L)

confiture *f.* jam (3)

conflit *m.* conflict

confort *m.* comfort

connaissance *f.* acquaintance (1-C; 2); knowledge

  faire la ~ de to meet (2-C)

connaître to know (4-L; 10)

consacré(e) devoted (15)

consacrer to devote

conseil *m.* piece of advice (11)

conseiller to advise (12)

conserver to keep, to preserve

conserves *f. pl.* canned foods (12)

consommer to consume (3)

constituer to form

construit(e) built (4-L)

consulter to consult (11)

contact *m.* contact (17)

conte *m.* tale (14)

contemporain(e) contemporary (11)

contenir to include, to contain (10)

content(e) happy (2)

continent *m.* continent (4)

continuer (à) to continue (1)

contravention *f.* traffic ticket

contre against

contrefaçon *f.* counterfeiting (12-L)

contribuer (à) to contribute (15)

contrôle *m.* test (14)

  ~ anti-doping drug test (14)

contrôler to control

convaincre to convince (15-L)

convenir to be suited (5-L); to be fitting, important (16-L)

convenu

  c'est ~ all right (9-C)

conversation *f.* conversation (1-C)

convertir to convert

copain *m.* friend *(male)* (2)

copine *f.* friend *(female)* (2)

coq *m.* rooster (18)

cordialement cordially (15-C)

cordonnier *m.* cobbler, shoe repair (17-L)

corps *m.* body (13)

correct(e) correct (15)

correspondance *f.* connection (6)

corriger to correct

Corse *f.* Corsica (4)

corse *m.* Corsican language

costume *m.* suit (5)

Côte d'Azur *f.* French Riviera (4)

Côte d'Ivoire *f.* Côte d'Ivoire (4)

côté *m.* side; aspect

  à ~ de next to (4)

côtelette *f.* chop (9)

cou *m.* neck (13)

se coucher to go to bed (13)

coude *m.* elbow (13)

couleur *f.* color (5)

coup d'œil *m.* glance

  jeter un ~ to take a quick look (15-L)

coupable guilty

couper to cut (3-L); to hang up, to disconnect (7)

courageux (-euse) courageous (2)

courant(-e) widespread

courir to run (18)

couronné(e) crowned

couronnement *m.* crowning (9-L)

courrier *m.* mail (8)

  ~ du cœur advice column (16-C)

  ~ électronique e-mail (8)

cours *m.* class, course (1)

  en ~ in class (1)

course *f.* errand (5); race (14)

  ~ de bicyclettes bicycle race (14)

  ~ de voitures car race (14)

  faire des ~s to shop (5)

court(e) short

couscous *m.* couscous (3)

cousin(e) *m., f.* cousin (2)

coût *m.* cost (3-L)

couteau *m.* (*pl.* -eaux) knife (9-C)

coûter to cost (5)

  ~... le kilo to cost . . . a kilo (14-C)

couvert *m.* table setting (9-C)

  mettre le ~ to set the table (9-C)

couvert(e) overcast (8)

  le ciel est ~ it's cloudy (8)

craie *f.* chalk (1)

craindre to fear, to be afraid of (14-L)

cravate *f.* tie (5)

crayon *m.* pencil (1)

créer to create (7-L; 17)

crème *f.* cream (3)

crémerie *f.* dairy store (12)

créole *m.* Creole (5)

crêpe *f.* crepe (5)

crevette *f.* shrimp (9)

criminalité *f.* crime (11)

crise *f.* crisis

  ~ de foie liver attack (13-C)

  ~ économique economic crisis (12-L)

critère *m.* criterion

critique critical

critiquer to critique (15)

croire to believe (14-C)

croisière *f.* cruise (4-L)

croissance *f.* growth

croix verte *f.* green cross (drug store sign) (13)

croquer une bouchée (sur le pouce) *(fam.)* to have a (quick) bite (17-L)

crudités *f. pl.* raw vegetables (9)

cuillère *f.* spoon (9-C)

  petite ~ teaspoon (9-C)

cuisine *f.* cooking, cuisine (3); kitchen (16)

  faire la ~ to cook (5)

cuisinier (-ère) *m., f.* chef, cook

cuisinière *f.* stove (16)

cuisse *f.* thigh (13)

cuisson *f.* cooking (3-L)

cure *f.*

  faire une ~ to go to a health spa (13-C)

curiste *m., f.* person going to a health spa (13-C)

D

d'abord *voir* abord

d'accord *voir* accord

dame *f.* lady (8)

Danemark *m.* Denmark (4)

dangereux (-euse) dangerous (2)

dans in (3); in *(time)* (16)

danse classique *f.* ballet (15)

danser to dance (1)

danseur (-euse) *m., f.* dancer (15)

d'après according to (12-L)

date *f.* date (9)

d'autant plus all the more (17-L)

davantage more (13)

de of, from, about (1); any (3); *contraction avec* le, les: du, des (3)

  ~ la (l') some (3)

début *m.* beginning (6)
décalage horaire *m.* time difference
décembre *m.* December (9)
déception *f.* disappointment (17-C)
décès *m.* death (13-L)
décider (de) to decide (to) (6)
déclarer to declare
découverte *f.* discovery
découvrir to discover
décrire to describe (3-L; 14)
décrocher to pick up (the phone) (7-C)
déçu(e) disappointed (17-C)
dedans inside
défaut *m.* fault
défendre to forbid (15)
défense *f.* prohibition (10-C)
déferler to unfold (14-L)
degré *m.* degree (14-C)
dégueulasse *(fam.)* disgusting (18-C)
déjà already (5)
déjeuner to have lunch (3)
déjeuner *m.* lunch (9)
délicieux (-euse) delicious (3)
délinquance *f.* delinquency (11)
délivré(e) freed (17)
deltaplane *m.* hang gliding (14)
demain tomorrow (4)
  à ~ see you tomorrow (1-C)
  ~ matin tomorrow morning (4)
  ~ soir tomorrow evening, tomorrow night (4)
demande *f.* request
demander (à) to ask for (1)
  ~ son chemin to ask for directions (4-C)
démarche *f.* step (13-L)
démarrer to start (car) (10)
demi(e) half (6)
démolir to demolish
déneiger to remove the snow from (17-L)
dent *f.* tooth (13)
dentiste *m., f.* dentist (13)
département *m.* administrative division of France (5)
se dépêcher (de) to hurry (13)
dépense *f.* spending
dépenser to spend (8)
depuis since, for (6)
dernier (-ère) last (5)
  le ~ the latest (2)

derrière behind (4)
des *voir* de; some (3)
dès from . . . on, as of (13-L; 16)
  ~ que as soon as (17)
désagréable unpleasant (2)
désastre *m.* disaster (11)
descendre to get off, to go down, to come down (6)
description *f.* description
se déshabiller to undress (13)
désirer to desire, to wish (2)
désobéir to disobey (7)
désolé(e) sorry (7)
désormais henceforth (6-L)
dessin animé *m.* cartoon (11)
dessinateur (-trice) *m., f.* cartoonist (15-L)
destruction *f.* destruction (15)
se détendre to relax (13)
détente *f.* relaxation
détester to hate (2)
  ~ faire to hate doing (2)
détresse *f.* distress
deux two (1)
deuxième second (2)
devant in front of (2)
développement *m.* development
développer to develop
devenir to become (10)
  qu'est-ce que tu deviens? what are you up to? (1-C)
deviens *voir* devenir
deviner to guess
devise *f.* motto (9-L)
devoir to have to, to owe (12)
devoir *m.* duty
  ~s homework (1)
  ~s écrits written work (8)
  faire ses ~s to do one's homework (5)
dialogue *m.* dialogue (1)
Dieu *m.* God (18)
différent(e) different (9)
difficile difficult (2)
diffuser to broadcast (13-L)
diffusion *f.* broadcast
dimanche *m.* Sunday (9)
diminuer to decrease, to diminish (17)
dîner to have dinner (3)
dîner *m.* dinner (9)
dingue *(fam.)* nuts (18-C)
diplomate *m.* diplomat (2)
diplôme *m.* degree

dire to tell, to say (14)
  cela veut ~ it means (1)
  ce qu'ils disent what people say
  on dit you say (1)
  pourriez-vous me ~... (1)? could you tell me . . . ? (4-C)
  qu'est-ce que... veut ~? what does . . . mean? (1)
directement directly
dirigeant(e) *m., f.* leader (18-L)
diriger to direct, to manage (4-L)
dis donc! say! (1-C)
discours *m.* speech
discrimination *f.* discrimination
discuter to have a chat; to discuss (11)
disent *voir* dire
disparaître to disappear
disparition *f.* disappearance
se disperser to scatter (17)
disposer de to have at one's disposal (10-L)
disquette *f.* diskette (8)
distance *f.* distance
distingué(e) distinguished (15-C)
distinguer to distinguish
distraction *f.* entertainment (2)
dit *voir* dire
divan *m.* sofa (16)
divisé(e) divided (1)
diviser to divide (14-C)
divorce *m.* divorce
dix ten (1)
dix-huit eighteen (1)
dix-neuf nineteen (1)
dix-sept seventeen (1)
dix-septième seventeenth (2)
doigt *m.* finger (13)
DOM (départements d'outre-mer) *m. pl.* overseas regions of France
domaine *m.* area
dommage *m.* damage, harm (11)
  il est ~ (que) it's too bad (that) (11)
  quel ~! what a shame! (17-C)
don *m.* gift, talent (15-L)
donc therefore (15)
donner to give (1)
  ~ sur to look out on (16)
  ~ un coup de téléphone to make a phone call (8-C)
dont whose, which (5-L)
dormir to sleep (7)

dos *m.* back (13)
douane *f.* customs
doubler to pass *(in traffic)* (10-C)
douche *f.* shower (16)
douter to doubt (11)
doux (douce) gentle
douzaine dozen
douze twelve (1)
doyen *m.* dean
drame *m.* drama (15)
drapeau *m.* flag (4-L)
drogue *f.* illegal drug (11)
droit *m.* law (1-L)
 tout droit straight ahead (4-C)
 à ~e right, to the right (4-C)
du *voir* de
durer to last (4-L)

E

eau *f.* water (3)
 ~ minérale *f.* mineral water (3)
 ~ naturelle *f.* tap water
échanger to exchange
échapper to escape
écharpe *f.* scarf (5)
échelle *f.* scale, size (10-L)
échouer (à) to fail (15)
éclair *m.* lightning (6-L)
éclairage *m.* lighting (17-L)
éclater to break, to explode
école *f.* school (3)
 ~ secondaire *f.* high school (3)
écologie *f.* ecology (17)
écologique ecological (11)
écologiste *m., f.* ecologist (17)
économies *f. pl.*
 faire des ~ to save money (8)
économique economical
économiser to save (12-C)
économiste *m., f.* economist (2)
écorce *f.* bark (17)
écouter to listen (1)
écran *m.* screen (10-L)
écrevisse *f.* crayfish
écrire (à) to write (to) (14)
écrit(e) written (8)
écrivain(e) *m., f.* writer (2)
éditorial *m.* editorial (16-C)
éducation *f.* upbringing;
 education
 ~ physique *f.* physical
 education (8)

éduquer to educate
effet *m.* consequence, result
égal(e)
 ça m'est ~ I don't care (17-C)
également also
égalité *f.* equality (11)
église *f.* church (2-L; 4)
eh ben *(fam.)* so (18-C)
eh bien well then (1)
électronique electronic (11-C)
élève *m., f.* pupil (3)
élevé(e) high
éliminer to eliminate
élision *f.* elision (18-C)
elle she, it (1); her (5)
elles they (1); them (5)
élu(e) elected
embêter to bother (11)
embouteillage *m.* traffic jam (10)
embrasser to kiss (2)
émission *f.* program, show (11)
emmener to take (someone) (13)
empêcher (de) to prevent (17-L)
emplacement *m.* location (10-L)
emploi *m.* job (11)
 ~ du temps schedule
employé(e) *m., f.* employee, clerk
 (6)
employer to use
emporter to take (5)
emprunter to borrow (8)
en to, in (4); some, any (11-C;
 15); of it (15); in *(time)* (16)
enchanté(e) delighted (2)
encombrement *m.* congestion,
 obstruction (10-L)
encore still, again (6); more (9-C)
 ne... pas ~ not yet (8)
s'endormir to fall asleep (13)
endroit *m.* place (4)
énergie *f.* energy (17)
enfance *f.* childhood
enfant *m., f.* child (1)
enfin at last, finally (16)
 m'~ *(fam.)* well (18-C)
engagement *m.* commitment
engin *m. (fam.)* thingamajig
 (11-C)
enlever to remove (3-L; 13)
enneigé(e) snow-covered (17-L)
ennuyeux (-euse) boring (2)
enquête *f.* survey (13-L)
enquêter to investigate (11-L)
enrichissement *m.* improvement

enseignement *m.* teaching, education (15)
enseigner to teach (15)
ensemble together (1)
ensuite then (4-C)
entendre to hear (6)
entier (-ère) whole
entre between (4)
 ~ autres among other things
 (17-L)
entrée *f.* entrance, hall (16)
entreprise *f.* company
entrer (à, dans) to enter, to go in
 (2)
entretenir to maintain (10-C)
enveloppe *f.* envelope (8)
envie *f.* wish, desire (9-L)
 avoir ~ de to feel like (11)
environ about (13-L)
environnement *m.* environment
 (17)
envoyer to send (8-C)
s'épanouir to flourish
épargner to save
épaule *f.* shoulder (13)
éphémère short-lived
épice *m.* spice
épicé(e) spicy (3-L)
épicerie *f.* grocery store (12)
épicier (-ère) *m., f.* grocer (12)
épier to watch, to spy on
épinards *m. pl.* spinach (9)
époque *f.* era
épris(e) enamored (16-L)
équipe *f.* team (14)
équitation *f.* horseback riding
 (14)
erreur *f.* mistake, wrong number
 (7)
escalope *f.* cutlet (9)
esclave *m., f.* slave
espace *m.* space (17)
 ~ vert *m.* park
Espagne *f.* Spain (4)
espagnol(e) Spanish (2)
espérer to hope (9)
espoir *m.* hope
esprit *m.* mind, spirit (14-L)
essayer (de) to try (12)
essence *f.* gas (10-C)
essentiel(le) essential
est *m.* east (4-C)
est-ce que... ? *question phrase* (1)
estimer to believe, to think

et and (P)
établi(e) established
étage *m.* floor (16)
étagère *f.* shelf (16)
étape *f.* stage; leg (of a journey) (6-L)
état *m.* condition, state (10-L)
  ~ de fait *m.* state of affairs (18-L)
Etats-Unis *m. pl.* United States (4)
été *m.* summer (5)
éteindre to turn off (7-L)
éternuer to sneeze
éthylotest *m.* blood-alcohol test (10-C)
étoile *f.* star (4-L)
étonné(e) amazed (11)
étonnement *m.* surprise (17-C)
s'étonner to be astonished, to wonder (15-L)
étranger (-ère) *m., f.* foreigner (8-L; 10)
étranger (-ère) foreign (8)
être to be (2)
  ça y est that's it (5)
  ~ à to belong to (5)
  ~ à... km de to be ... (kilometers) from (14-C)
étudiant(e) *m., f.* student (1)
étudier to study (1)
euh uh (18-C)
euro *m.* euro (12)
Europe *f.* Europe (4)
européen(ne) European (10)
eux they, them (5)
s'évader to get away, to escape
événement *m.* event (8-L)
évidemment obviously (18)
évident(e) obvious (11)
évier *m.* kitchen sink (16)
éviter (de) to avoid (11)
évoquer to evoke (17)
exactement exactly (8)
examen *m.* exam (1)
examiner to examine (13)
excusez-moi pardon me (1-C)
exemplaire *m.* unit
exemple *m.* example
  par ~ for example
exercice *m.* exercise (1)
  faire de l'~ to exercise (13)
exister to exist
expédier to mail (8)
expérience *f.* experience

expérimenter to try
expliquer to explain (1)
explorateur *m.* explorer
exprimer to express (14-C)
  s'~ to express oneself
extérieur(e) outside
  à l'~ outside (5)
extrait *m.* excerpt (15)
extrême extreme

F

fabriquer to manufacture
fac *abrév. de* **faculté**
face *f.* side (12-L)
  en ~ de across from (4)
fâché(e) angry (17-C)
se fâcher to get angry
facile easy (2)
facilement easily (18)
façon *f.* way
facteur *m.* mail carrier (8)
faculté *f.* university, school (1)
faim *f.*
  avoir ~ to be hungry (3)
faire to do, to make (4-L; 5)
  ~... mètres to be ... meters tall (14-C)
  ~... degrés to be ... degrees *(weather)* (14-C)
  ~ du, de la, de l', des to study (8); to play *(sport)* (14)
  ~ du... kilomètres à l'heure to go ... kilometers per hour (10-C)
  ~ du... aux 100 kilomètres to use ... *(liters of gas)* per 100 kilometers (14-C)
  faites... ! do ... ! (1)
fait *m.* fact (6-L)
faites *voir* **faire**
faits divers *m. pl.* human interest stories (16-C)
falloir must (12)
  il faut it's necessary (3-L; 4)
fallu *participe passé de* **falloir**
familier (-ère) colloquial (18-C)
famille *f.* family (2)
  en ~ as a family; at home
fantastique fantastic (2)
farine *f.* flour (3)
fascinant(e) fascinating (2)
fatigué(e) tired (2)

faut *voir* **falloir**
faute *f.* mistake (15)
fauteuil *m.* armchair (16)
faux (fausse) false (11)
  ~ ami *m.* false cognate
favori(te) favorite (2)
fédération *f.* federation
féminin(e) feminine (2)
femme *f.* woman (1); wife (2)
fenêtre *f.* window (1)
fermé(e) closed (2)
fermer to shut, to close (1)
  ne pas ~ l'œil not to sleep a wink (13)
ferroviaire relating to the railroad (6-L)
festival *m.* festival
fête *f.* holiday (9)
  ~ des Mères Mother's Day
  ~ du Travail Labor Day (9)
  ~ nationale Independence Day (9)
feu rouge *m.* red light
feuille *f.* leaf (17)
  ~ de laurier bay leaf (3-L)
feuilleton *m.* series (11)
février *m.* February (9)
ficher
  fiche-moi la paix! leave me alone! (17-C)
  je m'en fiche! I don't care! (17-C)
fiction *f.* television drama (11-L)
fier (-ère) proud (4-L)
fièvre *f.* fever (13)
figure *f.* face (18-L)
fil *m.* thread (12-L)
  au bout du ~ on the line (15-L)
filet *m.* filet (9)
fille *f.* girl, daughter (2)
film *m.* film (2)
fils *m.* son (2)
fin *f.* end
  en ~ de at the end of
finalement finally
financier (-ère) financial
fini(e) finished
finir (de) to finish (7)
Finlande *f.* Finland (4)
fixer to fasten
flâner to stroll (8-L)
fléau *m.* scourge (13-L)
fleur *f.* flower (9-C; 17)
fleuriste *m., f.* florist (12)

fleuve *m.* river (5-L)
flic *m. (fam.)* cop (11-L)
flotte *f. (fam.)* water (18-C)
flûte *f.* flute (15)
fois *f.* time
  une ~ once
fond *m.*
  au ~ in the back (5-C); at the bottom
fonder to found (5-L)
fondue *f.* cheese fondue
football *m.* soccer (2)
  ~ américain football (14)
forêt *f.* forest (17)
forme *f.* form
  en ~ in shape
former to train (13-L); to make up
formidable sensational, terrific (2)
fort strongly
fortuitement accidentally, by chance (11-L)
fou (folle) crazy
fougère *f.* fern (4-L)
se fouler le (la)... to sprain one's . . . (13-C)
four *m.* oven (16)
  ~ à micro-ondes microwave oven (16)
fourchette *f.* fork (9-C)
fournir to provide (7-L)
frais *m.* cost (10)
frais (-aîche) cool (4-L)
  faire ~ to be cool (8)
fraise *f.* strawberry (9)
français(e) French (1)
  en ~ in French (1)
Français(e) *m., f.* French person (2)
France *f.* France (4)
franchise *f.* frankness (11)
francophone French-speaking (5-L)
francophonie *f.* French-speaking communities (5-L)
frein *m.* brake (10)
freiner to brake (10)
fréquemment frequently (18)
fréquent(e) frequent (18)
fréquenter to go to, to go out with (2)
frère *m.* brother (2)

fric *m. (fam.)* money (18-C)
frigidaire *m.* refrigerator (16)
frites *f. pl.* French fries (3)
froid *m.* cold
  ~ mordant biting cold (17-L)
froid(e) cold (2)
  avoir ~ to be cold (3)
  faire ~ to be cold *(weather)* (5)
  il fait ~ it's cold (1-C)
fromage *m.* cheese (3)
frontière *f.* border
fruit *m.* fruit (3)
  ~s de mer shellfish (9)
fumer to smoke (1)
furieux (-euse) furious (11)
futur *m.* future (17)

G

gagnant *m.* winner
gagner to earn (8); to win (14); to reach (17-L)
galet *m.* smooth stone (4)
gant *m.* glove (5)
garagiste *m.* mechanic (10-C)
garantie *f.* guarantee
garçon *m.* boy (2); waiter (3)
garde-fou *m.* safeguard (14-L)
garder to keep
gare *f.* train station (4)
garer to park (2)
gaspiller to waste (10-L)
gastronomie *f.* gastronomy
gâteau *m. (pl. -eaux)* cake (3)
gauche
  à ~ on the left (4-C; 16)
gel *m.* frost (17)
geler to freeze
gendarme *m.* policeman (10)
général(e) *(pl. -aux, -ales)* general (18)
  en ~ in general (1)
généralement generally (13)
génération *f.* generation
généreux (-euse) generous (2)
Genève Geneva (4)
genou *m. (pl. -oux)* knee (13)
gens *m. pl.* people (10)
gentil(le) nice
géographie *f.* geography (8)
géologie *f.* geology (8)
gérant(e) *m., f.* manager (8-L)

gestion *f.* management (1-L)
gigot *m.* leg of lamb (9)
glace *f.* ice cream (3)
glissant(e) slippery (10-C)
gloire *f.* glory
godasse *f. (fam.)* shoe (18-C)
golf *m.* golf (14)
gorge *f.* throat (13)
gosse *m. (fam.)* child (18-C)
goût *m.* taste (3-L)
goûter to taste, to have an afternoon snack (3)
grâce à thanks to (11-L)
gramme *m.* gram (12)
grand(e) large, big, tall (9)
  ~es vacances summer vacation (10)
  ~ magasin department store (11)
grand-chose
  pas ~! not much! (5-C)
  ce n'est pas ~ it's no big deal (17-C)
Grande-Bretagne *f.* Great Britain (4)
grandir to grow up
grand-mère *f. (pl. grands-mères)* grandmother (2)
grand-père *m. (pl. grands-pères)* grandfather (2)
grands-parents *m. pl.* grandparents (2)
gratte-ciel *m.* skyscraper (17-L)
gratuitement for free (7-L)
grave serious (13)
  ce n'est pas ~ it's not serious (17-C)
grec (grecque) Greek (8)
Grèce *f.* Greece (4)
grippe *f.* flu (13-C)
gris(e) gray (5)
grogner to growl (15-L)
gros(se) large, big (6)
  ~ titre *m.* headline (16-C)
gruyère *m.* Swiss cheese
guerre *f.* war
  ~ mondiale world war
  ~ nucléaire nuclear war (11)
guillemets *m. pl.* quotation marks
guitare *f.* guitar (15)
Guyane *f.* French Guiana
gymnastique *f.* gymnastics (14)

H

s'habiller to get dressed (13)
habitable livable (17)
habiter to live (1)
habitude *f.* habit, custom (10)
***hacher** to chop (3-L)
***hamburger** *m.* hamburger (3)
***haricot vert** *m.* green bean (9)
***se hâter** to hurry (17-L)
***haut(e)** high
  en ~ at the top of
Havane (La) *f.* Havana (4)
hebdomadaire *m.* weekly publication (15-L)
héritier (-ère) *m., f.* heir (9-L)
hésiter (à) to hesitate (15)
heure *f.* hour, time (6)
  à l'~ on time (6)
  à quelle ~? at what time? (1-L)
  à tout à l'~ see you later (P)
  de bonne ~ early (12)
  ~ **conventionnelle** conventional time (6-C)
  ~ **officielle** official time (6-C)
  quelle ~ est-il? what time is it? (5-C; 6)
heureusement fortunately (6)
heureux (-euse) happy (2)
hier yesterday (5)
histoire *f.* history (8); story
  ~ **de l'art** art history (8)
hiver *m.* winter (5)
***hockey** *m.* hockey (14)
***Hollande** *f.* Holland (4)
homme *m.* man (1)
  ~ **d'affaires** businessman
  ~ **politique** politician
honneur *m.* honor (15-C)
horoscope *m.* horoscope (7-L; 16-C)
***hors-d'œuvre** *m.* appetizer (3)
hôte *m.* guest
hôtel *m.* hotel (1)
hôtesse *f.* hostess (4)
huile *f.* oil (3)
***huit** eight (1)
hypermarché *m.* giant supermarket (12)
hypocondriaque hypochondriac (13)
hypocrisie *f.* hypocrisy (2)
hypocrite hypocritical (2)

I

ici here (1)
idée *f.* idea (5)
identité *f.* identity
il he, it (1)
  ~ **y a** there is, there are (3); since, ago (8-L; 16)
  ~ **y a... que** it has been . . . that (16)
île *f.* island (4-L)
ils they (1)
imaginer to imagine
imam *m.* imam (Muslim prayer leader) (18)
immédiat(e) immediate
immédiatement immediately
immeuble *m.* apartment building (16)
immigré(e) immigrant (18)
imparfait *m.* imperfect tense (10)
imper *m.* raincoat (6)
imperméable *m.* raincoat (5)
impoli(e) impolite (2)
importance *f.* importance (11)
important(e) important (11)
impossible impossible (2)
impôt *m.* tax
imprécision *f.* imprecision (11-C)
impression *f.* impression
  avoir l'~ to have a feeling
impressionnant(e) impressive (8)
imprimante *f.* printer (8)
incarner to embody (17)
incertain(e) uncertain
incertitude *f.* uncertainty (11)
inclure to include (17)
incompétent(e) incompetent (2)
inconnu(e) *m., f.* stranger (1-C)
inconnu(e) unknown
inconvénient *m.* annoyance (11)
incrédule incredulous
indépendamment independently (18)
indépendance *f.* independence
indépendant(e) independent (2)
indifférence *f.* indifference (17-C)
indiquer to indicate (4-C; 9)
  pourriez-vous m'~... ? could you show me . . . ? (4-C)
indispensable indispensable (10)
individuel(le) individual
inflation *f.* inflation (11)

influence *f.* influence
informations *f. pl.* news (14)
informatique *f.* computer science (8)
ingénieur *m.* engineer (2)
injuste unfair (11)
inoubliable unforgettable
inquiéter to worry (13)
  s'~ (de) to be worried (13); to worry (15)
inscrire
  s'~ to sign up (14-L)
inspirer to inspire
installer to install
  s'~ to settle
instant *m.* moment (7-C)
instauration *f.* establishment (18-L)
instrument *m.* instrument (15)
  ~ **de musique** musical instrument (15)
insuffisamment insufficiently (18)
insuffisant(e) insufficient (15)
insupportable unbearable (8)
intelligemment intelligently (18)
intelligent(e) intelligent (2)
interdit(e) forbidden (10-C)
intéressant(e) interesting (2)
intéresser to interest (16)
  s'~ (à) to be interested (in) (15)
international(e) international
Internet *m.* Internet
interroger to ask questions
interrompre to interrupt
interrompu(e) interrupted
interview *f.* interview (11)
intolérance *f.* intolerance (2)
inutile useless (2)
invité(e) *m., f.* guest
inviter to invite (1)
Irlande *f.* Ireland (4)
Italie *f.* Italy (4)
italien(ne) Italian (2)
ivre drunk

J

jaillir to spring (17)
jalousie *f.* jealousy
jamais never (8)
jambe *f.* leg (13)
jambon *m.* ham (3)

janvier *m.* January (9)
Japon *m.* Japan (4)
japonais(e) Japanese (8)
jardin *m.* yard, garden (17)
jaune yellow (5)
jazz *m.* jazz (2)
je, j' I (1)
jean *m.* jeans (5)
se jeter dans to flow into
jeu *m.* (*pl.* **-eux**) game
  ~ télévisé game show (11)
jeudi *m.* Thursday (9)
jeune young (9)
  ~s gens *m. pl.* young people (2)
jeunes *m. pl.* young people
jeunesse *f.* youth
jogging *m.* jogging (14)
joindre to join
  se ~ à to join forces with (4-L)
joli(e) pretty (9)
jouer to play (1)
  ~ à to play *(game, sport)* (14)
  ~ de to play *(musical instrument)* (15)
  ~ un rôle to play a part
joueur *m.* player (14)
jour *m.* day (4-L; 9)
journal *m.* (*pl.* **-aux**) newspaper;
  TV news (11)
  ~ de mode fashion magazine
  (16-C)
  ~ télévisé TV news
journalisme *m.* journalism (8)
journaliste *m., f.* journalist (2)
journée *f.* day (13)
juillet *m.* July (9)
juin *m.* June (9)
jupe *f.* skirt (5)
jus de fruit *m.* fruit juice (3)
jusqu'à until (4-C; 6)
  ~ ce que until
jusque until
juste fair (11); just (16)
  ~ avant just before (8)
  ~ un peu just a little (1)
justement as a matter of fact (6)
justice *f.* justice (11)

K

kilogramme (kilo, kg) *m.* kilogram (2.2 pounds) (3-C)

kilomètre (km) *m.* kilometer (10)
  à... ~s de ... kilometers away
  (14-C)
  ~s/heure kilometers per hour
kiosque (de journaux) *m.* newspaper stand (16-C)
klaxon *m.* horn (car) (10)
klaxonner to honk

L

la *voir* **le**
là there (2)
là-bas over there (4)
laboratoire *m.* laboratory (4)
lac *m.* lake (17)
laid(e) ugly (2)
laïcité *f.* secularism (18-L)
laisser to leave, to allow (6)
lait *m.* milk (3)
lampe *f.* lamp (16)
lancement *m.* launching (5-L)
lancer to launch (6-L)
langue *f.* language (8)
lapin *m.* rabbit (9)
latin *m.* Latin (8)
lavabo *m.* sink (16)
se laver to wash, to bathe (13)
lave-vaisselle *m.* dishwasher (16)
le (la, l', les) the (1); him, her, it,
  them (8)
  ~ plus the most (11)
leçon *f.* lesson (1)
lecteur (-trice) *m., f.* reader (15)
  lecteur de disquettes disk drive
  (8)
  lecteur de CD CD player (7)
légumes *m. pl.* vegetables (3)
lent(e) slow (18)
lentement slowly (18)
lequel (laquelle, lesquels, lesquelles)
  which (12-L)
les *voir* **le**
lessive *f.*
  faire la ~ to do laundry (5)
lettre *f.* letter (8)
leur to them (9)
leur (le, la), leurs (les) theirs (14)
leur(s) their (5)
lever to raise (13)
  se ~ to get up (13)
librairie *f.* bookstore (4)

libre free (7)
lien *m.* link (15-L)
lieu *m.* place (8-L)
ligne *f.* line (6)
limiter to restrict
lire to read (14)
  lisez! read! (1)
Lisbonne Lisbon (4)
liste *f.* list (4)
lit *m.* bed (16)
litre (l) *m.* liter (3-C)
littéraire literary (15)
littérature *f.* literature (8)
livre *m.* book (1)
livre *f.* pound (3-C)
localité *f.* town, city
locataire *m., f.* renter (8-L)
location *f.* rental (10)
logement *m.* housing
logiciel *m.* software (8)
loi *f.* law (1-L; 10)
loin de far from (4)
loisirs *m. pl.* free time
Londres London (4)
longtemps a long time (6)
lors de during (12-L)
lorsque when (17)
louer to rent, to rent out (8-L; 10)
Louisiane *f.* Louisiana (16)
loyer *m.* rent (16)
lucide lucid (17)
lui to him, to her, to it (2, 9)
lumière *f.* light (17)
lundi *m.* Monday (9)
lune *f.* moon (17)
lunettes de soleil *f. pl.* sunglasses
  (5)
lutte *f.* fight, struggle (13-L)
luxe *m.* luxury
lycée *m.* high school (4)
lycéen(ne) *m., f.* high school
  student

M

ma my (5)
machin *m.* *(fam.)* thingamajig
  (11-C)
Machin-Chouette what's-his-
  name (11-C)
machine à laver *f.* washing
  machine (16)

Madame *f.* (*pl.* **Mesdames**) Mrs., Ms., ma'am (P)
~ **Unetelle** Mrs. So-and-So (11-C)
Mademoiselle *f.* (*pl.* **Mesdemoiselles**) Miss, Ms. (P)
magasin *m.* store (4)
grand ~ department store (11)
magazine *m.* (news) magazine (11-L)
Maghreb *m.* the Maghreb (Morocco, Algeria, Tunisia) (18)
Maghrébin(e) *m.*, *f.* person from the Maghreb (18)
magnétoscope *m.* VCR (7)
magnifique magnificent (2)
mai *m.* May (9)
maillot *m.* jersey (14)
~ **de bain** bathing suit (5)
main *f.* hand (13)
maintenant now (4)
maintenir to maintain
maire *m.* mayor (15-C)
mais but (1)
maison *f.* house (4)
maître d'hôtel *m.* maitre d' (9-C)
majorité *f.* majority
mal *m.* damage (15)
avoir du ~ **à** to have trouble (15)
avoir ~ **à** to have a sore . . . (13)
pas ~ not bad (P)
se faire ~ **à** to hurt one's . . . (13)
mal badly (5)
malade sick (2)
maladie *f.* illness (13)
malgré despite
malheureusement unfortunately (18)
malheureux (-euse) unhappy (2)
mandat *m.* money order (8)
manger to eat (1)
manière *f.* way
manifestation *f.* protest march (18-L)
manque *m.* lack (11-L)
manquer to miss
manteau *m.* (*pl.* -eaux) coat (5)
marchand(e) *m.*, *f.* merchant (9)
marchander to bargain (12-C)
marché *m.* market (6-L; 9)
~ **en plein air** open-air market (9)
marcher to work, to function (7)

mardi *m.* Tuesday (9)
mari *m.* husband (2)
Maroc *m.* Morocco (4)
marocain(e) Moroccan (18)
marquer to mark
marre
j'en ai ~! I've had it up to here! (17-C)
mars *m.* March (9)
masculin(e) masculine (2)
massif (-ive) massive
match *m.* match (2)
~ **de football** soccer game (2)
matérialiste materialistic (11)
matériel *m.* hardware (8)
mathématiques (maths) *f. pl.* mathematics (8)
matière *f.* subject (8); matter (17)
matin *m.* morning (4)
du ~ A.M. (6)
matinée *f.* morning (9)
faire la grasse ~ to sleep late (5)
mauvais(e) bad (2)
faire ~ to be bad (weather) (5)
mec *m.* (*fam.*) guy (18-C)
mécanicien *m.* mechanic (10-C)
méchamment out of meanness (18)
méchant(e) mean, bad (2)
médecin *m.* doctor (2)
médecine *f.* medicine (8)
médias *m. pl.* mass media
méditatif (-ive) pensive (17)
méfait *m.* negative effect, misdeed (13-L)
meilleur(e) better (18)
le ~, **la** ~**e**, **les** ~**(e)s** the best
membre *m.* member
même self (5); same (3-L); even
ménage *m.*
faire le ~ to do housework (5)
mener to lead (11-L)
mensonge *m.* lie (14)
mensuel *m.* monthly publication (16-C)
mentir to lie (7)
menu *m.* menu, fixed price meal (3)
méprisant(e) contemptuous (18-L)
mer *f.* sea (4)
merci thank you (P)
~ **mille fois** thanks a million (4)
mercredi *m.* Wednesday (9)

mère *f.* mother (2)
merguez *f.* North African spicy red sausage (3)
mes my (5)
Mesdames *f. pl.* ladies (1-C)
Mesdemoiselles *f. pl.* ladies (12)
message *m.* message (7)
messagerie vocale *f.* voice mail (7)
Messieurs *m. pl.* Gentlemen (4)
mesure *f.* measurement
mesurer to be . . . tall (14-C)
météo *f.* weather forecast (8)
métier *m.* occupation, career (15)
~ **artistique** career in the arts (15)
mètre *m.* meter (14)
métro *m.* subway (6)
metteur en scène *m.* director (18-L)
mettre to put (on), to set, to turn on, to take (*time to do something*) (6-L; 17)
se ~ **à** to begin (17)
meublé(e) furnished (16)
meubles *m. pl.* furniture (16)
mexicain(e) Mexican (2)
Mexico Mexico City (4)
Mexique *m.* Mexico (4)
midi *m.* noon (6)
Midi *m.* south of France
mien (le), **mienne (la)**, **mien(ne)s (les)** mine (14)
mieux better (18)
le ~ best (18)
milieu *m.* circle (15); middle
mille thousand (4)
milliard *m.* billion (4)
million *m.* million (4)
mine *f.*
avoir bonne ~ to look good, healthy (13)
avoir mauvaise ~ to look sick (13)
Ministère *m.* department
Minitel *m.* telephone computer (7-C)
minuit *m.* midnight (6)
minute *f.* minute (4)
mise en scène *f.* directing
moche (*fam.*) ugly (18-C)
modem *m.* modem (8)
moi me, I (2; 9)
moins less (1)
de ~ **en** ~ less and less

mois *m.*   month (5)
moitié *f.*   half (4-L)
moment *m.*   time
mon (ma, mes)   my (5)
monde *m.*   world (11)
mondial(e)   worldwide (15-L);
  international
moniteur *m.*   monitor (8)
  ~ de ski   ski instructor (9-L)
monnaie *f.*   change (12-C)
Monsieur *m.* (*pl.* Messieurs)   Mr.,
  sir (P)
  ~ Untel   Mr. So-and-So (11-C)
montagne *f.*   mountain (11)
montant *m.*   cost
monter   to get on, to go up (6)
montrer   to show (1)
monument *m.*   monument (8)
moral(e) (*pl.* -aux, -ales)   moral
morceau *m.* (*pl.* -eaux)   piece (3-C)
Moscou   Moscow (4)
mot *m.*   word (3-L)
  ~ clé   key word
  ~s croisés   crossword puzzle
  (16-C)
moto *f.*   motorcycle (6)
moufle *f.*   mitten (17-L)
mourir   to die (10)
moutarde *f.*   mustard (3)
mouton *m.*   mutton (3); sheep
  (18)
moyen *m.*   means (6-L)
Moyen Age *m.*   Middle Ages
Mozambique *m.*   Mozambique (4)
muezzin *m.*   muezzin (18)
multiplié(e) (par)   multiplied (1)
multiplier   to multiply (14-C)
mur *m.*   wall (3)
musée *m.*   museum (4)
musicien(ne) *m.*, *f.*   musician (2)
musique *f.*   music (2)
  ~ classique   classical music (2)

N

nager   to swim (14)
naissance *f.*   birth (2-L)
naître   to be born (6)
nana *f.* (*fam.*)   girl (18-C)
natation *f.*   swimming (14)
nationalité *f.*   nationality (2)
nature *f.*   nature (17)
naturel(le)   natural

naturellement   naturally
navette *f.*   shuttle (17)
navire *m.*   ship (4-L)
navré(e)   sorry (17-C)
ne (n')   (negation) (2)
  ~... jamais   never (8)
  ~... pas   not (2)
  ~... pas encore   not yet (8)
  ~... personne   nobody (12)
  ~... plus   no more (12)
  ~... que   only (12)
  ~... rien   nothing (12)
né(e)   born (6)
néanmoins   nonetheless (18-L)
nécessaire   necessary (7)
nécessairement   necessarily (18)
négatif (-ve)   negative (14)
neige *f.*   snow (8)
neiger   to snow (8)
n'est-ce pas?   isn't it so? (1)
nettement   clearly (15-L)
nettoyage à sec *m.*   dry cleaning
  (17-L)
neuf   nine (1)
neuf (neuve)   new (10)
neuvième   ninth (2)
neveu *m.*   nephew (2)
nez *m.*   nose (13)
nièce *f.*   niece (2)
n'importe   no matter (6-L)
Noël *m.*   Christmas
noir(e)   black (5)
noirci(e)   blackened (17)
noircir   to blacken (17)
nom *m.*   name (9)
nombrable   countable (17)
nombre *m.*   number (11)
nombreux (-euse)   numerous
non   no (1)
  ~ plus   neither
nord *m.*   north (4-C)
nord-africain(e)   North African
Norvège *f.*   Norway (4)
nos   our (5)
notamment   notably (10-L)
note *f.*   note (8)
noté
  c'est ~   I've got it (9-C)
notre   our (5)
nôtre (le, la), nôtres (les)   ours (14)
nourriture *f.*   food (3)
nous   we (1); us (11)
nouveau (nouvel), nouvelle, nouveaux, nouvelles   new (9)

Nouvelle-Angleterre *f.*   New
  England
Nouvelle-Orléans (La) *f.*   New
  Orleans (4)
nouvelles *f. pl.*   news (8)
  donnez-moi de vos ~   let me
  hear from you (8)
novembre *m.*   November (9)
nuage *m.*   cloud (8)
nucléaire   nuclear (11)
nuit *f.*   night (4-L; 13)
numéro *m.*   number (8-C)
  ~ de téléphone *m.*   phone
  number (7-C; 10)

O

obéir (à)   to obey (7)
objet *m.*   thing
  ~s trouvés   lost and found (6)
obligatoire   compulsory (10)
observer   to watch
obtenir   to obtain (3-L; 10)
occasion *f.*   opportunity
  d'~   used (10)
occupant(e) *m.*, *f.*   passenger
  (10-C)
occupé(e)   busy (7-C)
s'occuper de   to take care of (13)
octobre *m.*   October (9)
œil *m.* (*pl.* yeux)   eye (13)
œuf *m.*   egg (9)
œuvre *f.*   work (15)
officiel(le)   official
offrir   to offer
oiseau *m.* (*pl.* -eaux)   bird (17)
olive *f.*   olive (9)
olympique   olympic
ombre *f.*   shade
omelette *f.*   omelet (5)
on   one, we, they (1)
oncle *m.*   uncle (2)
ondoyer   to shimmer (17)
onze   eleven (1)
onzième   eleventh (2)
opéra *m.*   opera (15)
opinion *f.*   opinion (11)
s'opposer à   to oppose
optimiste   optimistic (2)
or   yet; now (13-L)
orage *m.*
  faire de l'~   to storm (8)
orange *f.*   orange (9)

orchestre *m.* orchestra (15)
ordinateur *m.* computer (7)
oreille *f.* ear (13)
orgueil *m.* pride (16-L)
origine *f.*
  à l'~ originally
orthographe *f.* spelling
ou or (1)
où where (2)
  ~ ça? whereabouts? (4)
oublier (de) to forget (5)
ouest *m.* west (4-C)
oui yes (P)
outre
  en ~ in addition (10-L)
ouvert(e) open (2)
ouverture *f.* opening time
ouvreuse *f.* usher
ouvrez votre livre! open your
  book! (1)

P

page *f.* page (1)
pain *m.* bread (3)
paix *f.* peace (11)
panneau routier *m.* (*pl.* -eaux)
  road sign (10-C)
pantalon *m.* pants (5)
papeterie *f.* stationery store (12)
papetier *m.* stationer (12-C)
papier *m.* paper
  ~ à lettres stationery (8)
  ~s documents (10)
paquet *m.* parcel (8)
par by (1)
  ~ contre however (3-L)
paraître to appear; to publish
  (15-L)
parapluie *m.* umbrella (5)
parc *m.* park (4)
parce que because (4)
pardon excuse me (1-C)
pardonnez-moi excuse me (1-C)
pare-brise *m.* windshield (10)
parents *m. pl.* parents (2)
paresseux (-euse) lazy (2)
parfait(e) perfect (5)
parfaitement perfectly (18)
parfois sometimes
pari *m.* bet, gamble (8-L)
parisien(ne) Parisian (2)
parking *m.* parking lot (4)

parler to speak (1)
parmi among (13-L)
parole *f.* word, utterance (15-L)
part *f.*
  c'est de la ~ de qui? may I say
    who's calling? (7-C)
participer to participate
partie *f.* game; part (13)
  faire ~ to belong
partir to leave (7)
  à ~ de leaving from, starting
    from (4-L)
partout everywhere (13-C; 18)
pas not (2)
  ne... ~ not (2)
  ~ du tout not at all (4)
  ~ encore not yet (5)
passage *m.* way
  de ~ passing (17-L)
passager (-ère) *m., f.* passenger
  (10-C)
passant(e) passerby
passé *m.* past
  ~ composé compound past tense
passer to take (*an exam*); to spend
  (*time*) (2); to be displayed (*on
  screen*), to pass (9-C)
  ~ un coup de fil (téléphone) to
    make a phone call (7-C)
  ~ par to pass by (10)
  se ~ to happen (7)
passionnant(e) exciting
pastis *m.* pastis (licorice-flavored
  drink) (14)
pâté *m.* pâté (9)
  ~ de foie liver pâté (12)
pâtes *f. pl.* noodles (5)
patience *f.* patience (3)
  avoir de la ~ to be patient (3)
patinage *m.* skating (14)
patiner to skate (14)
pâtisserie *f.* pastry shop (12)
pâtissier (-ère) *m., f.* pastry maker
  (12)
patron *m.* boss (8-L; 14)
patrouille *f.* patrol (15-L)
patte *f.* leg (animal) (9)
pauvre poor (2)
payer to pay (8-C; 10)
pays *m.* country (4)
paysage *m.* landscape, countryside
  (17)
paysan(ne) *m., f.* small farmer;
  peasant (9-L)

Pays-Bas *m. pl.* the Netherlands
  (4)
peau *f.* skin (18-L)
pêche *f.* peach (9); fishing (14)
peine *f.* trouble (7)
  ~ capitale capital punishment
  ce n'est pas la ~ it's not worth
    the trouble (7)
peintre *m.* painter (15)
peinture *f.* painting (15)
  ~ à l'huile oil painting (15)
pelouse *f.* lawn (17)
pendant during, for (8)
penser to think (5)
  ~ à to think about, to have in
    mind (5)
  ~ de to think of, to have an
    opinion about (15)
pensionnaire *m., f.* boarder (14-L)
pépinière *f.* breeding ground
  (14-L)
perdre to lose (6)
  ~ patience to lose patience (6)
père *m.* father (2)
Père Noël Santa Claus
péril *m.* danger (13-L)
  en ~ endangered (15)
permettre to allow (2-C; 17)
permis de conduire *m.* driver's
  license (10)
persil *m.* parsley (3-L)
personne *f.* person
  ne... ~ nobody (12)
  ~ ne nobody
personnel(le) private, personal
peser to weigh (14-C)
pessimiste pessimistic (2)
pétanque *f.* lawn bowling (14)
petit(e) small, little (9)
  ~ déjeuner *m.* breakfast (9)
  ~ gâteau *m.* (*pl.* -eaux) cookie
  ~ pois *m.* pea (9)
  ~(e) ami(e) *m., f.* boyfriend,
    girlfriend (2)
  ~e annonce *f.* classified ad (16)
Petites Antilles *f. pl.* Lesser
  Antilles (5)
petits-enfants *m. pl.* grandchildren (2)
peu little, few (3)
  ~ m'importe it doesn't matter
    (17-C)
  un ~ de a little, a few (3)
peuple *m.* people

peur *f.* fear
  avoir ~ de to be afraid of (11)
  faire ~ to scare (11)
peut-être maybe (9-C; 12)
phare *m.* headlight (10)
pharmacie *f.* drugstore (4)
  ~ de garde emergency drugstore (13)
  ~ de nuit all-night drugstore (13)
philosophie (philo) *f.* philosophy (2)
photo *f.* photo (3)
phrase *f.* sentence (14)
physique *f.* physics (8)
piano *m.* piano (15)
pichet *m.* pitcher (3)
pièce *f.* coin (12-C); play (14); room (16)
  ~ d'identité *f.* ID (8-C)
pied *m.* foot (13)
  à ~ on foot (6)
pierre *f.* stone (15)
piéton(ne) *m., f.* pedestrian (17-L)
pile *f.* battery (7)
piller to plunder (14-L)
pinard *m. (fam.)* wine (18-C)
pique-nique *m.* picnic
piquer to sting (17-L)
piscine *f.* swimming pool (4)
pizza *f.* pizza (3)
place *f.* square (9); seat (10); place (14)
  à ta (votre, sa) ~ in your (his, her) place (16)
  de la ~ room (4)
  ~ du marché *f.* market square (9)
placer to place (16); to put
plage *f.* beach (4)
plaindre to pity
  se ~ to complain (8-L)
plaire
  ça vous plaît? do you like it?
  s'il te plaît please (3)
  s'il vous plaît please (3)
plaisir *m.* pleasure (15-C)
plaît *voir* **plaire**
plan *m.* level
  sur le ~ de from the point of view of (16-L)
planche *f.*
  ~ à roulettes skateboarding (14)
  ~ à voile sailboarding (14)

plancher *m.* floor *(Quebec)* (16)
planète *f.* planet (17)
plat *m.* dish (3)
  ~ cuisiné prepared dish (12)
  ~ du jour special of the day (9-C)
  ~ principal main course (3)
plein *m.*
  faire le ~ to fill up (10-C)
plein(e) full (4)
  ~ air outdoor (9)
pleuvoir to rain (8)
plongée sous-marine *f.* scuba diving (14)
pluie *f.* rain (8)
  ~ acide acid rain (17)
plupart *f.*
  la ~ de... most . . .
  pour la ~ for the most part
pluriel *m.* plural
plus more (1); no longer
  de ~ furthermore; another
  de ~ en ~ more and more
  en ~ in addition (10)
  le ~ de the most (11)
  ne... ~ no more (12)
  ~ de more than
  ~ tard later (7)
plusieurs several (3-C; 15)
plutôt rather
pneu *m.* tire (10)
poche *f.* pocket (5)
poème *m.* poem (10)
poésie *f.* poetry (14)
poète *m.* poet (17)
poids *m.* weight (12-L)
poignée de main *f.* handshake (P)
point *m.* period
poire *f.* pear (9)
poisson *m.* fish (3)
poissonnerie *f.* fish market (12)
poissonnier (-ère) *m., f.* fishmonger (12)
poivron *m.* (green) pepper (3-L)
poli(e) polite (2)
politesse *f.* politeness
politique political
politique *f.* policy (5-L); politics (11)
pollution *f.* pollution (11)
polo *m.* polo shirt (5)
Pologne *f.* Poland (4)
pomme *f.* apple (9)
  ~ de terre potato (9)

pont *m.* long weekend
populaire popular (18)
porc *m.* pork (9)
portable *m.* cellular phone (7)
porte *f.* door (1)
portée *f.* reach (7-L)
  à la ~ de toutes les bourses within everyone's reach (14-L)
portefeuille *m.* wallet (7)
porter to wear (5); to bear, to show (12-L)
  se ~ bien to be in good health (13)
portière *f.* car door (10)
Portugal *m.* Portugal (4)
poser to put (9); to set down (11-C)
  ~ une question to ask a question (9)
positif (-ve) positive
posséder to own (13)
possession *f.* belonging
possibilité *f.* possibility (11)
possible possible (2)
poste *m.* extension *(phone)* (7-C); position
poste restante *f.* general delivery (8-C)
pot *m.* drink (6)
pote *m. (fam.)* friend, buddy (18-C)
poule *f.* hen (18)
poulet *m.* chicken (3)
pour to, in order to (4); for (11-L; 16)
  ~ rien for nothing (6)
pourboire *m.* tip (9-C)
pourcentage *m.* percentage
pourquoi why (4)
poursuivre to follow, to chase
pourtant however (18-L)
pourvoir to provide (4-L)
pouvoir *m.* power (1-L)
pouvoir to be able to (5-L; 7)
  il se peut que it's likely that (11)
pratiquer to practice (14)
prédire to predict (13-L)
préférable preferable (11)
préféré(e) favorite (3)
préférence *f.* preference
  de ~ preferably
préférer to prefer (13)
premier (-ère) first (2)

Premier ministre *m.* prime minister
prendre to take, to have (3); to have (meal) (9)
  ~ **part** to take part (16-L)
  ~ **le volant** to get behind the wheel (10-C)
  ~ **un pot** to have a drink (6)
prenez *voir* **prendre** (3)
préoccuper to preoccupy (11)
préparer to prepare (3)
préposé(e) *m., f.* employee (8-C)
près de near (4)
présent(e) present (2)
présenter to introduce (2-C; 9)
président(e) *m., f.* president (2)
presque almost (10)
presse spécialisée *f.* specialized publications (16-C)
pressé(e) in a hurry (17-L)
prêt(e) ready (5)
prêter to lend (8)
prévoir to predict, to foresee (8); to plan
prier to beg (2-L); to pray (18)
  je vous en prie don't mention it
prière *f.* prayer (18)
principal(e) main (5-L)
principalement mainly
printemps *m.* spring (9)
priorité *f.* priority
  ~ **à droite** right of way on the right (10)
prise de sang *f.* blood test (13)
privilège *m.* privilege
prix *m.* price (3); prize
  à tout ~ at all costs (16-L)
  ~ **fixe** menu (3)
probable probable (11)
  il est ~ it is likely (11)
  il est peu ~ it is unlikely (11)
probablement probably (18)
problème *m.* problem (6)
procès *m.* trial
prochain(e) next (4)
  à la ~e see you next time (1-C)
proche near
proclamer to proclaim (18)
produire to produce (14)
produit *m.* product (5-L; 12)
  ~ **surgelé** frozen food (12)
prof *m., f. abrev. de* **professeur**
professeur *m.* professor, teacher (1)

profession *f.* profession (2)
professionnel(le) professional
profiter (de) to take advantage of (8)
programme *m.* program (11)
programmeur (-euse) *m., f.* computer programmer (2)
projet *m.* plan, project
promenade *f.*
  faire une ~ to go for a walk (5)
promener to walk (13)
  se ~ to go for a walk (13)
promettre to promise (17)
propre clean; own (9)
propriétaire *m., f.* owner (16)
protéger to protect (12-L)
prouver to prove (7)
provençal(e) *(pl. -aux, -ales)* from Provence (9)
province *f.* province
provincial(e) provincial
provisions *f. pl.* grocery shopping
  faire ses ~ to do one's shopping (9)
prudemment carefully (18)
prudent(e) careful (2)
pseudonyme *m.* pseudonym
psychiatre *m.* psychiatrist
psychologie *f.* psychology (8)
public *m.* public (10-L)
public (-ique) public
publicité *f.* ads (11)
publié(e) published (15)
publier to publish
puis then
puisque since (6-L; 8)
puissance *f.* power
puits *m.* well (5-L)
pull *m.* sweater (5)
punir to punish (7)
pyjama *m.* pajamas (5)

Q

quai *m.* bank (of a river) (8-L)
qualité *f.* quality (11)
quand when (2)
quant à as for (12-L)
quantité *f.* quantity
quarante forty (2)
quart *m.* quarter (6)
quartier *m.* neighborhood
quatorze fourteen (1)

quatre four (1)
quatre-vingt dix ninety
quatre-vingts eighty
quatrième fourth (2)
que than (18); *(pron. rel.)* that, which, whom (16); what, which (7); how (18)
  ne... que only (12)
  ~ **veut dire... ?** what does . . . mean? (5-C)
québécois(e) from Quebec (5)
quel(le) what, which (5)
quelque some (2)
  ~ **chose** something (5)
  ~ **part** somewhere (11-C)
quelquefois sometimes (18)
quelqu'un someone (10)
qu'est-ce que what (7)
  ~ **c'est?** what is it? (1)
  ~**... veut dire?** what does . . . mean? (1)
  qu'est-ce qu'il y a? what's the matter? (5-C)
qu'est-ce qui what (7)
  ~ **ne va pas?** what's wrong? (5-C)
  ~ **se passe?** what's going on? (5-C)
  ~ **s'est passé?** what happened? (5-C)
question *f.* question (1)
queue *f.*
  faire la ~ to stand in line (5)
qui who (4-L; 7); *(pron. rel.)* who, that (16)
  à ~ to whom? (7)
  ~ **est-ce que** whom (7)
  ~ **est-ce qui** who (7)
quinze fifteen (1)
quitter to leave (9-L)
  Ne quittez pas! Hold on! (7)
quoi what (7)
  il n'y a pas de ~ don't mention it, you're welcome (1)
  ~ **de neuf?** what's new? (P)
quotidien(ne) daily (11-L)

R

raccourcir to shorten
raccrocher to hang up (the phone) (7-C)
race *f.* race

racines *f. pl.* roots, origins (3-L)
raconter to tell
radio *f.* radio (1)
radiocassette *f.* tape recorder (7)
raisin *m.* grape (9)
raison *f.* reason (17)
  avoir ~ (de) to be right (3)
raisonnable moderate, reasonable
ramener to bring back (14-L)
ranger to put away, to clean up (7)
rapide fast (2)
rapidement rapidly (18)
rappeler to call back (7)
  ~ (à) to remind (15)
  se ~ to remember (13)
rapport *m.* relationship
rapporter to bring back (6)
raquette *f.* snowshoe (17-L)
rare rare (11)
rarement rarely (18)
ras le bol
  j'en ai ~! I've had it up to here! (17-C)
ravi(e) delighted (17-C)
rayer to cross out
rayon *m.* department (12)
raz-de-marée *m.* tidal wave (14-L)
réaliser to produce (13-L)
réalité *f.* reality (4-L)
récemment recently (5)
récent(e) recent (18)
recette *f.* recipe
recevoir to receive (8-C; 12)
recherche *f.* search (9-L)
recherché(e) sought-after (14-L)
réclamer to demand
recommandé(e) registered (8)
recommander (à) to recommend (to) (3)
reconnaissance *f.* gratitude; recognition (11-L)
reconnaissant(e) grateful (15-C)
reconnaître to recognize (10)
recueillir to gather (18-L)
recyclage *m.* recycling (17)
rédaction en chef *f.* post of editor-in-chief (15-L)
réduire to reduce (3-L)
réel(le) real
réfléchir to think about (7)
reflet *m.* reflection (17)
refuser (de) to refuse (15)
regard *m.* glance

regarder to look at (1)
régime *m.* diet (13); regime
  être au ~ to be on a diet (13)
  faire un ~ to be on a diet (5)
région *f.* region, area
régional(e) (*pl.* -aux, -ales) regional
règle *f.* rule (10)
régler to pay (10); to solve
regretter (de) to regret, to be sorry (11)
régulièrement regularly (13)
relation *f.* relationship
  ~ d'affaires *f.* business acquaintance (2)
relier to connect (6-L)
religion *f.* religion
remarquer to notice
remercier to thank (11)
remettre to put on, to hand in, to hand back, to postpone (14-L; 17)
remise *f.* discount (12)
remonter to go back
remplacer to replace (3-L)
remplir to fill (12-L)
remplisseur de pause *m.* conversational filler (18-C)
rencontrer to meet (8)
rendre to return (something), to give back (6); to make (11)
  se ~ compte to realize (18-L)
  ~ visite à to visit (*a person*) (6)
renom *m.* renown (5-L)
renommé(e) famous
renseignement *m.* piece of information (4)
se renseigner to obtain information
rentrée *f.* beginning of the school year (8)
rentrer to go in, to come back (4)
renvoyer to expel (9-L)
  ~ à to reflect (18-L)
répandre to spread
réparation *f.* repair
réparer to repair (10)
repas *m.* meal (9)
repasser to retake (a test)
répéter to repeat (13)
  répétez! repeat! (1)
répondeur *m.* answering machine (7)
répondre to answer (6)
  répondez à... ! answer . . . !(1)

réponse *f.* answer (10)
reportage *m.* report (11)
se reposer to rest (13)
reprise *f.* time (18-L)
République démocratique du Congo *f.* Republic of the Congo (4)
réputation *f.* reputation (9-L)
requis(e) required (13-L)
réseau *m.* network (6-L)
réservation *f.* reservation
  faire une ~ to book a seat
réserver to reserve (10)
résidence *f.* residence (4)
  ~ universitaire university dorm (4)
résister to resist
résoudre to resolve
responsable responsible
ressembler à to resemble, to look like (9)
ressource *f.* resource
restaurant *m.* restaurant (3)
restaurer to restore (15-L)
restau-U *m.* university cafeteria (4)
rester to stay (4); to remain (7)
résultat *m.* result
retard *m.*
  en ~ late (2)
retenir to hold back; to remember (10)
retour *m.* return
retourner to return (10)
retrouver to find again, to meet (6); to encounter
  se ~ to meet
réunion *f.* meeting
se réunir to meet
réussir (à) to succeed, to pass (*a test*) (7)
réussite *f.* success (16-L)
se réveiller to wake up (13)
revenir to come back (10)
rêve *m.* dream (4-L)
rêver (de) to dream (9-L; 15)
revoir to see again (8)
  au ~ good-bye (P)
révolution *f.* revolution
revue *f.* magazine (14)
rez-de-chaussée *m.* ground floor (16)
riche rich (2)

rien nothing (5)
  ça (cela) ne fait ~ it doesn't matter (12-C)
  de ~ you're welcome (1)
  ne... ~ nothing (12)
  ~ d'important nothing much (5-C)
risque *m.* risk
rivière *f.* river (17)
riz *m.* rice (3-L; 9)
robe *f.* dress (5)
  ~ de chambre robe (5)
rock *m.* rock (2)
rôle *m.* part
roller *m.* in-line skating (14)
roman *m.* novel (10)
romancier (-ière) *m., f.* novelist (18-L)
rosbif *m.* roast beef (9)
rose pink (17)
rôti *m.* roast (9)
rouge red (3)
rougir to blush (7)
rouler à... km à l'heure to go . . . kilometers per hour (10)
route *f.* road
rubrique *f.* section of a newspaper (15-L)
rue *f.* street (4)
rugby *m.* rugby (14)
rumeur *f.* rumor (17)
russe Russian (8)
Russie *f.* Russia (4)

S

sa his, her, its (5)
sac *m.* bag (7)
  ~ à dos backpack (1)
Saint-Valentin *f.* Valentine's Day (9)
sais *voir* savoir
saison *f.* season (9)
salade *f.* salad (3)
salle *f.* room
  ~ à manger dining room (16)
  ~ de bains bathroom (16)
  ~ de classe classroom (1)
salon *m.* living room (16)
salut hi (P); so long (1-C)
salutation *f.* greeting (15-C)
samedi *m.* Saturday (9)
sandwich *m.* sandwich (5)

sans without (2)
sans-abri *m.* homeless (11)
sans-logis *m.* homeless (11)
sans-papiers *m.* undocumented aliens (11)
santé *f.* health (11)
  être en bonne ~ to be in good health (13)
  être en mauvaise ~ to be in bad health (13)
satisfaction *f.* satisfaction (17-C)
satisfait(e) satisfied (17-C)
saucisse *f.* sausage (3-L)
saucisson *m.* hard salami (9)
savoir to know (6-L; 10)
  à ~ that is to say (18-L)
  je ne sais pas I don't know (1)
savoir-faire *m.* know-how
sciences éco(nomiques) *f. pl.* economics (8)
sciences po(litiques) *f. pl.* political science (8)
sculpteur *m.* sculptor (15)
sculpture *f.* sculpture (15)
SDF (*abrév. de* **sans domicile fixe**) homeless (11)
sec (sèche) dry (12)
sèche-linge *m.* dryer (16)
sécher to dry (13)
  ~ un cours to cut class (13)
second(e) second (2)
secours *m.* help
secrétaire *m., f.* secretary (2)
sécurité *f.* security (11)
séduire to attract (5-L)
seize sixteen (1)
séjour *m.* stay (8)
séjourner to stay
sel *m.* salt (3)
selon according to (1-L; 11)
semaine *f.* week (4)
sembler to seem (11)
  il semble (que) it appears (that) (11)
semestre *m.* semester (8)
semoule *f.* semolina (3)
Sénégal *m.* Senegal (4)
sénégalais(e) Senegalese (8)
sens interdit do not enter (10-C)
sens unique one way (10-C)
sentiment *m.* feeling (15-C)
sentir to smell; to feel (7)
  se ~ to feel (13)
séparer to separate

sept seven (1)
septembre *m.* September (9)
série *f.* series (11)
sérieux (-euse) serious (2)
serveuse *f.* waitress (9-C)
service *m.* service
  ~ compris tip included (3)
serviette *f.* napkin (9-C)
servir to serve
  ~ à to be used for (3-L; 7)
ses his, her, its (5)
sésame *m.* key to success (14-L)
seul(e) alone (2); only (5-L)
seulement only (18)
short *m.* shorts (5)
si yes, of course (2); if (4)
sida *m.* AIDS (11)
siècle *m.* century
siège *m.* seat (10)
  ~ arrière back seat (10)
  ~ avant front seat (10)
sien (le), sienne (la), sien(ne)s (les) his, hers, its (14)
sieste *f.*
  faire la ~ to take a nap
signaler to indicate
signer to sign (10)
signification *f.* meaning
simple simple (2)
sincère sincere (2)
sincérité *f.* sincerity (2)
singulier *m.* singular
sinon if not
situation *f.* situation
six six (1)
ski *m.* skiing (14)
  ~ nautique water-skiing (14)
skieur (-euse) *m., f.* skier
snowboard *m.* snowboarding (14)
social(e) (*pl.* **-aux, -ales**) social (11)
société *f.* society (11)
sociologie *f.* sociology (8)
sœur *f.* sister (2)
soi-disant supposed (11-L)
soie *f.* silk (17-L)
soif *f.*
  avoir ~ to be thirsty (3)
soigner to treat
soin *m.* care
soir *m.* evening (3)
  ce ~ tonight (1)
  du ~ P.M. (6)
  à ce ~ see you this evening (1-C)

soirée *f.* evening (2)
soixante sixty (2)
solaire solar (17)
soldat *m.* soldier
solde *m.* sale (12)
  en ~ on sale (12)
sole *m.* sole (9)
soleil *m.* sun
  faire du ~ to be sunny (8)
sombre dark (17-L)
son his, her, its (5)
sondage *m.* poll (11)
  ~ d'opinion opinion poll (11)
sonner to ring (7)
sorte *f.* sort, kind (3)
  en ~ que such that (18-L)
  quelle ~ de what kind of (3)
sortir to go out (7)
souci *m.* worry (10-L)
soudain suddenly
souffler to blow
souffrir to suffer (15)
souhait *m.* wish
  à tes (vos) ~s! bless you! (13-C)
souhaiter to wish (7-L; 11)
soupe *f.* soup (3)
sous under (4)
sous-titré(e) subtitled (11-L)
souterrain(e) underground
souvent often (2)
spatial(e) (*pl.* **-aux, -ales**) space (5-L; 17)
spécial(e) (*pl.* **-aux, -ales**) special
spécialité *f.* specialty
spectacle *m.* performance, show
  ~s entertainment section (*of a newspaper*) (16-C)
sport *m.* sport (2)
  faire du ~ to play sports (5)
sportif (-ve) athletic (14)
stade *m.* stadium (4)
station *f.* stop (6); station (17)
  ~ service gas station (10-C)
  ~ spatiale space station (17)
  ~ thermale health spa (13-C)
stationnement interdit no parking (10-C)
stationner to park (10)
stop *m.*
  faire du ~ to hitchhike (6)
studieux (-euse) studious (2)
stupide stupid (2)
stylo *m.* pen (1)
succès *m.* success (11)

succursale *f.* branch (business) (17-L)
sucre *m.* sugar (3)
sud *m.* south (4-C)
Suède *f.* Sweden (4)
suffire
  ça suffit! enough! (17-C)
suffisamment sufficiently (18)
suffisant(e) sufficient (18)
Suisse *f.* Switzerland (4)
suite à following (18-L)
suivant(e) following (15)
suivre to follow; to take (courses) (8)
super super (5)
super *m.* premium (gas) (10-C)
supermarché *m.* supermarket (12)
supporter to tolerate (11)
suppression *f.* removal (12-L)
sur on (4)
sûr(e) certain (11)
sûrement surely (18)
surgelé(e) frozen (12)
surgir to appear, to occur (17-L)
surmenage *m.* overwork (11-L)
surnom *m.* nickname
surpris(e) surprised (11)
surtaxe *f.* fee (8-C)
surtout above all (6-L; 15)
survoler to tower over (4-L)
sus
  en ~ extra (9-C)
symbole *m.* symbol
sympathique nice (2)
symphonie *f.* symphony (15)
Syndicat d'Initiative *m.* tourist information bureau (4)
système *m.* system

T

ta your (5)
tabagisme *m.* nicotine addiction (13-L)
table *f.* table (16)
  à ~ food is ready (9-C)
  ~ de nuit bedside table (16)
  ~ ronde round table (discussion) (11)
tableau *m.* (*pl.* **-eaux**) chalkboard (1); painting (15)
tableur *m.* spreadsheet (8)
tâche *f.* task

taille *f.* size
talent *m.* talent (3)
  avoir du ~ to have talent (3)
talon aiguille *m.* high heel (17-L)
tant mieux! good! (17-C)
tant pis! too bad! (17-C)
tante *f.* aunt (2)
taper to type (8)
tapis *m.* carpet (16)
  ~ volant flying carpet
tard late (13)
  à plus ~ see you later (P)
tarte *f.* pie (3)
tasse *f.* cup (3-C)
taux *m.* rate (12-C)
  ~ de change exchange rate (12-C)
taxi *m.* taxi (6)
Tchad *m.* Chad (4)
technologie *f.* technology
tee-shirt *m.* T-shirt (5)
teinturerie *f.* dry cleaner's (12)
tel(le) such, like (3-L; 18)
télé *f.* TV (2)
télécarte *f.* pay phone card (7-C)
télégramme *m.* telegram (8)
téléphone *m.* telephone (7)
téléphoner (à) to telephone, to call (7)
  ~ avec préavis to make a person-to-person call (8-C)
  ~ en P.C.V. to call collect (8-C)
téléviseur *m.* TV set (7)
télévision (télé) *f.* television (1)
tellement so; so much (18)
témoignage *m.* testimony (18-L)
témoigner (de) to demonstrate, to bear witness (to) (15-L)
témoin *m.* witness (5-L)
température *f.* temperature (13-C)
temps *m.* weather (6); time (3-L; 6)
  de ~ en ~ from time to time
  il est ~ it's time (11)
  quel ~ fait-il? what's the weather like? (5)
tenir to hold (10)
  ~ à to be fond of; to be anxious to (10)
  ~ compte de to take into account (10-L)
  ~ de to take after (10)
tennis *m.* tennis (14); *f. pl.* tennis shoes (5)

tenue *f.*
  en petite ~   in light clothing (17-L)
terminale *f.*   senior year of high school
terminer   to end (1)
se terrer   to bury oneself (17-L)
terrible   terrible (13-L); super (17-C)
tes   your (5)
tête *f.*   head (9)
texte *m.*   text (14)
TGV *m.*   high-speed train (6-L)
thalassothérapie *f.*   seawater therapy (13-C)
thé *m.*   tea (3)
théâtre *m.*   theater (4)
ticket *m.*   ticket (6)
tien (le), tienne (la), tien(ne)s (les)   yours (14)
  à la ~ne   cheers, to your health (14)
tiens!   hey! (1-C; 2)
timbre *m.*   stamp (8)
timide   shy (2)
titre *m.*   title
toi   you (P)
  et ~   and you (P)
toilettes *f. pl.*   restroom (16)
TOM (territoires d'outre-mer) *m. pl.*   overseas regions of France
tomate *f.*   tomato (9)
tomber   to fall (10)
  ~ en panne   to break down (car) (10)
ton   your (2)
tonnerre *m.*   thunder (8)
tort *m.*
  avoir ~ (de)   to be wrong (3)
tôt   early (13)
toubib *m. (fam.)*   doctor (18-C)
toucher   to touch
toujours   always (2); still
tour *m.*
  faire un ~   to go for a walk (5)
tourisme *m.*   tourism
touriste *m., f.*   tourist (5)
touristique   touristic
tourner   to turn (4-C)
tout(e), tous, toutes   all, every; each (4)
  ~ les ans   every year (5)
  ~ les jours   every day (4)
  ~ le monde   everybody (12)

  ~ le temps   all the time (8)
tout   all; completely (8)
  ~ à coup   suddenly
  ~ de même   in any case (18-L)
  ~ de suite   immediately (3)
  ~ droit   straight ahead (4-C)
tradition *f.*   tradition
traditionnel(le)   traditional (18)
traditionnellement   traditionally (18)
traduire   to translate (14)
trafic *m.*   (drug) traffic (11)
tragédie *f.*   tragedy (15)
train *m.*   train (6)
  ~ à grande vitesse (TGV)   high-speed train (P-L)
traîneau *m.*   sleigh, sled (17-L)
trait d'union *m.*   hyphen
traitement *m.*   treatment
  ~ de texte *m.*   word processor (8)
trajet *m.*   trip (6-L)
tranche *f.*   slice (3-C)
transformer   to transform
transmettre   to hand down
transport *m.*   transportation (6)
transporter   to carry
travail *m.*   work (11)
travailler   to work (1)
travailleur (-euse) *m., f.*   worker
travers
  à ~   through, throughout (4-L)
traversée *f.*   crossing (6-L)
traverser   to cross (4-C)
treize   thirteen (1)
tréma *m.*   diaeresis
trente   thirty (2)
trentième   thirtieth (2)
très   very (P)
  ~ bien   very well (P)
trimestre *m.*   quarter (8)
triste   sad (11)
trois   three (1)
troisième   third (2)
trombone *m.*   trombone (15)
trompette *f.*   trumpet (15)
tronc *m.*   trunk (17)
trop   too much, too many (3)
trouver   to find (1-L; 3)
  comment trouvez-vous... ?   how do you like . . . ? (3)
  où se trouve... ?   where is . . . located? (4-C)
  se ~   to be located (4-C); to find oneself (13)

truc *m. (fam.)*   thingamajig (11-C); thing
truite *f.*   trout (9)
tu   you (1)
Tunisie *f.*   Tunisia (4)
tunisien(ne)   Tunisian (3)
TVA *f.*   value-added tax (10)
type *m. (fam.)*   guy (18-C)
typique   typical

U

un(e)   a, an, one (1; 3)
  à la ~e   on the front page (16-C)
union libre *f.*   living together
unir   to unite
universel(le)   universal
universitaire   university *(adj.)*
université *f.*   university (1)
usage *m.*   use, usage (15)
usine *f.*   factory (4)
utile   useful
utiliser   to use (8)

V

va   *voir* aller
vacances *f. pl.*   vacation (9)
  grandes ~   summer vacation (10)
vache *f.*   cow (18)
vague *f.*   wave
vais   *voir* aller
vaisselle *f.*
  faire la ~   to do the dishes (5)
valise *f.*   suitcase (5)
  faire les ~s   to pack the suitcases (5)
valoir   to be worth
  il vaut mieux   it's better (11)
  ~ la peine   to be worth (16-L)
vantard *m.*   braggart
varier   to vary
variété *f.*   variety (9)
  ~s   variety show (11)
Varsovie   Warsaw (4)
vas-y!   go ahead! (4)
veau *m. (pl. -eaux)*   veal, calf (9)
vedette *f.*   star
végétarien(ne)   vegetarian (9)
veille *f.*   eve (11-L)
vélo *m.*   bicycle (6)

vendeur (-euse) *m., f.* salesperson (12)

~ **de journaux** news dealer (16-C)

vendre to sell (6)

vendredi *m.* Friday (9)

venir to come (10)

~ **de** to have just (10)

vent *m.* wind

faire du ~ to be windy (8)

ventre *m.* stomach (13)

vérifier to check (10-C)

véritable true

vérité *f.* truth (14)

verre *m.* glass (3-C; 14)

vers toward, about, around (13)

vert(e) green (5)

veste *f.* jacket (5)

veston *m.* coat (5)

vêtements *m. pl.* clothes (5)

veut *voir* **vouloir**

viande *f.* meat (3)

victime *f.* victim

vide empty (14)

vidéo *f.* video

vie *f.* life (11)

~ **familiale** *f.* family life

vietnamien(ne) Vietnamese

vieux (vieil, vieille[s], vieux) old (9)

vif (-ive) lively (17)

village *m.* village

ville *f.* city, town (4)

en ~ in town, downtown (4)

vin *m.* wine (3)

vingt twenty (1)

~ **et unième** twenty-first (2)

vingtième twentieth (2)

violet(te) violet

violon *m.* violin (15)

violoncelle *m.* cello (15)

virgule *f.* comma

viser to target (13-L)

visiter to visit *(a place)* (4)

visiteur *m.* visitor

vite quickly (18)

vitesse *f.* speed (6-L)

vivace vivacious (15)

vivier *m.* breeding ground (14-L)

voici here is, here are (1)

Voie lactée *f.* Milky Way (17)

voilà there is, there are (1)

~... **que** it has been . . . that (16)

voile *f.* sailing (14)

voile *m.* veil

voir to see (5-L; 7)

voire even (14-L)

voisin(e) *m., f.* neighbor (11)

voiture *f.* car (2)

~ **d'occasion** used car (10)

~ **neuve** new car (10)

voix *f.* voice (7)

volant *m.* steering wheel (10)

voler to steal

volley-ball *m.* volleyball (14)

volonté *f.* will (15)

vos your (1)

votre your (1)

vôtre (le, la), vôtres (les) yours (14)

à la ~! cheers, to your health (14)

voudrais *voir* **vouloir**

vouloir to want to (7)

~ **bien** to be willing (7)

je voudrais I would like (2-C; 3)

qu'est-ce que... veut dire? what does . . . mean? (1)

vous you (P)

et ~ and you (P)

voyage *m.* trip (4)

~ **organisé** tour (5)

faire un ~ to take a trip (5)

voyager to travel (4)

voyons! let's see! come on! (8)

vrai(e) true (2)

c'est pas ~! no?! (17-C)

vraiment really, truly (9)

W

Walkman *m.* Walkman (7)

week-end *m.* weekend (4)

Y

y there, of it, to it (15)

yeux *m. pl.* eyes (2-L)

Z

zéro zero (1)

zut alors! darn! (17-C)

zydeco Louisiana music

Anglais-français

The English-French Vocabulary contains only active vocabulary.

A

a   un, une (3)
about
   it's ~   il s'agit de (15)
above all   surtout (15)
absent   absent(e) (2)
absolutely   absolument (11)
to accept   accepter (de) (15)
accident   accident *m.* (10)
according to   selon (11)
acquaintance   connaissance *f.* (2)
across from   en face de (4)
actor   acteur *m.* (2)
actress   actrice *f.* (2)
ad   publicité *f.* (11)
   classified ~   petite annonce *f.*
   (16)
addition
   in ~   en plus (10)
address   adresse *f.* (8)
to adore   adorer (1)
advantage
   to take ~   profiter (de) (8)
advice   conseil *m.* (11)
to advise   conseiller (12)
affectionate   affectueux (-euse) (2)
affront   atteinte *f.* (15)
afraid
   to be ~   avoir peur (11)
Africa   Afrique *f.* (4)
after   après (1)
afternoon   après-midi *m.* (4)
age   âge *m.* (3)
ago   il y a (16)
ahead   d'avance (14)
AIDS   sida *m.* (11)
air letter   aérogramme *m.* (8)
airplane   avion *m.* (6)
airport   aéroport *m.* (10)
alcohol   alcool *m.* (3)
Algeria   Algérie *f.* (4)
Algerian   Algérien(ne) *m., f.* (18)
all   tous, toutes (4)
   ~ right   d'accord (10)
to allow   permettre (17)
almost   presque (10)

alone   seul(e) (2)
along   au bord de (4)
alphabet   alphabet *m.* (1)
already   déjà (5)
also   aussi (2)
always   toujours (2)
A.M.   du matin (6)
amazed   étonné(e) (11)
ambitious   ambitieux (-euse) (2)
American   américain(e) (2)
an   un, une (3)
and   et (P)
   ~ you   et toi, et vous (P)
animal   animal *m.* (*pl.* -aux) (18)
ankle   cheville *f.* (13)
annoyance   inconvénient *m.* (11)
answer   réponse *f.* (10)
to answer   répondre (à) (6)
   answer!   répondez! (1)
answering machine   répondeur *m.*
   (7)
anthropology   anthropologie *f.* (8)
apartment   appartement *m.* (4)
to appear
   it appears (that)   il semble (que)
   (11)
appetizer   *hors-d'œuvre *m.* (3)
apple   pomme *f.* (9)
appliance   appareil électro-
   ménager *m.* (16)
to appreciate   apprécier (2)
April   avril *m.* (9)
Arabic   arabe *m.* (8)
architect   architecte *m.* (2)
architecture   architecture *f.* (8)
area   coin *m.* (9)
arm   bras *m.* (13)
armchair   fauteuil *m.* (16)
armoire   armoire *f.* (16)
arrival   arrivée *f.* (8)
to arrive   arriver (1)
art   art *m.* (8)
   ~ history   histoire de l'art *f.* (8)
article   article *m.* (15)
artist   artiste *m., f.* (2)
as . . . as   aussi... que (18)
Asia   Asie *f.* (4)

to ask   demander (à) (15)
   ~ for   demander (1)
   ~ a question   poser une question
   (9)
asleep
   to fall ~   s'endormir (13)
asparagus   asperges *f. pl.* (9)
at   à (1); au (2); chez (4)
athletic   sportif (-ive) (14)
attention
   to pay ~   faire attention (5)
August   août *m.* (9)
aunt   tante *f.* (2)
Australia   Australie *f.* (4)
Austria   Autriche *f.* (4)
author   auteur *m.* (2)
automatic   automatique (10)
to avoid   éviter (de) (11)

B

back   dos *m.* (13)
backpack   sac à dos *m.* (1)
bad   mauvais(e), méchant(e) (2)
   it is too ~ (that)   il est dommage
   (que) (11)
   to be ~ (weather)   faire mauvais
   (5)
badly   mal (18)
baker   boulanger (-ère) *m., f.* (12)
bakery   boulangerie *f.* (12)
ballet   ballet *m.*; danse classique *f.*
   (15)
banana   banane *f.* (9)
bank   banque *f.* (4)
   ~ account   compte en banque *m.*
   (11)
bark   écorce *f.* (17)
baseball   base-ball *m.* (14)
basketball   basket-ball *m.* (14)
bathing suit   maillot de bain *m.*
   (5)
bathroom   salle de bains *f.*;
   toilettes *f. pl.* (16)
bathtub   baignoire *f.* (16)
battery   pile *f.* (7)

to be être (2)
  it is c'est (1)
  they are ce sont (1)
beach plage *f.* (4)
beautiful beau (bel), belle, beaux, belles (9)
beauty beauté *f.* (15)
because parce que (4)
to become devenir (10)
bed lit *m.* (16)
  to go to ~ se coucher (13)
bedroom chambre *f.* (4)
beef bœuf *m.* (9)
beer bière *f.* (3)
before avant (6)
  just ~ juste avant (8)
to begin commencer (à) (1); se mettre à (17)
beginning début *m.* (6)
to behave se conduire (14)
behind derrière (4)
beige beige (6)
Belgium Belgique *f.* (4)
to belong to être à (5); appartenir à (10)
belt ceinture *f.* (5)
best le mieux; le meilleur, la meilleure, les meilleur(e)s (18)
better meilleur(e) (18)
  it's ~ (that) il vaut mieux (que) (11)
between entre (4)
bicycle bicyclette *f.*; vélo *m.* (6)
big gros(se) (6); grand(e) (9)
billion milliard *m.* (4)
biology biologie *f.* (8)
biotechnology biotechnologie *f.* (17)
bird oiseau *m.* (*pl.* -eaux) (17)
black noir(e) (5)
to blacken noircir (17)
blackened noirci(e) (17)
blood test prise de sang *f.* (13)
blouse chemisier *m.* (5)
blue bleu(e) (5)
to blush rougir (7)
board tableau *m.* (*pl.* -aux) (1)
boat bateau *m.* (*pl.* -eaux) (6)
body corps *m.* (13)
book livre *m.* (1)
  ~ of tickets carnet *m.* (6)
bookstore librairie *f.* (4)
boot botte *f.* (5)
boring ennuyeux (-euse) (2)

born
  to be ~ naître (6)
to borrow emprunter (8)
to bother embêter (11)
bottle bouteille *f.* (12)
bourgeois bourgeois(e) (15)
bowling
  lawn ~ pétanque *f.* (14)
boy garçon *m.* (2)
boyfriend copain *m.*; petit ami *m.* (2)
brake frein *m.* (10)
to brake freiner (10)
branch branche *f.* (18)
Brazil Brésil *m.* (4)
bread pain *m.* (3)
to break down tomber en panne (10)
breakfast petit déjeuner *m.* (9)
brilliant brillant(e) (18)
brilliantly brillamment (18)
to bring apporter (3); amener (13)
  ~ back rapporter (6)
bronze bronze *m.* (15)
brother frère *m.* (2)
brown brun(e) (5)
to brush (se) brosser (13)
Brussels Bruxelles (4)
building
  apartment ~ immeuble *m.* (16)
bus autobus *m.* (1); bus *m.* (6)
  ~ stop arrêt d'autobus (4)
business acquaintance relation d'affaires *f.* (2)
but mais (1)
butcher boucher (-ère) *m., f.* (12)
  ~ shop boucherie *f.* (12)
butter beurre *m.* (3)
to buy acheter (5)
by par (1); au bord de (4)

C

cable câble *m.* (11)
café café *m.* (1); bistrot *m.* (3)
café-restaurant brasserie *f.* (12)
cake gâteau *m.* (*pl.* -eaux) (3)
calculator calculatrice *f.* (7)
calendar calendrier *m.* (9)
to call appeler (13)
  ~ back rappeler (7)
  to be ~ed s'appeler (13)
can pouvoir (7)

Canada Canada *m.* (4)
Canadian canadien(ne) (2)
candy bonbon *m.* (9)
canned food conserves *f. pl.* (12)
capital capitale *f.* (8)
car voiture *f.* (2); auto *f.* (6)
  new ~ voiture neuve *f.* (10)
  used ~ voiture d'occasion *f.* (10)
card carte *f.* (14)
  orange ~ carte orange *f.* (6)
care
  to take ~ of s'occuper de (13)
career métier *m.* (15)
  ~ in the arts métier artistique (15)
careful prudent(e) (2)
carefully prudemment (18)
caretaker concierge *m., f.* (16)
carpet tapis *m.* (16)
carrots
  grated ~ carottes râpées *f. pl.* (9)
cartoon dessin animé *m.* (11)
cashier's caisse *f.* (12)
casino casino *m.* (4)
cassette cassette *f.* (7)
cat chat *m.* (18)
CD CD *m.* (7)
  ~ player lecteur de CD *m.* (7)
cello violoncelle *m.* (15)
cellular phone portable *m.* (7)
certain certain(e) (2); sûr(e) (11)
certainly certainement (18)
Chad Tchad *m.* (4)
chair chaise *f.* (1)
chalk craie *f.* (1)
champion champion(ne) *m., f.* (14)
championship championnat *m.* (14)
to change changer (de) (6)
charming charmant(e) (2)
cheers! à la tienne!, à la vôtre! (14)
cheese fromage *m.* (3)
chemistry chimie *f.* (8)
cherry cerise *f.* (9)
chicken poulet *m.* (3)
child enfant *m., f.* (1)
China Chine *f.* (4)
Chinese chinois(e) (8)
chocolate chocolat *m.* (3)
to choose choisir (de) (7)

chop côtelette *f.* (9)
church église *f.* (4)
cinema cinéma *m.* (4)
circle milieu *m.* (15)
city ville *f.* (4)
class cours *m.* (1)
 in ~ en cours (1)
classical classique (2)
classmate camarade de cours *m.*, *f.* (2)
classroom classe *f.*; salle de classe *f.* (1)
clean propre (9)
to clean faire le ménage (5)
 ~ up ranger (7)
clerk employé(e) *m.*, *f.* (8)
to close fermer (1)
closed fermé(e) (2)
clothes vêtements *m. pl.* (5)
cloud nuage *m.* (8)
club boîte *f.*, club *m.* (2)
coat manteau *m.* (*pl.* -eaux); veste *f.*; veston *m.* (5)
coffee café *m.* (3)
cola coca *m.* (3)
cold froid(e) (2)
 to be ~ avoir froid (3); faire froid (5)
color couleur *f.* (5)
column colonne *f.* (17)
to come venir (10)
 ~ back revenir (10)
 ~ down descendre (de) (6)
 come on! voyons! (8)
comedy comédie *f.* (15)
competent compétent(e) (2)
complete complet (-ète) (18)
completely complètement (18)
complicated compliqué(e) (2)
compulsory obligatoire (10)
computer ordinateur *m.* (7)
 ~ progammer programmeur (-euse) *m.*, *f.* (2)
 ~ science informatique *f.* (8)
concert concert *m.* (6)
concierge concierge *m.*, *f.* (16)
conductor chef d'orchestre *m.* (15)
connection correspondance *f.* (6)
to consult consulter (11)
to consume consommer (3)
contact contact *m.* (17)
to contain contenir (10)
contemporary contemporain(e) (11)

continent continent *m.* (4)
to continue continuer (à) (1)
to contribute contribuer (à) (15)
to cook faire la cuisine (5)
cooking cuisine *f.* (3)
cool
 to be ~ faire frais (8)
corner coin *m.* (9)
 at the ~ of au coin de (4)
correct correct(e) (15)
Corsica Corse *f.* (4)
to cost coûter (5)
Côte d'Ivoire Côte d'Ivoire *f.* (4)
countable nombrable (17)
country pays *m.* (4); campagne *f.* (8)
countryside paysage *m.* (17)
courageous courageux (-euse) (2)
course cours *m.* (1)
couscous couscous *m.* (3)
cousin cousin(e) *m.*, *f.* (2)
cow vache *f.* (18)
cream crème *f.* (3)
to create créer (17)
credit card carte de crédit *f.* (10)
Creole créole *m.* (5)
crepe crêpe *f.* (5)
crime criminalité *f.* (11)
to critique critiquer (15)
cross
 green ~ croix verte *f.* (13)
cucumber concombre *m.* (9)
cuisine cuisine *f.* (3)
to cut class sécher un cours (13)
cutlet escalope *f.* (9)

D

dairy store crémerie *f.* (12)
damage mal *m.* (15)
to dance danser (1)
dancer danseur (-euse) *m.*, *f.* (15)
dangerous dangereux (-euse) (2)
date date *f.* (*calendar*) (9)
daughter fille *f.* (2)
day jour *m.* (9); journée *f.* (13)
dear cher (-ère) (8)
December décembre *m.* (9)
to decide décider (6)
delicious délicieux (-euse) (3)
delighted enchanté(e) (2)
delinquency délinquance *f.* (11)
Denmark Danemark *m.* (4)

dentist dentiste *m.*, *f.* (13)
department département *m.* (5); rayon *m.* (12)
 ~ store grand magasin *m.* (11)
to describe décrire (14)
to desire désirer (2)
desk bureau *m.* (*pl.* -eaux) (1)
destruction destruction *f.* (15)
devoted consacré(e) (15)
dialogue dialogue *m.* (1)
to die mourir (10)
diet
 to be on a ~ faire un régime (5); être au régime (13)
different différent(e) (9)
difficult difficile (2)
to diminish diminuer (17)
dining room salle à manger *f.* (16)
dinner dîner *m.* (9)
 to have ~ dîner (3)
diplomat diplomate *m.* (2)
disaster désastre *m.* (11)
to disconnect couper (7)
discount remise *f.* (12)
to discuss discuter (11)
dish plat *m.* (3)
 prepared ~ plat cuisiné (12)
 to do the ~es faire la vaisselle (5)
dishwasher lave-vaisselle *m.* (16)
disk drive lecteur de disquettes *m.* (8)
diskette disquette *f.* (8)
to disobey désobéir (à) (7)
divided divisé (par) (1)
to do faire (5)
doctor médecin *m.* (2)
documents papiers *m. pl.* (10)
dog chien *m.* (18)
door porte *f.* (1); (of a car) portière *f.* (10)
dorm résidence universitaire *f.* (4)
to doubt douter (11)
downtown en ville (4); centre-ville *m.* (12)
drama drame *m.* (15)
to dream rêver (de) (15)
dress robe *f.* (5)
to dress
 to get dressed s'habiller (13)
drink pot *m.* (6)
 before-dinner ~ apéritif *m.* (3)
 to have a ~ prendre un pot (6)

to drink   boire (12)
  I drink   je bois (3)
  you drink   tu bois; vous buvez (3)
to drive   conduire (10; 14)
driver   chauffeur *m.* (10)
  ~'s license   permis de conduire *m.* (10)
drug   drogue *f.* (11)
  ~ testing   contrôle anti-doping *m.* (14)
drugstore   pharmacie *f.* (4)
  all-night ~   pharmacie de nuit (13)
  emergency ~   pharmacie de garde (13)
dry   sec (sèche) (12)
  ~ cleaner's   teinturerie *f.* (12)
to dry   sécher (13)
dryer   sèche-linge *m.* (16)
duck   canard *m.* (18)
during   pendant (8)

E

ear   oreille *f.* (13)
early   en avance (6); de bonne heure (12); tôt (13)
to earn   gagner (8)
easily   facilement (18)
easy   facile (2)
to eat   manger (1)
ecological   écologique (11)
ecologist   écologiste *m., f.* (17)
ecology   écologie *f.* (17)
economics   sciences éco(nomiques) *f. pl.* (8)
economist   économiste *m., f.* (2)
education   enseignement *m.* (15)
egg   œuf *m.* (9)
eight   huit (1)
eighteen   dix-huit (1)
elbow   coude *m.* (13)
eleven   onze (1)
eleventh   onzième (2)
elsewhere   ailleurs (18)
e-mail   courrier électronique *m.* (8)
to embody   incarner (17)
employee   employé(e) *m., f.* (6)
empty   vide (14)
end   bout *m.* (6)
to end   terminer (1)
endangered   en péril (15)

energy   énergie *f.* (17)
engineer   ingénieur *m.* (2)
England   Angleterre *f.* (4)
English   anglais(e) (1)
English (language)   anglais *m.* (1)
to enjoy
  ~ doing   aimer faire (2)
enough   assez (de) (3)
to enter   entrer (2)
entertainment   distraction *f.* (2)
entrance   entrée *f.* (16)
envelope   enveloppe *f.* (8)
environment   environnement *m.* (17)
equality   égalité *f.* (11)
equipment   matériel *m.* (8)
errands   courses *f. pl.* (5)
  to run ~   faire des courses (5)
euro   euro *m.* (12)
Europe   Europe *f.* (4)
European   européen(ne) (10)
evening   soirée *f.* (2); soir *m.* (3)
every   tout(e) (8)
  ~ day   tous les jours (4)
  ~ year   tous les ans (5)
everybody   tout le monde (12)
everywhere   partout (18)
to evoke   évoquer (17)
exactly   exactement (8)
exam   examen *m.* (1)
to examine   examiner (13)
excerpt   extrait *m.* (15)
exercise   exercice *m.* (1)
to exercise   faire de l'exercice (13)
expenses   frais *m. pl.* (10)
expensive   cher (-ère) (4)
to explain   expliquer (1)
expression   expression *f.* (7)
eye   œil *m.* (*pl.* yeux) (13)

F

factory   usine *f.* (4)
to fail   échouer (à) (15)
fair   juste (11)
fall   automne *m.* (9)
to fall   tomber (10)
false   faux (fausse) (11)
family   famille *f.* (2)
fantastic   fantastique (2)
far from   loin de (4)
fascinating   fascinant(e) (2)
fast   rapide (2); vite (18)

father   père *m.* (2)
father-in-law   beau-père *m.* (*pl.* beaux-pères) (2)
favorite   favori(te) (2); préféré(e) (3)
February   février *m.* (9)
to feel   sentir (7); se sentir (13)
  ~ better   aller mieux (13)
  ~ like   avoir envie (11)
feminine   féminin(e) (2)
fever   fièvre *f.* (13)
field   champ *m.* (17)
fifteen   quinze (1)
fifth   cinquième (2)
fifty   cinquante (2)
filet   filet *m.* (9)
film   film *m.* (2)
finally   enfin (16)
to find   trouver (3)
  ~ again   retrouver (6)
  ~ oneself   se trouver (13)
fine
  I'm ~   ça va bien, je vais bien (P)
finger   doigt *m.* (13)
to finish   finir (de) (7)
Finland   Finlande *f.* (4)
first   premier (-ère) (2); d'abord (7)
fish   poisson *m.* (3)
  ~ market   poissonnerie *f.* (12)
  ~monger   poissonnier (-ère) *m., f.* (12)
fishing   pêche *f.* (14)
five   cinq (1)
floor   étage *m.* (16); (*in Quebec*) plancher *m.* (16)
  ground ~   rez-de-chaussée *m.* (16)
florist   fleuriste *m., f.* (12)
flour   farine *f.* (3)
flower   fleur *f.* (17)
flute   flûte *f.* (15)
foggy
  to be ~   faire du brouillard (8)
to follow   suivre (8)
following   suivant(e) (15)
fond
  to be ~ of   aimer bien (2); tenir à (10)
food   nourriture *f.* (3)
foot   (*of animal*) patte *f.* (9); pied *m.* (13)
  on ~   à pied (6)
football   football américain *m.* (14)

for pendant (8); pour (16)
to forbid défendre (15)
foreign étranger (-ère) (8)
foreigner étranger (-ère) *m., f.* (10)
to foresee prévoir (8)
forest forêt *f.* (17)
to forget oublier (de) (5)
former ancien(ne) (2)
fortunately heureusement (6)
forty quarante (2)
four quatre (1)
fourteen quatorze (1)
fourth quatrième (2)
France France *f.* (4)
frankness franchise *f.* (11)
free libre (7)
freed délivré(e) (17)
French (language) français *m.* (1)
   in ~ en français (1)
French français(e) (1)
   ~ fries frites *f. pl.* (3)
French Riviera Côte d'Azur *f.* (4)
frequent fréquent(e) (18)
frequently fréquemment (18)
Friday vendredi *m.* (9)
friend ami(e) *m., f.* (1); copain *m.*, copine *f.* (2)
from de (1); dès (16)
front
   in ~ of devant (2)
frost gel *m.* (17)
frozen surgelé(e) (12)
fruit fruit *m.* (3)
   ~ juice jus de fruit *m.* (3)
full plein(e) (4)
fun
   to have ~ s'amuser (à) (13)
to function marcher (7)
furious furieux (-euse) (11)
furnished meublé(e) (16)
furniture meubles *m. pl.* (16)
future avenir *m.* (11); futur *m.* (17)

G

game show jeu télévisé *m.* (11)
garden jardin *m.* (17)
general général(e) (18)
   in ~ en général (1)
generally généralement (13)
generous généreux (-euse) (2)

Geneva Genève (4)
gentlemen Messieurs (4)
geography géographie *f.* (8)
geology géologie *f.* (8)
German allemand(e) (2)
Germany Allemagne *f.* (4)
to get
   ~ closer s'approcher (18)
   ~ off descendre (de) (6)
   ~ on monter (dans) (6)
   ~ up se lever (13)
girl fille *f.* (2)
girlfriend copine *f.*; petite amie *f.* (2)
to give donner (1)
   ~ back rendre (6)
glass verre *m.* (14)
glove gant *m.* (5)
to go aller (4)
   go ahead! allez-y!; vas-y! (4)
   ~ back rentrer (4)
   ~ down descendre (de) (6)
   ~ in entrer (2)
   ~ . . . kilometers per hour rouler à... km à l'heure (10)
   ~ out sortir (7)
   ~ out with sortir avec (7)
   ~ to fréquenter (2)
   ~ up monter (dans) (6)
   let's go! allons-y! (4)
   shall we go? on y va? (4)
God Dieu *m.* (18)
golf golf *m.* (14)
good bon(ne) (5)
   ~ evening bonsoir (P)
   ~ morning bonjour (P)
good-bye au revoir (P)
gram gramme *m.* (12)
grandchildren petits-enfants *m. pl.* (2)
grandfather grand-père *m.* (*pl.* grands-pères) (2)
grandmother grand-mère *f.* (*pl.* grands-mères) (2)
grandparents grands-parents *m. pl.* (2)
grape raisin *m.* (9)
gray gris(e) (5)
Great Britain Grande-Bretagne *f.* (4)
Greece Grèce *f.* (4)
Greek (language) grec *m.* (8)
green vert(e) (5)
   ~ beans *haricots verts *m. pl.* (9)

grocer épicier (-ère) *m., f.* (12)
grocery shop épicerie *f.* (12)
guitar guitare *f.* (15)
gymnastics gymnastique *f.* (14)

H

habit habitude *f.* (10)
hair cheveux *m. pl.* (13)
half demi(e) (6)
ham jambon *m.* (3)
hamburger *hamburger *m.* (3)
hand main *f.* (13)
to hand back/in remettre (17)
handshake poignée de main *f.* (P)
hang gliding deltaplane *m.* (14)
to hang up
   don't hang up! ne coupe(z) pas! (7)
to happen se passer, arriver (7)
happiness bonheur *m.* (11)
happy content(e), heureux (-euse) (2)
hat chapeau *m.* (*pl.* -eaux) (5)
to hate détester (2)
   ~ doing détester faire (2)
Havana La Havane (4)
to have avoir (3); prendre (9)
   it has been . . . that il y a... que, voilà... que (16)
   ~ a sore . . . avoir mal à... (13)
he il (1)
head tête *f.* (9)
headlight phare *m.* (10)
health santé *f.* (11)
   to be in bad ~ être en mauvaise santé (13)
   to be in good ~ être en bonne santé (13); se porter bien (13)
to hear entendre (6)
heat chaleur *f.* (8)
hello bonjour, bonsoir (P); *(on telephone)* allô, j'écoute (7)
hen poule *f.* (18)
her elle; son, sa, ses (5); la (l') (8); lui (9)
here ici (1)
   ~ is voici, voilà (1)
hers le sien, la sienne, les sien(ne)s (14)
to hesitate hésiter (à) (15)
hey! tiens! (2)
hi salut (P)

high school lycée *m.* (4)
him lui (2); le (l') (8); lui (9)
his son, sa, ses (5); le sien, la sienne, les sien(ne)s (14)
history histoire *f.* (8)
to hitchhike faire du stop (6)
hockey *hockey *m.* (14)
to hold tenir (10)
~ **back** retenir (10)
hold on! ne quittez pas! (7)
Holland *Hollande *f.* (4)
home
at the ~ of chez (4)
homeless sans-abri *m.,* sans-logis *m.,* SDF *m.* (11)
homework devoirs *m. pl.* (1)
to do ~ faire (ses) devoirs (5)
to hope espérer (9)
horn klaxon *m.* (10)
horrible affreux (-euse) (2)
horse cheval *m.* (*pl.* -aux) (18)
horseback
~ **riding** équitation *f.* (14)
on ~ à cheval (6)
hostess hôtesse *f.* (4)
hot chaud(e) (2)
to be ~ avoir chaud (3); faire chaud (5)
hotel hôtel *m.* (1)
hour heure *f.* (6)
house maison *f.* (4)
how comment (6); que (18)
~ **are you?** ça va?, comment ça va? (P)
~ **do you do?** comment allez-vous? (P)
~ **many?** combien (de)? (6)
~ **much?** combien? (1); combien de? (6)
~ **much is . . . ?** combien font... ? (1)
hundred cent (4)
hungry
to be ~ avoir faim (3)
hunting chasse *f.* (13)
to hurry se dépêcher (de) (13)
to hurt one's . . . se faire mal à... (13)
husband mari *m.* (2)
hypochondriac hypocondriaque (13)
hypocrisy hypocrisie *f.* (2)
hypocritical hypocrite (2)

I

I je (1); moi (2)
ice cream glace *f.* (3)
idea idée *f.* (5)
if si (4)
illness maladie *f.* (13)
imam imam *m.* (18)
immigrant immigré(e) *m., f.* (18)
impolite impoli(e) (2)
importance importance *f.* (11)
important important(e) (11)
impossible impossible (2)
impressive impressionnant(e) (8)
in à (1); dans (3); en (4); *(time)* dans, en (16)
to include inclure (17)
included compris(e) (16)
incompetent incompétent(e) (2)
to increase augmenter (17)
Independence Day Fête nationale *f.* (9)
independent indépendant(e) (2)
independently indépendamment (18)
to indicate indiquer (9)
indispensable indispensable (10)
inflation inflation *f.* (11)
information renseignement *m.* (4)
instrument instrument *m.* (15)
musical ~ instrument de musique (15)
insufficient insuffisant(e) (15)
insufficiently insuffisamment (18)
insurance
full collision ~ assurance tous risques *f.* (10)
intelligent intelligent(e) (2)
intelligently intelligemment (18)
to interest intéresser (16)
interested
to be ~ s'intéresser (à) (15)
interesting intéressant(e) (2)
Internet Internet *m.* (8)
interview interview *f.* (11)
intolerance intolérance *f.* (2)
to introduce présenter (9)
to invite inviter (à) (1)
Ireland Irlande *f.* (4)
isn't it so? n'est-ce pas? (1)
it il (1); le (l'), la (l') (8)
of ~ en (15)

Italian italien(ne) (2)
Italy Italie *f.* (4)
its son, sa, ses (5)

J

jackal chacal *m.* (18)
jacket veste *f.* (5)
jam confiture *f.* (3)
January janvier *m.* (9)
Japan Japon *m.* (4)
Japanese (language) japonais *m.* (8)
jazz jazz *m.* (2)
jeans jean *m.* (5)
jersey maillot *m.* (14)
jewelry store bijouterie *f.* (12)
job emploi *m.* (11)
jogging jogging *m.* (14)
journalism journalisme *m.* (8)
journalist journaliste *m., f.* (2)
July juillet *m.* (9)
June juin *m.* (9)
just juste (1)
to have ~ venir de (10)
justice justice *f.* (11)

K

key clé (1)
keyboard clavier *m.* (8)
kilometer kilomètre *m.* (10)
kiss baiser *m.,* bise *f.* (8)
to kiss faire une bise à (P); embrasser (2)
kitchen cuisine *f.* (16)
knee genou *m.* (*pl.* -oux) (13)
to know savoir; connaître (10)
I don't ~ je ne sais pas (1)

L

Labor Day Fête du Travail *f.* (9)
laboratory laboratoire *m.* (4)
ladies Mesdemoiselles *f. pl.* (12); Mesdames *f. pl.*
lake lac *m.* (17)
lamb agneau *m.* (*pl.* -eaux) (3)

leg of ~ gigot *m.* (9)
lamp lampe *f.* (16)
landscape paysage *m.* (17)
language langue *f.* (8)
last dernier (-ère) (5)
late en retard (2); tard (13)
later plus tard (7)
latest dernier (-ère) (2)
Latin latin *m.* (8)
laundry
   to do the ~ faire la lessive (5)
law droit *m.* (8); loi *f.* (10)
lawn pelouse *f.* (17)
lawyer avocat(e) *m., f.* (2)
lazy paresseux (-euse) (2)
leaf feuille *f.* (17)
to learn apprendre (à) (9)
to leave laisser (6); partir (7)
left
   on the ~ à gauche (16)
leg jambe *f.* (13)
to lend prêter (8)
less moins (1)
Lesser Antilles Petites Antilles
   f. pl. (5)
lesson leçon *f.* (1)
let's see! voyons! (8)
letter lettre *f.* (8)
library bibliothèque *f.* (4)
lie mensonge *m.* (14)
to lie mentir (7)
life vie *f.* (11)
light lumière *f.* (17)
lightning éclair *m.* (8)
like comme (3); tout comme (9);
   tel(le) (18)
to like aimer (1); aimer bien (2)
   how do you ~ . . . ? comment
     trouvez-vous... ? (3)
   I would like je voudrais (3)
likely probable (11)
   it's ~ (that) il est probable
     (que); il se peut (que) (11)
line ligne *f.* (6)
   to stand in ~ faire la queue (5)
Lisbon Lisbonne (4)
list liste *f.* (4)
to listen écouter (1)
literary littéraire (15)
literature littérature *f.* (8)
little peu (3)
   just a ~ juste un peu (1)
livable habitable (17)

to live habiter (1)
lively vivace (15); vif (-ive) (17)
living room salon *m.* (16)
London Londres (4)
to look
   ~ at regarder (1)
   ~ for chercher (4)
   ~ good avoir bonne mine (13)
   ~ like avoir l'air (5); ressembler
     (à) (9)
   ~ out on donner sur (16)
   ~ sick avoir mauvaise mine
     (13)
to lose perdre (6)
   ~ patience perdre patience (6)
lost and found bureau des objets
   trouvés *m.* (6)
Louisiana Louisiane *f.* (16)
love *(to conclude a letter)*
   affectueux baisers *m. pl.* (8);
   amour *m.* (11)
to love aimer (1)
lucid lucide (17)
luck chance *f.* (6)
   what ~! quelle chance! (6)
luggage bagages *m. pl.* (5)
   hand ~ bagages à main *m. pl.* (5)
lunch déjeuner *m.* (9)
   to have ~ déjeuner (3)

M

ma'am madame *f.* (P)
magazine magazine *m.* (14)
Maghreb Maghreb (Maroc,
   Algérie, Tunisie) *m.* (18)
   person from the ~
     Maghrébin(e) *m., f.*
magnificent magnifique (2)
maid's room chambre de bonne *f.*
   (16)
mail courrier *m.* (8)
to mail expédier (8)
mailman facteur *m.* (8)
main course plat principal *m.* (3)
man homme *m.* (1)
management gestion *f.* (8)
manager
   middle-level ~ cadre *m.* (11)
many beaucoup (1)
   as ~ autant (18)

map carte *f.* (1)
March mars *m.* (9)
market
   ~ square place du marché *f.* (9)
   open-air ~ marché en plein air
     m. (9)
masculine masculin(e) (2)
match match *m.* (2)
materialistic matérialiste (11)
math mathématiques (maths)
   f. pl. (8)
matter matière *f.* (17)
   as a ~ of fact justement (6)
may pouvoir (7)
May mai *m.* (9)
maybe peut-être (12)
me moi (2)
meal repas *m.* (9)
mean méchant(e) (2)
to mean vouloir dire
   it ~s cela veut dire (1)
   what does . . . ~? qu'est-ce
     que... veut dire? (1)
meanness
   out of ~ méchamment (18)
meat viande *f.* (3)
medicine médecine *(science) f.* (8)
to meet rencontrer (8)
mention
   don't ~ it il n'y a pas de quoi
     (1)
menu carte *f.*; menu *m.* (3)
merchant marchand(e) *m., f.* (9)
merguez sausage merguez *f.* (3)
message message *m.* (7)
meter mètre *m.* (14)
Mexican mexicain(e) (2)
Mexico Mexique *m.* (4)
Mexico City Mexico (4)
midnight minuit *m.* (6)
milk lait *m.* (3)
Milky Way Voie lactée *f.* (17)
million million *m.* (4)
mind
   to have in ~ penser (à) (15)
mine le mien, la mienne, les
   mien(ne)s (14)
mineral water eau minérale *f.* (3)
minute minute *f.* (4)
Miss Mademoiselle *f.* (P)
mistake faute *f.* (15)
modem modem *m.* (8)
modern art art moderne *m.* (2)

Monday   lundi *m.* (9)
money   argent *m.* (3)
   ~ order   mandat *m.* (8)
monitor   moniteur *m.* (8)
month   mois *m.* (5)
monument   monument *m.* (8)
moon   lune *f.* (17)
more   plus (1); davantage (13)
morning   matin *m.* (4); matinée *f.* (9)
Moroccan   Marocain(e) *m., f.* (18)
Morocco   Maroc *m.* (4)
Moscow   Moscou (4)
most   le plus (11)
mother   mère *f.* (2)
mother-in-law   belle-mère *f.* (*pl.* belles-mères) (2)
motorcycle   moto *f.* (6)
mountain   montagne *f.* (11)
   ~ climbing   alpinisme *m.* (14)
mouth   bouche *f.* (13)
Mozambique   Mozambique *m.* (4)
Mr.   Monsieur *m.* (P)
Mrs.   Madame *f.* (P)
Ms.   Madame *f.*, Mademoiselle *f.* (P)
much   beaucoup (1)
   as ~   autant (18)
muezzin   muezzin *m.* (18)
multiplied   multiplié (par) (1)
museum   musée *m.* (4)
music   musique *f.* (2)
musical   comédie musicale *f.* (15)
musician   musicien(ne) *m., f.* (2)
must   devoir, falloir (12)
mustard   moutarde *f.* (3)
mutton   mouton *m.* (3)
my   mon, ma, mes (5)

N

name   nom *m.* (9)
   what's your ~?   comment vous appelez-vous?, comment t'appelles-tu? (1)
   my ~ is . . .   je m'appelle... (P)
nationality   nationalité *f.* (2)
nature   nature *f.* (17)
near   près de (4)
necessarily   nécessairement (18)

necessary   nécessaire (7)
   it is ~ (that)   il faut (que) (4); il est nécessaire (que) (11)
neck   cou *m.* (12)
to need   avoir besoin (de) (10)
negative   négatif (-ive) (14)
neighbor   voisin(e) *m., f.* (11)
nephew   neveu *m.* (2)
Netherlands   Pays-Bas *m. pl.* (4)
neuvième   ninth (2)
never   ne... jamais (8)
new   nouveau (nouvel), nouvelle, nouveaux, nouvelles (9); neuf (neuve) (10)
   what's ~?   quoi de neuf? (P)
New Orleans   La Nouvelle-Orléans (4)
news   nouvelles *f. pl.* (8); actualités *f. pl.* (11); informations *f. pl.* (14)
next   prochain(e) (4)
next to   à côté de (4)
nice   bien; sympathique (2); beau (bel), belle, beaux, belles (9)
   to be ~ (weather)   faire beau (5); faire bon (8)
niece   nièce *f.* (2)
night   nuit *f.* (13)
   all ~ long   de la nuit (13)
nightclub   boîte de nuit *f.* (2)
nightgown   chemise de nuit *f.* (5)
nine   neuf (1)
nineteen   dix-neuf (1)
no   non (1)
   ~ more   ne... plus (12)
nobody   ne... personne (12)
noise   bruit *m.* (11)
   to make ~   faire du bruit (11)
noodles   pâtes *f. pl.* (5)
noon   midi *m.* (6)
North Africa   Afrique du Nord *f.* (18)
North America   Amérique du Nord *f.* (4)
Norway   Norvège *f.* (4)
nose   nez *m.* (13)
not   ne... pas (2)
   ~ at all   de rien (1); pas du tout (4)
   ~ bad   pas mal (P)
   ~ yet   pas encore (5); ne... pas encore (8)
note   note *f.* (8)

notebook   cahier *m.* (1)
nothing   rien (5); ne... rien (12)
   for ~   pour rien (6)
novel   roman *m.* (10)
November   novembre *m.* (9)
now   maintenant (4)
nuclear   nucléaire (11)
number   nombre *m.* (11)
   wrong ~   erreur *f.* (7)

O

to obey   obéir (à) (7)
to obtain   obtenir (10)
obvious   évident(e) (11)
obviously   évidemment (18)
October   octobre *m.* (9)
of   de (1)
   ~ course   bien sûr (5)
   ~ it   y (15)
office   bureau *m.* (*pl.* -eaux) (1)
often   souvent (2)
oh no!   ah non! (4)
oil   huile *f.* (3)
old   ancien(ne) (2); vieux (vieil), vieille, vieux, vieilles (9)
   how ~ are you?   quel âge avez-vous (as-tu)? (3)
   to be . . . years ~   avoir... an(s) (3)
olive   olive *f.* (9)
omelet   omelette *f.* (5)
on   sur (4)
one   on *m.* (1)
one   un(e) (1)
   the ~   celui, celle
   the ~s   ceux, celles (14)
only   ne... que (12); seulement (18)
open   ouvert(e) (2)
to open   ouvrir (1)
   open your book!   ouvrez votre livre! (1)
opera   opéra *m.* (15)
opinion   opinion *f.* (11)
   ~ poll   sondage d'opinion *m.* (11)
   to have an ~   penser (de) (15)
optimistic   optimiste (2)
or   ou (1)
orange   orange *f.* (9)
orchestra   orchestre *m.* (15)
order   commande *f.* (12)
   in ~ to   pour (4)

to order   commander (3)
other   autre (4)
our   notre, nos (5)
ours   le (la) nôtre, les nôtres (14)
outside   à l'extérieur (5)
oven   four *m.* (16)
  microwave ~
    four à micro-ondes *m.* (16)
over there   là-bas (4)
overcast   couvert(e) (8)
own   propre (9)
to own   posséder (13)
owner   patron(ne) *m., f.* (14);
    propriétaire *m., f.* (16)

P

to pack   faire les bagages (5)
  ~ the suitcases   faire les valises
    (5)
package   colis *m.* (8)
page   page *f.* (1)
painter   peintre *m.* (15)
painting   peinture *f.*, tableau *m.*
    (*pl.* -eaux) (15)
  oil ~   peinture à l'huile *f.* (15)
pajamas   pyjama *m.* (5)
pants   pantalon *m.* (5)
parcel   paquet *m.* (8)
parents   parents *m. pl.* (2)
Parisian   parisien(ne) (2)
park   parc *m.* (4)
to park   garer (2); stationner (10)
parking lot   parking *m.* (4)
part   partie *f.* (13)
to pass   *(an exam)* réussir (à) (7)
  ~ by   passer par (10)
pastis   pastis *m.* (14)
pastry maker   pâtissier (-ère) *m., f.*
    (12)
pastry shop   pâtisserie *f.* (12)
pâté   pâté *m.* (9)
  liver ~   pâté de foie *m.* (12)
patient
  to be ~   avoir de la patience (3)
to pay   payer, régler (10)
peace   paix *f.* (11)
peach   pêche *f.* (9)
pear   poire *f.* (9)
peas   petits pois *m. pl.* (9)
pen   stylo *m.* (1)
pencil   crayon *m.* (1)

pensive   méditatif (-ive) (17)
people   gens *m. pl.* (10)
perfect   parfait(e) (5)
perfectly   parfaitement (18)
pessimistic   pessimiste (2)
philosophy   philo(sophie) *f.* (2)
phone
  cellular ~   portable *m.* (7)
  ~ booth   cabine téléphonique *f.*
    (7)
  ~ number   numéro de téléphone
    m. (10)
photo   photo *f.* (3)
physical education   éducation
    physique *f.* (8)
physics   physique *f.* (8)
piano   piano *m.* (15)
pig   cochon *m.* (18)
pink   rose (17)
pitcher   pichet *m.* (3)
pizza   pizza *f.* (3)
place   endroit *m.* (4); place *f.* (14)
  in your (his, her) ~   à votre (ta,
    sa) place (16)
to place   placer (16)
planet   planète *f.* (17)
play   pièce *f.* (14)
to play   jouer (1); *(sports)* jouer (à)
    (14); *(musical instrument)*
    jouer (de) (15)
  ~ sports   faire du sport (5)
player   joueur (-euse) *m., f.* (14)
playwright   auteur dramatique *m.*
    (15)
pleasant   agréable (2)
please   s'il te plaît; s'il vous plaît
    (3)
to plug in   brancher (7)
P.M.   de l'après-midi, du soir (6)
pocket   poche *f.* (5)
poem   poème *m.* (10)
poet   poète *m.* (17)
poetry   poésie *f.* (14)
Poland   Pologne *f.* (4)
policeman   agent de police *m.* (2);
    gendarme *m.* (10)
polite   poli(e) (2)
political science   sciences
    po(litiques) *f. pl.* (8)
politics   politique *f.* (11)
pollution   pollution *f.* (11)
polo shirt   polo *m.* (5)
poor   pauvre (2)

popular   populaire (18)
pork   porc *m.* (9)
  ~ butcher   charcutier (-ère) *m., f.*
    (12)
  ~ butcher's shop   charcuterie *f.*
    (12)
Portugal   Portugal *m.* (4)
possessions   affaires *f. pl.* (7)
possibility   possibilité *f.* (11)
possible   possible (2)
post office   bureau de poste *m.* (4)
postcard   carte postale *f.* (8)
poster   affiche *f.* (1)
to postpone   remettre (17)
potato   pomme de terre *f.* (9)
to practice   pratiquer (14)
to pray   prier (18)
prayer   prière *f.* (18)
to prefer   aimer mieux (2); préférer
    (13)
preferable   préférable (11)
to preoccupy   préoccuper (11)
to prepare   préparer (3)
present   cadeau *m.* (*pl.* -eaux) (1)
present   présent(e) (2)
president   président *m.* (2)
pretty   joli(e) (9)
price
  fixed ~ *(menu)*   prix fixe *m.* (3)
printer   imprimante *f.* (8)
probably   probablement (18)
problem   problème *m.* (6)
to produce   produire (14)
product   produit *m.* (12)
profession   profession *f.* (2)
professor   professeur *m.*; prof *m.,*
    f. (1)
program   émission *f.*; programme
    m. (11)
to promise   promettre (17)
Provence   Provence *f.*
  from ~   provençal(e)
    (*pl.* -aux, -ales) (9)
psychology   psycho(logie) *f.* (8)
published   publié(e) (15)
pullover   pull *m.* (5)
to punish   punir (7)
pupil   élève *m., f.* (3)
purchase   achat *m.* (5)
purse   sac *m.* (7)
to put   mettre (17)
  ~ away   ranger (7)
  ~ on   mettre, remettre (17)

Q

quality   qualité *f.* (11)
quarter   quart *m.* (6); trimestre *m.* (8)
Quebec   Québec *m.*
   from ~   québécois(e) (5)
question   question *f.* (1)

R

rabbit   lapin *m.* (9)
race   course *f.* (14)
   bicycle ~   course de bicyclettes *f.* (14)
   car ~   course de voitures *f.* (14)
radio   radio *f.* (1)
rain   pluie *f.* (8)
   acid ~   pluie acide *f.* (17)
to rain   pleuvoir (8)
raincoat   imperméable *m.* (5); imper *m.* (6)
to raise   lever (13)
rapidly   rapidement (18)
rare   rare (11)
rarely   rarement (18)
rather   assez (18)
to read   lire (14)
   read!   lisez! (1)
reader   lecteur (-trice) *m., f.* (15)
ready   prêt(e) (5)
reason   raison *f.* (17)
to receive   recevoir (12)
recent   récent(e) (18)
recently   récemment (5)
to recognize   reconnaître (10)
to recommend   recommander (3)
recycling   recyclage *m.* (17)
red   rouge (3)
reflection   reflet *m.* (17)
refrigerator   frigidaire *m.* (16)
to refuse   refuser (de) (15)
registered   recommandé(e) (8)
to regret   regretter (de) (11)
regularly   régulièrement (13)
to relax   se détendre (13)
to remain   rester (4)
to remember   retenir (10); se rappeler (13)
to remind   rappeler (à) (15)
to remove   enlever (13)
rent   loyer *m.* (16)

to rent   louer (10)
rental   location *f.* (10)
   ~ agency   compagnie de location *f.* (10)
to repair   réparer (10)
to repeat   répéter (1; 13)
report   reportage *m.* (11)
Republic of the Congo
   République démocratique du Congo *f.* (4)
to reserve   réserver (10)
to rest   se reposer (13)
restaurant   bistrot *m.*; restaurant *m.* (3)
to return   rentrer (4); retourner (10)
   ~ (something)   rendre (6)
review   revue *f.* (14)
rice   riz *m.* (9)
rich   riche (2)
right
   ~ away   tout de suite (3)
   ~ of way on the right   priorité à droite (10)
   to be ~   avoir raison (de) (3)
to ring   sonner (7)
river   fleuve *m.*, rivière *f.* (17)
roast   rôti *m.* (9)
   ~ beef   rosbif *m.* (9)
robe   robe de chambre *f.* (5)
rock   rock *m.* (2)
room   place *f.* (4); pièce *f.* (16)
roommate   camarade de chambre *m., f.* (2)
rooster   coq *m.* (18)
rugby   rugby *m.* (14)
rule   règle *f.* (10)
rumor   rumeur *f.* (17)
to run   courir (18)
Russia   Russie *f.* (4)
Russian   russe *m.* (8)

S

sad   triste (11)
sailboarding   planche à voile *f.* (14)
sailing   voile *f.* (14)
salad   salade *f.* (3)
salami   saucisson *m.* (9)
sale
   on ~   en solde (12)
   ~s   soldes *f. pl.* (12)

salesperson   vendeur (-euse) *m., f.* (12)
salt   sel *m.* (3)
same   même (5)
sandwich   sandwich *m.* (5)
Saturday   samedi *m.* (9)
sauerkraut and assorted meat
   choucroute garnie *f.* (12)
to save   faire des économies (8)
to say   dire (14)
   how do you ~ ... ?   comment dit-on... ? (1)
to scare   faire peur (à) (11)
scarf   écharpe *f.* (5)
to scatter   se disperser (17)
school   fac(ulté) *f.* (1); école (3)
   secondary ~   école secondaire *f.* (3)
school year   année scolaire (8)
   beginning of the ~   rentrée *f.* (8)
scuba diving   plongée sous-marine *f.* (14)
sculptor   sculpteur *m.* (15)
sculpture   sculpture *f.* (15)
sea   mer *f.* (4)
seafood   fruits de mer *m. pl.* (9)
season   saison *f.* (9)
seat   banquette *f.* (6)
   back ~   siège arrière *m.* (10)
   front ~   siège avant *m.* (10)
   ~ belt   ceinture de sécurité *f.* (10)
   ~s   places *f. pl.* (10)
second   deuxième, second(e) (2)
secretary   secrétaire *m., f.* (2)
security   sécurité *f.* (11)
to see   voir (7; 8)
   ~ again   revoir (8)
   see you later   à plus tard, à tout à l'heure (P)
   see you soon   à bientôt (P)
to seem   sembler (11)
to sell   vendre (6)
semester   semestre *m.* (8)
semolina   semoule *f.* (3)
Senegal   Sénégal *m.* (4)
Senegalese   sénégalais(e) (8)
sensational   formidable (2)
sentence   phrase *f.* (14)
September   septembre *m.* (9)
series   feuilleton *m.*; série *f.* (11)
serious   sérieux (-euse) (2); grave (13)
to set   mettre (17)

seven   sept (1)
seventeen   dix-sept (1)
seventeenth   dix-septième (2)
several   plusieurs (15)
she   elle (1)
sheep   mouton *m.* (18)
shelf   étagère *f.* (16)
to shimmer   ondoyer (17)
shirt   chemise *f.* (5)
shoe   chaussure *f.* (5)
shop   boutique *f.* (12)
shopkeeper   commerçant(e) *m., f.*
   (12)
shopping
   to do one's ~   faire ses provisions
      (9)
   ~ center   centre commercial *m.*
      (4)
shorts   short *m.* (5)
shoulder   épaule *f.* (13)
to show   montrer (1)
shower   douche *f.* (16)
shrimp   crevette *f.* (9)
shuttle   navette *f.* (17)
shy   timide (2)
sick   malade (2)
to sign   signer (10)
simple   simple (2)
since   depuis (6); puisque (8)
sincere   sincère (2)
sincerity   sincérité *f.* (2)
to sing   chanter (1)
sink   lavabo *m.* (16)
   kitchen ~   évier *m.* (16)
sir   monsieur *m.* (P)
sister   sœur *f.* (2)
six   six (1)
sixteen   seize (1)
sixty   soixante (2)
to skate   patiner (14)
skateboarding   planche à roulettes
   f. (14)
skating   patinage *m.* (14)
   in-line ~   roller *m.* (14)
skiing   ski *m.* (14)
   water-skiing   ski nautique (14)
skirt   jupe *f.* (5)
sky   ciel *m.* (8)
to sleep   dormir (7)
   not ~ a wink   ne pas fermer l'œil
      (13)
   ~ late   faire la grasse matinée (5)
slow   lent(e) (18)

slowly   lentement (18)
small   petit(e) (9)
to smoke   fumer (1)
snack
   to have an afternoon ~   goûter
      (3)
snow   neige *f.* (8)
to snow   neiger (8)
snowboarding   snowboard *m.* (14)
so   tellement (18)
   ~ much   tellement (18)
soccer   football *m.* (2)
social   social(e) (*pl.* -aux, -ales)
   (11)
society   société *f.* (11)
sociology   socio(logie) *f.* (8)
sock   chaussette *f.* (5)
sofa   canapé *m.*, divan *m.* (16)
software   logiciel *m.* (8)
solar   solaire (17)
sole   sole *f.* (9)
some   certain(e), quelque (2); en
   (15)
somebody   quelqu'un (10)
someone   quelqu'un (10)
something   quelque chose (5)
   ~ else   autre chose (12)
sometimes   quelquefois (18)
son   fils *m.* (2)
song   chanson *f.* (10)
soon   bientôt (8)
   as ~ as   aussitôt que, dès que
      (17)
sorry   désolé(e) (7)
   to be ~   regretter (de) (11)
so-so   comme ci, comme ça (P)
soup   soupe *f.* (3)
South America   Amérique du Sud
   f. (4)
space   espace *m.* (17)
space   spatial(e) (*pl.* -aux, -ales)
   (17)
Spain   Espagne *f.* (4)
Spanish   espagnol(e) (2)
to speak   parler (1)
to spend   dépenser (8)
   ~ (time)   passer (2)
spinach   épinards *m. pl.* (9)
sporting goods   articles de sport
   m. pl. (12)
sports   sports *m. pl* (2)
   to play ~   faire du sport (5)
spreadsheet   tableur *m.* (8)

spring   printemps *m.* (9)
to spring   jaillir (17)
square   place *f.* (9)
stadium   stade *m.* (4)
stage   étape *f.* (14)
stamp   timbre *m.* (8)
to start   démarrer (10)
starting from   à partir de (16)
state   état *m.* (15)
station   chaîne *f.* (11); station *f.*
   (17)
   cable ~   chaîne câblée *f.* (11)
   space ~   station spatiale *f.* (17)
stationer's   papeterie *f.* (12)
stationery   papier à lettres *m.* (8)
stay   séjour *m.* (8)
to stay   rester (4)
steak   bifteck *m.* (9)
stepfather   beau-père *m.* (*pl.*
   beaux-pères) (2)
stepmother   belle-mère *f.* (*pl.*
   belles-mères) (2)
stereo system   chaîne stéréo *f.* (7)
still   encore (6)
stomach   ventre *m.* (13)
stone   pierre *f.* (15)
   smooth ~   galet *m.* (4)
stop   station *f.* (6)
to stop   arrêter (11); cesser (de)
   (15)
store   magasin *m.* (4)
stormy
   to be ~   faire de l'orage (8)
stove   cuisinière *f.* (16)
strawberry   fraise *f.* (9)
street   rue *f.* (4)
student   étudiant(e) *m., f.* (1)
studious   studieux (-euse) (2)
to study   étudier (1)
stupid   stupide (2)
subject   matière *f.* (8)
subway   métro *m.* (6)
to succeed   réussir, réussir (à) (7)
success   succès *m.* (11)
such   tel(le) (18)
to suffer   souffrir (15)
sufficient   suffisant(e) (18)
sufficiently   suffisamment (18)
sugar   sucre *m.* (3)
suit   costume *m.* (5)
suitcase   valise *f.* (5)
summer   été *m.* (5)
Sunday   dimanche *m.* (9)

sunglasses   lunettes de soleil *f. pl.* (5)
sunny
  to be ~   faire du soleil (8)
super   super (5)
supermarket   supermarché *m.* (12)
  giant ~   hypermarché *m.* (12)
surely   sûrement (18)
surprised   surpris(e) (11)
Sweden   Suède *f.* (4)
to swim   nager (14)
swimming   natation *f.* (14)
  ~ pool   piscine *f.* (4)
Switzerland   Suisse *f.* (4)
symphony   symphonie *f.* (15)

T

table   table *f.* (16)
  bedside ~   table de nuit *f.* (16)
  round ~   table ronde *f.* (11)
to take   emporter (5); *(courses)* suivre (8); prendre (9); emmener (13); *(time to do something)* mettre (17)
  ~ after   tenir de (10)
tale   conte *m.* (14)
talent
  to have ~   avoir du talent (3)
to talk   parler (1)
tall   grand(e) (9)
tape recorder   radiocassette *f.* (7)
tart   tarte *f.* (3)
taxi   taxi *m.* (6)
tea   thé *m.* (3)
to teach   apprendre (à) (9); enseigner (15)
teacher   professeur *m.*; prof *m., f.* (1)
teaching   enseignement *m.* (15)
team   équipe *f.* (13)
telegram   télégramme *m.* (8)
telephone   téléphone *m.* (7)
to telephone   téléphoner (à) (7)
television   télé(vision) *f.* (1)
to tell   dire (à) (14)
ten   dix (1)
tennis   tennis *m.* (14)
  ~ shoes   tennis *f. pl.* (5)
terrific   formidable (2)
test   contrôle (14)
  blood ~   prise de sang *f.* (13)

text   texte *m.* (14)
than   que (18)
to thank   remercier (11)
thank you   merci (P)
thanks a million   merci mille fois (4)
that   ce (cet), cette (7); ça (9); que *(pron. rel.)* (16)
  ~'s it!   ça y est! (5)
the   le, la, l', les (1)
theater   théâtre *m.* (4)
their   leur(s) (5)
theirs   le leur, la leur, les leurs (14)
them   eux, elles (5); les (8); leur (9)
then   alors (1)
there   là (2); y (15)
  ~ are   il y a (3)
  ~ is   voilà (1); il y a (3)
therefore   donc (15)
these   ces (7)
they   ils, elles; on (1)
thigh   cuisse *f.* (13)
thing   chose *f.* (11)
  dumb ~   bêtise *f.* (14)
to think   penser (5); réfléchir (à) (7)
  ~ about   penser à (15)
  ~ of   penser de (15)
third   troisième (2)
thirsty
  to be ~   avoir soif (3)
thirteen   treize (1)
thirtieth   trentième (2)
thirty   trente (2)
this   cela (1); ce (cet), cette (7)
those   ces (7)
thousand   mille (4)
three   trois (1)
throat   gorge *f.* (13)
thunder   tonnerre *m.* (8)
Thursday   jeudi *m.* (9)
ticket   billet *m.*, ticket *m.* (6)
tie   cravate *f.* (5)
time   heure *f.*, temps *m.* (6)
  all the ~   tout le temps (8)
  for a long ~   longtemps (6)
  on ~   à l'heure (6)
  to have ~   avoir le temps (8)
  to have a good ~   s'amuser (à) (13)
tip included   service compris (3)
tire   pneu *m.* (10)
tired   fatigué(e) (2)
to   à (1); pour (4)
  ~ it   y (15)

tobacco shop   bureau de tabac *m.* (7)
tobacconist   buraliste *m., f.* (12)
today   aujourd'hui (4)
together   ensemble (1)
to tolerate   supporter (11)
tomato   tomate *f.* (9)
tomorrow   demain (4)
  ~ evening   demain soir (4)
  ~ morning   demain matin (4)
  ~ night   demain soir (4)
tonight   ce soir (1)
too
  ~ many   trop (3)
  ~ much   trop (3)
tour   voyage organisé *m.* (5)
tourist   touriste *m., f.* (5)
  ~ office   Syndicat d'Initiative *m.* (4)
tooth   dent *f.* (13)
Tour de France   Tour de France *m.* (14)
toward   vers (13)
town   ville *f.* (4)
traditional   traditionnel(le) (18)
traditionally   traditionnellement (18)
traffic   circulation *f.* (10); *(drugs)* trafic *m.* (11)
  ~ jam   embouteillage *m.* (10)
tragedy   tragédie *f.* (15)
train   train *m.* (6)
  ~ station   gare *f.* (4)
to translate   traduire (14)
transportation   transport *m.* (6)
to travel   voyager (4)
travel agency   agence de voyages *f.* (4)
tree   arbre *m.* (17)
trip   voyage *m.* (4)
  to take a ~   faire un voyage (5)
trombone   trombone *m.* (15)
trouble
  to have ~   avoir du mal à (15)
trout   truite *f.* (9)
truck   camion *m.* (6)
true   vrai(e) (2)
truly   vraiment (9)
trumpet   trompette *f.* (15)
trunk   coffre *m.* (10); tronc *m.* (17)
truth   vérité *f.* (14)
to try   essayer (de) (12); chercher (à) (15)
T-shirt   tee-shirt *m.* (5)

Tuesday   mardi *m.* (9)
Tunisia   Tunisie *f.* (4)
Tunisian   tunisien(ne) (3)
to turn on   allumer (7); mettre (17)
TV   télé (2)
   ~ news   journal *m.* (*pl.* -aux) (11)
   ~ set   téléviseur *m.* (7)
twelve   douze (1)
twentieth   vingtième (2)
twenty   vingt (1)
twenty-first   vingt et unième (2)
two   deux (1)
to type   taper (8)

U

ugly   laid(e) (2)
umbrella   parapluie *m.* (5)
unbearable   insupportable (8)
uncertainty   incertitude *f.* (11)
uncle   oncle *m.* (2)
under   sous (4)
to understand   comprendre (9)
undocumented aliens   sans-papiers *m.* (11)
undressed
   to get ~   se déshabiller (13)
unemployment   chômage *m.* (11)
unfair   injuste (11)
unfortunately   malheureusement (18)
unhappy   malheureux (2)
United States   Etats-Unis *m. pl.* (4)
university   fac(ulté) *f.*, université (1)
   ~ cafeteria   restau-U *m.* (4)
unlikely   peu probable (11)
unpleasant   désagréable (2)
until   jusqu'à (6)
use   usage *m.* (15)
to use   utiliser (8)
used   d'occasion (10)
   to be ~ for   servir (à) (7)
useful   utile (2)
useless   inutile (2)
utilities   charges *f. pl.* (16)

V

vacation   vacances *f. pl.* (9)
   summer ~   grandes vacances *f. pl.* (10)

Valentine's Day   Saint-Valentin *f.* (9)
variety   variété *f.* (9)
   ~ show   variétés *f. pl.* (11)
VAT (value-added tax)   TVA *f.* (10)
VCR   magnétoscope *m.* (7)
veal   veau *m.* (9)
vegetables   légumes *m. pl.* (3)
   raw ~   crudités *f. pl.* (9)
vegetarian   végétarien(ne) (9)
very   très (P)
   ~ well   très bien (P)
violin   violon *m.* (15)
to visit
   ~ (a place)   visiter (4)
   ~ (people)   rendre visite à (6); aller voir (8)
voice   voix *f.* (7)
   ~ mail   messagerie vocale *f.* (7)
volleyball   volley-ball *m.* (14)

W

to wait (for)   attendre (6)
waiter   garçon *m.* (3)
to wake up   se réveiller (13)
walk
   to go for a ~   faire un tour, faire une promenade (5); se promener (13)
to walk   promener (13)
Walkman   Walkman *m.* (7)
wall   mur *m.* (3)
wallet   portefeuille *m.* (7)
to want   vouloir (7)
war
   nuclear ~   guerre nucléaire *f.* (11)
Warsaw   Varsovie (4)
washed
   to get ~   se laver (13)
washing machine   machine à laver *f.* (16)
water   eau *f.* (3)
watercolor   aquarelle *f.* (15)
way   chemin *m.* (16)
we   nous; on (1)
to wear   porter (5)
weather   temps *m.* (6)
   ~ forecast   météo *f.* (8)
Wednesday   mercredi *m.* (9)
week   semaine *f.* (4)

weekend   week-end *m.* (4)
welcome
   you're ~   il n'y a pas de quoi (1)
well   bien (P); alors (13)
   ~ then   eh bien (1)
what   quel(le) (5; 7); qu'est-ce qui?, qu'est-ce que?, quoi? (7)
   ~ is it?   qu'est-ce que c'est? (1)
   ~ kind of   quelle sorte de (3)
wheel   volant *m.* (10)
when   lorsque (17)
   ~?   quand? (2)
where   où (2)
whereabouts?   où ça?
which   quel(le) (5; 7) que, qui (*pron. rel.*) (16)
   of ~   dont (17)
white   blanc(he) (3)
who   qui, qui est-ce qui (7); qui (*pron. rel.*) (16)
   ~'s speaking?   qui est à l'appareil? (7)
whom   qui est-ce que (7); que (*pron. rel.*) (16)
   to ~?   à qui? (7)
whose   dont (17)
   ~ turn is it?   c'est à qui? (6)
why   pourquoi (4)
wife   femme *f.* (2)
will   volonté *f.* (15)
willing
   to be willing   vouloir bien (7)
to win   gagner (14)
window   fenêtre *f.* (1)
windshield   pare-brise *m.* (10)
windy
   to be ~   faire du vent (8)
wine   vin *m.* (3)
winter   hiver *m.* (5)
to wish   désirer (2); souhaiter (11)
with   avec (1)
without   sans (2)
woman   femme *f.* (1)
word processor   traitement de texte *m.* (8)
work   travail *m.* (11); œuvre *f.* (15)
to work   travailler (1); marcher (7)
world   monde *m.* (11)
worried
   to be worried   s'inquiéter (13)
to worry   inquiéter (13); s'inquiéter (de) (15)

worth
  it's not ~ the trouble ce n'est
    pas la peine (7)
wrestling catch *m.* (14)
to write écrire (à) (14)
writer écrivain(e) *m., f.* (2)
written écrit(e) (8)
wrong
  to be ~ avoir tort (de) (3)

Y

yard jardin *m.* (17)
year an *m.* (3); année *f.* (4)
  school ~ année scolaire *f.* (8)
yellow jaune (5)
yes oui (P); si (2)
yesterday hier (5)
you toi, vous (P); tu (1)
young jeune (9)
  ~ people jeunes gens *m. pl.* (2)

your votre, vos (1; 2); ta, ton, tes
  (5)
yours le tien, la tienne, les
  tien(ne)s; le (la) vôtre, les
  vôtres (14)

Z

zero zéro (1)

Index

Credits

Text and Illustrations

Text: p. 28, Reprinted from Université de Liège Administration de l'Enseignement et des Etudiants.

p. 28, Bac en anthropologie, cours obligatoires, cours à option—syllabi excerpted from www.ulaval.ca/sg/PR/C1/1.531.01.html. Reprinted by permission of Laval University.

p. 41, Puigro cartoon from *Le Français dans le monde,* #105, June 1994, p. 8.

p. 80, Jambalaya recipe. Reprinted by permission of Saveurs du Monde, http://www.saveurs.sympatico.ca.

p. 193, Article, «Le téléphone au féminine», *Journal Français,* April 1999.

p. 193, Article, «Le téléphone mobile est 'in'», *Journal Français,* June 2001.

p. 194, Web advertisement from Pagesmobiles.com.

p. 220, Excerpts from article, «Les scènes de la Seine», *Journal Français,* February 2001.

p. 222, Poem by Jacques Prévert, «Chanson de la Seine», from *Spectacles.* Copyright © Editions Gallimard. Reprinted by permission.

pp. 248–249, Excerpt from Dominique Ageorges, «Le chef Marc Veyrat, héritier de onze générations de paysans français». Copyright © 2001 Agence France Presse. Reprinted with permission.

p. 250, Description of Auberge de l'Eridan restaurant from viamichelin.com.

p. 281, Excerpts from article, «Visionaute, un système anti-embouteillages unique en Europe», *Journal Français,* October 1999.

p. 306, Descriptions of TV5 programming, from www.tv5.org/5tv/index.html.

p. 359, Excerpt from www.jamaislapremiere.org/pages/ch_03.html.

p. 383, Excerpts from article, «L'effet Mondial attire les jeunes footballeurs français», *Journal Français,* August 1999.

p. 388, Copyright by L'EXPRESS. Distributed by the New York Times Special Features.

p. 406, Biography, «Hergé–le Père de Tintin» from www.chez.com/tintinetmilou.

pp. 433–434, Excerpt, "Charles Alexis Henri Clérel de Toqueville," from the Encyclopédie Hachette (http://fr.encyclopedia.yahoo.com/articles/ni/ni_995_p0.html). Copyright © 2001 Hachette Multimédia/Hachette Livre, tous droits réservés. Notice légale. Copyright © 2001 Yahoo! France. Tous droits réservés.

p. 438, Poem by Robert Mélançon, «Neige» de *Peinture aveugle,* (Montréal: VLB Editeur, 1980). Copyright © by Robert Mélançon. Reprinted by permission.

pp. 455–456, Excerpts from article, «A Montréal sans mettre le nez dehors», *Journal Français,* January 2001.

pp. 476–477, Excerpts from article, «Vive la télé en couleur!» *Journal Français,* February 2000.

Illustrations: pp. 200, 237, Network Graphics; pp. 2 (bottom), 263, 290, Anna Veltfort; All other illustrations by George M. Ulrich.

Photographs and Realia

Photographs: p. 1, David R. Frazier Photolibrary; p. 3, David R. Frazier Photolibrary; p. 5, AP/Wide World Photos; p. 7, David R. Frazier Photolibrary; p. 9, Antman/The Image Works; p. 27, Beryl Goldberg; p. 32, David R. Frazier Photolibrary; p. 35, R. Lucas/The Image Works; p. 52, David R. Frazier Photolibrary; p. 58, Andrew Brilliant; p. 60, David R. Frazier Photolibrary; p. 80, Beryl Goldberg; p. 88, David R. Frazier Photolibrary; p. 91, Kip Brundy/Getty Images; p. 108, David

R. Frazier Photolibrary; p. 110, Beryl Goldberg; p. 112, David R. Frazier Photolibrary; p. 115, Paul Dalzell; p. 134, Beryl Goldberg; p. 138, Reuters/Getty Images; p. 139, Phyllis Picardi/Stock Boston; p. 143, David R. Frazier Photolibrary; p. 163, David R. Frazier Photolibrary; p. 170, David R. Frazier Photolibrary; p. 172, David R. Frazier Photolibrary; p. 192, David R. Frazier Photolibrary; p. 197, David R. Frazier Photolibrary; p. 217, IPA/The Image Works; p. 220, David R. Frazier Photolibrary; p. 225, Oscar C. Williams; p. 228, Steven Rothfield/Getty Images; p. 245, David R. Frazier Photolibrary; p. 257, David R. Frazier Photolibrary; p. 260, Beryl Goldberg; p. 278, David R. Frazier Photolibrary; p. 284, David R. Frazier Photolibrary; p. 304, David R. Frazier Photolibrary; p. 311, Ray Scott/The Image Works; p. 312, David R. Frazier Photolibrary; p. 328, David R. Frazier Photolibrary; p. 339, Anita Jensen/ Getty Images; p. 342, Matt Jacob/The Image Works; p. 349, Ulrike Welsch/Photo Researchers; p. 363, AP/ Wide World Photos; p. 366, A. Gyori/Sygma; p. 382, AP/Wide World Photos; p. 386, David R. Frazier Photolibrary; p. 402, Peter Menzel/Stock Boston; p. 414, Wolfgang Kaehler/Getty Images; p. 417, Oscar C. Williams; p. 437, Beryl Goldberg; p. 438, Jocelyn Boutin/Index Stock; p. 456, Pascal Quittemelle/Stock Boston; p. 459, Owen Franken/Stock Boston.

Realia design: Anna Veltfort: pp. 28, 53, 54, 80, 193, 194, 220, 222, 248–249, 250, 251, 281, 306, 307, 332-333, 357, 359, 383.

Realia: p. 17, courtesy *Télé 7 Jours;* p. 20, courtesy Paris Ile-de-France Comité Régional du Tourisme; p. 59, (left) courtesy Surya Restaurant Indien, (right) courtesy La Varangue Restaurant Réunionnais; p. 63, courtesy Palais Jamai Fes; p. 75 (right), courtesy Capital; p. 78, courtesy Le Plateau Rouge; p. 81, courtesy Häagen-Däas / Boutiques Aeorports de Paris Magazine; p. 152, courtesy Air France; p. 162, courtesy Thalys; p. 173, courtesy France Telecom; p. 177, courtesy Genesys; p. 187, courtesy Sélection Reader's Digest; p. 189, courtesy Télécarte; p. 199, courtesy Musée d'Orsay; p. 203, courtesy *Pariscope;* p. 206, courtesy *Le Figaro;* p. 258, courtesy Renault Eurodrive/TGV/SNCF; p. 280, courtesy Jaguar; p. 302, courtesy *Télé 7 Jours/On A Tout Essayé;* p. 308, courtesy *Télé 7 Jours;* p. 319, courtesy Ministère de L'Économie des Finances et de L'Industrie; p. 331, courtesy Mairie de Paris; pp. 346 and 357, *Francoscopie 2001:* Comment vivent le Français; p. 360, www.reul.ucl.ac.be/presse/communiques/tabac; p. 390, courtesy Espace Bonnard; p. 400, courtesy Sélection Reader's Digest; p. 407, Copyright © Casterman. Reprinted by permission; p. 447, courtesy *Pariscope;* p. 448, courtesy Tourisme Québec; p. 461, courtesy Sesame Café; p. 468, courtesy *Pariscope;* p. 473, «Les Triplés» by Nicole Lambert, originally published in *Figaro Madame,* March 9, 1991. Reprinted by permission.

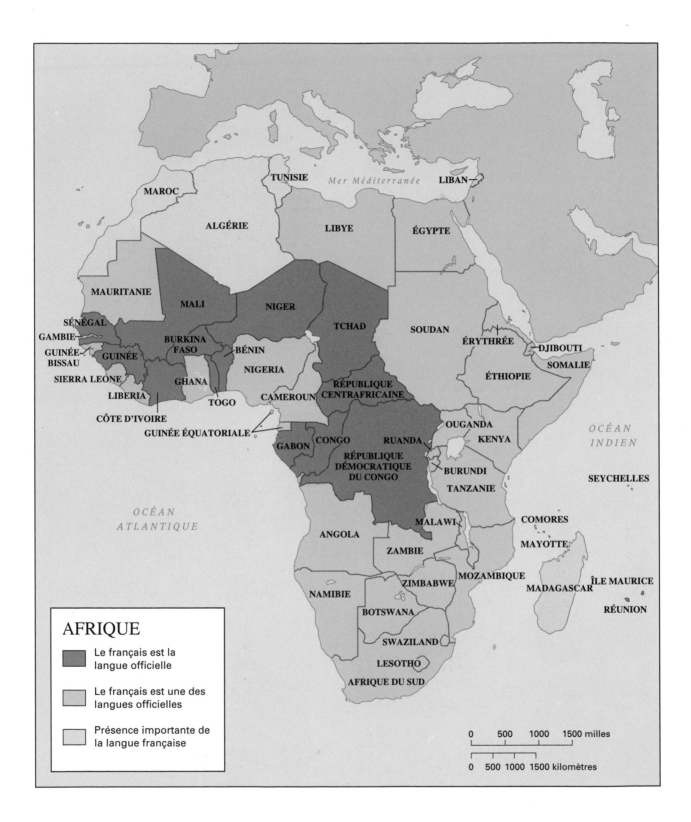

AFRIQUE

MAROC
TUNISIE
LIBAN
Mer Méditerranée
ALGÉRIE
LIBYE
ÉGYPTE
MAURITANIE
MALI
NIGER
TCHAD
SOUDAN
ÉRYTHRÉE
DJIBOUTI
SÉNÉGAL
BURKINA
FASO
SOMALIE
GAMBIE
BÉNIN
GUINÉE-
BISSAU
GUINÉE
NIGERIA
ÉTHIOPIE
SIERRA LEONE
GHANA
RÉPUBLIQUE
CENTRAFRICAINE
LIBERIA
CAMEROUN
TOGO
CÔTE D'IVOIRE
OUGANDA
GUINÉE ÉQUATORIALE
KENYA
CONGO
RUANDA
GABON
RÉPUBLIQUE
DÉMOCRATIQUE
DU CONGO
BURUNDI
OCÉAN
INDIEN
TANZANIE
SEYCHELLES
OCÉAN
ATLANTIQUE
MALAWI
COMORES
ANGOLA
MAYOTTE
ZAMBIE
MOZAMBIQUE
ÎLE MAURICE
ZIMBABWE
MADAGASCAR
NAMIBIE
RÉUNION
BOTSWANA
SWAZILAND
LESOTHO
AFRIQUE DU SUD

Le français est la langue officielle

Le français est une des langues officielles

Présence importante de la langue française

0   500   1000   1500 milles

0   500 1000 1500 kilomètres